THE WORLDS OF THE TRUST

Despite the common belief that they are found only in the common law tradition, trusts have long been known in mixed jurisdictions even where they have a civilian law of property. Trusts have now been introduced by legislation in a number of civilian jurisdictions, such as France and China. Other recent developments include the reception of foreign trusts through private international law in Italy and Switzerland and the inclusion of a chapter on trusts in Europe's Draft Common Frame of Reference.

As a result, there is a growing interest in the ways in which the trust can be accommodated in civil law systems. This collection explores this question, as well as general issues such as the juridical nature of the trust, the role and qualifications of the trustee and particular developments in specific jurisdictions.

LIONEL SMITH is James McGill Professor of Law and Director of the Paul-André Crépeau Centre for Private and Comparative Law at the Faculty of Law, McGill University, Montreal, Canada.

THE WORLDS OF THE TRUST

Edited by
LIONEL SMITH

CAMBRIDGE
UNIVERSITY PRESS

CAMBRIDGE
UNIVERSITY PRESS

University Printing House, Cambridge CB2 8BS, United Kingdom

One Liberty Plaza, 20th Floor, New York, NY 10006, USA

477 Williamstown Road, Port Melbourne, VIC 3207, Australia

314-321, 3rd Floor, Plot 3, Splendor Forum, Jasola District Centre, New Delhi - 110025, India

79 Anson Road, #06-04/06, Singapore 079906

Cambridge University Press is part of the University of Cambridge.

It furthers the University's mission by disseminating knowledge in the pursuit of education, learning and research at the highest international levels of excellence.

www.cambridge.org
Information on this title: www.cambridge.org/9781107032439

First published 2013

A catalogue record for this publication is available from the British Library

Library of Congress Cataloging in Publication data
Smith, Lionel, 1965–
The worlds of the trust / Edited by Lionel Smith.
pages cm
ISBN 978-1-107-03243-9 (Hardback)
1. Trusts and trustees. I. Title.
K795.S65 2013
346.05′9–dc23 2012049255

ISBN 978-1-107-03243-9 Hardback

Additional resources for this publication at www.cambridge.org/9781107032439

CONTENTS

to pass good title to, say, a bona fide purchaser even if he acts in breach is widely accepted in trust jurisdictions in common law and civil law. Despite its ubiquity, it is essential not because it is necessary for the trust to exist,[15] but rather because of its practical usefulness in realizing the economic value of the trust assets and maintaining the smoothness of commercial transactions.

Thirdly, it is also common in almost all trust jurisdictions that if the trustee unlawfully alienates trust assets in favour of volunteers or individuals in bad faith, the recipient has at least a liability (and the beneficiary a correlative power) that the alienation be annulled. Additionally, depending on the law of the jurisdiction concerned, the specific trust assets may also be immune from the claims of the recipient's creditors,[16] and the recipient may owe duties enforceable by the beneficiary to return the specific assets to the trust fund or to pay compensation. Such duties are not the same as those owed by the trustee to the beneficiary; for example, the recipient owes no duty to manage the assets, let alone one to act in the best interest of the beneficiaries, but only the duty to return them.[17] It is submitted that the beneficiary's power to annul the unlawful transaction is essential, because by strengthening the beneficiary's rights through (*in personam*) remedies enforceable against the transferee, it crucially makes the trust more useful; the costs it brings – of overriding the rights of, say, purchasers in bad faith and volunteers – are not excessive. After all, all jurisdictions subscribe to a system of rules for resolving competing rights pertaining to the use of property, such as the rule on bona fide acquisition.

In the final analysis, amongst the essential features of a trustee's powers over the trust assets, only that to manage the trust property is essential for the existence of the trust. However, since such a limited power will not make the trust practically useful, save in exceptional cases of property preservation mentioned above, it is also essential to give the trustee power to alienate trust assets lawfully and hence pass good title to a transferee that meets the requirements for obtaining such a title, such as a bona fide purchaser. For the same reasons of practical usefulness, it is

[15] If, as explained above, not even the trustee's right to alienate trust property is necessary for the existence of a trust, it must be doubly so for his right to alienate trust property free from the beneficiaries' rights when he acts in breach.

[16] Hayton, Kortmann and Verhagen, *Principles of European Trust Law*, above, note 5, p. 59.

[17] The rights of the beneficiary against these third-party recipients are not necessarily the same as those against the original trustee: R. Nolan, 'Property in a Fund' (2004) 120 L.Q.R. 108.

also essential for a beneficiary to have the right to annul unlawful dispositions vis-à-vis, say, a volunteer or purchaser in bad faith.

Common law jurisdictions and an overwhelming majority of civil law jurisdictions grant the power of management to the trustee through giving him titulary ownership of the same kind enjoyed by a full owner. However, the vesting of ownership rights with the trustee is only a common, if not an extremely efficient means to grant him the essential powers to administer and alienate the trust assets. A jurisdiction can choose to empower the trustee with the same essential powers, which are typically associated with ownership, rather than ownership itself. A well-known legislative example of this model is the Québec Civil Code, which does not give ownership of the trust assets to the settlor, let alone any party in the trust relationship.[18] The trustee is given powers of control and exclusive administration over the trust assets.[19] The Civil Code also gives him, in the broadest terms, the 'exercise of all the rights pertaining to the patrimony'.[20] Another example is the *bewind* trust under Dutch law and a similar form evolved in South Africa and recognized by legislation, albeit they are much less than trusts involving the transfer of ownership to trustees. In such forms, ownership is granted to the beneficiary but the trust property is 'placed under the control of [the trustee] to be administered or disposed of according to' the trust.[21]

B. *Third parties and trust assets*

If the trust arrangement had only consisted of granting the trustee with powers to manage the trust assets, it would have just been a variant of contract or agency. One of the distinguishing features of the trust that gives it comparative advantage over, say, agency or mandate, is the immunity or ring-fencing of the trust assets from the claims of the heirs, spouses and personal creditors of the trustee, particularly in the event of

[18] Civil Code of Québec, art. 1261 (C.C.Q.): 'The trust patrimony, consisting of the property transferred in trust, constitutes a patrimony by appropriation, autonomous and distinct from that of the settlor, trustee or beneficiary and in which none of them has any real right.' D. W. M. Waters, 'The Institution of the Trust in Civil and Common Law', *Recueil des Cours* (Boston / London / Dordrecht, 1995), vol. 252, pp. 396–407.

[19] See M. Cantin Cumyn, 'The Legal Power' (2009) 3 *European Review of Private Law* 345.

[20] C.C.Q., above, note 18, art. 1278.

[21] Trust Property Control Act, 1988 (South Africa), s. 1, discussed in M. J. de Waal, 'The Uniformity of Ownership, *Numerus Clausus* and the Reception of the Trust into South African Law' (2000) 3 *European Review of Private Law* 439, 449.

his death, divorce or bankruptcy.[22] This allows the settlor to relinquish ownership and possession of the trust property in favour of the trustee-manager without fear of the latter's insolvency, and distinguishes the trust from other institutions such as mandate, agency or contracts for the benefit of third parties.

To ring-fence the trust assets, it is both necessary and sufficient that the trustee's personal creditors be subject to a disability that prevents them from compelling the trustee to satisfy his personal liabilities with trust assets.[23] This gives the beneficiary a correlative immunity from the creditors' claims. It also entails – although it would be prudent for trust statutes to stipulate this separately and additionally – the trustee owing a duty to refrain from using trust assets to meet his personal liabilities.[24] The trust assets should only be used to satisfy his trust liabilities.[25]

Segregation of the trust assets could be achieved, in civil law jurisdictions, by the creation of two separate patrimonies held by the trustee, whereby trust creditors can only claim against trust assets, and the trustee's personal creditors can only claim against the trustee's own assets.[26] In common law jurisdictions, insolvency legislation typically provides that only assets beneficially owned by the bankrupt trustee owner will fall within the bankrupt estate.[27] In fact, since it is not the purpose of the trust to ring-fence the trustee's own assets from trust liabilities, the trustee's duty is also consistent with permitting

22 H. Hansmann and U. Mattei, 'The Functions of Trust Law: A Comparative Legal and Economic Analysis' (1998) 73 NYU L. Rev. 434.

23 This will need to be achieved by legal enactment.

24 *Bennet* v. *Wyndham* (1862) 4 De G F & J 259. Personal liabilities broadly include liability for the claims of heirs and spouses, and debts incurred by the trustee in all his other affairs outside of the relevant trust at issue.

25 Trust liabilities refer to debts incurred by the trustee for the management of trust affairs. This could be achieved by requiring the trustee to provide personal security: see, for example, Trust Property Control Act, 1989 (South Africa), s. 6(3).

26 See also, K. Reid, 'Conceptualising the Chinese Trust: Some Thoughts from Europe', SSRN Working Paper Series, available at http://papers.ssrn.com (last visited 4 April 2011). In fact, even when two separate patrimonies are created, the law of a particular jurisdiction can still allow trust creditors to claim against both patrimonies. For the position in Latin America, see N. Malumian, *Trusts in Latin America* (Oxford University Press, 2010), pp. 21–2.

27 See, for example, Insolvency Act 1986 (UK), s. 283(3)(*a*), in relation to individual trustees; the same assumption is adopted in relation to corporate trustees. Before express legislative provisions, the trustee for bankruptcy was treated as standing in exactly the same position as the bankrupt himself: P. Watts, 'Constructive Trusts and Insolvency' (2009) 3 J. Eq. 250, citing *Copeman* v. *Gallant* (1716) 1 P Wms 314; 24 ER 404.

trust creditors to claim from the trustee's personal assets, as is the approach taken in common law jurisdictions.[28]

In this connection, it needs to be clarified that even if the trust assets are protected from the claims of the trustee's personal creditors, this is not necessarily because the trust assets fall into the same pool of assets that are also available to the creditors, and that the beneficiary has *in rem* rights against the trust assets that defeat the creditors' *in personam* rights against the trustee in having their liability met by these assets. Rather, the beneficiary's rights can still be understood as personal rights against the trustee only. It is just that they belong to a partitioned part within all the assets of the trustee, and such a part is protected, in that assets falling within it are not available to meet the personal creditors of the trustee.[29] Accordingly, the creation of the separate (trust) patrimony readily explains why the beneficiary's rights are protected from the claims of the trustee's personal creditors. The beneficiary never needs to enforce his rights, let alone any *in rem* rights, against the personal creditors directly. All he needs are *in personam* rights against the trustee to be paid out of the protected trust patrimony.

A feature that is also practically essential for a trust to be a tool for managing a changing portfolio of assets is that the trust assets should not be limited to the initial settled sum, but should also include assets derived from and representing it from time to time.[30] To achieve this, the law can simply treat it as a standard implied term in the trust undertaking that the trustee holds the subsequent assets under the same terms as the original ones. Trust legislation can also define trust property to include assets derived from the original settled sum. The tracing rules that determine which new asset is treated as representing the original assets are just evidentiary in nature.

Seen in this light, the rights of the beneficiary to enforce the trust in relation to the new, traceable products of the original trust assets still do not require any *in rem* explanation. If the new assets are derived from a lawful exercise of the trustee's right to alienate trust assets, they are simply brought within the scope of the trustee's personal trust undertaking. If the new assets are the exchange products of an unlawful

[28] L. Smith, 'Trust and Patrimony' (2009) 28 E.T.P.J. 332; (2008) 38 R.G.D. 379.

[29] H. L. E. Verhagen, 'Trusts in the Civil Law: Making Use of the Experience of "Mixed" Jurisdictions' (2000) 3 E.R.P.L. 477, 488.

[30] Nolan, 'Property in a Fund', above, note 17, 108. There may also be mandatory rules in particular jurisdictions governing the type of property that may not be subject to a trust. Additionally, it is also essential that only present property (as opposed to a *spes*) can be trust property.

transaction, the beneficiary has the right to adopt or authorize them. Once the transaction is adopted, the benefits obtained from it are treated as falling within the trust assets.[31] Put another way, the trustee who owns or has powers of control over the benefits of the trust simply owes the same personal obligations in relation to these benefits as he does in relation to the original trust assets.

To summarize, the essential rights of a trust that are often treated as showing that it is a 'proprietary' institution can, on close examination, be explained as *in personam* rights. These include the immunity of the trust fund from the claims of the trustee's personal creditors, and the substitution of the original trust fund by its traceable products. Accordingly, in so far as the trust assets are still in the hands of the trustee, it is submitted that the trust can be fully accommodated within the law of obligations.

Thus far, this section has only discussed the position of one type of third parties to a trust arrangement, namely the trustee's personal creditors. The other major groups concerned are transferees of trust assets and parties who interfere with the trustee–beneficiary relationship through assisting in a breach of trust or otherwise intermeddling with trust affairs.[32] As the next section will seek to show, it is not an essential element of the trust that such parties stand in any particular legal relationship vis-à-vis the trust assets. Their position will be discussed in the next section on the relationship between the beneficiary and third parties.

C. Beneficiary and the trust assets / third parties

As a preliminary attempt in identifying the essential rights and duties of the parties to a trust, the present chapter only focuses on private express trusts for beneficiaries. In a private express trust, the beneficiary plays the ultimate role in enforcing obligations against the trustee and third parties. It is submitted, therefore, that for a practically useful trust to exist, it is only essential for the beneficiary (or anyone representing him in legal actions) to have the capacity to enforce rights.[33]

[31] If the unlawful transaction is a sale, the purchaser (who may be the trustee himself) will take free from the beneficiaries' rights; the proceeds from the sale will fall within the trust assets.

[32] In common law terminology, one who assumes the role of trustee is called a trustee *de son tort* and is subjected to the obligations of a trustee; this will not be discussed in this chapter.

[33] In so far as there is a mechanism for legally representing unborn, disabled or incapacitated beneficiaries, it is submitted that the law should not prohibit them from being beneficiaries.

Although the beneficiary is often spoken of as the beneficial owner of the trust assets, the analysis in this chapter suggests that it is not essential for him to have any proprietary rights in relation to the trust assets. This is because in so far as the trustee's personal creditors are prohibited from having any recourse to the trust assets, such assets are ring-fenced and hence only available to meet trust liabilities and the beneficiary's *in personam* claims against the trustee. Consequently, there is no priority conflict between the beneficiary and the trustee's personal creditors as such, and hence no necessity to give the former any proprietary claim over the trust assets. Bolstered by the ring-fencing mechanism, it is sufficient for the beneficiary to have *in personam* claims against the trustee to make distributions to him according to the terms of the trust.

In contrast, it is submitted that it is essential for the beneficiary to have some rights against some unauthorized transferees of trust assets, such as volunteers and purchasers in bad faith. Although such rights of enforcement are not essential for the trust to exist, they are crucial in protecting the beneficiary from the trustee's breaches, and some of them should be treated as essential. This is because if the beneficiary is unable to enforce any rights against any unauthorized transferee, his right to obtain the assets will be easily extinguished by the trustee's unauthorized disposition.

There is a wide range of beneficiary's rights against unauthorized transferees in trust jurisdictions around the world. These include, at the low end, annulling the unauthorized transfer and requiring the transferee to return the specific property or, where this is not feasible, paying compensation. At the high end, and typically found in common law jurisdictions only, the trust assets and their traceable products are also immune from the claims of the heirs, spouses and creditors of such transferees. This means that such transferees are also subject to duties to refrain from using the trust assets to meet their personal liabilities.

Since these rights are enforceable against an indeterminate class of persons, they might appear to resemble *in rem* rights at first glance. Nonetheless, not all of them need to be explained on the basis that the beneficiaries have *in rem* rights in the trust property. Nor is such an explanation without difficulty. It might be noted that the beneficiary's rights against the transferees are much more limited than his rights against the trustee. If the beneficiary is treated as having proprietary rights in the trust assets that are enforceable against an indeterminate class (including the trustee), justification will be needed to explain why the trustee's position differs from that of the transferees.

It is submitted that less extensive claims, such as those to have the transaction annulled, and to compel the transferee to return the trust property or its traceable products (or if not feasible, their monetary equivalent) to the trust fund, and pay compensation, if any, can be explained as personal in nature. In particular, the transferee's obligations can be seen as arising from the law of unjust enrichment[34] or wrongful interference with contractual or obligational rights.[35] For the former, the transferee has obtained an enrichment at the expense of the beneficiaries. The enrichment is unjust because it results from conduct that infringes the beneficiaries' right to receive the enrichment. It is therefore prima facie recoverable unless the transferee can invoke the defence of bona fide purchase, which is a policy-based exception to promote the smoothness of commercial transactions. In civil law terms, the beneficiary can be treated as having a *jus ad rem*, meaning a right to a thing enforceable against individuals who are subject to the law of obligation to deliver the property. But a *jus ad rem* is still a personal right rather than a right *in rem*, in the property. Such an analysis can adequately explain the personal rights of the beneficiaries vis-à-vis the transferee for the return of the traceable trust assets or their monetary equivalent.

Alternatively, if the transferee is required to pay compensation for loss of the trust fund arising from his receipt, such a personal duty can be explained on the basis of his wrongful conduct in interfering with the trustee's performance of his obligations towards the beneficiaries. This is similar to the economic tort of interference with contractual rights, whereby third parties can be subject to duties in relation to purely personal rights. Although it is plausible for such liability to be strict, it is more sensible for fault to be required, given that the defendant could easily be worse off than his prior position by paying compensation. By the same token, it is submitted that personal liability imposed on third parties for assisting with the breach of trust should be justified on the same basis of interference with the legal relationship of the trustee and beneficiary. In so far as such third parties have not received trust property, their liability cannot be based on unjust enrichment.

However, if, as in common law jurisdictions, the traceable trust assets are immune from the claims of the transferee's heirs, spouses and creditors in the event of his death, divorce or bankruptcy, it is submitted

[34] G. L. Gretton, 'Constructive Trusts and Insolvency' (2000) 3 E.R.P.L. 463, 464–5; G. L. Gretton, 'Trusts Without Equity' (2000) 49 I.C.L.Q. 599.

[35] Smith, 'Trust and Patrimony', above, note 28, 343–5.

that they cannot be explained purely on a personal basis. Firstly, at least in all civil law jurisdictions, the laws of unjust enrichment and wrongful interference with contractual (or obligational) rights only give rise to personal duties. They do not also impose a duty on the respondents to refrain from using the unjust benefits or funds to be used to pay compensation. Besides, since they are not the trustees themselves and have not undertaken any trust duties, it is not possible to imply any undertaking on the part of the transferee to refrain from using the trust fund to meet his personal liabilities. Accordingly, there is no basis to impose a further duty to refrain from using the relevant assets without stretching the existing laws of unjust enrichment and torts. An *in rem* justification will be necessary.

As explained above, the beneficiary's rights vis-à-vis third parties are not necessary for the existence of the trust, but they significantly enhance the protection of the beneficiary and hence also the attractiveness of the trust. It is submitted that unless they involve significant negative effects on third parties they should be treated as essential to a trust. In this light, since most jurisdictions have already adopted rules on bona fide acquisition, the imposition of restitutionary liability on recipients who are not bona fide purchasers to restore the trust assets is not draconian and should be essential. After all, the third party is only required to restore an enrichment he is not entitled to receive in the first place; he is not incurring expenses from his own funds to compensate the beneficiary's loss. Beyond that, it is not readily obvious whether it is also essential for such recipients (as well as knowing assisters) to be subject to compensatory liability. In so far as a jurisdiction contemplating the adoption of the trust already imposes fault based liability against third parties who interfere with contractual rights, it is not draconian to also impose similar liability in the context of trust. In contrast, rarely, if ever, do civil law jurisdictions also treat such third parties as subject to trusteeship in relation to the assets they receive.

D. *Trustee and beneficiary – check and balance*

Thus far, the present chapter has focused on the relationship, if any, between the respective parties to a trust (trustee, beneficiaries and third parties) on the one hand, and the trust assets on the other. This section considers the personal relationship between the trustee and beneficiary.

Upon giving the trustee powers of management and alienation, and hence control over the trust assets, it is essential that the trustee wield these powers for the best interest of the beneficiary, and not for his own benefit. To this end, a check and balance mechanism is needed to instruct the trustee as to how to exercise his powers, and to hold him accountable to such an instruction. It is submitted that these two purposes can be achieved by the following essential duties. First, the trustee should owe the duty to act honestly and in what he in good faith considers to be the best interest of the beneficiary, and not exercise these powers for his own benefit.[36] Secondly, to identify the scope of the assets subject to this duty, one needs to distinguish the trust assets from the trustee's own assets. Hence, the trustee should owe the duty to keep accurate financial records of the trust assets and to report them. Thirdly, in order that the beneficiary can hold the trustee to account, the latter should owe the duty to provide a minimum level of information to beneficiaries.[37]

Beyond these essential duties, the trustee is paradigmatically subject to duties of care, loyalty and compliance with the terms of the trust.[38] To the extent that breach of these latter duties is not dishonest or in bad faith, either liability can be excluded by exemption clauses, or the relevant transaction in breach can be subsequently ratified by the beneficiary.[39] Moreover, depending on the particular type of private express trust involved, such as fixed or discretionary trusts, the specific duties prescribed by the terms of the trust may differ. For example, a fixed interest trustee owes the duty to draw up a complete list of the beneficiaries and to use his best effort to contact individual beneficiaries. Such duties are essential for a trust to be recognized as a *fixed interest* trust, even though they are not essential for a trust to exist. It is also submitted that despite its widespread acceptance in common law jurisdictions, the *Saunders* v. *Vautier*[40] rule, which allows beneficiaries who are *sui juris* and together

[36] *Armitage* v. *Nurse* [1998] Ch 241, 253; *Citibank NA* v. *MBIA Assurance SA* [2006] EWHC Civ 3215 (Ch), upheld [2007] EWCA Civ 11, [82]. Hayton, 'The Irreducible Core Content of Trusteeship', above, note 1; Wei, 'The Irreducible Core Content of Modern Trust Law', above, note 1.

[37] *Schmidt* v. *Rosewood Trust Ltd* [2003] UKPC 26, [2003] 2 AC 709.

[38] There are also other specific duties such as the duty to get in trust property, to act personally and not to delegate, to act impartially between beneficiaries, to act jointly with co-trustees, to name but a few. All of these duties can be classified under the broad duties of care, loyalty and compliance with the terms of the trust.

[39] In other words, a trust deed may contain a clause to permit a trustee who acted in good faith to keep secret profits. The precise scope of permissible exemption varies depending on jurisdiction, but it is hardly conceivable that a jurisdiction would allow a trustee to exempt liability for breaches committed dishonestly or in bad faith.

[40] *Saunders* v. *Vautier* (1841) 4 Beav 115; 41 ER 482, affd Cr & Ph 240; 49 ER 282.

absolutely entitled to the entire beneficial interest to terminate the trust fund unanimously, need not be an essential feature. The right of such beneficiaries to terminate the trust prematurely is not necessary for a trust to exist; it merely allows their wishes to override that of the settlor. Nor does its abolition undermine the commercial utility of the trust. Finally, as the end of this section will seek to explain, it is submitted that these duties are personal in nature, meaning that they are owed by and enforceable against the trustee only.

1. Honesty and good faith

The trust deal or undertaking is that the trustee holds the assets for the beneficiary. To give substance to this deal, the trustee's most fundamental duty is, if he decides to exercise his powers, to do so for the best interest of the beneficiary, and not for his own benefit. This is but a broad statement about the duty, and needs to be refined in two aspects: the state of mind required in discharging this duty and the precise content of the duty.

Firstly, as to the state of mind required, it is clear that the duty is not strict. This is because the content of the trust undertaking is not to achieve a particular *result*, such as the presence of beneficial consequences from the exercise of the trustee's powers. It is an undertaking as to the *purpose or motivation* of one's action, namely acting *with the intention to* benefit the beneficiary.[41] Thus far, the bone of contention is whether it is only a duty to act honestly and in good faith for the best interest of the beneficiary, or whether it extends beyond that, to whether the trustee must also take a requisite degree of care.

The debate takes place in the context of the permissible scope of exemption clauses, namely whether liability for all losses except those arising from actual fraud can be excluded, or whether the non-excludable clauses also include liability arising from gross negligence.[42] In English law, this was settled in *Armitage* v. *Nurse* in favour of the former, and actual fraud is defined as acting with an intention 'to pursue a particular course of action, either knowing that it is contrary to the interests of the beneficiaries or being recklessly indifferent whether it is contrary to their interests or not'.[43] Millett LJ (as he then was) considered that the relevant essential obligation is the duty to act honestly and in what the trustee

[41] L. Smith, 'The Motive, Not the Deed', in J. Getzler (ed.), *Rationalizing Property, Equity and Trusts: Essays in Honour of Edward Burn* (London: Butterworths, 2003), p. 53.

[42] P. Matthews, 'The Efficacy of Trustee Exemption Clauses in English Law' (1989) Conv. 42.

[43] *Armitage*, above, note 36, 253.

considers in good faith to be to the benefit of the beneficiaries.[44] The Uniform Trust Code (of the United States) takes the same position. Section 1008 renders unenforceable exculpation clauses that seek to relieve liability for 'bad faith or . . . reckless indifference to the purpose of the trust or the interests of the beneficiaries'.[45] However, the *Restatement (Third) of Trusts* suggests, additionally, that the trustee should still owe a minimal degree of care.[46]

It is submitted that the duty of honesty and good faith is both necessary and sufficient for a trust to arise. It is necessary because the very concept of a trust is to manage property for the benefit of the beneficiary. A trust that does not require the trustee to manage trust assets in what he considers, in good faith, to be the best interest of the beneficiary is self-contradictory, and hence not a trust.[47] It is also sufficient because if the trustee acts with the bona fide intention to benefit the beneficiary, he will have done the minimum necessary to comply with his trust undertaking. Of course, even when the essential requirements of a trust are met, there may be extraneous considerations of policy for imposing a higher standard of care on the trustee. The law of a particular jurisdiction can still choose to disallow exclusion of these more stringent duties, but this would be due to policy reasons rather than the essential requirements for a trust to exist.

Secondly, as to the content of the duty, Millett LJ refers to it as one to act 'for the benefit of the beneficiaries'. His Lordship did not further require that the trustee act for the *best interest* of the beneficiaries. At first glance, it may appear that Millett LJ's formulation is sufficient, as the trustee is indeed intentionally seeking the benefit of the beneficiaries. However, the concept of benefit is problematic for two reasons. First, it can include benefits that are practicably negligible. Secondly, where, say, two alternative investments require equal effort on the part of the trustee,

[44] Ibid., 253–4.

[45] See also UTC, s. 105(b)(2). Section 801 of the Code requires the trustee to 'administer the trust in good faith, in accordance with its terms and purposes and the interests of the beneficiaries'.

[46] *Restatement (Third)*, above, note 2, s. 77(2) Comment d.

[47] See the debate between Langbein and Cooper on whether settlors are allowed to exempt this duty or even prescribe an investment practice that is harmful to the interest of the beneficiaries: J. H. Langbein, 'Burn the Rembrandt? Trust Law's Limits on the Settlor's Power to Direct Investments' (2010) 90 B.U.L.Rev. 375; J. A. Cooper, 'Empty Promises: Settlor's Intent, the Uniform Trust Code, and the Future of Trust Investment Law' (2008) 88 B.U.L.Rev. 1165; J. H. Langbein, 'Mandatory Rules in the Law of Trusts' (2004) 98 Nw. U.L.Rev. 1105.

but one can produce more substantial benefits than the other, which can still produce some benefits, the less stringent formulation means that the trustee can choose the latter investment with impunity. Put another way, a duty only to act with the intention to benefit the beneficiary is consistent with an intention to forego opportunities to obtain more benefits, even if the latter do not involve any more effort on the part of the trustee. It is bizarre to allow a trustee to take such an approach in managing the trust. In any event, one could also say that such a situation is not for the benefit of the beneficiaries, because they are worse off than they would have been for the same cost. Given these considerations, and the difficulty of defining what 'better' – as opposed to any – benefits means, the duty is best formulated as one to seek the 'best interest' of the beneficiary.

It might also be said that to accommodate usage of the trust in modern commerce, the trustee's essential duty is merely to exercise his powers *not* for his own benefit.[48] At first glance, the decision of the English Court of Appeal in *Citibank NA* v. *MBIA Assurance SA*[49] seems to support such a view. In *Citibank*, Arden LJ considered a securitization trust arrangement whereby the trustee was bound by a negative pledge clause to follow the directions of the monoline insurer in exercising the power to dispose of trust assets,[50] and the trust deed further precluded the trustee from taking the interest of the beneficiaries into account in following such directions. Her Ladyship opined, *obiter*, that such an arrangement was not repugnant to the irreducible core obligation of the trustee, because the trustee was still subject to a duty of good faith, and that the trustee still retained some discretion in relation to other matters.[51]

It is submitted that the *Citibank* decision does not undermine the existence of the trustee's essential duty to act in the best interest of the beneficiary. First, *Citibank* involved a constraint on the trustee's power to not dispose of the trust assets without the consent of the monoline insurer. The trustee still owed other essential duties towards the beneficiaries, such as those to account for the trust assets and to provide

[48] B. McFarlane, *The Structure of Property Law* (Oxford / Portland, Oregon: Hart Publishing, 2008), pp. 551 ff.

[49] *Citibank*, above, note 36.

[50] The negative pledge clause prohibits the trustee from, inter alia, disposing the charged trust assets without obtaining the consent of the insurer. The trust deed further provides that in following the instructions of the insurer, the trustee is 'not required to have regard to the interests of the [beneficiaries]' (*Citibank*, above, note 36, [54]).

[51] *Citibank*, above, note 36, [82].

information, and must still act in good faith for the best interest of the beneficiaries in relation to these duties as well as other aspects of its powers.[52] Secondly, since the constraint enabled the monoline insurer to preserve and enforce its security, it was an important factor in obtaining its agreement to guarantee the bonds and accordingly the setting up of the securitization. In this light, the constraint ultimately, albeit indirectly, benefited the note-holders.

Taking all these considerations into account, it is submitted that the essential duty of the trustee should be to act in what he considers in good faith to be the best interest of the beneficiary. This is in fact the duty of loyalty in its broadest and most general sense.[53] Although the duty of loyalty is often seen as comprising specific prohibitions that can be breached even if the trustee acted in good faith, such as the no-conflict rules and the self-dealing and fair-dealing rules, it is submitted that these rules merely give practical import to the fundamental fiduciary duty to act in what the trustee considers in good faith to be the best interest of the beneficiary. While the settlor or beneficiary may release the trustee from these specific rules, the fundamental fiduciary duty that justifies them is essential to a conceptually coherent trust, and cannot be excluded.

2. Duty to keep accurate financial records and provide information

Having identified the fundamental fiduciary duty of the trustee, a rule is needed to identify the subject matter to which his duty applies. Such a rule crucially distinguishes the evolving body of trust assets from the trustee's own assets throughout the life of the trust. Accordingly, the trustee should owe an essential duty to segregate the trust assets by maintaining a separate financial record of the trust assets.[54]

As a practical matter, if there is not even a beneficiary in the trust who has information about the financial records of the trust, there is no one

[52] For a contrary view, see A. Trukhtanov, 'The Irreducible Core of Trust Obligations' (2007) 123 L.Q.R. 342.

[53] Or, it may be put as the duty of good faith. See Langbein, 'Mandatory Rules in the Law of Trusts', above, note 47; J. H. Langbein, 'Questioning the Trust Law Duty of Loyalty: Sole Interest or Best Interest?' (2005) 114 Yale L.J. 929; Companies Act 2006 (UK), ss. 172, 175; R. Nolan and M. Conaglen, 'Good Faith: What Does It Mean for Fiduciaries and What Does It Tell Us About Them?', in E. Bant and M. Harding (eds.), *Exploring Private Law* (Cambridge University Press, 2010), p. 319.

[54] *Re Skinner* [1904] 1 Ch 289. In English law, the duty is often expressed in the language of a duty to keep accounts.

who can find out whether the trustee has breached trust obligations and enforce them accordingly.[55] The duty to provide reports of these financial records to the beneficiary should therefore also be essential. By extension of the same logic, for every part of the trust fund, there must at least be a beneficiary who knows that he is a beneficiary and is aware of the general nature of his rights under the right, or else there is no one to enforce the trustee's obligations in relation to all of the segregated trust assets.[56]

3. Rights *in personam*

For each essential duty of the trustee, there is a correlative right. They are the correlative rights that the trustee act in what he considers, in good faith, to be the best interest of the beneficiaries, keep accurate account of the trust property, and provide a minimum level of information. In allocating these rights to the beneficiary and powers of control over the trust assets to the trustee, a check and balance mechanism is created. The trustee has at least *in jure*,[57] if not also de facto powers to manage the property independently; at the same time, his powers are checked by rights to ensure that he does so in a good faith belief as to the best interest of the beneficiary.

In general, these essential rights are held by the beneficiary. However, there is no reason why some of these rights, such as the right to obtain information, cannot be held by, say, the settlor or the protector, whether jointly with the beneficiary or independently. Such an arrangement has the advantage of having an additional party to help monitor the trustee, without him having to expend the time and effort to act as a co-trustee.[58] Since the fundamental purpose of the trust is to seek the best interest of the beneficiary, these parties should also in turn exercise their rights in the best interest of the beneficiary.

These are also primary rights, which, if infringed, give rise to secondary rights such as the right that the trustee disgorge profits obtained from

[55] UTC, s. 402(a)(4); *Restatement (Third) of Trusts* (Philadelphia: American Law Institute, 2003), s. 2; *Armitage*, above, note 36, 253, Millett LJ remarking that, 'If the beneficiaries have no rights enforceable against the trustee there are no trusts.'

[56] See, for example, UTC, s. 105(b)(8) and (9); D. Hayton, P. Matthews and C. Mitchell, *Underhill and Hayton: Law of Trusts and Trustees*, 17th edn (London: LexisNexis Butterworths, 2006), p. 822; J. Mowbray et al., *Lewin on Trusts*, 18th edn (London: Thomson Sweet & Maxwell, 2008), p. 789.

[57] In a bare trust where the trustee is required to follow the intructions of the beneficiaries from time to time, he has *in jure* but not de facto control over the trust assets.

[58] R. H. Sitkoff, 'An Agency Costs Theory of Trust Law' (2004) 89 Cornell L. Rev. 621.

the breach, the right that he restore the trust property *in specie* or in value, and the right to adopt or annul a transaction in breach. Significantly, these secondary rights are *in personam* and only exigible against the trustee; they do not give the claimant any priority in payment in the event of the trustee's bankruptcy. The claimant will just rank *pari passu* with the other unsecured creditors.

III Conclusion

The trust has been recognized in English law for a few centuries. It is not until the past two decades that debate about its essential features has emerged. This is due in part to heightened interest in the reception of the trust in civil law jurisdictions, and hence the need to question the minimum steps needed to fit this new species into their existing private law frameworks. It is due, in another part, to the progressive approach of offshore practice in innovating new forms of trusts to meet client needs.

Thus far, discussion on the essential features of the trust has focused on the irreducible core. This chapter seeks to achieve two tasks: first, it distinguishes essential features that are necessary for a trust to exist from those that are most important for an effective and useful trust and are widely accepted in trust jurisdictions, and also between essential and merely paradigmatic features. It then seeks to formulate, in basic terms, the rights and duties necessary to put the essential features in place. Secondly, it argues that all of the essential features of a private express trust can be accommodated by creating personal rights and duties. It is hoped that such an approach would help demystify the view that the ring-fencing of trust assets can only be achieved in civil law jurisdictions by granting the beneficiary proprietary rights in relation to the trust assets.

2

The civil law trust: a modality of ownership or an interlude in ownership?

YAËLL EMERICH

How can the trust drawn from the common law take shape within a civilian context? Fiduciary ownership is not unthinkable within a civilian context. It may be considered as purposive ownership or, to be more precise, as a modality of ownership. Quebec's legislator, imagining the *fiducie* as a patrimony by appropriation, has impressed this purposive character within the very heart of the concept of patrimony, which emerges as a renewed concept. However, the question arises of discerning the extent to which Quebec's *fiducie* has severed all ties to ownership, and of the theoretical limits and challenges presented by a conception of this kind. Who is this 'other' whose property is administered by the trustee? From whom does one acquire property when it has been held in a *fiducie*? Should Quebec's *fiducie* be analysed as a modality of ownership or as an interlude in ownership?

I Introduction

The *fiducie*[1] was present within Roman law,[2] then gradually disappeared from most civilian systems, at least as a nominate institution.[3] However,

I thank Professor Lionel Smith for his invitation to the Worlds of the Trust conference where this paper was presented, and Ms Régine Tremblay for her help as research assistant. I also acknowledge the financial support of the Social Sciences and Humanities Research Council of Canada, which enabled me to participate in the conference and to produce this chapter.

[1] For the use of the word *fiducie*, see the 'Note on Translation', in this volume, p. xiv.

[2] Roman law recognized both the *fiducia cum creditore* (*fiducie* employed as security) and the *fiducia cum amico* (*fiducie* for administration). See, in particular, R. Monier, *Manuel élémentaire de droit romain*, 6th edn, 2 vols. (Paris: Montchrétien, 1947), vol. II, p. 120; J. Gaudemet, *Droit privé romain*, 2nd edn (Paris: Montchrétien, 2000), p. 268. The Roman *fiducie*, conceived in an era when the transfer of possession entailed a transfer of ownership, has been described as the 'ancestor of the institutions of deposit and pledge': F. Zenati-Castaing and T. Revet, *Les biens*, 3rd edn, coll. Droit fondamental (Paris: Presses Universitaires de France, 2008), p. 404, para. 252.

[3] L. Baudouin, *Le droit civil de la province de Québec: Modèle vivant de droit comparé* (Montréal: Wilson et Lafleur, 1953), p. 1244.

recent decades have given a new vitality to this mechanism in several countries with civilian or mixed legal traditions.[4] All the same, this renaissance of the civilian *fiducie* often draws inspiration less from the Roman *fiducie* than from the trust of the common law[5] – a situation which necessarily implies a certain degree of adjustment. While the common law trust is based on the division of ownership between the trustee and the beneficiary – the former having ownership in law, the latter having ownership in equity – fear of a split in the conception of ownership has often had the result of blocking the use of *fiducies* and, more specifically, fiduciary ownership in civil law.

The notion of ownership associated with the *fiducie* has often been met with condemnation in the civil law; some see it as a debased form of ownership, since fiduciary ownership would be limited in its duration and in its extent. However, it seems that several theoretical frameworks can be considered in order to understand and translate the *fiducie* within a civilian context, as can be shown through the examples of France and Quebec.

The first objective of the present chapter is to show that fiduciary ownership is a possibility within the civil law, both from the perspective of theory and that of practice. Fiduciary ownership is not unthinkable within a Romano-Germanic system. The French *fiducie*, which has recently appeared in the *Code Napoléon* as a nominate institution as a result of the enactment of the Law of 19 February 2007, seems to stand as an example within statutory law of just this sort of recognition. This fiduciary ownership, in which some have seen ownership with a charge, can be considered to rather be a modality of ownership; in other words, a particular mode of existence of ownership.

[4] For example, in Louisiana (first law on the *fiducie* in 1920 and Louisiana Trust Code of 1964, incorporated into arts. 1721ff of the Civil Code), in Japan (legislation of 1922), in Mexico (legislation of 1924); and, following the ratification of the Hague Convention of 1 July 1985 on the Law Applicable to Trusts and on their Recognition, in Switzerland (arts. 149a to 149d of the Federal Law on Private International Law), or in Luxembourg (Law of 27 July 2003 respecting *Fiducie* and *Fiducie* Contracts). However, this study is limited to the examples presented by the *fiducies* of France and Quebec.

[5] Zenati-Castaing and Revet, *Les biens*, above, note 2, p. 405, para. 252. On the links between France's *fiducie* and the trust see, in particular, C. Larroumet, 'La fiducie inspirée du trust' (1990) 1 *Dalloz* 119, 120, para. 4. On the links between Quebec's *fiducie* and the trust see, in particular, Office de révision du Code civil, Comité du droit de la fiducie, *Rapport sur la fiducie* (Montréal: Office de révision du Code civil, 1976), p. 2. See also, for a more nuanced approach to this question: M. Cantin Cumyn, 'La fiducie en droit québécois dans une perspective nord-américaine', in J. Herbots and D. Phillippe (eds.), *Le trust et la fiducie: implications pratiques* (Brussels: Bruylant, 1997), p. 74, para. 7.

As its second objective, this chapter explores the degree to which a *fiducie* detached from ownership is relevant. The Civil Code of Québec presents the *fiducie* as a patrimony by appropriation[6] in which none of the associated legal actors has a real right. However, this raises the question of discerning the extent to which Quebec's legislator completely severed *fiducie* from ownership through the optics of the patrimony by appropriation. Indeed, this sort of conception does not present itself without raising serious theoretical problems. Can it really be thought that the property transferred into a *fiducie* no longer has an owner? If this is indeed the case, from whom does one acquire property that was within a *fiducie*, and who is this other person whose property is administered by the trustee? While not attempting to resolve completely the contradictions posed by a *fiducie* severed from ownership, I will at least try to raise some questions tied to the potential break from ownership that Quebec's *fiducie* brings.

Thus, two solutions to the issue of adjusting the *fiducie* to the environment of a civilian system will be investigated here: on the one hand, that of analysing the *fiducie* in terms of fiduciary ownership, a straightforward modality of ownership (Section II), and, on the other hand, that of seeing the *fiducie* as an interlude in ownership or, in other words, the *fiducie* as bracketing ownership or providing an interval to it (Section III).

II *Fiducie* as a modality of ownership

The possibility of a fiduciary ownership in civil law from the point of view of theory will be proposed, as this theoretical possibility, which certainly resonated in the Civil Code of Lower Canada, henceforth finds a concrete illustration in the current law in France.

A. *The theoretical possibility of fiduciary ownership in civil law*

Fiduciary ownership can be analysed as an instance where the outlines of ownership have been redesigned. Fiduciary ownership is an ownership that has received a specific alignment towards a purpose. As Professors Zenati-Castaing and Revet write, 'ownership is fiduciary where a person becomes the owner in order to carry out a task, at the close of which the thing is transferred back to the legal actor who had

[6] A patrimony dedicated to a purpose (the corresponding French term is '*patrimoine d'affectation*').

made the initial alienation or to a third party designated by the latter' (our translation).[7] Yet, as has been rightly emphasized, 'the explanation, for the particular characteristics of the right of ownership, is the technical function that the right fulfils without calling into question its essence'.[8] Granted, the trustee is not free to act without any restriction, since he must carry out acts in line with the purpose of the *fiducie*; that is to say, the purpose fixed by the settlor.[9] However, ownership is far from being the perfectly absolute right that the civilian jurist is often tempted to describe; the legislator can, according to the very definition of property, set 'limits' on this right and set 'conditions' with respect to its use.[10]

Fiduciary ownership is not a source of wealth for the trustee, since he must act in the interest of a third person, the beneficiary, rather than in his own interest.[11] According to several authors, this justifies seeing in the institution of the *fiducie* only the presence of legal powers,[12] and not a subjective right[13] of ownership. Still, it remains uncertain whether subjective rights in general, and ownership in particular, must necessarily be exercised in one's own interest. In

[7] Translation of '[l]a propriété est fiduciaire lorsqu'une personne devient propriétaire afin d'exécuter une mission, à l'issue de laquelle la chose est rétrocédée à l'aliénateur initial ou à un tiers par lui désigné', Zenati-Castaing and Revet, *Les biens*, above, note 2, p. 404, para. 252.

[8] Translation of '[l]es spécificités du droit de propriété s'expliquent par la fonction technique qu'elle remplit sans remettre en cause son essence', B. Kan-Balivet, 'Les clés du contrat de fiducie-gestion' (2009) 185 *Droit et patrimoine* 70, 75. See also, with respect to ownership-for-administration, B. Kan-Balivet, *Les techniques de gestion des biens d'autrui*, Thesis in Private Law (University of Lyon, 2004), p. 172.

[9] On this idea: P. Marini, 'Enfin la fiducie à la française' (2007) 20 *Dalloz* 1346, 1347.

[10] Civil Code of Québec, art. 947 (C.C.Q.) and France's Civil Code art. 544 (C.C.). On this point see, in particular, P. de Vareilles-Sommières, 'La définition et la notion juridique de la propriété' (1905) 4 *Revue trimestrielle de droit civil* 444, 477–8; R. A. Macdonald, 'Reconceiving the Symbols of Property: Universalities, Interests and Other Heresies' (1994) 39 *McGill Law Journal* 761; G. Goldstein, 'La relativité du droit de propriété: enjeux et valeurs d'un Code civil moderne' (1990) 24 *Revue juridique Themis* 507.

[11] M. Grimaldi, 'La fiducie: réflexions sur l'institution et sur l'avant-projet de loi qui la consacre' (1991) 12 *Défrenois* 897, 913. See also on this point M. Cantin Cumyn, 'La propriété fiduciaire, mythe ou réalité?' (1984) 15 *Revue de droit de l'Université de Sherbrooke* 7, 13.

[12] On the notion of powers: E. Gaillard, *Le pouvoir en droit privé* (Paris: Economica, 1985), pp. 232–3; M. Cantin Cumyn, *L'administration du bien d'autrui* (Cowansville: Les Éditions Yvon Blais, 2000), p. 76, para. 91; M. Cantin Cumyn 'Le pouvoir juridique' (2007) 52 *McGill Law Journal* 225.

[13] A patrimonial or extra-patrimonial right. Subjective rights are contrasted with objective rights, the rules of State law which must be obeyed.

addition, the notion of a power has not achieved complete independence in relation to the concept of '*droit subjectif*'.[14]

No doubt, fiduciary ownership is temporary.[15] However, civilian scholarship has already demonstrated that perpetuity is not an essential feature of ownership.[16] The law in no way requires ownership to be perpetual; types of temporary ownership, for instance in the realm of intellectual property, have already been recognized.[17] Moreover, an idea has been put forward according to which it is only a modality of ownership or particular manner of existence for ownership, namely fiduciary ownership, that comes to an end when fiduciary ownership is extinguished, and not the ownership itself.[18]

Civil law ownership is truly a flexible institution and it is perfectly capable of adapting to the sorts of changes that follow from fiduciary ownership. As a type of ownership, fiduciary ownership is distinctive, since the trustee-owner comes under certain limits with respect to his powers over the thing. Nevertheless, the traditional attributes of

[14] The definition of a *droit subjectif* remains sufficiently broad that the notion of power can be encompassed by it; moreover, the notion of a power is commonly associated with that of a *droit subjectif*. See, e.g., G. Cornu, *Vocabulaire juridique*, 7th edn (Paris: Presses Universitaires de France, 2005), *s.v.* 'droit subjectif': 'individual prerogative recognized and protected by the law, this prerogative permits its holder to do, require or forbid something *in his own interest or, sometimes, in the interest of another*' (emphasis added). See also F. K. Savigny, *Traité de droit romain*, C. Guénoux (trans.), 8 vols. (Paris: Didot, 1851), p. 7, para. 4; R. Saleilles, *De la personnalité juridique: histoires et théories; 25 leçons d'introduction à un cours de droit civil comparé sur les personnes juridiques*, 2nd edn, 8 vols. (Paris: A. Rousseau, 1922), vol. I, pp. 547–8. See also, with respect to criticism of the employment of the notion of a power as a complete explanation of the trustee's situation, F. Barrière, *La réception du trust au travers de la fiducie*, coll. Bibliothèque de droit de l'entreprise (Paris: Litec, 2004), pp. 326–7.

[15] The duration of fiduciary ownership was increased from 33 to 99 years, following an amendment to the legislation on the *fiducie* which is now codified in art. 2019-2 C. civ. On this point, see in particular *Encyclopédie juridique Dalloz: Répertoire de droit civil*, 3rd edn, 'Fiducie' by F. Barrière, para. 56.

[16] C. Pourquier, *Propriété et perpétuité: Essai sur la durée du droit de propriété* (Aix-en-Provence: Presses Universitaires d'Aix-Marseille, 2000), p. 249, para. 294. See also C. Atias, *Droit civil: Les biens*, 6th edn (Paris: Litec, 2002), p. 111, para. 76.

[17] In French civil law, the intellectual property rights with respect to literary and artistic creations expire fifty years after the death of the author (even if the author's moral rights are perpetual): *Code de la propriété intellectuelle*, art. L. 121-1, para. 3. See also, on the temporary nature of patent rights, art. L. 611-2 C.P.I. Moreover, just as an item of property can be abandoned by its owner, parties to a contract can very well provide that the ownership under the contract will have a limited duration.

[18] F. Frenette, 'La propriété fiduciaire' (1985) 26 *Cahiers de droit* 727, 736. On this modality, see Section III.B below.

ownership, namely *usus*, *fructus* and *abusus*, can be found within fiduciary ownership, since the trustee has in principle all the powers over the property which is held in *fiducie*.[19]

The simple fact that the rights regarding the enjoyment, disposition and use of the trust property would be limited by the purpose of the *fiducie* does not negate the potential of the presence of these traditional attributes of ownership. Moreover, these limits are entirely compatible with the very definition of ownership, which does permit restrictions on the rights of the owner.[20] Indeed, ownership is less the actual exercise of all the prerogatives conferred by ownership than it is the status that would empower the owner to exercise them. Finally, the mark of ownership, namely exclusivity,[21] can also be seen to be present in fiduciary ownership, since the trustee may exercise his powers over the trust property without the assistance or consent of anyone else.[22]

B. The recognition of fiduciary ownership in the realm of practice: the example of France's civil law

After the failure of several bills to gain enactment,[23] France's Civil Code now includes a new title, a part of the code called *De la fiducie* introduced

[19] For example, art. 1265 C.C.Q., and above all art. 1278 C.C.Q. according to which the trustee 'has the control and exclusive administration of the trust patrimony [. . . and] the exercise of all the rights pertaining to the patrimony'. See also art. 2023 C.C.: 'In relation to third-parties, the trustee is deemed to have the broadest powers over the *fiducie* patrimony.' According to one interpretation, the trustee is deprived of the *fructus*. One can nevertheless maintain that since it is the trustee who collects the fruits, he has the right to them, even if the trustee does not have the enjoyment of them because 'the sole end for which he may use his prerogatives is to realize the purpose of the fiducie': F. Barrière, 'Commentaire de la loi n° 2007–211 du 19 février 2007 (deuxième partie)' (2007) 144 *Bulletin Joly Sociétés* 556.

[20] For scholarship that has already taken this position see Frenette, 'La propriété fiduciaire', above, note 18, 736; Vareilles-Sommières, 'La définition', above, note 10, 477–8.

[21] See, in particular, F. Zenati, *Essai sur la nature juridique de la propriété: Contribution à la théorie du droit subjectif*, Thesis in Law (University of Lyon, 1981), p. 543, para. 400; Y. Emerich, 'Propriété, relation et exclusivité: étude de droit comparé' (2009) 4 *Revue de la recherche juridique* 1841, 1848.

[22] See on this point Grimaldi, 'La fiducie', above, note 11, 916; F. Barrière, 'Commentaire de la loi n° 2007–211 du 19 février 2007 (première partie)' (2007) 119 *Bulletin Joly Sociétés* 440. See also, for comparison, art. 1278 C.C.Q.: 'A trustee has the control and *exclusive* administration of the trust patrimony' (my italics).

[23] See X. Delpech, 'Enfin une loi sur la fiducie!' (2007) 9 *Dalloz* 566, 566. However, innominate *fiducies* were recognized in French law prior to the enactment of Law no. 2007–211 of 19 February 2007 introducing the *fiducie*; these innominate *fiducies* were

in Book III, which in turn concerns the 'Different Ways by which the Right of Ownership is Acquired'.[24] Article 2011 of this Code defines *fiducie* as '*the arrangement by which one or more settlors transfer property*, rights or guarantees for the performance of an obligation, or an assemblage of property, rights or guarantees, present or future, *to one or more trustees* who, holding them *separate from their own patrimony*, act for a *determinate purpose* in favour of one or more *beneficiaries*' (my translation and italics).[25]

The concept of a patrimony by appropriation receives just an oblique reference in the French Civil Code by means of the trust patrimony.[26] Indeed, the French *fiducie* does not involve a genuinely autonomous patrimony, since the *fiducie* patrimony is not completely separated either from the personal patrimony of the trustee or the personal patrimony of the settlor. Accordingly, the second paragraph of article 2025 of the French Civil Code provides that where the *fiducie* patrimony is insufficient, the creditors of the *fiducie* can seek payment of their claim from the patrimony of the settlor. Moreover, the parties can establish by stipulation that the common pledge of the creditors of the *fiducie* will be limited to the patrimony of the trustee.[27] In that case, we would be in the presence of a form of division with respect to patrimony, creating a sub-patrimony within the trustee's personal patrimony rather than an actual patrimony by appropriation, totally severed from the personal patrimony of the trustee.

Questions have been asked about the legal character of the transfer of property into *fiducie*.[28] In particular, one question is whether or not the

with respect to, in particular, securitization (Code monétaire et financier, art. L. 214–43 s.) or assignments of claims deployed as security (ibid., art. L. 313–23 s.). See also C. Witz, *La fiducie en droit privé français* (Paris: Economica, 1981), p. 41.

[24] Law no. 2007–211 of 19 February 2007, introducing the *fiducie*, was amended by Law no. 2008–776 of 4 August 2008 on the modernization of the economy (the LME) as completed by ordinance no. 2009–112 of 30 January 2009. The 2008 law opened *fiducie* to natural persons and increased its maximum duration to 99 years.

[25] Three principal elements can be drawn from this definition: (1) *fiducie* is an arrangement by which a settlor transfers property to a trustee; (2) the trustee holds this property apart from his own patrimony; (3) the trustee acts for a determinate purpose in favour of a beneficiary.

[26] On the patrimony by appropriation, see Section III.A below.

[27] Art. 2025 para. 2 C.C.: 'Where the trust patrimony is insufficient, the patrimony of the *settlor* becomes the common pledge for these creditors, in the absence of stipulation in the fiduciary contract making the *trustee* bear all or part of these liabilities' (emphasis added).

[28] On this question see, in particular, R. Libchaber, 'Les aspects civils de la fiducie dans la loi du 19 février 2007 (2e partie)', (2007) 19 *Répertoire du Notariat Defrénois* 1194; P. Malaurie and L. Aynès, *Les biens*, 3rd edn (Paris: Defrénois, 2007), para. 757. For a

settlor merely 'puts the property into the care of' the trustee. However, the most plausible solution is to admit, in line with the classic analysis of a transfer of property,[29] that the transfer towards a *fiducie* brings about a transfer of the ownership of the property, which in both cases makes the trustee a type of owner. Moreover, this is the position of Senator Philippe Marini, the initiator of the bill respecting the *fiducie*.[30]

Some authors have seen this as a perversion of the concept of ownership,[31] particularly due to the fact that an ownership of this type is not deployed in the interest of the trustee. However, it is possible to see in it an ownership whose outlines have been redesigned, the rights of the trustee being exercised 'in a fiduciary fashion, namely in the interest of another'.[32] A substantial portion of civilian scholarship no longer has qualms about recognizing the existence of fiduciary ownership in French civil law;[33] in particular, the idea of a type of ownership 'with a charge' has come up.[34]

similar reflection within Quebec's civil law: Y. Caron, 'The Trust in Quebec' (1980) 25 *McGill Law Journal* 421, 425. And see also, for a comparison between the situation in France (transfer of right of ownership to the trustee) and Quebec (absence of real right): J.-P. Dunand, *Le transfert fiduciaire: 'donner pour reprendre' mancipio dare ut remancipetur – analyse historique et comparatiste de la fiducie-gestion*, coll. Genevoise: grands textes (Basle: Helbing & Lichtenhahn, 2000), p. 384.

29 See, in particular, H. Mazeaud et al., *Leçons de droit civil: Les Biens*, 8th edn, 4 vols. (Paris: Montchrestien, 1994), vol. 2, book II: *Biens, droit de propriété et ses démembrements*, p. 103, para. 1348.

30 According to P. Marini, 'La fiducie: enfin!' (2007) 36 *La Semaine Juridique – Entreprise et Affaires* 2050, paras. 3 and 4, the *fiducie* is a 'contract transferring ownership'; however, this 'transfer in full ownership' is 'limited, two times over, in duration and content'.

31 See P. Decheix, 'La fiducie ou du sens des mots' (1997) 35 *Dalloz* 36.

32 Translation of 'de manière fiduciaire, c'est-à-dire dans l'intérêt d'autrui', G. Blanluet and J.-P. LeGall, 'La fiducie, une œuvre inachevée' (2007) 26 *Droit fiscal* 676.

33 Senator Philippe Marini, the initiator of the bill on the *fiducie*, has himself described the *fiducie* as translative of ownership. Marini, 'Enfin la fiducie à la française', above, note 9, 1347. See also Barrière, 'Commentaire (2e partie)', above, note 19, 556; Malaurie and Aynès, *Les biens*, above, note 28, pp. 243ff; Grimaldi, 'La fiducie', above, note 11, 916. With respect to the links between classical ownership and fiduciary ownership, see M. Grimaldi and F. Barrière, 'La fiducie en droit français', in M. Cantin Cumyn (ed.), *La fiducie face au trust dans les rapports d'affaires* (Brussels: Bruyant, 1999), pp. 246ff.

34 With respect to the notion of ownership with a charge see P. Marini's report, Rapport au Sénat sur la proposition de loi sur la fiducie, para. 442 of 27 May 2009, article 6. See also A. Raynouard and F. Jourdain-Thomas, 'La fiducie, nouvel outil de gestion et de sûreté' (2010) 5 *Semaine Juridique Notariale et Immobilière* 1063, paras. 11–12. On the different expressions used to describe fiduciary ownership: B. Mallet-Bricout, 'Fiducie et propriété', in S. Bros and B. Mallet-Bricout (eds.), *Liber Amicorum Christian Larroumet* (Paris: Economica, 2010), pp. 297ff, paras. 21ff.

In order to account for France's *fiducie*, it can be useful to explore the notion of modalities of ownership. As Dean Jean Carbonnier emphasized, the modalities of the right of ownership 'are ways of being with which the right of ownership clothes itself; their result, in the final analysis, is always limits on the powers of the owner, yet without the right of ownership being dismembered, for all that'.[35] This learned author gave, as examples for these modalities of ownership, co-ownership and indivision, but also inalienable ownership and ownership that is subject to an appropriation – 'shaped by an appropriation'.[36] The fiduciary ownership put in place by the French legislation seems to fit perfectly within the mould of the concept of a modality, since it is a type of ownership that comes under an appropriation and is directed to a purpose.[37] It is indeed possible to find the traditional attributes of ownership within the fiduciary ownership of French law, since the trustee receives the right to make use of the property that comes within the *fiducie*, to collect the fruits of this property and to alienate them.[38]

However, a part of legal doctrine continues to have reservations regarding the employment of ownership as a characterization, which would account for *fiducie*. Thus, the idea has been mentioned that the trustee has limited powers and is less an absolute owner (sole master of his thing, and having free disposal of it) than an 'administrator', in the case of the management *fiducie*, or a 'custodian', in the case of a

35 J. Carbonnier, *Les biens: Droit civil*, 19th edn, 4 vols. (Paris: Presses Universitaires de France, 2000) vol. III: *Les Biens (monnaie, immeubles, meubles)*, p. 144, para. 78. See also S. Normand, 'La notion de modalité', in S. Normand (ed.), *Mélanges offerts au professeur François Frenette: Études portant sur le droit patrimonial* (Quebec: Presses de l'Université Laval, 2006), pp. 255ff.

36 Translation of 'modelée par une affectation', Carbonnier, ibid.

37 Barrière, 'Commentaire (2e partie)', above, note 19, para. 3; Y. Emerich, 'Les fondements conceptuels de la fiducie française face au trust de la common law: entre droit des contrats et droit des biens' (2009) 1 *Revue internationale de droit comparé* 49, 67. The notion of a modality of ownership had already been proposed by François Frenette to explain the ownership of the *fiducie* property in Quebec under the Civil Code of Lower Canada: Frenette, 'La propriété fiduciaire', above, note 18, 735–6. On the notion of modalities of ownership see, in particular, Normand, 'La notion de modalité', above, note 35, 255ff; Carbonnier, *Les biens*, above, note 35, p. 144, para. 78.

38 See art. 2023 C.C.; Barrière, 'Commentaire (1ère partie)', above, note 22, 555, para. 5 had already taken this position. See also Witz, *La fiducie*, above, note 23, p. 268, para. 276: 'The trustee is the only legal actor who is empowered to exercise all the attributes of ownership which pertain to the property which is to be administered or which has been appropriated as security, by virtue of her status as the owner of this property.'

security *fiducie*.[39] The issue has been raised whether exclusivity is present in fiduciary ownership, since the trustee can be shut out of his relationship with the property as a result of a decision made by the settlor or a beneficiary who is neither trustee nor settlor.[40]

These doubts, with respect to the deployment of the characterization of ownership – namely the notion of fiduciary ownership – can lead to the consideration of the hypothesis whereby the *fiducie* makes a free and clear break from the concept of ownership. Above all, the framework of Quebec's *fiducie*, as it is derived from the Civil Code of Québec, is not quite the same as the framework of France's *fiducie*, thus the issue of a severance of Quebec's *fiducie* from ownership arises there all the more pointedly. Would the *fiducie* thereby bring about a sort of interlude or bracketing in relation to ownership?

III The *fiducie* as interlude to ownership?

The Civil Code of Québec has made the *fiducie* a patrimony by appropriation detached from the notion of real rights, which raises the issue of knowing whether the civilian *fiducie* can sever all its ties to ownership.

A. The recognition of a patrimony by appropriation separated from the notion of a real right: the example of Quebec's civil law

Unlike its French counterpart, Quebec's *fiducie* has acknowledged the existence of a true patrimony by appropriation. It is however widely conceded that the concept of a patrimony by appropriation stands as an alternative to fiduciary ownership and as a protective wall against it, since fiduciary ownership would be a concept too heavily imprinted with the common law.[41] Above all, the *fiducie* of the Civil Code of Québec is

[39] See, in particular, B. Mallet-Bricout, 'Le fiduciaire propriétaire?' (2010) 8 *La Semaine Juridique – Entreprise et Affaires* 1193, para. 7; Mallet-Bricout, 'Fiducie et propriété', above, note 34, p. 304: 'the spirit that animates these dispositions is the opposite of the one which is recognized as animating art. 544 C.C.'.

[40] On this point see, in particular, Mallet-Bricout, 'Le fiduciaire propriétaire?', ibid., para. 8. However, it can be asked whether this is simply a case where that fiduciary ownership comes to an end, precisely by virtue of this setting aside of the exclusivity of powers over the thing.

[41] See on this point J. E. C. Brierley, 'Regards sur le droit des biens dans le nouveau Code civil du Québec' (1995) 47 *Revue internationale de droit comparé* 33, 45, para. 17; M. Cantin Cumyn, 'The Quebec Trust: A Civilian Institution with English Law

altogether detached from the notion of real rights, since by the very terms of article 1261, the *fiducie* patrimony is 'autonomous and distinct from that of the settlor, trustee or beneficiary and in which none of them has any real right'. This led Dean John Brierley to remark that the notion of real rights, with respect to the *fiducie* of the Civil Code of Québec, is simply 'obsolete'.[42] Lastly, the *fiducie* of the Civil Code of Québec refers to the rules on the administration of the property of another, which may well result in making the trustee merely an administrator of property.[43]

The patrimony by appropriation is an impersonal patrimony, detached from juridical personality. It owes its cohesion to the goal that has been impressed upon it.[44] This modern or objectivist conception of the patrimony, introduced by the German scholarly writers Brinz and Becker,[45] is a direct challenge to the nineteenth-century classical or subjectivist conception held by Aubry and Rau.[46] In the classical conception, patrimony denotes the 'aggregate composed of a person's property, considered as making up a legal universality'.[47] This conception saw the patrimony as inseparably tied to personhood in the eyes of the law and,

Roots', in J. M. Milo and J. M. Smits (eds.), *Trusts in Mixed Legal Systems* (Nijmegen: Ars Aequi Libri, 2001), p. 80.

42 Brierley, 'Regards sur le droit des biens', above, note 41, 42. Before the codification of 1994, the Civil Code of Lower Canada recognized a limited role for the management *fiducie*, in the context of liberalities, while the security *fiducie* was developed by employing the Special Corporate Powers Act (R.S.Q. 1977, c. P-16). The Civil Code of Québec expanded the domain of the *fiducie*, by providing a legal framework which structures personal *fiducies*, just as it does business *fiducies*, *fiducies* for other private purposes or *fiducies* for the public benefit: J. Beaulne, *Droit des fiducies* (Montreal: Wilson et Lafleur, 1998), p. 4, para. 7. On the security *fiducie* see, in particular, L. Payette, *Les sûretés réelles dans le Code civil du Québec*, 4th edn (Cowansville: Les Éditions Yvon Blais, 2010), pp. 944ff.

43 However, on the idea of an administrator-owner, and on the absence of incompatibility between the status of being an administrator and the status of being the owner of the property, rather than being an administrator and representative (although the latter pairing is the most common), see Kan-Balivet, *Techniques de gestion*, above, note 8, pp. 143ff.

44 See, in particular, Carbonnier, *Les biens*, above, note 35, p. 7, para. 4; P. Charbonneau, 'Les patrimoines d'affectation: vers un nouveau paradigme en droit québécois du patrimoine' (1983) 85 *Revue du Notariat* 491.

45 S. Ginchard, *Essai d'une théorie générale de l'affectation des biens en droit privé français*, Thesis in Law (University of Lyon 3, 1974), p. 1, para. 1.

46 F. Zenati, 'Mise en perspective et perspectives de la théorie du patrimoine' (2003) 4 *Revue trimestrielle de droit civil* 667. See also N. Kasirer, 'Translating Part of France's Legal Heritage: Aubry and Rau on the *patrimoine*' (2008) 38 *Revue générale de droit* 453.

47 C. Aubry, C. Rau and P. Esmein, *Cours de droit civil français*, 7th edn, 12 vols. (Paris: Librairies techniques, 1964), vol. II, p. 14.

as in the case of legal personhood, saw there to be one and only one patrimony per person, indivisible and inalienable.[48] By contrast to this conception, the patrimony by appropriation is comprised of two masses of property: a set of assets impressed with a purpose, and a set of liabilities that arise in the pursuit of this purpose.[49] Within this type of patrimony, the link between the property and obligations is no longer forged by their relation to a person, but rather by their common purpose.[50]

The patrimony put in place by Quebec's *fiducie* is a genuine patrimony by appropriation, according to the very terms of the Civil Code.[51] As Dean Sylvio Normand emphasizes, 'henceforth in Quebec law, an autonomous patrimony can accordingly be created without any person being able to claim to be at its head. This clashes with the subjectivist conception which shouted from the rooftops that the existence of a right of ownership over the property was absolutely necessary.'[52] According to the *Minister's Commentaries* on the Civil Code, Quebec's *fiducie* amounts to the recognition of a patrimony without a person at its head, since rights and property can henceforth be recognized in the absence of a person who would be their legal anchor. For all those reasons, the items of property which make up a trust patrimony are not things without an owner, 'since the trustee has control of the property and detention of it'.[53]

Moreover, the conception of a patrimony by appropriation that was taken up by the Civil Code of Québec has been considered by legal doctrine to differ from the European concept of patrimony by appropriation, seen as a de facto universality (in other words a mass of property without an associated set of liabilities). According to Professor Madeleine Cantin Cumyn, 'this way of conceiving of the patrimony by appropriation is the result of the preference in Europe

[48] For a critical perspective see A.-L. Thomat-Raynaud, *L'unité du patrimoine: essai critique* (Paris: Defrénois, 2007), pp. 16ff.

[49] Beaulne, *Fiducies*, above, note 42, p. 24.

[50] B. Roy, 'L'affectation des biens en droit québécois' (2001) 103 *Revue du Notariat* 383. See also T. Naudin, *La théorie du patrimoine à l'épreuve de la fiducie*, Master in Law (University of Caen Basse-Normandie, 2007), paras. 42 and 43.

[51] Art. 1261 C.C.Q.: 'The trust patrimony, consisting of the property transferred in trust, constitutes *a patrimony by appropriation*, autonomous and distinct from that of the settlor, trustee or beneficiary' (author's emphasis). See also, in particular, Brierley, 'Regards sur le droit des biens', above, note 41, 45ff.

[52] S. Normand, *Introduction au droit des biens* (Montreal: Wilson & Lafleur, 2000), p. 25. See also Québec, Ministère de la Justice, *Commentaires du Ministre de la Justice: Le Code civil du Quebec*, 3 vols. (Quebec: Les publications du Québec, 1993), vol. I, art. 1261 C.C.Q.

[53] Normand, ibid.

for a *fiducie* built on fiduciary ownership'.[54] This remark leads us to gauge the link between Quebec's *fiducie* and ownership.

When the Civil Code of Lower Canada was still in force, the Supreme Court in *Royal Trust* v. *Tucker*[55] explicitly recognized the existence of a type of fiduciary ownership, which it characterized as a '*sui generis* property right'. At the same time, some of the scholarly writers criticized this position. In their eyes, fiduciary ownership was in no way equivalent to what an owner is in the sense of the civil law. They even saw this position as the direct opposite of ownership[56] to such a degree that the notion of fiduciary ownership would have led to the distortion of the rules of the Civil Code.[57] From a theoretical point of view, this reaction seems too strong because it does not take into account the possibility of adapting civilian ownership, in particular by means of the notion of a modality of ownership.[58] The fact, however, remains that the conception of *fiducie* was markedly renewed in the Civil Code of Québec.

[54] M. Cantin Cumyn, 'Pourquoi définir la fiducie comme un patrimoine d'affectation?', in N. Kasirer (ed.), *Colloque du Trentenaire 1975–2005: regards croisés sur le droit privé* (Cowansville: Éditions Yvon Blais, 2008), p. 140 (notes omitted). See also E. Ravanas, 'Les difficultés d'introduction de la fiducie québécoise dans un pays de tradition civiliste connaissant l'institution de la réserve héréditaire' (2007) 109 *Revue du Notariat* 265, 283ff; M. Naccarato, 'La fiducie: réflexion sur la réception judiciaire d'un nouveau code' (2007) 48 *Cahiers de droit* 505, 510ff.

[55] See *Royal Trust Co.* v. *Tucker* [1982] 1 S.C.R. 250 and the conclusion of Beetz J. at p. 272: 'The [settlor] is no longer the owner of property conveyed in trust [. . .]. Ownership is not vested in the beneficiary of the income, who is only a creditor of the trustee. It also is not vested during the trust in the beneficiary of the capital: in a great many cases he ranks second or third and has not even been born or conceived. When the property held in trust is finally conveyed to him [. . .] the trust has terminated. That leaves only the trustee in whom ownership of the trust property can be vested. Clearly the right of ownership is not the traditional one, since, for example, it is temporary and includes no *fructus*. It is a *sui generis* property right.' For an analysis of the above see, in particular, M. McAuley and J. Talpis, 'The Quebec Trust in the Real World', in *Conférences sur le nouveau Code civil du Québec*, Actes des journées louisianaises de l'Institut canadien d'études juridiques supérieures (Cowansville: Les Éditions Yvon Blais, 1991), p. 58. See also J. E. C. Brierley, 'L'affaire "Tucker" sous les feux du droit comparé' (1984) 15 *Revue de droit de l'Université de Sherbrooke* 3.

[56] Cantin Cumyn, 'La propriété fiduciaire', above, note 11, 12. *Contra*: P.-B. Mignault, 'A propos de la fiducie' (1933–34) 12 *Revue du Barreau* 73, 76.

[57] Cantin Cumyn, 'La propriété fiduciaire', above, note 11, 13: 'it is not conceived, within civil law, that a person could be the holder of a real or personal right without this right presenting a pecuniary advantage for her and, by virtue of this, being an asset within her patrimony'.

[58] See Section II.A. above.

In present-day Quebec law, a majority of commentators agree that the *fiducie* has severed all ties to ownership.[59] The plain truth is that under the terms of article 1261 C.C.Q., none of the legal actors associated with the arrangement has a real right – this point is no doubt the most significant difference from France's *fiducie*. Several interpretations for this are possible and not all of them remove the tie to ownership.[60] Still, the majority opinion, both in the scholarship and in the decided cases, seems to see a Quebec *fiducie* that would henceforth be severed from ownership and real rights, by means of the concept of a patrimony by appropriation.[61]

Thus, the leading conception follows the theory which is set out in particular by Professor Madeleine Cantin Cumyn: it is no longer appropriate to reason in terms of *droits subjectifs* exercised in one's own interest (terms which bring in their train the division of patrimonial rights into real rights and personal rights); the reasoning must rather be in terms of powers of administration exercised in the interest of the beneficiaries.[62] Recently, the Quebec Court of Appeal seems to have taken up this view, in a decision rendered on 18 December 2009, with respect to a security *fiducie* which the court

[59] The *fiducie* created by the Civil Code of Québec seems to have avoided the connection to ownership: J. E. C. Brierley, 'De la fiducie', in Barreau du Québec and Chambre des notaires du Québec (eds.), *La réforme du Code civil* (Québec: Presses de l'Université Laval, 1993), para. 14. However, it is worth noting the location of *fiducie* within the Civil Code of Québec: the provisions which govern this institution are in Book 4, entitled 'Property', rather than in the next Book which concerns obligations.

[60] This may in particular mean that ownership is not a real right or at least not a real right as traditionally understood. See, on this point, Y. Emerich, *La propriété des créances: approche comparative* (Paris: Libraire générale de droit et de jurisprudence, 2007), pp. 298ff.

[61] Moreover, this was the view of the Civil Code Revision Office: Office de révision du Code civil, Comité du droit de la fiducie, *Rapport*, above, note 5, p. 4: 'If we analyse the fiducie in a civilian context, it is immediately apparent that *the rights that the trustee exercises with respect to the property placed in the fiducie are not those of an owner, even if he has all the powers of administration and alienation.* Neither can ownership of the property be in the hands of the beneficiary, who is rather in the situation of a creditor with respect to the *fiducie*. As for the settlor, it is essential that he rids himself of the property he puts under *fiducie*. *The report proposes that the things or rights put under fiducie be considered to make-up a patrimony which is separate from the patrimony of the trustee, who has exclusive administration over this separate patrimony*' (emphasis added).

[62] M. Cantin Cumyn, *Traité de droit civil: L'administration du bien d'autrui* (Cowansville: Éditions Yvon Blais, 2000), p. 4, para. 3: 'The administrator does not exercise a right, but rather a power over the property of another' (translation of '*L'administrateur n'exerce pas un droit, mais un pouvoir sur le bien d'autrui.*')

ordered be constituted, under article 591 C.C.Q., in the context of providing security for an obligation of support.[63]

Moreover, article 1278 C.C.Q. provides that the trustee 'acts as the administrator of the property of others charged with full administration', which is interpreted as a reference to Title 7 in Book 4 of the Code, dealing with the 'Administration of the Property of Others'.[64] According to the *Commentaries* of the Minister of Justice:

> *A trustee has the exclusive administration of the trust patrimony, and the titles relating to the property of which it is composed are drawn up in his name; he acts in all matters in accord with the act by which the* fiducie *was constituted and acts as an administrator of the property of others charged with full administration.* The reference to the rules on the administration of property of others has the effect, on the one hand, of conferring on the trustee the power to undertake all acts relating to the property which is under administration, in so far as he judges this necessary or useful in the interest of the *fiducie* or of the beneficiaries, and on the other hand has the effect of subjecting the trustee to a set of provisions intended to ensure his honesty and the quality of his administration.[65]

Even if it is taken for granted that the Civil Code of Québec has severed the ties between *fiducie* and ownership by means of the patrimony by appropriation and the reference excluding the notion of real rights, some questions remain open. This is especially due to the traditional link, in their essence, between the concept of patrimony and that of ownership.[66] According to the traditional view, the owner has a patrimony, in which

[63] *Droit de la famille – 093071*, 2009 QCCA 2460, para. 56, Kasirer JA: 'In Quebec law, the trustee has neither "legal ownership" of the trust property, [. . .], nor "sui generis ownership" [. . .]. This is important in imagining the limited character of the trustee's control over the trust assets where the potential for conflict is in the air. Instead of a proprietary entitlement, *the trustee has "powers" (pouvoirs) of administration to be exercised on behalf of the beneficiaries, as opposed to "legal rights" (droits subjectifs) to be exercised in his or her own interest*' (notes omitted and italics added).

[64] See also art. 1299 C.C.Q.: 'Any person who is charged with the administration of property or a patrimony that is not his own assumes the office of administrator of property of others.'

[65] Québec, Ministère de la Justice, *Commentaires*, above, note 52, p. 747 (emphasis added). See also F. Rainville, 'De l'administration du bien d'autrui', in *La réforme du Code civil*, 3 vols. (Quebec: Presses de l'Université Laval, 1993), vol. 1, p. 785: 'The full administration of the property of another presupposes that the administrator is able to exercise over the property all the rights and powers that a natural person, who is not under any incapacity, would *over his own property*' (emphasis added).

[66] See, in particular, M. Fabre-Magnan, 'Propriété, patrimoine et lien social' (1997) 3 *Revue trimestrielle de droit civil* 583.

can be found the items of property he owns, these items of property in turn being defined as subject to appropriation. However, the *fiducie* presents itself with a patrimony unmoored from the person, one which holds property over which no one has a right of ownership. Yet, this property had an owner[67] and will have one again once the *fiducie* comes to an end.[68] The question that can thus be posed is whether the *fiducie* creates a sort of interlude in ownership or, in other words, a bracketed ownership, providing an interval within which ownership and real rights no longer set the terms for our reasoning, while still taking into account the world of ownership since the ownership of the trust property will be transferred to a new owner when the *fiducie* comes to an end.[69] Thus, the notion of a *fiducie* severed from ownership does not present itself in the legal landscape without raising further questions.

B. *Can the* fiducie *cut all ties to ownership?*

The hypothesis of a patrimony by appropriation severed from ownership and *droits subjectifs* presents sizeable theoretical challenges to the civilian jurist. First of all, the question that can be posed relates to the identity of the 'other' whose property is administered by the trustee. By definition, the property is subject to an appropriation.[70] Yet, if the trustee 'acts as the administrator of the property of others', as article 1278 C.C.Q. provides, does this mean that there is an 'other' who is the owner of the property

67 Indeed, according to art. 1260 C.C.Q., the *fiducie* results from an act whereby the settlor transfers property from his patrimony to another patrimony constituted by him.

68 When the *fiducie* comes to an end, the trustee must, according to the provisions of art. 1297 C.C.Q., 'deliver the property to those who are entitled to it. Where there is no beneficiary, any property remaining when the trust is terminated devolves to the settlors or his heirs.' And 'property of a social trust that terminates by the impossibility of its fulfilment devolves to a trust, to a legal person or to any other group of persons devoted to a purpose as nearly like that of the trust as possible'. See also art. 1296: 'A trust is terminated by the renunciation or lapse of the right of all the beneficiaries, both of the capital and of the fruits and revenues. A trust is also terminated by the expiry of the term or the fulfilment of the condition, by the attainment of the purpose of the trust or by the impossibility, confirmed by the court, of attaining it.'

69 It can be asked whether *fiducie* brings into being a form of transmission for property alongside, in particular, contract and succession. Indeed, this is one of the possible ways to interpret France's *fiducie*, which was introduced within Book 3 entitled 'Different Ways in which Ownership is Acquired'.

70 P.-A. Crépeau, N. Kasirer et al., *Dictionnaire de droit privé: les obligations*, 3rd edn (Cowansville: Éditions Yvon-Blais, 2003), *s.v.* 'bien'. See also: G. Cornu, *Vocabulaire juridique*, 7th edn, coll. Quadrige (Paris: Presses Universitaires de France), *s.v.* 'bien'.

that comes within the trust? A scholarly writer once emphasized that 'it does not seem satisfactory or even coherent to explain that the trustee is a manager into whose hands is placed a power, in the strict sense of the term, namely that he would be exercising a prerogative based on a right held by another, and to assert at the same time that the property belongs to no one'.[71] It is thus legitimate to ask about the identity of this 'other', the owner, if it is not the trustee. It is certainly not the settlor: according to the very definition of *fiducie*, he is no longer the owner of the property transferred into a *fiducie*.[72] If we take literally the legislator's statement that the trustee really administers property that is not his own, then the shadow of ownership (ownership held by the beneficiary, or held by the *fiducie* itself?) falls once again upon the *fiducie*.

Another challenging theoretical question is the one that asks from whom someone acquires property from within a *fiducie*. This is not a new question and Dean François Frenette was already taken aback by the fiction that concedes, by way of a *fiducie* in the absence of an owner and in the absence of legal personhood, that 'whoever would acquire property from the trustee, would acquire it from no one'.[73] Granted, the titles to the property are in the name of the trustee (art. 1278 C.C.Q.). Is this however enough to conclude that the acquirer acquires the title, on which his right of ownership is based, from someone who is not the owner, given that this conflicts with the traditional principle of the civil law, according to which one cannot transfer more rights than one has?[74]

Legal doctrine has put forward the proposition that the *fiducie* should be recognized as a new '*sujet de droit*'.[75] To be more specific, this would mean 'considering that the *fiducie* is the *sujet de droit* with respect to the rights and obligations which are encompassed by the *fiducie* patrimony, even though the *fiducie* does not have the status of being a legal person'.[76] It would thus be appropriate to 'recognize this non-person as the *sujet de droit* with respect to the rights and obligations encompassed by the

[71] Kan-Balivet, *Les techniques*, above, note 8, 161.

[72] According to art. 1260 C.C.Q.: '[. . .] the settlor transfers property from his patrimony to another patrimony constituted by him [. . .]'.

[73] Frenette, 'La propriété fiduciaire', above, note 18, 737.

[74] On the adage *nemo plus juris*, see, in particular, A. Mayrand, *Dictionnaire de maximes et locutions latines utilisées en droit*, 4th edn, updated by M. Mac Aodha (Cowansville: Éditions Yvon Blais, 2007), *s.v.* 'nemo plus juris ad alium transferre potest quam ipse habet'.

[75] A bearer of private law rights and obligations.

[76] M. Cantin Cumyn, 'La fiducie nouveau sujet de droit?', in J. Beaulne, *Mélanges E. Caparros* (Montreal: Wilson and Lafleur, 2002), p. 142.

fiducie patrimony. Thus, the *fiducie* must be accepted as a third type of *sujet de droit*, alongside human beings and legal persons.'[77]

This theoretical approach shows how difficult it is to break completely from ownership and the tie of belonging, even if one employs the conception of a patrimony by appropriation which severs this patrimony from ownership. Indeed, the problem carries over elsewhere: whenever there are items of property in the legal landscape, a civilian jurist naturally looks for their owner, or at least the person or *sujet de droit* to whom he can link this property. If article 1261 C.C.Q. is interpreted in a manner which sees none of the participants to the *fiducie* arrangement as an owner, perhaps the *fiducie* itself would have the status of owner? [78] This idea has the merit of renewing, at least indirectly, the ties between *fiducie* and ownership, as well as, at the very least and more explicitly, of mending the ties between *sujet de droit* and the things that rights bear upon. However, it remains that this solution entails a fundamental revision to the conception of *sujet de droit*, which is traditionally linked to legal personhood. This step is taken to avoid the notion of legal person and the formalities that apply to this type of entity, which are precisely what the legislator sought to avoid.[79]

To date, this proposition has not been accepted. Accordingly, the question returns of who this other, this owner, might be, if the owner is not the trustee or the *fiducie* itself. Who is being referred to by the 'other', if it is neither the trustee nor the settlor, since the trustee administers the property of another, and the settlor has by definition ceased to be the owner of the property which he has transferred into the *fiducie*? Would this other be the beneficiary, who might be considered an owner,

[77] Ibid., p. 143.

[78] On the theory of the quasi-personification of the *fiducie* see also M. Faribault, *Traité théorique et pratique de la fiducie ou trust du droit civil dans la province de Québec* (Montreal: Wilson and Lafleur, 1936); P. Lepaulle, *Traité théorique et pratique des trusts en droit interne, en droit fiscal et en droit international* (Paris: Rousseau, 1932), p. 42; P. Lepaulle 'An Outsider's View Point of the Nature of Trusts' (1928–29) 63 *Revue du Notariat* 431, 435; M. Cantin Cumyn, 'The Trust in a Civilian Context: The Quebec Case' (1994) 3 *Journal of International Trust and Corporate Planning* 69, 71–2: 'Although the trust is not classified as a moral person it will, as a patrimony by appropriation, operate in a similar way. *It will be the owner of the trust property.* It will be able to enter into contracts and incur debts or other obligations.' See also the discussion of this subject by Beetz J. in *Royal Trust Co.* v. *Tucker*, [1982] 1 R.C.S. 250, 264–73.

[79] See J. E. C. Brierley, 'Substitutions, stipulations d'inaliénabilité, fiducies et fondations' (1988) 3 *Cours de perfectionnement du Notariat* 243, 267; Cantin Cumyn, 'La fiducie nouveau sujet de droit?', above, note 76, 139.

at least latently, and whose status has similarities to the substitute in the context of the civil law institution of substitution?[80] Would it thus be possible to think that if the beneficiary does not have a right of ownership over the course of the *fiducie* (as justified by the letter of article 1261 C.C.Q.), he at least is 'destined for ownership', this 'right established with certainty' which article 1265 C.C.Q. brings to mind? Is this shadow of the beneficiary's future ownership the factor that can explain the choice of words by the legislator when he says that trustees administer the property of others?

It does seem that the intention of Quebec's legislator was to set aside ownership (at least as ownership is traditionally meant) while the *fiducie* is in effect by means of the patrimony appropriated to a purpose. However, this setting aside is only partial and temporary since ownership will be reconstituted once the *fiducie* comes to an end,[81] as soon as the trustee hands over the property to the beneficiary.[82] Thus, Quebec's *fiducie* could be analysed less as a negation of ownership, and more as a bracketing of ownership or even as a new mode by which ownership is acquired.

IV Conclusion

Our initial question, which sought to find out whether the civilian *fiducie* can be understood as a modality of ownership or as an interlude in ownership, does not call for a univocal answer. The preceding discussion shows that ownership, as an institution, is sufficiently malleable to adapt

[80] As art. 1243 C.C.Q. provides, the substitute is 'seised of *ownership* of the property' by the opening of the substitution. But, as art. 1223 provides, before the opening of the substitution it is the institute who is 'the *owner* of the substituted property'.

[81] A link should be made here to what certain scholarly writers in Quebec, for example François Frenette and Sylvio Normand, have called the *vis attractiva*, a fourth attribute of ownership alongside the *usus*, *fructus* and *abusus*. *Vis attractiva* is the ability of the full ownership to reconstitute itself once a dismemberment comes to an end (see F. Frenette, 'Du droit de propriété: certaines de ses dimensions méconnues' (1979) 20 *Cahiers de droit* 439, 446; Normand, *Introduction au droit des biens*, above, note 52, p. 11). If this were the case, it would just confirm the fact that the shadow of ownership would then fall on Quebec's *fiducie*.

[82] This reasoning has in mind the typical case in the realm of *fiducie*, a case where the property is handed over to the beneficiaries when the *fiducie* comes to an end (art. 1297 C.C.Q.). However, in special cases the property will be handed over to the settlor or his successors, as provided by the second paragraph of article 1297 (the ownership thus reconstituting itself in their hands). It may even be handed over to another *fiducie*, a legal person or group of persons (art. 1298). Here the ownership would potentially reconstitute itself in favour of this new person or be once again postponed.

to fiduciary ownership. The law now in force in France is an example of this. As well, *fiducie* could be seen as an interlude in ownership, thus breaking, at least in part, the *fiducie*'s ties to the mould of ownership. This could be the solution chosen by the Civil Code of Québec.

Still, whatever path might be explored, the civilian jurist is faced with a struggle if he seeks to completely sever *fiducie* from ownership. This is clear from the model of France's civilian *fiducie*, due to its recognition of fiduciary ownership. Yet, this also transpires from the solution followed by Quebec's legislator, who made *fiducie* a patrimony by appropriation, while letting the shadow of ownership fall upon it.

Until the present time, the civilian conceptions of *fiducie* seem to be so firmly anchored in ownership – which is the pre-eminent connection between persons and property, as well as being the institution by which property is transferred from patrimony to patrimony – that if *fiducie* is thought of in terms severed from ownership, this will at the very least imply two things. On the one hand, this break could not be simple; it entails a series of changes at the level of legal analysis. The principal change would be the redefinition of the concept of patrimony, which emerges completely renewed. However, the changes could just as well extend to other fundamental concepts, stretching as far as the concept of *sujet de droit*, as certain scholarly writers have already suggested. On the other hand, this break could be neither total nor permanent, and could at most be seen as a bracketing of ownership or marking an interlude in it. As long as the *fiducie* is in existence, the shadow of ownership will continue to fall upon it, and ownership will revive in full force when a *fiducie* comes to an end.

3

How to square the circle? The challenge met by Swiss insolvency law in dealing with common law trusts

AUDE PEYROT

I Introduction

On 1 July 2007, Switzerland ratified the Hague Convention on the Law Applicable to Trusts and on their Recognition. While two comprehensive reports in the 1950s clearly stated that trusts were incompatible with the Swiss legal system,[1] the ratification of the Convention sixty years later was relatively uncontested. Granted, there were some developments in internal Swiss law that facilitated this result;[2] nonetheless, a progressive evolution of mentalities is what really made it possible. Today, generally speaking, given the ratification, it can no longer be said that trusts are incompatible with Swiss law.

One clarification must be made at the outset. As a result of adopting the Hague Convention on Trusts, Switzerland now recognizes and implements the effects of a *foreign trust*. However, trusts do not form part of Swiss domestic substantive law, so there is no such thing as a Swiss trust. In particular, we will see that the *fiducie* under Swiss law forms no equivalent to the common law trust.[3] Consequently, Switzerland only welcomes trusts with an international perspective by way of the Hague Convention.

New provisions on trusts were inserted into Swiss law to implement the Hague Convention: first, in the Private International Law Act of 19

[1] See the reports of C. Reymond, 'Le trust et le droit suisse' (1954) 73 *Revue de droit suisse* 119, and F. Gubler, 'Besteht in der Schweiz ein Bedürfnis nach Einführung des Instituts der angelsächsischen Treuhand (trust)?' (1954) 73 *Revue de droit suisse* 215. These two studies sought to determine whether the Anglo-Saxon trust could be introduced in Swiss law. Reymond, ibid., 209, concluded that the trust is irreconcilable with and contrary to the spirit of Swiss law.

[2] In particular, the introduction of legal concepts in Swiss law, which are considered to be true segregated estates. In this respect, see Section II.C below.

[3] See Section II.B below.

December 1987 (PILA),[4] second, in the Debt Enforcement and Bankruptcy Act of 11 April 1889 (DEBA).[5,6] This legislative action with respect to debt enforcement makes Switzerland a special, if not unique, case among civil law countries. This issue seems to be a relatively unexamined topic in both civil law and common law countries that have ratified the Hague Convention. It is therefore worth examining how Switzerland has managed to deal with insolvency in relation to trusts without prior experience in the field and while also having no real model available.

The present chapter proposes three areas of discussion in relation to common law trusts and Swiss insolvency law.[7]

(1) Section II will explore how the effect of ring-fencing, which is inherent to trusts, is compatible with the so-called 'unity of patrimony' (*unité du patrimoine*), a principle at the core of debt liability in Swiss law. Specifically, this section will evaluate whether the trustee is permitted to hold separate assets under a trust that are not vulnerable to his personal debts despite the insistence in Swiss law of general individual liability based on the whole of the estate. Further, this section will show how the matter was quite conveniently resolved in Swiss law and will review article 284b DEBA which was promulgated in this respect.
(2) Building on the first analysis, Section III will discuss whether or not the segregation of trust assets is compatible with the requirement in Swiss law for publication of trust relationships in public registers. In particular, it will examine whether the trust relationship must be published and whether the creditors must be aware of it for the segregation to take place. Article 149d PILA, which governs the publication of trusts, does not provide a clear answer. My analysis will propose an interpretation of the latter provision that departs from prevailing majority opinion in Switzerland.
(3) Section IV will discuss the position of creditors with regular monetary claims arising out of the management of a trust who seek debt collection in Switzerland. The issue is twofold. The debt liability

[4] *Recueil systématique du droit fédéral* (RS) 291. [5] RS 281.1.

[6] On 1 July 2007, arts. 149a to 149e were introduced into the PILA, together with an amendment to art. 21 PILA. Further, arts. 284a and 284b were added to the DEBA.

[7] For a more complete analysis on these topics, see A. Peyrot, *Le trust de* common law *et l'exécution forcée en Suisse* (Zurich: Schulthess, 2011).

regime represents a preliminary and material issue that is left to the law applicable to the trust, while debt enforcement proceeding is an implementation issue that is to be provided for by the Swiss insolvency law. For the case where – further to the law applicable to the trust – debts are directly attributable to the trust fund, a new provision had to be promulgated in Swiss law, that is, article 284a DEBA. It is interesting to see whether the solutions implemented by the latter rule comply with the existing logic of Swiss law and with that of trusts and how Switzerland has attempted to deal with both.

II Ring-fencing effect versus the principle of 'unity of patrimony'

Prior to ratifying the Convention, Swiss legislators had to broach the question of the possible coexistence of the trust's ring-fencing effect and the principle in Swiss law of the 'unity of patrimony'. The latter is common to other civil law countries and has been the subject of debate in those jurisdictions as well.[8] The following sub-section attempts to explain the fashion in which this question has been resolved within Swiss law.

A. *Ring-fencing: the heart of the concept of trusts*

The segregation of trust assets is one of the essential characteristics of the institution of trusts, as clearly stated at article 2 para. 2 lit. a of the Convention.[9] Its implementation is imposed on civil law countries having ratified the Convention as one of the minimum legal consequences of recognizing trusts (art. 11 para. 2).[10] In concrete terms, where trust law so requires, the assets of a trust must be recognized as distinct from the trustee's property in three ways: as they relate to the spouse of the trustee since they do not form part of his matrimonial regime; as they relate to the heirs of the trustee since they do not fall within his estate; and especially as they relate to the

[8] In France, see especially F. Barrière, *La réception du trust au travers de la fiducie* (Paris: Litec, 2004), pp. 338–47.

[9] See also art. III of D. J. Hayton, S. C. J. J. Kortmann, H. L. E Verhagen (eds.), *Principles of European Trust Law* (The Hague: Kluwer Law International, 1999).

[10] See art. 11 para. 2 and para. 3 lit. a–b of the Convention.

trustee's personal creditors in the event of his insolvency (art. 11 para. 3 lit. a–c of the Convention).

Legal scholars put forward the importance of the segregation of trust assets, particularly in the context of article 11 of the Convention. They consider it an essential element of trusts, without which its recognition would be devoid of sense.[11] Jonathan Harris argues, moreover, that the principle of segregation should not be affected or diminished by articles 15 or 16 of the Convention, for fear of rendering its recognition meaningless.[12]

B. *'Unity of patrimony' as illustrated in the* fiducie *of Swiss law*

The ring-fencing effect may be seen, at first sight, to be in direct conflict with the 'unity of patrimony' principle, which states that an individual who meets all his debts possesses only one estate upon which all his debts rely. It prohibits individuals from creating separate funds within a single estate.[13] This principle is derived from the subjective theory of patrimony developed in the nineteenth century by the French authors Aubry and Rau.[14] In France, the principle has become dogma[15] and continues to remain such despite stark criticism in French doctrine.[16] While the concept was not as fervently embraced in Switzerland, it is nonetheless a key principle in Swiss debt liability law[17] and has been expressed in doctrine both explicitly[18] and implicitly, though never codified. Debt liability is

[11] J. Harris, *The Hague Trusts Convention: Scope, Application and Preliminary Issues* (Oxford: Hart, 2002), p. 311; C. Jauffret-Spinosi, 'La Convention de la Haye relative à la loi applicable au trust et à sa reconnaissance (1er juillet 1985)' (1987) 114 *Journal du Droit International* 23, 55ff; A. von Overbeck, 'Rapport explicatif/Explanatory Report', in *Actes et documents de la Quinzième session, t. II: Trust – loi applicable et reconnaissance* (The Hague: Bureau permanent de la Conférence, 1984), p. 394, para. 108.

[12] Harris, *Hague Trusts Convention*, above, note 11, pp. 315ff, in particular p. 317.

[13] L. Thévenoz and J.-P. Dunand, 'La fiducie: droit des biens ou droit des obligations?', in *Rapports suisses présentés au XVème Congrès international de droit comparé: Bristol, 27 juillet au 1er août 1998* (Zurich: Schulthess, 1998), pp. 491ff.

[14] C. Aubry and C. Rau, *Cours de droit civil français d'après la méthode de Zachariae*, E. Bartin (ed.), 5th edn (Paris: Marchal et Godde, 1917), vol. 9; the first edition dates from 1839.

[15] Barrière, *Réception du trust*, above, note 8, p. 338 and the reference cited in note 1413.

[16] See in this respect F. Cohet-Cordey, 'La valeur explicative de la théorie du patrimoine en droit positif français' (1996) 4 *Revue trimestrielle de droit civil* 819.

[17] In this vein, P.-R. Gilliéron, *Commentaire de la loi fédérale sur la poursuite pour dettes et la faillite: loi du 11 avril 1889, texte en vigueur le 1er janvier 1997* (Lausanne: Payot, 1999), paras. 19ff, section 'remarques introductives: art. 1 à 37'.

[18] L. Thévenoz, 'La fiducie, cendrillon du droit suisse: propositions pour une réforme' (1995) 114 *Revue de droit suisse* 253, 322ff.

often described as general, personal and unlimited, which mirrors the concept of the uniform liability of the whole of an estate.[19]

The Swiss *fiducie* provides a good illustration of the 'unity of patrimony' mechanism.[20] Originating from business practice, the *fiducie* was admitted in Switzerland for the first time in the case law of the Swiss Federal Court at the beginning of the twentieth century.[21] It thus came into being and has evolved on the margins of the law according to case law. It has been shaped as an institution within contract law that implies the full and absolute transfer of title on fiduciary property. The settlor (*fiduciant*) transfers assets to the trustee (*fiduciaire*) who is required to hold the fiduciary assets for a certain purpose and duration and in accordance with the terms of the contract. The trustee is a full owner, even though he holds the property for others, usually for the settlor, who is the contractual partner of the trustee, or for third-party beneficiaries if there are any.

Specifically, Swiss case law has explicitly rejected the notion of a division of ownership between an external title for the trustee and an internal title for the settlor or third-party beneficiaries.[22] The property belongs indivisibly to the trustee. That is one salient feature that distinguishes the *fiducie* from the common law trust. Furthermore, the *fiducie*, in its common form, is subject to the principle of 'unity of patrimony', which prevents the formation of a separated fund within the estate of the trustee. Strictly applied, this means that the fiduciary assets – in the event of the bankruptcy of the trustee – form part of the bankrupt's

[19] See especially Gilliéron, *Commentaire*, above, note 17, para. 31; A. Von Overbeck, 'National Report for Switzerland', in Hayton et al., *Principles of European Trust Law*, above, note 9, p. 110.

[20] With respect to Swiss fiduciary transfer, see J.-F. Ducrest and S. Guex, 'La fiducie', in *Fiche juridique suisse* No. 732 (28 January 2002); J.-P. Dunand, *Le transfert fiduciaire: 'donner pour reprendre', mancipio dare ut remancipetur: analyse historique et comparatiste de la fiducie-gestion* (Basle: Helbing & Lichtenhahn, 2000); A. Peyrot, 'La fiducie en droit suisse' (2010) 47 *Revue Lamy du droit des affaires* 94; C. Reymond, *Essai sur la nature et les limites de l'acte fiduciaire*, Thesis (Lausanne: 1948); Thévenoz and Dunand, 'La fiducie', above, note 13; R. Watter, 'Die Treuhand im Schweizer Recht' (1995) 114 *Revue de droit suisse* 179.

[21] Arrêt du Tribunal fédéral (ATF) 31 II 105. Decisions of the Swiss Federal Court may be found online on the website www.bger.ch.

[22] ATF 31 II 105, cons. 3. The absence of division of property in Swiss law was also discussed in the celebrated case of *Harrison c. Crédit suisse* published in ATF 96 II 79, and translated into French in *Journal des Tribunaux* (JT) 1971 I 329, cons. 7a. See Thévenoz, 'Cendrillon du droit suisse', above, note 18, 265.

estate, since they are not ring-fenced. In this respect, the Swiss *fiducie* also significantly differs from the common law trust.

It should be noted however that the 'unity of patrimony' principle has been relaxed through case law in relation to the so-called '*fiducie-gestion*' (fiduciary transfer for management purposes). Based on an application by analogy of article 401 para. 3 of the Swiss Code of Obligation of 30 March 1911 (CO),[23] the Swiss Federal Court permits the settlor (or the beneficiaries, if any) to claim and segregate certain types of fiduciary assets in the event of the trustee's bankruptcy.[24] This preferential treatment is, however, only available to movable property and claims (to the exclusion of immovable property) that have been acquired against third persons for the account of the settlor (or beneficiaries), and not to the assets that have been originally transferred from the settlor to the trustee. This remedy is therefore relatively restricted in its scope and conditions for implementation.[25]

As such, the *fiducie* of Swiss law remains fundamentally tied to the principle of 'unity of patrimony', which is undoubtedly one of the institution's weaknesses and which prohibits it from being considered a functional equivalent to trusts. It is interesting to note that a project to codify the *fiducie* with the intent of bringing it in line with trusts was examined at the same time as the ratification of the Hague Convention. This attempt was abandoned, however, as it was seen as not necessarily desirable and likely to slow down the ratification process.[26]

C. Reconciling the principles: pre-existing ring-fenced funds under Swiss law

At first glance, the ring-fencing effect of trust law and 'unity of patrimony' of Swiss law seem irreconcilable. A careful examination of the

[23] RS 220. The rule comes from the law of mandate (art. 394 *et seq.* CO) which is broadly conceived under Swiss law and which partially applies to the '*fiducie-gestion*'.

[24] The leading case is *Feras Anstalt c. Banque Vallugano* decided in 1973 and published in ATF 99 II 393, JT 1974 I 588.

[25] Its implementation implies that fiduciary assets can be individualized. See especially ATF 102 II 103.

[26] See *Message du Conseil fédéral du 2 décembre 2005 concernant l'approbation et l'exécution de la Convention de La Haye relative à la loi applicable au trust et à sa reconnaissance*, in *Feuille fédérale* 2006, pp. 561–618 (hereinafter *Message*), p. 593. The German version was published in the *Bundesblatt* 2006, pp. 551–608, and the Italian version in the *Foglio federale* 2006, pp. 517–74.

latter, however, results in a more nuanced conclusion. This principle has never become a dogma under Swiss law and is subject to exceptions. The Swiss legal system is indeed already familiar with certain forms of ring-fenced funds, known as '*patrimoines séparés*' or '*patrimoines spéciaux*' in the Swiss French and '*Sondervermögen*' in the Swiss German terminology. Their legal status is distinct from the status of the personal assets of the legal owner: for example, they are not liable for the personal debts of the legal owner and they do not form part of his estate upon death.[27] One of the most fully developed types of ring-fenced funds in Swiss law is the 'contractual investment fund' (*fonds de placement contractuel*),[28] which I will briefly discuss below.

Investment funds under Swiss law were designed on the basis of a trust structure. This structure was chosen instead of other legal structures, such as co-ownership.[29] The fund assets belong legally to the company managing the funds, but they are held in a fiduciary capacity for the account of investors. Without specific legislative action, the investment fund's assets would be subject to the general principle of 'unity of patrimony', with the risk of being called to meet personal debts of the managing company, in solidarity with the general estate of the latter. To alleviate this concern, the Swiss legislator included an explicit right of segregation of the fund assets in the event of the fund management company's winding-up.[30] This right of segregation is broadly designed and operates automatically without any need to file a claim.[31] Furthermore, the law facilitates this segregation by imposing a requirement for separate holdings: the collective assets must be held separately in a depository bank[32] and the fund manager is required to keep separate accounting records.[33]

27 Such special estates exist most notably in the fields of matrimony and of succession. See in this respect D. Piotet, 'Les effets à l'égard des créanciers de la pluralité des patrimoines d'un même sujet de droit, notamment la question de la subrogation patrimoniale', in *Tradition mit Weitsicht: Festschrift für Eugen Bucher zum 80. Geburtstag* (Zurich: Schulthess, 2009), pp. 561–80; L. Thévenoz, 'Patrimoines fiduciaires et exécution forcée', in *Insolvence, désendettement et redressement: études réunies en l'honneur de Louis Dallèves* (Basle: Helbing & Lichtenhahn, 2000), pp. 345–69; D. Staehelin, 'Sondervermögen und Haftung', in *Festgabe für Franz Hasenböhler* (Zurich: Schulthess, 2004), pp. 87–113.

28 Regulated under arts. 25 to 35 of Collective Capital Investments Act (CCIA), RS 951.31.

29 Thévenoz, 'Cendrillon du droit suisse', above, note 18, 281.

30 Art. 35 CCIA.

31 German doctrine qualifies this automatic segregation as '*Absonderung*', as opposed to the segregation that only happens on request, which is known as '*Aussonderung*'.

32 Art. 73 CCIA. 33 Art. 87 CCIA.

Legal scholars see the legal regime for investment funds as having the characteristics of a true ring-fenced fund,[34] which is specifically and uniquely intended for investing for the account of the investors.[35] This example, alongside others,[36] thus provided reassurance that the 'unity of patrimony' was not an intangible concept and that it could be subject to exceptions without collapsing.[37] Trusts are but an additional derogation to the principle.

D. *Implementation of the ring-fencing effect of trusts in Swiss debt enforcement (art. 284b DEBA)*

Having overcome the dogmatic hurdle, legislators could tackle the implementation of the segregation of trust assets with Swiss debt enforcement law. To do so, article 284b DEBA was adopted, clearly anchoring this effect in the heart of the relevant law. The rule states succinctly that '[i]n the event of a trustee's bankruptcy, the trust assets shall be segregated from the trustee's estate, after deduction of any claims of the trustee against the trust'.[38]

In principle, upon the bankruptcy of a debtor, all of his assets form the estate in bankruptcy (*masse en faillite*) – regardless of the location of the property.[39] As the trust fund is a separated fund in the hand of the trustee, any assets therein do not become part of the estate in bankruptcy.

[34] Piotet, 'Les effets à l'égard des créanciers', above, note 27, p. 569; Staehelin, 'Sondervermögen und Haftung', above, note 27, p. 94; Thévenoz, 'Cendrillon du droit suisse', above, note 18, 281 and 315.

[35] Thévenoz, 'Cendrillon du droit suisse', above, note 18, 281.

[36] For example, the fiduciary operations of banks that also benefit from the automatic right to segregation. See current art. 37d of the Swiss Banking Act of 8 November 1934 (BA), RS 952.0, *cum* art. 16 BA, but for which the legal regime is less complete. Notably, the law does include an obligation to keep assets separately. See in this respect, Thévenoz, 'Cendrillon du droit suisse', above, note 18, 315–16; Von Overbeck, 'National Report for Switzerland', above, note 19, pp. 112ff.

[37] In addition, the Swiss Federal Court in 2001 decided – without going into a detailed analysis of the matter – that a right to segregation under foreign law (*in casu* the recognition of a constructive trust under American law) was not contrary to Swiss public order. See decision TF 5C.169/2001 of 19 November 2001 (unpublished).

[38] Unofficial translation by D. W. Wilson, in *Trusts.ch: Newsletter of December 21st 2006*, available on www.trusts.ch. The French text, considered an official version alongside the German and Italian, states: '*dans la faillite d'un trustee, le patrimoine du trust est distrait de la masse en faillite après déduction des créances du trustee contre ce patrimoine*'. The segregation of trust assets also applies to individual enforcement against the trustee, i.e. in case of seizure.

[39] See art. 197 DEBA.

Article 284b DEBA provides indeed for the *automatic* segregation of the trust assets. The segregation is *ipso jure*, without any claim or judicial action required. The competent authority must therefore *ex officio* ensure that the trust assets are kept out of the estate in bankruptcy. This is only true, however, if the ownership of these assets is made sufficiently clear. In practice, this means that the assets have been accounted for and held separately. Should the trust relationship not be self-evident, interested parties may seek judicial intervention to segregate the trust's funds.[40] The success of any such action ultimately relies on the evidence that the property is indeed held in trust.

III The ring-fencing effect and the publication of a trust in Swiss public registers

The second issue to be addressed is the relationship between the publication of a trust in Swiss public registers and the effective segregation of trust assets. The question lies in whether or not the trust relationship must be known by third parties for the segregation to take place in case of the trustee's bankruptcy. Article 149d PILA, which governs the publication of trust relationships, does not provide for a clear or definitive answer. The following considerations will explore this issue and will propose an interpretation of the law that differs from the views expressed by the Federal Council in relation to article 149d PILA[41] and from the majority opinion that has formed among scholars.[42] As discussed below, however, this approach seems justified in that it is more consistent with the Swiss legal system and with the Hague Convention.

Given its interest and complexity, this matter certainly deserves a detailed analysis.[43] Here, however, I will limit myself to a few general considerations. After a brief overview of article 12 of the Convention and article 149d PILA, I will explore the effects of publication and non-publication as they relate to third party purchasers in good faith. Thereafter, we will see whether this also has consequences for a trustee's personal

[40] *Message*, above, note 26, pp. 605–7, 611; P. M. Gutzwiller, *Schweizerisches Internationales Trustrecht* (Basel: Helbing & Lichtenhahn, 2007), p. 187, para. 284b-6. On the proceeding, see Peyrot, *Le trust de* common law, above, note 7, pp. 70ff.

[41] *Message*, above, note 26, p. 611.

[42] See authors cited below, note 56.

[43] For a further analysis of this topic, see A. Peyrot, 'La mention du trust dans les registres publics et la protection des créanciers de bonne foi: un regard critique' (2009) 5 *Revue suisse du droit des affaires* 366.

creditors, and, as a corollary, to the effective segregation of trust assets in case of bankruptcy of the trustee.

A. Publication of trusts under article 12 of the Convention and article 149d PILA

Article 12 of the Convention provides for the possibility of mentioning the trust relationship in the public register of a contracting State, stating that '[w]here the trustee desires to register assets, movable or immovable, or documents of title to them, he shall be entitled, in so far as this is not prohibited by or inconsistent with the law of the State where registration is sought, to do so in his capacity as trustee or in such other way that the existence of the trust is disclosed'. This rule seeks to facilitate the management of the trust by enabling the trustee to disclose the trust relationship to third parties.[44] This step can be essential in jurisdictions where publication of some form is required to ensure opposability of rights.

The publication of trusts in Swiss law is done under article 149d PILA, which reads as follows:

> (1) Where trust assets are registered in the trustee's name in the land register, the shipping register or the aircraft register, the existence of the trust may be mentioned in the said register.
> (2) Trust relationships concerning intellectual property rights registered in Switzerland shall, on request, be registered in the relevant register.
> (3) Trust relationships, which are not mentioned or registered, shall not be enforceable against bona fide third parties.[45]

[44] Jauffret-Spinosi, 'La Convention de la Haye', above, note 11, 60; E. Gaillard and D. Trautman, 'La Convention de la Haye du 1er juillet 1985 relative à la loi applicable au trust et à sa reconnaissance' (1986) 75 *Revue critique de droit international privé* 1, 29; H. Van Loon, 'The Hague Convention of 1st July 1985 on the Law Applicable to Trusts and on their Recognition', in A. Prüm et al., *Trust et fiducie: la Convention de La Haye et la nouvelle législation luxembourgeoise* (Paris: Montchrestien, 2005), p. 31.

[45] Unofficial translation by D. W. Wilson, in *Trusts.ch: Newsletter of December 21st 2006*, available on www.trusts.ch. The French text, considered an official version alongside the German and Italian, states: '(1) Lorsque les biens d'un trust sont inscrits au nom d'un trustee dans le registre foncier, le registre des bateaux ou le registre des aéronefs, le lien avec un trust peut faire l'objet d'une mention. (2) Le lien avec un trust portant sur des droits de propriété intellectuelle enregistrés en Suisse est, sur demande, inscrit dans le registre pertinent. (3) Le lien avec un trust qui n'a pas fait l'objet d'une mention ou qui n'a pas été inscrit n'est pas opposable aux tiers de bonne foi.'

Being the legal titleholder of the trust assets, the trustee is registered in his personal name in the various public and private registers (see art. 2 para. 2 lit. b of the Convention). Having no legal personality, a trust does not have this capacity on its own. Therefore, the mention of the trust relationship in the register allows third parties to see that the trustee owns the relevant trust asset as trustee and not in his private capacity.[46] This is the goal of article 149d PILA, which provides Swiss law with an explicit legal basis for publication of trusts and thereby ensures its compatibility with domestic laws, as set out by article 12 *in fine* of the Convention.

Swiss law requires publication of property and rights ordinarily subject to a tabular publication in a public registry, such as immovable property, vessels and aircraft, as well as intellectual property rights. Movable property and claims subject to a trust are excluded from publication.[47] Immovable property is published through a mention that the property in question 'forms part of a trust estate'.[48] The settlor is entitled to require the trust mention upon the initial transfer of the immovable property to the trustee, as is the trustee once the transfer is complete. Further, should an instrument or a law provide for the publication of a trust and the trustee refuses to do so, the beneficiaries may request that a judge order publication.[49] This seems to be the only possibility for the beneficiaries to obtain publication.

Under Swiss law, publication of a trust relationship is optional. The parties therefore have the choice of whether or not to reveal to third parties the existence of a trust relationship on a given asset. Looking more closely, however, publication is not in fact optional, since the law penalizes non-publication. Article 149d para. 3 PILA states that any trust

[46] F. Guillaume, 'Trust, réserves héréditaires et immeubles' (2009) 1 *Pratique juridique actuelle* 33, 43.

[47] Note that the first draft legislation initially provided for the creation of a register of movable property held in trust. This idea was ultimately abandoned given the numerous criticisms thereof. See in this respect *Message*, above, note 26, p. 605.

[48] *Lignes directrices destinées au traitement des affaires liées à un trust*, Federal Land Registry and Real Estate Law Office, 28 June 2007 (updated 28 August 2007), p. 4. It should be noted that these guidelines were written for cantonal offices responsible for the land register. They are only indicative and non-binding.

[49] Ibid., p. 3; B. Foëx, 'La mention du trust au registre foncier' (2009) 90 *Revue suisse du notariat et du registre foncier* 81, 84ff; S. Wolf and N. Jordi, 'Trust und schweizerisches Zivilrecht – insbesondere Ehegüter-, Erb- und Immobiliarsachenrecht', in S. Wolf (ed.), *Der Trust: Einführung und Rechtslage in der Schweiz nach dem Inkrafttreten des Haager Trust-Übereinkommens* (Berne: Stämpfli, 2008), p. 73.

relationship not mentioned in the appropriate public register is not enforceable against good faith third parties. In other words, the existence of a trust relationship is not in question, but it cannot be invoked to the detriment of such good faith third parties without having been published. Article 149d PILA thereby goes further than article 12 of the Convention, as the latter does not attach any legal effect to non-publication.

Under Swiss law, good faith implies that the person was unaware of the trust and could not have been aware of its existence despite the exercise of the diligence required by the particular circumstances.[50] Good faith, therefore, is lacking in the case of a person who knows of the trust relationship by other means, notwithstanding the lack of publication.

B. *Effects of publication and non-publication on good faith third-party purchasers*

The effects of publication and non-publication of trusts will here be discussed with respect to the land register. These considerations are applicable *mutatis mutandis* to other public registers relevant to trusts (vessel and aircraft register, registers relating to intellectual property).

The land register provides for publication of immovable property. It is managed at the cantonal level, is organized based on strict rules and is overseen by the State. It aims to record the various property rights or legal relationships on immovable property (including ownership, existence of a lien, etc.) and permits them to be enforceable against third parties. A real right (*right in rem*) can only benefit from its inherent *erga omnes* effect if third parties are aware of its existence.

Upon publication of trusts in the land register, the good faith of third parties is eliminated in that they are no longer able to claim ignorance of a trust relationship on the immovable property in question.[51] As such, anyone acquiring immovable property that has mention of a trust relationship in the register must ensure that the trustee has the power to alienate the immovable property. Should the trustee thereafter be shown

[50] Art. 3 para. 2 of the Swiss Civil Code of 10 December 1907 ('CC'), RS 210. On good faith, cf. ATF 127 III 440, JT 2002 I 543, cons. 2c. See also H. Deschenaux, *Traité de droit privé suisse, vol. V/II/ 2: Le registre foncier* (Fribourg: Éditions universitaires, 1983), pp. 637ff.

[51] See art. 970 para. 4 CC, which applies by analogy to mentions in the land register, such as the mention of a trust relationship. See *Lignes directrices*, above, note 48, p. 3; Foëx, 'La mention du trust au registre foncier', above, note 49, 85ff; Guillaume, 'Trust, réserves héréditaires et immeubles', above, note 46, 43ff; Wolf and Jordi, 'Trust', above, note 49, p. 73.

not to have had the requisite powers or authorities, the third party's acquisition is not protected, for want of good faith. The third party is thereby exposed to the beneficiaries' right to trace the immovable property as publication effectively guarantees this right.[52]

Conversely, where the trust relationship is not published in the land register, the purchaser of immovable property has legitimate reasons for believing that it belongs to the trustee proper, who has the necessary power to sell the property. If it later becomes clear that this is not the case, the third party retains ownership regardless. Article 149d para. 3 PILA renders unpublished trusts not enforceable against good faith third parties. In this case, the existence of a trust relationship is not in question, but it cannot be set up against the bona fide purchaser.[53] The purchaser acts in good faith if, at the time of acquisition, he was unaware of the trust and could not have known of its existence despite the exercise of the diligence required by the particular circumstances. From the beneficiaries' perspective, failure to mention the trust in the land register paralyses their right to trace the immovable property alienated to a third party in violation of the trust.[54] In other words, the trustee can choose not to mention the trust in the register and keep the relationship confidential, but he does so at the peril of the beneficiaries.

This valid acquisition of property from an unauthorized party departs from the principle of *nemo plus juris ad alium transferre potest quam se ipse habet* (no one can transfer to another a larger right than he himself has), a concept justified in Swiss law through the principle of 'public faith' (*'foi publique'*), partially expressed in article 973 CC.[55] The principle creates a legal fiction whereby the land register is complete and accurate even if it does not correspond with reality. The principle of public faith thereby serves to secure transactions of immovable property. As such, where the trustee appears to be the true owner in the land register and this publication is considered

[52] See *Lignes directrices*, above, note 48, p. 3; Foëx, 'La mention du trust au registre foncier', above, note 49, 86; D. Pannatier Kessler, *Le droit de suite et sa reconnaissance en Suisse selon la Convention de La Haye sur les trusts* (Zurich: Schulthess, 2011), p. 146.

[53] Foëx, 'La mention du trust au registre foncier', above, note 49, 86.

[54] Ibid.

[55] Art. 973 para. 1 CC: 'Whoever acquires, in good faith, ownership or any other right in rem relying upon a registration in the Real Estate Register, shall be protected in such acquisition.'

complete and accurate, the purchaser acquires the property rights on the immovable, even if the trustee was not in a position to sell it under the restrictions imposed by the trust.

From the foregoing, it becomes clear that the good faith purchaser benefits from explicit protection under Swiss law. It is therefore a matter of course that the expression 'good faith third parties' in article 149d para. 3 PILA should include third party purchasers. This is uncontroversial in Swiss legal scholarship.

A more complex and live issue is whether or not creditors can equally be considered 'good faith third parties' under article 149d PILA and whether the effective segregation of trust assets published in the trustee's name depends on the trust relationship being mentioned.

C. Effects of publication and non-publication of the trust on the segregation of trust assets

The mention of a trust relationship in the appropriate register shows that the property is not part of the trustee's estate proper, but is a separate asset for the benefit of the trust's beneficiaries. Personal creditors of the trustee are thereby advised that the property in question is not available to meet the trustee's personal debts. The simple mention has an informative effect. What happens, on the other hand, if there is no mention of the trust relationship in the register? Does this hinder the effective segregation of the trust assets? In other words, can a creditor who extends credit to a trustee personally, having been led to believe in good faith that the property published in the trustee's name in the relevant public register was indeed his personal property, ask for the forced sale of the property in question to his benefit?

Swiss courts have not yet had an opportunity to consider this matter. As for the Swiss Federal Council, the views expressed in the *Message* on approval and implementation of the Hague Convention are the following: if the existence of a trust is not mentioned in the relevant register, the beneficiaries' right to segregation fails, with the result that it may be seized in favour of creditors who made loans to the trustee, in his private capacity, based upon the good faith understanding that he personally owned the published property. In other words, article 149d para. 3 PILA would protect not only bona fide purchasers of alienated trust assets but also good faith personal creditors of the trustee.[56] The majority of Swiss legal scholars have embraced these views.[57]

This interpretation of article 149d para. 3 PILA however deserves to be questioned. As shown below, it has three shortcomings. First, it relies on a premise, i.e. the bona fide credit granting, that is not in line with Swiss law and the functioning of Swiss public registers. Second, it is contrary to the spirit of the Hague Convention, which places particular importance on the ring-fencing effect. Third, its implementation would give rise to inextricable practical difficulties.[58]

On the first point, under Swiss law, the principle of 'public faith' is enshrined in article 973 CC.[59] Yet this legal provision, which is of general scope, only protects those who acquire in good faith a real right over a property, to the exclusion of those who have a mere claim against the registered owner.[60] In particular, Swiss public registers are not intended or designed to protect whatever creditors believe as to the solvency of a

[56] *Message*, above, note 26, p. 606: '*L'al. 3 dispose qu'une relation de trust qui n'a pas été inscrite dans un registre public n'est pas opposable aux tiers de bonne foi. Cette règle sert à protéger tant les créanciers de bonne foi du trustee que les acquéreurs de bonne foi de biens du trust qui ont été aliénés. Dans le premier cas, elle a pour effet de permettre aux créanciers de faire saisir les éléments du patrimoine du trust qui n'ont pas fait l'objet d'une inscription, dans le cadre d'une procédure d'exécution forcée ouverte à l'encontre du trustee.*' 'Paragraph 3 states that a trust relationship that has not been mentioned in a public register is not enforceable against bona fide third parties. This rule protects both bona fide creditors and bona fide purchasers of alienated trust assets. In the first case, the rule permits creditors in an enforcement proceeding against the trustee to seize elements of the trust fund that were not registered.'

[57] M. Eichner, *Die Rechtsstellung von Treugebern und Begunstigten aus Trust und Treuhand* (Basle: Helbing & Lichtenhahn, 2007), p. 200; Foëx, 'La mention du trust au registre foncier', above, note 49, 86ff; R. Gassmann, arts. 149a–149e PILA, in *Handkommentar zum Schweizer Privatrecht* (Zurich: Schulthess, 2007), pp. 3479–86, paras. 6ff, section 'art. 149d PILA'; P. M. Gutzwiller, *Schweizerisches Internationales Trustrecht* (Basel: Helbing & Lichtenhahn, 2007), p. 176, para. 149d-20; J. Schmid, Arts. 942–77, in *Basler Kommentar: Zivilgesetzbuch II*, 3rd edn (Basel: Helbing & Lichtenhahn, 2007), para. 47a, section 'art. 946 CC'; N. P. Vogt, Arts. 149a–149e PILA, in *Basler Kommentar: Internationales Privatrecht*, 2nd edn (Basel: Helbing & Lichtenhahn, 2007), para. 16, section 'art. 149d PILA'; Wolf and Jordi, '*Trust*', above, note 49, p. 73.

[58] For a further analysis on the topic, see references under notes 4 and 43. Of the same opinion under Swiss law: Pannatier Kessler, *Le droit de suite*, above, note 52, pp.156ff.

[59] This legal provision applies to the land register, which is the most comprehensively regulated public register. It is also applicable *mutatis mutandis* to the other public registers. See Pannatier Kessler, *Le droit de suite*, above, note 52, p. 123.

[60] See especially A. Homberger, Arts. 919–77, in *Kommentar zum Schweizerischen Zivilgesetzbuch, IV. Bd: Das Sachenrecht* (Zurich: Schulthess, 1938), para. 11, section 'art. 973 CC'; F. Jenny, *Der öffentliche Glaube des Grundbuches nach dem schweizerischen ZGB* (Bern: Stämpfli, 1926), p. 36. See also ATF 72 II 358 which asserts that Swiss bankruptcy

debtor or the effective composition of his estate. Specifically, public registers provide lenders no guarantee that the registered property is truly part and will remain part of the debtor's estate, so as to serve to pay them off in the event of a debtor's default or his bankruptcy.[61] The only means by which a creditor can secure his right over a particular asset is to seek a collateral on that property. Any creditor who lists his debtor's assets without taking out a security interest must assume the risk that the property will become unavailable. Good faith, even when based on the relevant public register, shall by no means compensate for the lack of collateral.[62] Since article 149 para. 3 PILA does not explicitly depart from the general rule of article 973 CC, it needs to be construed in accordance with it, for fear of distorting the system and creating a difference of treatment. It would indeed be unsatisfactory if protection of bona fide creditors through public registers were to be denied on a general level but were to be admitted in the case where creditors are faced with an unpublished trust.

Furthermore, protection of good faith causes a departure from the real material situation, so that it must be admitted restrictively. According to

law does not recognize a principle whereby third-party property is in the possession of the debtor, thereby giving the appearance of belonging to said debtor. The argument of abuse of rights is nevertheless available. Of another opinion: G. Gautschi, in *Berner Kommentar, VI. Bd: Das Obligationenrecht, 4. Abt.: Die einzelnen Vetragsverhältnisse, 2. Teilbd: Der einfache Auftrag: Art. 394–406 OR* (Bern: Stämpfli, 1960), para. 6b, section 'art. 401 CO'; J. Hofstetter, *Traité de droit privé suisse, vol. VII, t. II/1: Le mandat et la gestion d'affaires* (Fribourg: Editions Universitaires, 1994), pp. 126ff, in particular note 23.

61 With reservation to the clawback action, the debtor may for example, at any time and without adequate consideration, alienate the assets upon which the creditor has – by assumption – based his decision to extend credit, thereby depriving the creditor to obtain a forced sale on these assets in the event of the debtor's personal bankruptcy. This shows that public registers provide no adequate protection to creditors.

62 See L. Thévenoz, *Trusts in Switzerland: Ratification of the Hague Convention on Trusts and Codification of Fiduciary Transfers* (Zurich: Schulthess, 2001), p. 285: 'Certainly, the protection of the trustee's personal creditors is a legitimate concern, as they could be misled by the apparent solvency of their debtor if his trustee status is not revealed in the public registers. This fear is unfounded. Where a debtor's solvency is based on assets such as real estate, aircraft, vessels or industrial or intellectual property rights, a lender who is anxious about the debtor's worth will not be content to verify his assets at the time the loan is made, but will seek collateral, which alone guarantees the possibility of realizing it for his benefit in the event of the debtor's default. The validity of the security interest on real estate not identified in the land register as subject to a trust will then depend entirely on the lender's good faith (as a bona fide purchaser). If the register is silent about the trust, it may prejudice the beneficiaries' interests, but not those of the secured creditor.'

case law, good faith is solely protected under a specific legal provision that defines its scope.[63] Clearly article 149d para. 3 fails to meet these requirements, as protection of good faith is only expressed in general terms without any reference to bona fide creditors.

Second, the interpretation of article 149 para. 3 PILA, as put forward by the Federal Council message, is not in line with the spirit of the Hague Convention. Contracting States have to construe their internal provisions in accordance with the Convention, leaving aside the effects of articles 15, 16 and 18, which reserve – respectively – imperative rules, laws of immediate application and public order. Given the importance of the ring-fencing effect, the segregation of trust assets must be recognized to as great an extent as possible by contracting States. In our view there is no ground to invoke any of the above-mentioned rules to safeguard an interest that is not formally protected under Swiss domestic law, i.e. bona fide credit granting.[64]

Third, assuming one had to admit such a concept, the protection of bona fide creditors gives rise to major difficulties associated with its implementation as well as the equal treatment of creditors. Such a concept would require determining whether a creditor is indeed 'bona fide' under article 149d para. 3 PILA, based upon unknown criteria, as consulting the register is not a condition for protection under Swiss law.[65] If we are to protect lenders, are we not also required to protect the trustee's other contractual creditors who would not have consulted the register? If not, how do we justify the inequality in treatment? Similarly, how do we protect creditors resulting from wrongdoing, for whom the publication in public registers is not intended? Indeed, protecting bona fide creditors is reminiscent of Pandora's box: once open, there is no control over what follows. The moment we grant prerogatives on specific property for ordinary loans that do not naturally enjoy such a privilege (as opposed to real rights) – based on nothing more than the creditor's good faith – no objective attachment criteria on the property in question remain and the scope of legal protection could extend *ad*

63 ATF 96 II 161, JT 1971 II 76, cons. 4c. See also P. Piotet, 'La bonne foi et sa protection en droit privé suisse' (1968) 64 *Revue suisse de jurisprudence* 81–8 and 100–3.

64 For another perspective, see Gassmann, *Handkommentar*, above, note 57, para. 6, section 'art. 149d PILA'.

65 In the context of the land register, the effects of publication operate independently of an effective consultation of the register, as entries made therein are deemed to be known by third parties (see art. 970 para. 4 CC). The law thereby creates a fiction of knowledge. Cf. Deschenaux, *Traité de droit privé*, above, note 50, p. 638.

infinitum. In conclusion, by contrast with the position of the Federal Council and the majority view amongst Swiss scholars, the solution proposed here is that the effective segregation of trust assets in case of the trustee's bankruptcy should not depend on the trust relationship being mentioned in the relevant public register. It is worth mentioning that different authors in other civil jurisdictions support an equivalent view.[66] In any event, the courts will be the definitive forum to settle this delicate issue.

IV Collection of debts regularly incurred in the management of the trust

Here we will venture into our third topic, that of creditors' rights with respect to a trustee acting in that capacity, be such rights a result of contract, wrongdoing or other means. Should the trustee default on payment, these creditors must be able to recover their debts through debt collection proceedings. Swiss legislators found it necessary to set up specific enforcement procedures for debts regularly incurred in the management of a trust.

This phenomenon is likely to remain relatively marginal as we can expect a trustee to carry out his trust-related obligations with diligence. Nevertheless, debt enforcement remains pertinent if the trustee is negligent or cannot cover the debt, for example, due to insufficient liquidity. Exploring this topic is all the more interesting in that it shows how Switzerland, as a civil law jurisdiction without a tradition of trusts, has proceeded to regulate debt collection in this context.

We will first examine the debt liability regime for trusts, as this is a necessary preliminary issue for Swiss law. We will then see how debt enforcement works in Switzerland, where the debts are against the trustee's personal estate and where the debts are directly attributed to the trust assets.

A. Debt liability regime under the law applicable to the trust

Initiating enforcement proceedings for debts resulting from a trust requires first determining what estate is liable for those debts. In view

[66] In Dutch law, cf. M. Koppenol-Laforce, 'The Trust, The Hague Trusts Convention and Civil Law Countries: A Mission Impossible' (1998) 3 *Notarius International* 27, 39 and also from the same author, *Het Haagse Trustverdrag* (Deventer: Kluwer, 1997), pp. 196ff. In Luxembourgish law, see A. Prüm, T. Revet and C. Witz, 'La ratification de la Convention de la Haye par le Grand-Duché de Luxembourg', in Prüm et al., *Trust et fiducie*, above, note 44, p. 59.

of its material nature, this issue relies on the foreign law applicable to the trust, i.e. in the first place the law chosen by the settlor under article 6 of the Convention or – if none is chosen – on the objective criteria set forth in article 7 of the Convention. As we know, the trustee formally holds two separated estates, his own estate and the trust fund. Debts can be attributed to either depending on the applicable provisions.

Debt liability under various trust laws seems to follow one of two main trends: the 'traditional approach' and the 'modern approach', discussed in the following sub-sections. These trends will be examined very generally and concisely.

1. Traditional approach to debt liability

The traditional approach remains, even today,[67] that of English law: the trustee bears personal and unlimited liability to third parties for debts incurred in the management of a trust. This personal liability is based on the trustee's position as owner of the trust assets. The trustee's position is thereby distinguishable from that of the agent in that the trust, lacking legal personality, is simply unable to be represented.[68] The actions of the trustee, as such, do not bind the trust itself but him personally on his own property. This is the case regardless of whether the debts were incurred by regular means or otherwise.

The personal liability of the trustee is subject to various corrective measures. First, the trustee enjoys a right of indemnity against the trust assets, enabling him to directly deduct the amounts due or to be reimbursed.[69] However, this right is subject to strict conditions. For

[67] See however Trust Law Committee, *A Consultation Paper: Rights of Creditors Against Trustees and Trust Funds* (London: Tolley Publishing, 1997) and Trust Law Committee, *Report: Rights of Creditors Against Trustees and Trust Funds* (London, 1999), www.kcl.ac.uk/law/research/centres/trustlawcommittee/otherpapersandreports/TLCCreditorsRights-AgainstTrusteesReport.pdf. These documents contain various proposals for reform to improve the position of creditors. The proposals are before the Law Commission, but to date no concrete action has been taken.

[68] See in this respect J. Mowbray et al., *Lewin on Trusts*, 18th edn (London: Sweet & Maxwell, 2008), p. 677, para. 21–10: 'A trustee is in a different position from an agent. In general terms an agent acts on behalf of his principal and does not incur any personal liability provided that he acts within the scope of his authority: it is the principal, not the agent, who is liable. By contrast, a trustee acts as principal in connection with the administration of the trust and consequently does incur personal liabilities to third parties, whether or not he is acting in accordance with his powers and duties as trustee.'

[69] See especially in England s. 31(1) Trustee Act 2000. D. Hayton, P. Matthews and C. Mitchell, *Underhill & Hayton: Law Relating to Trusts and Trustees*, 18th edn (London: Butterworths, 2010), pp. 1063ff, paras. 81.1ff.

example, it is only available if the debt was incurred by regular means and was in the interests of the trust. Further, the trustee cannot be indebted to the trust assets for a violation of his duties in other circumstances.[70] Should this occur, indemnification is only possible for the portion in excess of the amount the trustee himself owes to the trust. Second, the trustee may in a contractual matter (though not one of wrongdoing) limit, or even exclude, his personal liability in a contract with a third party. Such a limitation or exclusion clause is permissible within certain limits and under certain conditions.[71] For example, the trustee may limit his personal liability to a determined amount or to an amount not exceeding the trust assets available.[72]

Creditors whose claims arise out of the management of a trust can, as a general rule, only satisfy them out of the trustee's personal estate, excluding the trust assets.[73] Under certain conditions, the traditional approach gives them a right to be subrogated to the trustee's right of indemnity against the trust property. This is, however, a secondary right that relies on the existence of a concrete right of indemnity on the part of the trustee, with the result that it is not always available.[74] As such, due to circumstances beyond his control or knowledge, a creditor may not be able to have recourse against the trust assets and can rely only on the trustee's personal property, leaving the said creditor in a delicate situation if the trustee is insolvent.

Despite these corrective measures, notably the right of indemnity and contractual limitation of liability, the basic scenario under the traditional approach remains that the trustee is personally liable for debts incurred in the management of the trust. Any debt collection proceeding must therefore be against the trustee in relation to his personal property. Generally, the traditional approach is beneficial to the trust, but rather unfavourable to the trustee and to creditors.

[70] On the limits of a trustee's right to indemnity, see Trust Law Committee, *Report*, above, note 67, pp. 5ff.

[71] Especially if compatible with the contract in question where the trustee specifies he is acting 'as trustee only' or 'as trustee and not otherwise'. See in this respect Mowbray et al., *Lewin on Trusts*, above, note 68, p. 678, para. 21–11.

[72] C. Mitchell, *Hayton & Mitchell: Commentary and Cases on the Law of Trusts and Equitable Remedies* (London: Sweet & Maxwell, 2010), p. 350, para. 8–81; Mowbray et al., *Lewin on Trusts*, above, note 68, p. 678, para. 21–11.

[73] L. Smith, 'Trusts and Patrimony' (2009) 28 *Estates, Trusts & Pensions Journal* 332, 339ff.

[74] Trust Law Committee, *Report*, above, note 67, pp. 4ff; Mowbray et al., *Lewin on Trusts*, above, note 68, pp. 694ff, para. 21–39.

2. Modern approach to debt liability

The second approach to debt liability is found in American law, as illustrated by the Uniform Trust Code,[75] as well as in some offshore jurisdictions, such as Jersey, Guernsey or Anguilla.[76] This approach provides – if conditions are met – for full exoneration from liability of the trustee on his personal estate and (the corollary) for a direct liability of the trust fund. In a contractual matter, this presupposes that the contract was duly concluded in the trustee's fiduciary capacity and that it disclosed this capacity.[77] In matters of wrongdoing or for obligations resulting from ownership or control of property, this implies that the trustee would not be personally at fault.[78] We can therefore say that the modern trend enables the trust's creditors to have recourse directly against the trust assets.

B. Debt collection proceedings in Switzerland

Part of the challenge faced by Swiss legislators was to provide for debt enforcement proceedings implementing the diverse approaches of trust laws to debt liability, in particular the traditional and modern trends seen above. Swiss law now provides for two distinct debt enforcement proceedings depending on the estate held liable for the debt, be it the trustee's personal estate or the trust fund.

1. Debt collection against the trustee's personal estate

If, under the applicable trust law (as under the base model of the traditional approach), debts incurred in the management of a trust are those of the trustee's personal estate, Swiss law would proceed as though the trustee were being sued for his private debts, like any natural or legal person. Since the existing legal provisions were deemed sufficient,

[75] See especially §1010(a) Uniform Trust Code: 'Except as otherwise provided in the contract, a trustee is not personally liable on a contract properly entered into in the trustee's fiduciary capacity in the course of administering the trust if the trustee in the contract disclosed the fiduciary capacity.' For liability for wrongdoing and that resulting from ownership or control of trust assets, see §§1010(b) and (c).

[76] See for example s. 32(1)(a) Trusts (Jersey) Law (1984): 'Where a trustee is a party to any transaction or matter affecting the trust – if the other party knows that the trustee is acting as trustee, any claim by the other party shall be against the trustee as trustee and shall extend only to the trust property.'

[77] §1010(a) UTC. [78] §1010(b) UTC.

Swiss legislators saw no reason to adopt specific provisions to regulate such a case.[79]

The sole peculiarity of the proceedings is that trust assets have to be kept out of reach of creditors (as not being liable for the debts under the law applicable to the trust), in which case article 284b DEBA will permit their segregation.[80]

2. Debt collection against the trust fund (art. 284a DEBA)

(a) General Article 284a DEBA governs the collection of debts that are attributed to the trust fund itself, as this may be the case in the modern approach to debt liability. This is a new type of debt enforcement proceeding under Swiss law. As we will see, Swiss legislators demonstrated creativity in this regard, adopting innovative solutions. However, these solutions, it must be noted, do not always line up with the traditional logic of Swiss insolvency law and that of the trust.

Article 284a DEBA, titled 'Debt collection proceeding for debts of a trust fund', reads as follows:

> (1) Where a trust in the sense of Chapter 9a PILA is liable for a debt, the proceedings must be brought against the trustee as representative of the trust.
> (2) The forum for such proceedings shall be the trust's seat in the sense of article 21 § 3 PILA. Where the trust's designated place of administration lies outside Switzerland, the proceedings shall be brought where the trust is effectively managed.
> (3) The debt collection proceedings shall be continued by way of bankruptcy. The bankruptcy shall be limited to the trust assets.[81]

Article 284a para. 1 DEBA governs the organization of proceedings. While the debt is one of the trust fund itself, the proceedings must formally be brought against the trustee (or one of the trustees) in his capacity as 'representative of the trust'. This expression is problematic as, strictly speaking, a trust cannot be 'represented' as it lacks legal personality.[82] This is sufficient, however, to show that the trustee is not

[79] *Message*, above, note 26, p. 608. [80] Ibid.

[81] Unofficial translation by D. W. Wilson, in *Trusts.ch: Newsletter of December 21st 2006*, available on www.trusts.ch.

[82] The laws of certain American States tend, however, to view the trustee as an 'agent'. See *Restatement of the Law Second Trusts* (St Paul: American Law Institute Publishers, 1959), §271A, comment (a): 'In a few States, it is expressly provided by statute that a trustee is a general agent for the trust property and that his acts, within the scope of his authority, bind the trust property to the same extent as the acts of an agent bind his principal.'

being sued in his personal capacity, but as trustee. The Swiss rule is thereby consistent with the American Uniform Trust Code that provides that the proceedings be brought against the trustee 'in his fiduciary capacity' even when trust assets are directly liable for the debt.[83] From the Swiss perspective, it may be noted that such debt collection proceedings brought against a person 'as representative' of a segregated fund are a novel legal solution that was designed specifically for the trust and that departs from the existing solutions under Swiss law.[84]

Article 284a para. 2 DEBA sets out where the proceedings may take place, that is the forum of the debt collection proceeding (*forum de la poursuite*). According to this provision, proceedings can be brought at the 'trust's seat'. This concept was taken directly from corporate law and its definition modelled on that of the seat of a company.[85] This borrowing was not necessarily desirable, since it refers to a concept foreign to the logic of trust. Be that as it may, the 'trust's seat' is primarily understood as being the location where the trust is to be managed.[86] According to article 284 para. 2 DEBA, debt collection proceedings may be commenced in Switzerland so far as either the designated or the trust's effective place of management lies in Switzerland.

Continuation of the proceedings is set out in article 284a para. 3 DEBA, where the trust is subject to bankruptcy proceedings.[87] Here, Swiss legislators opted for a collective and general form of enforcement, meaning that where bankruptcy is adjudged, all the trust's assets form an estate in bankruptcy ultimately designed to benefit all the creditors of the trust. The alternative would have been to subject the trust to seizure, an individual and special form of enforcement, which seeks to realize

[83] §1010(c) UTC: 'A claim based on a contract entered into by a trustee in the trustee's fiduciary capacity, on an obligation arising from ownership or control of trust property, or on a tort committed in the course of administering a trust, may be asserted in a judicial proceeding against the trustee in the trustee's fiduciary capacity, whether or not the trustee is personally liable for the claim.'

[84] On this topic, see Peyrot, *Le trust de* common law, above, note 7, pp. 151–69, in particular pp. 162ff.

[85] *Message*, above, note 26, pp. 597ff and 609: 'As proposed in the draft, para. 2 of art. 284a DEBA provides that the forum of proceedings is the seat of the trust in the meaning of new art. 21 para. 3 PILA or the place where the trust is effectively managed. We thereby come close to the regulation applicable to legal persons and associations of persons, which is logical if we consider that enforcement is de facto against the trust itself which is, similar to a legal person or an association, a distinct and autonomous fund.'

[86] See art. 21 para. 3 PILA.

[87] With exception to debts listed in art. 43 DEBA (notably, taxes and other public contributions) and to securities (art. 151 DEBA).

only as much of the debtor's assets as is necessary to pay off the creditors who initiated the proceedings. The main consideration for choosing bankruptcy was to ensure equal treatment, as it was said to be the only way to ensure that a trust's creditors could be simultaneously and equitably satisfied.[88] As such, the trust was compared to a legal entity that is regularly set off against multiple creditors.[89]

The choice of bankruptcy is in many ways problematic. First, its justification is unfounded. Other than the fact that comparing trusts to a legal entity is inadequate,[90] trusts are rarely subject to a large number of creditors, especially since they are generally created for estate planning purposes. A situation of excessive debt – the common scenario justifying bankruptcy – is atypical of trusts.[91] Seizure would likely have been better adapted to the insolvency of a trust and would better retain its substance, especially in light of a trust's potential future beneficiaries.[92] Second, it is unclear what would become of a bankrupt trust. Generally, bankruptcy results in the liquidation of the legal entity at issue. What happens in the case of a trust? Does it dissolve *ipso facto* or can it last beyond bankruptcy? Such questions do not rely on Swiss domestic law but on the foreign law applicable to the trust, which we can assume does not envision the eventuality of a trust being bankrupt. Finally, it is equally uncertain how a judgment of bankruptcy under Swiss law affecting the assets of a trust would be perceived abroad and whether it would be recognized if required.

(b) 'Personification' of the trust? From the preceding, it appears that article 284a DEBA somehow 'personifies' the trust as it confers on it various characteristics of legal persons:[93] the use of the term 'representative of the trust' to describe the trustee at article 284a para. 1 DEBA, the reference to the 'trust' s seat' at article 284a para. 2 DEBA, the concept of 'effective management' of the trust, and making the trust fund subject to

88 *Message*, above, note 26, p. 611.

89 See the French (*'entité juridique'*) and the Italian (*'entità giuridiche'*) texts. The German version, which is the original one, refers to *'Rechtsgebilde'*, which is a more neutral formulation.

90 As in the French and Italian versions of the *Message*.

91 L. Thévenoz, 'L'avant-projet suisse de ratification de la convention sur les trusts', in *Le trust en droit international privé: Perspectives suisses et étrangères: Actes de la 17ème Journée de droit international privé du 18 mars 2005 à Lausanne* (Zurich: Schulthess, 2005), p. 100.

92 Ibid.

93 See also P. Panico, *International Trust Laws* (Oxford University Press, 2010), p. 272, para. 6.119.

bankruptcy are each examples of this personification. We must acknowledge that this trend is not a general one, but applies only in the context of debt enforcement and relates to a specific type of proceeding (set up to meet the requirements of the modern approach to debt liability).

Nevertheless, this move towards a 'personification' of the trust for the need of debt enforcement is not necessarily desirable, as it is not in line with the traditional logic of the institution. In treating trusts so similarly to legal persons, Swiss law goes even further than certain common law jurisdictions.[94] In addition, even though contracting States enjoy a certain discretion in implementing the recognition of foreign trusts – especially in relation to debt enforcement – it is more advisable to avoid the attribution of novel characteristics to a foreign institution, in order not to jeopardize its overall coherence.

Part of the reason for this move towards a 'personification' may be found in the difficulty of making trusts fit within civilian logic. In this respect, it may seem simpler for civil law jurisdictions to bring trusts closer to legal persons, whose legal context is well defined and for which the rules are ready for use (with respect to insolvency, taxation, etc.).

V Conclusion

I conclude this brief overview of the treatment of trusts in Swiss enforcement law with three final comments based upon the preceding analysis.

First, as with other civil law systems, Swiss debt liability law is based on the principle of the 'unity of patrimony'. Recognition of trusts as ring-fenced funds under the Hague Convention, however, did not cause any great difficulties, primarily because Swiss law never saw this principle as immutable and inflexible dogma and because derogations to the concept in various forms and means existed in Swiss law beforehand. The 'unity of patrimony' remains the basic model, even if trusts added another major exception thereto, which is now anchored at article 284b DEBA. Generally, should further exceptions to this principle be introduced in

[94] Notably the United States. See in this respect *Restatement of the Law Third Trusts* (St Paul: American Law Institute Publishers, 2003), §2 comment (a): 'Increasingly, modern common-law and statutory concepts and terminology tacitly recognize the trust as a legal "entity", consisting of the trust estate and the associated fiduciary relation between the trustee and the beneficiaries. This is increasingly and appropriately reflected both in language (referring, for example, to the duties or liability of a trustee to "the trust") and in doctrine, especially in distinguishing between the trustee personally or as an individual and the trustee in a fiduciary or representative capacity.'

the future,[95] it may be opportune to reflect on the role and place of 'unity of patrimony' in the various legal systems that subscribe thereto.

Second, we have seen that Swiss law deals, at article 149d PILA, with publication of trust relationships in public registers. However, it leaves it unclear whether this publication is a prerequisite to the effective segregation of the concerned property in the event of the trustee's personal bankruptcy. As argued herein, contrary to the current majority opinion of Swiss legal scholars, we believe it does not. In our view, public registers do not protect creditors with personal rights, as opposed to acquirers of rights *in rem* over the concerned property. Article 149d PILA must therefore be interpreted under the law as it stands. Accordingly, a trust relationship (and the segregation of a particular trust's assets) is enforceable against the trustee's personal creditors independent of any publication. This solution promotes the ring-fencing effect of trusts imposed under the Hague Convention as a minimum requirement of recognition and avoids practical problems.

Finally, Swiss law tackled the complex issue of debt enforcement proceedings where debts incurred in the management of the trust are – according to the modern approach to debt liability – attributable to the trust fund itself. Swiss legislators clearly demonstrated some creativity in adopting innovative solutions at article 284a DEBA. However, it must be said that these solutions do not always line up with the traditional logic of the Swiss insolvency law and that of the trust. As for the latter, it may be pointed out that article 284a DEBA tends towards a certain 'personification' of the trust in submitting it to the collective debt collection proceedings and using concepts applicable to legal persons. Admittedly, this trend is not a general one, as it is limited to debt enforcement. However, neither is it harmless since it evokes a more general risk: that civilian jurisdictions may treat trusts as (quasi-) legal persons upon any sign of difficulty in integrating or implementing them in their domestic law![96]

[95] Such as the proposal for directives on 'protected funds'. See in this respect S. C. J. J. Kortmann et al. (eds.), *Towards an EU Directive on Protected Funds* (Deventer: Kluwer, 2009).

[96] Panico, *International Trust Laws*, above, note 93, p. 272, para. 6.119 notes a similar trend in Italian law with respect to the tax treatment of trusts.

4

Can a modern legal system do without the trust?

REINOUT WIBIER

I Introduction

When civil lawyers and common lawyers communicate, there is always a high risk of talking at cross purposes. I remember a conference where Professor Robert Stevens was defending a paper before a group consisting mainly of civil lawyers from the Netherlands, Germany and many other jurisdictions where private law has been codified in a civil code. Professor Stevens argued that it is conceptually impossible that one person is the owner of a contractual claim but another person is entitled to receive payment because ownership of a claim and entitlement to payment are in fact one and the same thing. This of course is perfectly possible in many civil law jurisdictions, simply because the civil code says so.[1] Professor Stevens' argument was that ownership of a claim is simply the same thing as being entitled to payment, whereas in many civil law jurisdictions these questions are treated as separate. The background to this discussion was the question of whether the legal transfer of a claim is possible without giving notice to the debtor. From an English law perspective this would be unthinkable but in the Netherlands a claim can be legally transferred without giving notice to the debtor. Failure to give notice means that the debtor will continue to be able to validly discharge the claim by paying the original creditor. The assignee then has recourse against this original creditor (but not against the debtor). Since there is no trust concept in the Netherlands, the assignee now runs a credit risk against the assignor. This, however, is not the case under English law because the proceeds are (probably) held on trust by the

A version of this contribution was published in (2011) 5:1 *Law and Financial Markets Review* 37.

[1] As an example, on the basis of art. 94(3) of Book 3 of the Civil Code, Dutch law permits the legal transfer of a claim without giving notice to the debtor. The debtor will still be able to validly discharge its debt by paying the original creditor, however, unless notice of the transfer has been given.

assignor for the benefit of the assignee. I must admit that this English law solution may very well lead to the more equitable result and the common law probably owes this to the trust.

What this story also shows, in my view, is that common law solutions are often very practical and business-friendly, whereas having a civil code which purports to solve all (potential) legal issues may often lead to solutions that may seem a bit odd or even downright contrary to common sense. The trust is a case in point because it often allows the person with the 'real' or economic interest in an asset to pursue its rights against a person who happens to be the legal owner even if the latter is bankrupt. In contrast: in civil law jurisdictions, including the Netherlands, this often proves to be difficult or even impossible due to a hostility to trusts and trust-like concepts.

In this chapter I will argue that it is very difficult indeed to leave trust concepts out of modern jurisdictions, precisely for the reasons shown by the above example. Without a trust concept there will be many unjust results and a civil law jurisdiction very often is only able to partially mitigate these unfortunate results. But we must start at the beginning. In Section II, I will discuss the question of why Dutch law has become so hostile to trusts and trust-like concepts. In Section III, I will describe a number of legal problems that arise due to this hostility to trusts. Subsequently (Section IV) I will describe a number of instances where the trust is creeping back into the Dutch legal system, and I will end this chapter with my conclusions in Section V.

II Keeping the trust out of the new Dutch Civil Code

There are two main reasons why the Dutch legal environment is relatively hostile to trusts. The first can be found in article 3:84(3) of the Civil Code, prohibiting fiduciary ownership. This will be further discussed in Section II.A. The second reason is found in articles 3:276 and 3:277 of the Civil Code, requiring that a creditor take recourse against the entire estate of its debtor (and thus prohibiting different creditors from having recourse against different parts of an estate). This reason will be further discussed in Section II.B.

A. *No fiduciary ownership*

In 1992 the Netherlands introduced a brand new civil code. The main drafter of the new code was Professor E. M. Meijers (1880–1954), who was an outspoken opponent of trusts, as the following quotation illustrates:

> The English notion that, he who manages property for the benefit of another and has the right to dispose of that property qualifies as the legal owner, is without a doubt inferior to our view that the person for whose benefit the property is being administered is the exclusive owner of that property.[2]

Professor Meijers' views had great influence on the Dutch Civil Code, although apparently he was one of the few scholars to hold such strong views against ownership that was only of a temporary nature (as the trust was seen by Meijers).[3] It may be useful to note in this context that fiduciary ownership in the Netherlands mainly developed to avoid certain rules regarding the creation of rights of pledge on assets. Fiduciary ownership was used as an alternative way to create security over movables and receivables to avoid certain formalities for the creation of pledges.[4] Under the Civil Code in force before 1992, creating a right of pledge on a movable asset required taking this asset out of the possession of the pledgor. This was viewed as inconvenient, especially if the relevant assets needed to be used in the pledgor's business. In practice, the parties tried to avoid these formalities by transferring the asset to the secured party instead of creating a pledge on the asset.[5] The Dutch Supreme Court confirmed the validity of this structure in 1929. The most important case in this respect was in relation to the famous Dutch Heineken breweries.[6]

The complete inventory of a bar had been 'pledged' to Heineken as security for a loan granted by Heineken to the owner of the bar. Instead of actually using the right of pledge, the parties chose to transfer the inventory to Heineken by way of security. The main advantage of this was that for a transfer there was no need to take the assets out of the

[2] Taken from A. C. F. G. Thiele, *Collective Security Arrangements* (Deventer: Kluwer Legal Publishers, 2003), p. 279. See E. M. Meijers, WPNR 2998 (1927), 414 for a Dutch language overview of his objections to the trust.

[3] W. J. Zwalve, 'Regelgeving in het vermogensrecht' (2009) 2009–1 *RM Themis*, 24–5.

[4] It is important to note that as a matter of Dutch law a right of pledge is conceptually and legally very different from an ownership right even if the latter (mainly) serves a security purpose.

[5] Similarly, rights of pledge over receivables required giving notice to the debtor. This notice requirement could be avoided if instead of creating a pledge, the receivable was transferred by way of security to the secured party.

[6] Supreme Court decision of 25 January 1929, *NJ* 1929, p. 616 (*Bierbrouwerij*).

possession of the owner of the bar. A transfer of ownership can also be effected by way of *constitutum possessorium*, leaving the owner of the bar in the possession of the assets, a possibility that did not exist for creating rights of pledge. In this way a new security right (that was not mentioned in the Civil Code at all) was created by the Supreme Court: ownership for security purposes or fiduciary ownership.[7]

This then of course triggered the question of what the exact rights and obligations of a fiduciary owner were. The Civil Code did not provide an answer simply because fiduciary ownership was nowhere to be found in it. In a later case the Supreme Court ruled that as a general principle a fiduciary owner should not have any more rights than a pledgee would have had in cases where the transfer was for security purposes.[8] A fiduciary owner should not have more rights in relation to the assets than the holder of a right of pledge in relation to those assets would have had if the transfer did not serve any other purpose than to provide the new owner with a security right. This meant, for instance, that a fiduciary owner was obliged to sell the relevant asset upon a default of the borrower and was not allowed to simply keep the asset. The proceeds of the sale that exceeded the secured liabilities needed to be handed back to the transferee. As a consequence of these Supreme Court decisions, fiduciary ownership became a hybrid form of ownership. The fiduciary owner was the legal owner of the asset but there were certain restrictions to the ownership right. These restrictions then of course corresponded with certain rights the transferee had, most importantly the right to the assets being returned upon payment of the secured liabilities and the right to receive any excess proceeds from a sale. It was this division of rights between the fiduciary owner and the transferor that Professor Meijers did not like. Ownership should be one and indivisible. Moreover, his view was that a person that wanted to create a security interest should use a right of pledge and not a hybrid form of ownership.

Meijers did, however, acknowledge that the requirement of taking the asset out of the possession of the pledgee was not very practical. In his draft for the new Civil Code, Meijers did two things to solve this problem. First, he introduced the possibility to create non-possessory rights of pledge, i.e. a right of pledge where the pledgor could keep the

[7] It is not difficult to see that this is not easily reconciled with a *numerus clausus* principle for proprietary rights.

[8] Supreme Court decision of 3 January 1941, *NJ* 1941, p. 470.

assets in its possession.[9] Secondly, he tried to ban fiduciary ownership by introducing a specific prohibition in the Civil Code.[10] It is against this background that article 84(3) of Book 3 of the Dutch Civil Code, which is one of two provisions that would seem to be an obstacle to trust-like structures in the Netherlands, must be viewed. It translates as follows:[11]

> A juridical act which is intended to transfer property for purposes of security or which does not have the purpose of bringing the property into the patrimony of the acquirer, after transfer, does not constitute valid title for transfer of that property.

Dutch law sets three requirements for a valid transfer of an asset: (i) delivery (ii) by a person who is authorized to dispose of the asset (iii) pursuant to a valid legal title (art. 84(1) of Book 3 of the Civil Code). This shows that transfers that lack a valid legal title are void as a matter of Dutch law. Consequently, a transfer of an asset for security purposes or a transfer to a trustee for an asset to be held on trust[12] would be void as a matter of Dutch law due to lack of a valid legal title. This is generally seen as an important obstacle to the introduction of trusts in the Netherlands.

B. No separate estates

The second rule that may be an even bigger obstacle to the introduction of trusts in the Netherlands can be found in articles 3:276 and 3:277(1) of Book 3 of the Civil Code. In translation they read as follows:

> Unless otherwise provided by law or contract, a creditor can take recourse for his claim against all the property of his debtor.

[9] The possibility, which previously did not exist, to create a right of pledge over receivables without giving notice to the debtor was introduced at the same time. Both security rights require a notarial deed of pledge or a non-notarial deed that then needs to be registered with the tax authorities.

[10] Art. 84(3) of Book 3 of the Civil Code.

[11] An English (and French) translation of Book 3 of the Dutch Civil Code that has been prepared by Peter P. C. Haanappel and Ejan Mackaay is available at: http://papers.ssrn.com/sol3/papers.cfm?abstract_id=1737823. I have copied all translations of Civil Code articles in this chapter from that source.

[12] Here is a point where confusion between common lawyers and civil lawyers may easily arise. I have been given to understand that the creation of a trust over an asset should perhaps not be viewed as a transfer of the relevant asset but as the creation of a new right over the asset. However, art. 84(3) of Book 3 of the Dutch Civil Code would still be an obstacle for creating this right because it prohibits split ownership.

> Except for the causes of preference recognized by law, after payment of the costs of execution, creditors have, amongst themselves, an equal right to be paid from the net proceeds of the property of their debtor in proportion to their claims.

These articles prevent the creation of separate estates. One of the main features of the trust (at least from a civil law perspective) is that it enables beneficiaries to separate assets from the personal estate of the trustee, particularly in case of the trustee's insolvency.[13] The trust assets are not available to the trustee's general body of creditors. This is seen as a major problem of the trust from a Dutch law perspective because it would violate the above rule, which is seen as fundamental. All assets of a debtor should be available to its creditors. Reasons for not accepting exceptions to this rule vary from the fear of fraud to the fundamental uneasiness with any ability to create separate estates that are only available to a number of creditors but not to others.

Other arguments that have been used against introduction of trusts in the Netherlands are that they would be ideally suited for fraud, that they would not fit in the Dutch legal system which has a *numerus clausus* of proprietary rights and that Dutch law has sufficient alternatives that enable parties to reach a very similar result.[14] In the next section I will focus on this last point because I think that there is a good case to be made for the view that, whatever the objections to the introduction of a trust in the Netherlands, the statement that there are adequate alternatives is simply too optimistic.

III The main trouble with having no trust

Reading the above, a common lawyer may well think that the Dutch legal system is not very practical. There are in fact a number of common

[13] From the perspective of a trust-friendly jurisdiction this may be quite different. I have been given to understand that insolvency of the trustee is seen by some as an atypical situation which really should not be used as the standard for developing trust law, mainly because trustees almost never go bankrupt and the trust has been developed for entirely different purposes such as wealth management. From a civil law perspective, however, the way in which trust-friendly jurisdictions deal with insolvency of the trustee is the most interesting feature of the law of trusts.

[14] See S. C. J. J. Kortmann, 'Past "de trust" in het Nederlandse Recht?', in David J. Hayton et al. (eds.), *Vertrouwd met de Trust: Trust and Trust-like Arrangements* (Deventer: W. E. J. Tjeenk Willink, 1996), pp. 169–93. Professor Kortmann argues in his article that there are no fundamental reasons why the trust could not be introduced into Dutch law.

instances where the lack of a trust instrument is indeed felt. Perhaps atypically from a common lawyer's perspective all these cases involve what should happen if the person who might be seen as a de facto trustee becomes insolvent. From the perspective of a civil lawyer, the ability to separate assets from the trustee's estate in favour of the beneficiaries is the most useful aspect of the common law trust.

A. *Monies held for third parties*

There are various commercial relationships where A keeps money belonging to B in its (A's) own bank account. Collection agencies, for instance, sometimes collect receivables of service providers (doctors, lawyers, dentists, etc.). The monies are directly paid by the clients into a bank account that is in the name of the collection agency. The proceeds of exploitation of certain intellectual property rights might also be streamlined in this way. In the Netherlands there is an organization called Buma/Stemra that collects monies due to composers. Each time a song is played on the radio, the songwriter is entitled to a small fee and Buma/Stemra collects these fees on the songwriter's behalf. Moreover, there are also legal service providers such as civil law notaries and bailiffs who have statutory duties that require holding money that belongs to their clients. For civil law notaries the most important example is money held for the purchaser or the seller in real estate transactions. Real estate can only be delivered through a notarial deed and there is a practice in the Netherlands whereby the purchaser pays the purchase price to the civil law notary who then disburses this sum to the seller once delivery of the real estate to the purchaser has been effected. As a consequence of this practice neither the seller nor the purchaser runs a credit risk against the other. What they often do not realize is that they may instead run a credit risk against the civil law notary.[15] The same is true for the other two examples provided in this section. Professionals that have their receivables collected by a special collection agency run an insolvency risk against the agency and songwriters run an insolvency risk against Buma/Stemra.

If these entities were to become insolvent, their clients would only have a contractual claim in the estate which would rank *pari passu* with all

[15] This is not the case due to special legislation protecting the clients of civil law notaries. I will discuss this special legislation in the next section.

creditors' claims, irrespective of whether the monies belonging to their clients can be identified. Perhaps a common lawyer would have the means to separate the monies held for clients by concluding that these monies are held on trust, but due to the Dutch system described above no such option would exist under Dutch law. Unfortunately this position is confirmed by case law.

In a well-known case a collection agency, ProCall, collected invoices originated by doctors of the Beatrix Hospital. The amounts collected were held in a bank account in ProCall's name but bearing the name 'ProCall re Beatrixhospital', thus clearly indicating that the amounts standing to the credit of the account economically belonged to the hospital. ProCall became bankrupt and the hospital requested release of the funds from the bankruptcy trustee. The bankruptcy trustee, however, took the view that the hospital only had a contractual claim against ProCall and that this claim should be treated no differently from any other contractual claims. As I pointed out above, this would mean that the claim would rank *pari passu* with all other unsecured claims against the estate on the basis of article 277(1) of Book 3 of the Dutch Civil Code.[16] The likely result of this approach would of course be that the hospital would only receive partial payment and that the money standing to the credit of the account would be divided on a *pro rata parte* basis between all of ProCall's creditors.

The Supreme Court agreed with the bankruptcy trustee. It explicitly rejected the view that the bank account held by ProCall qualified as a trust account that enabled the hospital to separate the money held in it from the rest of the estate as this view would be contrary to articles 276 and 277 of Book 3 of the Civil Code.[17]

B. *Fungible securities held for third parties*

A very similar situation arises for fungible securities that are held through an intermediary. In a controversial Supreme Court case,[18] securities broker Van Loosbroek & Co (Loosbroek) held securities through its intermediary Kas-Associatie N.V. (Kas), a bank. Kas was an institution that had been admitted by Euroclear Netherlands, the Dutch Central Securities Depository. In its account with Kas, Loosbroek held securities for its own

[16] See Section II.B above.

[17] Supreme Court decision of 13 June 2003, *NJ* 2004, 196 (*Beatrix Hospital/ProCall*).

[18] Supreme Court decision of 23 September 1994, *NJ* 1996, 461 (*Kas-Associatie*).

clients, including Drying Corporation N.V. (Drying). When Loosbroek became insolvent, Kas claimed to have a right of pledge on securities held in the account as security for loans provided to Loosbroek by Kas. Drying, however, claimed that no such pledge could possibly exist because the securities held in the account were not Loosbroek's own but were merely held by Loosbroek for the benefit of Drying. Since the concept of the trust is unknown to Dutch law, there could be no solution for Drying based on Loosbroek holding the securities on trust for Drying. The argument that the securities had been directly acquired by Drying through delivery to Loosbroek was also rejected because this type of direct acquisition (based on article 110 of Book 3 of the Civil Code) is only available for tangible assets under Dutch law. As a matter of Dutch law it is possible that delivery of movable property to A (a de facto trustee) for the benefit of B (a de facto beneficiary) leads to a direct acquisition of ownership by the beneficiary.[19] The ultimate result was that Drying had to accept that its securities had been validly pledged to Kas by its (now insolvent) intermediary Loosbroek. I will come back to this point presently. What is important to note here is that the *Kas-Associatie* case shows that clients with a securities account may very well run an insolvency risk against their intermediary – again – because Dutch law fails to accept the trust.[20]

C. *Security trustee in loan transactions*

A rather specific case is security that is held by a security agent in a syndicated loan transaction for the benefit of a large group of banks. Syndicated loans are contracts where two or more banks agree to grant a loan to one or more borrower(s) on common terms governed by a single agreement between all parties.[21] This is a practical way of preventing one

[19] This possibility is opened by art. 110 of Book 3 of the Dutch Civil Code, which states that if there is a legal relationship between two persons from which it follows that person A will hold certain movables for the benefit of person B, then delivery to person A will lead to the direct acquisition of ownership by person B.

[20] Of course this is unacceptable. The Dutch legislature again intervened to create special rules that would prevent this effect. These rules will be further discussed in the next section. They mainly show that solutions that may come naturally to trust-friendly jurisdictions require complicated solutions and specific action by the legislature in the Netherlands.

[21] Philip R. Wood, *Law and Practice of International Finance*, University edn (London: Sweet & Maxwell, 2008), § 7–03.

single bank from running all the credit risk in relation to one borrower in cases where the amount is too high for a single bank to bear. If the loan is secured, the security will usually be created in favour of a security agent as it is a lot more practical if the security is held by one party for the benefit of the syndicate members than creating security for the benefit of all the banks jointly – for example, when banks wish to sell their participation and in enforcement scenarios.

As there remains uncertainty under Dutch law about whether security interests can be held by a party that is not the creditor of the secured obligations, security is provided to a security agent through the creation of a parallel debt. Under the parallel debt arrangement, the borrower undertakes an obligation to pay the entire amount due to all syndicate banks to the security agent and this debt obligation (i.e. the debt payable to the security agent) is subsequently secured. The parallel debt documentation provides that the borrower will only have to pay the secured liabilities once and that payments towards the parallel debt will lead to discharge of the borrower's obligations to the individual banks (and vice versa).

The syndicate banks may run an insolvency risk against the security agent holding the security interest which secures their claims against the borrower – a risk that would not exist if the security were deemed to be held on trust by the security agent for the benefit of the syndicate banks as beneficiaries. In addition, due to the parallel debt, monies may be collected by the security agent that need to be passed on to the economic owners of the money, i.e. the relevant lenders. Again, because there is no trust under Dutch law, this may lead to problems.

D. General concluding remarks

The above examples are all similar in certain respects. They all deal with situations where the legal owner of an asset is different from the economic owner, where there is a de facto trustee who holds the asset for the benefit of one or more beneficiaries. The trouble is that the legal situation does not match economic realities in these instances. Unlike the common law, civil law (at least in the Netherlands) would seem to be insufficiently flexible to deviate from strict ownership analysis to reach just and equitable results. Consequently, the beneficiary of the relevant asset runs an insolvency risk against the legal owner.

A thing to note here is that the problem seems to be particularly pressing if the relevant assets are intangible. As a matter of Dutch law it is possible that delivery of movable property to a person fulfilling the role of trustee for a beneficiary leads to a direct acquisition of ownership by the beneficiary. This possibility arises from article 110 of Book 3 of the Dutch Civil Code, which states that if there is a legal relationship between two persons from which it follows that A will hold certain movables for the benefit of B, then delivery to A will lead to the direct acquisition of ownership by B. This is not a trust, because A simply never obtains ownership; B will become the owner immediately upon delivery. But it does solve the problem of the insolvency risk. However, the Supreme Court has determined that this provision does not apply to intangibles such as claims, as in the *Kas-Associatie* case[22] (see above). However, in a world where intangible assets seem to become more important almost on a day-by-day basis, the thought that the problem is limited to these types of rights is not very reassuring.

In the next section, I will discuss a number of instances where the trust is creeping back into the Dutch legal system to mitigate the effects of the rules described in this section. It will show that trust-like concepts are almost unavoidable in modern jurisdictions and it will trigger the question whether it would not be simpler to give up resistance to the trust in general and instead happily accept it is a useful or even indispensable legal structure.

IV Examples where the trust is creeping back in

A. *Client monies held by specific professionals*

As observed above, civil law notaries regularly hold money for the benefit of their clients, for instance in real estate transactions. The Dutch legislature has provided a specific tailor-made solution to prevent monies held by civil law notaries for their clients from getting stuck in the bankrupt estate of the civil law notary concerned. Article 25 of the Law on the Notarial Profession determines that (i) civil law notaries are obliged to open one or more special accounts for holding client monies and (ii) monies held in these accounts (i.e. the claim against the financial institution where the account is maintained) are owned by the clients for whom the money is held. Consequently, the claim against the relevant financial institution is jointly owned by a large number of persons. Should a civil law notary go bankrupt, these joint clients would

[22] *Kas-Associatie*, above, note 18.

be able to separate the account from the rest of the estate (they own the claim against the bank) and they would not be adversely affected by the civil law notary's insolvency (except maybe for practical issues such as the question how they should proceed in distributing the monies held in the account). A similar regime exists for monies held by bailiffs, another profession that regularly calls for holding monies that do not belong to the professional but to beneficiaries. But as the *Beatrix Hospital/ProCall* case discussed above shows, no such rule exists for the clients of collection agencies.[23] In this case the Dutch Supreme Court incidentally did in fact accept the possibility for attorneys and accountants to open trust accounts while at the same time rejecting any other occupational groups' right to do so. This means that some people who entrust money to third parties are protected, but others are not. The distinction is not entirely random (civil law notaries, bailiffs, attorneys and accountants are all professional practitioners, subject to professional conduct rules, and they all regularly hold monies belonging to third parties, often when performing statutory duties), but this does not seem sufficient to warrant these different levels of protection. Another issue with this solution is that it gives the clients of the relevant professional joint ownership of the account. This may cause problems if they need to exercise their rights, especially if they are to act jointly in order to effect these rights. This would be rather impractical, to put it mildly.

The Dutch Supreme Court seems to have accepted only one exception to these strict rules – in a case involving a payment by the tax authorities which was made by mistake into an insolvent estate.[24] The general rules would dictate that this money, now being part of the estate, would be distributed equally between creditors having claims directly against the estate. The resulting claim for repayment of the money would not enjoy any preference in relation to other post-insolvency estate claims. Other claims would include the bankruptcy trustee for its fees, tax and salary claims incurred during the bankruptcy and other costs of the bankruptcy. In other words: the claim for return of the money would not have any preference. In fact, some of these claims (e.g. the claim for the trustee's salary) would have priority over the claim for return of the money that was mistakenly paid into the estate. The Supreme Court, however, determined that the money had to be returned immediately to the tax authorities because there had been no legal relationship at all between the

[23] See *Beatrix Hospital/ProCall*, above, note 17.
[24] Supreme Court decision of 5 September 1997, *JOR* 1997, 102 (*Ontvanger/Hamm q.q.*).

insolvent party and the tax authorities and payment into the estate had obviously been a mistake. It has been argued in Dutch legal literature that by providing this solution the Supreme Court accepted at least the concept of the money being held on trust for the benefit of the tax authorities. But the case continues to be an exception to the rule that there is generally no separation of estates under Dutch law, and it seems unlikely that the Supreme Court meant to introduce trusts in the Netherlands through this case. This is confirmed by its aversion to the concept in the more recent *Beatrix Hospital/ProCall* case, as discussed above.

B. Fungible securities held for third parties

Under English law the position of an investor that holds fungible securities through a chain of financial institutions (often called intermediaries in this context) is protected because the intermediary is a trustee for the securities account holders who are the beneficial owners of the securities held in the account. As a result, the investors are not affected by the insolvency of their intermediary.[25] However, as the trust concept is alien to Dutch law a different solution has had to be found to prevent the holders of securities entitlements from having to share with the general creditors of the intermediary upon its insolvency.

The problem has been addressed in the Netherlands by way of a special statute, the Securities Transfer Act,[26] which deals with the holding and transfer of securities that are held through intermediaries. In addition to providing the legal structure for the transfer of securities through book entries, the statute determines that the joint investors that hold their securities through an account with a registered intermediary (i.e. an intermediary admitted to Euroclear Netherlands)[27] are the joint owners of the securities that they are credited with in the intermediary's books. The joint ownership structure that is used for this protection is rather complicated: what could have been achieved with relative ease by

[25] Philip R. Wood, *Set-off and Netting, Derivatives, Clearing Systems*, 2nd edn (London: Sweet & Maxwell, 2007), § 18–032; R. Goode, *Legal Problems of Credit and Security*, 3rd edn (London: Sweet & Maxwell, 2003), § 6–10.

[26] *Wet giraal effectenverkeer*. For ease of reference I will refer to this act as the 'Securities Transfer Act'. It contains both rules to protect investors against the insolvency of their intermediary and rules for transferring securities by way of book entries. For the purpose of this chapter, the investor protection rules are the most important.

[27] Euroclear Netherlands itself determines which institutions are admitted.

intermediary needs to be admitted by Euroclear Netherlands or (and this is where the scope is widened) fall within the broad definition of an investment firm under the Dutch Act on Financial Supervision.[31] However, only those investment firms that are allowed to perform investment services in the Netherlands under the Dutch Act on Financial Supervision will qualify for the protection offered by the Securities Transfer Act. This includes two main categories: (i) banks or investment funds with a Dutch licence and (ii) banks or investment funds with a European passport.

Going back to the *Kas-Associatie* case discussed in Section III.B, the proposed legislation should solve the problem that arose there. Loosbroek probably would have qualified as an investment firm allowed to perform investment services under the Dutch Act on Financial Supervision. In addition, Loosbroek obviously administered a securities account in the Netherlands, namely the account through which it had credited its client Drying with the securities. Consequently, its clients (including Drying) would have obtained a proprietary interest in the pool of securities offering them protection in case of Loosbroek's insolvency.

The common law reader may well suffer some confusion after this overview of how clients of intermediaries are protected under Dutch law against their intermediary's insolvency. In my view, the above solution is ridiculously complicated. Simply introducing the trust as a legal structure would probably make these kinds of solutions obsolete. The absence of a trust triggers the need to grant full ownership rights to the clients of financial intermediaries. It would of course be much simpler to accept that intermediaries often hold securities for the benefit of their clients and to offer these clients proprietary protection against the insolvency of their intermediary by using the concept of a trust, where the intermediary is the trustee and the investor the beneficiary.

C. *Agency*

A truly interesting trust-like structure can be found in the Dutch law of agency. Agency, or mandate, is defined in article 400 of Book 7 of the Civil Code as follows:

[31] The definition of 'investment firm' in the Dutch Act on Financial Supervision reads as follows: an investment firm is 'the party providing an investment service'. This definition includes, amongst others, brokers, asset managers, investment advisers and placement agents.

> Mandate is a contract whereby one party, the mandatary, binds himself toward the other party, the mandator, to perform one or more juridical acts on account of the mandator without there being a relationship of employment.[32]

An example would be the collection agency that is hired by a professional services provider. If a doctor hires a collection agency to collect her bills, the collection agent will not only collect money but will also enter into a contract with a bank to open an account where the monies can be collected. The collection agency may also itself hire a bailiff to assist with collection if certain amounts remain unpaid. Consequently, in agency relationships the agent often enters into contracts, thus obtaining contractual rights against third parties, for the account of the principal. The contractual party is the agent, but the benefits of the contract and the economic interest accrue to the principal. The question then arises of what will happen if the agent goes bankrupt. Above it was shown that monies held by an agent (i.e. contractual rights against banking institutions) will generally form part of the bankrupt estate and that the principal will not have any priority in relation to this money.[33]

From my perspective, the most interesting aspect of these types of agency contracts is article 421 of Book 7 of the Civil Code. On the basis of this article if the agent goes bankrupt the principal is able to acquire for himself any contractual rights[34] that the agent has obtained against third parties by simply sending a notice to both this third party and the agent. Here the concept of one person (the agent) being the legal owner of certain contractual rights whereas another (the principal) is the actual or economic owner of those rights is clearly acknowledged by allowing the latter to separate the rights from the former's insolvent estate. This would in my view include the contractual rights against a bank, i.e. the money held in a bank account by the collection agency for the benefit of the professional service provider. In a trust-friendly jurisdiction the solution in these types of situations would probably be found in the agent holding money on trust for the principal. In the Netherlands, a separate solution is required to remedy the unjust results that would otherwise occur. The solution of article 421 of Book 7 of the

[32] Translation taken from Peter P. C. Haanappel and Ejan Mackaay's translation of Book 7 of the Dutch Civil Code, above, note 11.

[33] *Kas-Associatie*, above, note 18, and, even more relevant here, *Beatrix Hospital/ProCall*, above, note 17.

[34] The relevant contractual rights should not be purely personal or non-transferable.

Civil Code does, however, seem a rather elegant solution and is perhaps the closest that Dutch law comes to having an actual trust.

D. *Collective investment schemes*

The final example of trust-like structures creeping back into the Dutch legal system is in relation to collective investment schemes. These can take a number of legal forms. For instance, participants in a collective investment scheme may be the shareholders in a company that purchases the investment assets. Sometimes the investment scheme is not in the form of a legal entity issuing shares but in the form of a number of contracts between a management company, a depositary and the participants in the investment scheme. Each participant then purchases one or more units in the fund, which are basically contractual rights entitling the holder to the profits of the fund. Financial supervision rules require that the assets of the fund are kept by the depositary. Moreover, there is a special rule in the Act on Financial Supervision which states that the assets of the fund shall only be used to cover liabilities relating to the management and custody of the fund, and units.

This means that any other liabilities, e.g. personal debts of the depositary, cannot be covered by the assets of the fund. The situation is at least somewhat similar to the position of a trustee. A trustee's private creditors do not have recourse against the trust assets. Again, this would seem to be an example where the lack of a trust in the Netherlands has been remedied by a specific rule for a specific situation and where introduction of a trust-like structure in the Netherlands would have been an alternative.

E. *The Hague Trusts Convention*

One of the more favourable portents for introducing the trust into the Dutch legal system might be that the Netherlands has ratified the Hague Convention on the Law Applicable to Trusts and on Their Recognition (the Convention).[35] The Convention obliges the Netherlands to recognize certain aspects of the trust that have been validly created in a trust-friendly jurisdiction: 'Such recognition shall imply,

[35] Convention on the Law Applicable to Trusts and on Their Recognition, The Hague, 1 July 1985, in force 1 January 1992, 23 ILM 1389. Available at: www.hcch.net/upload/conventions/txt30en.pdf.

as a minimum, that the trust property constitutes a separate fund, that the trustee may sue and be sued in his capacity as trustee, and that he may appear or act in this capacity before a notary or any person acting in an official capacity.'[36]

As a practical matter the impact of the Netherlands being a party to the Convention is rather limited. First, it does not introduce the trust into the Dutch legal system; it simply obliges the Netherlands to recognize certain legal consequences of trusts that have been validly created in accordance with the laws of jurisdictions that do have trusts. Secondly, it remains uncertain whether it would be possible to subject Dutch assets to even an English law trust, because this subjection itself would probably be governed by Dutch property law. Consequently, the full force of article 84(3) of Book 3 of the Civil Code, containing the prohibition on transferring assets without the intention for the asset to form part of the transferee's estate, would be felt. Is this not exactly what the transfer of an asset to a trustee would entail? And even if the English law analysis would allow for assets being held on trust without those assets being transferred to a trustee, it is still hard to see how this could be translated back to the Dutch system where subjection to a trust would seem difficult without such a transfer. An additional hurdle would be article 13 of the Convention, which allows jurisdictions to refuse recognition of trusts 'the significant elements of which, except for the choice of the applicable law, the place of administration and the habitual residence of the trustee, are more closely connected with States which do not have the institution of the trust'.[37] In cases where all the assets are subject to Dutch property law, this exception to the need to recognize a trust may well apply.

On closer inspection it would seem safe to conclude that the Convention does not offer any immediate or easy solutions for the advocates of the introduction of a trust-like structure in the Netherlands.

This conclusion may, however, need to be revisited due to a recent change in Dutch private international law. The Dutch legislature has determined specifically in a statute on conflict rules for proprietary rights that a transfer of an asset to a trustee is not considered to violate article 84(3) of Book 3 of the Civil Code. This provision of private international law means that an important hurdle for subjecting assets to a foreign law trust seems to have been eliminated. It introduces at least the theoretical

[36] Ibid., art. 11. [37] Ibid., art 13.

possibility to use English law trusts to achieve objectives that cannot currently be achieved through Dutch law alternatives. Only time will tell whether foreign law trusts can actually be used for this purpose in the Netherlands pursuant to this change in legislation.[38]

F. Concluding remarks

Most of the examples that were discussed in the previous sections have one thing in common. They all try to correct legal outcomes that are deemed to be unacceptable, using concepts similar to trusts, but without actually introducing the trust in the Netherlands. Thus, they also show that there are a number of cases where the lack of the trust concept leads to unacceptable results. This clearly raises the question whether it would not be far simpler to introduce a general trust concept in the Netherlands, perhaps even by introducing a special section on trusts in the Civil Code. Otherwise there may continue to be cases where inequitable results occur. Why, for instance, are the clients of a civil law notary protected, while the clients of a collection agency are not?[39]

Three main reasons are generally given as to why the introduction of a general concept of the trust in Dutch law would not be a good idea. One reason that is often put forward is that trusts may be easily abused to hide monies from creditors and thus to evade paying one's debts. The second reason is that trusts are a convenient way to avoid taxes. Both these reasons are not very convincing in my view. Trusts set up for these reasons would evidently be void and people set on avoiding taxes and other debts hardly need a trust to do so. The third reason, however, does have some merit. Trust law is complex. The trust is a difficult concept and it leads to various interesting but difficult questions. In the common law the trust has a very long tradition and many of these problems and issues have been solved in case law precedents. New problems can be solved building on the centuries-long experience with the trust as a legal concept. The Netherlands, of course, has no such tradition. The introduction of the trust in the Netherlands would thus potentially lead to a chaotic situation and much legal uncertainty. For that reason it may be best to continue to find solutions on a case-by-case basis in situations where the legal outcome is unacceptable.

[38] And it would still not seem to be possible for Dutch entities to act as a trustee.

[39] Ignoring the possibility of protection through art. 421 of Book 7 of the Civil Code for the moment. This option is in my view legally sound, but has not yet been confirmed in case law.

It would be convenient, however, if the Dutch courts and legislature would show some flexibility in this regard in applying the existing rules. For instance, it should generally be possible to protect persons with an economic interest in an asset against the insolvency of the legal owner. This can be achieved in many ways as the above examples show (agency, trust accounts, etc.) and the most straightforward option might often be to simply conclude that during the 'trustee's' insolvency these assets do not form part of the bankrupt estate and are thus not subject to private creditors of this 'trustee'. A way of achieving this goal without too much trouble would be for the legislature to simply specify assets that fall outside the scope of the 'trustee's' insolvency in certain specific instances, for example securities held by financial intermediaries for investors and monies held in collection accounts by collection agencies for the benefit of their clients. A way of dealing with fears of abuse of the trust concept might be by limiting the ability to act as a trustee to professional parties that are subject to regulation, such as banks. The ability to hold monies on trust could then be combined with regulatory oversight, limiting the risks of trusts being used to avoid paying creditors. Professor Meijers would probably not have liked this solution. Times have changed significantly, however, since he reworked the beautiful Dutch Civil Code.

V Conclusion

My conclusion can be brief. At the beginning of this chapter I posed the question whether trusts can be kept out of a modern legal system. I believe they cannot. There are simply too many instances where economic and legal interests, especially in intangible assets, will not run parallel. In these instances failure to accept the concept of one person being the legal owner and another the beneficial owner will often lead to unacceptable and unjust results. This does not mean, however, that I think that the common law trust should be introduced in the Netherlands.

Doing so would introduce all sorts of complex problems into the Dutch legal system for which it would have no answer. Of course, eventually the answers would come, but only at great cost and through lengthy litigation. The ensuing legal uncertainty would be unacceptable. The solution for this problem is fairly simple. The Dutch legal system should, on a case-by-case basis, try to find solutions to problems that arise due to the lack of the trust as an accepted legal concept. These solutions could be based on trust-like structures as in the case of the rules allowing a principal to obtain rights owned by its agent against third parties.[40] I personally would like to take a welcoming view towards the common law trust and use solutions provided by it because the common law shows that it is possible to offer practical results without opening the floodgates to fraud, tax evasion and selective payment only to some creditors.

[40] Art. 421 of Book 7 of the Civil Code, discussed in Section IV.C above.

5

Stateless trusts

LIONEL SMITH

I Introduction

The jurist trained in the common law may have difficulty imagining a legal system without the trust. Pierre Lepaulle spoke of common law jurisdictions as places 'where trusts accompany the rhythm of life, from the cradle to the grave, where everyone knows what it is from seeing it functioning at the home as in the office'.[1] Many of the chapters in this volume discuss the different ways in which trusts can be welcomed into civilian systems. Such a development, it seems, necessitates careful doctrinal effort, whether or not it benefits from a legislative foundation.

But there are other possibilities. Can trusts migrate from one place to another?[2] Can trust *law* migrate from one place to another, or simply be imported ad hoc, so that a settlor can establish a trust that is entirely governed by a foreign legal system? If so, the settlor may not care whether or to what extent her own legal system has a trust; she merely chooses one that does, and in particular she may choose the one that offers the features that best suit her particular wishes.

The Hague Trusts Convention[3] requires the courts of countries where it is in force to recognize trusts, whether or not their legal system has any kind of trust at all. This is a rather extraordinary reality: the Convention is not, like most Hague Conventions, an agreement on choice of law rules, but also imposes an obligation to recognize what would otherwise be unrecognizable. If the courts of one legal system are confronted with

[1] P. Lepaulle, 'An Outsider's View Point of the Nature of Trusts' (1928) 14 Cornell L.Q. 52, 52–3. Those who teach the subject might, however, think that Lepaulle exaggerated a little bit.

[2] For the common law principles on this question, see P. Matthews, *Trusts: Migration and Change of Proper Law* (London: Key Haven Publications, 1997), a book that is small but mighty; R. A. Hendrickson, *Changing the Situs of a Trust* (New York: Law Journal Press, looseleaf).

[3] Hague Convention on the Law Applicable to Trusts and Their Recognition, The Hague, 1 July 1985, in force 1 July 1992.

a legal construction from another legal system that simply does not exist in the local system of the forum, there is a problem. Not only does the local system not have rules about that foreign construction; but, as a result of that, it probably does not have any relevant choice of law rules. The natural and normal solution is to recharacterize this foreign construction in terms that are known to the forum law.[4] Like any translation, this is inevitably imperfect, but the forum legal system cannot engage with legal constructions that it does not recognize.

The need for non-trust jurisdictions to recharacterize trusts as contracts, legal persons or other institutions, and the problems to which this was thought to give rise, were among the primary reasons for the adoption of the Convention.[5] If the Convention is brought into force in a country, its courts then must recognize foreign trusts as trusts, even if the forum law has no such institution;[6] and it will no longer be true that the forum law has no choice of law rules for trusts, because the Convention provides them.[7]

In 2007, Switzerland decided to ratify the Convention without creating, in its domestic law, an institution that falls within the Convention's definition of a trust.[8] Other states that did the same thing, much earlier, are Italy and the Netherlands, and as we will see, there are reasons to think that at least some features of the Swiss ratification were informed by the Italian experience.

II It's my trust, I'll choose the legal system

As far as choice of law is concerned, the Convention's starting point in its article 6 is that the settlor can choose the governing law.[9] There are a

[4] K. Lipstein, 'Characterization', in *International Encyclopedia of Comparative Law* (Tübingen: Mohr, 1994), vol. III, ch. 5; M. Graziadei, 'Recognition of Common Law Trusts in Civil Law Jurisdictions under the Hague Trusts Convention with Particular Reference to the Italian Experience', in L. Smith (ed.), *Re-imagining the Trust: Trusts in Civil Law* (Cambridge University Press, 2012), p. 29, pp. 40–4.

[5] A. E. Von Overbeck, 'Explanatory Report on the 1985 Hague Trusts Convention', in *Proceedings of the Fifteenth Session (1984), volume II, Trusts – Applicable Law and Recognition* (The Hague: Hague Conference, 1985), p. 370, para. 14.

[6] Hague Convention, above, note 3, art. 11.

[7] Ibid., ch. II.

[8] See A. Peyrot's contribution to this volume (Chapter 3), and also A. Peyrot, *Le trust de* common law *et l'exécution forcée en Suisse* (Geneva: Schulthess, 2011); D. P. Kessler, *Le droit de suite et sa reconnaissance selon la Convention de La Haye sur les trusts:* Tracing *en droit civil suisse* (Geneva: Schulthess, 2011). For the earlier argument that Swiss domestic law should be amended when the Convention should be ratified, see L. Thévenoz, *Trusts in Switzerland: Ratification of the Hague Convention on Trusts and Codification of Fiduciary Transfers* (Zurich: Schulthess, 2001).

[9] Hague Convention, above, note 3, art. 6.

number of limits on this. One of them is built into article 6 itself: if the settlor manages to choose a legal system that 'does not provide for trusts or the category of trust involved', then the choice is not effective.[10] That is not surprising and one might hope that this will not occur very often. In such a case, just as in a case in which the settlor does not choose a governing legal system, the judge must decide with which legal system the trust is most closely connected, applying a set of objective connecting factors.[11] All of this is subject to the general provision in article 5 that states:

5. The Convention does not apply to the extent that the law specified by Chapter II does not provide for trusts or the category of trusts involved.	5. La Convention ne s'applique pas dans la mesure où la loi déterminée par le chapitre II ne connaît pas l'institution du trust ou la catégorie de trust en cause.

This provision, however, must be one with very little scope. Because of the features of article 6 that we have just noticed, article 5 would seemingly only cover the case where the judge is required to determine choice of law by objective factors, and that process points to a legal system without the trust, or the category of trusts, involved. It would be unusual for a trust to be, objectively, most closely connected to a non-trust system.

More important is article 13:

13. No State shall be bound to recognise a trust the significant elements of which, except for the choice of the applicable law, the place of administration and the habitual residence of the trustee, are more closely connected with States which do not have the institution of the trust or the category of trust involved.	13. Aucun Etat n'est tenu de reconnaître un trust dont les éléments significatifs, à l'exception du choix de la loi applicable, du lieu d'administration et de la résidence habituelle du trustee, sont rattachés plus étroitement à des Etats qui ne connaissent pas l'institution du trust ou la catégorie de trust en cause.

This article was included as a kind of protection for non-trust states against the recognition obligations of the Convention.[12] It *permits*

[10] Ibid. [11] Hague Convention, above, note 3, art. 7.

[12] Von Overbeck, 'Explanatory Report', above, note 5, para. 123: 'The option offered by article 13 is open to the judges of all the Contracting States, but it is clear that it is in fact

(it does not require) the courts of such a state to withhold recognition of a trust that falls within the description in article 13. Take the case of a trust created in the Netherlands, of Dutch property, with Dutch trustees and beneficiaries, but for which the settlor chooses Quebec law. Article 13 applies, because all the significant elements are more closely connected with the Netherlands than with Quebec – except the choice of governing law, but article 13 excepts that from consideration.

The other elements on the list of factors to be disregarded in article 13 – the place of administration, and the habitual residence of the trustee – are a little harder to understand. These are objective factors in the sense that unlike a choice of law clause, they are not determined by mere words in a document. Indeed, they are both on the list of objective connecting factors that a judge must look to when there has been no express choice of law.[13] So if a trust were created with Dutch beneficiaries, but the trust property were located in Quebec, and the trustees were resident in Quebec, and the settlor chose Quebec law as the governing law, article 13 is apparently just as applicable as in the earlier example. This seems a little odd, but since article 13 is only permissive, it may not be very important.[14]

The permissive nature of article 13 has been a matter of great importance in Italy. Professor Maurizio Lupoi stressed that the starting point of the Convention is settlor autonomy in choice of law, and he has succeeded inasmuch as Italian courts do not on the whole make use of article 13 in situations in which they could.[15] Instead, they permit settlors to create trusts which are basically Italian trusts in every way, except that they are governed by a foreign legal system.[16] In this way, Italians can make use of the Convention effectively to import foreign trust law into Italy, when it permits them to accomplish goals that cannot be achieved within Italian law. This has been described by a delegate to

an escape clause in favour of States which do not have trusts. The clause will be used above all by judges who think that the situation has been improperly removed from under the application of their own laws.'

13 Hague Convention, above, note 3, art. 7.

14 The complicated drafting history of art. 13 is explained in Von Overbeck, 'Explanatory Report', above, note 5, paras. 125–33.

15 See M. Lupoi, *Trusts: A Comparative Study*, trans. S. Dix (Cambridge University Press, 2000), pp. 357–62; M. Lupoi, 'A Civil Law Perspective on Trusts and the Italian Case' (2005) 11(2) *Trusts & Trustees* 10.

16 See Graziadei, above, note 4; A. Braun, 'Italy: The Trust Interno', in D. Hayton (ed.), *The International Trust*, 3rd edn (Bristol: Jordans, 2011), p. 795.

the Conference at which the Convention was drafted as 'one of the most remarkable outcomes that the Convention has triggered'.[17]

The Convention is also in force in the Netherlands. It is, however, not clear that the solutions adopted in Italy would be followed there. Commentators seem to think that the Dutch courts would use article 13 to refuse recognition to what was, in every way except choice of law, a Dutch trust.[18]

What of Switzerland? The federal Swiss Private International Law Act of 18 December 1987, in its article 149c,[19] now provides:

1. The law governing trusts is regulated by the Hague Convention of 1 July 1985 on the Law Applicable to Trusts and Their Recognition.	1. Le droit applicable aux trusts est régi par la Convention de La Haye du 1er juillet 1985 relative à la loi applicable au trust et à sa reconnaissance.
2. The law specified by that Convention also governs where, under its art. 5, the Convention is not applicable and where, under its art. 13, the State is not obliged to recognize a trust.	2. Le droit désigné par ladite convention est également déterminant dans les cas où, conformément à son art. 5, elle n'est pas applicable, et où, conformément à son art. 13, l'Etat n'est pas tenu de reconnaître un trust.

The result is that the choice given by article 13 has basically been made by the legislature, in the sense that the option not to recognize a trust that falls within article 13 has been taken away from the courts. Even article 5 has been, in a sense, disapplied. More precisely, article 5 is in force in Switzerland; but when article 5 applies, it says that the Convention does not apply; and article 149c para. (2) then steps in to say that after all, the Swiss choice of law rule in this situation is the one yielded by the Convention that does not apply.

These legislative choices – particularly, the disapplication of article 13 – seem to point in the direction of a version of settlor autonomy with respect to choice of law that surpasses the text of the Convention, and

[17] D. W. M. Waters, 'The Hague Trusts Convention Twenty Years On', in M. Graziadei, U. Mattei and L. Smith (eds.), *Commercial Trusts in European Private Law* (Cambridge University Press, 2005), p. 56, p. 80.

[18] See R. Wibier's contribution to this volume (Chapter 4), at pp. 85–6, noting however a recent change to Dutch private international law; and Graziadei, Mattei and Smith, *Commercial Trusts*, above, note 17, pp. 422–3.

[19] The French text is official, as are the German and Italian texts available at www.admin.ch. The English text here is my own translation from the French.

surpasses the law as it has developed in Italy. The inference must be that the Swiss legislator – being surely conscious of the Italian experience and the discussions surrounding article 13 – deliberately chose to create an environment with the widest possible latitude for the choice of the governing law.

The United Kingdom arguably did something similar, although not necessarily so consciously. It was one of the first states to sign the Convention. In its legislative incorporation of the Convention into domestic law, it simply omitted article 13.[20] This omission was based on the assumption that article 13 was only potentially relevant to non-trust states.[21] But this seems to have been a mistake, if only because article 13 refers to 'States which do not have the institution of the trust *or the category of trust involved*'.[22] Some countries, for example, allow non-charitable purpose trusts, which do not generally exist in English law. English law has trusts, but does not have that category of trust. But by choosing not to enact article 13, the UK Parliament has apparently taken away from UK courts the possibility of withholding recognition of such a trust, even if all of the significant elements of that trust (except the choice of a foreign governing law) are most closely connected with a UK jurisdiction.[23]

As a final example, we may consider Quebec, where the Convention is not in force. The Civil Code of Québec, however, enacts as a starting

[20] See the Schedule to the Recognition of Trusts Act 1987 (UK). It is not wholly clear that this is appropriate under the Convention, which allows states to make reservations as to particular articles, and stipulates that 'no other reservation shall be permitted' (art. 26). The Convention does not allow reservations in relation to art. 13. The Swiss technique, as we have seen, was to bring into force the whole Convention, including art. 13, and then to enact as a matter of Swiss law that the option given by art. 13 was not to be exercised by Swiss courts.

[21] This assumption is visible in Von Overbeck, 'Explanatory Report', above, note 5; see the quotation from para. 123, above, note 12, and also para. 124: 'this provision allows a judge of a State which does not have trusts to refuse recognition to the trust because he thinks that the situation involved is internal to his State. In contrast this possibility does not exist for those States which have trusts, but those States do not seem to feel the need for it.'

[22] Emphasis added. The reference to 'the category of trust' appears to have been added quite late in the evolution of art. 13: Von Overbeck, 'Explanatory Report', above, note 5, paras. 132–3.

[23] This is the opinion of M. Lupoi, 'The Effects of the Hague Convention in a Civil Law Country' (1998) 4(7) *Trusts & Trustees* 15, 16 and J. Harris, *The Hague Trusts Convention: Scope, Application and Preliminary Principles* (Oxford: Hart, 2002), p. 343: 'the Recognition of Trusts Act 1987 appears to have the surprising effect of authorising an English settlor in an otherwise wholly domestic context to create a trust unknown or unauthorised in English domestic trust law, by the simple expedient of choosing a foreign law to govern it'.

point the Convention principle that a settlor is free to choose the governing law of a trust.[24] Here too, the courts have begun to recognize trusts of Quebec property, governed by a foreign legal system.[25]

How are we to assess this trend in favour of unrestricted settlor autonomy respecting choice of law? Is there any objection to it? We can notice, first, that not every system follows this approach. The common law, where the Convention has not replaced it, is not wholly deferential to the settlor's choice. The most striking example is seen where the trust property is immovable: the usual view is that the trust's validity, effects and administration will be governed by the law of the *situs* of the immovable.[26] This is a mandatory rule that is not subject to settlor choice. We can also notice that Belgium has rejected unrestricted settlor autonomy. The Convention is not in force there, but many of its principles appear in the Belgian Code of Private International Law.[27] The settlor may choose the applicable law;[28] if, however, all of the significant elements of the trust (except for the choice of law) are in a jurisdiction that does not have trusts, then the express choice is ineffective.[29] No discretion is given to the court.

In relation to choice of law regarding contracts, a consensus emerged some years ago in favour of party autonomy.[30] This, arguably, informed

[24] Civil Code of Québec, art. 3107.

[25] Investment trusts of movables governed by Ontario law were recognized in *Fonds Norbourg Placements équilibrés (Liquidation de)* [2007] R.J.Q. 1890 (C.A.), noted by J. Claxton (2008) 27 E.T.P.J. 341; a trust of immovable property in Quebec governed by California law was accepted in *Re Piccini*, 2006 QCCS 7939, noted by J. Talpis, (2007) 27 E.T.P.J. 78.

[26] D. W. M. Waters, M. Gillen and L. Smith, *Waters' Law of Trusts in Canada*, 4th edn (Toronto: Thomson/Carswell, 2012), pp. 1462, 1469; A. W. Scott, W. F. Fratcher and M. L. Ascher, *Scott and Ascher on Trusts*, 5th edn (Boston: Aspen, 2006), §46.1. In the Convention, by contrast, there is nothing that turns on the distinction between movable and immovable property.

[27] Loi portant le Code de droit international privé, 16 July 2004. See P. Matthews, 'Trusts in Belgian Private International Law: Selected Provisions from the New Belgian Code of Private International Law, Translated into English, with an Introductory Note', (2005) 19 Trust L.I. 191.

[28] Code de droit international, ibid., art. 124 §1, first sentence: 'Le trust est régi par le droit choisi par le fondateur.'

[29] Ibid., art. 124 §1, para. 2: 'Lorsque tous les éléments significatifs du trust, à l'exception du choix du droit applicable, sont localisés dans un Etat dont le droit ne connaît pas l'institution du trust, ce choix est sans effet.'

[30] In the EU context, see the Rome I Regulation (Regulation (EC) No 593/2008), replacing the Convention on the Law Applicable to Contractual Obligations 1980, Rome, 19 June 1980. See the analogy drawn by Lupoi, 'Effects of the Hague Convention', above, note 23,

the choices made in the drafting of the Hague Convention. But this requires us to ask whether the two situations are comparable.[31] A contract has only very limited juridical effects beyond its effects on the parties; so to let them choose the juridical regime is to let them make a choice that substantially only affects them. We do not, however, let them choose which law will govern the rights of others, such as the law governing creditors' recourses, or the law regarding what is necessary to make a transfer of property that is effective *erga omnes*.

How does this distinction apply to trusts? It threatens to bring us back to the old question of whether trusts are part of the law of obligations, or of the law of property. The question is either unanswerable or uninteresting, in the sense that the answer is probably 'a bit of both'. Similarly, the tendency among some civilians to try to understand the common law trust as a kind of contract has led to certain misunderstandings.[32] Among the many aspects of (at least) the common law trust that cannot be duplicated by contractual arrangements between settlor and trustee are the insulation of the trust assets from the trustees' creditors; the nature of trusteeship as an office, independent of the person or persons who may occupy the office from time to time; and the court's supervisory jurisdiction, which allows the court to be consulted on the administration of a trust without the need for an allegation of wrongdoing or an actual legal dispute.[33]

These issues do not need to be resolved in order to assess critically the position taken in the Hague Convention. Instead, we can look at what effects the Convention actually brings about, in relation to the recognition of foreign trusts that it requires of those states that ratify it. An argument in favour of the settlor autonomy granted by the Hague Convention could be built on a claim that the Convention is not primarily concerned with the third-party or proprietary effects of trusts; in

19–20 and also in M. Lupoi, *Trusts: A Comparative Study*, trans. S. Dix (Cambridge University Press, 2000), pp. 349–50, to the Rome Convention and to other conventions concerning contracts.

[31] See Harris, *Hague Trusts Convention*, above, note 23, pp. 167–8.

[32] D. Hayton, P. Matthews and C. Mitchell, *Underhill and Hayton: Law Relating to Trusts and Trustees*, 18th edn (London: LexisNexis, 2010), pp. 16–18, list twelve distinct reasons why a common law trust is not a contract. John Langbein has noted that express trusts have features in common with contracts: J. Langbein, 'The Contractarian Basis of the Law of Trusts' (1995) 105 Yale L.J. 625, but has more recently explored some of the limits of settlor autonomy: J. Langbein, 'Burn the Rembrandt? Trust Law's Limits on the Settlor's Power to Direct Investments' (2010) 90 BU L. Rev. 375.

[33] See L. Smith, 'The Re-imagined Trust' in Smith, above, note 4, p. 258, pp. 271–3.

other words, that the freedom of choice that it grants to settlors does not allow them to impose legal consequences on third parties. Is this true?

In the absence of the Convention, the typical non-recognition problem that might arise in a non-trust state is in relation to the trustee's powers. The trustee presents himself, in such a jurisdiction, as a rather odd character: he claims to be at once the owner of property, but only its administrator, which in a civilian system may well amount to a contradiction in terms.[34] Moreover, he presents himself as having effectively unlimited *power* to deal with the trust property, vis-à-vis the world, even if, vis-à-vis his own beneficiaries, he has a limited *authority*. And he so presents himself not only to courts, but to notaries, land registrars, securities registrars and other officials. Hence the argument that one of the key goals of the Convention was to ensure that the powers of the trustee were acknowledged.[35] But the recognition of the wide powers of trustees, so far from potentially harming third parties, favours their protection, and it channels problems created by trustees who exceed their authority and misuse their powers into claims that must be brought against the trustee by the beneficiaries.

If this recognition of trustees' powers were the real goal and effect of the Convention, one might say that there is little objection to settlor autonomy. But if this were the real goal, it is not at all clear that it is the ultimate effect. The Convention almost certainly requires that when a trust is recognized, then the personal creditors of the trustee shall have no recourse against the trust assets, regardless of whether such a result is possible under local law.[36] This creates some internal tension in that the Convention also states that mandatory rules of the forum cannot be avoided under the Convention, in particular mandatory rules regarding 'the protection of creditors in matters of insolvency'.[37] How these provisions are to be reconciled is, to some extent, a matter for the future.[38]

[34] F. Weiser, *Trusts on the Continent of Europe* (London: Sweet & Maxwell, 1936), pp. 4–8; H. Motulsky, 'De l'impossibilité juridique de constituer un "Trust" anglo-saxon sous l'empire de la loi française' (1948) *Revue critique de droit international privé* 451, esp. 460–1.

[35] Lupoi, 'Effects of the Hague Convention', above, note 23, 15: 'the Conference had two basic aims: the recognition of the trustee's powers and the laying down of conflict rules concerning the validity of trusts. On the first topic, the objective was set from the very beginning of the proceedings: trustees should enjoy the same powers as that which the law governing the trust would confer on them.'

[36] Hague Convention, above, note 3, art. 11(a); see also art. 2(a).

[37] Ibid., art. 15(e).

[38] See Harris, *Hague Trusts Convention*, above, note 23, pp. 376–7, and also pp. 317–18.

But if the Convention protects trust assets against personal creditors of the trustee, then this alone means that it cannot be viewed as a document that is concerned only to ensure the recognition of trustees' powers in relation to trust property. On the contrary, it potentially revises central elements of the private law of states that bring it into force; namely, the availability of assets to answer debts, which is to say, the understanding of the patrimony, which is nothing less than a fundamental aspect of the law of persons.[39] In that perspective, it is not at all clear why full settlor autonomy as to governing law was thought to be appropriate.

And indeed, it is not so clear that unrestricted settlor autonomy *was* thought to be appropriate. The view that article 13, for example, serves as a genuine limiting factor on settlor autonomy is not wholly untenable; on its face, it gives courts a discretion, with little direction as to how to use it.[40] Switzerland has taken this discretion away from its courts; the UK also, although in this case, arguably by mistake.[41] Elsewhere, a different view of its scope may be taken; and this could arguably be good for the success of the Convention, which to date has been adopted in a significant, but not an overwhelming, number of jurisdictions. In this respect, Lupoi's arguments may reveal a paradox: the more successfully he contends that the Convention grants full settlor autonomy, even in relation to trusts that have no international character, the less some countries may be willing to ratify the Convention.[42]

[39] C. Cassagnabère, 'De la division du patrimoine au démembrement de la personnalité: étude du concept de patrimoine d'affectation à travers l'exemple québécois' (2012) 92 *Revue Lamy droit civil* 63.

[40] As we have seen, Professor Lupoi's argument is that the best interpretation of the Convention as a whole is that art. 13 has a narrow scope; he does not clearly state when he thinks it can be appropriately used to deny recognition of a trust. He mentions 'exceptional cases' and suggests that tax evasion may be one: Lupoi, 'Effects of the Hague Convention', above, note 23, 21; see also 20: 'an exceptional rule for exceptional circumstances'.

[41] Above, note 20 and accompanying text. It would be possible for Parliament, of its own motion, to amend the Schedule to the Recognition of Trusts Act 1987, giving UK courts access to art. 13.

[42] See the discussion in M. W. Galligan, 'United States Trust Law and the Hague Convention on Trusts' (2000) *NYSBA Trusts and Estates Law Section Newsletter* 37, 39–40, attempting to minimize the difference between settlor autonomy and the common law rules relating to immovable property. The United States signed the Convention in 1988 but has never ratified it.

III Conclusion

Although the Convention aims at generating some level of consistency of results, the outcome of these differing approaches to its provisions may well be the emergence of a range of understandings of the question of settlor autonomy. Considering its subject matter – which has always been regarded, to some extent, as a fundamental point of difference between the common law and the civil law – the signing of the Convention was an extraordinary achievement.[43] One way to reach a compromise is to ensure that every party can see its position reflected in the final product.

This suggests another dimension to the theme of the conference that gave rise to this volume, 'The Worlds of the Trust / *La fiducie dans tous ses États*': not only do we find a range of conceptualizations and implementations of the trust, but also a range of approaches to the extent to which a settlor can freely choose to import the trust law of one jurisdiction into another. Those that offer the widest latitude in choice of law may find that they have deterritorialized their law; or, more precisely, delegalized their territory, unhitching it from the local legal system. In the anthropological context, Marc Augé has opposed the everyday understanding of a 'place', which has its own social history, traditions and associations, with the 'non-place':

> Clearly the word 'non-place' designates two complementary but distinct realities: spaces formed in relation to certain ends (transport, transit, commerce, leisure), and the relations that individuals have with these spaces. Although the two sets of relations overlap to a large extent, and in any case officially (individuals travel, make purchases, relax), they are still not confused with one another; for non-places mediate a whole mass of relations, with the self and with others, which are only indirectly connected with their purposes. As anthropological places create the organically social, so non-places create solitary contractuality.[44]
>
> Alone, but one of many, the user of a non-place is in contractual relations with it (or with the powers that govern it). He is reminded, when necessary, that the contract exists.[45]

There is an interesting echo with the arguments in favour of settlor autonomy for choice of law in trusts, many of which are built on analogies with contract law.

[43] See generally Waters, 'Hague Trusts Convention Twenty Years On', above, note 17.

[44] M. Augé, *Non-places: Introduction to an Anthropology of Supermodernity*, 2nd edn, trans. J. Howe (London: Verso, 2008), p. 76; original: M. Augé, *Non-lieux: introduction à une anthropologie de la surmodernité* (Paris: Seuil, 1992).

[45] Ibid., p. 82.

At the opposite extreme, those jurisdictions that refuse to participate in the Convention, or that preserve a significant role for article 13, signal a desire to remain an anthropological place; in other words, an insistence that juridical relationships among people with respect to property in that place must be governed by the law *of* that place, as it has evolved *for* that place.

In this perspective, the evolution of trust law, particularly under the Hague Convention, is perhaps a metaphor for the evolution of all of law in a world in which the dominance of the nation state as the sovereign giver of law is, according to some, increasingly tenuous.

6

The security *fiducie* in French law

FRANÇOIS BARRIÈRE

I Introduction

A. *The security* fiducie: *a triangular plot with multiple variations*

In the French *fiducie*, one person – the settlor – transfers rights to another person[1] – the trustee – who holds them not as his or her ordinary property, but rather in order to fulfil a particular purpose, for the benefit of the settlor, the trustee or a third party. If the transferred property – movables or immovables, corporeal or incorporeal – is appropriated to secure the repayment of a debt (with the creditor as beneficiary of the *fiducie*), the *fiducie* then has the role of a security. The security *fiducie* thus comes within the category of title-based security, but has the feature that it can involve any type of property and secure any type of claim. The plot of the *fiducie* story can have a number of variations: the settlor can be a debtor of the principal debt, but need not be (in which case the security will secure the repayment of the debt of another); the trustee can, but need not, be a creditor in relation to the debt, thus combining the status of trustee with the status of beneficiary; the *fiducie* can, but need not, involve putting the trust property into the hands of a third party; the trust property can, but need not, remain available to be used by the settlor. Accordingly, the characterization of something as a 'security' is not synonymous with a fixed arrangement, and it does not rule out a dynamic administration of the property which has been appropriated as security, just as the pledge in relation to an investment account can involve the disposition of some investments.

This article is based on articles of the author, including 'La fiducie-sûreté' (2009) JCP-E 1808; (2009) JCP-N, Rép. civ. Dalloz, v° fiducie (January 2008).

[1] The transfer of the rights is not essential to the institution of *fiducie*. It is conceivable that no transfer from the settlor takes place, as is the case of *fiducies* found in other countries, for example Luxembourg.

'The security *fiducie* in French law' is a title that might well come as a surprise at an international conference where a good number of the titles refer to aspects of comparative law. We have decided to premise our analysis on French law given the apparent dearth of scholarly writing in many countries on this aspect of the *fiducie* (and of the common law trust, for those who would see them as two institutions and not just one). But the comparative aspect will not be forgotten for all that and, at the risk that some will see in this a touch of provocativeness (and reasonably so), is it not possible to ask – after having been behind in development for many years by contrast to so many other countries from Latin America to Asia, obviously including the Anglo-American countries – whether French law is at the stage of becoming a pioneer with respect to the *fiducie*? At the very least, we will explore the interest of the *fiducie* and of its use as security for a debt.

B. *Advantages of the security* fiducie

During times when credit is scarce, and when more and more enterprises are undergoing restructuring, the advantages of an effective security in favour of the lender stands out even more clearly. Financing should be granted more easily and at a lower cost if the security offered is effective, reducing to that extent the risk undertaken by the lender. The title-based security which is afforded by the *fiducie* should therefore offer an ideal way to give lenders the safety that they seek and should thereby contribute to the thawing of the credit cycle, or even to ease the restructuring of certain enterprises. But the interests of the debtor who is under 'bankruptcy' must not be neglected either, and a balance must be sought between the restructuring of the insolvent enterprise and the protection that is linked to the security.[2]

There is a threefold advantage to the security *fiducie*. First, the creditor is particularly well protected by virtue of the exclusivity of the right of ownership transferred to him. Secondly, this kind of security is easily created. Thirdly, the enforcement of a security *fiducie* offers its beneficiary favourable treatment in any collective insolvency proceeding. Thus, this kind of security could easily become very popular, both during and outside of times of credit crisis.

[2] Bankruptcy as a legal concept does not exist in the French legal system, so the word is placed in inverted commas, as a reference to factual insolvency and the various kinds of collective proceedings that may follow.

C. *The duality in categories of security* fiducies

Sometimes the *fiducie* is presented as something recently introduced into French law. Granted, the legislation introducing it under this name – as a nominate institution – only dates back to 2007. Yet, long before that date, the *fiducie* existed without bearing this name; that is, in innominate form. The world of practice, in particular that of banking and finance, did not wait until the end of the first decade of the twenty-first century to have in hand legal tools equivalent to those available in certain neighbouring countries. *Fiducies* did appear, in particular situations, with a restricted field of operation. They did not bear the name *fiducie*, but they had all the characteristics of one. In particular, *fiducie*-type mechanisms whose purpose was to guarantee the performance of obligations had already been quietly put into place in France a good number of years ago.

D. *The characteristic common to all security* fiducies: *ownership appropriated to a purpose*

The website announcing the conference[3] that was the genesis of this volume stated that 'until recently, the trust was often described as foreign to the logic of the law of property in the civilian tradition'. An analysis of the security *fiducie* provides an opportunity to test whether 'this assertion is increasingly untenable'.[4] The present contribution does not seek to be a study which would claim to definitively settle this debate: the rich field of the subject in the realm of civil law is illustrated by the competing contentions in Quebec scholarly writings under the Civil Code of Lower Canada, by the judgments of the Supreme Court of Canada, and by the novel reform brought about by the Civil Code of Québec which came into force in 1994. This contribution seeks only to employ the optics of security – and thus of the analysis of a type of ownership which is 'accessory' to a guarantee – and to frame some reflections on the conference theme, without engaging in a broader analysis.

[3] 'La fiducie dans tous ses États' / 'The Worlds of the Trust' (McGill University, 23–25 September 2010). The original website is no longer online, but a summary (including the quoted text) is available at www.mcgill.ca/centre-crepeau/activities/trust/ last consulted 7 February 2012.

[4] Ibid.

The security *fiducie*, a variety of title-based security, involves a transfer of the property from the settlor to the trustee.[5] The right of ownership held by the trustee is thus impressed with a purpose; it is devoted to guaranteeing the payment of the claim. Thus, while the trustee has prerogatives, he must not exercise them in his own interest, but rather to fulfil the objective of the *fiducie* in the interest of the beneficiary (who may be the trustee). The prerogatives of (fiduciary) ownership must be exercised so that the objective for which the property was transferred is fulfilled.[6] The exclusivity that results from this transfer makes it particularly attractive for the beneficiary:[7] she will not have to claim alongside the other creditors of the creator of the security – while most secured creditors can be outranked by a creditor who has a greater preference, and moreover they may not be able to execute directly on the collateral if the debtor is subject to a collective proceeding.

This is not the ordinary ownership of article 544 Civil Code (C.C.), which involves 'the right to enjoy and dispose of things in the most

[5] The French *fiducie* did not follow the model of its Quebec cousin, where no real right exists once the property has been put in a patrimony by appropriation with no titulary. Perhaps this is because there is a greater attachment in France to a subjective conception of the patrimony. It may also be due to various practical issues which can arise from a *fiducie* along the Quebec model, including registration in the land register, the ability to create accessory real rights in the absence of a principal real right, as well as the ability to identify whose shoulders would bear the personal obligations which arise from the administration of the *fiducie* (in the absence of someone at the head of the patrimony). The Quebec solution relied on the first thesis put forward by P. Lepaulle (*Traité théorique et pratique du trust en droit interne, droit fiscal, et en droit international privé* (Paris: Rousseau, 1932), in particular pp. 31ff), which had also met with success in Mexico and Uruguay, as well as inspiring a draft law in Catalonia. See E. Arroyo i Amayuelos (ed.), *El Quebec, Un model de dret comparat per a Catalunya* (Barcelona: Publicaciones de la Universidad de Barcelona, 2001).

[6] An alternative, whose adoption would have limited debates on the nature of ownership with respect to the *fiducie*, was the proposal to make the *fiducie* a legal person. Lepaulle suggested this at a second stage ('La notion de trust et ses applications dans les divers systèmes juridiques', in *Acte du Congrès international de droit privé*, vol. 2, *L'unification du droit* (Rome: UNIDROIT, 1951), p. 197). This idea was recently revived and expanded by Professor Cantin Cumyn, who proposes, in a novel and stimulating analysis, to see in *fiducie* a '*sujet de droit*' (a bearer of private law rights and obligations), while preserving the distinction between a *fiducie* and a legal person. See M. Cantin Cumyn, 'Rapport général', in *La fiducie face au trust dans les rapports d'affaires* (Brussels: Bruylant, 1999), pp. 11ff, para. 26 and, from the same author, 'La fiducie, un nouveau sujet de droit?', in *Mélanges E. Caparros* (Montreal: Wilson & Lafleur, 2002), pp. 129ff.

[7] The beneficiary's right with respect to the trust should be characterized as personal. C. de Lajarte is also of this opinion: 'La nature juridique des droits du bénéficiaire d'un contrat de fiducie' (May 2009) RLDC 71.

absolute manner', but rather a 'fiduciary'[8] ownership. It was characterized in this manner in the law introducing the *fiducie*, as well as in the proposed text for a paragraph 2 of article 2011 C.C. discussed in the context of the law to promote access to credit for small and medium-sized enterprises.[9] This does not just affect the extent of the right, but the very nature of the right itself. Fiduciary ownership is limited in duration, limited by the fragmenting of the prerogatives of the settlor which are received by the trustee, and limited by the purpose with which the ownership is impressed. Hence fiduciary ownership will, in principle, neither be perpetual nor be absolute, just as ownership under a reservation of title is not an ordinary sort of ownership.[10] Indeed, a person who remains owner under a reservation of title cannot make use of the thing, nor may she enjoy it or dispose of it. The owner under a reservation of title lacks the attributes of ordinary ownership: *usus*, *fructus*, *abusus*. Still, she holds a title-based security with, as its sole attribute, the right to revendicate the property. Conversely, a trustee has in her hands the *usus*, *fructus* and *abusus* of the property (even if she must exercise these attributes in line with the appropriation); the trustee seems more like an owner than does an owner by reservation of title. If the character of owner were to be denied to the trustee, how then could this term still be applied to the person who benefits from a reservation of title? But what, then, would a reservation of title amount to, in the absence of ownership or an owner? Both in the case of security *fiducie* and of reservation of title,[11]

[8] This characterization of what the trustee has as 'ownership', even 'fiduciary ownership', does not meet with unanimous agreement. While some scholarly writers are of the opinion that 'this issue is beyond doubt' (F. Zenati-Castaing and Th. Revet, *Les biens*, 3rd edn (Paris: PUF, 2008), para. 255), the opinions of others are more qualified. See, in particular, B. Mallet-Bricout, 'Le fiduciaire propriétaire?' (2010) JCP-E 1191; from the same author, 'Fiducie et propriété', in S. Bros and B. Mallet-Bricout (eds.), *Liber amicorum Christian Larroumet* (Paris: Economica, 2009), p. 297. More generally, see Y. Emerich, 'Les fondements conceptuels de la fiducie française face au trust du common law: entre droits des contrats et droit des biens' (2009) 1 RIDC 49. Disagreements with respect to the content of the trustee's right also exist in other countries, for instance China: see R. Lee, 'Conceptualizing the Chinese Trust' (2009) 58 ICLQ 655, in particular 660ff.

[9] Which was struck down by the Conseil constitutionnel because it had no relation to the principal objective of this legal text.

[10] M. Grimaldi, 'Réflexions sur les sûretés propriétés (à propos de la réserve de propriété)', in *Études offertes à Jacques Dupichot* (Brussels: Bruylant, 2005), pp. 169ff; Ph. Malaurie and L. Aynès, *Les biens*, 4th edn (Paris: Defrénois, 2010), para. 413.

[11] Which could be characterized as a *fiducie*, since a transfer of rights is not essential to this latter institution.

ownership is not meant to supply the owner with the economic advantages that the thing can furnish, but rather to secure a claim.

In my view, appropriating property to a purpose does not result in a negation of ownership. Granted, the functional aspect of fiduciary ownership does not match the ordinary conception of ownership, conceived as absolute and paramount. Still, the holder of a right can validly subject it to restrictions when she transfers it, provided on the one hand that the restrictions are temporary, and on the other hand that the restrictions do not amount to a negation of the prerogatives of the owner.[12] The possibility of a clause which renders property inalienable shows that the right to dispose of property can be removed; *a fortiori* must it be possible to modify the ability to alienate the property, or to limit ownership's other attributes (*usus* and *fructus*). The legislator goes even further in limitations on the exercise of the attributes of ownership. Thus in the field of special purpose vehicles for the securitization of claims (at one time called 'common claim funds' (*fonds commun de créances*), now dubbed 'common securitization funds' (*fonds commun de titrisation*)), the law confers the status of owner upon the holders of units in these entities, all the while not granting them the prerogatives tied to the status.[13] While the legislator can confer a status without any of the usual attributes, a private agreement should not be able to go that far. Thus, a *fiducie* which conferred no independent prerogative upon the trustee should be recharacterized (in most cases, the appropriate characterization would be a contract of mandate). The limitations on the exercise of the attributes of fiduciary ownership can vary in extent. They may even be practically absent, upon the fulfilment of the purpose for which the transfer was undertaken. The same is also often the case where the transferred property comes to be mingled with property of the same kind in the personal patrimony of the trustee. Hence, the trustee can be authorized to dispose of the property she receives, with just a duty upon her to hand back equivalent property. In this case, which matches some of the configurations of security *fiducies*, the fiduciary character of the property does not seem to be obviously incompatible with the character

[12] Zenati-Castaing and Revet, above, note 8, paras. 237 and 263. See also F. Barrière, *La réception du trust au travers de la fiducie*, preface by M. Grimaldi (Paris: Litec, 2004), paras. 387ff.

[13] Th. Bonneau, 'Les fonds communs de placement, les fonds communs de créances et le droit civil' (1991) RTDC 1, para. 35; H. Hovasse and N. Martial-Braz, 'La titrisation', in *JurisClasseur Banque-Crédit-Bourse*, fasc. 2260, para. 19.

of ordinary ownership: there are practically no restrictions on the use of an owner's prerogatives. A possible exception to this absence of restriction would be the obligation which lies on the fiduciary owner to hand back an equivalent thing.[14] She would thus be required to avoid entering into juridical acts which could interfere with the performance of this obligation (for example, alienation of *fiducie* property when the market for this type of property is not liquid and so does not ensure that it will be possible to perform the obligation to hand back equivalent property). Under fiduciary ownership, the autonomy of the ordinary owner can thus reappear in good measure. Moreover, just as in the case of an ordinary owner, the fiduciary owner will have the benefit of an exclusive right to the trust property, freeing her from having to claim alongside the settlor's (other) creditors.

Fiduciary ownership is something other than ordinary ownership, with its own distinct legal framework. For example, in the realm of the nominate *fiducie*, the trustee is bound to render an account of her trusteeship; she is obligated to disclose her role as trustee to third parties; she may be subject to criminal sanction for abuse of trust; and the law provides for the possibility of replacement of the trustee. By comparison, an ordinary owner is not bound by an obligation to render accounts, nor is she subject to criminal sanction with respect to how she puts her property to use. It would be even more foreign to the status of an ordinary owner for her to be excluded from her rights of ownership because she has been replaced. The appropriation of the *fiducie* property justifies all this, including the expropriation from a replaced trustee of a type of ownership that is different from ordinary ownership, different from the ownership protected by the Declaration of the Rights of Man and of the Citizen or the the European Convention on Human Rights. This is not a unique state of affairs, as an owner can be compelled to transfer her ownership in certain circumstances which do not draw their justification from the public interest. For example, the forced transfer of shares can be imposed as a penalty on an officer of a company in a state of insolvency, and exclusion clauses can be included in the articles of certain companies.[15] Since the

[14] Thus, the French *fiducie* is distinct from the institution of mandate (whereas other countries have chosen a legal framework for *fiducie* that relies in part on the rules of mandate).

[15] See also the cases of forced withdrawal, where the minority holders, in certain situations, can be forced to transfer their listed financial instruments to the majority shareholder, according to D. Schmidt, 'Réflexions sur le retrait obligatoire' (1999) RDBF 213, 214. However, this position was not followed by the Cour de cassation (Com. 29 April 1997, case 95-15220, *Bull. civ.* IV, para. 108).

transfer from a replaced trustee is not an ordinary transfer of ownership, surely it should not trigger rights of first refusal.

E. Outline

The *fiducie* is not monolithic when it is deployed as a security. Indeed it presents multiple configurations that have greater or lesser importance depending on the particular case. While the security *fiducie* so named in the Civil Code must receive particular attention here and be the subject of the major part of the discussion (in section III below), this should not lead us to overlook the innominate, non-codal security *fiducie*.

II The innominate security *fiducie*

While the trend in the case law has at times been to refuse to recognize types of *fiducie* that are not specifically governed by legislation, the legislator did not wait for a law bearing the name to introduce *fiducies*. No patrimony by appropriation is created in the case of either of these two types of innominate *fiducie*. The transferred property is mingled within the personal patrimony of the trustee, unlike what occurs in the case of a nominate *fiducie*. A common law trust requires a separation within the trustee's assets, between his personal property and the property which is subject to the trust. An innominate *fiducie* does not necessarily subject the assets to this sort of separation; the *fiducie* will then be similar to the *fiducia* of Roman law. This absence of a separation could seem like a flaw in the legal framework of the innominate *fiducie*, yet it is not necessarily so. On the contrary, this absence is what certain economic actors seek.

A. Difficulties in gaining recognition by the courts

1. The pledge of ready money, a security *fiducie* well established in case law

The case law has not always been hostile to security *fiducies* invented in the realm of practice. Accordingly, courts found the handing over of sums of money by a debtor to a creditor so as to secure the claim of the latter party to be valid.[16] Since the sums of money are fungible

[16] Com. 17 May 1994, case 91-20083, *Bull. civ.* IV, para. 178; Com. 3 June 1997, case 95-13365, *Bull. civ.* IV, para. 165.

property,[17] they become the property of the creditor. Thus, the creditor was allowed to return equivalent property and so had the ability to dispose of what she had received from the debtor.[18] This creditor was also freed of the need to claim alongside the other creditors if her debtor became insolvent. This arrangement, which the realm of practice had long dubbed 'the pledge of ready money' (*gage-espèces*), establishes a fiduciary transfer of property entered into as a security.[19] This pledge involves minimal formality, both as to its creation – there is no requirement that the sums be set apart – and in relation to enforcement of the security, which takes place outside of any collective proceeding. The debtor does not transfer the sums to the creditor by way of ordinary ownership, which would allow the creditor to make use of the sums without having to account for them. The transfer is rather in terms of an ownership impressed with the purpose of securing the claim, with the particular feature that the obligation to return the property relates to an equivalent to the original sum of money, due to money's fungible nature. The debtor transfers ownership to the creditor as security for a claim: this arrangement matches the features of the security *fiducie*, even if it does not bear this name. Since the property, whose ownership was transferred, has mingled within the creditor's patrimony and become indistinguishable from her other ready money, this property can be freely used, subject to the obligation which lies on the creditor to hand over its equivalent. But if the creditor had gained ordinary ownership, no such obligation would have existed. This is not the *propter rem* obligation brought about by the *fiducie*, but rather an obligation that arises at the moment of the transfer of the property. One hesitates to suggest that this fiduciary ownership is incompatible with the foundations of property law, particularly since the mingling of the transferred sums with the creditor's own money makes it impossible to distinguish the sums that had been acquired by an ordinary transfer from those which come from a fiduciary transfer. The coexistence of the fungible sums in one and the same

17 Unless the sums in question would have been given a specific character and unless the law would allow the revendication of fungibles: see D. R. Martin, 'De la revendication des sommes d'argent' (2002) *Dalloz* 3279.

18 S. Torck, 'Les sûretés sur sommes d'argent après l'ordonnance du 23 mars 2006 portant réforme du droit des sûretés et la loi sur la fiducie du 19 février 2007' (Jan.–Feb. 2008) 1 RDBF 8 (*étude* 2), para. 10.

19 This arrangement is now recognized by the first paragraph of art. 2341 C.C. with respect to currency and by the second paragraph of art. 2741 C.C. with respect to money on deposit.

patrimony, whatever the nature of the transfer might be, suggests that the rights which result are not incompatible in nature. In any case the fungibility of the sums is based on the presumption that if they were all that different in nature, they would not be interchangeable.

2. The legal framework of the pledge of ready money

The situation of the creditor is particularly favourable should the debtor become subject to a collective proceeding: the creditor is exempted from the proceedings carried out to discharge the debtor's liabilities. If the underlying obligation owed to the creditor is not performed, she will remain the ultimate owner of the sums that she had received. The creditor can keep the money up to the amount of the debt that they secured, and there will be extinction of the creditor's obligation to return the same amount. While it can be granted that the creditor, who becomes owner of the sum of money, is in turn a debtor bound by an obligation to return that sum, this second-order debt could seem to be subject to compensation in relation to the debt owed by the first-order debtor. However, there is some doubt about this understanding. Compensation involves reciprocal claims which are exigible (whose payment is due), certain and liquid. But the claim to receive back the sum of money never coexists with the exigibility of the secured claim. On the contrary, the claim to have the property returned is extinguished at the instant that it would come due, if the first-order obligation is not paid.[20] This seems less a case of compensation and more a mode of realization which is particular to this innominate security *fiducie*: the ownership which was temporarily impressed with a purpose is automatically transformed into ordinary ownership upon the resiliation of this security. This definitive transfer of ownership in favour of the unpaid creditor is inherent to the enforcement of this security *fiducie*, subject to the obligation to pay to the debtor any surplus, should the amount of the secured claim be less than the sum which served as security.

3. The assignment of claims as a security, a security *fiducie* discounted by the courts

Innominate security *fiducies* were otherwise less favourably received by the courts, however. In a decision of 19 December 2006, the commercial division of the Cour de cassation set out the principle that 'aside from the

[20] S. Bros, 'Gages sur sommes d'argent', in *Lamy droit des sûretés*, fasc. 268-51.

cases provided for by statute, a juridical act by which a debtor assigns and transfers to his creditor all his rights bearing on claims, to serve as security, brings about a pledge of claims'.[21] An assignment of claims entered into as a security – a fiduciary alienation – is thus reclassified as a pledge by the Cour de cassation, even though the intention of the parties was clear. The party who thought she had the status of assignee of a claim thus sees herself reduced to being merely the holder of a right of preference, and is not holder of the claim itself. Thus, according to this set of decisions, the assignment of claims governed by the general law can apply in relation to an immediate and absolute assignment.[22] This line of cases, which transforms into a pledge the assignment of claims by way of security, is similar to past decisions that reduced a security *fiducie* into a pledge with a taking-in-payment clause.[23] Yet the factors justifying the limitations on taking-in-payment clauses are not present when the collateral consists of claims for sums of money. In this context, the valuation of the collateral is not open to debate, and there is little risk that unfair advantage will be taken of the debtor. This serves as an illustration of how difficult it is for French law to accept a transfer of a right with only a part of the right's prerogatives, a temporary ownership that would only become conclusive where the debtor fails to perform her obligations, an ownership which is not an end unto itself but above all a means. Perhaps it also shows that the courts intend to leave the extension of this type of arrangement to the legislator, given its significant impact on collective insolvency proceedings. This policy is in other respects open to debate: there is no *numerus clausus* of the types of contracts transferring property; the *numerus clausus* of real rights does not stand in the way of a new use of the right of ownership; this is not a case which would result in perpetual inalienability; nor would it result in the disassociation of the elements of ownership.[24]

[21] 'En dehors des cas prévus par la loi, l'acte par lequel un débiteur cède et transporte à son créancier, à titre de garantie, tous ses droits sur des créances, constitue un nantissement de créance': case 05-16395, *Bull. civ.* IV, para. 250. See also Com. 26 May 2010, case 09-13388, *Bull. civ.* IV, para. 94.

[22] To contrary effect, a draft proposal to reform the law of obligations considers recognizing assignments of claims as a security.

[23] Civ. 1°, 8 July 1969, para. 268; J. Derrupé, 'Note' (1970) JDI 916; Ph. Fouchard, 'Note' (1970) RCDIP 75. A taking-in-payment clause purports to allow the pledgee to take full ownership of the pledged property in payment of the debt.

[24] On this point, see P. Crocq, *Propriété et garantie*, preface by M. Gobert (LGDJ, 1995), paras. 153ff, 238ff and 252ff. See also Civ. 3° (31 October 2012), N° 11-16304, Bull. civ. III.

B. *Its repeated recognition by legislation*

1. The security *fiducie*, an institution with widespread approval in the field of banking and finance

The world of finance did not wait until 2007 to employ mechanisms which offer the safety of deploying ownership as a security, granting a creditor exclusive title to property until she is paid.

The employment of this sort of mechanism in French law stretches back several decades. After these beginnings, the practice gained support from certain arrangements which had their origins in European Community law. The innominate *fiducie* saw notable growth and development in the realm of incorporeal property whose value can be determined objectively (claims for sums of money, financial instruments traded on a regulated market). Employment of the security in that realm avoids any risk of unfair exploitation of the debtor and unfair enrichment of the creditor when the security is realized, without needing to involve an expert evaluator. Now the provisions governing these security *fiducies* can be found in the Monetary and Financial Code (M.F.C.), an indication of the field in which these arrangements are used. Indeed, it is in the world of financial dealers that these mechanisms developed, where one person more often than not wears both the hat of trustee and that of beneficiary. If the financial institution which receives the transfer were no longer recognized as having the character of (fiduciary) owner, the effects on the prudential assessment of the assets would be such that the transactional structure would lose its interest. The *exclusivity* accorded to the creditor, and thus the fact that it avoids having to claim along with other creditors, leads to the characterization of the creditor as owner, which in turn means that this mechanism has a very favourable treatment in the calculation of the financial ratios of banking institutions, since the credit risk is correspondingly reduced.

Two examples can serve as illustrations of this type of security. The first is drawn from the world of banking and the second from the sector of financial markets.

2. Assignment of business claims as a security

Since 1984, financial institutions can take an assignment of the claims of their customers that were generated in the course of the customers' business (this is dubbed a 'Dailly' assignment, due to the name of the author of the law which created this measure, now governed by articles L. 313–23ff. M.F.C.). An assignment of claims, entered into as a security under this measure, transfers to the assignee the ownership of the claims. If the debt secured by this assignment ceases to exist, the claims which come within the assignment must be transferred back to the client. Conversely, if the debtor fails to pay the debt, the creditor's ownership of the assigned claim becomes conclusive and is free of restriction. Here we have a fiduciary transfer by way of security: the assignee becomes the owner of the property as security for a debt, and can only have the free enjoyment of it if the debtor fails to perform her obligation. Other civil law countries, for example Madagascar, take care to expressly characterize this mechanism as a fiduciary assignment.

The legal framework of this innominate security *fiducie* is particularly favourable. The formalities are reduced to the bare minimum. All that needs to be drawn up is a list of the claims. The transfer of ownership to the assignee can be set up against third parties as of the date indicated by the financial institution as assignee, without any need for publication by registration.[25] Thus, the formalities required to create and realize this security are inexpensive.

3. Financial collateral arrangements: characterization as security *fiducie*

In the realm of financial instruments, the legislator introduced various innominate security *fiducies*. While others exist,[26] this is particularly the case with respect to financial instruments as collateral, following the European Directive of 6 June 2002 respecting financial collateral arrangements (in good part reproducing a legal framework that already existed, at least in French law). Accordingly, in order to secure certain financial obligations, a debtor may transfer 'in full ownership' collateral that is 'financial instruments, negotiable instruments, claims, contracts or sums of money' (article L. 211–38 M.F.C.) to a creditor that is a financial institution. Depending on the nature of the property transferred, the property will mingle with other property of the same nature held by the financial institution (for example, sums of money or financial instruments held in paperless form). Once again, this mechanism is based on

[25] This does not avoid conflicts between the assignee and a seizing creditor, or involving successive assignees.

[26] Mention could be made, for example, of the secured loans of financial instruments, based on the law of 17 June 1987, or the security which can be granted in interbank systems since the law of 2 July 1998. Please see, more generally, H. de Vauplane, 'La fiducie avant la fiducie: le cas du droit bancaire et financier' (2007) JCP-E 2051.

ownership impressed with a purpose: the assignee can only make use of the ownership in line with the governing purpose, namely as a security. However, once this ownership has been received, the ownership is not frozen and, unless the contract provides otherwise, the property can be more or less freely deployed (which may assist in the financial institution's refinancing). However, this deployment will be subject to the assignee's obligation to make sure that it will be able to return equivalent property. Once again, this is an example of how elements within the sphere of obligations accompany the transfer of ownership. This case also brings out the practical non-existence of restrictions on the prerogatives of the fiduciary owner: the trustee can pretty freely dispose of the property transferred to her. Moreover, due to the property's fungibility, sometimes the trustee cannot even distinguish between the items of property which she holds in ordinary ownership and those which she acquired from a fiduciary transfer.

Once again, the legal framework of this innominate security *fiducie* is particularly attractive. Only a small amount of formality is involved in creating a financial collateral arrangement and rendering it so that it can be set up against third parties. All that is required is the drawing-up of a document which makes the relevant property identifiable and attests to the transfer. In addition, the realization of the collateral arrangement is free of the constraints which are ordinarily imposed on secured creditors when their debtor is insolvent; the realization can take place by compensation, by taking the property in payment or by sale of the property, depending on the mode of evaluation that the parties stipulate.

4. The advantage which comes from the absence of a patrimony by appropriation

Moreover, this brings out a special characteristic of the innominate *fiducie*: it involves a transfer by way of security, but it does not bring about the isolation of the transferred property in a patrimony by appropriation. On the contrary, the collateral merges into the general patrimony of the creditor (temporary owner) and mingles with her own property of the same kind. This increases the creditor's protection, while she wears both the hat of trustee and of beneficiary, since it allows her to be direct owner of the property and frees her from any restriction in case of non-payment or of insolvency on the part of her debtor (if the property has been transferred to a patrimony by appropriation the realization of the security can be delayed). The situation of the creditor is particularly strong where the property used to secure her claim is in her own patrimony and not a patrimony by appropriation, the patrimony of her debtor or the patrimony of a third party. Thanks to the ownership transferred to the creditor as trustee, it is the creditor (a participant in the financial and banking markets) who is privileged, to the detriment of the debtor. The creditor avoids the risk of having to claim alongside debtors' other creditors, thereby avoiding the need to take an action in revendication[27] (explaining the favourable treatment in the calculation of the financial ratios of banking institutions). This ownership also means that, beyond the creditor, the banking and financial marketplace as a whole is protected. It is here that this market's logic of certainty and stability will predominate and justify the development of the innominate security *fiducie*.

III The nominate security *fiducie*

The nominate *fiducie* was long-awaited in France, and was preceded by a number of innominate forms of the institution of *fiducie*. It was introduced into the Civil Code by Law 2007–211 of 19 February 2007. It might have been expected that this long-delayed birth would be easy. This turned out not to be the case: the birth was chaotic and somewhat accidental. The parliament was meant to discuss class actions, but this subject was withdrawn at the last minute from the orders of the day. A bill introducing the *fiducie* came to fill this vacuum. Far from allowing it to have general application, the legislation initially introduced just a small-scale *fiducie*: settlors had to be legal persons subject to company tax, only 'banks' and 'insurers' could be trustees, and it was forbidden for a *fiducie* to be donative in nature.[28] At the time, the French nominate *fiducie* was quite a runt, overshadowed by its neighbours within the legal systems of the European continent and its Anglo-American cousins.[29]

27 Unlike the situation of the creditor who has stipulated for reservation of title.

28 Thus, the French *fiducie* is geared to have a largely commercial field of deployment, comparable to the contemporary common law trust. See J. H. Langbein, 'The Secret Life of the Trust: The Trust as an Instrument of Commerce' (1999) 107 Yale LJ 165. See also H. Hansmann and U. Mattei, 'The Functions of Trust Law: A Comparative Legal and Economic Analysis' (1998) 73 NYU L Rev 434 and M. Graziadei, U. Mattei and L. Smith (eds.), *Commercial Trusts in European Private Law* (Cambridge University Press, 2005).

29 P. Matthews, 'The French Fiducie: And Now for Something Completely Different?' (2007) 21(1) T.L.I. 17, even if this author concedes that the French *fiducie* is more closely related to the trust than Luxembourg's *fiducie* (p. 31).

When the candle on the nominate *fiducie*'s first birthday cake had just been blown out, Law 2008–776 of 4 August 2008 on the modernization of the economy corrected certain flaws in the initial legislation. This was perhaps a new indication of the instability of law and of how it can evolve in successive strata; better a correction in the short-term than none at all. The ability to be the settlor of a *fiducie* was extended to all persons, bringing to an end an unjustified discrimination.[30] In particular, this allows natural persons, especially individuals carrying on a business, to establish security *fiducies*, as legal persons were already able to do, re-establishing a level competitive playing field between business owners who have chosen to operate their business through the vehicle of a legal person and those who have not. This 2008 law also simplified what needed to be done so that the transfer of claims to the trustee could be set up against third parties (the original legislation was discouragingly complex in requiring formalities involving bailiffs or notaries). In addition, the law authorized lawyers to be trustees[31] and extended the maximum duration of the terms of a *fiducie* from 33 to 99 years.

The provisions on the *fiducie* were further altered by Order 2008–1345 of 18 December 2008 reforming the law with respect to enterprises in difficulty, and clarified by Order 2009–112 of 30 January 2009 implementing several measures respecting the *fiducie*. The latter, in particular, introduced provisions with respect to ownership transferred by way of security.[32] Finally, Law 2009–526 of 12 May 2009 improved the provisions on the security *fiducie* by simplifying and clarifying the law, and streamlining procedures. After this marathon of legislative fine-tuning, the legal framework of the security *fiducie* was firmly established.

[30] This is a bit like how the ability to be a partner within a simplified shareholder-owned company (*société par actions simplifiée*) was at one time limited just to legal persons before it was opened to any person.

[31] Oddly, notaries are still not authorized to be trustees, even though their role with respect to the mandate for future protection could have suggested that they would also be called to become trustees on behalf of vulnerable people.

[32] They were respectively inserted in the sub-title on security over immovables and the sub-title on security over movables. In fact, these provisions are nearly identical; the reason for this duplication lies in the structure of the code. They will apply to 'ownership transferred as security' or to *fiducies*, leading to a patrimony by appropriation and being governed by articles 2011ff of the Civil Code. The provisions on the outcome of the security – including the absence of enrichment on the part of the creditor – are doubtless meant to become the general law with respect to innominate *fiducies*, for example the 'pledge of ready money'. The legal framework of the innominate *fiducies* will be firmly established by this.

Despite the flaws in the initial 2007 legislation (for instance, the law's silence with respect to the modes of enforcement in the security *fiducie*), legal practitioners employed it and continue to sing its praises. The first two *fiducies* were announced in February 2008,[33] precisely a year after the law introducing the *fiducie* was enacted. Both were security *fiducies*. One involved Gaz de France (settlor) and the *Caisse des dépôts et consignations* (trustee), to secure certain undertakings in favour of the employees of Gaz de France. The other involved a company which was experiencing difficulties and owed a tax debt (settlor), the Natixis Bank (trustee) and the State (beneficiary). These deployments confirmed that this institution responds to a need in the practical realm, whether it is used to secure monetary debts or to secure undertakings which are not the result of loans. In 2009, the press revealed that Plysorol, an enterprise specializing in plywood sheets and which was at the time under court-supervised restructuring, had put in place a security *fiducie* over its inventory in order to obtain a loan and thus avoid judicial liquidation.[34] Still in 2009, a big-box store, in order to obtain a loan, transferred to a trustee the shares of the company which held the ownership of its building.[35] More recently, in 2010, the CPB company (which manages the petrochemical installations at l'Étang de Berre and is a member of the LyondellBasell group) established a *fiducie*, with the *Caisse des dépôts et consignations* as trustee, to secure payment with respect to the rights that its salaried employees had by virtue of a company-level agreement.[36] Analogously, the Rol Pin company established a *fiducie* in the first quarter of 2010 in favour of the beneficiaries of its 'plan for the conservation of employment' (a plan required by the Labour Code in case of a layoff of employees), with Equitis as trustee.[37] A security *fiducie* was also put in place in 2010 to ensure the repayment of a fresh loan from a shareholder

[33] See V. de Senneville, 'Première application de la fiducie', *Les Echos*, 8 February 2008; 'Coup d'envoi pour les trusts à la française', *Option finance*, para. 968, 18 February 2008, p. 5; 'Premier contrat de fiducie en France' (2008) D 469; 'Premier faire-part pour la fiducie' (March 2008) RLDC 30; R. Dammann, G. Podeur and V. Roussel, 'Fiducie: des débuts prometteurs', *Option finance*, para. 971, 10 March 2008, pp. 37ff.

[34] F. Anselmi, 'La fiducie-sûreté pourrait faciliter les restructurations d'entreprises', *L'Agefi*, 29 October 2009.

[35] O. Delaunay, 'Première application de la fiducie gestion en restructuring', *Option Droit & Affaires*, 16 December 2009, p. 1: this arrangement also put in the hands of the trustee an aspect of administration of the premises.

[36] LJA, para. 961, 8 February 2010, p. 4.

[37] Th. Brun and B. Teston, 'Un exemple de fiducie: la sécurisation des paiements dus au titre d'un PSE', *Option finance*, para. 1103, 6 December 2010, pp. 32ff.

to a company that distributes photos (and which was under court-supervised restructuring).[38] This *fiducie* was with respect to photo libraries including resale or licence rights (however, the settlor was to continue to have the use and legal enjoyment of the libraries and rights). On 4 November 2010, the Court of Appeal of Paris confirmed that the property which had been transferred could not be included in the scope of the court-supervised plan for assignment of the enterprise in favour of a new owner[39] (who takes all or part of an enterprise, as a going concern). Legal practitioners also raised as an example of deployment of the security *fiducie* 'the creation of a strictly controlled plan for project financing' or 'security in favour of a new owner for the completion of the decontamination of a piece of land'.[40]

In the absence of a public register, it is impossible to know how many contracts of *fiducie* have been entered into since 2007. Following the birth of the *fiducie*, this institution may have been slowed in spreading its wings by the lack of a national register of *fiducies*, until the register was created by the decree of 2 March 2010. It also may have been slowed by the reforms, announced by ordinances, to the law of *fiducie* (enacted under authorizations based on the law on the modernization of the economy).[41]

Let us distinguish in turn the legal nature (A) and the legal framework (B) of the nominate security *fiducie*.

A. *The legal nature of the nominate security* fiducie

The characteristics of the nominate security *fiducie* can be summed up as a type of title-based security with a patrimony appropriated to a purpose (1). The principal complaints that are usually made against title-based security instruments of various kinds cannot be made against the nominate security *fiducie* (2).

[38] A. Feitz, 'L'agence photo Gamma reprise pour 100.000 euros', *Les Echos*, 7 April 2010, p. 22.

[39] Cour d'appel de Paris, 4 November 2010, case 10/07100; (2011) JCP-G 71.

[40] Colloque du 24 juin 2010, Conseil National des Barreaux, *Avocats & Droit*, Sept.–Oct. 2010, p. 10.

[41] One legislative instrument altered the legal framework which governs *fiducie* during a collective proceeding; the other specified the framework which applied with respect to natural persons.

1. A title-based security with a patrimony by appropriation: a protected exclusive right

(a) The exclusivity of the right of ownership Unlike innominate *fiducies*, the ownership of any type of property can be transferred to the trustee of a nominate *fiducie* to secure a claim against the settlor. For example, the law deals with assignments of claims in order to confer on these assignments an exceptional and particularly attractive legal framework with respect to setting them up against third parties.[42] Even if certain conflicts can still arise (for example, with a sub-contractor who can take a direct action, where the contractor transferred his own claim against the owner-client to a trustee),[43] this arrangement should enjoy definite success. After all, the decided cases have refused to grant validity to assignments of claims entered into as security, other than in the situations permitted by enacted law.[44] Aside from movable rights, it will also be possible to put under *fiducie* rights bearing on immovables, so long as the transfer meets the formal requirements with respect to an authentic act and the publication of land rights. Unlike other security directed at securing a particular type of claim, the *fiducie* can secure claims of any type.[45]

Ownership of the property comes to be exclusively in the trustee's hands.[46] This allows her to avoid any need to claim alongside the settlor's creditors. However, the settlor is not completely deprived of a right of oversight, since she can bring about the appointment of a third party as protector (article 2017 C.C.). As for the trustee, the transfer of ownership is not a mechanism which provides her with absolute protection. In a case where the settlor continues to have the actual possession of the movables, and there is thus an absence of publicity with respect to the movables, third parties seizing the property will be able to rely on the apparent legal possession of the debtor, to the disadvantage of the beneficiary of the *fiducie*, just as the titleholder of a clause reserving ownership can have a third-party claim set up against their good faith

[42] Departing from the legal framework set by article 1690 C.C.

[43] B. Mallet-Bricout, 'Quelle efficacité pour la nouvelle fiducie-sûreté?' (2009) 185 *Droit & Patrimoine* 79, note 24.

[44] See Sections II.A.3, 'The assignment of claims as a security', and II.B.2, 'Assignment of business claims as a security', above.

[45] Even if the rights have been transferred out of the patrimony of the settlor, her creditors will be able to seize these rights if the creditors have a right to follow which was published before the transfer into the *fiducie* or if there was fraud with respect to their rights.

[46] See Section I.D, 'The characteristic common to all security *fiducies*', above.

entry into possession. The conflict is of the same kind and resolves itself in an equivalent fashion. For both institutions this is thus only a relative disadvantage; since the success of reservation of title is not undermined by this disadvantage, there is no reason to think that it would have any more effect on the success of the security *fiducie*.

More often than not the trustee will be charged with the custody and care of the thing which was transferred as security for a claim. But the trustee could hold all of the powers that an ordinary owner holds, just as in the realm of innominate *fiducies*. As in the case of an innominate *fiducie*, the trustee would accordingly be under the obligation to hand over an equivalent set of rights to the settlor-debtor or to the third-party beneficiary when the security is extinguished by payment of the underlying debt or when the security is realized for non-payment of the debt. This means that the trust property cannot be rendered unavailable, which could be advantageous where the security lasts for a long period of time. Thus, the trustee's fiduciary ownership will receive a distinct shape, to a greater or lesser degree, respecting any restrictions on the usual attributes of ownership with which she has to comply, and always shaped by the appropriation of the property as a security.

(b) Patrimony by appropriation The beneficiary of the nominate *fiducie* avoids having to claim alongside the personal creditors of the trustee, thanks to the establishment of a patrimony by appropriation, which receives the transferred ownership (the separate interest of the patrimony by appropriation clarifies that the rights have been transferred to it, making it difficult to argue that a real right is conferred upon anyone other than the trustee).[47] The insulation of the assets which have been transferred into the *fiducie* patrimony also means that the beneficiary is spared having to bear the risk of an insolvency of the trustee; the question whether the beneficiary should properly be paid is assessed by taking into account solely the assets and liabilities of the *fiducie* patrimony.[48] Indeed, the trust property does not come within the personal patrimony of the trustee, but rather comes to rest in the patrimony by

[47] Unless the law accepts a patrimony with no titulary, in which no one has a real right, as in Quebec. However, this was not the option chosen by France's legislator.

[48] Without a doubt, the combination of ownership impressed with a purpose and a patrimony appropriated to a purpose is the key aspect which allows close comparisons, at the very least, or even equivalences to be drawn between the *fiducie* and the common law trust. This is not so much because trust would involve a patrimony by appropriation (although the Uniform Trust Code moves towards this), but rather because the *fiducie*

appropriation. Admittedly, the provisions of the Civil Code do not say this in so many words, unlike the black letter of the draft bill introducing the *fiducie*. The first article of this bill was conceptually richer and was careful to characterize the trust patrimony in this way. But this characterization is a necessary implication from the provisions of the Civil Code. Article 2011 C.C. sets out that the property which comes within the *fiducie* is kept apart from the 'personal patrimony' of the trustee, and article 2024 C.C. says that the opening of a collective proceeding 'with respect to the trustee does not affect the *fiducie* patrimony'.

Thus, the property which has been appropriated is, in principle, exclusively appropriated to payment of the secured debt. The settlor is divested of her property by the translatory effect of the *fiducie*, but the transfer does not take place in favour of the trustee personally. Instead it takes place to carry out a specified purpose. This explains why the property does not enter the personal patrimony of the trustee. The nominate *fiducie* seems more respectful of the appropriation of the property than the innominate *fiducie*, where the property merges with the personal property of the trustee and where the trustee's obligations amount to an obligation to return equivalent property. Since the property under a nominate *fiducie* is not absorbed into the trustee's personal patrimony, she cannot use the property as she wishes. The trustee can only put the property to a use which accords with its appropriation and which is within the limits of the prerogatives that were transferred. This patrimony by appropriation is useful since the characterization of the trustee as an owner creates a risk that third parties will fail to distinguish between the property held in *fiducie* and the ordinary property which belongs to the trustee, with the result that the personal creditors of the trustee could attempt to seize the trust property. When the trustee is the beneficiary of the security *fiducie*, this separation may at first glance seem to be less advantageous. It does remain useful, how-

patrimony offers a protection similar to that which equity offers to the beneficiary of a trust. Accordingly, trust could survive beyond the bounds of the common law, in a legal system which does not recognize equity. Compare G. Gretton, 'Trusts without Equity' (2000) 49 ICLQ 599. Compare also Barrière, *La réception du trust au travers de la fiducie*, above, note 12. Please see also J. H. Langbein, 'The Contractarian Basis of the Law of Trusts' (1995) 105 Yale L.J. 625; L. Ho, 'The Reception of the Trust in Asia: Emerging Asian Principles of Trust' (2004) Sing. J.L.S. 287, which analyses the reception of the trust in China, in South Korea, in Taiwan and in Japan, all countries without equity.

ever: the debtor must in principle perform her obligation, and it is only subordinately that the security will be called upon to extinguish the principal debt. Keeping the *fiducie* property in a separate fiduciary patrimony further ensures that the debtor's security is not at risk should the trustee herself go bankrupt, unlike in the case of innominate security *fiducies*.

The assets of the *fiducie* must also answer for the *fiducie*'s liabilities: creditors who have claims which arose from the custody of the *fiducie* property or its management will be able to recover them from the *fiducie* patrimony. In the case of a security *fiducie*, these claims should generally be minor.[49]

The extent of the strain on the principle of a unitary patrimony should not be exaggerated. Granted, one and the same person who has been empowered to act as a trustee can be at the head of several patrimonies: her own and one or more *fiducie* patrimonies. But it was already the case that a person could appropriate some of her property to a particular purpose through a legal person, in particular one with a sole shareholder. Through this legal person, she would have been appropriating some of her assets – outside of her personal patrimony – to the fulfilment of a specific purpose. The law also provides that the assets of a determinate compartment of a securitization organization only answer for the debts of that compartment (article L. 214–42–1 M.F.C.), and not the entirety of the debts of this organization, breaking once again with the dogma of the unitary patrimony. Finally, in the present day, following the enactment of Law 2010–658 of 15 June 2010 respecting limited liability individual entrepreneurs, any individual carrying on a

[49] Under the law, the creditors will have a subsidiary right of action against the settlor if the assets of the *fiducie* are insufficient, unless the trustee takes the burden of this subsidiary right onto her own patrimony, in place of the settlor, or unless the creditor renounces this subsidiary right. Thus, in the French conception the *fiducie* patrimony is not watertight. But this should not present an insuperable disadvantage. In principle, the trustee of a trust under the common law is liable on her own property for the debts which arose from the administration of the trust (see L. Smith, 'Trust and Patrimony' (2008) 38 RGD 379). This mechanism does have the virtue of preventing a situation where the trustee of a *fiducie* would unduly weigh it down with liabilities. The mechanism makes her sensitive to her responsibilities, with respect to not generating more expenses than the *fiducie* patrimony could bear. It can also be imagined that a creditor whose claim arose from the administration of the *fiducie* could renounce seeking the recovery of her claim elsewhere than against the *fiducie* patrimony. This would be exactly like the creditor of a limited liability company recovering her claim just against the patrimony of the company without requiring that the chief administrator stand as a surety for the company, and thus without a subsidiary recourse.

business can appropriate property to her commercial or professional activities, isolating the property – as well as the related debts – from her personal patrimony. Thus, there is no longer any doubt that the appropriation of property can now be carried out without having recourse to a legal person. Moreover, the novelty of *fiducie* is perhaps less the trustee's multiple patrimonies, but rather the possibility it offers for the settlor to isolate certain assets for a particular purpose. This is less a case of the trustee breaking with the unity of her patrimony, than of the settlor breaking with the unity of her own.

2. Title-based security without prohibitive disadvantages

(a) Making the property available in favour of the settlor Transferring ownership of the property to the trustee presents some (non-prohibitive) disadvantages for the settlor. The first is the loss of the ability to use the property. This problem can easily be remedied by stipulating in the terms of the *fiducie* that the trustee will let the settlor have the enjoyment or use of the property,[50] somewhat as in a sale and lease-back. Moreover, the security *fiducie* without delivery is explicitly addressed by the legislator. However, when the *fiducie* bears upon movables that are not subject to publicity by registration and the settlor remains in possession thereof, the beneficiary of the *fiducie* faces the risk of competition between her rights and those of the legal successors of the settlor. The absence of publication – even optional publication – appears here as a weakness of the French legal framework. As has already been mentioned, in a case where the property is made available to the settlor and there is no publication of the beneficiary's rights, there is a risk that a third party will seize or acquire the property and then set up her possession in good faith against any subsequent claims. But this risk is of the same kind as the one faced by the owner under title reservation, a risk which has not been a hindrance to the success of the latter institution.

(b) Recharging The second disadvantage is the risk of wasting credit, since the trust property may be worth more than the amount of the debt. This difficulty is solved by the power to recharge[51] the *fiducie*,[52] following

[50] The legal framework for commercial leases or leases of a business (a contract giving the lessee control over the management and stock-in-trade) will not apply (art. 2018-1 C.C.).
[51] Which will need to be stipulated in the terms of the *fiducie*.
[52] See Section III.B.2, below.

the model of the rechargeable hypothec.[53] The trust property can be appropriated to secure a new claim, whether held by the original creditor or another. The power to recharge avoids leaving unused the value which remains and it maximizes the available amount of wealth. In this way, the security departs from the principle which ties the fate of the accessory to that of the principal, since the extinction of the initial debt does not necessarily lead to disappearance of the security. The power to recharge also adapts the principle which requires a security to be for a claim of a specific amount. The amount may well only be determined following the establishment of the security, without a requirement that it be determined from the start. In addition, the power to recharge the *fiducie* allows it to avoid coming under fire under the provision for disproportionate security in article L. 650–1 Comm.C. If a power to recharge is accepted, it raises the possibility that a trustee, who is also first in rank as a beneficiary and thus a senior secured creditor, will find herself under the obligation to continue carrying out the office of trustee for the benefit of a beneficiary who is second in rank and thus a junior secured creditor, even after payment of the claim owed to the trustee.

B. *The legal framework of the security* fiducie

Now that the nature of the security *fiducie* has been clarified, an analysis can be made, in turn, of the establishment (1), the recharge (2) and the realization (3) of this institution.

1. Establishment of the *fiducie*

(a) The people involved Today any person can establish a *fiducie* (unless they are resident in a tax haven[54]), while at the beginning only certain legal persons could be settlors. But only a 'bank', an insurance company or a lawyer can be a trustee. Some observers will see in this restriction the opposite of confidence, even though this is the etymological origin of the term *fiducie*. The settlor is not able to choose the person in whom she has the greatest confidence to carry out a task by virtue of the transfer of ownership to that person. The fear that *fiducies* would be used for money laundering explains this restriction – shared by

[53] Ph. Dupichot, 'La fiducie-sûreté en pleine lumière: à propos de l'ordonnance du 30 janvier 2009' (2009) JCP-G I 132, para. 10.

[54] A State which does not have a tax treaty with France providing for assistance to combat tax fraud or tax evasion.

other countries, for example Luxembourg – of the office of trustee to professionals already experienced in the obligations of diligence which apply in this field. This limitation has not proved to be a hindrance to the growth of the security *fiducie*. The loans that are secured are often granted by financial institutions; if a person who is not qualified to be a trustee wishes to employ a *fiducie* in her favour, she can do so freely so long as she calls upon a qualified trustee. It is most often the case that the task of the trustee can be summed up as custody of the property, securing her claim (or that of the beneficiary of the *fiducie*). Yet, as in the realm of innominate *fiducies*, nothing forbids granting the trustee the right to dispose of the property. Property acquired in turn would become part of the patrimony by appropriation, via real subrogation. It is possible to hold the office of trustee and concurrently to be a beneficiary of the *fiducie*, but this does not imply that the trustee can act beyond the scope of the conditions set on the exercise of her rights by the contract with the settlor. Since the trustee must carry out her task carefully and loyally, some observers may see, in the two hats worn by such a trustee, a conflict of interest which might violate the trustee's obligation of loyalty. However, as in the realm of the common law trust, nothing stops the terms of the *fiducie* from foreseeing certain intersecting interests of the trustee and authorizing them.[55] Moreover, the obligation of loyalty is owed not only to the beneficiary, but also to the settlor with respect to the purpose which is to be fulfilled.

(b) Particulars which must be included Certain distinct features can be seen in the establishment of the security *fiducie*: while it must comply with the 'general law'[56] of *fiducie*, other provisions must also be put into practice.

There are particulars which must be included in the terms of any *fiducie*[57] – description of the property transferred; duration; identification of the settlor, beneficiary and trustee; 'task' to be pursued by the

[55] J. H. Langbein, 'Questioning the Trust Law Duty of Loyalty: Sole Interest or Best Interest?' (2005) 114 Yale L.J. 929, 963ff.

[56] One example is if a natural person wishes to transfer, as a security, property owned jointly or property held in undivided co-ownership. According to the second paragraph of article 2012 C.C., she will only be able to do this by notarial act. This is just as would be the case for any other type of *fiducie*.

[57] If the property under *fiducie* is held in undivided co-ownership or comes within the community of property between spouses, there must also be compliance with the formal requirements of article 2012 C.C.

trustee; the prerogatives of the trustee (article 2018 C.C.) – which, in principle, any contract would have set out in any case apart from this legal requirement. In addition, a contract which establishes a security *fiducie* must state what debt is secured and the estimated value of the assets which are transferred (articles 2372–2 and 2488–2 C.C.).

The requirement to state the debt secured is not problematic: the *fiducie* is complying with the same requirements as the other types of real security and is expressing the principle that a security must be for a claim of a specific amount. The trust property enters the scene to secure a claim, whether determinate or determinable.

More novel is the requirement to state the estimated value of the property, upon pain of nullity with respect to the establishment of the *fiducie*. Perhaps this is a sign of the evolution of the concerns of public authorities, for whom the problem of excessive debt burdens is becoming more salient. But the argument here is open to question. After all, it is not the security which creates the debt burden; payment of the debts can be sought against all property owned by the debtor, whether or not it is charged with a security. Could the motivating factor be the fear that the settlor will lose the ownership of her property, which had a greater value that she thought? This risk is minimized by the possibility open to the settlor of keeping the enjoyment of the property (the transfer of ownership is then painless for the settlor in terms of the usefulness of the thing, since she continues to have it in her hands). It is also minimized by the possibility of recharging the security *fiducie* by appropriating it as security for another debt[58] (and thus employing the value of the property), and it is minimized above all by the impossibility of the creditor enriching herself upon the realization of the security. The appropriateness of this requirement thus seems doubtful, unless it could be seen as a protective measure in favour of the creditor. But if this would be the justification, why would this sort of requirement, bearing this sort of penalty, be limited only to this particular security device?

(c) The formalities with respect to taxation Upon pain of nullity, the contract of *fiducie* is subject to the formality of being registered with the Civil Service's tax authority within a month of the contract's conclusion, for a fixed fee of €120. When this formality, which

[58] Granted, this possibility exists only if it was stipulated in the contract of *fiducie*.

necessarily implies a written contract, is added to the particulars which must be stated in a contract of *fiducie*, all doubts are dissipated on where the *fiducie* should be classed among the types of contract: it comes within the category of formal contracts. Modifications to the contract are subject to the same requirements. Apparently, it is from this registration that the relevant information is transmitted to the national register of *fiducies*, to which only some divisions of the Civil Service have access, in particular to combat money laundering. Moreover, a declaration that the *fiducie* exists must be filed with the appropriate department of the tax authority within fifteen days of the conclusion of the contract. In sum, the formalities to establish a nominate security *fiducie* are greater than those for innominate *fiducies*, even if it is best not to overstate the costs and formalities. Moreover, the transfer of the rights arising from the security contract must, once again upon pain of nullity, be recorded in writing and registered with the tax authority within a month. The latter formality means that there is no practical effect to the automatic transfer of the security with the claim, which would usually occur by virtue of the principle that the fate of the accessory follows that of the principal, since in the absence of an express act which is registered, the transfer will be deemed never to have occurred.

(d) The irrevocability of the security A security's effectiveness depends on its irrevocability. The security *fiducie* is novel in this respect, since the legislation does not expressly make it irrevocable. A creditor who is a beneficiary of a security *fiducie* faces the risk that the general legal regime for revocation of the terms of a *fiducie*, in article 2028 C.C., will come into play. But the impact of this situation must not be exaggerated. Article 2028 C.C. draws a distinction between two cases. In the first situation, the beneficiary has not accepted the contract of *fiducie*: it can be revoked. This basis for revocation is analogous to the one applicable to the institution of stipulation for another (of which *fiducie* is a variety). To be forearmed against this risk, all the creditor-beneficiary has to do is to accept the security *fiducie*. In the second situation, the terms have been accepted and can be modified or revoked, whether with the consent of the beneficiary (which is not problematic) or by decision of the court, according to the black letter of the article. Thus a court could, at least in theory, revoke an established *fiducie*, to the disadvantage of the creditor-beneficiary. In reality, this provision must not be given too wide an effect. There is no ambiguity with respect to the intention of the legislator; it

provision which was actually enacted departs markedly from this logic: it put in place a potential nullity for any *fiducie*, whatever its purpose might be, since a third-party beneficiary or the trustee would find it impossible, in practical terms, to know whether the settlor is meeting her obligations as they come due when she enters into the *fiducie* contract, and thus to be certain that this basis for automatic nullity is not present. The ordinance of 18 December 2008 was a very timely measure, removing this flaw with respect to security *fiducies*: a transfer into a *fiducie* 'as security for a debt undertaken concurrently' will not be null.[63]

2. Recharging the *fiducie*

(a) The principle The economic advantage of rechargeable securities can be understood when borrowed money is repaid and a credit reserve is re-established; when the underlying value of the collateral increases, a new reserve arises.[64] This advantage increases in the case of title-based security, like the *fiducie*: the ability to recharge the security avoids a situation where part of the value of the property could not be appropriated for securing credit.[65] The law permits a *fiducie* to be rechargeable under certain conditions, some of them particular to settlors who are natural persons.

(b) The modalities The ability to recharge a *fiducie* must always be stipulated in the terms of the *fiducie*. This means that the trustee will not find herself unexpectedly obliged to continue pursuing her task once the initial debt – perhaps owed to her – has been extinguished. The recharging agreement is subject to the same conditions with respect to its form, and its publication by registration, as the contract of *fiducie*. It is entirely in the interest of the creditor-beneficiary to see to the publication of the recharging agreement as soon as possible, since this is the date which determines her ranking among the creditors.

The law requires that in the recharging of a security *fiducie*, when the latter was established by a natural person, 'the trust patrimony can be appropriated to secure a new debt only up to the limit of the estimated value [of the trust property] on the day of recharge' (articles 2372–5 para.

[63] The same criterion applies to the 'recharging' of a *fiducie*.

[64] Compare N. Jachiet et al., Inspection générale des finances et inspection générale des services judiciaires, *Rapport d'enquête sur l'hypothèque et le crédit hypothécaire* (Ministère de l'économie, des finances et de l'industrie, November 2004).

[65] See Section II.B.2, 'Assignment of business claims as a security', above.

2 and 2488–5 para. 2 C.C.).[66] This rule avoids a situation where a settlor (who is a natural person) would indebt herself in the expectation that (with time) the value of the property will rise.[67] On the contrary, this rule requires her to take notice of the property's latent additional value at the time the security is recharged. Yet it can be asked whether this limit is enough, and whether behind the intention to use the value of the property to secure new debt there lurks the risk that any borrower (including lay natural persons) would be encouraged to take on excessive debt, without being able to repay it when the property goes down in value. This concern is answered by the retort that the banker's or notary's duty to advise should minimize cases of this kind.

This obligation with respect to an estimate of the value was initially required of all settlors, but the legislator then reduced its application so that it would only be required of natural persons. Perhaps the reasoning behind this is that legal persons deserve less protection than natural ones. This argument is only partly convincing. As has already been mentioned, it is not the appropriation of property as a security that creates the indebtedness; the debt will allow the creditor to seize any property. Thus, it will not have a major impact on the debtor if she provides as security property that has a monetary value less than was claimed for it: her patrimony is and remains the common pledge of her creditor, who has, in addition, the trust property as security (it is the state of being overly indebted which has an unfortunate impact on the debtor). It is more the creditor than the debtor who may have to bear its repercussions. By taking as security property that has a value which is actually lower than the value hoped for, the creditor is under the risk that her security only provides her with partial assurance. Still, this disadvantage[68] exists where the debtor is a natural person just as it does where the debtor is a legal person; it exists where the security is recharged just as it does where the security is newly established. After all, the property can go down in value from the moment the security is established. Besides, why require from a legal person an estimate of the value of the property when the security *fiducie* is established[69] yet free the legal person from that restriction when it subsequently appropriates this selfsame property to secure another

[66] 'Le patrimoine fiduciaire ne peut alors être affecté en garantie d'une nouvelle dette que dans la limite de sa valeur estimée au jour de la recharge.'

[67] L. Aynès, 'Le régime juridique de la fiducie' (May 2009) RLDC 67, 69 in particular.

[68] See also Ph. Théry, 'L'hypothèque rechargeable' (May 2007) *Droit & Patrimoine* 42.

[69] See Section III.B.1(b), 'Particulars which must be included', above.

debt, where there is a 'recharging' of the security? This lack of parallelism in treatment is puzzling. Perhaps some benefit can be seen in this provision by drawing a parallel with a phenomenon that contributed to the subprime crisis:[70] among the people who had borrowed to buy a home, some of them later recharged the real security on the home to secure other loans, in particular for purposes of everyday expenses. When the downturn in the real estate market occurred, creditors found themselves unable to recover their claims from the immovable on which their security bore. If the intention of the legislator was to combat this risk, the obligation to have an estimate of the property's value should also apply to legal persons, which is no longer the case since the law of 12 May 2009. Moreover, the obligation should apply just as well to the rechargeable hypothec, which is also at risk from a decline in the value of the property on which the security bears; the mere mention of a maximum sum in the act establishing the security is not sufficient to eliminate this risk.

3. Enforcement of the security

If the secured debt has been extinguished, the security no longer has a purpose and the contract will be brought to an end, save in the case of a recharge of the security. If the security needs to be enforced, a distinction must be drawn between an enforcement that takes place outside (a) or at the time of (b) a collective proceeding. The two situations have in common that the beneficiary of the security *fiducie* has a particularly privileged position in relation to the creditors who hold other types of security; this is no doubt one of the reasons for the success of this security device.

(a) Enforcement outside of a collective proceeding When the enforcement of the security is triggered, as provided by the governing contract, this presents one of two possible situations. In the first, the trustee is also the beneficiary: in this case, the trust property leaves the trust patrimony for the trustee's personal patrimony. Thus, she goes from being a fiduciary owner to being an ordinary owner,[71] free of any encumbrance or appropriation. The second possibility is that the security is for the benefit of a third party. In this case this creditor, as beneficiary

[70] P. Crocq, 'La nouvelle fiducie-sûreté: une porte ouverte sur une prochaine crise des subprimes en France?' (2009) *Dalloz* 716.

[71] M.-P. Dumont-Lefrand, 'Le dénouement de l'opération de fiducie' (June 2008) *Droit & Patrimoine* 63, 66 in particular.

of the *fiducie*, will have property transferred to her,[72] and will hold the ordinary type of ownership. The creditor-beneficiary can also provide in the contract that the trustee will sell the property and hand over the price to her, avoiding being burdened with an item of property which may not necessarily be of use to her. The way will have been prepared in advance for this transfer of ownership from the trustee to the beneficiary or to the third party. Indeed, this prospect will have required, at the time the *fiducie* is established, that no limitation on the right of ownership will present an obstacle to it. The property will be freed of rights of first refusal and obligations requiring that permission will be obtained for a transfer. Thus, there is no prohibition either of a taking-in-payment clause or of a clause which permits a private sale. The absence of these prohibitions makes the security *fiducie* a security whose mode of enforcement is flexible,[73] keeping in mind as well that it does not require any seizure proceeding before the enforcement can take place, since the trustee is already the owner of the property.

In order to avoid any enrichment of the creditor and plundering of the debtor, the value of the property will have to be estimated by an expert[74] when the security is realized (articles 2372–3 and 2488–3 C.C.). The exception to this is property whose value is beyond question: assets that are listed on an organized market (for example, Euronext or Alternext) and, *a fortiori*, sums of money. Any surplus by which this valuation exceeds the secured debt must be returned to the debtor-settlor.

However, before transferring any surplus to the debtor-settlor, the beneficiary must first pay out of that amount those creditors whose debt arose from the administration of the *fiducie* (articles 2372–4 and 2488–4 C.C.). It might have been thought that these trust creditors should be paid before there is any transfer out of the *fiducie* patrimony,[75] but the legislator was not of this opinion.

[72] Should the creditor wish to sell the property, she would not be subject to the prohibition on clauses of private sale (a contractual clause which frees the creditor from the obligation to employ a public auction to sell the property on which her security bears).

[73] By not setting a limit on taking-in-payment clauses bearing on the principal residence of a settlor who is a natural person, the law could even seem excessively accommodating. Aside from this, the advantages of the security *fiducie* can be seen, by comparison to the pledge of inventory or the pledge securing the repayment of a consumer loan, where taking-in-payment clauses are forbidden.

[74] Designated by private agreement or by the court.

[75] F. Barrière, 'La loi instituant la fiducie: entre équilibre et incohérence' (2007) JCP-E 2053, para. 31.

(b) Enforcement at the time of a collective proceeding While the law with respect to collective proceedings is an area of dangerous liaisons between the interests of the creditor and those of the enterprise in difficulty,[76] the law introducing the *fiducie* seemed, in its original version, highly favourable to creditors who are the beneficiaries of a security *fiducie*, thanks to the exclusivity that fiduciary ownership confers upon them. At a time when the general law forbade the exercise by a creditor of a contractual right to take ownership of the collateral, and so removed any real advantage to a taking-in-payment clause, no provision of the 2007 law limited the enforcement of a security *fiducie* during the time when the debtor-settlor was subject to a collective proceeding. The ordinance of 18 December 2008 changed the game somewhat, advancing an interesting compromise between the interests at play. First of all, let us cast our eyes on the advantages of the security *fiducie* when the settlor is in a state of 'bankruptcy', and then let us study the enforcement of the *fiducie* in this situation.

The position of the beneficiary of the security *fiducie* is particularly stable in a case where the settlor is in a state of 'bankruptcy'.[77] The contract of the security *fiducie* is not considered a contract 'in progress', as this term is used with respect to collective proceedings. Thus the contract is not subject to being resiliated by the officials of the collective proceedings. The creditor who is favoured by a *fiducie* is excluded from the committees of creditors, thus avoiding delays and abandonment of debts which might otherwise be required of her.[78] Where there is a transfer of an enterprise in the collective proceedings, this can entail neither the transfer of the trust property (which is logical, since it is no longer owned by the bankrupt settlor), nor even a transfer of the availability agreement by which the debtor may have retained the use of the collateral (which means that the trustee will be able to recover the enjoyment of the collateral even before the end of the duration agreed for the availability agreement). If the settlor wishes to regain the ability to make use of the collateral, she can pay her creditor early. This is a

[76] F.-X. Lucas and M. Sénéchal, 'Fiducie ou sauvegarde, il faut choisir' (2008) *Dalloz* 29; M. Farge and O. Gout, 'L'impact du nouveau droit des entreprises en difficulté sur le droit de sûretés' (March 2009) RLDC 25ff, para. 3

[77] More generally, see F. Barrière, 'La fiducie-sûreté' (2009) JCE-E 1808, paras. 37ff; (2009) JCP-N 1291, paras. 37ff; (January 2010) *Trusts e attività fiduciarie* 5, paras. 37ff.

[78] This also avoids the possibility that the secured creditor might block the adoption of a plan submitted to the committees of creditors, where the secured debt is substantial.

departure from the principle that forbids the payment of prior creditors, but it is justified by the advantage for the settlor in being able to make use of the collateral.[79]

Now that the general setting has been described, the time has come to study first the legal framework which applies to the enforcement of a security *fiducie* when the debtor is under bankruptcy protection (a framework inspired by the Chapter 11 process in American law), or under court-supervised restructuring, and then to study the framework for enforcement during a judicial liquidation.

The legal framework which applies during bankruptcy protection splits in two, depending on whether or not an agreement was concluded in favour of the settlor for making use of the property or for its enjoyment.

If the trustee, having become the owner of the collateral, agreed to allow the settlor to continue to make use or have the benefit of it, so as to facilitate the settlor's bankruptcy protection or restructuring, then the law provides that the property must remain at the disposal of the settlor. One might say that the law has an irrebuttable presumption that the property is essential to the settlor's enterprise, and so avoids having to characterize this or that asset as essential (and avoids the litigation that a subjective criterion of this sort would have entailed). In this spirit, if a *fiducie* is accompanied by an availability agreement, article L. 622–23–1 Comm.C. forbids any enforcement triggered by the failure to pay a debt or by an acceleration clause depriving the settlor of the benefit of the agreed duration upon the opening of this sort of collective proceeding, when the debt preceded the opening of the collective proceeding. Thus, it will only be possible to pay the creditor after the period of monitoring or of the restructuring plan. The rule could have been more flexible: as soon as the property is no longer owned by the settlor, nothing should have prevented the trustee from transferring it to the beneficiary, so long as it was clear that the debtor-settlor would still have the benefit of the agreement for use of the collateral (if the settlor has the use or enjoyment of the property, it should be a matter of indifference for the settlor what person owns the property). This is comparable to the way in which a contract of lease can be set up against the person to whom the ownership of an immovable has been transferred.

[79] This power should be rarely needed. If the property is of use to the settlor, she will have stipulated an availability agreement in her favour from the beginning.

If, on the other hand, there was no agreement for the availability or enjoyment of the property by the settlor, then article L. 622–23–1 Comm.C. is interpreted, *a contrario*, to permit the enforcement of the security, and the trustee should be able to transfer the property to the beneficiary. Since the property is no longer in the patrimony of the settlor nor is the settlor making use of it, it would be illogical to freeze the trust patrimony. On the contrary, there is reason to allow the enforcement of the security and to free up the property, which up to that time will have been held in the trust, from the appropriation with which it was charged. In any case, the non-possessory security *fiducie* seems to be the 'best of securities', once a collective proceeding has been commenced, which suggests that it will become much used in practice.[80]

In bankruptcy protection or court-supervised restructuring, the enforcement of the security *fiducie* can take place as soon as the period for observation or for the restructuring plan has ended (or in case the plan is not complied with[81]), including if a judicial liquidation[82] has begun. There is no limitation which would interfere with its enforcement. This allows the creditor to be paid more quickly than if she needed to wait for an enforcement organized by the officials of the collective proceeding. As a result, 'a comparison with the situation of a hypothecary creditor, for example, or of a creditor with a possessory pledge of the stock-in-trade, speaks for itself, since the *fiducie* is so obviously superior during a judicial liquidation'.[83] Indeed, unlike the situation with those two securities, the beneficiary of a *fiducie* can be paid as soon as the judicial liquidation opens (thus without having to wait), and without being outranked by preferred creditors. Yet, until that moment, the beneficiary of the *fiducie* will have left the enjoyment

[80] P. Crocq, 'L'ordonnance du 18 décembre 2008 et le droit de sûretés' (2009) JCP-E 1313, para. 37.

[81] Para. 2 of art. L. 626-27 Comm.C.

[82] Art. L. 641-11-1, VI Comm.C.

[83] 'La comparaison avec la situation d'un créancier hypothécaire par exemple ou d'un créancier nanti sur le fonds de commerce se passe de commentaires tant la supériorité de la fiducie est manifeste au cours de la liquidation judiciaire': F. Pérochon, 'A propos de la réforme de la liquidation judiciaire par l'ordonnance du 18 décembre 2008' (March 2009) 8–10 *Gazette du Palais* 3, para. 40. See also J.-J. Ansault, 'Fiducie-sûreté et sûretés réelles traditionnelles: que choisir?' (May 2010) *Droit & Patrimoine* 52, 66 in particular. It can also be noted that whereas a taking-in-payment clause is rendered inoperative when the hypothec bears on the principal residence of the debtor, the *fiducie* does not labour under an analogous restriction. This may seem to be insufficiently protective of debtors who are natural persons.

of the property to his debtor, just as if the debtor had pledged her stock in trade or hypothecated her immovable in a way which permitted her to continue to make use of it. The security *fiducie* could also come to be chosen in practice over the pledge of an investment account containing financial instruments. Granted, this pledge benefits from a type of exclusivity due to the right of retention which it grants, but it does not allow the creditor to realize her security when she pleases during a collective proceeding.[84] Indeed, the right of retention is as effective as it is frustrating. Granted, the creditor who has a right of retention will end up receiving a complete and exclusive payment of her claim, as the counterpart to handing over the thing at the request of the court-supervised liquidator. But it is at the very least paradoxical that the creditor has to wait for the exclusive payment intended for her, according to the sequential playing out of the proceedings for judicial liquidation, without being able to obtain her payment as soon as the proceedings open. Since the security *fiducie* allows the creditor to obtain payment right away, it has a definite advantage over the right of retention. Perhaps there will be a loss of interest in employing real rights of retention, with more use made of security *fiducies*; both institutions offer a type of exclusivity, but one has an ease of enforcement that the other lacks. And if there is transfer of the enterprise, the interests of the creditor of the security *fiducie* will not be impaired. Not only will the availability agreement, if any, be brought to an end, the property itself will be liquidated so as to pay the creditor. This is better than other kinds of real security, where the creditor's rights are only over some part of price realized from the collateral, which does not always reflect its market value.

Finally, this legal framework preserves the chances of restructuring the enterprise by not depriving the enterprise of an important asset (one which is presumed to be useful due to the availability agreement). But the framework still leaves the creditor with the possibility of enforcing his security, without being required to claim along with other creditors, when the property is not useful to the enterprise or when there is no chance that the enterprise can be restructured (and so passes into judicial liquidation). In these situations, French law is particularly competitive compared to other countries, which are often thought to give more protection to their creditors.

[84] M. Grimaldi and R. Dammann, 'La fiducie sur ordonnances' (2009) *Dalloz* 670, para. 15.

IV Conclusion

Despite its tumultuous awakening, could the nominate security *fiducie* become the queen of securities?[85] Other effective types of security exist. Among those which come to mind are the innominate *fiducies* – the security assignment dubbed 'Dailly', securities for financial obligations governed by the Monetary and Financial Code – as well as pledges of claims.[86] But the range within which these securities can apply is so narrow that they cannot prosper more generally. This is also the case for the reservation of ownership, since that security is only of interest to the seller or supplier of property.[87] As for the pledge of ready money, another type of innominate *fiducie*, the absence of a separate trust patrimony means that it is not necessary to earmark the money held as collateral. This might seem to make things easier, as compared with the nominate *fiducie*. Still, this pledge makes the debtor-pledgor bear the risk of the bankruptcy of her creditor. Thus, what seems an advantage could at times be analysed as a prohibitive drawback. Conversely, since any property can be put into a nominate *fiducie* by complying with a fairly simple set of formalities required to establish this security, the exclusivity conferred by fiduciary ownership as well as the modes for the enforcement of the security *fiducie* could attract numerous creditors. In addition, the *fiducie*'s flexibility in relation to the debtor's continued use of the collateral, even while proceedings for bankruptcy protection or restructuring are under way, could reassure the debtor. Thus, the use of securities which confer a right of retention, and therefore a protective situation

[85] Crocq, above, note 80, para. 37; J.-J. Ansault, 'La fiducie ressuscitée!' (May 2009) *Journal des sociétés* 22, 23 in particular; Lajarte, above, note 7, p. 86: 'France's *fiducie* ensures sufficient protection for the interests of the beneficiary. Let us wish that this pledge of effectiveness will give a brilliant future to *fiducie*' ('la fiducie française assure au bénéficiaire une protection suffisante de ses intérêts. Souhaitons que ce gage d'efficacité donne à la fiducie un brillant avenir').

[86] L. Aynès, 'Le nantissement de créances, entre gage et fiducie' (September 2007) *Droit & Patrimoine* 66; D. Legeais, 'La réforme des sûretés, la fiducie et les procédures collectives' (2007) *Revue des sociétés* 687, 694. With this pledge, the creditor has the right to have the claim paid directly to her, once the debtor of the claim has notice of the pledge (art. 2363 C.C.). This offers her a type of exclusivity with respect to the claim.

[87] Mallet-Bricout, above, note 43, 85 in particular: 'it is likely that the security *fiducie* of movables will become the ownership-based security of choice for incorporeal movables, while the reservation of ownership will remain the gold standard in this area for corporeal movables' ('il est probable qu'elle [la fiducie-sûreté mobilière] devienne la sûreté-propriété privilégiée pour les meubles incorporels, tandis que la réserve de propriété resterait la référence en ce domaine pour les meubles corporels').

for the creditor, could eventually recede in favour of the security *fiducie*. *A fortiori*, the other types of security will have to compete with the security trust, given its ability to be used for any type of property.

However, the French nominate security *fiducie* has some drawbacks. Three will be mentioned here. First, the absence of publication is a factor which has the potential to create conflicts, which may be resolved to the detriment of the beneficiary of a non-possessory security *fiducie*, and to the advantage of the third party who relied on the appearances created by the possession of the debtor-settlor. However, this disadvantage only pertains to security *fiducies* over movables that are not publicly registered and in which the debtor retains possession. It is equivalent to the disadvantage borne by a seller who reserves title: she also risks finding herself in conflict with a third party who entered into possession of the property in good faith. Yet experience shows that this risk is not prohibitive to the employment of reservation of ownership. Second, if it attaches to collateral which has greater value than the amount of the debt which it secures, the security may turn out to be disproportionate; there is therefore a risk of wasting credit. However, the rechargeable nature of a nominate *fiducie* limits the scope of this concern. Third, the remuneration of the trustee introduces a cost avoided by other types of security which do not involve an intermediary. However, this cost should remain limited, since the 'task' of the trustee essentially consists of preserving the property and keeping it safe, and even this component will not exist in the case of a transfer of incorporeal property, as a security with the trustee as its sole beneficiary. Accordingly, we may wonder whether the advantages of the security *fiducie* will outweigh its disadvantages.

The future will tell whether the transplant of this nominate structure will ultimately be rejected. The security *fiducie* upsets some of the principles of the law of security. The idea of a security as merely an accessory to the claim does not have its usual vigour in this field. Indeed, when the secured claim is assigned, the transfer of the security to the assignee requires a writing which is entered in the register; it is not transferred to the assignee automatically. When the debt has been extinguished, the security is not automatically extinguished and can persist if it is rechargeable. The nominate *fiducie* also adapts the principle that requires a security to be for a claim of a specific amount, since the amount can only be determined subsequent to the establishment of a rechargeable *fiducie*. The security *fiducie* also elicits further thought with respect to certain aspects of its legal framework, whether it be the lack of an express provision setting out that this security is irrevocable, the requirement that a statement be included of the estimated value of the property (a condition for validity of the security) or the employment of the estimated value of the property as a limit for the recharging of the security for settlors who are natural persons.

The security *fiducie* also leads to further development with respect to some classical legal principles. The theory of a unitary patrimony has suffered a setback from the counter-example of the *fiducie* patrimony. The traditional notion of ownership also needs to be reviewed in light of the developing concept of fiduciary ownership. The *fiducie* is based on a novel type of transfer of ownership, impressed with a definite purpose and excluding the claims of others in the thing. Since the *fiducie* partakes of ownership and its exclusivity, this results in a favourable treatment in case of bankruptcy of the debtor and, in the case of lending institutions, a favourable treatment with respect to their prudential ratios. The analysis of innominate *fiducies*, which often confer ownership upon the trustee, with all the attributes of ordinary ownership – ownership transferred for fiduciary purposes but which partakes of ordinary ownership where fungible property is concerned – presumes that there are no incompatibilities between innominate *fiducies* and the law of property. Such compatibility presages that the type of ownership shaped by the nominate *fiducie*, an example of the flexibility of ownership as an institution, is indeed acceptable in the law.

The National Association of Business Corporations (*Association Nationale des Sociétés par Actions* or ANSA) declares that this '*fiducie* ... [could] foreshadow a promising future for the institution'.[88] Its acceptance by the world of practice will confirm or disprove this prediction. The future will tell whether the nominate security trust will meet with a level of success equivalent to that of its innominate stepsisters. It can be assumed that the latter will continue to be widely used in practice, since their modes of establishment, third-party effectiveness and enforcement are just as attractive, except for the innominate *fiducie*'s lack of a *fiducie* patrimony which some creditors will prefer. Could it be that the nominate security *fiducie* might in time serve as an inspiration to some common law countries,[89] where there seems to be less use of security trusts? This would be a signal example of the cross-influences among legal systems.

[88] ANSA, 'La fiducie', April 2009, para. 09–020, p. 6 ('*fiducie (. . .) [peut] augurer d'un avenir prometteur pour l'institution*').

[89] With respect to the possibility that the Civil Code of Québec might influence Canadian common law in the realm of *fiducie* and trust, see A. Grenon, 'Of Codifications, the Uniform Trust Code and Quebec Trusts: Lessons for Common Law Canada' (2003–2004) 23 *Estates, Trusts & Pensions* 237, 263 and, by the same author, 'La fiducie canadienne issue de la common law: le droit comparé peut-il favoriser son évolution?' (2006) Ottawa L. Rev. 83, 97ff.

7

The trustee: mainspring, or only a cog, in the French *fiducie*?

BLANDINE MALLET-BRICOUT

I Introduction

A. *Are trusts and French law sibling rivals?*

A French law journal took up this provocative question a few years ago in a special edition devoted to trusts and their reception in French law.[1] This international conference on the confrontation of Anglo-Saxon trusts and civilian *fiducies* (in their varied forms) happily leads us to answer the question in the negative: trusts and French law are certainly not siblings,[2] nor, however, are they rivals. The recent enactment of the French *fiducie* (under Law 2007–211 of 19 February 2007) was undoubtedly influenced by the Anglo-American trust, though this influence is by necessity qualified.

This chapter brings us back to the broad theme of the role of the trustee, a matter which has also been addressed in other contributions: is the trustee the mainspring, or only a simple cog, in the French *fiducie*?

Whether we consider the trustee in civilian *fiducies*, or in the Anglo-American trust, there is no doubt that this legal entity is central – indeed indispensable – to the operation of *fiducies* and of trusts.[3]

B. *Concept*

In French law, the trustee (*fiduciaire*) is the one to whom the settlor (*constituant*) entrusts a present or future asset or grouping of assets,

1 'Trust et droit français: les frères ennemis? Perspectives, réflexions croisées' (March 2006) RLDC 57.

2 As evidenced by France's non-ratification of the Hague Convention on the Law Applicable to Trusts and on Their Recognition of 1 July 1985.

3 See M.-F. Papandreou-Déterville, *Droit anglais des biens* (Paris: LGDJ, 2004), p. 513. In the author's opinion, 'the trustee is most certainly the fulcrum of the institution' even though a common law trust never fails for want of a trustee.

rights or security interests with the intention that the trustee 'acts for a specific purpose for the benefit of one or more beneficiaries' (article 2011 Civil Code (C.C.)).

The settlor can name one or several trustees. The list of possible trustees is restricted, however, to credit establishments, investment companies, insurance companies and lawyers.[4] Private individuals are notably excluded from this list.

The trustee does not fit any existing legal classification in French law; it is simply not categorized, neither as a mandatary, nor as an administrator, nor as belonging to any other legal category. The trustee is simply an 'actor' (*agissant*) in relation to the trust property, but a particular actor in that it acts within the novel framework of a patrimony that is separate from its own (article 2011 C.C.), which French doctrine calls a 'trust patrimony' (*patrimoine fiduciaire*).[5]

The trustee is therefore not a classic manager or administrator, but has a novel position in French positive law as the titulary of two patrimonies – its own patrimony and the trust patrimony – a concept that derogates completely from the classical theory of patrimony in French law.[6]

[4] Art. 2015 C.C. For further details on the requirements for being a trustee, see B. Gouthière et al., *La fiducie, mode d'emploi*, 2nd edn (Levallois: Francis Lefebvre, 2009), no. 720. For comparison, Luxembourgish law also specifies that the title of trustee can be applied only to a credit institution, an investment firm, an investment company with variable or fixed share capital, a securitization company, a management company of common funds or of securitization funds, a pension fund, an insurance or reinsurance undertaking or a national or international public body operating in the financial sector (Law of 27 July 2003, art. 4).

[5] The existence of a patrimony separate from the personal patrimony of the trustee is not reflected in all civilian *fiducies*, notably in Switzerland where the trustee administers the fiduciary assets within its own patrimony without the creation of a 'trust patrimony' (see B. Chappuis, 'L'incidence de la convention de La Haye relative à la loi applicable au trust et à sa reconnaissance sur la fiducie en droit suisse', in Centenaire du Code civil suisse, colloque du 5 avril 2007 (Société de législation comparée, 2008), vol. 8, pp. 201ff). The Roman *fiducia* also did not recognize the existence of a separate patrimony. Luxembourgish law, on the contrary, provides for an autonomous fiduciary patrimony (Law of 27 July 2003, art. 6).

[6] This theory is often called the 'Aubry and Rau theory', named after the two authors at its origin. Under this theory, which is fundamental to French law, every legal person has a patrimony and can have only one patrimony. This classical theory excludes all possibility of a patrimony by appropriation. The law of *fiducie* clearly puts this theory into question, as does the recent Law 2010–658 of 15 June 2010 on limited liability individual entrepreneurs (*entrepreneur individuel à responsabilité limitée*), which created a status for the benefit of entrepreneurs who are physical persons providing for two patrimonies to be attached to a single legal person – a personal patrimony and a patrimony specific to professional activities. On this matter, see especially F. Terré (ed.), *EIRL: L'entrepreneur individuel à responsabilité limitée, Droit 360°* (Litec, 2011).

C. *Diversity of the trustee's roles*

Further, the trustee may have several 'fiduciary roles', as French law permits management trusts (*fiducie-gestion*) and security trusts (*fiducie-sûreté*). The trustee may therefore be administering assets in the interests of an objective determined by the settlor; these assets are to be remitted, upon fulfilment of the terms of the trust, to a third-party beneficiary (or several beneficiaries). Alternatively, it may be managing a patrimony consisting of a security for the benefit of a third-party creditor, or even for itself if it is a creditor of the settlor.

There are therefore multiple French *fiducies*, making it difficult even to attempt to analyse the way it works. Whether a *fiducie* is created for management or security purposes is not a trivial matter, not even when the two functions are combined, where the trustee is not the settlor's creditor but remains responsible for managing the fiduciary patrimony as security for a third-party creditor.[7] Here, we can already see the limits of the doctrinal distinction between management trusts and security trusts. The legislator has decided officially to retain this dichotomy, even though many provisions of the French Civil Code are now devoted exclusively to the security *fiducie*.[8]

D. *The trustee as key element of the* fiducie *mechanism*

The trustee is therefore seen as a unitary figure in the French Civil Code and, at first blush, is a key element of the *fiducie* mechanism. Indeed, of the twenty-one articles relating to the *fiducie* in Book III of the Civil Code, two-thirds concern the trustee, one-third exclusively so.

Despite this, gaps remain in the French legislation with respect to the core of the matter, that is, with respect to the nature of the relationship between the trustee and the settlor on the one hand and between the trustee and the beneficiary on the other. In addition, fiduciary liability is covered only in a single, rather vague, article.

Clearly, the French legislator still has work to do (despite the numerous amendments relating to the *fiducie* that came out in the three years

[7] The first *fiducies* settled in France after the coming into force of the Law of 19 February 2007 were of this type.

[8] See arts. 2372–1ff. and 2488–1ff. C.C., on securities, inserted into Book IV by Order 2009–112 of 30 January 2009. The general provisions on *fiducies* are found in Book III, dedicated to special contracts, at arts. 2011ff.

following the 2007 enactment[9]), and judges will need to clarify matters. Practitioners, however, are likely to remain apprehensive of the *fiducie* in France – since its adoption on 19 February 2007, the *fiducie* has been sparingly used.

Nevertheless, at first glance the trustee seems to be the indisputable mainspring of the French *fiducie*: the trust property is transferred to the trustee, who must simultaneously respect the settlor's will while acting in a way that is proper to one who is both an owner and an administrator.

E. An array of legal capacities

The trustee combines a number of legal capacities, through which its functions and its role can be studied. It is at once the settlor's co-contracting party for a period of time, the owner of the trust property, the administrator of the trust patrimony, and sometimes even the creditor of the settlor. This novel position makes it difficult to harmonize the *fiducie* with traditional civilian legal categories: how can the law allow for the same entity to be both the recognized owner of assets as well as a simple administrator thereof for the benefit of a third party? We must have recourse to the characterization – a strange one for French law – of 'temporary owner on behalf of another', leading us to imagine an owner that is required to act only within the limits of the objectives assigned to it by another (the settlor) for the benefit of a third party (the beneficiary).

Here we can see how the difficulties that surround the French *fiducie* are not easily understood outside civil law systems.

Indeed, contrary to the French *fiducie* that finds its foundation in both contract law and property law, historically the Anglo-American trust is based on property law alone.[10] This essential difference enables us better to grasp the diversity of approaches to civilian *fiducies* and Anglo-American trusts. Some have even gone so far as to consider the comparison of the trust to the *fiducie* to be impossible; and, in any case, that the transposition of the rights known under trust law into civilian categories is unworkable.[11]

[9] Specifically: Law 2007–211 of 19 February 2007 on the *fiducie* (the foundational text), Law 2008–776 of 4 August 2008 on the modernization of the economy, Order 2008–1345 of 18 December 2008 reforming the law of collective proceedings, Orders 2009–112 and 2009–104 of 30 January 2009, Law 2009–526 of 12 May 2009 on the simplification of the law. These texts are easily found on http://legifrance.gouv.fr using their numbers.

[10] See Papandreou-Déterville, *Droit anglais des biens*, above, note 3, pp. 425ff.

[11] See especially H. Motulsky, 'De l'impossibilité juridique de constituer un trust anglo-saxon sous l'empire de la loi française' (1948) RCDIP 451; C. Witz, *La fiducie en droit*

I believe, on the contrary, that a useful comparison can be made that focuses on the civil law trustee, which shares a number of common traits with its common law counterpart. At the very least, many questions surrounding the role of the trustee in civil law can equally be asked about the trustee in common law and vice versa. There is clearly a certain 'universality' with respect to the problems, if not to the legal solutions, relating to the powers, duties and liabilities of trustees. The goals that one seeks to achieve through a civilian *fiducie* or an Anglo-American trust are probably the closest link between the two.

F. Outline

While seeking to introduce points of comparison with the Anglo-American trust and other civilian *fiducies*, we will see how the French *fiducie* clearly stretches the classical civilian concepts of administrator and of owner. This leads us to question whether the trustee is really the mainspring in the mechanism of the *fiducie*, or is only a simple cog, dependent on many other cogs in the workings of the trust.

To do so, we will first look at the trustee as a contractual administrator who is crucially dependent on the settlor (Section II) and, second, we will discuss the trustee as a limited owner of the fiduciary assets (Section III).

II The trustee as dependent contracting party

There is nothing immediately strange or shocking in the assertion that a contracting party could be seen to be 'dependent': any bilateral contract necessarily creates a relationship involving some dependency on the will of the other contracting party. In the French *fiducie*, however, the trustee's position is more nuanced. The dependence of the trustee on the other parties in the *fiducie* has multiple facets.

In addition to the concept of dependence, which results from the mechanism of the French *fiducie* (A below), there is the matter of the settlor's actual domination in several situations (B below). The legal uncertainty around the trustee's liability remains equally paradoxical: despite this state

privé français, preface by D. Schmidt (Paris: Economica, 1981), p. 6, no. 8, that speaks of a 'chasm' (fossé) between Anglo-American trust and continental laws. Also, on the difficulties of harmonization in Europe of the different forms of *fiducie* and trust, see A. Braun, 'The Framing of a European Law of Trusts', in this volume, p. 277.

of dependency, the trustee's liability is addressed by the French legislator in only a cursory fashion (C below).

A. *The concept of dependence*

As in the common law trust, the *fiducie* mechanism rests on the idea that the trustee works for the benefit of a third party selected by the settlor. At the end of the day, it is the beneficiary who acquires the assets in the trust patrimony.

The trustee therefore acts as the administrator of the trust property entrusted to it. However, unlike an Anglo-American trustee – who is not fundamentally subject to the terms of a contract[12] – the French trustee is necessarily bound by the terms of the trust contract with the settlor. In French law, the *fiducie* is a special contract, placed alongside other contracts such as the contract of sale, loan or deposit. This contract of administration is autonomous in juridical nature: it bears no relationship with the contract of mandate, unlike in Swiss law, for example, which relies specifically on the law applicable to mandate to define the rules around the Swiss *fiducie.*[13] Luxembourgish law is similar.[14] In French law, the *fiducie* is a stand-alone form of contract. Some authors have recently considered the role of the beneficiary in the French *fiducie* as relying on a stipulation regarding third parties under article 1121 C.C.,[15] but this remains a matter of debate.

In any case, the trustee is the interface between the settlor and the beneficiary on the basis of a contract concluded between it and the settlor. This three-party *fiducie* operation relies at its core on a contract

[12] See R. David and C. Jauffret-Spinosi, *Les grands systèmes de droit contemporain*, 11th edn (Paris: Dalloz, 2002), no. 259, note 2: 'The category of trust developed outside the contractual realm and has remained completely distinct therefrom.' This analysis must, however, be qualified as certain Anglo-American writers have a much more contractarian approach to the trust in positive law: see specifically J. H. Langbein, 'The Contractarian Basis of the Law of Trusts' (1995) 105 Yale L.J. 625ff.

[13] See Chappuis, 'L'incidence de la convention de La Haye', above, note 5, p. 203: the author presents this reference to the law of mandate as being the 'fundamental framework' (*cadre fondamental*) of the Swiss *fiducie*, which itself is not regulated by any legal text.

[14] Law of 27 July 2003, art. 7: 'The rules governing mandates, in so far as they are not based on representation, are applicable to the relationship between the fiduciant and the fiduciary, to the extent the present title or the parties do not derogate therefrom.' In Luxembourgish law, the *fiduciant* corresponds to the *constituant* (i.e., settlor) in French law.

[15] See especially Gouthière et al., *La fiducie*, above, note 4, para. 751.

between two of the three parties. In this contractual context, the trustee seems to have a major role to play as the mainspring of the operation.

The reality, however, is in many ways different.

First, the French law on *fiducie* prohibits the use of a *fiducie* as a liberality (article 2013 C.C. imposes nullity as a matter of public order). Doctrinal writers criticize this approach, which can be explained only by the legislator's fears that the *fiducie* could be used for misguided purposes. The *fiducie* as liberality may eventually make its way into French law, which would give the trustee an essential role as an intermediary between respect for the wishes of the settlor, and the preservation of the beneficiary's interests.

Secondly, French law permits conflation of roles among the three parties to the *fiducie* operation. The trustee can also be the beneficiary of the *fiducie*, as permitted under article 2016 C.C. This is most notably the case where the trustee is a creditor of the settlor and a security *fiducie* is created to guarantee the settlor's debt to the trustee. This is therefore not just a hypothetical case.

The settlor can also be the beneficiary (article 2016 C.C.). This could occur in the case of a management trust comprised of the assets of a settlor who is an incapable major. This is a more classic case that the common law trust also recognizes.[16] Under French law, such a *fiducie* leads to a presumption of 'concerted action' under commercial law (article L. 233–10 II 5° Commercial Code).

The *fiducie* can thereby concretely be reduced to two parties instead of three, one of which plays two roles, that of trustee or settlor and that of beneficiary. The *fiducie* structure is thereby maintained (three distinct functions), if somewhat warped (two actors). In these – possibly frequent – cases, the trustee is no longer an interface between the settlor and the beneficiary, but exists face-to-face with its co-contractor, the settlor, which modifies the initial spirit of the *fiducie* mechanism and distances the French *fiducie* from the trust. The contractual basis of the *fiducie* comes to the fore in such cases.[17]

[16] R. Legeais, *Grands systèmes de droit contemporain: approche comparative*, 2nd edn (Paris: Litec, 2008), para. 476.

[17] This contractual foundation also means the settlor and the trustee cannot be one and the same since, according to some authors, a contract cannot be concluded with oneself. However, contracting with oneself generally seems possible under French law, as several authors have discussed (C. Larroumet, *Droit civil, Les obligations, Le contrat, 1re partie*, 6th edn (Paris: Economica, 2006), no. 257ff; F. Terré, P. Simler, Y. Lequette, *Droit civil, Les obligations*, 10th edn (Paris: Dalloz, 2009), paras. 182ff). Some authors have stated that such

A similar comment can more broadly be made with respect to the position of the beneficiary in the *fiducie* mechanism (indirectly shedding light on the role of the trustee).

This is because, thirdly, the beneficiary is in some ways no more than the recipient of the results of the trustee's actions based on the will of the settlor (who through the *fiducie* transfers one or several 'assets, rights or security interests').

The beneficiary is not a party to the *fiducie* contract. Article 2028 C.C. makes only rather allusive mention of the beneficiary's acceptance of the *fiducie*: 'The *fiducie* contract may be revoked by the settlor as long as it has not been accepted by the beneficiary.' However, other consequences of this acceptance are not clearly laid out. In particular, the Civil Code provides no insight into the fate of the fruits and revenues of the assets, rights or security interests in the trust patrimony. It seems that they do not go to the beneficiary unless otherwise provided for in the terms of the trust.[18] The beneficiary is thereby the recipient only of the assets placed in *fiducie*, as stipulated, upon fulfilment of the terms of the trust. Historically, the common law did not provide any better position for the beneficiary, who was 'completely ignored';[19] only by means of equity did its situation improve.

On the model of stipulations for another in French law,[20] the settlor remains the master of the *fiducie*'s existence for as long as the beneficiary has not accepted the terms of the trust.

Under French law, then, the beneficiary – who indeed remains very discreet in the text of the Civil Code – is no more than a secondary and relatively passive player. The beneficiary is always free to refuse the *fiducie* (not necessarily ending it thereby, however[21]) and more

a possibility would very likely leave the settlor's creditors open to fraud, as the settlor could simply protect a portion of its assets by creating a second patrimony that it itself manages. However, a recent law now recognizes just such a situation: Law 2010–658 of 15 June 2010 on limited liability individual entrepreneurs authorizes entrepreneurs who are physical persons to create a patrimony by appropriation dedicated to their professional activities. Further, the trust recognizes the possibility of the settlor naming itself as trustee, but to the benefit of a third party (see A. M. Honoré, *Droit des trusts et droit des biens, course mimeograph no. 645* (Strasbourg: Faculté internationale pour l'enseignement du droit comparé, 1967), p. 10).

[18] On this topic see Gouthière et al., *La fiducie*, above, note 4, para. 3600.

[19] Witz, *La fiducie*, above, note 11, no. 6. Also, David and Jauffret-Spinosi, *Les grands systèmes*, above, note 12, para. 259.

[20] Which, in particular, is the theoretical basis for life insurance contracts.

[21] Art. 2029(2) C.C.: the terms of the *fiducie* may provide for 'the conditions under which the contract continues' thereafter.

importantly can seek judicial action to name a provisional trustee or to replace the trustee, in certain cases defined by the terms of the trust or by operation of law (see article 2027 C.C.).

Clearly, the beneficiary is not considered an essential cog in the *fiducie* mechanism. While the beneficiary must indeed be named by the settlor, this party has no choice but to remain passive (if it accepts the terms of the trust); apart from refusing the *fiducie* or requesting the replacement of the trustee, no other explicit rights are provided to the beneficiary. Notably, the beneficiary has no means to require that the trustee render accounts unless otherwise explicitly provided for in the *fiducie* contract (article 2022 C.C.).

This legal structure leads to the question of possible recourses by the beneficiary against the trustee, should the trustee misuse its administration powers or act against the interests of the beneficiary. On what bases can the beneficiary pursue action against the trustee? French doctrine has broached the subject in the absence of any general provisions in the Civil Code.[22] In particular, what action can the beneficiary take should the trustee misappropriate trust assets? There is no textual basis for the beneficiary to benefit from a right to follow or a right of preference. If it has accepted the *fiducie,* the beneficiary enjoys only personal rights against the trustee. Some writers afford the beneficiary the possibility of taking conservatory measures if the trustee's administration threatens the beneficiary's interests.[23] The possibility of specific recovery of trust property is *a priori* excluded, except where restitution is sought from the trustee itself, in the case of a security trust where the debt has been paid.

Under French law, the beneficiary effectively enjoys no real rights. The trustee is considered the owner of the trust property and French law does not recognize any dismemberment of ownership in the creation of a *fiducie.*[24] The beneficiary can seek action only to enforce the trustee's accepted duties,[25] in particular, the transfer of ownership of the property upon conclusion of the *fiducie*. The beneficiary cannot seek termination of the

22 Book IV of the Civil Code does, however, stipulate that the beneficiary has rights in the specific case of the security trust: on default of payment of the secured debt, the legislator has given third-party beneficiaries who are the settlor's creditors the right to demand from the trustee 'the handing over of the property, which the creditors then have at their disposition' (arts. 2372–3(2) and 2488–3(2) C.C.).

23 Gouthière et al., *La fiducie*, above, note 4, para. 3750.

24 See Section III below.

25 On this topic, Witz, *La fiducie*, above, note 11, para. 284. See also C. de Lajarte, 'La nature juridique des droits du bénéficiaire d'un contrat de fiducie' (May 2009) RLDC 71.

fiducie contract for breach, because it is not party thereto, nor can it require restitution from a third-party purchaser of an asset improperly disposed of by the trustee, since the beneficiary has no real rights in such property.[26]

The gaps and uncertainties in French law in this regard are in contrast to the breach of trust action that was created in common law specifically to protect the beneficiary. In England, the historical evolution of the trust led to the beneficiary – who initially had no rights (other than a beneficial interest, less than a right) – having personal rights and eventually rights *in personam ad rem acquirendam*.[27] The French *fiducie* also contrasts with the trust with respect to the rule by which a donee of trust property, or a purchaser in bad faith thereof, having become the owner at law, nonetheless becomes itself a trustee and must hold the assets in the beneficiary's interest.[28] The trust assets, in other words, are charged with the equitable rights of the beneficiary, who enjoys a right to follow them.[29]

Further, what happens, in the case of multiple trustees, should one depart? Would the beneficiary suffer any consequences in such a situation? Again, the French Civil Code is silent, leaving it up to the parties to provide for such a case, if they wish, in the terms of the trust. The parties could thereby stipulate that the *fiducie* would continue under the remaining trustees and outline how the possible redistribution of powers among them would take place.

English law, on the contrary, foresees such a possibility and protects the beneficiary by means of joint tenancy: if a trustee departs, the remaining trustees continue validly to administer the trust in the interests of the beneficiary. They thereby jointly take on, in some way, the powers of the departed trustee.

These issues, then, lead us to question the role of the trustee in French law: it seems that the trustee is in a *face-to-face* relationship with the settlor, more so than being an *interface* between the settlor and

26 As the trustee has never transferred ownership of the asset to the beneficiary, the beneficiary has no means to bring an action in revendication on the ownership of an asset. It never belonged to the beneficiary. Could it bring such an action as a future or potential owner? Further, art. 2023 C.C. states: 'In its relationship with third parties, the trustee is deemed to have the widest powers with respect to the trust patrimony, unless it is demonstrated that the third parties had knowledge of the limitation of its powers.'

27 See D. Hayton, 'The Distinctive Characteristics of the Trust in Anglo-Saxon Law', in A. Prüm and C. Witz (eds.), *Trust et fiducie (colloque du 11 décembre 2003)* (Paris: Monchrestien, 2005), esp. p. 11.

28 On this topic, David and Jauffret-Spinosi, *Les grands systèmes*, above, note 12, no. 259.

29 Papandreou-Déterville, *Droit anglais des biens*, above, note 3, p. 547.

beneficiary. The absence of legal provisions to resolve the many obvious questions bears witness to this: the French legislator has left these matters to the *fiducie* contract; in practice, to the will of the settlor.

This brings us to an essential part of the *fiducie* mechanism as envisioned in French law: it is the settlor who seems to play an essential role in the *fiducie* regime. The settlor is the contracting party through which everything begins and, in some ways, everything happens.

B. *The pre-eminence of the settlor*

We have seen that, under French law, the beneficiary's position is relatively secondary and rather unclear. What of the other actor with whom the trustee must interact? The mission of the trustee is generally understood to be the dynamic administration of the assets held in *fiducie*,[30] a rather gratifying view of its duties. However, in studying its actual administration powers, we are forced to move from myth to reality.

The Myth: The trustee can act freely with respect to the trust property, especially as sole owner of these assets[31] and as French law provides no details as to the obligations of the trustee in its 'mission'. There is no theorization of the trustee's duties in French law nor, indeed, any theorization of reinvestment, should the trustee decide to sell assets in the trust patrimony.[32]

The trustee is certainly expected to respect the same general obligations of care and diligence as any asset manager. The only clear limit on the trustee's powers enshrined in the Civil Code is that it must act 'for a specific purpose for the benefit of one or more beneficiaries' (article 2011 C.C.). Article 2018(6) C.C. further states that the terms of the *fiducie* 'determine the mission entrusted to the trustee or trustees and the scope of their powers to administer or to dispose'.[33] Here we can see the material role of the settlor, the trustee's co-contractor.

30 For a nuanced approach to the various techniques for the administration of the property of another through the lens of dynamic administration, see B. Balivet, 'Les techniques de gestion des biens d'autrui' (PhD thesis, University of Lyon 3, 2004).

31 See Section III below.

32 In comparison, English law has adopted a principle of subrogation, as much real as personal: David and Jauffret-Spinosi, *Les grands systèmes*, above, note 12, para. 259.

33 The mission must appear in the terms of the *fiducie* 'on pain of nullity' (*à peine de nullité*) (article 2018 C.C.). It is especially important as it enables an appreciation of the trustee's responsibility in case of difficulty.

The Reality: The settlor certainly has some obligations to the trustee, but these are few and far between: to transfer the ownership and deliver the assets to the trustee;[34] if necessary, to follow the approval procedure laid out in French corporate law where the assets placed in *fiducie* are shares; and, if the contract is onerous, to pay the trustee.

As for the trustee, it does what the settlor has empowered it to do – 'that which is required for the beneficiary's interest'[35] – which can mean, in some cases, no more that conserving the assets placed in *fiducie* (in the case of a security trust for its own benefit as trustee-creditor, for example).

As such, from the mythic idea of dynamic administration, we may come to a simple conservation of assets, over which the trustee has no real powers. The administration of the *fiducie* tends to be rather similar to a simple deposit, with only the qualification (albeit a fundamental one) that the trustee is supposed to be the owner of the relevant assets.

Further, under article 2018–1 C.C., the *fiducie* contract may provide that the settlor retains the right to the use and enjoyment of the assets placed in *fiducie,* which greatly limits the trustee's administration.

The French law of *fiducie*, guided by a clear desire for flexibility, has created the possibility of *fiducies* that are arrangements composed of extremely abstract relationships. More concretely, the trustee, especially in the case of a security trust, could thereby have no other mission than to conserve an asset, or abstractly to administer property that is not in its possession. This is a coherent model in that it allows the settlor to retain the right to use the trust property,[36] but it makes it difficult to maintain the perceived coherence of the mechanism as a whole.

In the most extreme of cases, could the trustee be stripped of all powers? It seems possible, as the French Civil Code places no limits on the contours of the mission and powers of the trustee. Some authors however believe that the trustee, as owner, must at minimum retain the power to take conservatory measures in relation to the assets.[37]

Could a requirement be imposed on the trustee that prior approval, by the settlor or the beneficiary, was required for certain acts? It seems

[34] The *fiducie* contract may however provide for the trustee to retain possession of the fiduciary assets (art. 2018–1 C.C., respecting disposition agreements).

[35] On this topic, O. Fille-Lambie and L-J. Laisney, 'La fiducie: nouvelle garantie des crédits syndiqués?' (May 2010) *Droit et patrimoine* 76.

[36] Especially in the case of a security trust.

[37] Gouthière et al., *La fiducie*, above, note 4, para. 3280.

possible, as the law is again silent in this respect, and in the light of the autonomy of the parties with respect to the terms of the *fiducie*. Fraud could be the only limit to such a reduction of the trustee's powers, especially in the case of a management trust.

The preponderant role of the settlor in the French *fiducie* is thus clear: the settlor's wishes are enshrined in the terms of the *fiducie*, and the settlor remains to a considerable degree the master of the situation, be it in a management trust or a security trust.

This is a legitimate possibility in the case of the management trust, where the idea is to permit a person to entrust the administration of all or some of their property to a third party, with a specific goal in mind to which the administrator must adhere. Similarly, in the case of a security trust, the settlor could understandably seek to specify (in agreement with the creditor as beneficiary) the acts the trustee may carry out in order to maximize the value of the security. However, even if the desired goal is understandable and legitimate, it remains difficult to reconcile it with the characterization of the trustee as owner in French law.[38]

Further, the settlor can emphasize its pre-eminence in the *fiducie* relationship, reinforcing its control over the trust patrimony by naming a third party to 'ensure the preservation of its interests in executing the contract and who may dispose of the powers conferred upon the settlor by law' (article 2017 C.C.). This third-party figure finds its inspiration in the 'protector' role sometimes found in foreign trust law, even though the prerogatives are not the same. In the French *fiducie*, this third party can control the trustee's administration, solicit its replacement (article 2027 C.C.) and even exercise all the powers of the settlor – essentially becoming the settlor's 'eyes and ears'.

It becomes clear from the French legislation that the trustee's actions are thereby controlled. Despite this – and this may seem paradoxical – the liability regime around the trustee remains no more than a sketch in the French Civil Code.

C. *The trustee's liability: a paradoxical sketch*

The question of the trustee's liability to the settlor and the beneficiary is linked to the underlying and important matter of protecting the settlor and the beneficiary of the *fiducie*.

[38] See Section III below.

This same issue also arises in the debate around the place, be it marginal or essential, of the trustee in the *fiducie*, since the greater the role of the trustee, and the broader its obligations, the greater the legislative attention that should rightly be paid to its liability.

That being said, the French Civil Code gives the trustee's liability short shrift. A single – fundamental yet succinct – article is devoted to this liability: 'the trustee is personally liable for faults that it commits during the performance of its mission' (article 2026 C.C.).

The trustee can be held both civilly and criminally liable (in particular on the basis of breach of confidence). However, many aspects of the trustee's civil liability are not addressed in the Civil Code.

1. Nature of the trustee's liability

There is no doubt that the trustee is liable contractually to the settlor should it not respect the terms of the *fiducie* contract.

There is also no doubt that the trustee can be liable extra-contractually for wrongs committed against a third party to the *fiducie* contract.

But what of the trustee's liability to the beneficiary? This is a delicate question as there is an ongoing doctrinal debate as to the nature of the rights that the beneficiary enjoys under French legislation.

As we have seen, in principle the beneficiary has only personal rights against the trustee; but this unsatisfactory position of insufficient protection has pushed some French doctrinal writers to attempt to provide more effective rights to the beneficiary. Some authors consider that the beneficiary should enjoy personal rights on the trust property comparable in effectiveness to real rights.[39] Personal rights would thereby slide into the category of real rights.[40] A recent work defends such an idea, whereby the *fiducie* would include a stipulation for another, with concomitant rights of action, to the benefit of the beneficiary.[41]

The Civil Code remains silent on these issues, however.

[39] See especially F. Barrière, *La réception du trust au travers de la fiducie*, preface by M. Grimaldi (Paris: Litec, 2004), nos. 626ff, who retains the concept of *jus ad rem*.

[40] See J. de Guillenschmidt, 'La France sans la fiducie?' (1991) RJC 49, who evokes 'a right with shades of the real'.

[41] Gouthière et al., *La fiducie*, above, note 4, no. 751: in the case of a stipulation for third-party action to the benefit of the beneficiary, if the beneficiary has accepted the *fiducie* it may bring a direct action against the trustee to seek performance of the contract and seek reparation for any damages resulting from the nonperformance or improper performance of the terms of the trust. If the beneficiary has not accepted the *fiducie*, the beneficiary retains the possibility of an action in extracontractual liability against the trustee.

2. Conditions on the trustee's liability

Article 2026 C.C. restricts the trustee's liability to the existence of a fault. This is an abstract concept that is not necessarily welcome in the world of contractual liability toward the settlor, as debate is ongoing in French doctrine over whether there is even a notion of 'contractual fault' in contract law.[42]

There are therefore no clearly defined *fiduciary obligations* in French law.[43] The Civil Code does indeed require that the trustee provide accounts to the settlor (and even to the beneficiary or to third parties under article 2017 C.C.), but otherwise its obligations remain vague: the trustee has to act according to the 'interests entrusted thereto' (failure of which could lead to replacement: article 2027 C.C.), to the extent that a 'mission' and 'powers' have been entrusted (see articles 2018(6) and 2023 C.C.).

The general idea seems to be that the trustee is trustworthy and must therefore respect its mission. Failure to do so is undoubtedly a 'fault' under article 2026 C.C.

Many questions remain, however:

- Does the trustee have an obligation of means or an obligation of ends in defending the 'interests entrusted thereto'? One can hope that the terms of the trust specifying its mission also lay out the scope of the obligations to the settlor.
- Can the trustee's liability be limited, for example only to cases of fraud or gross negligence? There is nothing to suggest that such a limitation of liability is impossible, especially in a juridical relationship between professional settlors and trustees. However, from the perspective of the beneficiary, such a clause could be without effect if we allow that the trustee is liable extracontractually to the beneficiary.[44] In effect, it is impossible effectively to limit the trustee's delictual liability in French law.

[42] See especially D. Tallon, 'Pourquoi parler de faute contractuelle?', in *Ecrits en hommage à Gérard Cornu* (PUF, 1995), p. 429; P. Rémy, 'La "responsabilité contractuelle": histoire d'un faux concept' (1997) RTDC 323ff.

[43] In comparison, the obligations of the trustee are well developed in Anglo-American law. For example, the Australian trust recognizes a duty of care on the part of the trustee which is not subject to exoneration by contract. The trustee's duties include a duty to avoid conflicts between the obligations arising from the trust and the trustee's personal interests, a duty to inform the beneficiary of all matters relating to its interests, a duty to transfer ownership to a capable beneficiary and a duty to be loyal to the beneficiary: D. Ong, *Trusts in Australia*, 3rd edn (Sydney: Federation Press, 2007), pp. 219ff.

[44] As discussed above.

Not all foreign *fiducie* or trust laws provide for such a transfer of ownership of the trust property. Russian law, for example, created in its new Civil Code the regime of 'trust management of property', inspired by the Anglo-American trust, except that it is a nominate contract and not an institution of property law. The Russian Civil Code, although it draws on the idea of a transfer of property in relation to trust management,[49] clearly states that 'the transfer of property to trust management shall not entail the transfer of the right of ownership thereto to the trustee manager' who 'shall be obliged . . . to effectuate the management of this property in the interests of the founder of the management or person specified therein (beneficiary)'.[50]

Similarly, Chinese law does not transfer ownership of the property to the trustee. Article 2 of the Chinese trust law states that the settlor 'entrusts its property rights to the trustee', which must be distinguished from a transfer of ownership.[51]

Further, some legal systems provide for a transfer of ownership to the trustee as in French law, but without the creation of a trust patrimony separate from the personal patrimony of the trustee. This is the case in Swiss law, which is based on the Roman *fiducia*.[52]

In 2007 France made what was, in the light of its legal tradition, a radical choice: not only did it accept that the *fiducie* could entail a double transfer of ownership, from the settlor to the trustee and then from the trustee to the beneficiary; it also adopted the theory of patrimony by appropriation.[53]

This adoption, at a theoretical level, logically entails that the trustee will have access to a remarkable range of prerogatives, namely those that are held by an owner in a civil law system. As such, the trustee indeed seems

[49] 'Under a contract of trust management of property one party (founder of management) shall transfer to the other party (trustee manager) property in trust management . . .': *Civil Code of the Russian Federation*, W. E. Butler, trans. & ed. (London: Wildy, Simmonds & Hill, 2010), art. 1012. On this contract, see David and Jauffret-Spinosi, *Les grands systèmes*, above, note 12, para. 210.

[50] Butler, ibid.

[51] R. Lee, 'Convergence and Divergence in the Worlds of the Trust: Duties and Liabilities of Trustees under the Chinese Trust', Chapter 17 in the present volume.

[52] The Roman *fiducia* also heavily influenced the German trust, called *Treuhand* (or *fiduziarisches Rechtsgeschäft*), whose legal framework developed through case law based on art. 903 *Bürgerliches Gesetzbuch* (BGB) (according to the *Kommentar* of the BGB).

[53] In reality, characterizing the trust patrimony as a 'patrimony by appropriation' is problematic. The settlor of a *fiducie* does not create a second patrimony alongside its personal patrimony in which some of its assets are appropriated; it empowers a third party (the trustee) to manage some of its assets, which then creates a patrimony segregated from its own. A few doctrinal writers have picked up on this subtle distinction.

to play the role of mainspring in the French *fiducie*, as an indispensable 'ownership transferor' between the settlor and the beneficiary.

In reality, however, there are many arguments that demonstrate that the trustee is no more than a diminished owner, as the classical prerogatives of an owner can be deeply curtailed, if not ignored completely.

The French *fiducie* leaves gaping holes in the classical attributes of ownership (A below). Given its precarious position as owner, the trustee essentially has the sword of Damocles hanging over its head (B below). Further, the French legislator sought to strike the ultimate blow to the trustee's ownership rights by imagining the possibility of dividing ownership between the trustee and the beneficiary, as occurs in the common law trust (C below).

A. *Gaping holes in the attributes of trustee as owner*

As we have seen, the *fiducie* is often presented as the implementation of a double transfer of ownership:[54] first, from the settlor's patrimony to the trust patrimony administered by the trustee and, second, upon termination of the *fiducie*, to the beneficiary's patrimony (be it a third party or the trustee itself), unless the assets return to the settlor's patrimony.

This transfer of ownership is what makes the French *fiducie* so important, the objectives being, on the one hand, to prevent third parties from having access to the trust property (in a security trust) and, on the other hand, to encourage a dynamic administration of the property by the trustee (in a management trust).

That being said, the substance of the French law of ownership is found in article 544 C.C. A unanimously accepted definition of ownership is difficult to find in French doctrine, but the majority of authors agree that ownership comprises all of the benefits of the owned property, that it is the fullest real right that one may have over a thing, and that it is characterized by the exclusivity conferred upon its holder, and by its

[54] See F. Zenati-Castaing and T. Revet, *Les biens*, 3rd edn (Paris: PUF, 2008), paras. 255, 261 and 287; P. Malaurie and L. Aynès, *Les biens*, 3rd edn (Paris: Defrénois, 2007), para. 757; P. Puig, 'La fiducie et les contrats nommés' (June 2008), *Droit et patrimoine* 72; more nuanced, R. Libchaber, 'Les aspects civils de la fiducie dans la loi du 19 février 2007' (2007) *Defrénois* 38631, paras. 2 and 19ff; M. Grimaldi, 'La fiducie: réflexions sur l'institution et sur l'avant-projet de la loi qui la consacre' (1997) *Defrénois* 897, esp. para. 13 ('we must be careful in treating the *fiducie* as a contract of transference of ownership, as no actual wealth is transferred in a *fiducie*').

perpetuity.[55] As the sole master of the property, an owner can use the property, benefit from its fruits and, above all, dispose of it.

What, then, is going on in the *fiducie*?

The trustee may be very limited in the exercise of its prerogatives over property (*usus, fructus, abusus*). While the provisions of the French Civil Code relating to *fiducies* do not explicitly suppress any of the traditional prerogatives of ownership, these provisions contain the seeds of many substantial limitations on the attributes of ownership. The Civil Code views the trustee's prerogatives restrictively. Whatever prerogatives of ownership over a thing the trustee enjoys exist only insofar as they are provided for by the settlor.

The trustee's position is in spirit contrary to the ordinary law of ownership. Instead of being an owner with sole mastery over property, the trustee is foremost a manager (management trust) or a conservator (security trust), with an imperative to respect the 'specific purpose' of the operation (article 2011 C.C.) and the powers given to it by the settlor.

Granted, the trustee is not the only type of owner to have its prerogatives limited, at least for a period of time. For example, there is a necessary limitation of ownership prerogatives in the case of reservation of title.[56] It is worth noting a major difference between these two situations of instrumentalized ownership: in the first case (title reservation) the seller accepts that it is in its own interest that its prerogatives be limited for a time, whereas in the case of a *fiducie* these limitations are in the interests of a third party.[57] This is what has led commentators to describe the trustee as an owner on behalf of another.[58]

[55] See notably J.-L. Bergel, M. Bruschi and S. Cimamonti, *Traité de droit civil. Les biens* (Paris, LGDJ, 2000), paras. 79ff; Malaurie and Aynès, *Les biens*, above, note 54, paras. 431ff; F. Terré and P. Simler, *Droit civil. Les biens*, 7th edn (Paris, Dalloz, 2006), paras. 74ff; G. Cornu, *Droit civil. Les biens*, 13th edn (Paris: Montchrestien, 2007), paras. 26ff; compare with F. Zenati, 'Pour une rénovation de la théorie de la propriété' (1993) RTDC 305.

[56] Art. 2367(1) C.C.: 'Ownership of a thing may be retained as security through a clause of retention of title which suspends the translatory [transfer of ownership] effect of a contract until payment in full of the obligation which constitutes the counterperformance.'

[57] With the exception of the security trust where the beneficiary is the trustee, in which case the *fiducie* is settled in the interests of the trustee. As such, we can then go on to question the unity of the French *fiducie*, as this case of security trust is not fundamentally distinguishable from other mechanisms of ownership for security purposes (*sûretés-propriété*) that French law recognizes without difficulty.

[58] V. L. Kaczmarek, 'Propriété fiduciaire et droits des intervenants à l'opération' (2009) *Recueil Dalloz* 1845, esp. para. 11; also, F. Danos, *Propriété, possession et opposabilité*,

Can we still speak of ownership, however, if the trustee loses the classical prerogatives of ownership, definitively and in the interest of another person?

B. *The sword of Damocles hanging over the trustee as owner*

Considering the fundamental characteristics of ownership as generally understood by doctrine – exclusivity and perpetuity[59] – what are we to make of 'fiduciary ownership'?

First, there is no perpetuity to trust ownership: the *fiducie* is by its nature temporary (limited to ninety-nine years from the date the contract is signed: article 2018(2) C.C.), and trust ownership has no reason to last beyond the term of the trust.

Further, the trustee may find its ownership withdrawn against its will in several situations: article 2027 C.C. provides for the replacement of the trustee, either through the contract, whose terms can freely specify conditions for such replacement, or (more likely) for legal reasons (failure in its obligations, jeopardizing the entrusted interests, or through the institution of procedures for reorganization or receivership). Also, article 2028 C.C. permits the settlor to revoke the status of trustee, who thus loses ownership of the trust property.

Exclusivity is equally difficult to reconcile with trustee ownership. Exclusivity implies a 'privative relationship' and confers on the owner the 'right to exclude', that is, to deny power over the property to anyone else.[60] The general idea underlying the exclusive character of ownership is therefore that the sole owner of property has power over the owned thing and its benefits, since he is its sole master.[61]

preface by L. Aynès (Paris: Economica, 2007), para. 43, which discusses '"ownership" in service of another' (*'"propriété" au service d'autrui'*).

59 The absolute nature of ownership rights, affirmed in art. 544 C.C., is subject to so many exceptions in positive law that it is often no longer considered a distinctive characteristic of ownership. On this topic, see Cornu, *Droit civil*, above, note 55, para. 29; C. Larroumet, *Droit civil*, vol. 2, *Les biens: droits réels principaux*, 5th edn (Paris: Economica, 2006), paras. 211ff; Bergel, Bruschi and Cimamonti, *Traité de droit civil*, above, note 55, paras. 93ff; Grimaldi, 'La fiducie', above, note 54, paras. 16ff; more nuanced, Terré and Simler, *Droit civil*, above, note 55, paras. 140ff; *contra* Malaurie and Aynès, *Les biens*, above, note 54, nos. 431 and 455. In any case, it seems difficult to state that the trustee has absolute ownership rights on the trust property given the many limits on its authority.

60 Zenati-Castaing and Revet, *Les biens*, above, note 54, pp. 315ff.

61 On this topic, J.-L. Bergel, *La propriété* (Dalloz (Connaissance du droit collection), 1994), p. 31; Terré and Simler, *Droit civil*, above, note 55, para. 143.

This being the case, 'fiduciary ownership' seems not at all to confer on the trustee such mastery over the trust patrimony. The trustee, in fact, may be excluded from such a relationship to the property by the decision of the settlor or the third-party beneficiary.

As we have already seen, several provisions allow an extraordinary supervisory authority on the part of the settlor over the administration of the trust property: the trustee must above all remain true to the 'mission'[62] entrusted to it by the settlor. Further, the trustee must render accounts to the settlor (article 2022 C.C.) and remains liable for any wrongs it commits in carrying out its mission (article 2026 C.C.). In addition, article 2017 C.C. highlights the organization of this supervision of 'trust ownership', as it provides that the settlor may, at any time, 'designate a third-party charged with ensuring the preservation of [the settlor's] interests in connection with the performance of the contract'. The trustee thereby acts under the eye of a censor who represents the settlor.

Trust ownership is therefore in no way an unfettered ownership. Thus it has been characterized as 'a new type of ownership, a burdened ownership'.[63]

True, the idea of burdened ownership is not new in French law and does not negate its characterization as ownership; however, 'fiduciary ownership' is particular in that it places major burdens on the trustee, not in its own interest, but in the interest of another.

What, then, is this 'ownership' that can be lost, be it by replacement or revocation, upon request by a third party? Above all, the trust is an operation aimed at a defined goal, in which the (supposed) principal actor is in fact subservient to the decisions and choices of the other parties to the operation. Having said this, if we hold onto the classical

[62] Evocative of the *fiducie* as foremost a notion of representation or of delegation of authorities instead of a notion of ownership, this term is used on multiple occasions in the French Civil Code, at arts. 2018(6), 2022 and 2026. It also occurs in Legislative decision 2009–001 ('Trustee activities' (*L'activité de fiduciaire*)) on the reform of the national regulations on the legal profession.

[63] See P. Marini, Rapport au Sénat no. 442 of 27 May 2009, art. 6 series B (nouveau) available on www.senat.fr. French doctrine is ever imaginative in describing this new form of ownership, using multiple adjectives to attempt to describe its uniqueness, with the trustee being a 'bound owner' (*propriétaire obligé*) and the fiduciary ownership being 'sketchy' (*modelée*), 'imperfect' (*imparfaite*), 'diminished' (*amoindrie*) or even 'ephemeral' (*éphémère*).

idea of ownership – a 'pillar' of the civil law[64] – it becomes difficult to accept the notion of a subservient owner.[65]

As some authors have discussed, this leads us to question even whether the trustee can properly be called an owner.[66]

Moreover, recognition of the trustee as a genuine owner leads to unresolved practical consequences. For example, should commercial assets be placed in the trust patrimony, what would be the right way to publish the ownership of such assets in the commercial and corporate registry? Is the trustee registered as 'owner', even if it is unlikely that the trustee will be managing the assets?[67] Registration of the trustee as the owner of commercial assets held in a *fiducie* would not in any way reflect the economic reality of the situation.

Another example: what would happen should the trustee alienate property from the trust patrimony without having the requisite authority? The sanction associated with the sale of another's goods cannot apply,[68] because the trustee is the 'owner' of the asset. What action could then be brought against the trustee by the settlor or even the beneficiary? An action for revendication seems to be excluded, so only a personal action against the trustee could be brought, which would be meagre consolation.

Finally, we see clearly how these difficulties essentially arise from the fact that the *fiducie* is also and above all a *contract* – a nominate contract that is officially based on a transfer of ownership, but one that is marked

[64] See J. Carbonnier, *Flexible droit: pour une sociologie du droit sans rigueur*, 10th edn (Paris: LGDJ, 2001), p. 255.

[65] On the philosophical connections between ownership and liberty, see notably M. Xifaras, *La propriété: étude de philosophie du droit* (Paris: PUF, 2004), pp. 90 and 280ff; also, A-M. Patault, 'V° Propriété', in D. Alland and S. Rials (eds.), *Dictionnaire de la culture juridique* (Paris: PUF Lamy, 2003).

[66] R. Libchaber, 'Une fiducie française, inutile et incertaine', in *Mélanges en l'honneur de Philippe Malaurie: Liber amicorum* (Paris: Defrénois, 2005), p. 303, esp. paras. 13ff; Libchaber, 'Les aspects civils de la fiducie', above, note 54, esp. para. 25; see also, Danos, *Propriété, possession et opposabilité*, above, note 58, para. 43; P. Crocq, *Propriété et garantie* (Paris: LGDJ, 1995), para. 242. To the contrary, M. Bouteille, 'La propriété fiduciaire, une modalité externe de la propriété' (September 2010) RLDC 64, where the author defends the idea of the trustee's rights as an 'external modality of ownership' that confirms the existence of the trustee's ownership, thereby ensuring compatibility with the classical theory of ownership in civil law.

[67] In particular, a trustee who was a lawyer could not manage the corporate assets, given the professional restrictions attached to his profession. Further, art. 2018–1 C.C. allows for the trust contract to provide that the settlor will maintain the use and enjoyment of the assets.

[68] Art. 1599 C.C. provides for the nullity of the sale in this case.

by a heavy obligational burden. In the *fiducie*, then, the contract is not simply the means by which ownership is transferred – which seems to be its function in general – but is the core of the mechanism. Fiduciary ownership is nothing more than an instrument to achieve a clearly defined economic end.[69]

Ownership in this way becomes a tool of relationships that are primarily obligational, at the risk of losing its essential nature, with the trustee being no more than a 'diminished' owner at best.

The French legislator even sought to strengthen this development by proposing to divide fiduciary ownership between the trustee and the beneficiary, as in the Anglo-American trust.

C. *The aborted attempt at divided ownership in the* fiducie

In October 2009, the French legislature addressed the uncertainties around the idea of fiduciary ownership with an attempt to cast a new light on it. The French Parliament passed into law a second paragraph to article 2011 C.C.[70] This new provision had a very specific meaning, which was spelled out in the *travaux préparatoires* of the law relating to access to credit for small and medium enterprises.[71]

Through this new provision, the French legislator sought to encourage the introduction of Islamic finance in the financial markets of Paris,[72] as Islamic finance has specific requirements under Islamic law, deriving from the requirements of *sharīʿa*.[73] The French legislator believed the

[69] B. Mallet-Bricout, 'Fiducie et propriété', in *Liber Amicorum Christian Larroumet* (Paris: Economica, 2010), pp. 297–327.

[70] Art. 2011(2) C.C.: 'The trustee has fiduciary ownership of the assets in the trust patrimony, for the benefit of one or more beneficiaries as stipulated in the terms of the trust.'

[71] Law 2009–1255 of 19 October 2009 with respect to encouraging access to credit for small and medium enterprises. See specifically Marini, Rapport, above, note 63.

[72] The development of Islamic finance in France was advocated by Paris Europlace in its 2009 action plan (see the report by E. Jouini and O. Pastre, 'Enjeux et opportunités du développement de la finance islamique pour la place de Paris' (2009), available on the Paris Europlace website at www.paris-europlace.net/links/doc063972_fr.htm). See also J. Arthuis, 'La finance islamique en France: quelles perspectives?', Rapport fait au nom de la commission de finances 329 (2007–2008). French doctrine has also recently shown interest in this topic: G. Brayer, *La finance islamique: l'autre finance* (Société de législation comparée, 2009); F.-X. Lucas, 'La fiducie au pays de l'Or noir' (2009) *Bulletin Joly Sociétés* 825.

[73] For details on these principles, see J. Charlin, 'Fiducie, sukuk et autres murabaha ou ijara' (2009) JCP-E 1946.

fiducie to be the 'appropriate instrument' (*l'instrument idoine)*[74] to meet the requirements of one of the financial instruments of Islamic finance, the *sukuk*.

As adapted to this instrument, the *fiducie* would have been based on the principle that the beneficiary thereof – the investor in the *sukuk* – has a direct right in the assets of the fiduciary patrimony, and not simply a personal right against the trustee.[75] Senator Philippe Marini's report concluded in this sense that fiduciary ownership reflected a 'new concept of ownership' (*nouveau concept de propriété*), one which is divided between the trustee and the beneficiary: 'In summary, the trustee would benefit from the juridical ownership of the assets whereas the beneficiary would benefit from the economic ownership thereof.'

Here we can clearly see the influence of Anglo-American law, which has long accepted a distinction between legal ownership and beneficial interests.[76] This explains the mechanism of the common law trust, which certainly inspired the French *fiducie*. Aligning French law with the legal foundations of Anglo-American property law is hard to imagine, however: the juridical dissociation of the titulary of a right from the benefit of that right does not exist in French law.[77] This notion is in direct contradiction of the fundamental civilian principle of unity of ownership which appears in article 544 C.C.

Under the proposed article 2011(2) C.C., the trustee would be no more than the 'juridical owner' of the fiduciary assets. Such a shake-up of the civilian theory of ownership is not trivial. It is one thing to permit evolutions in the functions of property law, be it through ownership for

[74] Marini, Rapport, above, note 63.

[75] The argument is developed clearly in Marini, Rapport, above, note 63.

[76] The concept of ownership is not a unitary concept in Anglo-American law. In the case of the trust, the trustee is vested with legal ownership whereas the beneficial interests fall to the beneficiary. This dissociation of ownership is rooted in the distinction in English law between common law and equity. For a comparison of the Anglo-Saxon and civilian conceptions of ownership, see P. Matthews, 'The Compatibility of the Trust with the Civil Law Notion of Property', Chapter 13 in the present volume.

[77] This has, however, been the object of some doctrinal study, though the authors do not agree on the legal foundations of the possibility of such a dissociation: see in particular C. Goyet, *Le louage et la propriété à l'épreuve du crédit-bail et du bail superficiaire* (Paris: LGDJ, 1983); G. Blanluet, *Essai sur la notion de propriété économique en droit privé français: recherches au confluent du droit fiscal et du droit civil* (Paris: LGDJ, 1999); S. Ravenne, 'Les propriétés imparfaites: contribution à l'étude de la structure du droit de propriété' (PhD thesis, University of Paris-Dauphine, 2007); also, Grimaldi, 'La fiducie', above, note 54, no. 18; A. Bénabent, 'La fiducie (analyse d'un projet de loi lacunaire)' (1993) JCP-N 275.

a purpose, collective ownership or ownership for security purposes; it is another to contemplate the explosion of the concept of ownership itself, such that it would include both the classical ownership (*plena in re potestas*) of article 544, and this new form of divided fiduciary ownership.

Some French doctrinal writers questioned this legislative text[78] and the Constitutional Council struck down the provision (for reasons outside the present discussion[79]), effectively closing the debate for the time being. Since then, the French legislator seems to have come to the conclusion that there are legal structures other than the *fiducie* that could be conducive to introducing Islamic finance in France.

As such, the trustee remains the sole owner of the trust property, without any division of ownership, which at the very least preserves the unity of ownership in French civil law.

IV Conclusion

The contractual relationship clearly predominates over the patrimonial relationship when a *fiducie* is created. The contractual terms can hollow out the fiduciary function, either from the point of view of the administration of the assets, or from the point of view of the ownership thereof.

The trustee thus seems not so much to be the mainspring of the *fiducie*, but only a simple multi-functional cog. The legal characteristics of the French *fiducie* remain unclear and overly elastic, and this, along with the gaps in the *fiducie* regime, leads to unfortunate difficulties that the judiciary will be left to remedy.

78 L. Aynès and P. Crocq, 'La fiducie préservée des audaces du législateur' (2009) *Recueil Dalloz* 2559; Mallet-Bricout, 'Fiducie et propriété', above, note 69, pp. 319ff.

79 Decision of the Conseil constitutionnel 2009-589 DC of 14 October 2009. The Conseil constitutionnel considered the new article 2011(2) C.C. to have no relationship to the purpose of the law relating to access to credit for small and medium enterprises, in which it was included.

8

British colonial law and the establishment of family *waqfs* by Arabs in the Straits Settlements, 1860–1941

NURFADZILAH YAHAYA

I Introduction

In 2009, members of the Arab Alsagoff family in Singapore challenged the decision of the Islamic Religious Council of Singapore, also known as the Majlis Ugama Islam Singapore (MUIS), to appoint one of their family members who would identify the beneficiaries of the religious family trust known as a *waqf*.[1] In order to ascertain the testator's original

Versions of this chapter were presented at the European Social Science History Conference in Ghent in April 2010, and at the American Society for Legal History in Philadelphia in November 2010. I am grateful to Stuart Banner, Rohit De, Beshara Doumani, Michael Gilsenan, Michael Laffan, Hannah Müller, Intisar Rabb, Mitra Sharafi and Muhammad Qasim Zaman for their feedback. I would especially like to thank conference participants at The Worlds of the Trust conference at McGill University in September 2010 for all their comments, especially Tina Piper.

[1] A *waqf* is the act of establishing a charitable trust and, hence, the trust itself according to Islamic law. The genesis of the institution known as *waqf* could be traced back to the time of the Prophet Muhammad who instructed a caliph to alienate his property so that the income could be distributed for charity. R. Peters et al., 'Wakf (a.)', in P. Bearman et al., *Encyclopaedia of Islam*, 2nd edn (Brill, 2010), available at www.brillonline.nl/subscriber/entry?entry=islam_COM-1333>. For more on the early origins of the *waqf*, see M. Gill, 'The Earliest Waqf Foundations' (1998) 57 *Journal of Near Eastern Studies* 125.

The following abbreviations are used in the notes to this chapter:

CO = Colonial Office
1 KY = Kyshe's Reports (Civil Cases)
2 KY = Kyshe's Reports (Ecclesiastical Cases)
MC = Magistrate's Court (Straits Settlements)
MLJ = Malayan Law Journal
SGHC = Singapore High Court
SLR = Singapore Law Review
SSLR = Straits Settlements Law Report

wishes in establishing the trust, the court pored over the text of the will of Raja Siti binte Kraying Chanda Pulih dated 29 November 1883. Subsequently, on 17 December 2009, Judge Andrew Ang ruled that the Islamic Religious Council of Singapore would retain management of the religious endowment, which allowed them to appoint any member of the Alsagoff family as the person to identify the trust beneficiaries.[2] This case was one of the latest links in several chains of lawsuits that had been filed periodically by Arab clans in Singapore since the late nineteenth century, when Singapore was under colonial rule as part of the Straits Settlements along with Penang and Malacca.[3] Legal cases adjudicated by colonial courts set binding precedents for future cases involving the same religious trusts. Not only that, Islamic law concerning the *waqf*s as conceived by the British legal administration also carried over into the postcolonial nation-state almost completely.

In contrast to the constrained and defined style of the law report of the 2009 case, colonial reports on cases involving the *waqf* were often rife with uncertainty, and reflected a spectrum of legal opinions regarding the compatibility of Islamic law with English law in the colony. This chapter demonstrates how colonial legal practitioners faced a daunting task in administering family *waqf*s as they were forced to debate the meanings of family, descent and charity, while grappling with translation complications in documents written in three languages – English, Malay and Arabic.[4] Although the law of England was taken to be the governing law in the colony, religious laws could be applied within the realm of family law, namely in matters of inheritance, marriage, divorce and guardianship. Since legal practitioners generally claimed that the legal system of the Straits Settlements was unlike other British colonies, each case brought before the courts became especially significant, since each legal ruling contributed to an authoritative corpus of law reports that formed the basis for future rulings on similar cases.

[2] *Syed Abbas bin Mohamed Alsagoff and Another* v. *Islamic Religious Council of Singapore (Majlis Ugama Islam Singapura)* [2009] SGHC 281.

[3] There were at least four lawsuits involving the Alsagoff family *waqf* from 1918 to 2009. They were filed in 1918, 1956, 1958 and 2009.

[4] It was highly likely that colonial legal authorities were aware of the huge significance of the institution in the lives of Muslims across the British Empire. In 1895, Lord Stanley of Alderley pointed out in his weighty question to the House of Lords that the *waqf* was 'one of their most cherished institutions, upon which depends the prosperity of their individual families which have rendered important services to the State in times of danger'. House of Lords question on Muslim law relating to endowments, IOR/L/PJ/6/400, File 1104, 5 July 1895.

II Charitable endowments in the British Empire

Legal scholar F. W. Maitland famously referred to the trust as the 'quintessential English institution'.[5] Within the British Empire, several entities which shared sufficient similar traits with the English trust came to be referred to as such.[6] These included Chinese trusts, Hindu trusts and Muslim trusts also known as *waqfs*. The *waqf* was a common device utilized by Muslims to organize and maintain wealth.[7] Historians such as Gregory Kozlowski imply that English law created a distinction between public and private endowments, and thus affected Muslim subjects minimally in British India. Conversely, this chapter will demonstrate that English law directly impinged upon private family endowments by blurring the line between private and public arenas in the Straits Settlements.[8] Recently, two works on religious endowments have emerged that support the view that English law in the colonies intruded upon the management of local endowments, both public and private. The first is Stephanie Po-Yin Chung's recent article that compares the Chinese law of trusts (*tong*) with the English law of trusts in Hong Kong from the 1860s to the 1980s.[9] Chung contrasts Chinese business conduct that values joint ownership based on kinship and communal bonds with Western conceptions of business based on individual ownership. The second is Ritu Birla's book, *Stages of Capital: Law, Culture, and Market Governance in Late Colonial India*, which traces colonial impositions of standardized rational markets through the formulation and implementation of law on the Hindu trust. She demonstrates how British legal authorities changed the notion of charitable giving within Hindu

[5] F. W. Maitland, *Equity: A Course of Lectures* (Cambridge University Press, 2003), p. 23.

[6] Muslim *waqfs* throughout the British Empire have been examined separately in several cases, although *waqfs* in Mauritius, Malaya and the Aden Protectorate have yet to be examined in detail. For more on *waqfs* in India, the Middle East and East Africa, see G. C. Kozlowski, *Muslim Endowments and Society in British India* (Cambridge University Press, 1985); Y. Reiter, 'Family Waqf Entitlements in British Palestine (1917–1948)' (1995) 2:2 *Islamic Law and Society* 174; J. N. D. Anderson, 'Waqfs in East Africa' (Autumn 1959) 3:3 *Journal of African Law* 152; N. Oberauer, 'Fantastic Charities: The Transformation of Waqf Practice in Colonial Zanzibar' (2008) 15:3 *Islamic Law and Society* 315.

[7] Timur Kuran even labels the *waqf* 'a defining feature of Islamic civilization': T. Kuran, 'The Provision of Public Goods Under Islamic Law: Origins, Impact and Limitations of the Waqf System' (2001) 35 *Law and Society Review* 841, 848.

[8] Kozlowski, *Muslim Endowments and Society in British India*, above, note 6, p. 194.

[9] S. Po-Yin Chung, 'Chinese *Tong* as British Trust: Institutional Collisions and Legal Disputes in Urban Hong Kong, 1860s–1980s' (November 2010) 44:6 *Modern Asian Studies* 1409.

communities despite an official policy of non-intervention in the cultural conventions and practices of Indian subjects. In India, the English legal distinction between public charitable trusts and private trusts (which includes family trusts) mistranslated customary social welfare practices that were traditionally directed at both families and broader communities. Such family trusts clearly defied the public/private distinction.[10] Both Chung and Birla highlight that Hindu and Chinese customs clashed with British colonial administrations on a legislative and core institutional level. Like the Muslim *waqf*, the Chinese *tong* and the Hindu trust were simply not compatible with the notion of English trusts no matter how much British administrators tried to equate them linguistically and in practice. By imposing British legal conceptions of Chinese and Indian traditions, British authorities significantly altered local cultural and religious practices by intruding upon the sphere of the family trust.

III Background of British knowledge on the *waqf*

In order to administer local endowments in the colonies, British authorities actively gathered knowledge about this vital institution in its various forms. By the first half of the twentieth century, British colonial authorities had amassed crucial knowledge on a wide range of *waqfs*, such as family endowments, mosques, schools, burial grounds, shrines and tombs which were located within British spheres of influence including British India, Palestine, Iraq, Egypt, Mecca, Madina and Syria. Correspondences on *waqfs* by colonial officials were widely circulated amongst the Colonial Office, the India Office and the various offices in particular colonies.[11]

In contrast to indirect rule in some territories, British colonial courts in the Straits Settlements directly administered all aspects of religious laws without ceding authority to local religious elites. By the first half of the twentieth century, two trends that would drastically transform the *waqf* in the British Straits Settlements began to emerge. Firstly, the relatively limited English legal concept of charity deeply impinged upon the broader Islamic concept of charity that included many more acts than

[10] R. Birla, *Stages of Capital: Law, Culture, and Market Governance in Late Colonial India* (North Carolina: Duke University Press, 2009), p. 71.

[11] These included the colonial governments of Palestine, Iraq, Malay states, Kenya, Zanzibar, Somaliland, Nigeria, Cyprus, Gold Coast and Ceylon. CO 732/26/2, Draft 49052/27 Arabic, March 1927.

the English legal definition. Secondly, the English rule against perpetuities stated that 'no interest is good unless it must vest, if at all, no later than twenty-one years after some life in being at the creation of the trust'. The English rule against perpetuities effectively led to the abolition of the *waqf* as a perpetual trust in favour of a more limited temporal trust.[12] This temporal restriction was strictly enforced such that once a *waqf* was scrutinized by legal practitioners in colonial courts, it risked dissolution, either partially or completely, for the reasons stated above.

The *waqf* was in effect a species of trust within British colonies, being a dedication or consecration of property either in express terms, or by implication for any charitable or religious object or to secure any benefit to human beings. The establishment of a *waqf* was comparable to establishing a trust in England. In order to establish a *waqf*, the settlor would sequester the property such that it became perpetually inalienable, and appoint a trustee to manage the property.[13] According to *sharīʿa*, the act was deemed legally irrevocable as it entailed the complete transfer of the right to ownership from the hands of the founder (also known as *wāqif*) to those of God.[14] In this way, the *waqf* was a thoroughly religious and pious concept and a material institution that was a charitable act of the first order.[15] Henceforth, the property sequestered could not be sold, inherited or given away as a gift.[16] The property would also potentially be free from the claims of other family members and other heirs. This ensured the physical and economic integrity of the estate across multiple generations who were appointed

12 The historical background of the rule against perpetuities is highly complex. It could be traced back to the medieval period, when feudal lords became suspicious of state property held by the dead hand (*mort main*). In order to avoid such alienation of property, which would lead to a valuable loss of tenure for an indefinite period of time, the rule against perpetuities gradually developed in Western Europe. In England specifically, the Statutes of Mortmain were enacted in 1279 and 1290 to circumscribe the Church's property holdings. The modern version of the rule against perpetuities was contained in the Mortmain and Charitable Uses Acts of 1888 and 1891 that effectively repealed the Mortmain Act of 1736. An exception to this rule was the charitable trust.

13 The trustee was entitled to more than ten per cent of the income of the *waqf* for his efforts.

14 The purpose was after all to do good for the sake of God. W. Hallaq, *Sharīʿa: Theory, Practice, Transformations* (Cambridge University Press, 2009), p. 143.

15 F. B. Tyabji, *Muhammadan Law: The Personal Law of Muslims*, 3rd edn (Bombay: N. M. Tripathi & Co., 1940), p. 541.

16 D. S. Powers, 'Orientalism, Colonialism, and Legal History: The Attack on Muslim Family Endowments in Algeria and India' (July 1989) 31:3 *Comparative Studies in Society and History* 535, 536.

beneficiaries of the *waqf*.[17] Theoretically, upon extinction of the family line, entitlement to the usufruct would consequently pass to a religious or charitable institution.

Considering the basic similarities between the English trust and the *waqf*, it was not surprising that Arab inhabitants of the Straits Settlements felt confident in establishing an Islamic institution within English legal jurisdictions which, after all, already possessed a similar establishment. On the whole, Arab testators demonstrated a high degree of juridical flexibility as they deftly manipulated colonial understandings of Islamic legal practice, even when colonial conceptions of the *waqf* appeared to deviate fundamentally from Islamic doctrine and reasoning concerning the institution. Legislative attempts to interfere with the terms and substance of the divine law, regarded as the embodiment of God's immutable will, would have normally been impermissible in the lives of these Arabs if they resided within Muslim jurisdiction.[18] In light of restrictions imposed by English common law, it was remarkable that during the colonial period several Arab litigants voluntarily and repeatedly brought *waqf* disputes to colonial courts in the Straits Settlements, sometimes even with the hope that *waqfs* would indeed be dissolved – an act against strict Islamic legal precepts since *waqfs* were constantly established as perpetual endowments.[19]

Law reports strongly suggest that the ostensible purpose of litigation was financial. There were two main classes of litigants in legal disputes. They were either members of the testator's descent group included in the class of beneficiaries, or members of the same clan outside the lineal descent group excluded from the class of beneficiaries. In courts, both groups of litigants stressed a re-examination of the testator's will and trust deed. Non-beneficiaries of a particular *waqf*, who would have otherwise inherited according to the formula prescribed in the Quran if there had been no *waqf*, tended to focus on the wording of the *waqf* in their efforts to include themselves within the class of beneficiaries. The number of cases involving *waqfs* in the Straits Settlements suggested that *waqfs* proved to be highly contentious institutions, according to not

[17] Several *waqfs* established in the nineteenth century are still in existence today.

[18] The law concerning the *waqf* is highly developed with meticulous precision. J. N. D Anderson, 'Recent Reforms in the Islamic Law of Inheritance' (1965) 14 *International and Comparative Law Quarterly* 349, 349.

[19] In fact, the establishment of a *waqf* for a limited period of time is not valid according to Islamic law.

just English law but Islamic law as well. Although the act was legal according to Islamic law, by alienating part of his property (a maximum of a third, according to Islamic law), a founder could prevent the otherwise rightful inheritors and their descendants from partaking in the alienated property forever.

On the other hand, beneficiaries themselves could profit from questioning trustees' competence and good faith or disputing their fellow beneficiaries' shares in the settlement. In the event that a *waqf* was declared a failure, the money earned from sale of the endowment would go to beneficiaries named in the founding testament. In this way, these beneficiaries stood to immediately gain a lump sum of money derived from the entire trust instead of the relatively small instalments they were receiving from the estate from time to time. Moreover, *waqf* failure was an attractive outcome as it would effectively end all other external claims to the *waqf*, such as those made by the testator's other descendants not named as beneficiaries by the testator. Since legal costs of a *waqf* dispute were borne out of the *waqf* estate, dissolution could prevent its worth from being whittled away over time.

By disputing *waqfs* in colonial courts, Arab litigants were in fact challenging the key anchor of family property holdings. Alterations to an existing *waqf* could lead to significant repercussions on kinship relations, since the *waqf* often bound not only members of a particular clan in the Straits Settlements, but also members of the same clan residing further afield elsewhere, whether on the Malay Peninsula, in Burma, the Netherlands Indies, India, or even Arabia. Often, the family *waqf* functioned as the resilient linchpin of a clan with far-flung members scattered across the Indian Ocean. Hence, within the context of precarious diasporic family relations, challenging the status of an existing *waqf* that had been purposefully established by a deceased patriarch was a rather bold act.

Yet, *waqfs* were relentlessly disputed in colonial courts. Arab *waqfs* were, in fact, disproportionately represented in colonial courts. Despite constituting only 0.34 per cent of the population in Singapore during the nineteenth century, at least forty cases involving *waqf*s owned by Arab families were brought to courts in the Straits Settlements from 1868 to 1963. The number of cases involving Indian Muslim *waqfs* trailed a distant second with fewer than ten disputes in colonial courts during the same period. The reason for this discrepancy lies in the fact that Arab residents owned much larger amounts of immoveable property, which they were able to convert into *waqf* property. After all, by 1936, they were the richest group in terms of ownership of assets per head in Singapore.[20]

Considering the severe legal limitations imposed by colonial courts on family trusts, it was significant that several wealthy Arab patriarchs chose to subsequently establish their *waqfs* in the Straits Settlements. Since the diaspora originated from Hadhramaut and settled in various places in East Africa, the Netherlands East Indies and on the Malay Peninsula, the choice of *waqf* locations was certainly large. The choice of the Straits Settlements was even more remarkable considering the fact that by the beginning of the twentieth century Arab testators seemed to be largely aware that laws regarding immoveable property were subject to the law of the jurisdiction where the property was located according to common law conventions in the Straits Settlements. By sequestering property in the Straits Settlements, Arab testators were knowingly subjecting their pious and religious endowments to English law. Arab patriarchs' choice of the Straits Settlements as the location of their *waqfs* suggested that the colony had become a suitable permanent anchor point for the diasporic community by the second half of the nineteenth century. It also meant that they found the British colony to be sufficiently accommodating for the establishment of *waqfs*, which was rather curious considering the harsh restrictions on temporal limits and a more limited definition of charity.

IV Dominance of colonial law

Just as their descendants would later attempt to utilize colonial law to wrest more control over existing *waqfs*, testators too had their own reasons for establishing *waqfs* in the British colony. The default application of English law in the colony had its own advantages for Muslim testators as it granted more testamentary freedom than a strict application of Islamic law would allow.[21] For example, they could pass the whole of their property in the form of a *waqf*, and not just a third of it as prescribed by Islamic law.[22] It was not until 1 January 1924 that property was devolved by default according to Islamic law should a Muslim die

[20] W. G. Clarence-Smith, 'Hadhrami Arab Entrepreneurs in Indonesia and Malaysia: Facing the Challenge of the 1930s Recession', in P. Boomgaard and I. Brown (eds.), *Weathering the Storm: The Economies of Southeast Asia in the 1930s Depression* (Singapore: Institute of Southeast Asian Studies, 2000), p. 229.

[21] A. Layish, 'Family Waqf and the Shari'a Law of Succession' (1997) 4:3 *Islamic Law and Society* 352, 355–6.

[22] *In the Goods of Abdullah, deceased* [1835] 2 Ky 8.

intestate.[23] Even after 1924, if a testator so wished, he or she could still devolve his or her property contrary to Islamic law, in accordance with English law.[24] In other words, the default colonial administration of Islamic law allowed an Arab testator more liberty in disposing of his property than Islamic law would otherwise allow.

Perhaps Arab testators' confidence arose from a perceived general colonial policy of non-intervention in religious affairs. Colonial courts might have been severe, but they were not particularly attentive to the various endowments being established in the colony. In fact, colonial courts rarely challenged the status of a particular *waqf* on their own, although from 1886 onwards, land granted or leased by or on behalf of the Crown free of rent or of nominal value for religious purposes required the Governor's written consent.[25] Most of the time, family *waqfs* were brought to the court's attention by Arab litigants interested in the *waqf* in the first place.[26] Up until the point of litigation, the management of family *waqfs* remained firmly in the hands of private trustees appointed by testators without any interference from the state.[27] If private trustees were incompetent or untrustworthy, the onus was upon beneficiaries to inform the court by enacting some form of legal action. A valuable *waqf* established by a wealthy Arab merchant name Syed Shaik Alkaff in 1923 was in existence for a full thirteen years before its terms were challenged in court by some of his descendants, while the *waqf* of Syed Ahmed Alsagoff was established forty-three years prior to being in English courts. Most *waqfs* were critically examined only after they were challenged and disputed in colonial courts, usually by the testators' descendants and relatives. This implies that these *waqfs* would have been allowed to exist as they were had Arab litigants not brought them to the attention of the colonial courts in the form of various lawsuits.

23 Ordinance 1923 came into force on 1 January 1924, after which the estate and effects were administered according to Islamic law by default, as long as it did not run counter to English law. A. Ibrahim, *The Legal Status of the Muslims in Singapore* (Singapore: Malayan Law Journal Ltd, 1965), p. 27.

24 'English law' refers to the English law in force in the colony at the time.

25 Ordinance II of 1886, Section 9, *The Acts and Ordinances of the Legislative Council of the Straits Settlements from the 1st April 1867 to the 7th March 1898*, Vol. II (London: Eyre and Spottiswoode, 1898), p. 876.

26 *Re Syed Shaik Alkaff, deceased; Alkaff & Anor* v. *Attorney-General* [1923] 2 MC 38.

27 Trustees could be members of the family, usually the brother of the deceased. At times, it could be someone in the testator's employ prior to his death.

Consequently, colonial courts divorced the *waqf* from the domestic sphere of the family by only discussing the *waqf* from the perspective of state land, without referring to the family at all.[35] Active litigation on the part of Arab communities allowed the colonial court to directly regulate familial and kinship relations for the benefit of the colonial state. Not surprisingly, litigation strategies involved a fundamentally different power dynamic outside the family. Arguments in law reports tended to focus on semantics in legal terms and clauses, while neglecting the role of kinship relations, most probably because such familial bonds had no place in colonial courts which had already placed the family *waqf* in the realm of the public.

V Law reports

The wide availability of law reports strongly indicated a strong legalist-professional approach to dispute resolution concerning the Islamic institution in colonial courts. Law reports reveal that most of the court cases involving Arab family endowments appeared in the early twentieth century, right after the period of wide proliferation of works on Islamic law by European colonialists during the late nineteenth century.[36] Within the British Empire, 'Anglo-Muhammadan law' emerged in British India in the late eighteenth century. It was a mixture of English and Islamic laws, concepts, institutions and jurisprudence, markedly different from both Islamic law and English law, being a fluid combination of the two.[37] However, since it was a product of specifically Indian legislation, legal authorities in the Straits Settlements displayed great uncertainty as to whether it was applicable to Muslims living in the Straits Settlements and Arabia in the first place. Moreover, the form of 'Anglo-Muhammadan law' that emerged in British India was derived from the *Hanafi madhhab* or juridical school, while Muslims in Southeast Asia and Hadhramaut Arabia belonged to the *Shāfi'i madhhab*.[38] There are

[35] Kozlowski, *Muslim Endowments and Society in British India*, above, note 6, p. 150.

[36] David S. Powers points out that this colonial phenomenon sparked off interests in Islamic law after the middle of the nineteenth century, which produced translations, monographs and comprehensive works on the subject. D. S. Powers, 'Wael B. Hallaq on the Origins of the Islamic Law: A Review Essay', (2010) 17 *Islamic Law and Society* 126, 131.

[37] M. K. Masud, 'Anglo-Muhammadan Law', in *Encyclopaedia of Islam, THREE*. G. Krämer et al. (eds.) (Brill, 2010) available at http://referenceworks.brillonline.com.

[38] *Madhhab* (pl. *madhāhib*) refers to a juridical-religious school of law. The four schools of law are Shāfi'ī, Ḥanafī, Ḥanbalī and Māliki.

variations between the two *madhhabs* with regards to the *waqf*, something which judges in the Straits Settlements were aware of. Besides, in general, al least some judges in the Straits Settlements were keen on articulating a new legal course for the colony, separate from British India. They therefore preferred to underscore its differences from other colonies, not necessarily of a religious nature, in order to justify their deviation from Indian rulings.[39]

Rules concerning the *waqf* remained vague during the colonial period. Throughout the British Empire, the terms of the substantive laws of *waqf* were not defined in any enactment. According to an explanatory report attached to legislation of the *waqf* in Mauritius in 1941, it was actually up to local colonial courts to discover what the laws were and apply them to the *waqf*.[40] Courts however, rarely offered their own takes on substantive laws of *waqf*. The same report revealed that British courts applied religious laws by reference from time to time to 'recognized textbooks' on the issue, as well as to the 'steadily growing body of judicial decisions, reinforced from time to time by important decisions of the Judicial Committee of the Privy Council'.[41]

In the Straits Settlements, decisions were made independent of Indian precedents even when court decisions ultimately aligned with Indian court decisions. The most glaring omission in law reports was the famous Indian case of *Abul Fata Mahomed Ishak* v. *Russamoy Dhur Chowdry* in 1894, in which the Privy Council affirmed a High Court ruling that the *waqf* in question was not a valid charitable endowment, but only a ruse to aggrandize the family holdings.[42] The case quickly acquired political valence as several Muslim subjects rightfully saw it as symptomatic of a broader colonial attack on *waqf* as an economic hindrance for growth in a market economy. Used as a rallying point by discontented Muslims, the case led to the Wakf Validating Act of 1913, which dramatically

39 For example, the fixed rate of five per cent on receipts and payments to be received by the trustee was not binding in the Straits Settlements unlike in British India and England. *Wanchee Incheh Thyboo & Anor.* v. *Golam Kader* [1883] 1 Ky 611.

40 CO 167/919/14, C. A. Hooper, Procureur and Advocate General, Explanatory Report on Ordinance no. 9 of 1941, 9 May 1941.

41 Ibid.

42 The object of this suit was to establish whether a settlement of property effected by deed dated 21 December 1868 was a valid *waqf*. In July 1895, the House of Lords ruled that the poor had been added as beneficiaries to the settlement merely to give it 'a colour of piety'. Parliament believed that the only real beneficiaries of the *waqf* were members of the family which meant the trust was invalid. IOR/L/PJ/6/400, File 1104, House of Lords question on Muslim law relating to endowments, 5 July 1895.

overturned the Privy Council decision. While both Ali Jinnah, then a barrister in Bombay who was an unofficial member of the Governor General's Council, and later lawyers like Asaf Fyzee claimed that the Act triumphantly restored Islamic law, it was actually more likely to be a political act, according to Michael R. Anderson.[43]

The ambiguity of the status of the family *waqf* in the Straits Settlements was reflected in the lengthy and intricate discussions in colonial law reports that arose in no small part from general uncertainty in legal administration of the Islamic endowment, both public and private, in British colonies. Public *waqf*s consisting of mosques, schools or burial grounds were clearly a sensitive topic amongst Muslims who gave these endowments particular attention.[44] In the Straits Settlements, charitable endowments of land or money given to support a mosque or Hindu temple, shrine or school were under the 'Mahomedan and Hindu Endowments Ordinance no. 92, formerly Ordinance XVII of 1905'.[45] Subsequently, the Mohamedan Advisory Boards in each settlement supervised the management of public *waqf*s. Municipal Commissioners ensured that public *waqf*s, especially burial grounds, were properly run.[46] Concern was expressed by local Muslims in numerous published letters and articles in the press, calling for the government's attention to these public *waqf*s.[47] Although private family *waqf*s were not discussed in the mass media as much, they were clearly not exempted from governmental control.

[43] M. R. Anderson, 'Islamic Law and the Colonial Encounter in British India', in D. Arnold and P. Robb (eds.), *Institutions and Ideologies – A SOAS South Asia Reader*, Collected Papers on South Asia (Richmond: Curzon Press, 1993), p. 183; A. A. A. Fyzee, *Cases in the Muhammadan Law of India and Pakistan* (Oxford University Press, 1965), p. 334.

[44] 'Council Representation: Letter from A Malay Muslim to the Editor', *The Singapore Free Press and Mercantile Advertiser*, 2 November 1920, p. 12; The Mohamedan Advisory Board, *The Singapore Free Press and Mercantile Advertiser*, 29 September 1924, p. 9.

[45] For a complete text of the ordinance, see 'Mahomedan and Hindu Endowments. Ordinance no. 92', *The Laws of the Straits Settlements, Volume 2* (London: Waterlow, 1920), pp. 222–9.

[46] 'Bidadari: Letters from "A Muslim" to the Editor of the Straits Times', *Straits Times*, 4 February 1925, p. 10; 'Burial of Indigent Muslims – The Trust Fund's Work', *The Singapore Free Press and Mercantile Advertiser*, 23 November 1926, p. 2; Muslim Correspondent, 'Burial Ground Committee', *The Singapore Free Press and Mercantile Advertiser*, 16 March 1927, p. 15; 'Dispute over Land Used as Burial Ground', *Straits Times*, 30 October 1936, p. 16.

[47] 'Letter from "A Mohamedan" to the Editor', *Straits Times*, 2 December 1911, p. 10; 'Letter from S to the Editor', *The Singapore Free Press and Mercantile Advertiser*, 28 October 1926, p. 16.

Law reports are certainly valuable in providing a better understanding of colonial realities, but they omitted certain key elements in legal culture which directly affect the way that they can be read historically. From the narrative of these law reports, it is clear that the court decision was not the main event. Rather, the specific circumstances of the case that led up to the ruling were emphasized in each law report concerning the *waqf*. The *raison d'être* of the corpus of law reports was, after all, to supply the courts and litigants with a formal document that they could refer to in future similar cases.[48] Law reports recorded judicial proceedings as a whole instead of addressing every issue presented in court. In the interest of setting and recording legal precedents in the Straits Settlements, they selected the most relevant points of argument that emerged during trial proceedings. Even excellent but well-worn arguments tended to be merely alluded to but not elucidated upon in law reports.[49] Hence, despite possessing a formal and uniform structure, law reports form a rather limited historical source.

The content of law reports was discursively embedded in larger discourses of power and authority, which determined its form and structure.[50] Law reporters, usually young lawyers yet to gain enough experience, would take notes during legal proceedings and organize their notes to form a law report, which would include the final ruling as well. Law reports could influence future rulings to a considerable degree by acquiring a certain slant, mainly by highlighting certain aspects of the case in the summary and list of catchwords contained in the headnote of each law report.[51] Law reports adhered very closely to a certain formal structure, being part of a long tradition of official documentation. For example, they possessed a narrative structure that was consistently neat and logical so as to facilitate more efficient reading. Verdicts and conclusions to complicated cases were often presented as inevitable. Some law reports even suggest that legal decisions were arrived at within one single setting, when in reality, court sessions often ran over several weeks or

[48] I. Agmon, 'Text, Court, and Family in Late-Nineteenth-Century Palestine', in B. Doumani (ed.), *Family History in the Middle East – Household, Property and Gender* (Albany: State University of New York Press, 2003), p. 204.

[49] For example, see judge's remarks in the law report of *In Re Abdul Kader's Settlement, Aisha Binte Mohamed Ali* v. *Udmansah bin Mohamed Ali* [1928] SSLR 37.

[50] B. Doumani, 'Adjudicating Family: The Islamic Court and Disputes between Kin in Greater Syria, 1700–1860', in B. Doumani (ed.), *Family History in the Middle East – Household, Property and Gender* (Albany: State University of New York Press, 2003), p. 174.

[51] I am indebted to Mitra Sharafi for pointing out the importance of headnotes to me.

even months. Furthermore, law reports provided the sense that judges who handled court cases dealt with court proceedings single-handedly in performing their tasks as arbitrators. However, in reality, judges frequently engaged with other judges who adjudicated the same or similar cases in the past. This was evident in the way judges often imitated each other's language to bolster their own legal authority in particular rulings. Being intentionally derivative, judges' legal decisions concerning the *waqf* did not waver much from each other and soon a dominant narrative began to emerge, which meant that alternative rulings had to be justified at great length. Judges also participated in debates with lawyers who represented their clients in law. Nonetheless, the critical role of lawyers was largely missing in law reports for these reports did not offer a thick description of legal proceedings much to the historian's dismay, although lawyers definitely played a key role in arguing cases in a manner that was most beneficial to their clients.[52] In association with this, legal procedure and protocols were also not expounded upon. Judges preferred to sum up arguments without attribution to specific sides, although one can, of course, surmise the identity of the lawyers from the content of specific arguments.

Lastly, law reports generally do not indicate the level of knowledge possessed by Arab litigants who evidently argued their cases exclusively through their lawyers in colonial courts. Despite the stark absence of individual Arab voices in law reports, it was highly likely that Arab litigants had a big say in legal strategy and representation. Yet, the language of law reports made it extremely difficult to distinguish between agency and representation. It is a challenge to differentiate litigants' intentions and line of argument from that of a lawyer's legal strategy in court. Unfortunately, mention was rarely made of Arab or any other local witnesses being called to the stand in cases involving *waqfs*. Law reports indicated that courts scrutinized trustees' actions solely by examining documentary evidence including ledgers, financial statements and bank accounts.[53] This absence raises many key questions. Were litigants actually present in courts, or did this imply that they simply authorized their attorneys to be present in court on their behalf?

[52] The unjust omission of lawyers has been crucially addressed in F. Tuerkheimer, 'A Short Essay in the Editing of Cases in Casebooks' (2008) 58 *Journal of Legal Education* 531. Mitra Sharafi's article on colonial lawyering foregrounds the role of lawyers during the colonial period: M. Sharafi, 'A New History of Colonial Lawyering: Likhovski and Legal Identities in the British Empire' (Fall 2007) 32:4 *Law and Social Inquiry* 1059.

[53] In contrast, *sharīʿa* often privileges spoken testimony.

Similarly, when dealing with particular Islamic legal terms and precepts, judges and lawyers preferred to refer to well-worn Islamic legal textbooks rather than ask local religious authorities such as *qadis*.[54] When cases were brought to colonial courts, judges did not delegate any real authority to local translators or religious leaders in courts. In law reports, judges rarely displayed a sense of being overwhelmed by the intricacies of Islamic law or by the complexity of individual family disputes.

Documentary evidence was particularly important in *waqf* disputes. Insistence on documentary evidence was a marked feature of common law courts, as opposed to Islamic courts which placed much more importance on actual oral deposition.[55] Judges referred almost exclusively to textual evidence which consisted mainly of wills, but also occasionally included codicils and *waqf* deeds, all of which had to be notarized.[56] The wills were often those which had been accepted into probate by the courts several years prior to the suit. Every instrument purporting to be testamentary and executed in accordance with the formal statutory requirements was entitled to probate if it purported to dispose of property or contained the appointment of an executor. However, the document had to fulfil certain conditions. According to Ordinance no. 26 of 1921 and Ordinance no. 3 of 1926 of the Laws of the Straits Settlements, a will includes 'a testament and an appointment by will or by writing in the nature of a will in exercise of a power and also a disposition by will and testament or devise of the custody and tuition of any child'.[57] For a will made by a Muslim to be accepted on probate, it had to comply with the provisions with regard to execution and attestation contained in

[54] In deciding questions of Islamic law, judges were at liberty to accept as proof of the 'Mohammedan Law' made in the following books: (1) Any English translation of the Koran, (2) *Mohammedan Law*, by Syed Ameer Ali, (3) Howard's translation of Van den Berg's French translation of the *Minhaj Et Talibin, a Manual of Mohammedan Law according to the School of Shāfi'i*, by Nawawi, (4) *A Digest of Moohummudan Law*, by Neil B. E. Baillie, (5) *Anglo-Muhammadan Law*, by Sir Roland Knyvet Wilson. 'The Governor in Council may vary from or add to the list of books by publishing notifications in the Straits Settlements Government Gazette': Chapter 57 Section 29, *Laws of the Straits Settlements, Volume 2* (Singapore: Government Printing Office, 1936), p. 254.

[55] Anderson, 'Islamic Law and the Colonial Encounter in British India', above, note 43, pp. 178–9.

[56] Existing *waqfs* that were established orally by a testator risked being declared null without exception. See CO 167/919/14, above, note 40.

[57] The will could also include a codicil. Ordinance no. 3, Section 2, *Laws of the Straits Settlements, Volume 1* (London: Waterlow, 1926), p. 11; Chapter 121, Section 2, *Laws of the Straits Settlements, Volume 3* (London: Waterlow, 1926), p. 329.

the Wills Ordinance.[58] Section 101 of the Evidence Ordinance provided that 'wills should be construed according to the rules of construction which would be applicable thereto if they were being construed in a court of justice in England'.[59] According to principles of English law in the Straits Settlements, the will had to be in written form, although in Islamic law a verbal will is acceptable.[60] In addition, even though it was not explicitly mentioned in government gazettes and Laws of the Straits Settlements, legal documents including wills and codicils had to be in English since there was a chance they might not be fully accepted by all government offices if they were written in another language.[61] However, in a case involving an Arab will, the court maintained that although it had discretion, it would not revoke an appointment without sufficient cause.[62] Once a will was 'proved', authenticated and subsequently accepted into probate, it was not taken lightly by the court. The will hence became a binding document.

Just like ecclesiastical courts in England, which were courts of verification and record,[63] colonial courts functioned as a crucial repository of important documents for Hadhrami clans. The amount of documentary evidence produced in *waqf* disputes highlighted the official textual memory of the colonial legal system. Trust that had been vested in the courts by Arab communities who purposefully created wills which conformed to rules instituted by courts ultimately paid off in these legal

[58] 'Every will should be signed at the foot or end thereof by the testator or by some other person in his presence and by his direction, and such signature shall be made or acknowledged by the testator as the signature to his will or codicil in the presence of two or more witnesses present at the same time, and such witnesses shall subscribe the will in the presence of the testator, but no form of attestation shall be necessary.' Ordinance 3, Section 6, *Laws of the Straits Settlements, Volume 1* (London: Waterlow, 1926), p. 14.

[59] Ibrahim, *The Legal Status of the Muslims in Singapore*, above, note 23, p. 32.

[60] A. Ibrahim, *Islamic Law in Malaya* (Singapore: Malaysian Sociological Research Institute, 1965), p. 300.

[61] For example, one law report revealed that an informal document could not be registered in the Land Office precisely because it was in Malay. *In the Goods of Hajee Mahomed Thaib* [1886] 4 Ky 178. In Mauritius, a French document was recognized in British colonial courts, although accounts still had to be produced in the English language. CO 167/919/14, above, note 40.

[62] In the case, the eldest living son of the testator wished the court to revoke the appointment of the testator's brother as executor. *In re Shaik Abdullah bin Ahmad bin Ali Al Tway Basalamah, Deceased* [1941] MLJ 6.

[63] R. B. Outhwaite. *The Rise and Fall of the English Ecclesiastical Courts, 1500–1860*, Cambridge Studies in English Legal History (Cambridge University Press, 2006), p. 7.

disputes. In this way, the textual memory possessed by the courts usefully spanned several generations, both familial and legal. Written records played a particularly critical role in the resolution of disputes over family endowments since they usually arose one or more generations after the death of the founder.[64] Since these documents made dispositions that did not follow a specific prescribed formula and produced highly particular configurations of devolution of property, which frequently departed from Islamic regulations specifically stated in the Quran, it was all the more crucial that written documents exist to prove testators' precise intentions in establishing *waqfs*.[65]

VI Posterity denied: rule against perpetuities

Documentary evidence was consulted extensively by legal practitioners who parsed every line in order to determine its legal validity. The *waqf* suffered from the same limitations as the English trust, namely the restrictions denoted by the English concept of charitability, and the rule against perpetuities which provided that no contingent or executory interest in property can be validly created, unless it must necessarily vest within the maximum period of one or more lives in being, and twenty-one years afterwards.[66] Although the rule against perpetuities influenced judges' decisions to a great extent eventually, it did not automatically prevent the perpetual establishment of *waqf*s in courts, as evident in judges' lengthy, contrapuntal ruminations and discussions with their predecessors and contemporaries on the *waqf*. This is because the wording of terms in Arab wills incorporated elements from Islamic law which called for more attention from the English judge who was understandably less familiar with the highly specific terminology. In fact, judges rarely set out to sidestep testators' wishes on their way to implementing the rule against perpetuities. For example, judges often took a

[64] In contrast, Muslim jurists tended to view written documents with a generous measure of suspicion as the written word can be manipulated in a manner that the oral testimony of trustworthy persons cannot. D. S. Powers, 'Islamic Family Endowment (Waqf)' (1999) 32 *Vanderbilt Journal of Transnational Law* 1167, 1182–3.

[65] A common tactic was the addition of several witnesses to attest to each document signed by the testator. *In the Matter of the Estate of Kulsome Bee, Deceased. Che Puteh and Rahimah Fatimah Bee* v. *Syed Omar Alsagoff and Others* [1930] SSLR 64.

[66] The relevant period is the same as that which obtains against remoteness of vesting, which governs trusts for persons (as opposed to trusts for purposes): Ibrahim, *The Legal Status of the Muslims in Singapore*, above, note 23, p. 25.

considerable amount of time to determine who should be included in the class of beneficiaries termed 'heirs as then ascertained according to Mohammedan Law'. Lawyer Ahmad Ibrahim erroneously implied that judges routinely assumed that this phrase referred to the testator's heirs, according to Islamic law, if the testator had died, at the expiration of twenty-one years from the actual date of death.[67] In actual fact, court judges often took their time to determine what was meant by the testator in each case, even to the point of challenging their predecessors' rulings on the same *waqf*. In other words, colonial courts did not merely dismiss the testator's intentions straightaway by imposing their own English legal definitions. Each case involving a *waqf* or any other form of perpetual trust in the Straits Settlements reopened the debate on the applicability of the rule in the Straits Settlements in the first place.

Nonetheless, in effect, the English rule against perpetuities influenced the establishment of the *waqf* to a great extent by effectively eradicating the perpetual aspect of these *waqf*s. Advised by English lawyers who familiarized their clients with the pitfalls of English law, Arab testators became more mindful of significant potential legal limitations posed by English law. Consequently, they took great measures to institute the *waqf* in a manner that was acceptable to English law. This precaution was necessary in order to ensure that the *waqf* was not declared void from the outset. One of these wealthy patriarchs who took measures to ensure the posthumous establishment of his *waqf* was Syed Ahmed bin Abdul Rahman Alsagoff. In 1868, he attempted to establish a perpetual trust in the form of a *waqf*, and specifically directed that his freehold and leasehold property should not be sold or mortgaged or in any way encumbered, but should be held in perpetuity by his trustee upon trust, to let the same from year to year or for any term not exceeding five years at the best rent, to manage and receive the rents and profits after payment of the incidental outgoings and expenses.[68] However, he astutely added the following:

67 Ibid.

68 According to the law report, the expenses included repairs of the houses and buildings and the construction of new buildings when judged beneficial to the interests of the estate and including the rebuilding of any houses or buildings which had become decayed or had been destroyed or injured by fire or tempest, to distribute $1,000 annually at the discretion of the trustee for charitable purposes (*sedikah*) according to 'Mohammedan customs and uses', and to divide the clear residue of such rents and profits annually amongst the testator's wife and children above-named and their descendants according to the shares prescribed by the 'Mohammedan law'.

And whereas I am advised that it is uncertain whether or not the rule of the English law against perpetuities extends to the Colony of the Straits Settlements and that if it should be found so to extend that the hereinbefore mentioned trusts in regard to my freehold and leasehold property may be held to be void and ineffectual. Now therefore I hereby declare and direct that, in the event of its being found that the said rule against perpetuities extends to the Colony and that the trusts hereinbefore declared in regard to the said freehold and leasehold property are in consequence inoperative and may be set aside; the trustee or trustees of this my will for the time being shall stand possessed of and entitled to the said freehold and leasehold property upon trust from time to time and during the lives of all such of the children and more remote issue of me the said Testator as shall be living at the time of my decease and during the lives and life of the survivors and survivor of such children and issue and also for and during the further term or period of twenty years to commence and be computed from the time of the decease of the survivor of the said children and issue to manage the said freehold and leasehold property and to apply the income and produce thereof in the manner hereinbefore directed and so long as the trusts herein before declared regarding the same are capable of taking effect and from and after the end or expiration of the said term or period of twenty years commencing from the decease of the survivor of the several persons hereinbefore described or referred to as aforesaid then I empower and direct the trustee or trustees for the time being of this my will or of the said freehold and leasehold premises to make sale and dispose of the same and to divide the proceeds thereof between and amongst the several persons then entitled to receive the net income and produce thereof in proportion to their several rights and interests thereon according to the Mohammedan law.

The alternative trusts in accordance with English law were established but subsequently contested by the founder's descendants who argued that trusts of the will, both as to corpus and income, were void for remoteness.[69] By 1917, there were two grandchildren (who were income beneficiaries) who were born after Syed Alsagoff's death and who had died leaving children. If these great-grandchildren succeeded to their parents' shares, there would be two successive unborn generations taking life interests in the income.[70]

69 The other plaintiffs were the executors of the trust and the Attorney-General who represented the charitable objects of the trusts.

70 The deceased testator had, at the time of the suit, eighteen great-great-grandchildren (children of some one or more of the great-grandchildren of the testator), and he had also one great-great-great-grandchild, the child of one of the eighteen great-great-grandchildren above.

The case did not revolve around the applicability of Islamic law. Instead the case turned mainly upon the question of old and new versions of the rule against perpetuities. The rule in *Whitby* v. *Mitchell*, sometimes called the 'old' rule against perpetuities, was often invoked. It prevented the creation of a settlement by giving a series of life estates from father to son for generations.[71] Eventually, the judge held that *Whitby v. Mitchell* (1889) had no application on the ground that the legal conditions applicable to the transmission and devolution of real property in Singapore were different from those applicable in England. The judgment was eventually upheld unanimously by the Court of Appeal.

Legal uncertainty of the *waqfs* stemmed from the absence of formal legal codes on the *waqfs*. From the outset, it seemed that the general lack of formal codification of laws concerning the *waqf* gave judges much potential leeway in their legal decisions. In other words, the absence of specific legal codes and case law concerning legal administration of the trusts and *waqfs* in the Straits Settlements presented judges, at least theoretically, with the opportunity to perform a new set of legal gestures in colonial courts. During this tentative period of legal codification, there was understandably considerable room for legal manoeuvre for legal practitioners. Unfettered by established legal codes in the Straits Settlements, judges potentially possessed much flexibility. Judges were forced to act upon their own initiatives in the absence of specific legislation on the *waqf* in the Straits Settlements. The judicial interpretation of concepts and applications of charity law in *waqf* cases in the Straits Settlements was a particularly subjective approach with no clear definitions in English and Irish court decisions that formed the main body of precedents alongside a handful of Indian decisions.[72]

However, it seems that judges in the courts of the Straits Settlements preferred not to exploit this judicial freedom in the end, actively opting to

[71] The rule had in fact been accepted and practised by conveyancers for two centuries prior to 1889 when it became the subject of judicial decision. For a discussion of the case and the legal concept of 'perpetuity', see C. Sweet, 'The Rule in *Whitby* v. *Mitchell*' (March 1912) 12:3 *Columbia Law Review* 199. *Whitby* v. *Mitchell* (1890) was discussed extensively in the following case: *Syed Ali Bin Mohamed Alsagoff and Others* v. *Syed Omar Bin Mohamed Alsagoff and Others* [1918] SSLR 2.

[72] Irish and English courts actually disagreed on key issues involving charity such as the question of whether gifts to a closed order of nuns were legitimate. While courts in Ireland held such gifts to be charitable, English courts did not. T. B. Lian, 'The Meaning of "Charity" in Malaya – A Comparative Study' (1969) 11:2 *Malaya Law Review* 220, 222.

align themselves with decisions in British India.[73] No matter how keen the judges might have been in wishing to chart their own legal course in the Straits Settlements, the parochial nature of the legal system is such that a legal decision consistent with previous rulings elsewhere in the Empire was preferred to an inconsistent one. In this manner, previous legal rulings provided a basis of authority for later ones in the Straits Settlements. Ultimately, law reports revealed that judges' judicial discretion was consistently tempered by previous colonial rulings as well as English statutes that had been enforced in the United Kingdom and/or elsewhere in the Empire. In producing law reports, judges adopted a confident tone and carefully implied that their rulings were arrived at more or less independently of cases elsewhere in the Empire or in the United Kingdom.[74]

VII Charity

Despite the emphasis on the English law of perpetuities, the perpetual nature of trusts did not automatically render the trust void, for the establishment of public trusts clearly meant a trust for charity was actually permitted in the Straits Settlements. The English law of perpetuities did not apply to charitable trusts. Understandably, *waqf*s often aspired to the status of charitable trust. Due to the fact that charitable *waqf*s could run perpetually, English courts paid extra attention to *waqfs* that were labelled 'charitable' since they might just be a shrewd tactic to circumvent limitations on perpetuity that were imposed on family *waqf*s. Wills and *waqf* deeds produced by Arab testators however did not differentiate between public and private charity throughout the colonial period, thus forcing judges to pore meticulously over individual terms dictated by testators in order to parse the terms according to English legal conceptions of charity to determine whether the trust was viable or not. This led to a seemingly subjective system of determining what was 'charitable' and what was not in colonial courts. Subsequently, certain terms in wills and deeds were consistently deemed uncharitable by court judges. These

[73] Judge-made law was frowned upon, being subject to the temper of the individual judge. Thomas Macaulay, India's first Law Member, referred to it disparagingly. E. Kolsky, 'Codification and the Rule of Colonial Difference: Criminal Procedure in British India' (Fall 2005) 23:3 *Law and History Review* 631, 639.

[74] The confident tone of law reports could be misleading as they were produced only after cases were closed.

included *kandoories*, feasts which were given to relatives, friends and the poor in the name of the deceased testator. Judges reasoned that these ceremonies were intended to be held in honour of an individual, and did not lead to any public advantage or utility. In addition, pilgrimages to Mecca done in the testator's name were also considered uncharitable since they were conducted for the sole benefit of the testator.[75]

Waqfs often ran aground, partially or completely, on the English common law definition of charity in the colonies.[76] In contrast, the Islamic definition of charity is extremely broad and wide-ranging, including all actions which are benevolent and 'doing good for humanity in general'.[77] 'Charity' was indeed a malleable concept, which colonial courts continually tried to fix from the perspective of colonial benefits at the time – social, economic and political. However, charitable giving is above all the heroic act of an individual, perhaps spurred on by religion, conscience or social concern, but only contingently related to either the reproduction or imagination of social order; its meanings as a social act are diluted, secondary and obscure. Charity is, in other words, context-dependent, rooted in practices of sociability, irreducible to a core principle of application.[78] However, charity could be regulated

75 *Re Hadjee Esmail bin Kassim, Deceased; Mohamadeen and Others* v. *Hussain Beebee Bintee Shaik Ali Bey* [1911] 12 SSLR 74.

76 The preamble to the Statute of Charities in 1601, also known as the Charitable Uses Act of 1601 or Elizabeth Statute (Statute 43 Eliz. c. 4), limited the classes of legal charities. However, the preamble was meant to be hortatory rather than definitive. The list included: (1) the relief of aged, impotent and poor people; (2) the maintenance of sick and maimed soldiers and mariners; (3) the maintenance of schools of learning, free schools and scholars in universities; (4) the repair of bridges, ports, havens, causeways, churches, sea-banks and highways; (5) the education and preferment of orphans; (6) the relief, stock or maintenance of houses of correction; (7) marriages of poor maids; (8) the supportation, aid and help of young tradesmen, handicraftsmen and persons decayed; (9) the relief or redemption of prisoners or captives; (10) the aid or ease of any poor inhabitants concerning payment of fifteens, setting out of soldiers, and other taxes. The statute remained unrepealed until the Mortmain and Charitable Uses Acts of 1888. For a full text of the preamble in old English, see Lian, 'The Meaning of "Charity" in Malaya', above, note 72, 220–2.

77 For a discussion of the differences between English trusts and *waqfs*, including an explanation of the different conceptions of charity, see A. White, 'Breathing New Life into the Contemporary Islamic Waqf: What Reforms can Fiqh Regarding Awqaf Adopt from the Common Law of Trusts without Violating Shari'ah?' (2006–2007) 41 *Real Property, Probate and Trust Journal* 497.

78 Schmidt specifically traces the concept of charity in the public statements made about charity in the context of the early eighteenth-century charity schools linked to the discourse on social and moral discipline of the poor. In light of Schmidt's study of

by courts and, as we shall see, certain charitable characteristics of the *waqf* were firmly banned from taking root in the Straits Settlements despite being well-established in the Islamic legal tradition.

Within the colony, the meaning of charity in English courts was influenced by two related factors: the role of the judiciary and the interpretation of the concepts of charity law.[79] Although both family and public forms of trusts were equally valid according to Islamic law, family *waqfs* were regarded as markedly different from public *waqfs* according to English law.[80] Unlike family *waqfs*, public *waqfs* (*waqf khayri*), where the founder dedicates property to a religious or charitable institution, were deemed charitable according to English law, and therefore faced fewer legal impediments in the Straits Settlements.[81] This was because according to the principles of the English law of charities, a purpose is not charitable unless it was for public benefit,[82] although British authorities recognized that the Muslim definition was different.[83] By the late 1880s, the legal definition of charity in England referred specifically to the act of giving with clear intention of public benefit.[84]

English openness towards several conceptions of 'charity' in England, it is rather jarring that the Muslim concept of 'charity' was not recognized in British colonies. J. Schmidt, 'Charity and the Government of the Poor in the English Charity-School Movement, circa 1700–1730' (October 2010) 49:4 *Journal of British Studies* 774, 774–5.

79 Although deemed problematic, this legal framework carried over to postcolonial Malaysia: Lian, 'The Meaning of "Charity" in Malaya', above, note 72, 221–2.

80 In fact, colonial courts administered family *waqfs* more extensively than public *waqfs*. Unlike family *waqfs*, public *waqfs* could be administered, at least partly, by Mohamedan Advisory Boards established by the government, headed by a British colonial official with several local Muslims under his charge. Indeed, endowments in land or money given or to be given for the support of any mosque or other pious, religious, charitable or beneficial purpose were to be managed by the Mohamedan and Hindu Endowments Board from 1 January 1906 onwards. Ordinance no. 92, Section 2, *Laws of the Straits Settlements, Volume 1* (London: Waterlow, 1926), p. 92. This did not mean that public *waqfs* escaped the courts' attention altogether during the colonial period. For more details on the administration of public *waqfs*, see *Haji Salleh Bin Haji Ismail and Another* v. *Abdullah Bin Haji Mohamed Salleh and Others* [1934] SSLR 7; *Re Shrine of Habib Noh* [1957] MLJ 139.

81 As part of the wealthy Muslim elite in the Straits Settlements, rich Arabs frequently established public trusts which consisted mostly of mosques and schools. Public *waqfs* have various uses. They have been used to supply weapons to warriors fighting in God's service; provide funds for the establishment of mosques, schools and hospitals; and pay the salaries of scholars, religious functionaries and students: Powers, 'Orientalism, Colonialism, and Legal History', above, note 16, 536.

82 Ibrahim, *The Legal Status of the Muslims in Singapore*, above, note 23, p. 34.

83 W. H. Rattigan, 'The English Law and Legislation upon the Native Laws of India' (1902) 3:1 *Journal of the Society of Comparative Legislation* 46, 60.

84 Birla, *Stages of Capital*, above, note 10, p. 70.

In contrast, family endowments benefited only a relatively small, select group of people, i.e. members of a particular family or clan, instead of the general, more abstract, public. An exception would be gifts meant for the testators' poor relatives which were regarded as charitable in courts.[85] Although the concept of charity was never properly defined, judges cited four specific divisions of charitable trusts: trusts for the relief of poverty, for the advancement of education, for the advancement of religion, and trusts for other purposes beneficial to the community not falling under any of the preceding categories. Although Arab testators paid much attention to the English rule against perpetuities by significantly modifying their *waqfs* in this respect, they opted not to alter charitable clauses in their wills to suit English legal definitions of charity. Rather, they stuck to a list of clauses deemed charitable according to Islamic law. It was for this reason that Arab *waqfs* partially or completely failed.

VIII Diasporic complications

Despite the high level of confidence in the English legal system held by legal practitioners, as well as Arab testators and litigants alike, courts sometimes found themselves having to justify the application of English law in the Straits Settlements as opposed to Islamic law. Not surprisingly, some judges professed astonishment that the question of law applied to Muslim subjects should even be considered by their colleagues and lawyers. Yet, law reports indicated that one of the primary concerns of colonial courts was the status of Islamic law in the administration of *waqfs* established by Arabs specifically. After all, a diasporic family structure that spanned huge geographical expanses guaranteed that a complex trans-legal existence was prevalent amongst Arab clans. Hence, British judges frequently wavered between *lex situs* (law of the place in which property is situated) and *lex domicilii* (law of domicile) and had to address this dilemma at the beginning of law reports.[86] In all of the cases

85 Interestingly, Wael Hallaq points out that the understanding of many Muslim jurists is that the charitable nature of the *waqf* dictated that the rich could not benefit from charitable endowments. However a minority of later Shāfi'ites came to approve of establishing endowments for the benefit of the well-to-do. Hallaq, *Sharīʿa*, above, note 14, p. 145.

86 *Re Syed Shaik Alkaff, Deceased; Alkaff & Anor* v. *Attorney-General, S.S.* [1923] MC 1; *Re Syed Abdulrahman Bin Shaikh Bin Abdulrahman Alkaff, Deceased* [1953] MLJ 68; *Re Syed Hassan Bin Abdullah Aljofri Deceased; The Estate & Trust Agencies (1927) Ltd* v. *Syed Hamid Bin Hassan Aljofri & 2 Ors* [1949] MLJ 198.

examined, *lex situs* ultimately triumphed.[87] Eventually, judges consistently concluded that since the immoveable property that constituted the *waqf* was situated in the Straits Settlements, it should be subjected to English law. With regards to a ruling over the Alkaff family *waqf* in Singapore, an English judge emphatically stated in 1923 that

> The trustees, having chosen Singapore as the site of the trust estate, we have only to consider the law administered by these Courts. That law is municipal in the strictest sense. The domicile of a testator, or the religious sect to which he belonged, is never allowed to interfere with the destination of his immovables ... it is so firmly embedded in our law that no Court can venture to break in upon it.[88]

Since the religious peculiarities of the *waqf* were not considered relevant, judges had little problem using the more generic term of 'trust' despite actual key differences between the two institutions.[89] In fact, any mention of testators' religious intentions was notably absent in later cases that revolved around the same *waqf*, as if Straits judges were increasingly distancing themselves from the litigants' religious orientation in administering such trusts.[90] However, as mentioned before, to equate a *waqf* with the English legal definition of a 'trust' was actually rather problematic, for it obscured the differences between the English common law trust and the Islamic *waqf*.[91] Asaf Fyzee, a specialist in Islamic law on the Indian

[87] At least one scholar has pointed out that it is commonly known that wills involving immoveable property were clearly subject to *lex situs* in Britain. If so, it is curious that judges grappled with this question well into the twentieth century. This pointed towards the wide judicial discretion that judges in the Straits Settlements seemed to possess. E. J. Cohn, 'The Form of Wills of Immovables' (1956) 5 *International and Comparative Law Quarterly* 395.

[88] *Re Syed Shaik Alkaff, Deceased; Alkaff & Anor* v. *Attorney-General* [1923] MC 1.

[89] One particular law report referred to the '*wakaf*' only when citing an Arabic will. *The Attorney-General (On the Relation of Shaik Ali Bin Ahmad Al Tway) and Shaik Ali Bin Ahmad Al Tway* v. *Shaik Ali Bin Awath Altway and Shaik Omar Bin Abdullah Al Tway* [1926] SSLR 11. For a close examination of the key differences between 'trust' and '*waqf*', see J. A. Schoenblum, 'The Role of Legal Doctrine in the Decline of the Islamic Waqf: A Comparison with the Trust' (1999) 32 *Vanderbilt Journal of Transnational Law* 1191.

[90] For example, subsequent law reports on lawsuits involving the Alsagoff *waqf* did not mention the testator's faith and religious intentions in establishing the *waqf*. *Re Syed Ahmed Alsagoff Deceased* [1960] MLJ 147; *Re Syed Ahmed Alsagoff, Deceased* [1962] MLJ 361; *Re Syed Ahmed Alsagoff, Deceased* [1963] MLJ 39.

[91] For an examination of the early relationship between 'trust' and '*waqf*' which began in the Crusades, see M. M. Gaudiosi, 'Comment: The Influence of the Islamic Law of Waqf on the Development of the Trust in England: The Case of Merton College' (April 1988) 136:4 *University of Pennsylvania Law Review* 1231.

subcontinent during the colonial period, emphasized that the Muslim trustee of a *waqf*, specifically known as the *mutawalli*, was in fact not a 'trustee' in the English legal sense of the word, but a 'manager' of the property that had been alienated to form a *waqf*.[92] Fyzee argued that the property that comprised the *waqf* was never vested in the figure of the *mutawalli*.[93] Unlike in an English trust, no property was ever 'conveyed' to a *mutawalli* precisely because all rights of property for the *waqf* the *mutawalli* managed were vested in divine authority.[94] Yet, the word 'trustee' constantly appeared in law reports involving the *waqfs*, instead of *mutawalli*. In contrast to Fyzee's exacting appraisal, historian Ritu Birla, took this to mean that the definition of the trust had been expanded to include those that did not require ownership of the property by the trustee. She points out how legislative debates preceding the enactment of the Indian Trusts Act of 1882 recognized that while Hindu and Islamic law was not commensurate with the English concept of 'trust', managers of indigenous endowments could be understood to be trustees in the more general sense adopted by the Act.[95] This could explain why little distinction was made between trusts and *waqfs* in law reports.

Multiple translations of wills

Rather predictably, Arab *waqfs* ran aground due to language complications. Arab testators often produced multiple wills – either simultaneous versions of the same will in different languages, or completely different wills produced at separate times which supplemented or cancelled earlier versions. Sometimes, a testator's final will would emerge to challenge another version of his will that had already been accepted by legal authorities in the Straits Settlements, although this was surprisingly rare in cases involving Hadhramis.[96] To complicate matters further,

92 According to Fyzee, '*mutawalli*' could also be translated as governor, superintendent or curator: Fyzee, *Cases in the Muhammadan Law of India and Pakistan*, above, note 43, p. 384. Historian Stephen Dale opts to use the word 'custodian' instead: S. F. Dale, 'Empires and Emporia: Palace, Mosque, Market, and Tomb in Istanbul, Isfahan, Agra, and Delhi' (2010) 53:1–2 *Journal of the Economic and Social History of the Orient* 212, 214.

93 Fyzee, ibid., p. 384.

94 Ibid., p. 386.

95 Birla, *Stages of Capital*, above, note 10, p. 82. In any case, family *waqfs* were not included in the Indian Trusts Act of 1882. F. N. Daruvala, *The Doctrine of Consideration treated Historically and Comparatively* (Calcutta: Butterworth, 1914), p. 269.

96 A will by an Indian Muslim who died in Singapore was challenged by a later version in India. *In the Estate of Vavena Katha Pillay Marican, Deceased* [1934] SSLR 281.

translations were often made by several translators, often due to testators' highly mobile lifestyle which made them subject to multiple jurisdictions that possessed their own respective official languages – both local and colonial. Sometimes, testators died in one place having established trusts in another. Even when the testator had settled in the Straits Settlements for a considerable amount of time, he tended to bear in mind his far-flung relatives connected with his trust or will and produced multiple, though not necessarily identical, versions of the same will. Complications arose due to the lack of capable translators in one location who could translate directly, or due to locations of documents and originals.

The problem of interpretation of wills in Arabic arose due to the multiple layers of translation that the will underwent before finally being accepted in probate.[97] Wills written in Arabic were often translated into Malay by one translator, then from Malay into English by another translator in the Supreme Court.[98] Not surprisingly, translations were often not identical. For example, the two wills of an Arab man named Shaik Abdullah bin Ahmad bin Ally bin al Tway Basalamah who died on 18 June 1925 in Singapore created much confusion in court as they were not identical.[99] Needless to say, erroneous probate copy of wills could have widespread repercussions through time. In the case of Syed Sheik Alkaff's will of 1910 the Malay rendering was deemed inaccurate and 'too free' by one of the judges in 1923. As a result, one of the plaintiffs' lawyers was forced to tender a revised translation of the trust deed.[100] However, even this revised translation failed to satisfy one of the judges, Judge Sproule, who was unimpressed by the oral evidence of the Malay translator, Haji Wan Abdullah, who had been called to correct the earlier translation. Sproule lamented that the man was more disposed to give opinions on Islamic law than Arabic grammar, which was his recognized area of expertise. On the other hand, he praised another Arabic translator named J. N. Mobaied, a commission agent in Singapore most probably from the Levant, who apparently knew Arabic and French very well, and

97 *Re Syed Shaik Alkaff, Deceased; Alkaff & Anor* v. *Attorney-General* [1923] MC 1.

98 In general, legal practitioners often complain about the difficulty of getting proper translations of documents written in Arabic.

99 It was not known when the English will was dated. The will in Arabic dated 31 May 1923 was proved in the Supreme Court of the Straits Settlements on 17 July 1925 while the will in English was proved separately on 18 November 1925. *The Attorney-General (On the Relation of Shaik Ali Bin Ahmad Al Tway) and Shaik Ali Bin Ahmad Al Tway* v. *Shaik Ali Bin Awath Al* [1926] SSLR 11.

100 *Re Syed Shaik Alkaff, Deceased; Alkaff & Anor* v. *Attorney-General* [1923] MC 1.

whose evidence he found to be very reliable. However, while they might be experts in Arabic grammar and etymology, translators were certainly not experts in Islamic law. In fact, translators sometimes inaccurately framed understandings of certain highly specialized legal terms with their own prejudice or ignorance. Even the supposedly reliable Mobaied was not exempted from making literal translations, oddly removed from the context of the trust deed that was heavily imbued with highly specialized Islamic legal terms.[101] For example, Mobaied emphasized to the court that the term *amur-al-khaira*, which he literally translated as *bonnes oeuvres*, meant 'nothing religious', and simply denoted 'giving something without return' or 'generosity'. By contrast, all the court judges recognized the religious intentions of establishing *waqf* and the concomitant *amur-al-khaira* specified in the deeds. Judges in the Court of Appeal sought to further refine juridical exactitude in their legal definition of the concept of *waqf* by referring to legal textbooks instead of merely relying on translators. Consequently, all three judges in the Court of Appeal consistently defined the phrase more comprehensively as 'being good works in the eyes of God as perceived by a devout Muslim'.

The case turned upon yet another crucial translation error. Mobaied translated the Arabic word *awlad* as 'children', and *ibna* as 'sons', but Judge Sproule crucially pointed out that both words were translated simply as *anak-anak* in Malay, which in fact only meant 'children' without taking gender into consideration. Gender distinction was crucial due to the different inheritance shares for male and female progeny under Islamic law. Syed Shaik Alkaff himself took pains to list the names of his sons under *ibna* and all the names of his children, male and female, under *awlad* in his will.[102]

No case reflected the complexity of multiple wills in different languages more than the case revolving around the multiple wills of an Arab merchant who made his fortune in Singapore named Syed Ahmed bin Abdul Rahman Alsagoff who died in Singapore on 27 March 1875.[103] On

101 It was likely that this was due to his lack of familiarity with the highly specific legal institution of the *waqf*.

102 One of the terms of the verdict in fact turned upon this very point. The original will stated that the condition for a granddaughter of Syed Shaik to partake from the corpus was that Syed Shaik's son had to die before him or prior to the date of the agreement. Thus although one of the testator's daughters had died, the judge ruled that her share should not go to the daughter of the deceased who was one of the defendants in this case.

103 *Syed Ali Bin Mohamed Alsagoff and Others* v. *Syed Omar Bin Mohamed Alsagoff and Others* [1918] SSLR 2.

21 December 1868 he made a will in Arabic which was annexed to his English will dated nine days later, 30 December 1868, which was subsequently proved by his son who was also his executor, Syed Mohamed Alsagoff. Both documents were admitted to probate. Rather interestingly, in the law report, the judge implied that he regarded the main will to be the one in English, with the Arabic as addendum, despite being aware that the English document was created several days after the Arabic one. It was even suggested in court that the Arabic will formed 'part of the English will' as if it was not sufficient to stand on its own.[104] The original Arabic will, produced earlier, was thus relegated to a secondary status, and the English will became the sole document referred to during more than half the trial. However, the Arabic will subsequently acquired a more important status as the Alsagoff *waqf* continued to be challenged in court through the rest of the twentieth century. During court proceedings, the judge appreciated the fact that the Arabic will contained much more precise details that clarified certain vague but key terms in the English will. For example, the term 'descendants' could only be ascertained by reading both the English and the Arabic together.[105]

IX Female testators and heirs

The class of descendants that was often the subject of debate in court was female descendants and, by extension, the issue of female descendants. Indeed, several Arab family *waqfs* tended to exclude daughters from the settlement or deliberately limit the amounts they could reap from the trust, although as long as they lived on the estate they could gain from the *waqf*.[106] In general, lineal descendants formed the main class of beneficiaries of *waqfs* established by Arab families.[107] The exclusion of

[104] *Re S A A Alsagoff, Deceased; Syed Zakaria Alsagoff & Ors* v. *R D Stewart & Ors* [1958] MLJ 264.

[105] The judge held that the testator had intended to use that expression to include the remotest generation coming into being during the prescribed period, and that on the death of the parent each succeeding generation should take, *per stirpes*, a life interest in the income until the time of distribution (subject only to the share of every male being twice that of every female, as directed by the Arabic will).

[106] Upon marriage, women tended to leave the estate and therefore lost their right to benefit from the *waqf*.

[107] Nonetheless, on the whole Tyabji's *Muhammedan Law* emphasized that a *waqf* often benefited two classes of descendants, namely women and orphans, who were often excluded from inheritance. Perhaps, in general, women did benefit more from *waqfs* established by Hadhramis in the Straits Settlements, but this was not obvious from

living daughters and granddaughters was due to the expectation that women would marry and leave the family home.[108]

Law reports indicated that women tended to reserve for themselves the right to be the first administrators of their own property, including endowments. They used this right to establish *waqf*s, and sue against infringements to their property. However, the number of cases involving female settlors was certainly small compared to that of male settlors, although women were deemed as qualified as men in their capacity as managers of endowments and it is likely that they too established *waqf*s if they had the means.[109]

There were certainly key differences between trusts established by female testators and male testators in law reports. Firstly, cases centred on female settlors tended to stand alone with little, if any, follow-up in court. In contrast, most of the other cases referred to in this chapter tended to be revisited often, as heirs periodically renewed their claims to dissolve a *waqf*, either to take advantage of changing legal administrations, or to argue against existing trustees' ineptitude or untrustworthiness in managing the trust. For example, the legal dispute involving the Alkaff family settlement was renewed about every ten years up to 2001.

Secondly, law reports indicated that a large number of widows preferred to act through proxies. These women rarely acted on their own in any capacity apart from the original act of conferring authority, either partial or complete, on their chosen representative. Often, their brothers, brothers-in-law, sons and other more distant relatives acted on their behalf in a legal capacity as powers of attorney. Hence, although law reports purported to represent the woman's voice in court, it was more likely that they were recording her representatives' claims instead. Women's independence was somewhat curtailed by the fact that male witnesses were required to be present at the preparation of official documents. The will of Raja Siti binte Kraying Chanda Pulih, the rich widow of the Arab merchant Syed Ahmad bin Abdulrahman Alsagoff, listed the names of three of her male relatives for example, although it seemed that she had full control over her property.[110]

the *waqf*s disputed in Straits Settlements courts. Tyabji, *Muhammadan Law*, above, note 15, p. 539.

108 Kozlowski, *Muslim Endowments and Society in British India*, above, note 6, p. 56.

109 Hallaq, *Sharīʿa*, above, note 14, p. 195.

110 *Syed Abbas bin Mohamed Alsagoff and Another* v. *Islamic Religious Council of Singapore (Majlis Ugama Islam Singapura)* [2009] SGHC 281.

Thirdly, law reports of cases involving female settlors' wills and deeds were more detailed than other law reports. Such attention to detail could be because female settlors were less common than male settlors. Thus their intentions might understandably need further explication. In addition, a wife had more leeway in dispersing her income as she was not bound like her husband to provide for her family. In fact, she could keep her income to herself if she so desired. Truly, it seemed that women tended to continue to disperse their income differently from male settlors when establishing a *waqf*. As a result of this freedom, a female settlor's instructions were likely to be less formulaic, and open to several permutations that had to be elucidated more explicitly.

Raja Siti's will, for example, differed from male testators' wills. Her will stated that she created a *waqf* from her houses and her mother's estate.[111] Half of the estate mentioned in the will was to go to her 'next-of-kin' according to 'laws of God and his apostle'. This was different from most *waqfs* which deliberately departed from Quranic inheritance formulas, as testators usually exploited the opportunity to specifically name the beneficiaries that often consisted of patrilineal descendants. In addition, women founded trusts that tended to benefit other women to a significant degree proportional to their entire estate.[112] Raja Siti directed the other half to be given to the mosque of her mother Alhajjah Fatima, and to mosques in the Hijaz and Taif.[113] Female settlors tended to establish trusts that benefited female relatives including parents and daughters, but also female strangers in their wills. Raja Siti bequeathed a significant portion of her estate to female descendants of the Prophet in Mecca, Madina and Taif for example. Likewise, in November 1911, another wealthy woman named Sharifah Shaikah bte Syed Omar bin Ali Aljunied bequeathed a third of her estate to be applied to purchase a house or shop and apply the income of the property to hold memorial celebrations for her, her parents and her daughter.[114] This could be

[111] It was unclear what portion this estate occupied relative to her entire property not mentioned in this particular document. Since she only delegated half of her property to her kin in her will, it was possible that she had made a separate settlement which was not addressed in the law report. Ibid.

[112] Hallaq, *Sharīʿa*, above, note 14, p. 195.

[113] The balance was to be distributed amongst her poor relatives in Singapore or elsewhere or on other charitable deeds which her executors deemed to be beneficial to her.

[114] In addition she directed that free supply of ten vessels of *zamzam* water be provided to the holy mosque of Mecca, furnishing a mat for Quran reciters every night for the period

construed as an attempt to create a sort of matrilineal system of property devolution on the part of female settlors.[115]

X Conclusion

The legal status of the *waqf* remained a contentious issue in the Straits Settlements throughout the colonial period. On 12 December 1955, lawyer J. C. Cobbett beseeched local courts to clarify laws regarding Muslim subjects in the local newspaper.[116] One of the questions he asked was 'Can a Mohammedan create a trust?'. He answered his own question by responding 'I rather doubt it unless by wakf.' This led to another related question, 'Is a wakf to be regarded as a testamentary instrument?'. Cobbett again responded to his own query, this time in the affirmative, since he believed 'there is some case authority for it'. Although the word *waqf* had often been equated with 'trust' in numerous trials, Cobbett clearly deemed the two entities to be distinct. Cobbett's second response implied that case law reinforced the status of a *waqf* as a testamentary instrument. This implied that the legal status of a *waqf* within the Straits Settlements was mainly, and perhaps only, reinforced by the several *waqf* disputes in colonial courts.

Despite their high mobility across the Indian Ocean and within the Malay Archipelago that granted them a wide array of legal avenues and jurisdictions, wealthy Arab patriarchs chose to link their families to a British colony by rooting a significant source of family wealth in the Straits Settlements. By entering their wills into probate at English courts in the Straits Settlements, and by alienating their immoveable property to form their family *waqf*s, Arab migrants constantly subjected themselves to English law which in turn significantly shaped the establishment and administration of these religious institutions. Although family *waqf*s were private religious establishments, they were not automatically relegated to the realm of personal law as they consisted of immoveable property, i.e. precious land resources in the colony. Ultimately, laws concerning the *waqf* were developed within the context of the common

between the third and the fourth prayers and engaging annually somebody to perform the pilgrimage on her behalf. *LS Investment Pte Ltd* v. *Majlis Ugama Islam Singapura* [1998] SGHC 51.

115 Unfortunately, there are insufficient law reports to corroborate this in the case of the Straits Settlements. Hallaq, *Sharīʿa*, above, note 14, p. 195.

116 J. C. Cobbett was offering a few comments on the new Marriage Bill relating to Muslims. 'The Muslim Marriage Bill', *Straits Times*, 12 December 1955, p. 6.

law trust without taking into account Islamic law at all. This was evident from the legal restrictions imposed on family *waqfs* that were derived from the common legal tradition. Firstly, *waqfs* were restricted from the outset by the English rule against perpetuities. While Hindu religious endowments were exempted from the English rule against perpetuities, the Muslim *waqfs* were not. Secondly, clauses in a family *waqf* that were deemed unambiguously charitable according to Islamic legal precepts were instead denounced as being uncharitable in English courts. The bases of these rulings were clearly not Islamic law but English common law. Influential precedents cited in these cases often involved English, Irish and Indian trusts which were already limited by English law. Not surprisingly, it was rare for *waqfs* in the Straits Settlements to be approved of in colonial courts entirely in accordance with the wishes of the testator.

By repeatedly denying posterity to family *waqfs* which could potentially alienate property perpetually, the courts functioned as state agents intent on generating as much revenue as possible for the colonial power.[117] This outright ban on perpetual trusts noticeably represented direct state intervention into the family and religious domain.[118] Here, we see a tension between the political goal of placating religious communities and the practical desire to conserve modes of production, in which the structures of family and community, organized labour, investment

117 After all, even when freehold and leasehold property was privately owned by individual residents, it was usually held under either 99 years' or 999 years' lease from the government. In his seminal book on *waqfs* in British India, Gregory Kozlowski touches upon the debate on trusts in England which had two opposing poles represented by John Stuart Mill, who supported trusts, and Lord Hobhouse, at the other end. It was Adam Smith's influential idea that the interest of the state requires that lands should be as much in commerce as any other goods, for when land is in commerce and frequently changes hands it is most likely to be well managed. Needless to say, this belief is the antithesis of the *waqf*. However, wealthy landowners in England were able to circumvent this restriction by agreeing to accept a specific income from an estate while renouncing the right to sell or alienate the property that formed the basis of the family's wealth. This was renewed every third generation and limited in force to thirty years after the death of the most junior participant in the entail. Technically this did not therefore violate the rule forbidding perpetuities. However, in the colonies, legal authorities were more mindful of such wily tactics. Kozlowski, *Muslim Endowments and Society in British India*, above, note 6, pp. 148–9.

118 Nicholas Dirks debunked the colonial myth that law was autonomous in practice by arguing that law was a powerful arm of the state because it appeared to be autonomous, seemingly separate from the government arm of the colonial state. N. B. Dirks, 'From Little King to Landlord: Property, Law and the Gift under the Madras Permanent Settlement' (April 1986) 28:2 *Comparative Studies in Society and History* 307, 322–3.

and exchange had to balanced.[119] As a compromise, *waqfs* that started out as perpetual trusts were mostly allowed to continue to exist, but in a limited fashion, in order to abide by English law.

The legal structure in the Straits Settlements, which allowed the testator to establish the *waqf*, simultaneously paved the way towards its dissolution. As a result of the peculiar status of the *waqf* that mainly consisted of immoveable property in the Straits Settlements, litigants who wished to challenge the status of an existing *waqf* were guaranteed a legal forum in the form of colonial courts that could potentially be hostile to *waqfs*. Nonetheless, it could not be said that litigants wholeheartedly embraced the colonial court's power to adjudicate *waqf* matters. After all, the colonial court was the only formal legal recourse sanctioned by the ruling government in the Straits Settlements for any kind of legal dispute, a colonial reality that Muslim subjects were aware of. English law was appealed to in other issues as well, outside the scope of this chapter.[120] Only rulings meted out by colonial courts were legally binding in the Straits Settlements. In light of colonial legal realities, Arab litigants perhaps had no choice but to subject the *waqf* consisting of immoveable property to a colonial legal system devoid of religious considerations. In any case, there were no clear winners or losers in each legal dispute since English law would have benefited some, while Islamic law would have allowed others to gain.

119 M. R. Anderson, 'Classifications and Coercions: Themes in South Asian Legal Studies in the 1980s' (November 1990) 10:2 *South Asia Research* 158, 163–4.

120 In one particular case involving an absent trustee of an Islamic religious *waqf* (a mosque), a Muslim letter-writer cited an English law that stated that a trustee must be consecutively absent for more than 12 months before he lost his position: 'Letter from A Mohamedan to the Editor', *Straits Times*, 2 December 1911, p. 10.

9

Zionist settlers and the English private trust in Mandate Palestine

ADAM HOFRI-WINOGRADOW

I Introduction: colonized settlers and the colonizer's law

The basic colonial encounter involved a colonizing power and colonized locals. Some colonial situations were more complex, involving a third element: settlers of non-local stock originating in an ethnos, or nation, different from that with which the colonizer was identified. Two prominent examples from the annals of the British Empire are the French inhabitants of Nouvelle France after France ceded it to the British in 1763, and the Dutch inhabitants of the Cape Colony after the British conquest of 1806. The British typically permitted such settler populations to retain at least parts of the laws to which they were accustomed, which laws were often based on the laws of the settlers' jurisdiction of origin. As regards settler use of English law, the English sometimes provided for the application of parts of it to non-British settlers, while blocking such settlers' attempts to use other parts. The part of English law most commonly applied to non-British colonial subjects, both settlers and natives, was commercial law, in order to facilitate commerce between different parts of the Empire. The parts least commonly applied to such inhabitants were family law, land law and the law of inheritance.[1]

[1] For colonial powers' conservative bias, keeping much of pre-conquest law in place as regards both the native population and settlers unassociated with the conquering power, see L. Benton, *Law and Colonial Cultures: Legal Regimes in World History, 1400–1900* (Cambridge University Press, 2002), p. 2; for the British colonial preference for installing English commercial law in the colonies, see T. O. Elias, *British Colonial Law: A Comparative Study of the Interactions Between English and Local Laws in British Dependencies* (London: Stevens & Sons, 1962), p. 128; for the British colonial preference for keeping the pre-conquest family law, land law and law of inheritance in place, see ibid., pp. 50–1, 143, 199, and S. E. Merry, 'From Law and Colonialism to Law and Globalization' (2003) 28 *Law & Social Inquiry* 572. For the 'continuum with respect to the likelihood of transplantation', starting with commercial law as likeliest to be transplanted and ending with family law as the least likely, see R. Harris and M. Crystal, 'Some

Trust law, at the intersection of those four disciplines, was a special case. This essay describes the attempts of the Zionist settler population of Mandate Palestine to use the common law private trust, the Mandate government's response and the settlers' resulting preference for trust companies over individual trusteeship, while occasionally using the latter despite the government's disapproval. Other British-ruled non-British settler populations, such as the French of Lower Canada and the Dutch of the Cape Colony, had the English private trust available to them as a result of their British rulers having made it available to the British settlers in the same territories.[2] Native populations, too, such as those of British-controlled India and Ceylon, were eventually permitted to use the English trust, both private and charitable. Building on the Indian and Ceylonese examples, one can construct a model of the typical process by which the English trust has been received in colonial legal systems. Non-British inhabitants' use of the English trust was first legitimized and facilitated by the colonial courts' applying the English law of trusts to disputes regarding natives' trusts. Concurrently, colonial draftsmen made incidental references to the trust in colonial legislation. Eventually, comprehensive trust codes were enacted.[3] As regards the reception of the English private trust in Mandate Palestine, only the second element of this model – incidental legislative references to the trust – occurred. Case-law-based reception was stopped in its tracks by an unsympathetic Chief Justice. While judicial hostility did not stop Zionist settlers in Palestine from actively using the English private trust, it did prevent codification of the subject for the duration of the Mandate.

Zionist settlers in Palestine had fewer reasons to abstain from using the English trust than settler populations such as the Canadian French or the South African Dutch. Unlike those populations, Zionist settlers were not attached to any pre-existing legal system or tradition to which the English trust did not belong. The Zionists had no metropole, from which they ventured to Palestine and to the law of which they were attached.

Reflections on the Transplantation of British Company Law in Post-Ottoman Palestine' (2009) 10 *Theoretical Inquiries in Law* 561, 562–4 and sources cited therein.

2 For the reception of the English trust in Lower Canada (later the province of Quebec), see D. W. M. Waters, M. R. Gillen and L. D. Smith, *Waters' Law of Trusts in Canada*, 4th edn (Toronto: Thomson-Carswell, 2012), p. 1413; for its partial reception in the Cape Colony, see T. Honoré and E. Cameron, *Honoré's South African Law of Trusts*, 4th edn (Cape Town: JUTALaw, 1992), pp. 15–16; T. Honoré, 'Trust', in R. Zimmermann and D. Visser (eds.), *Southern Cross: Civil Law and Common Law in South Africa* (Oxford University Press, 1996), pp. 849, 851–63.

3 See discussion at p. 226 below.

Zionist immigration to Palestine came, during the Mandate era, principally from the USSR, Poland, Germany, and other Eastern and Central European countries, where Jews often suffered persecution, some of which was brought to bear by legal officers and was even directly expressed in the law.[4] The Jews exiting those countries generally had no attachment to their law. Neither were they attached to the late-Ottoman law which prevailed in Palestine before the British conquest. Nor were they attached to any form of Jewish law: most Mandate-era Zionist immigrants to Palestine had no intention of submitting to either the traditional Rabbinical law (*halacha*) or the Rabbis who controlled it. Attempts to fashion a Westernized, up-to-date version of Jewish law, rebranded as 'Hebrew law', failed. As Ronen Shamir put it, 'at the height of establishing, reinventing, and dreaming the resurrection of a Jewish nation in Palestine, many Zionists rejected Jewish law, even at its renewed Hebrew-national appearance, and enthusiastically embraced the law of the British-governed colonial state of Palestine'.[5] At least some of them wanted this embrace to include the common law private trust.

That unusually ravenous Zionist appetite for the forms of English law met, in Palestine, a circumscribed, tentative and cautious British colonial government. The British, having conquered Palestine in 1917–18, governed it from 1922–48 as an 'A' Mandate entrusted to them by the League of Nations. Under that Mandate they undertook both to 'facilitate Jewish immigration ... and ... encourage ... close settlement by Jews on the land' and 'ensur[e] ... that the rights and position of other sections of the population are not prejudiced'.[6] They further promised that '[r]espect for the personal status of the various peoples and communities and for their religious interests shall be fully guaranteed. In particular, the control and administration of Wakfs [Islamic trusts] shall be exercised in accordance with religious law and the dispositions of the founders.'[7] Accordingly, the British largely left in place the existing panoply of religious community courts, each vested with exclusive jurisdiction over its community members' matters of personal

[4] For the history of Jewish Zionist immigration to Palestine during the Mandate era, see M. Lissak et al. (eds.), *The History of the Jewish Community in Eretz-Israel since 1882: The British Mandate Period: Part One* (Jerusalem: Mossad Bialik, 1993).

[5] R. Shamir, *The Colonies of Law: Colonialism, Zionism and Law in Early Mandate Palestine* (Cambridge University Press, 2000), p. 4.

[6] Mandate for Palestine and Transjordan, s. 6. The text of the Mandate is printed in N. Bentwich, *The Mandates System* (London: Longmans, 1930), pp. 137–45.

[7] Ibid., s. 8.

status.[8] Private law matters were, in principle, left to be governed by the *shari'a*-based Ottoman Civil Code, the Mejelle.[9]

Straddling the part of the law which has been most deeply Anglicized in Palestine (commercial law) and those parts which have been least Anglicized (family law, land law and the law of inheritance), trust law provided a challenge for the territory's British rulers.[10] The law as it stood on the eve of the British conquest knew one key form of trust, the Islamic *waqf*; even Palestinian Jews and Christians made, during the Ottoman era, use of the *waqf*.[11] The British gave Palestine's Jewish (Rabbinical) and Christian religious courts exclusive jurisdiction over the 'constitution and internal administration' of Rabbinical trusts (*hekdeshim*) and Christian religious trusts, respectively.[12] As Palestine's Muslim majority continued, during the Mandate era, to prefer the *waqf* over other forms of trust,[13] it was the Zionist settlers in Palestine who, more than other parts of its population, used the English private trust and trust company. Law reports, court files, period newspapers and archival materials show those settlers using them frequently, energetically and effectively for a great variety of purposes. Much, though by no means all, of the use of the common law trust and trust company by Zionist settlers in Palestine was focused on facilitating Zionist settlement in Palestine: private initiatives and official Zionist organs

[8] Palestine Order in Council 1922, ss. 47, 51–7, 64–5 (hereafter: 'Palestine Order in Council'). The text of the instrument is printed in Bentwich, *The Mandates System*, above, note 6, pp. 146–65.

[9] A. Likhovski, *Law and Identity in Mandate Palestine* (Chapel Hill: University of North Carolina Press, 2006), pp. 55–8.

[10] The process of partial Anglicization and the development of Mandate-era Palestinian law more generally have been the subject of several essays and monographs. Three highlights are E. Malchi, *The History of Law in Eretz-Israel*, 2nd edn (Tel Aviv: Dinim, 1953); Shamir, *Colonies of Law*, above, note 5; and Likhovski, *Law and Identity*, above, note 9.

[11] Ron Shaham, 'Christian and Jewish "Waqf" in Palestine during the Late Ottoman Period' (1991) 54 *Bulletin of the School of Oriental and African Studies* 460.

[12] The Palestine Order in Council gave non-Muslim communities' religious community courts exclusive jurisdiction over the 'constitution and internal administration' of religious trusts constituted before those courts according to the religious legal traditions they applied: §53(3) of the Palestine Order in Council, concerning Rabbinical Courts, §54(3) of the Palestine Order in Council, concerning Christian Ecclesiastical Courts. The *shari'a* courts were, similarly, granted exclusive jurisdiction in cases regarding the constitution or internal administration of a *waqf* constituted for the benefit of Muslims before a Muslim Religious Court: ibid., §52.

[13] For the development of Palestinian *waqfs* during the Mandate era see Y. Reiter, *Islamic Endowments in Jerusalem under British Mandate* (London: Frank Cass, 1996).

competed in funnelling both Jews and Jewish funds from the Jewish Diaspora to the site of the promised 'National Home'.[14]

Part of the value of this study, then, is in providing a particularly sharp example of a colonial population adopting more of the colonizer's own law than that colonizer was willing to have it use. This dynamic is one reason for my exclusive focus on Zionist settlers' engagement with the common law private trust. The Arab and non-Zionist Jewish populations preferred trust forms (the *waqf* and *hekdesh* respectively) which were not derived from the Mandatory power's metropolitan legal system. It may have not been accidental that the English trust, which, as Maitland noted, 'perhaps forms the most distinctive achievement of English lawyers',[15] proved a major sticking point in the Anglicization of the law of Palestine: the Mandate government never intended that Anglicization to be complete, and perhaps some British colonial officials saw the trust as too peculiarly Anglo-Saxon for such a blatantly non-Anglo-Saxon population, which already had its own indigenous forms of trust. On the other hand, as we shall see, it may be that the British colonial courts of Palestine's eventual rejection of settlers' attempts to use the common law private trust was largely a result of the wrong test case having been ill-argued before the wrong judge.[16] One key English legal idea the British did introduce to Palestine was the doctrine of precedent. A single Supreme Court decision rejecting the use of the English private trust in Palestine could thus bring about, if cited and applied in later cases, a complete derailment of the reception process.[17]

Part II describes how one of the leading lawyers of Palestine's Zionist settler community, Mordechai Eliash, tried and failed to have a conveyance of land to trustees on a conventional family trust of the English type registered at the Jerusalem land registry. Eliash having taken his case to the Supreme Court of Palestine, the Court produced an oblique decision, which could be construed as saying that the English private trust had not

[14] The British government had, in a declaration made on 2 November 1917, and again in the text of the Mandate for Palestine and Transjordan, declared its favourable view 'of the establishment in Palestine of a national home for the Jewish people': see Bentwich, *The Mandates System*, above, note 6, p. 137 (preamble).

[15] F. W. Maitland, 'Uses and Trusts', in *Equity: A Course of Lectures*, revsd. by J. Brunyate (Cambridge University Press, 1936).

[16] See text accompanying notes 77–9 below.

[17] For the workings of Mandate-era Palestinian case law, and their impact on the reception of English legal ideas in the law of Palestine, see Likhovski, *Law and Identity*, above, note 9, pp. 61–83.

been received into the law of Palestine. Eliash's attempts to correct this result by legislative action failed. Some Mandate-era Palestinian legislation did, nevertheless, refer to the trust concept in private, rather than charitable, contexts, and the courts did occasionally use the concept as if it was part of the law of Palestine, thus creating an uneven and unpredictable 'partial reception'. I compare the British authorities' Palestinian approach with their greater readiness to introduce the English private trust into the law of other colonies and mandated territories. In Part III, I describe the use Zionist settlers in Palestine made of private trusts and trust companies throughout the 1930s and 1940s, for business, investment, land-purchase and construction purposes. Trust companies were also key to the Zionist movement's 1930s effort to help Germany's Jews escape Nazi Germany with as much as possible of their property intact. During the 1940s, trusts became, as I show in Part IV, a key locus of debate among Palestine's burgeoning community of Zionist settler jurists. Leading legal academics and practitioners debated both whether English-style private trusts were part of Palestine's then-current law, and whether they should be a part of the law of the future Jewish state. Part V concludes.

II A lawyer rebuffed: Mordechai Eliash's family trust and the Mandate authorities

Mordechai Eliash was born in the Russian Empire in 1892, attended law school in both Berlin and Oxford, and immigrated to Palestine in 1919. A prominent figure of Religious Zionism at a time when most Zionists were not observant and most observant Jews were not Zionist, he quickly became one of the leading lawyers of Mandate Palestine.[18] Having in 1925 purchased 5.04 *dunums* of land in Ram, a village north of Jerusalem, he sought in 1931 to transfer the land to trustees – his brother, banker Alexander Eliash, and his employee, Adv. Moshe Kehati – on trusts fairly similar to those of a conventional English

[18] For Eliash's professional status see, e.g., N. Brun, *Judges and Lawyers in Eretz Israel, between Constantinople and Jerusalem, 1900–1930* (Jerusalem: Magnes, 2008), p. 360, note 51. For biographical information see G. Strassman, *'Ote ha-Glima: Toldot Arikhat ha-Din be-Eretz Yisra'el* [Wearing the Robes: A History of the Legal Profession to 1962] (Tel Aviv: Israel Bar Press, 1984), pp. 26–31, 303–4. For the Eliash papers see Central Zionist Archives (CZO), Mordechai Eliash Private Archive File List, available at www.zionistarchives.org.il/ZA/showpad.aspx?PageId=25&ParamId=A417Eliash,Mordecai&-Flag=4. The Eliash papers make up class A417 at the CZO.

family trust.[19] In February, the trustees applied to the Director of Lands, Jerusalem, asking that he register the transaction.[20] Five months later, the Acting Director of Lands, Moshe Doukhan, denied their application.[21]

Doukhan did not provide reasons for his decision. A property law textbook he published in 1935 hints at what may have been his reasoning. The land Eliash sought to dedicate was *miri* land, the full ownership of which was (according to Ottoman land law, which still applied, subject to Mandate-era amendments, in Palestine) vested in the Sultan or state. Private 'owners' of *miri*, like Eliash, were the state's tenants, though able to sell their land, mortgage it and pass it to their heirs. Ottoman statutes specifically provided that 'owners' of *miri* could neither bequeath it nor dedicate it as a *waqf*, and Doukhan extended this rule to the English trust, noting that '[i]n practice the Land Registry refuses to allow the registration of a trust of Miri, relying upon the general provisions of the Ottoman Law'.[22] He may have been referring to his own decision in Eliash's application. Other features of the legal background provide further likely reasons for Doukhan's decision. The trustees' petition, seeking to transfer land in Palestine to trustees of an English-style private

[19] The trusts were: first to Alexander Eliash, to secure his collection of debts Mordechai owed to him; next the income to be paid to Mordechai for 20 years (his then-expected lifespan); then the income to be paid, in equal shares, to Mordechai's two children for life (his widow was to have a quarter of the income for her lifetime); and finally a share of capital equivalent to the share of income allocated to each of the two children to be distributed, on the death of each child, to his or her issue, in shares as that child should in his or her will direct or, in the absence of a direction, equally. Some drafting imperfections, such as the repeated use of 'settler' for 'settlor', may be evidence for the draftsman's inexperience with such trusts. The draft trust deed is in Israel State Archives (ISA), case file for HCJ 77/31 *Eliash* v. *Director of Land* (hereafter: *Eliash* case file). On Alexander Eliash see Y. Rephael, 'Alexander Eliash', in *Encyclopedia of Religious Zionism* (Jerusalem, Rav Kook Institute, 1972), vol. IV, pp. 185–6.

[20] Letter of 23 February 1931, in *Eliash* case file.

[21] Letter of 10 July 1931, in *Eliash* case file.

[22] F. M. Goadby and M. J. Doukhan, *The Land Law of Palestine* (Tel Aviv: Shoshany's Printing Co., 1935), p. 94. The 'general provisions' referred to were article 121 of the Land Code of 7 Ramadan, 1274 A.H., and article 8 of the Provisional Law on Holding Real Estate of 5 Jamada Awal, 1331 A.H. Both provide that *miri* land may not be dedicated as *waqf*. An English translation of the Ottoman Land Code is available: *The Ottoman Land Code. Translated from the Turkish by Frederick Ongley* (London: Clowes and Sons, 1892). I thank one of the reviewers for the *Law and History Review* for referring me to Doukhan's book. For a discussion of the Ottoman *miri* regime see M. Bunton, *Colonial Land Policies in Palestine, 1917–1936* (Oxford University Press, 2007), pp. 36–7.

family trust, was at least rare and possibly unprecedented.[23] Its legal basis was shaky, as the reception of the English private trust into the law of Mandate Palestine was, at the time, an open question. Palestinian law knew some other types of trust. Islamic *waqfs* had been commonplace for centuries.[24] The Mandate administration had in 1924 created, by Ordinance, a civil (non-religious) legal regime to govern charitable trusts.[25] This Charitable Trusts Ordinance, drafted by Doukhan's 1935 co-author, Frederic Goadby, Director of the Mandate government's law school, in consultation with Palestine's first Attorney-General, Norman Bentwich, was 'modeled on the Ceylon Trusts Ordinance of 1917', carefully stripping this source of the majority of its provisions, which dealt with private, rather than charitable, trusts.[26] The decision to restrict Palestine's English-inspired statutory civil trusts regime to charitable trusts was explained by Herbert Samuel, High Commissioner at the time:

> It is believed that only a small number of English persons in the country will desire to create private trusts. Palestinians regularly use the institution of the wakf for the purpose of family settlements; and it does not appear expedient to encourage the introduction of a different system.[27]

Not anticipating the frequent use of private trusts for business and investment purposes in 1930s Palestine, this reasoning, focused exclusively on family settlements, made for the omission of the private trust from Palestine's Trusts Ordinance. That Ordinance was not the only one, however, to mention the trust: incidental use was made of the term 'trust' in several other ordinances enacted by 1931. Six of those references seem to refer to non-charitable trusts: the Companies

23 I have found no trace of an earlier application of this sort; later attempts would have been stymied by the *Eliash* precedent.

24 There is a rich literature on the use of *waqfs* in Palestine. The key work for the Mandate era is Reiter, *Islamic Endowments*, above, note 13.

25 Ordinance to Regulate Charitable Trusts Established Otherwise than in Conformity with Religious Law 1924, 1 *Legislation of Palestine, 1918–1925* (Norman Bentwich compiler, 1926), p. 120.

26 The modelling of the Palestinian Ordinance on the Ceylonese one is mentioned in N. Bentwich, 'Memorandum on the Amendments of the Charitable Trusts Ordinance proposed by the Chief Justice', UK National Archives (hereafter: UKNA), CO 733/75, 188. Bunton, *Colonial Land*, above, note 22, at 15, mentioned the Ceylonese origins of the Palestinian ordinance, referring to page 185 of the same collection of minute sheets which contains Bentwich's Memo. Goadby's draftsmanship is established by R. H. Drayton, Assistant Attorney General, 'Memorandum Regarding the Amendments Proposed by the Chief Justice', UKNA, CO 733/73 (9 September 1924), 1.

27 Letter of 27 March 1925, UKNA, CO 733/91/15719, 152, pp. 1–2, paragraph 3.

Ordinance of 1929 specifically grants all companies the power to act as trustees, as well as referring to the use of trustees in the employee compensation scheme, debenture and winding-up contexts.[28] The Partnerships Ordinance of 1930 discusses first the consequences of 'a partner being a trustee improperly employ[ing] trust property in the business or on the account of the partnership', and later notes that while on the death of a partner, 'legal interest[s] in any land which belongs to the partnership' shall pass according to the law of succession, the heirs shall hold that interest 'in trust' for the surviving partners.[29] While the first and fifth of those six instances can be reasonably read to refer to charitable rather than private trusts, the other four, three of which use the term 'trust' in specific company law contexts, cannot.[30]

28 Companies Ordinance No. 18 of 1929, *Official Gazette*, 15 May 1929, 378, gives, in subsections (o) and (w) of Schedule II, all companies the power to act as trustees unless that power is specifically excluded in a company's memorandum of association. Section 98(1)(b) permits 'the provision by a Company ... of money for the purchase by trustees of fully-paid shares in the Company to be held by or for the benefit of employees of the Company'. Ss. 124 and 128 mention trustees in the debenture context, and s. 180 mentions them in the winding-up context. The term 'trust' is further mentioned in ss. 29(2) ('No notice of any trust express, implied or constructive shall be entered on the register or receivable by the Registrar in respect of any Company'), 77, voiding provisions exempting officers of companies from, or indemnifying them against, liability in respect of, e.g., breaches of trust in relation to the company, 78(1) and (3), giving the Court power to exempt directors and trustees from liability for, e.g., breaches of trust, and 79(1) and (3), which create two kinds of statutory constructive trusts. For the history of the Ordinance see Harris and Crystal, 'Some Reflections', above, note 1.

29 Partnership Ordinance, No. 19 of 1930, *Official Gazette*, Gazette Extraordinary, 8 August 1930, 646, at ss. 20 and 29(2) respectively. For discussion of s. 29(2) see Z. Tzeltner, 'The Private Trust in Israel' (1960) 15 *Ha'Praklit* 214, 225–7.

30 The term 'trust' was further mentioned in legislation referring to public-owned land. The parent provision in this context was §12(1) of the Palestine Order in Council, which provided that '[a]ll rights in or in relation to any public lands shall vest in and may be exercised by the High Commissioner for the time being in trust for the Government of Palestine'. Another prominent Mandate-era use of the term 'trust' was in C. A. Hooper's much-used translation of the *Mejelle*, the Ottoman Civil Code: C. A. Hooper, *The Civil Law of Palestine and Trans-Jordan* (London: Azriel Press, 1938). Hooper translated the title to Book VI as 'Trusts and Trusteeship' (ibid., p. 185), despite its subject matter being, more generally, possession of another's effects, as of a found object by the person finding it; the Ottoman Turkish title to Book VI is 'émanet', Young's French translation being 'Des choses confiées à autrui': G. Young, *Corps de Droit Ottoman*, vol. VI (Oxford: Clarendon Press, 1906), p. 278. The term was used in other Mandate-era English translations of Ottoman legislation applicable in Mandate Palestine: see article 236 of the Ottoman Penal Code of 1859, in both: (i) C. G. Walpole, trans. (from the French), *The Ottoman Penal Code, 28 Zilhijeh 1274* (London: Clowes and Sons, 1888), and

Only two of the six seem, however, to have been the results of a conscious decision to use the English concept of a trust in the law of Palestine, outside the charity context. Palestinian legislation on issues not unique to Palestine was largely put together by cutting and pasting provisions from existing English and colonial enactments. This method of legislation was prone to inadvertent reception: the incorporation of English and colonial legal concepts, formulations and rules into Palestinian statute absent an explicit, considered decision to do so. While Government of Palestine and Colonial Office personnel seem to have generally been quite careful in composing Palestinian Ordinances, some details appear to have slipped in inadvertently. This may have been most likely to happen with the longest and most technical of Ordinances, such as the Companies Ordinance.[31] Though much documentation having to do with the drafting of this Ordinance has been lost,[32] we know it was drafted by Henry Nathan, of the London law office of Oppenheimer and Nathan, based, principally, on the UK Companies (Consolidation) Act 1908, and the 1926 Report of the UK Company Law Amendment Committee of 1925–6.[33] Nearly all the Ordinance's provisions where trusts are mentioned can in fact be traced, either to equivalent provisions in the 1908 Act, or to recommendations in the Report.[34] Nathan, who repeatedly expressed an agenda of conforming the commercial law of Palestine as nearly as may be to that of England,[35] seems to have

(ii) J. A. S. Bucknill and H. Apisoghom, trans. (from the Turkish), *The Imperial Ottoman Penal Code* (London: Humphrey Milford, 1913). Both translators used the term 'trust'.

31 The post-1931 case of the elaborate Income Tax Ordinance of 1941 seems to have been similar: see discussion at text to notes 61–2.

32 '[T]he Government of Palestine files on the drafting of that Ordinance have been lost . . . [t]he first in a series of four files created at the Colonial Office in London is also lost. The second covers . . . a stage at which the third draft of the ordinance was already distributed and a fourth was being drafted': Harris and Crystal, 'Some Reflections', above, note 1, 571.

33 Cmd. 2657. For the drafting of the Palestinian Ordinance and its sources see Harris and Crystal, 'Some Reflections', above, note 1, 571–3.

34 S. 29 of the Palestine Ordinance is derived from s. 27 of the Companies (Consolidation) Act 1908, 8 Edw. 7, c. 69; s. 78(1) of the former is derived from s. 279 of the latter; s. 124(2) from s. 102(2); and s. 180 from s. 164. S. 98(1)(b) of the Palestine Ordinance originated in para. 31 of the Report; s. 77 originated in para. 47, and s. 128 in para. 66.

35 He professed himself 'certainly inclined to the opinion that it is desirable that the English and the Palestinian Law should, so far as possible, be formulated in the same phrases': his letter to Lloyd of the Colonial Office, Middle East Department, 20 October 1927, in UKNA, CO 733/133. He took for granted that the law of the metropole and the law of the Mandated territory should be substantially identical. As Nathan sent his fifth and final draft to Sir John Shuckburgh of the Colonial Office, he wrote, '[Y]ou will observe that I have revised [the draft Ordinance] so as to bring

regarded the uses of the trust in the commercial sphere as of a piece with the rest of English commercial law. Though the Ordinance went through five elaborate drafts, with Bentwich and a 'committee of local [Palestinian] advocates' criticizing various details as too complex for the circumstances of Palestine, or otherwise inappropriate, there seems to have been no discussion regarding the references to the trust.[36]

There was, contrastingly, some such discussion apropos the two references to the trust in the Partnerships Ordinance, which was also drafted by Nathan, 'based on the English Partnership Act 1890, and certain provisions of the English common law'.[37] As to one of those two references, Bentwich noted that 'it would be better to omit this section because the notion of trust property, save in regard to charitable trusts, is scarcely developed in Palestine'. Colonial Office staff replied that '[t]rust may arise from many other circumstances than [sic] from express creation and is certain to be evolved in Palestine. Though the idea may be [better?] explained, it is recommended that the section be retained.' As to the other draft section that mentioned the trust, Bentwich noted that the '[s]ection . . . should be omitted because the terms used are not current in the law of Palestine and may lead to confusion; while the courts should apply the general principle which is embodied in the subsection without express direction'. Colonial Office staff replied that '[t]he terms may not now be in use in Palestine but they are convenient terms and represent circumstances which certainly may exist in Palestine. The section might be retained.'[38] Both sections were retained in the Ordinance as promulgated. A 'London' approach, adopted by Nathan and the Colonial Office, favouring the transplantation of the whole of English commercial law, including the commercial uses of the trust, into Palestine, thus prevailed over Samuel's and Bentwich's 'Palestinian' approach, which saw no need in burdening the already-complicated Palestinian legal system with the English law of private trusts. Colonial office staff, replying to Bentwich,

it as far as possible into accord with the English law as it now stands amended by the recent Companies Act 1928': letter dated 28 November 1928, entitled 'Your Ref. 57037/28', UKNA, CO 733/145.

36 The correspondence is in UKNA, CO 733/145.

37 N. Bentwich, 'Explanatory Note on the Partnership Ordinance', ISA, file M-283/26.

38 Bentwich's comments are in his 'Note on the Draft Partnership Ordinance', in UKNA, CO 733/145/18, at 23–4; the first refers to s. 19 of Nathan's draft (the later s. 20), and the second to s. 28(2) (the later s. 29(2)). The comments in reply are in a document in the same file entitled 'Memorandum upon Mr. Bentwich's Note on the Draft Partnership Ordinance', at 6–7.

predicted that the judicially imposed, remedial forms of trust, resulting and constructive, shall be the most useful in Palestine.

While some commercial uses of the English private trust were thus legislatively transplanted into Palestine, the private family trust, such as Eliash attempted to create, was quite consciously left out of the Palestinian (Charitable) Trusts Ordinance. This lack of legislative transplantation did not necessarily mean, however, that the private family trust could not be used in Palestine; there were other means of transplantation. In legal systems, like Mandate Palestine's, which recognize judicial decisions as a source of law, legal institutions can also be received into the local system by way of judicial decisions recognizing and legitimating their use. On explaining the decision to omit the private trust from the Palestinian Trusts Ordinance, Samuel noted that

> [a]ny person is free to constitute a trust in the English form, and should a question arise in the Courts about such a trust, the English law would doubtless be applied in accordance with the provisions of Article 46 of the Palestine Order in Council.[39]

Article 46 provided that subject to Ottoman law and to legislation enacted by the Mandate Government, the civil courts of Palestine were to apply 'the substance of the common law, and the doctrines of equity in force in England'.[40] Until 1931, the civil courts seem not to have met with an attempt to 'constitute' a private family trust 'in the English form'. They did, in at least two cases, employ the English private variety of trust; but one, a District Court decision later decisively reversed by the Supreme Court of Palestine, was a partnership case, and the other, a decision of the Supreme Court itself, dealt with a bankruptcy.[41] Neither

39 Samuel, letter, above, note 27.

40 The Palestine Order in Council, article 46. For a careful study of this provision and its construction by Mandate-era courts, see Likhovski, *Law and Identity*, above, note 9, pp. 61–83; id., 'In Our Image: Colonial Discourse and the Anglicization of the Law of Mandatory Palestine' (1995) 29 *Israel L Rev* 291.

41 Both decisions are unreported. The district court decision is quoted in the report of the Supreme Court decision which reversed it: CA 35/31 *Israel Lieber* v. *Jacob and Sheftel Mirenberg* 5 COJ 1811 [1931]. The following description is based on materials in the case files (now in the ISA) for that case and CA 131/30 *Israel Lieber* v. *Jacob and Sheftel Mirenberg*. The parties had entered into partnership 'for the manufacture of chocolate' and the partnership agreement set up a 'Board of Managers' of which Lieber and Sheftel Mirenberg were members, but Lieber acted without his partners' consent in managing the firm, having physically expelled them from the factory. They filed suit, asking that the Tel Aviv district court either order Lieber to manage the firm subject to Sheftel Mirenberg's consent, or 'restrain [Lieber] from the management of the undertaking and ... appoint

dealt with a private family trust. Against this background, and considering that the Mandate regime had by 1931 legislated many other institutions, rules and principles of English law into the law of Palestine, 'receiving' them in no uncertain terms,[42] the reception of the English private trust was, at best, halting, and was confined to the commercial context. Doukhan's dismissal of the would-be trustees' application fits this trend.

Why, then, did Eliash attempt what he must have known was an extremely unusual step? His private correspondence provides a clue. Nine days after Doukhan sent his response, Eliash responded to an enquiry by a relative, Yosef Eliash of Hadera, who asked Mordechai to find a way to have Yosef's land pass, after his death, other than to his heirs-at-law. Mordechai's response, in which he refers to his attempt to transfer his own land to trustees and have the transfer registered, makes clear that the grounds for that attempt were, precisely, that like Yosef's

a receiver in order to manage [the factory]'. The Court held that '[i]n view of the security [Lieber gave] and of the nature of the business we are of opinion that to appoint a receiver would not be a proper remedy . . . [n]either do we think it proper to restrain [Lieber] from the management', and chose instead to constitute Lieber 'trustee for all parties'. The Supreme Court reversed, holding that '[w]e know of no power either under English or Ottoman Law whereby such an appointment can be made, nor indeed, do we understand the effect of such an appointment' (all quotations from the Supreme Court decision in CA 35/31, p. 1812). The Supreme Court decision referred to in the text is CA 50/31 *Ibrahim Eff. Kamal (Syndic in the Bankruptcy of Abdel Mou'ti Ghneim)* v. *Adib Eff. Daudi*, unreported, delivered 14 October 1931. As this decision was described in CA 92/29 (Jaffa) *Arieh Gurevitz* v. *Anglo-Palestine Co. Ltd*, 1 COJ 228, 230–1 [1932]. '[i]n that case . . . Respondent . . . received and collected the proceeds of bills drawn in his favour by one Taher el Masri . . . Appellant, who was the Syndic in the bankruptcy of Abdel Mu'ti Chnesim, alleged that the Respondent [was] acting under instructions from Taher, who owed money to the bankrupt [and] was applying the proceeds of the bills for the benefit of the bankrupt, in fraud of his creditors . . . It was held in so far as it might be proved that the Respondent held such proceeds in trust, he did so as trustee not for the bankrupt but for Taher . . .'. The final sentence, from 'in so far', appears verbatim in the original decision, which I have located in the case file, available in the ISA. The courts used the term 'trust' in at least two more cases, but not in ways clearly implying their reception and use of the English concept of a private trust. In CA 42/29 *Olaf Erickson Lind* v. *Vester & Co., the American Colony Stores* 5 COJ 1808 [1930], the parties having agreed that defendants held property on trust for appellants, both the District and Supreme Courts held the trust not to be charitable, but did not specify what type of trust it was. Trusteeship was also mentioned in LJa 191/21 *Arthur Henry Finn* v. *Government of Palestine* 5 COJ 1802 [1929] but in the context of the law of deeds of arrangement rather than in that of private trusts.

42 For a general description of the reception process, see Malchi, *History of Law*, above, note 10, pp. 77–180.

land, Mordechai's land was *miri*. Since *miri* land could not be bequeathed, Mordechai attempted to structure the provision he wanted to make for his children out of his land by creating a private trust of that land.[43] He must have hoped that the Director of Lands, or, if need be, the courts, would not extend the prohibition on bequeathing *miri* and dedicating it as *waqf* to constituting a private trust of it.

In late December 1931 Mordechai applied, as he wrote to Yosef he would, to the Supreme Court of Palestine, sitting as a High Court of Justice, asking that the Court order the Director of Lands to show cause for not registering the trustees' rights in the land. He supported his application with two arguments. One was technical. The other was:

> Nor can it be maintained that a private trust is an institution foreign or repugnant to the law in force in Palestine. The Companies Ordinance 1929 contains many clauses mentioning trusts in respect of property.[44]

Arguing that the English private trust had already been introduced into the law of Palestine by way of the incidental references to it in the Companies Ordinance, Eliash asked the Supreme Court to reinforce that introduction and make it explicit. But the Court and its officials were less than obliging. The rule nisi boded ill: it directed the respondent to show cause why 'the disposition of Waqf lands of Special category, should not be registered in the Land Registry Office'.[45] From Eliash's point of view, this was the wrong question: the land in question was *miri*, not *waqf*, and Eliash wanted to declare an English-style private trust of it and have the trustees' title registered, not to register a disposition in any sort of *waqf*.

[43] Yosef Eliash's letter dated 16 Tammuz 5691 (according to the Hebrew calendar) and Mordechai's response dated 19.7.1931 are in CZO, A 417, file 749. In his response, Mordechai pretended that he was pursuing the matter for a client rather than on his own behalf. The rule that *miri* land could not be bequeathed appeared both in the Provisional Law on Holding Real Estate, article 8, referred to in note 22 above, and in the Succession Ordinance, No. 4 of 1923, *Official Gazette*, no. 88, 1 April 1923, s. 19, which lent renewed force to the Provisional Law Regulating the Right to Dispose of Immovable Property of 1329/1913. Article 8 of the latter provided (in R. C. Tute's translation: *Ottoman Land Laws* (Jerusalem: Greek Convent Press, 1927)), that 'Mirie land owned by virtue of a formal title deed cannot be constituted *waqf* or left by legacy unless the State confers the absolute ownership by Imperial mulknama according to Sharia law.' The final section of the Charitable Trusts Ordinance emphasized that *miri* land could not be devised for charitable purposes: Ordinance to Regulate Charitable Trusts, above, note 25, s 43.

[44] The application is in the *Eliash* case file. Eliash referred to s. 29(2), for which see note 28 above, as a particularly striking example.

[45] The rule is in the *Eliash* case file.

That whoever phrased the rule rephrased Eliash's application, originally put in the language of English trust law, in the language of *waqf*, boded ill regarding the court's willingness to permit Palestinians to declare and register English-type private trusts.

At the subsequent hearing, held on 18 May 1932, the Government Advocate, Elliott, appearing for the Director of Lands, addressed not the question whether the English private trust had been received into the law of Palestine, but whether such a trust could be constituted out of *miri* land. He argued that it could not, since *miri* was, under Ottoman land law, still in force in Mandate Palestine, publicly-owned land. Private holders of *miri* land – even those registered as its 'owners', like Eliash – were thus, in effect, lessees, and though they could, in principle, alienate their rights in the land, they could not transfer them to trustees, rather as they could not dedicate the land as *waqf*. Eliash countered with an attempt to drive a wedge between Palestine's Ottoman land law and its Mandate-era law of land registration, arguing that registering *miri* land as subject to a trust did not change its nature as *miri*. Such land was, he said, being registered as subject to (civil) charitable trusts, so why not private ones?[46]

Judgment was handed down on 15 June, and thoroughly disappointed Eliash. Sir Michael McDonnell, the Chief Justice, wrote:

> [T]here is a presumption that the legislator does not intend to make any substantial alteration in the law beyond what it explicitly declares either in express terms or by clear implication, or . . . beyond the immediate scope and object of the statute . . . I do not think one can seriously hold, knowing the nature of the Legislation with which we are dealing [the Companies Ordinance], that the Legislature intended by a mere side-wind to introduce a new principle of law, such as the doctrine of private trusts, into Palestine.[47]

This clear rejection of the applicability of the English private trust in Palestine – contradicting High Commissioner Samuel's confidence that should a case like Eliash's come before the courts, the English law of private trusts would 'doubtless be applied' – was unnecessary to decide the case. Eliash's application for an order that the Director of Lands

[46] My analysis of the oral arguments is based on the handwritten notes of Chief Justice McDonnell and Justice Khayat, in English and Arabic respectively; they are found in the *Eliash* case file. Doukhan's note in his property law textbook of 1935 (note 22 above), 94fn, that the question whether charitable trusts could be dedicated out of *miri* land was not argued in this case, is thus not quite accurate.

[47] HCJ 77/31 *Eliash* v. *Director of Land* 1 PLR 735 [1932] (hereafter: *Eliash* case report).

register his trustees' rights in the land could have been rejected by holding, more restrictedly, that *miri* land could not be made a trust. McDonnell held this, too,[48] and Justice Khayat added that the proposed trust was not a *waqf*, as it was not charitable. This last statement seems puzzling, as *shari'a* recognizes dedications of property as *waqf* to benefit the founder's descendants, known in Palestine as the *waqf dhurry*, to be no less charitable than dedications intended to benefit the wider public.[49] The dedication of such private family *waqfs* was common in Mandate Palestine; most *waqfs* dedicated in Mandate-era Jerusalem were of this type.[50] Khayat is unlikely to have been ignorant of the basic *shari'a* notion that family *waqfs*, too, were charitable in nature. Further, one wonders why Khayat raised the question whether Eliash's proposed trust was a *waqf*. Neither Eliash nor Elliot claimed that it was. Khayat may have relied on the rule nisi, which did, erroneously, refer to Eliash's trust as a *waqf*. Khayat further noted that 'there is no provision that allows the registration of immoveable property in the name of a person by way of trust except, as stated by petitioner, in the Companies Ordinance', and that the proposed trust was 'equal' to a bequest of *miri* land and so should be encompassed by the prohibition on the latter.[51]

It appears there was, for more than a decade after the *Eliash* case was decided, considerable confusion regarding the actual holding in the case. To go by reported decisions, Palestine's courts do not seem to have applied *Eliash* until 1945.[52] Three reported decisions, and at least one unreported decision, all of 1945–6, applied it, citing as the rule in *Eliash* McDonnell's general refusal to admit the English private trust into the law of Palestine rather than the more restricted point of whether such a trust could be dedicated out of *miri* land.[53] Doukhan, in his 1935

[48] *Eliash* case report, 736.

[49] Reiter, *Islamic Endowments*, above, note 13, p. 13.

[50] Reiter, ibid., lists in his Table 3.1, on pp. 50–1, all 61 *waqfs* established by Muslims in Jerusalem during the Mandate period for which data was found in the records (*sijill*) of the Jerusalem *sharī'a* Court. 52 of them were 'family' *waqfs*, dedicated to benefiting the founder's relatives.

[51] *Eliash* case report, 736–7; see also his pencilled draft judgment, in Arabic, in the *Eliash* case file.

[52] Israel State Archives policy currently makes a general search of unreported Mandate-era decisions very difficult.

[53] The three were: CC 125/43 *Malatzky* v. *Bawly*, Selected Cases of the District Courts (SCDC) 265 [1945]; LC 20/45 *Albert Missri* v. *Itzhaq Raphael Eliashar*, SCDC 180, 182 [1946]; and CA 16-24/45 *Bracha Ben-Ya'acov & ors.* v. *Joseph Forer*, 2 ALR 628 [1945] (reversed, on points irrelevant to present concerns, in Privy Council Appeals 30–32/47

textbook, took a similar view of the case, but noted that '[t]he case only decided that a disposition creating a [private] trust could not be registered at the Land Registry', not that such a disposition was wholly ineffective and void.[54] Eliash himself, when arguing a different case in 1942, representing an orphanage beneficiary of a charitable trust of *miri* land, argued that the decision in *Eliash* should be read as limited to the rejection of private trusts, and that McDonnell's statement that *miri* land could not be dedicated as *any* kind of trust was made *obiter*. The Supreme Court, however, rejected the latter part of Eliash's argument, holding that the *miri* point 'appears . . . to be one of the main grounds for the judgment'.[55]

His application to the Supreme Court having been rejected, Eliash wrote on 5 October 1932 to Harry Trusted, the Attorney-General, urging that '[t]here can be no doubt that the creation of private trust[s] is envisaged by other legislation as well as by such general principles as are laid down in article 46 of the Palestine Order in Council'. Noting that '[t]he judgment in question points . . . to the necessity of special legislation in this regard', Eliash asked 'that such legislative steps as may be necessary . . . be taken without delay'.[56] Trusted passed Eliash's letter to Elliott, who appeared for the government in the case, for comments. Elliott's response showed a very different understanding of the holding in *Eliash* from that evident in the 1940s decisions applying it. He wrote:

Bracha Ben-Ya'acov & ors. v. *Joseph Forer*, 2 Psakim 498 [1948]). None of the three was concerned with a family trust. The unreported decision was Estate Case 472/46 (Tel Aviv) *In Re Estate of Ya'acov Blum* (unreported). Robert Eisenman cited *Eliash* and *Ben-Ya'acov* in his *Islamic Law in Palestine and Israel: a History of the Survival of Tanzimat and Sharia in the British Mandate and the Jewish State* (Leiden: E. J. Brill, 1978), pp. 95–6, note 41 and text, attributing the courts' rejection of the English private trust to their '[c]onscious[ness] of the great evil family *waqf* had become in the Middle East and the endless controversy surrounding them'. There is no trace of such consciousness, or indeed any mention of the family (*dhurry* or *ahli*) *waqf*, in the decisions discussed; but the judges concerned may have been conscious of the issue nevertheless.

54 Goadby and Doukhan, *Land Law*, above, note 22, p. 90 (footnote and accompanying text). It was certainly Doukhan's own view – as distinct from his view of the holding in *Eliash* – that '[a] trust of Miri is, therefore, merely void': ibid., p. 94. The phrase appears in a discussion of charitable trusts, but Doukhan's view of private trusts of *miri* seems, from context, to have been similar.

55 CA 117/40 *Agudath Batey Yetomim Veyetomoth* v. *A-Gl*, 9 PLR 291, 297 [1942]. The Court (Gordon-Smith CJ) noted that according to both legislation and case law, *miri* land could not be dedicated for charitable purposes, either by will or *inter vivos*.

56 ISA, file M-269/10.

> The Supreme Court in discharging the order decided that a private trust could not be created of Miri Land. So far as the judgment refers to Trusts, other than Trusts of Miri Land, it should be read with caution.

'The Court was never called upon', noted Elliott, 'to discuss the effect the introduction of Equitable principles might have upon the law affecting' several areas of law which were in English law impacted by such principles, from the administration of decedents' estates and the wardship of infants to the rectification of deeds and the specific performance of contracts. The rest of Elliott's comments are of great interest:

> Had the Court had to decide under the Companies or Partnerships Ordinances whether the principles governing Private Trusts as we understand them were applicable in Palestine it might very well have held such principles applicable on the ground that the Ordinances referred to adumbrated such principles apart altogether from any consideration of what was meant by article 46 of the Order in Council, 1922.
>
> If I were asked whether in the view of the Supreme Court the principles governing Private Trusts were applicable in Palestine my answer would be 'Yes, but their application differs with the law applicable to the particular case under review'.
>
> In other words, the principles may be directly applicable where an Ottoman Law, Order in Council, Ordinance or Regulation so provide and indirectly in cases falling under article 46 of the Order in Council where there is no such provision.[57]

Here was a 1932 view joining Samuel's 1925 recognition that Palestinian attempts to establish private family trusts on the English model could be accommodated, by way of article 46 of the Palestine Order in Council, to the implications of the references to the trust in commercial legislation enacted since 1925. On this reading of the decision in *Eliash*, its impact on the emergent Palestinian law of private trusts was minimal: it merely held that 'owners' of *miri* land could not dedicate it as a private trust, extending the Ottoman-era statutory prohibition on dedicating such land from the Islamic form of trust to the English one. Doukhan's very different reading of the case, which, unlike Elliot's, was made public (in a published book), was not unduly restrictive of the Palestinian law of private trusts, either: the case merely decided, he wrote, that private trusts of land could not be registered in the Land Registry.[58] This did not rule out private trusts of personalty, even beyond the companies and partnerships contexts.

[57] ISA, file M-269/10. [58] See text to note 54 above.

Eliash's attempt to have the English law of private trusts introduced into Palestine by legislation, reversing the earlier decision not to do so, was, however, unsuccessful. The failure was due to the government's limited manpower being employed on more pressing issues, rather than to a governmental decision rejecting his attempt. The government file containing his request travelled to and fro for several years to little avail. The final substantive minute on the subject, dated August 1936, during the severe disturbances of that year, noted that '[t]here seems no hope of dealing with this at present'.[59]

While Mandate draftsmen continued to incidentally refer to trusts in legislation enacted after 1932, those references all appear to have entered the law of Palestine as an inadvertent result of the copying of the provisions which contain them from UK, colonial and model legislation. Though Mandate-era materials preserved in UK and Israeli archives reveal, in most cases, the source of each provision of the numerous Palestinian Ordinances enacted, I have found no explicit discussion of the appropriateness of the references to the private trust contained in several provisions. And so the Bankruptcy Ordinance of 1936 provided that '[t]he property of the bankrupt divisible amongst his creditors ... shall not comprise ... property held by the bankrupt on trust for any other person', language taken from the UK Bankruptcy Act 1914.[60] The Income Tax Ordinance of 1941 contained the largest number of references to the trust since the Companies Ordinance of 1929. It referred to a married woman's trustee (a reference to the English practice, prevalent among the upper classes before married women were granted the right to own property at law, of granting property to trustees on trust for such women for their separate use notwithstanding coverture), to a trustee 'having the direction, control or management of any property or concern on behalf of any incapacitated person', to the local trustee for a 'person not resident in Palestine', to 'two or more persons acting in the capacity of trustees of a trust', and defined 'disposition' to include 'trust'.[61] All but

[59] ISA, file M-269/10.

[60] Bankruptcy Ordinance, No. 3 of 1936, *Palestine Gazette*, Gazette Extraordinary, No. 566, 24 January 1936, Supplement No. 1, s. 37(1). The origin of this section – the fact that it 'follows s. 38 of the English Act'– is made clear in a 'Note on the Bankruptcy Bill, 1935', in the UKNA, CO 733/284, 4. The 'English Act' referred to is identified as the Bankruptcy Act 1914 in a letter by Hall, Officer Administering the Government, from 12 October 1935, in the same file. The English s. 38 is identical in relevant detail to the Palestinian s. 37.

[61] Income Tax Ordinance, No. 23 of 1941, *Palestine Gazette*, No. 1126, 22 August 1941, ss. 21 (married woman's trustee), 27 (trustee for an incapacitated person), 28(1) (trustee for

two of the sections containing those references were copied from the Model Income Tax Ordinance drafted by the 1922 Inter-Departmental Committee on Income Tax in the Colonies not Possessing Responsible Government, while the remaining two sections were taken from the Kenya Income Tax Ordinance of 1940.[62] Moving further away from commercial law, the expression 'breach of trust' appears in the Civil Wrongs Ordinance, enacted in 1944 and brought into force in 1947, the provision containing it having been copied from the UK Law Reform (Miscellaneous Provisions) Act 1934. While thought was given to this provision – it was one of a minority of the Palestinian Ordinance's provisions which were not based on the Cypriot Civil Wrongs Law of 1932 – the reference to the trust is not a central element thereof, and seems to have slipped in without discussion.[63]

Considering this plethora of legislative references to the English private trust, one is struck by Robert Drayton, the Mandate Government's

a 'person not resident in Palestine'), 29 (refers again to the two latter types of trustee), 34 (two or more joint trustees of one trust), and 22(1) (defines 'disposition'). Gabriel Eichelgrün, a noted Palestine 'tax consultant' of the 1940s, noted in his *Palestine Income Tax Guide* (Haifa: Paltax, 1945) that the definition of 'disposition' in s. 22(1) 'is one of the standard-phrases of the Palestine Legislator "swallowed virtually holus-bolus" (HC 77/31, *Eliash* v. *Director of Lands*) from English statutes (cf. 1920 Finance Act, sect. 20(5))' (p. 143). The best study of married women's separate property under English law remains S. Staves, *Married Women's Separate Property in England 1660–1833* (Cambridge, MA: Harvard University Press, 1990); see also R. J. Morris, 'Men, Women, and Property: the Reform of the Married Women's Property Act 1870', in F. M. L. Thompson (ed.), *Landowners, Capitalists, and Entrepreneurs: Essays for Sir John Habakkuk* (Oxford University Press, 1994), pp. 171–91.

62 Ss. 21, 27, 28(1) and 29 of the Palestine Ordinance are identical to ss. 20, 26, 27(1) and 28 of the Model Income Tax Ordinance, for which see Report of the Inter-Departmental Committee on Income Tax in the Colonies not Possessing Responsible Government, Cmnd. 1788 (Dec. 1922), 19ff. Ss. 22(1) and 34 of the Palestine Ordinance are identical to ss. 23 and 41, respectively, of the Kenya Income Tax Ordinance, No. II of 1940, and were taken therefrom: 'Income Tax Ordinance, 1941. Comparative Table', in UKNA, CO 733/444, Part II. For the origins and Mandate-era history of the Palestine Income Tax Ordinance see A. Likhovski, 'Is Tax Law Culturally Specific? Lessons from the History of Income Tax Law in Mandate Palestine' (2010) 11 *Theoretical Inquiries in Law* 725, 738, 747, 748, 751.

63 Civil Wrongs Ordinance, No. 36 of 1944, *Palestine Gazette*, No. 1380, 28 December 1944, Supplement No. 1, s. 14(6). That this clause, numbered 15(6) in the bill version of the Ordinance, published in 1942, was based on s. 1(6) of the English Law Reform (Miscellaneous Provisions) Act 1934, 24 & 25 Geo. 5, c. 41, is noted in a 'Memorandum on Draft Civil Wrongs Ordinance', ISA, file M-279/29. That most of the Ordinance was based on the Cyprus Civil Wrongs Law 1932 is noted in 'Civil Wrongs Ordinance, 1942. Objects and Reasons', dated 20 December 1941, signed by W. J. FitzGerald, Attorney General, in the ISA, same file.

Legal Draftsman since 1931, having commented in 1933, while explaining a clause he redrafted according to which 'rights to land which are not established by any claimant shall be registered in the name of the High Commissioner in trust for the government of Palestine', that '[i]n Palestine . . . trusts in the English sense do not exist'.[64] It seems that legislative references to trusts in the land settlement and registration context were not intended to refer to the technical English concept, but to a vaguer notion of holding *ex officio* for public purposes. Legislative use of the term in many other contexts, such as in the Income Tax, Bankruptcy and Civil Wrongs Ordinances, does, contrastingly, seem to refer to the English technical concept of a trust. While some of the references to trusts in those three Ordinances can be construed so as to cohere with the theory that the only variety of the English trust available under the law of Mandate Palestine was the charitable one, others, such as the reference in the Income Tax Ordinance to a married woman's trustee, cannot be so construed; and in all cases, such a construction appears, from context, to be distinctly artificial.

The Mandate-era Supreme Court itself delivered, post-*Eliash*, at least two decisions which cohere with Elliott's permissive reading of that case, permitting the creation of private trusts other than of *miri* land. In one case, the Court saw no difficulty in a contract 'for the transfer of certain shares' which provided that 'until the cheque and promissory note are paid, the shares remain in trust with the Belgo-Palestine Bank Ltd, Tel-Aviv' and laid certain obligations on that bank, as 'trustee'.[65] In another case, an Income Tax Appeal, the Court held, applying the section of the Income Tax Ordinance that referred to the local trustee for a 'person not resident in Palestine', that United Artists (Export) Ltd, an

[64] The clause in question is s. 29 of the Land (Settlement of Title) Ordinance 1928, *Official Gazette*, 1 June 1928, 201–75, as amended by the Land (Settlement of Title) (Amendment) Ordinance, No. 48 of 1939, published in Supplement No. 1 to the *Palestine Gazette*, 23 November 1939. Similarly, s. 29A, inserted in the amending Ordinance, provided that land used for, or assigned for, public purposes, shall be registered 'in the name of the High Commissioner in trust for the government of Palestine'. For Drayton's explanation, see 'Memorandum by the Legal Draftsman, R. H. Drayton, on the first drafts of the [1933 versions of] the Land (Partition) Ordinance, Land (Settlement of Title) Ordinance and Land (Registration of Title) Ordinance, dated 29 September 1933', para. 23, in the ISA, file M-711/15. For Drayton's appointment in October 1931, see Report by His Majesty's Government [. . .] to the Council of the League of Nations on the Administration of Palestine and Trans-Jordan for the year 1931, available here: http://domino.un.org/UNISPAL.NSF/a47250072a3dd7950525672400783bde/c2567d9c6f6ce5d8052565d9006efc72.

[65] CA 93/41 *Hausdorf* v. *Metzger* 1 SCJ 260, 261 [1941].

American film exporter, 'are ... assessable in the name of appellants [a Palestinian film distributor] as trustees'.[66] The position taken in these cases, recognizing the use of private trusts in Palestine, seems to have been formulated as a direct inference from the references to the trust in the Companies and Income Tax Ordinances, respectively. Judge Tzeltner of the Tel Aviv District Court went further, realizing Samuel's and Elliott's expectation that in contexts where no Palestinian Ordinance referred to the use of trusts, the courts would apply English trust law by way of article 46 of the Palestine Order in Council: he had no qualms about applying section 61 of the (English) Trustee Act 1925, which empowers the court to relieve trustees from liability for breaches of trust where they had 'acted honestly and reasonably, and ought fairly to be excused', to custodians of an absentee's property who made a mistaken payment to the Tel Aviv municipality.[67]

Thus, the Mandate Government and courts' position regarding the reception of the English private trust, other than of *miri* land, into the law of Palestine remained unclear after the *Eliash* decision. The pertinent sources fall into a pattern: English private trusts were suffered to exist in commercial contexts, while their applicability in the context of non-commercial landholding was repeatedly denied – by McDonnell in the *Eliash* decision, by Doukhan in his textbook and by Drayton in a memorandum. As we shall see in Part III, the continuing indeterminacy regarding the positive standing of the common law private trust did not prevent use of such trusts in practice by Palestine's growing Jewish settler population, although they responded to the emergent pattern by preferring trust companies, which could point to the many references to the trust in the Companies Ordinance, over individual trusteeship. The Supreme Court's cold-shouldering of Eliash may have been enough to prevent any further attempts to have *family* trusts of land on the English model approved by state authorities. Jewish Palestinian use of trusts and

[66] Income Tax Appeal 8/42 *Ideal Motion Pictures* v. *Assessing Office of Income Tax, Tel-Aviv* 9 PLR 481, 487 [1942].

[67] CC 673/46 *In Re Esther Baum, of Siberia, Russia, Absentee* v. *Rachel Avivi*, 2 District Court Decisions 418 [1950]. The decision in this case was given after the establishment of the state of Israel, which fact had no impact on the jurisdiction's law of private trusts: s. 11 of the Law and Government Ordinance, 2 *Official Gazette*, 19 May 1948, Appendix A, 1, issued by the provisional government of Israel four days after the state was established, provided that the law of Mandate Palestine, as it stood on the termination of the Mandate, was to continue in force, subject to express changes introduced by the new regime. No changes regarding private trusts had been introduced by 1950.

trust companies was, as we shall see, focused on business, investment, the purchase, sale and development of land and the facilitation of Jewish immigration to Palestine.

Such use may have developed even had the Mandate authorities been more clear-cut in their rejection of the common law private trust; as is the case with contracts, where the parties to a private trust effectively cooperate, resolving their differences (if any) by negotiation, arbitration or before non-state judicial fora, such a trust can, in many contexts, be effectively used without ever alerting a court, or any other arm of the state, to its existence. The use of the English trust started in medieval England as a non-state phenomenon, directed at bypassing and evading the state's rules (such as the feudal dues due on a tenant's death and tenants' inability to bequeath their land), long before the Chancery, or any ecclesiastical court, ever enforced a trust.[68]

Despite the various views which developed regarding the actual holding in *Eliash*, and the use of private trusts and trust companies in practice, the British were undeniably less facilitative of Zionist settlers' attempts to use English private trusts than they were of similar attempts by the non-British population of other colonies. In India, Ceylon and (applying Indian cases) the mandated territory of Zanzibar, Anglo-colonial courts facilitated native use of English private trusts, including in family contexts. According to those courts, such facilitation did not contradict the application of natives' personal (often religious) laws to their family affairs: trusts were, at least in India and Ceylon, seen as a non-personal-law subject.[69] Natives certainly had non-Western trust forms at their disposal: Indians of all creeds, for example, used and use *benami* transactions, a form of bare trusteeship under which one person is a merely formal, or ostensible, owner of property in which another is beneficially interested.[70] Muslims in both India and Ceylon made use of

[68] J. Biancalana, 'Medieval Uses', in R. H. Helmholz and R. Zimmermann (eds.), *Itinera Fiduciae: Trust and Treuhand in Comparative Perspective* (Berlin: Duncker & Humblot, 1998), p. 111.

[69] I thank Mitra Sharafi for her advice on this point.

[70] For an exhaustive treatment of the law of *benami*, see the Law Commission of India, 57th Report, *Benami Transactions* (1973); id., 130th Report, *Benami Transactions – a Continuum* (1988). The Indian courts of the Raj enforced *benami* transactions, noting their similarity to English resulting or bare trusts, which were also enforced in India. However, the Indian legislator, both under the Raj and since India's independence, has repeatedly acted to repress, first, fraudulent *benami* transactions, and, eventually, any such transaction: the Benami Transactions (Prohibition) Act, No. 45 of 1988, made entering into a *benami* transaction an offence punishable with imprisonment of up to three years. See

the *waqf*,[71] and Hindus of charitable trusts under Hindu law.[72] The availability of non-Western forms of trust did not stop the Indian and Ceylonese courts from applying English trust law to natives' trusts. In both India and Ceylon, Anglo-colonial facilitation of native use of English private trusts started in the courts, along with incidental references to the trust in colonial legislation; eventually comprehensive trust codes were enacted for both colonies, conceiving of the trust as an obligatory relationship rather than as a double ownership structure, but otherwise loyal to the English model.[73] Non-British European settler populations in British colonies, such as the Dutch of the Cape and the French of Lower Canada, were similarly allowed by their British rulers to use the English trust.[74] This despite the fact that they, too, had at their disposal non-English trust forms: the tutors, curators, administrators, usufructs, fiduciary substitutions, modus and foundations of the pre-Napoleonic civil law, and, in the South African case, the Dutch *bewind*.[75] The reception

ibid. Interestingly, some courts have held the *benamidar* – the ostensible owner – not to have legal title, and thus rejected the English trust analogy: see cases quoted in Law Commission of India, 57th Report, above, pp. 10–11.

71 For India, see G. C. Kozlowski, *Muslim Endowments and Society in British India* (Cambridge University Press, 1985); for Ceylon see A. Cooray, 'Oriental and Occidental Laws in Harmonious Co-existence: The Case of Trusts in Sri Lanka' (2008) 12 *Electronic Journal of Comparative Law*: www.ejcl.org/121/art121-5.pdf, 15.

72 For which, see A. C. Sen, *B. K. Mukherjea's Hindu Law of Religious and Charitable Trusts*, 5th edn (Calcutta: Eastern Law House Private Ltd, 2003). For their use in Ceylon, see Cooray, 'Oriental and Occidental Laws', above, note 71, 13.

73 W. F. Agnew, *The Law of Trusts in British India*, 2nd edn (Calcutta: Thacker, Spink & Co., 1920), pp. 14–29; B. M. Gandhi, *Equity, Trusts and Specific Relief* (Lucknow: Eastern Book Company, 1983), pp. 33, 236–40; and see cases like *Umes Chunder Sircar* v. *Mussumat Zahor Fatima* 17 L.R., I.A. 201 [1890]; *Moosabhai Mohamed Sajan* v. *Jaccobhai Mohamed Sajan* 29 I.L.R. 267 (Bom.) [1904]; and *Mumtaz-Un-Nissa* v. *Tufail Ahmed* 28 I.L.R. 264 [1905]. The Indian law of (non-religious, English-type, private) trusts was eventually codified in the Indian Trusts Act, Act II of 1882. For Ceylon, see discussion in L. J. M. Cooray, *The Reception in Ceylon of the English Trust* (Colombo: Lake House Printers and Publishers, 1971), pp. 3–9, 21; the Ceylonese law of trusts was eventually codified in the Trusts Ordinance of 1917, adding significantly to the Indian model. For Zanzibar, see Case 28/30 *Public Trustee* v. *H. H. the Sultana* 4 Zanzibar LR 14 [1930]; and see discussion in Elias, *British Colonial Law*, above, note 1, p. 117. Interestingly, an obligational understanding of the trust relationship reminiscent of that of the Indian and Ceylonese codes has recently come into vogue among scholars of the common law: L. D. Smith, 'Trust and Patrimony' (2008) 38 *Revue générale de droit* 379, 398–402; B. McFarlane and R. Stevens, 'The Nature of Equitable Property' (2010) 4 *Journal of Equity* 1.

74 See sources in note 2 above.

75 For the non-English trust forms available in British-governed Quebec, see Waters et al., *Law of Trusts*, above, note 2, pp. 1424–7. For South Africa, see F. W. D. Fischer, 'Trust,

process of the English private trust in South Africa and Quebec followed a roughly similar pattern to that found in India and Ceylon, though the presence of significant English settler populations in the former means the processes are not easily comparable: much of the greater legislative activity noticeable in Quebec and South Africa was consequent on the use of the trust by English settlers.[76] Palestine, too, experienced one element of the standard three-stage reception process: it had its incidental legislative references to the trust. But the reception process was derailed by *Eliash*, which, at least on one reading, decisively rejected the use of English private trusts by Palestinians. The process never got back on track until the end of the Mandate.

Why did the British display, intermittently as least, such a discouraging attitude towards attempts to use English private trusts in Palestine, while permitting them elsewhere? Several reasons come to mind. *First*, the derailment produced by *Eliash* may have been, at least partly, a product of Mordechai Eliash's insistence that his *miri* land be registered as held by persons who were trustees of an (English) trust; *miri* land was subject, as we have seen, to special complications. Had the test case on Palestinian use of English private trusts been concerned with assets of a less problematic type, such as *mulk* (fully-owned) land, shares or money, the result may well have been different. *Second*, a comparative colonial perspective hints that not only the substance of Eliash's application, but also the arguments he chose to support it, may have been less than felicitous: he, in effect, requested – one could say challenged – the Supreme Court to directly declare that Palestinians could, as a matter of colonial law, use English private trusts. That a less direct approach may have led to a different result is illustrated by a near-contemporary case, decided in 1930 by the Sultan's Court for Zanzibar, another Muslim-majority territory under

Fiducia, *Bewind* (administration), *Stichting* (foundation)' (1957) 20 *Tydskrif vir Heedendaagse Romeins-Hollandse Reg* 25.

[76] The general codification of trust law, which came relatively early (Act relating to Trusts, S.Q. 1879, c. 29) in Quebec and late (Trust Property Control Act, Act 57 of 1988) in South Africa, was preceded, in both jurisdictions, by a great number of special Acts making use of the trust for particular purposes. A key context of this early legislative activity in the private trusts field was the use of trustees for holding assets securing loans to companies; see the Cape Ordinance no. 13 of 1846 and, in Quebec, hundreds of private Acts enacted from the mid-nineteenth century until the eventual enactment of a general Act on the subject in 1914. See, for South Africa, Honoré, 'Trust', above, note 2, pp. 851–9; for Quebec, J. B. Claxton, *Studies on the Quebec Law of Trust* (Toronto: Thomson, 2005), pp. 10–12.

certificate under the hand of the High Commissioner' to do so.[83] While the continuing practice of establishing both charitable and private *waqfs*, which the British were obliged to continue according to the terms of their Mandate, meant that a considerable amount of Palestinian land was controlled by 'dead hands', the British may have felt that introducing another legal form which tends to perpetuity – the private trust – was unwise.[84] And *finally*, once *Eliash* was decided, it was, at least potentially, a precedent, which later courts could ill ignore, and which, on one reading, negatived Palestinian use of English private trusts.

III Trusts in action: private trusts in Zionist settler practice

On 14 February 1946, Dr Aharon Barth, a lawyer and Vice-Chair of the Board of the Anglo-Palestine Bank, then owned indirectly by the Zionist movement, wrote to the directors of 'Himnuta', a Jewish National Fund subsidiary established in 1938, which, as we shall see, functioned as a trustee:

> I wish to draw your attention to [one of the three decisions of 1945–46 applying *Eliash*] ... Applying an antiquated decision of 1931, and absent any *de novo* argument, this decision provides that a 'trust' is illegal in Palestine. This necessitates, I believe, a fundamental review of your company's legal status ... I should add that [in 1938, when Barth took care of the paperwork establishing and registering Himnuta] I consulted with [leading Palestinian lawyer Solomon] Horowitz, who believed, much

83 With the Companies Act 1862, 25 & 26 Vict., c. 89, s. 18, English company law started providing that every company incorporated under the Companies Acts, except charities, could hold land. This exception to the Mortmain Acts was repeated in later recodifications of English company law, down to and including the Companies Act 1948, 11 & 12 Geo. VI, c. 40, s. 14(1). The abolition of the law of mortmain in the Charities Act 1960, 8 & 9 Eliz. II, c. 58, ended the need for such an exception. For more detail on the decline and end of the English law of mortmain see A. H. Oosterhoff, 'The Law of Mortmain: An Historical and Comparative Review' (1977) 27 *University of Toronto Law Journal* 257, esp. 288–95; I. Dawson, 'The Rule against Inalienability – a Rule without a Purpose?' (2006) 26 *Legal Studies* 414, esp. 426–9. For the more restrictive Palestinian regime see Companies Ordinance, above, note 28, s. 15, which provided that 'the Registrar shall not register any Company which has as its object or one of its objects the acquisition and development of land generally in Palestine unless such Company produces a certificate under the hand of the High Commissioner empowering it to hold lands generally'.

84 For the use of *waqfs* in Mandate Palestine see Reiter, *Islamic Endowments*, above, note 13, pp. 49–50. Arguments five and six build on comments by a reviewer for the *Law and History Review*, for which I am thankful.

> like myself, that this decision of 1931, which was the only one of its kind, cannot be seen as a binding precedent. As Palestinian practice, including the establishment of trust companies being approved by the government's legal apparatus, has long since established, contradicting that decision, that the trust does indeed exist in Palestine, we did not see that decision as preventing the establishment in Palestine of trust companies.[85]

As Barth observed, the Zionist settler population in Palestine had during the 1930s and '40s, notwithstanding the Mandate legal system's unclear position regarding the reception of the English private trust, made frequent, varied use of trusts and (especially) trust companies. As observed above, I have found no trace of family trusts on the English model;[86] but trust companies were frequently used in various business, land-purchase, banking, investment and immigration contexts. Plain, unincorporated trusts were also occasionally used. Here follows a description of the uses to which trusts and trust companies were put, starting with pure 'private sector' uses and ending with uses of private, non-charitable trust structures by Zionist organizations for purposes related to building the Zionist state-in-waiting.

The unclear positive legal standing of individual trustees on the classical English model, and the contrasting express grant of power to act as trustees, in a Schedule to the Companies Ordinance, to companies incorporated according to the Ordinance,[87] channelled most Zionist settler use of private trusts into trust companies. Zionist settlers' trust companies acted as trust companies were then acting in England, the United States, Australia, South Africa and other jurisdictions: they performed the functions of an individual, unincorporated twentieth-century trustee, acquiring, holding, investing, managing and distributing money

[85] CZA, file KKL5/14060 (original in Hebrew; my translation). Barth's letter was mentioned by G. Alexander, 'The Foundation of Himnuta Ltd and Its Earliest Uses (1938–1940)' (1992) 68 *Kathedra* 80, 87. The history of the Anglo-Palestine Bank was described in N. Gross et al., *Banker to an Emerging Nation: the History of Bank Leumi Le-Israel* (Jerusalem: Masada, 1977); for Barth and his career at the bank, see ibid., pp. 173–4. For Himnuta see text to notes 123–32 below.

[86] Evidence of such family trusts, which could easily be created without having been brought to the attention of any public authority, may certainly elude researchers working in public, rather than private, archives. My searches, however, included the dozens of private archives, including those of leading Mandate-era lawyers, which have been deposited in the Israel State Archives and the Central Zionist Archives. Still I found no evidence of family trusts on the English model.

[87] Note 28, above. In England, the same power was only legislatively recognized in 1906: Public Trustee Act 1906, 6 Edw. VII, c. 55, s. 4(3).

and other assets. While the aforementioned local reasons may have been key to the Palestinian preference for trust companies over individual trustees, the move to corporate trusteeship was a key twentieth-century trend in the principal common law jurisdictions: as trustees' responsibilities and liabilities became increasingly burdensome, the corporate trustee, often a trusteeship arm of a larger financial service provider such as a bank or insurance company, came increasingly into use. Many settlors and beneficiaries were eager for the accumulated expertise often found at corporate trustees and the easy solution of the replacement trustee issue they provide.[88] As Palestinian trusteeship was modelled on foreign, principally Anglo-American, models, the local popularity of the trust company may have reflected this larger trend. As in the nineteenth-century United States and turn-of-the-century Japan, not every company with the term 'trust' in its name in fact provided trusteeship services; structured as companies rather than as trusts, and producing profit (or loss) for their shareholders rather than distributing income and capital to beneficiaries, some Palestinian 'trust companies' were trusts in name only.[89] So, for example, when the Jaffa riots of 1936 drove the establishment of a utility corporation for the purpose of building port facilities at Tel Aviv, the company was named 'Marine Trust Company', but the only feature differentiating it from a plain public (i.e. traded) corporation was a Board of Trustees tasked with easing the company into existence, safe-keeping monies subscribed until the company was ready to receive them.[90]

[88] On the rise of corporate trusteeship in the United States see L. M. Friedman, 'The Dynastic Trust' (1964) 73 Yale L.J. 547, 563–72; on the equivalent process in the United Kingdom see D. R. Marshall, *Corporate Trustees* (London: Europa Publications, 1952); G. Moffat et al., *Trusts Law*, 5th edn (Cambridge University Press, 2009), pp. 429–30. Trust companies first appeared in Massachusetts 'in 1818 or 1822', and then, a decade or two later, in South Africa, where '[t]he management of private trusts was often [since the mid-nineteenth century] undertaken by trust companies': Honoré, 'Trust', above, note 2, p. 855.

[89] For the free nineteenth-century American use of the term 'trust', see A. W. Scott, 'Fifty Years of Trusts' (1936) 50 *Harvard Law Review* 60, 73–5. For the 'trust [*shintaku*] companies' of early twentieth-century Japan, which were, in substance, lending institutions rather than trusts, see Hiroto Dogauchi, 'Trusts in the Law of Japan', in M. Cantin Cumyn (ed.), *La Fiducie face au trust dans les rapports d'affaires* (Brussels: Bruylant, 1998), pp. 105, 106; see further Makoto Arai, 'Japan', in A. Kaplan (ed.), *Trusts in Prime Jurisdictions*, 3rd edn (London: Globe Business Publishing, 2010), pp. 233, 234–6.

[90] *Palestine Post*, 'Trust Company for Tel Aviv Port Development: Utility Corporation opens Subscription Lists', 28 May 1936, 1. Similarly, the Builders' Trust Limited was a

The Mandate era did see use of non-incorporated private trusts. One such was the Palestine Orchestra Trust, established by trust deed as the body administering the orchestra's affairs. The trust deed, setting up a ten-member Board of Trustees, was authored in December 1935 by Bronislaw Huberman, the orchestra's founder, and lawyer Solomon Horowitz, who three years later advised Barth that *Eliash* 'cannot be seen as a binding precedent'.[91] Another instance of the use of individual trusteeship was the practice of registering all the flats in a condominium as owned by a 'committee' made up of the owners of certain of them, the non-registered flat-owners having previously agreed by contract that the committee-members 'hold [all the flats] in favor of all the purchasers of the flats' [that is, hold each flat for its respective purchaser]. This practice was contrived to bypass the inability, from 1937–53, of Palestinian flat-owners to register their rights in their flats; only owners of plots, in whole or in part, could register their rights. While the practice was in 1945 held illegal and void by the Supreme Court, *because* it amounted to registering land in the name of trustees, which was, under *Eliash*, impossible (it was this decision that alerted Barth to the potential destructive force of *Eliash*), it seems to have been quite popular in practice.[92] Individual

bank, not a trust: *Palestine Post*, 'Help for the House-owner: Builders' Trust Limited formed in Tel-Aviv', 26 January 1938, 3. Other trust companies with few, if any, traits distinguishing them from non-trust companies were the Ramelana Trust Co., Carmel Investment Trust and Joseph Loewy & Co., for records of which see ISA, files P-7/919, P-8/919 and P-9/919. Joseph Loewy or Löwy, a Jewish engineer and entrepreneur of German birth, active in the Palestinian land market since before World War I, was instrumental in the 1930s extension of Jewish Haifa and the establishment of settlements to the north, such as the town of Nahariya: Y. Gelber, *New Homeland: Immigration and Absorption of Central European Jews, 1933–1948* (Jerusalem: Ben Tzvi Institute, 1990), pp. 358–9, 364; the Carmel Investment Trust purchased and developed land on the central Carmel plateau: *Palestine Post*, 'Central Carmel Plateau between Athlit and Nesher', 12 November 1948, 14. The archival materials the three companies left make possible a characterization of their activities. No activities particularly characteristic of a trust – rather than of a company or corporation – were found.

91 For the Palestine Orchestra Trust, see U. Teplitz, *The Story of the Philharmonic Orchestra* (Tel Aviv: Keter, 1992), pp. 15–16; *Palestine Post*, 'Reply to Musicians' Complaints', 28 June 1946, 3. The orchestra's musicians rebelled in 1946, deciding not to renew their contracts with the trust, but rather to form a self-governing cooperative to replace the trust as the orchestra's managing body: *Palestine Post*, 'Palestine Orchestra to turn into Cooperative', 28 May 1946, 3.

92 Several construction projects where this practice was used provided the factual background to *Ben-Ya'acov* (above, note 53), where Shaw J declared it to be ineffective (the quoted phrase is drawn from the Court's quotations from contracts signed by individual purchasers; ibid., at 631). Eliash, appearing for the purchasers, argued that the

trusteeship was also used as an interim solution for registering, for the duration of construction, rights to land purchased by co-owners, none of whom were able to take care of obtaining permits necessary for construction. The trustee, the wife of one co-owner, seems to have actively taken care of construction.[93] The purchase, development and registration of land and flats appear to have been the primary contexts in which individual, unincorporated trusteeship was used.

Trust companies were, from the mid-1930s, used with an impressive frequency for investment and other business purposes, some specializing in real estate.[94] The 'certificates under the hand of the High Commissioner' which were, under the Companies Ordinance, necessary for

committee-members could be seen as trustees for every purpose except registration, but the court, unsurprisingly, rejected this contention. The registration of rights in flats, separately from the rights in the land they stood on, first became possible during the Ottoman era, by way of analogy from s. 25 of the Ottoman Land Code of 1858 (which referred to rights in gardens, orchards and vineyards rather than in flats). The possibility of such registration was abolished by the British in the Land Law (Amendment) Ordinance, 1937, s. 1, though existing registered rights in 'trees', 'buildings' and 'rights to build or add to existing buildings' were preserved. Flat-owners were thus left in need of devices such as the scheme described in the text, until the enactment of the Condominium Act 1952. See a brief review of the history of the subject in S. Ben-Shemesh, 'On the Abolition of the Separate Registration of Buildings and Plants' (1970) 26 *HaPraklit* 403.

93 This trust, created in 1935, provided the factual scenario behind CA 87/50 *Liebman* v. *Lifshitz* 6 PD 57 [1952].

94 See, e.g., the Palonath Trust and Agency Ltd, incorporated in order to 'manage a trust investment company business': *Palestine Gazette*, Hebrew Version, No. 517, 6 June 1935. The English version of that same issue of the Gazette included, e.g., a notice of the incorporation of OTIC, the Oriental Trust & Investment Company Ltd, incorporated in order 'to account lands and any estate or interest therein and to develop and turn to account same'. These were not the only trust companies whose incorporation was noticed in this issue of the Gazette, which I have picked as a sample. The *Palestine Post* published a weekly report on the 'weekly list of new enterprises' published in the Gazette; many of those reports feature trust companies. See, e.g., the following reports: 'Incorporation of 13 Private Companies', 14 January 1937, 10 [one trust company]; 'New Companies and New Investments', 23 July 1937, 12 [two trust companies]; 'LP.64,000 Invested in Local Industry and Trade', 16 March 1939, 9 [four trust companies]; 'Investments of LP.200,000 in August: 10 New Firms Commence Business', 27 September 1939, 6 [four trust companies]; 'Investments', 18 May 1941, 4 [one trust company]; and the apparent record holder, 'New Financing in Palestine: 23 Investment Trusts Formed at One Time', 13 June 1935, 1. The archives yield many further examples, e.g. the following trust companies, all of which specialized in purchasing, holding and selling real estate: the Union Holding and Trust Co., Ltd: ISA, files M-24/319, M-21/856, M-11/857, M-52/4355; Ramelana Trust Co., Ltd, Carmel Investment Trust Ltd, and Joseph Loewy & Co., Ltd (for which see note 90 above); Fidelity Emun Investment and Trust Co. Ltd: CZA, file KH4 7626; and the Palestine Trust Corporation: ISA, file M-20/309.

companies to hold land, were generously issued by Registrar of Companies Henry Kantorovich, to whom this power of the High Commissioner had been delegated. Kantorovich later recalled that he used to 'issu[e] certificates to companies to hold land where on the scanty evidence before him he was satisfied that the company was a genuine land development company'.[95] The Anglo-Palestine Bank incorporated its trust subsidiary, A.P.B. Trust Company Limited, in 1939; Barth was a member of its Board of Directors. The company 'was established for the purpose of engaging in every description of trustee business ... act[ing] as trustees for persons residing abroad who invest their capital here, as trustees for debenture holders, and undertak[ing] executorships under wills, etc'.[96] Where 'capitalists who still reside abroad' invested money in 'property or land' in Palestine, the company promised to establish a 'separate private limited compan[y] ... in respect of each property in order to facilitate its transfer to its rightful owner after his arrival in Palestine'.[97] A few years later the company 'reported good progress' in its business of acting 'for people living in Great Britain, the Empire and America, who entrust it with management of their Palestine investments and business', as well as acting 'for debtors' and 'administer[ing] the trusteeship in the name of groups of banks which participate in joint loans'.[98] The Eretz Yisrael Discount Bank, a prominent Palestinian privately owned bank, established its trust subsidiary in 1944.[99] Banks also provided trust and escrow services directly.[100]

95 For the requirements of the Companies Ordinance, s. 15, see note 83 above and accompanying text. Kantorovich's description of his pre-war practice is in the ISA, file M-714/19: Minutes of meeting held in office of Administrator General on Monday, 29th April, 1946. Participating were Administrator General Kantorovich, H. E. Baker, Acting Solicitor General, and J. F. Spry, Assistant Director of Land Registration.

96 *Palestine Post*, 'A.P.B. Trust Company Established: £P.50,000 Fully Paid Share Capital', 13 August 1939, 7; a Hebrew version of the same story was published in *Davar*, 14 August 1939, 3.

97 *Palestine Post*, 'Foreigners' Local Property: Activity of A.P.B. Trust Company', 8 September 1939, 4.

98 *Palestine Post*, 'Local Deposits for Financing War: Anglo-Palestine Bank's 1943 Report', 11 May 1944, 2.

99 Gross et al., *Banker*, above, note 85, p. 269.

100 As illustrated by the facts of *Hausdorf* v. *Metzger*, above, note 65. Banks also served as debenture trustees: see, e.g., notice of a general meeting of the debenture holders of Teltsch House Ltd, *Palestine Post*, 10 August 1939, 4, mentioning the Kupat Am Bank Ltd serving as trustee.

Insurance companies, too, formed trust company subsidiaries,[101] while some trust companies functioned as insurers.[102]

Private Palestinian demand for professional investment services appeared in the early 1930s with the immigration to Palestine of Jews from the Balkans and from Germany, who were accustomed to investing in securities. This demand led to the 1935 establishment of the 'Securities Exchange Bureau' (later the 'Tel Aviv Securities Clearing House'), the future Tel Aviv stock exchange.[103] It also led to the establishment of numerous investment trust companies, at least some of which operated as unit trusts: a well-known example was the Palestine Investment Association (PIA), a unit trust established in 1936 by Ernst Kahn, an immigrant from Germany.[104] The Yefet family's private bank also established a closed unit trust at about this time.[105] Palestinian investment practice was thus distinctly advanced for the time, at least compared to English practice: unit trusts were only 'introduced into England from America in 1932'.[106] The Anglo-Palestine Bank established what it called 'Palestine's second investment trust', the A.P.B. Investment Company Ltd, in 1945; Barth was again a Director, along with the Bank's other top managers. Having introduced its preference shares and debentures at the Tel Aviv Securities Clearing House, the company had already, on its registration, 'invested or loaned a total of around LP.400,000' in

[101] Insurance company 'Tzion' participated in the forming of the 'Mortgage Trust Company, Ltd', to which some mortgages 'Tzion' held were transferred: *Davar*, '"Tzion" Rising: Incomes Doubled in 1941', 26 April 1942, 4.

[102] E.g. the 'Zorfan' Trust Company, established to offer 'prompt mutual assistance for war-time damage from a special Compensation Fund formed through the cash subscriptions of members': *Palestine Post*, 'War Risk Fund', 20 September 1940, 6 (properties in Palestine were damaged during World War II by Italian air bombings, which also claimed numerous Palestinian lives). At the end of the 'first accounts period', 'allocation of compensation will be made or, if the property registered with the Fund is not damaged, money will be repaid': ibid. The directors included Shmuel Tolkowsky, MBE, Ernst Kahn, the founder of PIA (see text to note 104), and Menachem Dunkelblum, a leading lawyer and future Justice of the Supreme Court of Israel.

[103] For its history see S. Doron, 'From Exchange Bureau to Stock Exchange (1933–1962)' (1997) 137 *Riv'on Le'Banka'ut* 43.

[104] For the appearance of demand for investment opportunities and services, and the establishment of the Tel Aviv stock exchange, see Gross et al., *Banker*, above, note 85, pp. 178–9; Gelber, *New Homeland*, above, note 90, pp. 419–23. For the establishment of PIA see Gelber, ibid., p. 422; A. P. Michaelis, 'A Hundred Years of Banking and Money in Eretz-Yisrael' (1984) 91 *Riv'on Le'Banka'ut* 87.

[105] Gelber, *New Homeland*, above, note 90, pp. 419–20; Michaelis, 'Hundred Years of Banking', above, note 104, 88.

[106] L. C. B. G., 'Fixed and Flexible Trusts' (1937) 1 *Modern Law Review* 68, 69.

preference shares of local undertakings, in debentures and in loans to Jewish municipalities and local councils.[107] Its claim to being 'Palestine's second investment trust', after PIA, is only plausible if only investment trusts traded on the Securities Clearing House are counted.[108]

Attempts at establishing trust companies offering a wide repertoire of trust services were not limited to banks: the Palestine Trust Company Ltd held itself out as 'afford[ing] guidance on all financial and business problems', 'procur[ing] sound and profitable investment possibilities', 'perform[ing] all necessary operations towards execution of clients' undertakings', 'secur[ing] favorable investments in mortgages and other securities', 'assist[ing] in the purchase and development of land, plantations, farms, and urban property', 'undertaking the formation and establishment of companies and participat[ing] in their management', 'provid[ing] openings for capital in new or established business', 'creat[ing] strong economic units through the union of individual efforts having limited resources', 'assist[ing] in the prompt transfer of funds from Central Europe', and 'manag[ing] estates as executor, trustee, administrator or guardian'.[109] Activities promised were not always carried out, however; while the company did lend money,[110] function as a real estate agent,[111] serve as middleman in the sale of distributing houses of electrical appliances[112] and organize other companies,[113] many other aspects of its apparent multifaceted aptitude seem to have remained unexercised.

[107] *Palestine Post*, 'Half-Million Pound A.P.B. Trust', 30 September 1945, 2; see also Gross et al., *Banker*, above, note 85, p. 209.

[108] Many earlier investment trusts, such as those mentioned in note 94 above, were evidently disregarded, perhaps for marketing purposes, by A.P.B. top brass. S. Hoofien, General Manager from 1925–47, seems to have thought of establishing A.P.B.-controlled trust companies for several years before the first such company was eventually formed in 1939. In 1935 he proposed that the bank sell its Palestine Electric Company stock to a trust company formed for that purpose. The scheme was supposed to enable the bank to realize its profits on its P.E.C. holdings without relinquishing its voting rights. It was dropped on the advice of London solicitors, Cazenove, Akroyds & Greenwood & Company, and Linklaters and Paines. See correspondence in CZA, file L51\404.

[109] *Palestine Post*, Advertisement, 18 May 1934, 20.

[110] It advertised in February 1936 that it had 'Funds available for conservative mortgage loans to responsible building owners': *Palestine Post*, 16 February 1936, 2.

[111] It advertised an 'exquisite family home in Rehovoth': *Palestine Post*, 30 May 1935, 12.

[112] 'Business Offer', *Palestine Post*, 24 December 1936, 11.

[113] Such as the Palestine Plate Glass and Paint Works (Shepherd, Tobias and Co.) Ltd of Haifa: *Palestine Post*, 'Glass and Paint Factory: New £15,000 Company for Haifa', 4 November 1935, 5.

Similarly ambitious was the General Trust Corporation Ltd (GTC), founded in April 1939 by Siegfried Moses, a leader of German Zionism and recent immigrant from Nazi Germany. It held itself out as offering investment advice, property administration services ('especially on behalf of persons residing abroad'), expertise in setting up, reconstituting and winding-up enterprises, accounting services, advice on business restructuring, estate administration services, 'as well as assuming the trusteeship in those cases provided for in the Companies Law' (e.g. debentures and employee compensation schemes).[114] Data on the GTC's actual activities include its serving, from 1940, as trustee for PIA, registered that year as the Palestine Independent Trust Association Ltd; PITA itself focused on managing its portfolio.[115] The GTC also lent money.[116]

Mandate-era use of trust structures also extended to various Zionist organizations, which used the trust for both charitable and mixed, public–private purposes. Some uses of the trust form by Zionist organizations were plainly non-charitable – in effect, private trusts, set up and administratively supported by 'Zionist public sector' institutions, components of the Zionist state-in-waiting of the Mandate era. Use of trust structures by Zionist organizations started before the Mandate, during the Ottoman era. The Jewish National Fund (JNF), for example – Zionism's most prominent land-purchasing arm – was in effect a Zionist *waqf*, intended to purchase land in Palestine, hold it for the Jewish people, and never let it go: Jewish users of JNF land, such as *kibbutzim*, received leases or tenancies at will, the title to the land staying with the JNF. The JNF was registered in England in 1907 as an Association Limited by Guarantee. The English trust form, suggested by Herbert Bentwich (Norman's father and a prominent English solicitor and Zionist), was rejected, because as the Fund was to have, inter alia, powers to cultivate the land it purchased, lease it and develop industry, it could not,

114 See a letter by Moses to potential clients, marketing his services, in CZA, file S7\2108. Moses, chairman of the Organization of German Zionists (Zionistische Vereinigung für Deutschland) from 1933–7, later became the first Comptroller of the State of Israel, serving from 1949–61.

115 Gelber, *New Homeland*, above, note 90, p. 422; and see the 'company history' page on the PIA website: www.pia.co.il/pia/Front/Document.asp?ID=520505. PIA paid a dividend of 8.4% p.a. for 1940: *Palestine Post*, 'Progress of Palestine Unit Trust', 30 December 1941, 2.

116 As to Kibbutz Beit-Alpha, see contract of May 1941 between the Kibbutz and Palinvest, the Palestine Investment Service Ltd, and Deed of Charge granting the GTC a charge over the Kibbutz's crop of wheat and barley: both in CZA, file A376\288.

had it been established as a trust, be seen as purely charitable, and would thus have been subject to the rule against perpetuities, while its founders wanted it to be, precisely, a perpetuity.[117]

I will describe three particularly interesting examples of the use of trust forms by Zionist organizations, starting with the notorious and ending with the secret.

A. *Ha'avara*

Germany's Jews came under threat on the establishment of the Nazi government in early 1933. Many German Jews were relatively wealthy, and Nazi government policy, until the War years, supported their emigration. Wealthier Jews could immigrate to Mandate Palestine more easily than the less fortunate, as the Mandate government was, until 1937, prepared to issue an unlimited number of 'A-1' Visas, granted to immigrants who could demonstrate their ownership of property worth at least £1,000. Before the Nazis' rise to power, the number of such relatively wealthy Jewish immigrants to Palestine was limited: the prosperous Jews of Central and Western Europe – not to mention those of the Americas – were generally intent on staying in their host societies. The Nazis' rise to power brought a relatively prosperous Jewish population under direct threat for the first time since the late nineteenth-century rise of Zionism; and as other options for emigration were increasingly closed off, the Palestinian option became more attractive.

Prosperous immigrants, however, generally wanted to take their wealth along with them. German legislation enacted in 1931–2, before the Nazi takeover, in an effort to stem capital flight from Germany, limited the amount of funds those leaving German territory could take with them, absent special permission, to 200 Reichsmarks (then about £13). Such a sum did not suffice in order to obtain an 'A-1' visa, far less to settle in Palestine. Various commercial enterprises took advantage of German Jewry's plight by offering, for example, insurance policies

117 For the debate regarding the legal form to be given to the JNF, see H. Bentwich, 'Zur Legalisierung des jüdischen Nationalfonds', *Die Welt*, 28 September 1906, 27–32; M. Bodenheimer, 'Zur Legalisierung des jüdischen Nationalfonds', *Die Welt*, 3 October 1906, 13–14; 12 October 1906, 12–14. See further L. Doukhan-Landau [Moses Doukhan's daughter], *The Zionist Companies for Land Purchase in Palestine* (Jerusalem: Yad Izhak Ben- Zvi, 1979), pp. 63–85; T. Shiloni, *The Jewish National Fund and Settlement in Eretz-Israel, 1903–1914* (Jerusalem, Ben Zvi Institute, 1990), pp. 26–9; M. and N. Bentwich, *Herbert Bentwich: The Pilgrim Father* (Jerusalem, Hozaah Ivrith, 1940), pp. 139–40.

which could be purchased in Germany, then cashed abroad after emigration, at a significant discount. Under those circumstances, the leaders of the small German-Jewish community of pre-Nazi-era Mandate Palestine, principally Felix Rosenblüth and Werner Senator, along with the then-head of the Jewish Agency's political department, Chaim Arlosoroff, conceived of a trust operation for the extraction of Jews, along with their property, from Germany to Palestine. Negotiations between private Jewish businessmen, German-Jewish banks, representatives of the German Zionist movement, and the Nazi Wirtschaftsministerium proved successful, and in late 1933 two self-described trust companies were set up and registered, in Germany and Palestine respectively. The German trust company, PALTREU – Palästina Treuhandstelle zur Beratung Deutscher Juden, or the Palestine Trust Office for Advising German Jews, was a partnership of the Anglo-Palestine Bank and two major German-Jewish banks, owned by the Warburg and Wassermann families. The Palestinian trust company, the Trust and Transfer Office 'Ha'avara' (transfer), was, at first, a Tel Aviv subsidiary of the Anglo-Palestine Bank; the bank later transferred its holding to the Jewish Agency for Palestine, the local arm of the World Zionist Organization. The scheme worked as follows. German Jews deposited Reichsmarks in excess of the Reichsmark equivalent of £1,000 in one of two specially earmarked accounts at the Reichsbank. Having received a certificate for doing so, they were able to prove their ownership of funds in the sum deposited to the Mandate immigration authorities and receive an 'A-1' visa for Palestine. Palestinian merchants and industrialists, meanwhile, placed orders for German products – typically products German manufacturers had trouble selling on the free market – with the Ha'avara office in Tel Aviv. Monies taken from the PALTREU Reichsbank accounts were channelled to the German manufacturers as payment. As the Palestinian purchasers repaid Ha'avara, through Palestinian banks, for the credit extended, Ha'avara paid the counter-value to the newly-arrived immigrants from Germany. In this way the German need for export markets for German products was exploited to permit German Jews to escape Hitler's noose with at least some of their property intact: 25% of the Ha'avara monies were deducted from payments made to depositors, and used to cover the travel costs of poor immigrants from Germany and support immigrants during their absorption in Palestine. Depositors lost the applicable exchange commission for purchasing sterling; another fraction of the sums deposited was deducted to reimburse Palestinian purchasers of German goods for the extortionate prices demanded by

German manufacturers. On top of those losses, Ha'avara-PALTREU charged a 4% commission to cover their administrative costs. The terms worsened as Nazi repression deepened and Germany's Jews became more desperate to leave.[118]

Ha'avara served general Jewish and Zionist purposes.[119] It increased the Jewish population of Palestine, swelled the Jewish-Palestinian middle class and Palestine's industrial infrastructure, and saved some 50,000 to 60,000 German, Austrian and Czechoslovak[120] Jews from likely murder

[118] The archive of Ha'avara now forms Class L57 at the CZA. For the history of the Ha'avara transfer operation see: W. Feilchenfeld, *Five Years of Jewish Immigration from Germany and the Haavara-transfer* (Tel Aviv: Haaretz Press, 1938); W. Feilchenfeld et al., *Haavara-transfer nach Palästina und Einwanderung Deutscher Juden 1933–1939* (Tübingen: Mohr, 1972); L. Pinner, 'Vermögenstransfer nach Palästina, 1933–1939', in H. Tramer (ed.), *In Zwei Welten: Siegfried Moses Zum Funfundsiebzigsten Geburtstag* (Tel Aviv: Bitaon, 1962), p. 133; Gelber, *New Homeland*, above, note 90, pp. 26–35, 154–75; R. Bondi, *Felix: Pinchas Rosen and his Time* (Tel Aviv: Zmora Bitan, 1990), pp. 120, 247, 290; R. N. Rosenzweig, *The Economic Consequences of Zionism* (Leiden: E.J. Brill, 1989), pp. 81–9; H. A. Strauss, 'Jewish Emigration from Germany, Nazi Policies and Jewish Responses (II)' (1981) 26 *Leo Baeck Institute Yearbook* 343; Gross et al., *Banker*, above, note 85, pp. 176–8; E. Black, *The Transfer Agreement: the Dramatic Story of the Pact Between the Third Reich and Jewish Palestine* (New York: Carroll & Graf, 2001). For the subsidy Ha'avara paid Palestinian purchasers of German goods to reimburse them for the prices demanded by German vendors, see the documents in CZA file A417/422, including statements of claim and judicial decisions in lawsuits depositors filed against Ha'avara for deducting a larger fraction of sums deposited than was agreed; Ha'avara had to pay larger subsidies as the Germans demanded higher and higher prices.

[119] In furthering those purposes it established other trust companies, such as the Near East Trust Co., established in 1934 as an Ha'avara affiliate. In 1937 the Near East Trust Co. proposed 'to grant second-transfer mortgages . . . from money placed at its disposal by . . . Ha'avara', and 'issue LP.30,000 of 6% certificates which will be offered to transfer immigrants'. 'Preference [was to] be given to prospective immigrants who can thereby obtain an [immigration] certificate': *Palestine Post*, 'Second-Transfer-Mortgages managed by the Near East Trust Co.', 14 April 1937, 10. Once immigration from Germany was cut short by the war, the Near East Trust Co. shifted its activities to supporting the 'middle class' farming settlements founded in Palestine by Jewish emigrants from Germany (being 'middle class' principally meant, among late Mandate-era Palestinian Jews, not being a member of the powerful Jewish Labourers' Federation, the *histadrut*). It became 'a purchasing organization for a number of grocery stores', 'a subsidiary enterprise of the Rural and Suburban Settlement Company (RASSCO)', itself an Ha'avara affiliate: *Palestine Post*, 'LP.50,000 Debenture Issue of "Rassco"', 25 June 1945, 2. It collectively marketed the produce of 'middle class' communities to both grocery stores and industrialists, who contracted with the trust to buy this produce exclusively from the trust: see overview, dated 16.12.1943, of the trust's first year of renewed operations, and other pertinent documents, in CZA, file 415\422.

[120] After the *Anschluss* of March 1938, operations similar, though not identical, to Ha'avara were put in place for Austrian and (later) Czechoslovak Jews. These operations, like

at the hands of the Nazis. It provided a sizeable chunk – slightly more than 9 million Palestinian Pounds – of the influx of private funds, running to 54.2 million P.P., which was imported into Palestine between 1933 and 1939, driving its economic growth and facilitating the establishment of a modern infrastructure and economy.[121] Ha'avara resembles charitable trusts in that its beneficiaries were distressed persons, and in that it was administered through a mechanism set up by public-sector Zionist organizations; private trusts are usually the creation of their settlor and his legal and tax advisers, and are administered by them. Still, the essence of Ha'avara was a series of special-purpose private family trusts. Its purpose was to let German-Jewish immigrants *keep* as much as possible of their money; charitable trusts are a means of giving one's assets away. The unique nature of Ha'avara reflected the unique characteristics of its user population: still relatively wealthy, and yet distressed by a menacing regime and the restrictions it put on the exportation of money.

Strikingly, while the transfer mechanism functioned as a hybrid, public–private trust, neither of its two arms was, in point of form, a pure trust. Though 1930s German law knew a form of trust in the *Treuhand*,[122] it was seen as more appropriate to establish PALTREU as a partnership. The Tel Aviv arm of the operation, the Trust and Transfer Office Ha'avara, was a trust company, though one which did in fact function as a trustee. A further peculiarity of the transfer operation was that the monies distributed to its beneficiaries in Palestine did not derive directly from monies its settlors deposited in Germany, despite the settlors and beneficiaries being the same persons. Monies deposited in Germany were paid to German manufacturers. Monies distributed in Palestine came from credit extended by Palestinian banks to Palestinian purchasers of German goods. Of the familiar types of trust, the Ha'avara operation most resembles, perhaps, the pension fund: a standardized,

Ha'avara itself, only lasted until the opening of World War II: see sources in note 118 above.

121 For data on the sums transferred through Ha'avara and on capital imports to 1930s Palestine generally, see Gelber, *New Homeland*, above, note 90, pp. 152, 172; M. Michaely, *Foreign Trade and Capital Imports in Israel* (Tel Aviv: Am Oved, 1963), pp. 1, 3; M. Beenstock et al., 'Immigration and the Jewish Economy in Mandatory Palestine' (1995) 15 *Research in Economic History* 149–213; T. Gozansky, *Formation of Capitalism in Palestine* (Haifa: University Projects Press, 1986), pp. 99–107.

122 On the *Treuhand* see, e.g., S. Grundmann, *Der Treuhandvertrag: insbesondere die werbende Treuhand* (Munich: C. H. Beck, 1997); M. Löhnig, *Treuhand: Interessenwahrnehmung und Interessenkonflikte* (Tübingen: Mohr Siebeck, 2006); H. Kötz, 'Trusts in Germany', in *La Fiducie*, above, note 89, p. 175.

collective trust fund intended for a specific, pre-defined class of beneficiaries, where employee and employer contributions to the fund are made at time X (during employment) and disbursed at time Y (retirement). The Ha'avara-transfer substituted the physical distance between Germany and Palestine for the distance in time in the pension fund model, and the difficulties of Nazi repression, German exchange controls and Mandate immigration controls for the hardships of old age.

B. *Mheiman and Himnuta*

The extraction of Jewish monies from Nazi Germany was also the principal motive for the establishment of two more 'Zionist public sector' trust companies: Mheiman and Himnuta, both JNF subsidiaries. The two companies' unique names – Aramaic forms of 'trustee' – were chosen by Dr Barth, who took care of their registration: Barth was an observant Jew, conversant in Judaism's Aramaic sources.[123] The JNF established them as one element of a complex plan formed to facilitate the transfer to Palestine of monies the JNF itself accumulated in German banks, the fruits of donations by German Jews. Money owned by an organization, rather than an individual, could not be transferred to Palestine by way of Ha'avara. A solution was found once the Berlin offices of the JNF were indirectly contacted in April 1936 by Hermann Ferdinand Keller, a former inhabitant of the (non-Jewish) 'German Colony' of Haifa, newly arrived in Germany; some of the Templer inhabitants of Palestine's 'German Colonies' were, as a result of the deterioration of German–Jewish relations, keen to return to Germany and liquidate their property in Palestine.[124] Despite his emigration, Keller still owned a significant amount of land in Haifa, and was interested in selling it to the JNF. As both the German branch of the JNF and Keller were domiciled in Germany, the sale was not subject to German exchange controls: it was to be a sale between two Germans. The JNF did not, however, wish to hold Keller's land, on the periphery of Haifa, as part of its ever-growing fund of land, which its statutes barred it from selling: during this period, the Fund focused on acquiring rural land for agricultural development, and did not wish to hold urban land. The solution was found in the

123 Alexander, 'Himnuta', above, note 85, 86.

124 For the non-Jewish German community of late-Ottoman and Mandate-era Palestine, and its 'German Colonies', see Y. Ben-Artzi, *From Germany to the Holy Land* (Jerusalem: Ben Tzvi Institute, 1996).

establishment, in the Fall of 1936, of Mheiman, a trust company, so that it could hold Keller's land on trust for the JNF. Unlike the JNF itself, Mheiman was not barred by its statutes from selling its land. The consideration for the eventual sale of land held by Mheiman would then continue to be held on trust for the JNF, which could, as beneficiary, call for the monies when it saw fit. Registration of the land as owned by an unknown company rather than the JNF was also useful in preventing the anti-Zionist clerks of the Haifa land registry from derailing the plan.[125]

Mheiman was, however, limited, according to both its memorandum of association and statutes, to purchasing and acquiring Keller's Haifa land. It was made use of in three more purchases of land in Haifa from H. F. Keller and other German owners of Haifa land.[126] Still, when a sale of German-owned land in the Bet-Shean valley, by the Jordan River, was proposed, another company, on the Mheiman model but not limited to purchases in Haifa, was established in the Summer of 1938: Himnuta. While the last significant transaction in which Mheiman was involved was completed in 1938, and the company was eventually wound up in 1950, Himnuta has since its establishment served the JNF for a large variety of transactions: it was (and is) used whenever the JNF purchases land with a view to reselling it.[127]

Interestingly, the memoranda and statutes of both companies do not mention their trusteeship role. They define the companies' objects as purchasing, administering and holding real estate, and expressly give them extended powers to deal with the property they purchase, including, significantly, powers of sale. The establishment of each company was, however, accompanied by the conclusion of a contract between the newly established company and the JNF, according to which the company was to hold its assets in trust for the JNF. The contract concluded

125 For Mheiman, see G. A. Alexander, 'Land Transactions in Haifa between Germans and the Jewish National Fund, 1936–1937' (1988) 48 *Kathedra* 164; Y. Katz, *The Battle for the Land: the Jewish National Fund before the Establishment of Israel* (Jerusalem: Magnes, 2002), pp. 56–9. My description omits several additional complexities which characterized the transactions to which Mheiman was a party, but are unnecessary for present purposes.

126 Alexander, 'Land Transactions', above, note 125, 178–81.

127 On Himnuta, see generally Alexander, 'Himnuta', above, note 85, *passim*. For the winding-up of Mheiman, see Alexander, 'Land Transactions', above, note 125, 175 note 43. For the many 1940s uses of Himnuta, see Alexander, 'Himnuta', above, note 85, 93–5; Katz, *Battle*, above, note 125, pp. 196–8, 242–55. For later (post-1967) uses of Himnuta, see A. Ehrlich, 'West Bank Land Fraud' (1986) 15 *Journal of Palestine Studies* 161.

between Himnuta and the JNF made clear Himnuta's role as a passive trustee. It undertook to receive, release and transfer any asset upon receipt of instructions from the JNF. The JNF undertook to defray any transaction costs. Himnuta was not to undertake any obligation to a third party absent JNF consent in writing.[128]

The care Barth took to disguise the two companies' function as trustees in their memoranda and statutes is striking, especially if he believed in the late 1930s, as he described his belief of that time in his 1946 letter, that Chief Justice McDonnell's seeming rejection of the applicability of the English private trust in Palestine could not 'be seen as a binding precedent'. Barth's further 1946 statement, that *Eliash* did not prevent 'the establishment in Palestine of trust companies' and their approval by 'the government's legal apparatus', meaning the registrar of companies, was correct, since as we have seen, companies expressly called 'trust company', and even a 'General Trust Corporation', were successfully registered in Palestine both before and after the registration of the two JNF subsidiaries. Some of those 'trust companies' specialized, like Mheiman and Himnuta, in the purchase and resale of land in Palestine.[129] It was probably the identity of the beneficiary – the JNF – that made Barth disguise the subsidiaries' role as trustees for that organization. Both companies were registered during the disturbances known as the 'Arab Revolt' (1936–9); the JNF's controversial land purchases were a central cause of Arab alarm. In response to Arab pressure, British support for Zionism was weakening.[130] Strikingly, the two companies' very nature as JNF *subsidiaries* was also disguised: each company issued, on its establishment, 20 shares, held in equal parts by Barth and Dr Sally Hirsch. Both were then working as private lawyers, rather than for the JNF or any other public Zionist institution (16 of the 20 Himnuta shares were in 1939–40 transferred to the JNF).[131] The two companies' identity as JNF subsidiaries was thus kept from the Registry's staff. While Barth admitted, in his letter of 25 April 1938 to the Registrar of Companies,

[128] The memoranda and statutes of Mheiman have been lost, but not the contract it concluded with the JNF; I follow Alexander, 'Land Transactions', above, note 125, 175–6. For the memoranda and statutes of Himnuta, see Alexander, 'Himnuta', above, note 85, 86. The contract Himnuta concluded with the JNF is quoted by Katz, *Battle*, above, note 125, p. 59; the original is at the CZA, file L1/597.

[129] See examples in notes 90 and 94 above.

[130] T. Segev, *Palestine under the British* (Jerusalem: Keter, 1999), pp. 353–9.

[131] For the share allocation, see Alexander, 'Land Transactions', above, note 125, 176; Alexander, 'Himnuta', above, note 85, 91–3.

applying for the registration of 'Hinmuta', that the company was being established as a trustee for German Jews who were having difficulties transferring their property out of the Third Reich, he remained silent regarding Himnuta's being a trustee for the JNF.[132] Barth may have estimated that Mandate government officials would be less likely to obstruct what was presented as a humane effort to help Germany's oppressed Jews than JNF purchasing activity, presented as such.

C. *Use of nominee landowners*

My final example of the use of private trust forms by Zionist organizations involves JNF use of what were, in effect, individual passive trustees of land, in the increasingly adverse, from the JNF's perspective, circumstances of the 1940s. The Land Transfers Regulations of 1940 having forbidden, as regards 95% of the land in Palestine, the transfer of land owned by Palestinian Arabs other than to Palestinian Arabs,[133] the JNF resorted between 1940 and 1948 to legal subterfuge, in order to continue extending its landholdings. Key to several of the strategems adopted was a loophole in the regulations which facilitated Jewish purchases of Arab land if the latter were made in satisfaction of a mortgage. To take advantage of this loophole, the JNF arranged for land it purchased from Arab sellers – many continued to sell, despite the regulations and Arab agitation against such sales[134] – to be purchased and held by its Arab nominees. Such nominees, referred to in at least one JNF document as 'trusted persons', gave the JNF a mortgage on the land, a durable power of attorney and a notarized bill in recognition of a (fictional) debt owed by the nominee. The nominee would then fail to repay his purported debt, and the land would be subjected to a judicial sale by public auction, in which JNF representatives would appear and win. This trusteeship practice was fully concealed from the Mandate government, including its land registry and courts. It operated, at great risk of default on the nominees' part, absent the involvement of any government body. It continued to the end of the

[132] For Barth's letter, see Alexander, 'Himnuta', above, note 85, 88.

[133] Land Transfers Regulations, 1940, *Palestine Gazette*, Gazette Extraordinary, No. 988, 28 February 1940, Supplement No. 2.

[134] For Palestinian Arabs' sales of land to Zionist settlers, both individuals and organizations, throughout the Mandate period, and for Arab agitation against such sales, see H. Cohen, *An Army of Shadows: Palestinian Collaborators in the Service of Zionism* (Jerusalem: Ivrit, 2004).

Mandate, despite the applicability, in Palestine, of the English private trust having, in 1945–6, been explicitly rejected by the courts.[135]

The above three examples of the use of private trust forms by Zionist organizations demonstrate both the trust's eminent utility for effecting complex transactions and moving funds between territories, and its characteristic walking of the line between legality and the lack thereof. Zionist organizations made use both of trust types which were plainly legal – as trust companies were according to the Companies Ordinance – and, when driven to extremes by the government's limitations on Jewish land-purchase activities, of trust types which were wholly subterfuge, echoing the beginnings of the trust in late medieval England as a strictly private, passive nomineeship, played out outside the state's purview.[136]

If some British colonial judges, then, tended to deny the natives of Palestine and Zionist settlers there the use of the English private trust form, some of those settlers used it nonetheless, though trust companies, serving as trustees, were more popular than individual trusteeship. The Zionist settler population thus appropriated more of the colonizer's law than the latter was willing to have it use (at least on the more restrictive reading of *Eliash*). As is often the case with the uses to which trusts are put, Zionist settler use of private trusts and trust companies was often directed at evading inconvenient elements of positive law, such as the impossibility of registering title to a flat (rather than to a plot of land), Germany's limitations on the exportation of money, the quotas the Mandate authorities applied to Jewish immigration to Palestine, and the restrictions put on Jewish purchases of Arab-owned land. Much of the use of trusts and trust companies, both private initiatives such as Kahn's Palestine Investment Association and Moses' General Trust Corporation and initiatives of the Zionist establishment, such as Ha'avara and the JNF-controlled trust companies, was dedicated to the funnelling of Jews and Jewish money to Palestine. Other trusts were dedicated to using that money in purchasing land in Palestine. Jewish immigrants from Germany, as were Barth, Moses, Kahn, Rosenblüth and Senator, were as key to the burgeoning supply of trusteeship services in 1930s

135 For the practice described, see CZO, file KKL5/15927, minutes of a meeting between Y. Stroumza, T. Wolf and A. Danin (all JNF operatives), held 5 November 1947 (the phrase 'trusted persons' appears in this document); ibid., file KKL5/15929, letter dated 4 January 1948, by JNF land dept. to Adv. Yoav Sugarman. See also Katz, *Battle*, above, note 125, pp. 129, 232, note 87 and text; Y. Katz, *Jewish Settlement in the Hebron Mountains and the Etzion Bloc* (Ramat Gan: Bar-Ilan University Press, 1992), p. 31.

136 See note 68 above and accompanying text.

Palestine as to the simultaneously growing demand for them.[137] A 1936 listing, by trade or profession, of the Jewish immigrants from Germany then living in the town of Haifa, a major concentration of such immigrants, shows thirteen 'transferberater [transfer advisers], trustees usw.'.[138] Downtown Haifa's financial district, now largely derelict, still features a 'Trustees St.'.[139] The trust was not only important in practice, however; it was also, as we shall see in the next Part, an important focus of debate among Mandate Palestine's Zionist jurists.

IV Zionist settler jurists debate the trust

The common law trust, seen, despite its functional equivalents in other legal traditions, as unique to the common law, often seems foreign to jurists of other traditions. Civil law jurists in Quebec and South Africa, faced with the undeniable presence of the trust in their jurisdictions, repeatedly struggled with the technical difficulties of fitting the common law trust into civil law-based systems of private law.[140] The very advisability of such a reception was also debated. Some accepted that their systems have received something very similar to the English trust;[141] others insisted that though the terms 'trust', 'trustee' and other terms originating in English trust law were in common use in their systems, those terms were to be interpreted according to the principles of the receiving system, rather than as importing the English law of trusts.[142]

137 This prominence of lawyers and bankers principally familiar with German law and finance made for curious Anglo-German hybrids, such as the Fidelitas Investment & Trust Co. Ltd advertising its *Treuhand* services in the *Palestine Post*, 9 March 1934, 7.

138 Statistics of the German immigrants in Haifa, 1936, found in CZA, file S7\377. The data quoted is from Table 8.

139 Banks St., Deposit St. and Account St. are nearby.

140 See, for Quebec, Claxton, *Studies*, above, note 76, pp. 12–25.

141 See, e.g. Quebecois jurist P.-B. Mignault's essay 'A propos de fiducie' (1933) 12 *Revue du droit* 78, and the opinions by Chief Justice De Villiers of the Cape Colony discussed by Honoré, 'Trust', above, note 2, at p. 860 (incorporating into the law of the Cape 'the English conception of a trustee *de son tort*') and p. 862 (incorporating into the law of the Cape the English rule that on the insolvency of a registered owner of land, who held it as a trustee although the register did not reflect this fact, the beneficiaries have priority over the trustee's private creditors as regards the trust land). De Villiers clothed his reception of English ideas in civilian terminology; there was no explicit reception.

142 See, e.g., decisions by James Rose Innes, Chief Justice of South Africa, cited in Honoré, 'Trust', above, note 2, at pp. 862 and 868 ('the English law of trusts forms, of course, no portion of our jurisprudence ... but it does not follow that testamentary dispositions couched in the form of trusts cannot be given full effect in our own law').

1940s Palestine knew a similar debate, focused on both the advisability of receiving the English trust into the law of Palestine and the technical means for doing so. The trust was at the centre of a controversy which raged, throughout the decade, in the pages of the Journal of the Palestinian Association of Jewish Lawyers, *HaPraklit* [the lawyer]. The debate, caused by the co-existence of prevalent use of trusts and trust companies and incidental legislative references to private trusteeship with judicial decisions denying the applicability of the common law private trust in Palestine, was ignited by a lecture given at the 1942 conference of the Association, and later published in the inaugural issue of its organ, by Guido Tedeschi, a Jewish-Italian professor of law. Tedeschi was then lately arrived from Italy after having been fired from his post at Siena University following Mussolini's anti-semitic legislation of 1938. Tedeschi's piece did not directly address the reception of the private trust in Palestine: in reviewing the common law trust and civilian *fiducia*, he noted early instances of the adoption of the trust in largely civilian systems: Quebec, South Africa and Japan.[143]

Tedeschi's brief piece attracted several ripostes, focusing, unlike Tedeschi's piece, on the applicability and use of the private common law trust in Mandate Palestine. One was by Alfred Witkowski, then a leading Jewish-Palestinian lawyer of German birth, who received his legal education in both Germany and England. Witkowski, who was to be appointed in 1954, as Alfred Witkon, to the Supreme Court of Israel, served as its undisputed tax expert until his 1980 retirement.[144] His article pointed out how trust law was developing in Palestine under conditions similar to those which drove its development in late-medieval England. Since most land in both the agricultural and urban areas of Palestine was (state-owned) *miri*, its possessors could not bequeath it or dedicate it as *waqf*. Much as in England before the Statute of Wills of 1540, the impossibility of making wills of land proved a fertile ground for the adoption and popularization, in practice, of the common law trust. As is well known, a further reason for the medieval employment of the

[143] G. Tedeschi, 'Contemporary Trust Business' (1943) 78 *HaPraklit* 1. He could also have cited Ceylon, which adopted the English trust on top of a Roman-Dutch legal stratum: Cooray, *Reception*, above, note 73. For biographical information on Tedeschi see Y. Sagy, 'Interview with Gad Tedeschi', in Aharon Barak et al. (eds.), *Essays in Private Law, in Memory of Gad Tedeschi* (Jerusalem: Sacher Institute, 1995), p. 23.

[144] For biographical information see M. Landau, 'In Memory of Alfred Witkon', in Aharon Barak et al. (eds.), *Justice and the Judiciary* (Tel Aviv: Schocken, 1988), p. 11 (a collection of Witkon's articles); H. Cohn, 'On Alfred Witkon', ibid., p. 15.

English trust was the feudal burdens accompanying intestate succession, which were, in effect, a medieval form of taxation.[145] Witkowski was understandably vague, in print, in his treatment of this aspect of the parallelism between late-medieval and Mandate Palestinian circumstances, noting that 'though feudal burdens are not now imposed on property owners in Palestine, it is certainly possible that under modern conditions, too, a need will occasionally arise for the legal owner to be other than the beneficiary'.[146] Witkowski concluded, echoing Herbert Samuel's expectations of 1925, that article 46 of the Palestine Order in Council, which permitted the application of English law, excepting (probably) statute but including 'the doctrines of equity', so far as Ottoman and specifically Mandate law did not 'extend or apply', did permit the reception of the common law private trust into the law of Palestine. In particular, since most land in Palestine was state-owned, out of which *waqfs* – the only form of trust Ottoman law knew – could not be declared, there was an evident need, not satisfied by existing Ottoman law or Mandate legislation, for an alternative form of private trust.[147]

Reinforcing Witkowski's arguments, Tedeschi noted in a second piece on the subject, now addressing the applicability of the common law private trust in Palestine, that in light of the promulgation of the Charitable Trusts Ordinance and the references to the trust in other Ordinances, the common law trust could not be seen as contradicting any pre-existing principles of Palestinian law, and thus did not fall foul of the restrictive clauses of article 46.[148] Tedeschi further argued that instead of seeing the common law private trust as received into the law of Palestine by way of article 46, the trust should be seen as permitted as one result of the freedom of contract, which had been a basic principle of Palestinian law since late Ottoman times.[149] Arguing for the reception of the English private trust by way of article 46 had the disadvantage that a common reading of that article understood it to permit, subject to its several restrictive clauses, the importation of English case law while blocking that of English statutes (it permitted the importation of 'the substance of

145 See a listing of 'the chief custodial purposes of [medieval] uses' in J. Getzler, 'Duty of Care', in P. Birks and A. Pretto (eds.), *Breach of Trust* (Oxford: Hart, 2002), p. 43. Wielding power to dispose of land, including testamentary disposition, and escaping the Crown's fiscal claims are the last two.

146 A. Witkowski, 'Private Trusts in Palestine' (1947–48) 3 *HaPraklit* 99, 102.

147 The quotations are from the Palestine Order in Council, article 46.

148 Ibid.

149 For the introduction of this principle into Ottoman law, see Malchi, *History of Law*, above, note 10, pp. 62–3.

the common law, and the doctrines of equity'). Contracting parties, however, could agree to adopt, as between themselves, not only that part of the English law of trusts which was contained in the cases, but also its statutory part.[150]

Once the Italian-born Tedeschi, who studied law in Rome, and the German-born Witkowski, who received a PhD from Freiburg University, advocated the reception of the common law private trust into the law of Palestine, it was left to Professor Paltiel Dickstein of the Tel Aviv School of Law and Economics, a generation older than both and a product of Russian Zionism, to oppose that reception.[151] Echoing Chief Justice McDonnell, Dickstein argued that ill-drafted legislation does not prove that a foreign legal form has been received into local law. Difficulties, such as most of the land in Palestine being impossible to bequeath, should be corrected by direct amendment rather than by the importation of means for circumventing them. The chief reason for Dickstein's negative attitude towards the reception of the common law private trust into the law of Palestine was his ideological support for the fundamental refashioning of the law of the fast-increasing Jewish population of Palestine along lines drawn from ancient Jewish law, refashioned for the twentieth century. In such a worldview there was no place for the importation of the English private trust, and Dickstein emphasized the trust's deep roots in English culture and history. In the 1940s, when the adoption of the Anglo-American trust by non-Anglophone jurisdictions was less advanced than it is today, describing the trust as somehow peculiar to the English national character and history could, perhaps, have seemed plausible.[152]

[150] G. Tedeschi, 'On English-Style Private Trusts in Eretz-Yisrael' (1947–1948) 3 *HaPraklit* 306.

[151] For Dickstein, see Likhovski, *Law and Identity*, above, note 9, pp. 127–53.

[152] P. Dickstein, 'On Ways for Completing Our Law and on the Private Trust' (1948) 4 *HaPraklit* 4. Another group of 1940s publications which discuss the applicability of the common law private trust in Palestine were textbooks and practitioners' manuals on income tax law. The juxtaposition of the references to private trusteeship in the Income Tax Ordinance with *Eliash* and the mid-1940s cases applying it made for great uncertainty, which is reflected in the income tax literature. Some treatises, looking squarely at the provisions of the 1941 Ordinance, simply assumed, without argument, that private trusteeship was part of the law of Palestine: S. Moses, *The Income Tax Ordinance of Palestine* (Jerusalem: Tarshish, 1942), p. 96; A. Fellman, *The Palestine Income Tax Law and Practice* (Tel Aviv: Lapid, 1946), pp. 82, 128–9, 232, 254, 288, 292, 378. Other works, being aware of the conflicting line of case law, were driven to ambiguous statements on the subject. G. Eichelgrün opined in 1945 that 'One can say that the applicability of the English law of trusts is not yet explored at all in Palestine . . . It is . . . not impossible that the Palestine courts might today be more inclined to accept the substance of the English

V Conclusion: the law of trusts as a liminal site of legal transplantation

The career of the common law private trust in Mandate Palestine provides examples of several types of legal transplantation under colonial conditions. Jonathan Miller's typology of legal transplants was created with transplants between sovereign states in mind,[153] and requires adaptation before it is used to classify transplants under colonial conditions, where the recipient territory is not independent. A typology of legal transplants under colonialism, focused on transplantation to colonized territories, could identify two groups, according to the transplanting agents' identity: (i) transplants initiated by persons representing the colonizer or applying the colonizer's power and (ii) transplants initiated by others, such as the inhabitants of the colonized territory concerned who are not employed by, or do not otherwise serve, the colonizing power. A finer classification emerges once we take into account the motives of and reasons for transplantation. Colonizer-initiated transplantation can take place because its agents are convinced that the legal ideas they are transplanting are superior, and their transplantation will benefit the recipient population. Or it can take place as a cost-saving measure: colonial rule according to principles with which colonizing personnel are already familiar is cheaper (or 'more efficient') than requiring that personnel to familiarize itself with unfamiliar legal rules, ideas, principles and practices. Colonizer-initiated transplantation can also, as this chapter demonstrates, take place absent a full consideration of its appropriateness: colonizing personnel sometimes transplant large masses of legal ideas wholesale (as in copying lengthy, codifying enactments), without separate consideration of the appropriateness of transplanting each and every idea transplanted. Or they can act under an unverified

law of trusts in Palestine' (*Palestine Income Tax Guide* (Haifa: Paltax, 1945), p. 136). Moses reflected in the second edition of his treatise that '[t]he legal possibility of validly creating in Palestine a trusteeship in cases other than those provided for in statutes ... has been in the past somewhat doubtful, but in general assumed as existing. This view has been confirmed by section 21A, introduced by [the Income Tax (Amendment) Ordinance, 1945], which pre-supposes the possibility of creating a trusteeship for the purpose of a "settlement" in favour of minors' (S. Moses and W. Schwarz, *The Income Tax Ordinance of Palestine*, 2nd edn (Tel Aviv: Bitaon, 1946), p. 78).

[153] J. M. Miller, 'A Typology of Legal Transplants: Using Sociology, Legal History and Argentine Examples to Explain the Transplant Process' (2003) 51 *American Journal of Comparative Law* 839.

assumption that local law on a certain point must be similar or identical to the law they know, ignoring the very possibility of legal diversity.

Transplantation initiated by persons unconnected to the colonizing power can also take place as a result of myriad motives and causes. Transplantation other than by the colonizer is a matter of private persons and non-governmental groups and associations choosing to use legal forms and practices which have hitherto been foreign to them. While such choices were not always respected by colonizing personnel, this sort of transplantation could continue despite the absence of consent on the part of the colonizer, especially if respected by all the relevant (non-governmental) parties. As to the motives for and causes of this sort of transplantation, transplanting agents unconnected with the colonizer may seek to import legal ideas they see as superior, whether originating in the metropolitan legal system of the colonizing power in question or elsewhere. Cost-saving could play a role in this type of transplantation too, some colonized persons being anxious to take the shortest and cheapest route available to forming a social order independent of the colonizer. Such transplantation could even take place as a form of anti-colonial protest or struggle, its agents choosing legal imports from sources unconnected with, or seen as rivals of, the power colonizing them, as in British-controlled Egypt's use of French legal ideas.[154]

The Mandate-era Palestinian career of the common law private trust also included several decisions, which proved influential in varying degrees, to block its transplantation. The motives for such decisions were various: a belief that locals would have no use for the institution; that as the local pre-Mandate legal system included comparable institutions, transplanting the English private trust would unnecessarily clutter the legal landscape; that transplantation would impede Government policies, such as land settlement; and finally, a general abhorrence of transplanting English legal ideas into Palestine, stemming from a perception of the injustice wrought by British rule and a consequent desire to minimize its footprint. My study thus provides a vivid example of a struggle of two British colonial juristic mentalities: one supported the dissemination of English law in the Empire for native and non-British settler use, while the other believed in the preservation of the ante-colonial legal status quo.

The complexity of the transplantation story I have told reflects the trust's nature as a particularly complex and conflicted legal site. Its

[154] For which see G. Bechor, *The Sanhuri Code, and the Emergence of Modern Arab Civil Law (1932 to 1949)* (Leiden: E. J. Brill, 2007).

situation at a crossroads of family law, the law of succession and the law of commerce, business and investment placed it, in the British Empire, on the margins of the Empire's various personal law reserves. In India and Ceylon trusts were generally seen as outside that reserve, though the Ceylon Ordinance recognized Buddhist and Muslim 'religious trusts', exempting them from its charitable trusts regime.[155] The trust's situation in Palestine was yet more complex, as religious trusts – Moslem, Jewish and Christian – were explicitly included in the personal law reserve.[156] The fact that Muslim and Jewish religious trusts could be both charitable, in the sense of being dedicated to purposes of public benefit, and private family trusts, may have contributed to Chief Justice McDonnell's choice to block the transplantation of the English family trust into Palestine. That Jewish, Christian and Muslim religious trust law does not include commercial trusts may have, under those circumstances, contributed to this part of English trust law being successfully transplanted into Palestine.

The end result of the transplantation processes I have described was a partial reception of the English trust, on top of the existing religious trust regimes: while the English law of charitable trusts was received in a special Ordinance, that of commercial trusts was received through a combination of an official zeal for uniformity in commercial law, official oversight and settler enthusiasm. However, reception of the English family trust was blocked by the status-quo-minded Chief Justice. This result, while not reflecting any consciously settled and coherent government policy regarding transplantation of the English private trust into Palestine, does cohere with general British policy on the Anglicization of the law of Palestine: commercial law was Anglicized, land law was not. Zionist settlers' trust practice was discouraged where trusts were sought to be employed to create purportedly long-standing landholding arrangements: thus the discountenancing of the Eliash family trust and of the flat-owners' trust arrangement. Trust companies, on the other hand, were formed as commercial entities, often for investment purposes. The British, who scrutinized each one of them as their registration was sought, approved them, even when the subject of their commercial

[155] The Ordinance exempts 'religious trusts regulated by the Buddhist Temporalities Ordinance' and 'religious trusts regulated by the Muslim Intestate Succession and Wakfs Ordinance': An Ordinance to Define and Amend the Law Relating to Trusts, No. 9 of 1917, 4 of 1918, s. 109.

[156] Palestine Order in Council, articles 52, 53(3), 54(3)

activities was land. Landholding for commercial purposes was treated differently from the long-term holding of estates.

The trust's liminal character was reflected in the disagreement and confusion evident, on this subject, among British colonial personnel concerned with Palestine throughout the period of British rule. The private trust provisions of the Ceylon Trusts Ordinance were dropped from its early 1920s Palestinian descendant based on an expectation that should a private family trust on the English model come before the Courts of Palestine, they would apply the English law of private trusts, receiving it by way of the Palestine Order in Council, article 46. When, less than a decade later, such a trust did come before the Supreme Court of Palestine in the *Eliash* case, the Court acted contrary to this expectation. In the interim, English commercial law, including some commercial practices involving private trusts, was legislatively transplanted into Palestine as part of a Colonial Office drive to homogenize the commercial law of the Empire. Attorney-General Bentwich, often a champion of Anglicization, wrote to London that at least some of those practices were unknown in Palestine and legislative references to them were thus superfluous, but his advice was left unheeded. Come the 1930s, the *Eliash* decision amplified the accumulating confusion, as different official readers formed different views regarding the decision's import and consequences. Some Mandate officials were convinced that the English law of private trusts was no part of the law of Palestine. Others thought otherwise; so did, for example, the Registrar of Companies, who was registering trust companies by the dozen. Later in the decade, new Ordinances multiplied the legislative references to private trusts, a tendency which culminated in the 1941 Income Tax Ordinance. Though every word of this Ordinance was repeatedly scrutinized prior to enactment, those involved appear not to have been aware that private trusts were not necessarily a part of the law of Palestine. No thought appears to have been given to the issue. A few years later, contrastingly, the Courts of Palestine decided at least four cases based on the view that *Eliash* firmly excluded the English private trust from the law of Palestine.

Much of this confusion seems to have been a product of two tendencies. One was a tendency to treat each specific question separately as it arose, deciding it on the basis of its immediate doctrinal context. This tendency, which may have been a fruit of many colonial officials never having fully mastered the admittedly complex and multi-layered law of Palestine, seems to have prevented the formation, by any one official, of a full view of the common law private trust's evolving status under the law

court remarked regarding a will prepared by an English lawyer for a testator domiciled in South Africa regarding which property had been bequeathed to trustees who were to administer such property in favour of *cestuis que trust*:

> This [*cestuis que trust*] is a term which is unknown to our law, though the constitution of trusts and the appointment of trustees are matters of common occurrence in South Africa at the present day ... The [trust] idea is now so firmly rooted in our practice, that it would be quite impossible to eradicate it or to seek to abolish the use of the expression trustee.[4]

Despite the *Kemp* court's acknowledgement of the reception, from English law, of the trust into South African law, the court pointed out pertinently that the English legal rules pertaining to trusts were not received commensurately into South African law – English trust law, as a body of law, forms no part of South African law.[5] The Appellate Division, in its seminal judgment in *Braun* v. *Blann and Botha*,[6] ascribed South African law's aversion to English trust law to the fact that English law's notion of dual or divided ownership – a trust beneficiary's equitable ownership distinct from, but co-existing with, a trustee's legal ownership – is foreign to South African law's adherence (in typically civilian tradition) to single or unitary ownership in the form of dominium.[7] The non-reception into South African law of English trust law notwithstanding, English law remains an important source of comparative jurisprudence for the development of South African trust law; indeed, South African courts and academic commentators rely abundantly on English trust rules when addressing novel trust problems in South African law.

A further significant aspect of the *Braun* judgment is the court's criticism of earlier judicial attempts to 'civilianize' the trust through 'Romanist reconfiguration'[8] by casting the trust in a familiar Roman-Dutch guise. Typical of such purported domestication of the trust was the equation in *Kemp* of the testamentary trust with the testamentary

[4] *Estate Kemp* v. *McDonald's Trustee*, 1915 AD 491 at 507–8. [5] Ibid., at 499, 508.

[6] *Braun* v. *Blann and Botha*, 1984 (2) SA 850 (A) at 859E–F.

[7] See the discussion by M. J. de Waal, 'The Uniformity of Ownership, *Numerus Clausus* and the Reception of the Trust into South African Law', in J. M. Milo and J. M. Smits (eds.), *Trusts in Mixed Legal Systems* (Nijmegen: Ars Aequi Libri, 2001), pp. 43ff.

[8] Ibid., p. 48, referring to the term used by E. Cameron, 'Why No Constructive Trust in South African Law? The Experience of Another Mixed Legal System', paper read at a seminar on constructive trusts organized by the Universities of Edinburgh and Strathclyde and the Scottish Law Commission, 19 October 1996, p. 9.

fideicommissum and, consequently, the testamentary trustee with a fiduciary.[9] Such identification of the trust with the *fideicommissum* was authoritatively rejected by the Appellate Division in the *Braun* case. The *Braun* court reasoned it to be both historically and jurisprudentially wrong to identify the trust with the *fideicommissum* and to equate a trustee with a fiduciary;[10] instead the court labelled the (testamentary) trust, for purposes of South African law, a legal institution *sui generis* – an independent institution of its own kind.[11]

Given the reception of the trust as an institution from English law into South African law, though without the body of English trust law, and, moreover, given the operation of the trust, rooted in English common law, in South Africa's largely uncodified legal system with its strong civilian tradition, it stood to reason that a principle-based trust law unique to the South African condition had to be developed if the trust were to survive as more than a legal instrument operating on the outskirts of legal and commercial practice. This chapter traces some of the jurisprudential milestones in the development of South African trust law. It highlights the methodology followed towards the establishment of a coherent body of trust law that is, although still developing and far from comprehensive, nevertheless for the greater part conceptually pure and functionally responsive. To this end, this chapter contextualizes the contributions of the three principal constructors of South Africa's trust law – the courts, the legislature and writers – and shows how the contribution of each underpins the South African trust from an operational perspective.

II The courts – principal constructors

The judgment in *Braun* leaves no doubt that the primary development of South African trust law rests firmly with the courts. The court stated:

> Our Courts have evolved and are still in the process of evolving our own law of trusts by adapting the trust idea to the principles of our own law.[12]

In *Land and Agricultural Bank of South Africa* v. *Parker*, the Supreme Court of Appeal contextualized this statement with the following observation on the development of South African trust law:

> It may be said . . . that the English law trust, and the trust-like institutions of the Roman and Roman-Dutch law, were designed essentially to protect

[9] *Estate Kemp*, above, note 4, at 499, 512–3. [10] *Braun*, above, note 6, at 859C, 866B.
[11] Ibid., at 859E. [12] Ibid., at 859F–G.

> the weak and to safeguard the interests of those who are absent or dead. This guiding principle provided the foundation for this Court's major decisions over the past century in which the trust form has been adapted to South African law: That the trustee is appointed and accepts office to exercise fiduciary responsibility over property on behalf of and in the interests of another.[13]

The methodology of adapting the trust idea to the principles of South African law is manifest in two particular judicial practices that can be termed, first, alignment and, secondly, innovation. The former refers to South African courts' utilization of acknowleged common-law (Roman-Dutch) legal principles applicable to other fiduciary constructs to solve trust-law problems, in so doing aligning trustees' role as fiduciary functionaries, emphasized so explicitly in the aforementioned dictum from the *Parker* case, to South African law's general prescripts on fiduciary conduct. As indicated earlier, South African courts frequently fortify their findings effecting alignment with express reference to the corresponding English-law position. The judicial practice of innovation, on the other hand, refers to the courts' modernization of South African trust law where changing legal, social or economic conditions demand the renewal of trust law in order to secure the trust's optimal functionality and, moreover, to ensure that the trust remains true to its design as an instrument of protection, highlighted in the aforementioned dictum from the *Parker* case. To this end, too, South African courts rely copiously on apposite English trust rules to support their innovation of South African trust law.

A. *Alignment*

Three examples from South African case law serve to illustrate the judicial practice of alignment. First, in *Sackville West* v. *Nourse*, the issue for decision was whether trustees acted negligently in making a poor investment that occasioned patrimonial loss to the sole beneficiary under a trust. In determining the standard of care expected of trustees in effecting trust investments, the court relied expressly on the Roman-Dutch legal position regarding tutorship over a ward's property:

> Now, in dealing with the administration of the property of others by persons in a fiduciary position, our courts have adopted the rule of the

[13] *Land and Agricultural Bank of South Africa* v. *Parker*, 2005 (2) SA 77 (SCA) at paras. 19 and 20.

> Roman law, as expounded by the commentators and by the Dutch jurists. They have followed and applied the precept laid down by Paulus in the *Digest* (18.1.34.7), where we are told that 'the same principles which apply to a tutor in dealing with the property of his ward, should also be extended to other persons acting under similar circumstances; that is to say, to curators, procurators and all those who administer the affairs of others.' A trustee, therefore, is to be included in this category.[14]

Drawing on the Roman-Dutch legal position on tutorship, the court proclaimed that a trustee, like a tutor, must conduct investment with diligence and safety; moreover, that the standard of care to be observed in this regard is not that which a person ordinarily observes in the management of his or her own affairs, but rather that of the prudent and careful man – in Roman-law terms: the standard that can be expected of the *bonus et diligens paterfamilias*. The court concluded, therefore, that trustees, in conducting trust investments, may not expose the trust to any risk and, consequently, must avoid all investments that are speculative or otherwise attendant with risk or hazard.[15] Significantly, the court concludes with the following observation: 'In principle our law agrees with that of England.'[16]

A second example of alignment is found in *Doyle* v. *Board of Executors*, where the court was called upon to adjudicate on a trustee's refusal to provide a comprehensive account to a capital trust beneficiary of the trustee's administration of the trust from the time of the trustee's appointment. The trustee based its refusal to furnish the beneficiary with the requested account on the contingency of the beneficiary's right to trust capital during the greater part of the period of the trustee's administration of the trust.[17] The court, in rejecting the trustee's argument, pointed out that a trustee's office is fiduciary in nature; moreover, that, by reason of a trustee's occupation of a fiduciary office, a trustee owes the utmost good faith to actual and potential (contingent) trust beneficiaries.[18] The court resolved the trust law issue on a trustee's accountability by aligning trust law with the law of agency. Before attending to a relevant dictum from the *Doyle* judgment, it must be pointed out that South African law acknowledges that a trustee is not the agent of the trust founder, nor of the trust beneficiaries – a trustee's

[14] *Sackville West* v. *Nourse* 1925 AD 516 at 533–4.

[15] Ibid., at 534. See Section II.B below on a relaxation of this strict approach to trust investments.

[16] Ibid., at 535.

[17] *Doyle* v. *Board of Executors*, 1999 (2) SA 805 (C) at 810I–811H.

[18] Ibid., at 813B.

authority to act on behalf of a trust does not derive from a principal, but rather from the trust instrument at hand.[19] This notwithstanding, the law of agency (particularly given an agent's role as a fiduciary functionary) has proven fertile ground for judicial alignment of South African trust law with the general principles of South African law. In *Doyle* the court remarked:

> The duties of good faith, which are owed by an agent to his principal, are no different in kind to those that fall on a trustee . . . the duty [that] falls on an agent [is] to demonstrate that he acted with whatever care and skill the occasion demanded . . . Inextricably bound up with this by no means exhaustive compendium of obligations is the agent's duty to *give an accounting* to his principal of all that he knows and has done in the execution of his mandate and with the principal's property.[20]

On the above reasoning, the court ordered that the trustee *in casu*, in the discharge of its duty of good faith, could not deliver to the capital beneficiary mere unexplained and unvouched opening balances to trust accounts; instead, the trustee had to furnish the beneficiary with a comprehensive exposition of how the trust capital lay invested from time to time and of what undistributed income stood to be capitalized.[21] The *Doyle* court, like that in *Sackville West* before it, found fortification in English law for its principled stance on an agent's duty to account:

> It is not without significance that one finds similar statements of principle in the law of England . . . Indeed, it seems to me that on this matter our law and that of England are at one.[22]

A third example of alignment is found in *Hoosen* v. *Deedat*, where the court had to determine whether a trustee of a trust created to propagate the Islamic faith validly bestowed a power of attorney onto his daughter-in-law to take over his role as one of the trust's co-trustees. Having found that the trust deed in question did not provide expressly for the delegation by any of the trust's individual trustees of his rights, duties or powers,[23] the court proceeded to inquire whether the trust deed contained implied authorization to such effect. In answering this trust law question in the negative, the court again effected alignment between trust law and the law of agency:

> In considering the issue one may also, by analogy, draw usefully from an established principle in the law of agency, while not losing sight of the essential differences between trustee and agent. That principle states that

[19] *Hoosen* v. *Deedat*, 1999 (4) SA 425 (A) at paras. 21 and 22.
[20] *Doyle*, above, note 17, at 813D–H. [21] Ibid., at 815F–H. [22] Ibid., at 814F–G.
[23] *Hoosen*, above, note 19, at para. 23.

> where the identity and personal attributes or skills of the performer of an act are of material importance, delegation is not permitted.[24]

The trust *in casu* was established in the interests of the Muslim community to promote and propagate the Islamic faith. In the opinion of the court, the trustees would have to be imbued with the spirit of Islam in order to best give effect to the objects of the trust; indeed, the personal attributes of the trustees would have played a significant, if not conclusive, role in their selection as such.[25] The person of each trustee, therefore, assumed determinative importance in the overall design and functioning of the trust; this consideration militated against any suggestion of implied authorization for delegation in the trust deed.[26] Accordingly, the court held the purported delegation under the power of attorney to be legally impermissible.[27]

B. Innovation

Two examples from South African case law illustrate the judicial practice of innovation, in each instance the court importing precedent-setting renewal into trust law so as to achieve the functional sophistication of the legal rules governing the trust. However, a third example illustrates that, at times, innovation born out of frustration does not necessarily occur in consonance with legal principle and practical realities. The first (and arguably the most significant) instance that serves to illustrate the judicial innovation of South African trust law occurred in *Braun. In casu* the Appellate Division extended testamentary powers of appointment, well known in Roman and Roman-Dutch law as an exception to the rule prohibiting the delegation of testamentary power in the context of, inter alia, the testamentary *fideicommissum*, to trustees of testamentary trusts. The court founded its ruling in this regard expressly on the innovation of South African trust law necessitated by changing societal demands:

> It is one of the functions of our law to keep pace with the requirements of changing conditions in our society. To recognize the validity of conferring our common law powers of appointment on trustees to select income and/or capital beneficiaries from a designated group of persons would be a salutary development of our law of trusts ... The approach of our Courts is to apply the principles of our law to the development of our law of

[24] Ibid., at para. 26.
[25] Ibid., at para. 27.
[26] Ibid., at para. 28.
[27] Ibid., at para. 29.

> trusts. I am accordingly of the opinion ... that this Court should in principle recognize the validity of the conferment of our common law powers of appointment on trustees.[28]

Powers of appointment in the above sense are, per definition, discretionary in nature; hence the labelling of trusts under which trustees are enjoined with such powers as 'discretionary trusts'. The discretionary trust has, subsequent to its recognition in the *Braun* case, established itself as the foremost testamentary institution in modern South African trust practice[29] – a fact that bears testimony to the visionary development of South African trust law by the *Braun* court.

A second example of judicial innovation of South African trust law is found in *Administrators, Estate Richards* v. *Nichol*, which provided an opportunity for re-evaluation of the strict view on trustee investment taken in *Sackville West*.[30] Subsequent to the *Sackville West* judgment it became generally accepted practice for trustees who had not been given wide powers of investment under the trust instrument at hand, to confine the investment of trust property to so-called trust or trustee investments. These typically included government or municipal stocks, fixed deposits, loans on mortgage bonds and immovable property – investment platforms devoid of risk or hazard. In the *Nichol* case the court, finely attuned to the economic realities that define the modern investment milieu and, moreover, the fundamental changes in investment strategy since the handing down of the *Sackville West* judgment, opted for a more flexible approach to trust investment:

> An investment considered prudent in earlier times may rightfully be regarded as quite imprudent in the context of modern conditions. The ongoing and rapid decline in the value of money brought about by inflation, which has become a feature of our economy in the course of the past few decades, may well result in a sharp decline in the value of a monetary security within a relatively short period of time. In order to preserve the capital of the trust in real terms and so ensure the continued production of income, particularly in the case of a trust intended to be of long duration like the present, a trustee in such circumstances is of necessity obliged to invest in real assets with potential for capital growth. Such an investment, viz one where the capital is not fixed, necessarily involves some element of risk; but the risk may be unavoidable if the capital of the trust is to be preserved in real terms. The acceptance of this

[28] *Braun*, above, note 6, at 866H–867B.

[29] F. du Toit, 'Current Trends in Testamentary Succession' (2004) 25:2 *Obiter* 336, 354.

[30] See Section II.A above.

> element of risk as being unavoidable if the trust is to serve its purpose has inevitably led in more recent times to a change in investment thinking which involves a movement away from the more conservative approach developed in an age when inflation was either non-existent or of little consequence. In principle, therefore, I can see no justification at this stage for a hard and fast rule which precludes the investment of trust funds in quoted shares or licensed unit trusts; nor do I understand the *ratio* in *Sackville West v Nourse and Another (. . .)* as imposing such a limitation on the investment of trust property.[31]

In addition to innovating the South African legal position on trustee investment, the view enunciated in the *Nichol* case is aligned to the trustee investment philosophy in English law under the Trustee Act 2000; indeed, it has been suggested by South African commentators that the Trustee Act's prescripts should guide future South African legal development on this matter.[32] This recommendation underscores further South African trust law's receptiveness to English law influences, particularly to enhance the trust's functionality, provided that guidance from English law is compatible with the predominantly civilian-based legal tradition within which the South African trust operates.

A third example illustrates that not every judicial innovation of South Africa's trust law has been entirely successful. In *MAN Truck and Bus (SA) Ltd* v. *Victor* the High Court utilized, without precedent, the common-law *Turquand* rule in a trust dispute. The court used the rule to thwart the defence of a trustee that he lacked the requisite authorization by the trust's board of trustees to enter into a deed of suretyship on behalf of the trust and that the trust was, consequently, not bound as creditor to the plaintiff.[33] The High Court subsequently followed the *MAN Truck and Bus* decision in *Vrystaat Mielies (Edms) Bpk* v. *Nieuwoudt*.[34]

[31] *Administrators, Estate Richards* v. *Nichol*, 1999 (1) SA 551 (SCA) at 557G–558E.

[32] L. E. Balden and C. Rautenbach, 'Die sorgsaamheidsplig van trustees in die uitvoer van hulle beleggingsbevoegdhede: Kan ons by die Engelse trustreg leer?' ('Trustees' Duty of Care in the Execution of Their Powers of Investment: Can We Learn From English Trust Law?') (2005) 30:1 *Journal for Juridical Science* 91.

[33] *MAN Truck and Bus (SA) Ltd* v. *Victor*, 2001 (2) SA 562 (NC). The *Turquand* rule is taken from *Royal British Bank* v. *Turquand* (1856) 119 ER 886 (Ex Ch) and prescribes, in short, that a party dealing in good faith with a company can assume, if the company's affairs appear to be being conducted in a manner permitted by its memorandum and articles, that all internal managerial formalities required by the aforementioned documents have been duly complied with. In *MAN Truck and Bus* the court regarded conferment of authorization by the trust's board of trustees on the contracting trustee as such an internal managerial formality.

[34] *Vrystaat Mielies (Edms) Bpk* v. *Nieuwoudt*, 2003 (2) SA 262 (O).

The application of the *Turquand* rule to trusts has been subjected to considerable criticism. First, both commentators[35] and the courts[36] questioned whether it is appropriate to apply the rule, pertaining, as it does, to corporate entities endowed with legal personality, to trusts which, under South African law, are generally, save when legislation stipulates otherwise, not legal persons.[37] Secondly, subsequent courts expressed doubt as to the High Court's view in *MAN Truck and Bus* that a trustee's authorization to transact on behalf of a trust constitutes a matter of internal management for purposes of the *Turquand* rule.[38] Significantly, in the appeal in the *Vrystaat Mielies* case the court,[39] although leaving the question open, also expressed practical reservations regarding the applicability of the *Turquand* rule to trusts. The court pointed out that the *Turquand* rule operates hand-in-hand with actual or constructive notice. The rule applies,[40] for example, to companies by reason of public access to their founding documents.[41] Trust instruments are, in terms of South African law, not of an equally public nature. Section 4(1) of the Trust Property Control Act 57 of 1988, the statute that currently regulates certain aspects of trust administration, requires the lodgement of trust documents with the Master of the High Court who holds jurisdiction. Section 18 of the Act orders the Master to furnish a certified copy of any document under its control relating to trust property to a trustee, his surety, his representative or any person who in the opinion of the Master has sufficient interest in such a document. The Supreme Court of Appeal, in the *Vrystaat Mielies* case, pointed out that in South Africa there is no central register for trusts as is the case with companies.[42] A member of the public who wishes to transact with trustees and who wishes to ascertain the particular trust instrument's prescripts on, for example, trustee authorization will, therefore, first have to determine at which Master's office the trust deed was lodged.[43] Having found the correct

35 E.g. Cameron et al., *Honoré's South African Law of Trusts*, above, note 2, pp. 95, 324–5.

36 E.g. *Parker* v. *Land and Agricultural Bank of SA*, [2003] 1 All SA 258 (T) at 264c.

37 *Commissioner for Inland Revenue* v. *MacNeillie's Estate*, 1961 (3) SA 833 (A) at 840F–G.

38 *Nieuwoudt* v. *Vrystaat Mielies (Edms) Bpk*, 2004 (3) SA 486 (SCA), at para. 20.

39 Ibid. 40 Ibid., at para. 18.

41 S. 14 of the Companies Act 71 of 2008 provides for the registration of companies with the Companies and Intellectual Property Commission. The Commission is obliged, in terms of s. 187(4)(c) of the Act, to make the information contained in the companies register efficiently and effectively available to the public and to other organs of state.

42 *Nieuwoudt*, above, note 38, at para. 18.

43 S. 3(1) of the Administration of Estates Act 66 of 1965 determines that each Master, a functionary that holds administrative and interventionist powers regarding trusteeship, shall have its office at the seat of the provincial division of the High Court in respect of

Master's office, such member of the public would have to make an application to the Master for permission to inspect the trust instrument; something the Master, in the exercise of the discretion conferred by section 18 of the Act, may refuse. The court concluded, therefore, that whether knowledge of the contents of trust instruments is in law attributable to the public seems 'less than obvious'.[44]

Despite the above reservations and criticisms expressed on the applicability of the *Turquand* rule to trusts, the Supreme Court of Appeal in *Land and Agricultural Bank of South Africa* v. *Parker*,[45] patently frustrated by the trustees *in casu*'s flagrant disregard of the trust form and the prescripts of the trust deed, again proffered it, albeit in an *obiter dictum*, as a developmental solution to prevent the abuse of the trust. In *Parker* the court was confronted with an identity of interests between trustees and beneficiaries (because the trustees are all beneficiaries and, moreover, were all related to each other), which occasioned the trustees to conduct trust affairs with disregard of the trust's existence, especially in binding the trust to third parties, and then unscrupulously to deny the trust's liability by alleging a lack of authority. However, the *Parker* court's proposal on the utility of the *Turquand* rule received little support when, in *Van der Merwe* v. *Hydraberg Hydraulics CC; Van der Merwe* v. *Bosman*, the court declared:

> In *Nieuwoudt and Another NNO v Vrystaat Mielies (Edms) Bpk* 2004 (3) SA 486 (SCA) ([2004] 1 All SA 396) the Supreme Court of Appeal did not find it necessary to determine the question whether, as held by the Northern Cape High Court in *MAN Truck and Bus (SA) Ltd v Victor en Andere* 2001 (2) SA 562 (NC), the *Turquand* rule applies to trusts. I have some difficulty with the proposition in the absence of evidence of actual or constructive knowledge by the third party with the provisions of the trust instrument. In *MAN Truck* [the judge] proceeded on the understanding that, when a third party deals with a trust, it is deemed to be aware of the content of the trust instrument. I am not aware of any such legal fiction, and counsel did not refer me to any reasoned authority which might support it. There is no public record identifying at which of the several offices of the Master throughout the country a particular trust instrument is lodged, and even then the Master must decide whether any person seeking access to it should be permitted to inspect it.[46]

whose area of jurisdiction it has been appointed. Given that some of South Africa's provinces have more than one seat of a provincial division of the High Court, there are numerous Master's offices spread throughout the Republic.

44 *Nieuwoudt*, above, note 38, at para. 19.

45 *Land and Agricultural Bank of South Africa*, above, note 13, at para. 37.1.

46 *Van der Merwe* v. *Hydraberg Hydraulics CC; Van der Merwe* v. *Bosman*, 2010 (5) SA 555 (WCC), at para. 27.

Here, therefore, is an example of a somewhat dubious innovation of South African trust law through the application of the *Turquand* rule to trusts. Despite a clear need that has arisen to preserve the integrity of the trust as an instrument of protection where a negation of the divide between, on the one hand, trustees' control over trust property and, on the other, the benefit derived by trust beneficiaries from the trustees' exercise of such control, moved trustees to deny a trust's liability towards a third party, the *Turquand* rule appears a less than ideal solution to the problem in the context of South African trust practice. It will, therefore, be interesting to follow future development in this regard. It is submitted that three possibilities exist: the Supreme Court of Appeal can reject the application of the *Turquand* rule to trusts out of hand (for the reasons mentioned above); the courts and/or legislature can mould and transform the *Turquand* rule into suitability for application to trusts; or the legislature can amend trust law to render the *Turquand* rule in its present form fully applicable to trusts.

III The legislature – limited contribution

The South African legislature has made a relatively limited contribution to the development of trust law. The first statute regulating the trust institution was the Trust Moneys Protection Act 34 of 1934, significant principally for its directives regarding the furnishing of security by trustees. The South African legislature's most important (and most recent) contribution in the trust sphere is the Trust Property Control Act 57 of 1988.[47] It is generally accepted that this Act is not a legislative attempt at codification of the body of South African trust law; rather the Act seeks to establish firmer control over trustees and their stewardship of trusts by the Master of the High Court.[48]

From the perspective of the trust's operation in South Africa's mixed legal system, two provisions of the Trust Property Control Act deserve mention: first, the definition of a trust in section 1 of the Act and, secondly, the legislative codification of a trustee's duty of care in section 9(1) of the Act.

[47] The Act commenced on 31 March 1989.

[48] M. M. Corbett, 'Trust Law in the 90's: Challenges and Change' (1993) 56:2 *Journal of Contemporary Roman-Dutch Law* 262, 267.

A. *'Trust' legislatively defined*

The definition of 'trust' in section 1 of the Trust Property Control Act reads a follows:

> 'trust' means the arrangement through which the ownership in property of one person is by virtue of a trust instrument made over or bequeathed –
>
> (*a*) to another person, the trustee, in whole or in part, to be administered or disposed of according to the provisions of the trust instrument for the benefit of the person or class of persons designated in the trust instrument or for the achievement of the object stated in the trust instrument; or
>
> (*b*) to the beneficiaries designated in the trust instrument, which property is placed under the control of another person, the trustee, to be administered or disposed of according to the provisions of the trust instrument for the benefit of the person or class of persons designated in the trust instrument or for the achievement of the object stated in the trust instrument, but does not include the case where the property of another is to be administered by any person as executor, tutor or curator in terms of the provisions of the Administration of Estates Act, 1965 (Act No. 66 of 1965).

It is evident from the above defintion that the Act recognizes two forms of the so-called trust in the strict sense: first, the arrangement where the trustee is vested with the ownership in trust property and, secondly, where the ownership in trust property vests in the trust beneficiaries with the trustee as mere administrator. The former, by far the more prevalent of the two, is generally known as the so-called 'ownership trust', but has also been labelled, inter alia, the 'ordinary trust'[49] and the 'most common type' of trust.[50] The latter corresponds with the institution known as the '*bewind*' in modern Dutch law and that of the '*bewindhebber*' in Roman-Dutch law, and is correspondingly known as the '*bewind* trust' in South African law.[51] South African law recognizes that the term 'trust' can be used in a strict (narrow) sense, as well as in a

49 *Bafokeng Tribe* v. *Impala Platinum Ltd*, 1999 (3) SA 517 (BHC) at 545E.

50 *Commissioner, South African Revenue Service* v. *Deyfin Textiles (Pty) Ltd*, 2002 (4) SA 606 (N) at 611H.

51 *Bafokeng Tribe*, above, note 49, at 541J–542D. In Roman-Dutch law, it was possible to couple a *fideicommissum* with *bewind* (*administratio*) by appointing a *bewindhebber* to administer the fideicommissary property. The ownership of the property did not vest in the '*bewindvoerder*'; the latter held mere control over *res aliena* for purposes of administration: *Braun*, above, note 6, at 864G–H.

wide sense. Within its latter meaning, the term 'trust' denotes fiduciary arrangements under which one is entrusted with the affairs of another without being vested with the ownership of the property to be administered. Examples of trusts in the wide sense include executorship, tutorship, curatorship,[52] agency[53] and the like. In the former sense, a trust is generally constituted when the trustee becomes owner of the trust property for the purposes of the administration thereof. However, in *Conze* v. *Masterbond Participation Trust Managers (Pty) Ltd* the court opined that the definition of 'trust' in section 1 of the Trust Property Control Act describes the trust in the strict sense as a single institution[54] – it is evident, therefore, that the legislature intended both the ownership trust and the *bewind* trust (with its civilian roots) to be included under the Act's regulatory framework and that both, irrespective of the residence of ownership under the particular trust arrangement, are trusts in the strict sense for purposes of the Act.[55]

The legislative formulation of the ownership trust arrangement in section 1 of the Act corresponds greatly with one of the first judicial formulations of the trust idea in South African law. In *Estate Kemp* v. *McDonald's Trust*, the court described the arrangement in the will at hand as follows:

> The trustees, to whom the estate is directly bequeathed, are vested with the legal ownership in the assets. That is clear; but it is also clear that the testator never intended that they should have any beneficial interest; they were instituted not to enjoy but to administer the property. And their designation in its English meaning denotes persons entrusted (as owners or otherwise) with the control of property with which they are bound to deal for the benefit of others.[56]

The court's unfortunate use of the term 'legal ownership' (evocative of a trustee's ownership under English law) aside, this description of the trust idea emphasizes the trustee as owner of the trust property, however

[52] Significantly, these three fiduciary arrangements are excluded expressly in the definition of 'trust' in s. 1 from the regulatory ambit of the Trust Property Control Act; they are regulated, for historical reasons, by the Administration of Estates Act 66 of 1965.

[53] Agency is not regulated legislatively in South Africa; rather, common law rules govern the fiduciary relationship between principal and agent.

[54] *Conze* v. *Masterbond Participation Trust Managers (Pty) Ltd*, 1996 (3) SA 786 (C) at 794D–G.

[55] See Section IV below on the impact of Tony Honoré's view on this legislative definition of a trust in the strict sense.

[56] *Estate Kemp*, above, note 4, at para. 499.

devoid of any beneficial interest in such ownership. A trustee's ownership of trust property under an ownership trust is, therefore, characterized as 'bare' because trust property forms no part of the assets or estate of the trustee.[57] Indeed, in *Land and Agricultural Bank of South Africa* v. *Parker*, the court identified 'the core idea of the trust' in South African law as the functional separation between, on the one hand, a trustee's ownership (or control) of trust property and, on the other, the enjoyment derived (by the trust beneficiaries) from the trustee's exercise of such ownership (or control).[58] This conceptualization of the South African trust, evident in the early description of the trust in the above dictum in the *Kemp* case, prevailed in South African law and is reflected pertinently in the legislative definition of the trust – pertaining to both ownership and *bewind* trusts – in section 1 of the Trust Property Control Act.

B. *Duty of care codified*

A pertinent example of the inclusion of civil law notions into the Trust Property Control Act is found in section 9 thereof. Section 9(1) lays down the standard of care, diligence and skill expected of trustees and is essentially a codification of the common law position, gleaned from Roman-Dutch law, enunciated in *Sackville West*.[59] Section 9(1) stipulates:

> A trustee shall in the performance of his duties and the exercise of his powers act with the care, diligence and skill which can reasonably be expected of a person who manages the affairs of another

A trustee who fails to meet the above standard and, in so doing, causes patrimonial loss to trust beneficiaries, can incur personal liability for breach of trust and can be sued in delict by such beneficiaries to make good the loss sustained.[60] The question as to the liability of co-trustees for breach of trust posed (and, to some extent, still poses) some difficulty in South African law. In *Gross* v. *Pentz* the Appellate Division accepted,

[57] W. Geach and J. Yeats, *Trusts: Law and Practice* (Cape Town: Juta & Co. Ltd, 2007), p. 2. Section 12 of the Trust Property Control Act prescribes that trust property shall not form part of the personal estate of a trustee except insofar as such trustee is entitled to such property as a beneficiary under the trust.

[58] *Land and Agricultural Bank of South Africa*, above, note 13, at para. 19.

[59] See Section II.A above.

[60] See generally on trustee liability for breach of trust under South African law, F. du Toit, *South African Trust Law: Principles and Practice* (Durban: LexisNexis, 2007), pp. 103–6.

for purposes of deciding the plaintiff's *locus standi*, that co-trustees are liable jointly and severally, even when not all the co-trustees participated in the maladministration of the trust.[61] In coming to this conclusion the court again drew on common law authority:

> Inasmuch as the trust was not a legal institution known to Roman-Dutch law (see *Braun v Blann and Botha NNO and Another* 1984 (2) SA 850 (A) at 858H-859D), there is no Roman-Dutch authority on the point. In *Sackville West v Nourse and Another* [1925 AD 516] this Court, in considering the duties and liabilities of a trustee, sought assistance from the principles of the common law applying to the duties of tutors in dealing with the property of their wards and of other persons acting under similar circumstances, viz. curators, procurators and 'all those who administer the affairs of others' . . . As I understand the position, the general trend of Roman-Dutch law was to hold co-guardians jointly and severally liable to their ward for the maladministration of the estate. This was subject to the rule that if the administration had been divided, each guardian was liable only in respect of the share which he administered, and also to certain rules as to the order of excussion and rights of contribution as between guardians. (See generally *Niekerk v Niekerk* 1 Menz 452; *Voet* 27.8.6; *Grotius* 3.26.8 and 9; Van der Linden *Institutes* 1.5.6.)[62]

The court next somewhat dubiously distinguished what it perceived to be the English legal position, relied upon by the appellant's counsel:

> Appellant's counsel urged us rather to follow the English law relating to the liability of co-trustees which renders each trustee, in general, liable for the whole loss when caused by the joint default of all the trustees, even though all may not have been equally blameworthy, and a decree against all may be enforced against one or more only; but which holds that a trustee is not otherwise answerable for the receipts, acts or defaults of his co-trustee, but only for his own acts or defaults. These would include where he hands over the trust property to his co-trustee without seeing to its proper application or where he allows his co-trustee to receive the trust property without making due enquiry as to his dealing with it or where he becomes aware of a breach of trust, either committed or meditated, and abstains from taking the needful steps to prevent the wrong or to obtain restitution and redress. (See Underhill and Hayton *Law of Trusts and Trustees* 14th ed at 748–9, 791–2.)
>
> It seems to me, *prima facie*, that there appear to be differences between our law and English law in this sphere. It may be that a re-evaluation of our law could result in a relaxation of the rule as to joint and several liability in cases

[61] *Gross* v. *Pentz*, 1996 (4) SA 617 (A) at 629C, 630I. [62] Ibid., at 629F–H.

> where the maladministration was the sole work of one trustee and the other trustee had been innocent of any wrongdoing or neglect. In my view, however, this is not the appropriate occasion for such a re-evaluation.[63]

Here is another example of a prescript on trustee conduct in a fiduciary capacity – a trustee's duty of care, diligence and skill, acknowledged under the common law and in terms of the Trust Property Control Act – where trust law was judicially aligned to acknowledged principles of South African law. However, the *Gross* court's distinguishing of the English legal position appears questionable and it has been argued that South African law and English law are indeed not at odds on the issue of the liability of co-trustees. De Waal, in an instructive article on the topic, showed that in English law, a trustee is not vicariously liable for the acts of co-trustees: trustees' liability is personal, and the fault principle operates in respect of co-trustees' liability for breach of trust. Where two or more trustees are guilty of such a breach, their liability under English law is joint and several.[64] This conclusion corresponds with Moffat's exposition on the English law position:

> The fact that co-trusteeship is common and that the different trustees may have varying levels of expertise poses a compelling question: 'who is personally liable and for what?' In the present context 'personally liable' refers to equity's long-standing recognition (*Townley v Sherborn* (1634) J Bridg 35) that a trustee is liable only for his own breaches of trust, not for those of his co-trustees. But too much reliance cannot be placed on this limitation since a trustee may in some respects find himself at fault, even where a co-trustee causes the breach of trust . . . [The repeal of] s. 30(1) [of the Trustee Act 1925] by the Trustee Act 2000 [had] the effect that a passive trustee may now be liable if he or she fails to act in accordance with the duty of care . . . Where more than one trustee is liable for breach of trust, liability is joint and several, i.e. the beneficiary can claim the complete loss from any one trustee separately or from all or several of them jointly.[65]

De Waal's conclusion, therefore, rings true, and underscores the alignment between South African and English law on the issue:

> It needs to be stressed that, in my view, [South African] co-trustees are not vicariously liable for each other's acts . . . Once one has concluded that the liability of co-trustees in South African law is not vicarious in nature,

63 Ibid., at 630E–H.

64 M. J. de Waal, 'The Liability of Co-Trustees for Breach of Trust' (1999) 10:1 *Stellenbosch Law Review* 21, 28–9.

65 G. Moffat, *Trusts Law* (Cambridge University Press, 2009), pp. 588–9.

> the biggest potential difference with English law falls away. In both systems the liability of co-trustees for breach of trust is based on the individual fault of the trustees. The liability of those trustees who are indeed liable for breach of trust is joint and several, with the possibility of recourse or contribution among co-trustees.[66]

IV Writers – critical impetus

South African writers and academic commentators have made significant contributions to the development of South African trust law. Quite understandably, the trust and trust law have proven fascinating topics for academic comment and evaluation in the South African legal sphere. It is impossible to provide a comprehensive exposition on the contribution of writers and commentators to the development of South African trust law in the brevity afforded by a single chapter. Therefore, only the contribution of undoubtedly the foremost author on South African trust law, Tony Honoré, in his seminal work, *Honoré's South African Law of Trusts*, will be evaluated briefly.

The first edition of Honoré's work appeared in 1966 and the book is currently in its fifth edition, published in 2002; since the fourth edition it has been co-authored by a number of leading South African trust specialists (Honoré himself did not co-author the latest edition). *Honoré's South African Law of Trusts* provides a comprehensive and authoritative exposition of South African trust law and many of the constructs of modern South African trust law have a firm footing in Honoré's conceptualization of the operation of the trust in South Africa's mixed legal system. The work is cited extensively in other writings on South African trust law and the courts rely abundantly on the book's analysis of trust law principles.[67]

Arguably the two most important contributions to the development of South African trust law emanating from Honoré's work are, firstly, the construct of trusteeship as a quasi-public fiduciary office and, secondly, the notion that the residence of ownership is not the determining factor in establishing a trust in the strict sense. The authors themselves state it

[66] De Waal, 'The Liability of Co-Trustees', above, note 64, 34–5.

[67] A search on Jutastat Online, Juta Law Publishers' electronic database, at http://products.jutalaw.co.za/nxt/gateway.dll?f=templates&fn=default.htm (accessed on 18 December 2010), revealed at least 60 references to *Honoré's South African Law of Trusts* in reported South African cases since 1966.

best in the foreword to the book's fourth edition, published shortly after the enactment of the Trust Property Control Act 57 of 1988:

> It is agreeable to note that the new legislation stresses some of the themes developed in this book over the last twenty-five years. Central to trusteeship as a world-wide phenomenon which has evolved a specifically South African form is the fact that the trustee holds an office. This fact makes it impossible to identify the trust with any purely private law institution such as a contract or fideicommissum. It explains why in other civil law systems attempts to develop a law of trusts on the basis of such private law institutions have largely failed. From the trustee's position as an office holder follows the separation of the trust estate from the trustee's personal estate, to which the Trust Property Control Act s 12 now gives full effect. The character of the beneficiary's right as a protected right in personam is the obverse of the trustee's position as an office holder. This explains why the simple choice between a right in personam and one in rem does not fit the trust beneficiary's position. The same official character of trusteeship leads to the conclusion that it is immaterial whether the trustee owns the trust property (ownership-trust) or whether, while the trustee in his official capacity administers the property, the beneficiary owns it (bewind-trust). This wide view of the office of trustee as spanning both owners and non-owners, a view described by one writer as an 'ernstige flater' [serious error], was adopted in this book from the outset. If the critic was right, the passage of time has cured the error, which is now expressly endorsed by the legislature in its definition of 'trust' in the 1988 Act.[68]

Honoré's ground-breaking work on the basic constructs of South African trust law, readily followed by the courts and embraced by the legislature, provides fertile ground for present-day South African trust scholars to develop further some of the themes emanating from *Honoré's South African Law of Trusts*. Examples of such modern scholarship are de Waal's legal-comparative contributions on the South African trust as a true trust[69] and constructing a model for the introduction of the trust into civilian jurisdictions[70] as well as my own work on key aspects of a trustee's fiduciary office[71] and constitutionally founded public-policy

[68] T. Honoré and E. Cameron, *Honoré's South African Law of Trusts*, 4th edn (Cape Town: Juta & Co. Ltd, 1992), p. vi.

[69] M. J. de Waal, 'The Core Elements of the Trust: Aspects of the English, Scottish and South African Trusts Compared' (2000) 117:3 *South African Law Journal* 548.

[70] M. J. de Waal, 'In Search of a Model for the Introduction of the Trust into a Civilian Context' (2001) 12:1 *Stellenbosch Law Review* 63.

[71] F. du Toit, 'The Fiduciary Office of Trustee and the Protection of Contingent Trust Beneficiaries' (2007) 18:3 *Stellenbosch Law Review* 46; F. du Toit, 'A Trustee's Duty of Independence' (2009) 72:4 *Journal of Contemporary Roman-Dutch Law* 637.

constraints on the exercise of freedom of testation in setting up charitable testamentary trusts.[72] This modern scholarship, building upon many of Honoré's fundamental propositions on the South African trust, has been cited extensively in recent South African judgments[73] as well as in national trust law books[74] and international works on comparative law,[75] thus contributing further to the ongoing development and sophistication of South African trust law.

V Conclusion

The jurisprudential milestones in the development of the trust in South Africa's mixed legal system highlighted in this chapter show that the trust, having been received from English law, gained a firm footing in South Africa's legal and commercial landscape. South African courts are the principal constructors of a uniquely South African trust law; they do so by adapting the trust idea to the principles of South African law, whilst, at times, also invoking apposite English trust law rules to fortify their principled stance on trust matters. The South African legislature and writers have also made significant contributions to the development of a uniquely South African law of trusts. However, the development of South African trust law is far from complete and the truism stated by the eminent South African academic H. R. Hahlo more than half a century ago remains as true today as it was when originally penned:

> [W]hen it comes to 'trusts' in our law, even the most elementary propositions cannot be regarded as settled ... [I]t will take the work of several generations of judges and text writers before the law of trusts reaches maturity.[76]

[72] F. du Toit, 'The Constitutionally Bound Dead Hand? The Impact of Constitutional Rights and Principles on Freedom of Testation in South African Law' (2001) 12:2 *Stellenbosch Law Review* 222; F. du Toit, 'Constitutionalism, Public Policy and Discriminatory Testamentary Bequests: A Good Fit between Common Law and Civil Law in South Africa's Mixed Jurisdiction?' (2012) 27:1 *Tulane European and Civil Law Forum* 97.

[73] See, e.g., *Minister of Education* v. *Syfrets Trust Ltd*, 2006 (4) SA 205 (C); *Curators, Emma Smith Educational Fund* v. *University of KwaZulu-Natal*, 2010 (6) SA 518 (SCA).

[74] See, e.g., du Toit, *South African Trust Law*, above, note 60, pp. 14–16, 44–6.

[75] See, e.g., M. J. de Waal, 'Comparative Succession Law', in M. Reiman and R. Zimmermann (eds.), *The Oxford Handbook of Comparative Law* (Oxford University Press, 2008), p. 1088.

[76] H. R. Hahlo, 'Revocation of Trusts' (1952) 69:2 *South African Law Journal* 348, 349–50.

11

The framing of a European law of trusts

ALEXANDRA BRAUN

I Introduction

Since the Hague Convention on the Law Applicable to Trusts and on their Recognition came into force in 1992, trust law within the European Union has undergone an interesting evolution.[1] Some European legislatures have reformed already existing trust instruments, while others have introduced new domestic devices aimed at rendering their financial markets more competitive. As a consequence, in the course of the past twenty years, the list of fiduciary instruments available within Europe has increased. This growing diversity of devices has become cause for some concern. In particular, the complexity of the spectrum of trust law within Europe has been seen by some as an obstacle not only to the free movement of capital and services but also to mutual recognition. It has therefore been suggested that trust law should be rendered uniform within Europe.

In fact, in 2009, the outcomes of two academic research projects, both conducted by international groups of legal scholars, were published, suggesting that uniform instruments be introduced in the European Union. One is the by-product of an ambitious research project aimed at harmonizing European private law, which was carried out by two working groups of legal scholars, partly financed by the EU. Although the EU Commission had only envisaged the improvement of the coherence of European contract law, the scholars involved in the project prepared a draft for a future Common Frame of Reference that includes also a book (Book X) on trusts. The second, much smaller, project consists of an unofficial proposal for new European Union legislation on protected funds in the commercial sphere. This project was carried out by a working group, successor to the one that had previously produced the *Principles of European Trust Law.*

I would like to thank Michele Graziadei, Kenneth Reid, Ruth Sefton-Green and Lionel Smith for their invaluable comments on an earlier draft of this chapter.

[1] Hague Convention on the Law Applicable to Trusts and on Their Recognition, The Hague, 1 July 1985, in force 1 July 1992.

Although the two projects are inherently different, they both suggest a uniform fiduciary device for Europe and start from the premise that there is a need for such a device. It would thus seem that the Hague Trusts Convention, aimed at harmonizing trust law at the level of conflict of laws, has ultimately prepared the ground for proposals envisaging the harmonization of trust law at a substantive level. But is there a need for a European law of trusts? Do we have enough evidence to support such a claim and, if so, is the time ripe for an intervention of the European legislature?

This chapter addresses these questions by taking a closer look at the events that have occurred within Europe in the aftermath of the coming into force of the Hague Trusts Convention. Starting from an examination of the developments at a national level (Part II), the chapter moves onto an analysis of the objectives and scope of the recent academic projects aimed at unifying trust law within Europe (Part III). Having looked at the nature and essential features of the instruments propounded, it examines not only the feasibility of the two devices, but also the need for a unification of this area of the law (Parts IV and V).

II The Hague Trusts Convention and its impact within the EU

The aim of the drafters of the Hague Trusts Convention was substantially twofold. One objective was to establish common principles of conflict of laws on the law applicable to trusts, and the other to facilitate the recognition of trusts in States which do not provide for such instruments. It follows that the Convention determines not only what law governs the trust but also describes the consequences that derive from the recognition of the trust for jurisdictions that are unfamiliar with the concept. Thus, the Convention was not intended to introduce the trust into legal systems that do not already embrace the notion.[2] Neither was the Convention meant to provide a uniform substantive law. Its objective was rather to build a bridge between common and civil law systems by creating a uniform set of conflict of law rules.

Despite the initial enthusiasm, thus far relatively few States have ratified the Convention.[3] Within the European Union, only Italy,

[2] A. E. von Overbeck, 'Explanatory Report', in *Proceedings of the Fifteenth Session, vol. II, Trusts – Applicable Law and Recognition* (The Hague, 1985), p. 373, para. 14.

[3] A. E. von Overbeck, 'Law Applicable to, and Recognition of Trusts in Switzerland: The Possible Future under the Hague Convention' (1996) *Trusts & Trustees* 5; D. Waters, 'The Hague Trusts Convention Twenty Years On', in M. Graziadei, U. Mattei and L. Smith

Luxembourg, Malta, the Netherlands and the UK have undertaken the step.[4] Other countries such as Austria, Belgium, France, Germany, Spain or Portugal have not ratified the Convention and it is not clear whether this will change in the near future. As a consequence, the mutual recognition of trusts within Europe still poses certain problems.

There are probably several reasons why the Convention has not been more widely adopted. Some countries do not seem to see any advantage in doing so, while others are apparently concerned about the effect the ratification may have within their legal system.[5] Another important reason would seem to lie in the fear that national investors would take their money abroad. In other words, the ratification of the Convention bears the risk that citizens of legal systems which do not have a competing domestic device will set up a trust abroad on the reassurance that it will then be recognized under the Hague Convention in their own legal system. This was a danger the French and the Luxembourgish legislatures were aware of, and explains why both countries, together with other European countries, have since started reforming their law in this area.[6] Sometimes this has even led to the establishment of a new domestic device that is either functionally equivalent to the trust, or shares some of its basic structural characteristics.

A. *Recent developments*

Although Austria never signed or ratified the Hague Trusts Convention, in 1993 it passed a law introducing a new device, entitled *Privatstiftung*

(eds.), *Commercial Trusts in European Private Law* (Cambridge University Press, 2005), pp. 56, 88.

4 The Convention was also ratified by non-EU Member States within Europe such as Liechtenstein, Monaco, San Marino and Switzerland. Outside Europe, the Convention was ratified by Australia and by Canada, on behalf of most of its provinces (which decide individually whether to bring the Convention into force). The USA has signed the Convention, but not yet ratified it.

5 At present, Germany does not seem to envisage ratification of the Convention. It would appear that the legal profession does not see any advantage in doing so. See Waters, 'The Hague Trusts Convention', above, note 3, pp. 89–90. It would further seem that legal academics are concerned about the fact that German judges would have to apply foreign law. In favour of a ratification see J. Pirrung, 'Zur Ratifikation des Trust-Übereinkommens', in *Festschrift für Andreas Heldrich zum 70. Geburtstag* (Munich: C.H. Beck, 2005), p. 925. Against, H. Coing, 'Übernahme des Trusts in unser internationales Privatrecht?', in *Festschrift für Theodor Heinsius zum 65. Geburtstag am 25. September 1991* (Berlin/New York: Walter de Gruyter, 1991), p. 79.

6 For France see Rapp. Sénat no. 11 (2006–7) by Senator M. Henri de Richemont, p. 7.

(private foundation), which somewhat resembles the common law trust and which has met with widespread success in legal practice.[7] Since its establishment, in fact, more foundations seem to have been created than public limited companies, though this success can be largely ascribed to its tax advantages. Whether the passing of the statute can be indirectly linked to the adoption of the Hague Trusts Convention is not clear. It is probably more likely a response to the fear of losing business to Liechtenstein. In any event, it is interesting to notice that Austria has felt the need to introduce such a device at a time when other countries have also taken similar initiatives in order to attract investors.

In 1983, before the Hague Trusts Convention was signed, Luxembourg had introduced a new device, the *contrat fiduciaire*, allowing banks and investment companies to enter into fiduciary transfers of property.[8] The device was reformed in July 2003 with a law entitled *Loi sur la Fiducie* which not only ratified the Hague Convention, but also improved the status and flexibility of the instrument so as to be more in line with the common law trust. Thus, Luxembourg wanted to have in place a device that could compete with the common law trust and be recognized under article 2 of the Hague Convention.[9] It was, indeed, hoped that international investors and banks would opt for the *fiducie*, and that the instrument would become more widely used within Europe.[10]

In France attempts to develop a national device have been undertaken since 1989, but only in 2007 was it possible to pass a law introducing the *fiducie*, a special type of contract that can be employed for commercial purposes, be they management or security.[11] Concerns, especially those of French tax authorities, had brought previous proposals to a halt. The reason why France made the ratification of the Convention dependent on

[7] S. Kalss, 'Privatstiftung', in S. Kalss, C. Nowotny and M. Schauer (eds.), *Österreichisches Gesellschaftsrecht* (Vienna: Manzsche Verlags- und Universitätsbuchhandlung, 2008), pp. 1295 ff. For a comparison of the trust with the Privatstiftung see E. Micheler, 'Der Englische Trust im Vergleich zur österreichischen Privatstiftung – Allgemeine Bemerkungen und ausgewählte Fragen zur corporate governance von Trust und Privatstiftung', in P. Doralt and S. Kalss (eds.), *Aktuelle Fragen des Privatstiftungsrechts* (Vienna: Linde Verlag, 2001), pp. 291ff.

[8] Royal Decree of 19 July 1983.

[9] *Exposé des motifs* of Bill no. 4721, p. 4. On this point see H. van Loon, 'The Hague Convention of 1st July 1985 on the Law Applicable to Trusts and on their Recognition', in A. Prüm and C. Witz (eds.), *Trust et fiducie: la Convention de La Haye et la nouvelle législation luxembourgeoise* (Paris: Montchrestien, 2005), pp. 19, 25 and 31.

[10] Ibid., pp. 31–2. [11] Law no. 211 of 19 February 2007.

introducing a domestic device was the fear that it would cause businesses to flee from France and the grip of French lawyers to foreign jurisdictions. The parliamentary documents and reports of the statute introducing the *fiducie* illustrate, indeed, that the French legislature intended to introduce a device that could compete with the common law trust, before considering the ratification of the Convention, which as yet has still to happen.[12] Whether that goal was ultimately achieved is doubtful. The fact that since its introduction in 2007 the provisions have undergone numerous amendments and modifications gives reason to think that its use in practice has not been as successful as envisaged.

San Marino, on the other hand, passed a first law on trusts in March 2005,[13] a year after having ratified the Hague Convention.[14] This law introduced a comprehensive set of trust provisions which seem to have met with success in legal practice. The trust provisions were reformed again in 2010, mainly in order to allow settlors to choose the law of San Marino even when the trust fund is managed by trustees who are not resident or do not have their seat in San Marino.[15] Together with the amended version another statute was passed introducing a new fiduciary device, entitled *affidamento fiduciario*, that seems to represent a civilian response to the trust.[16] Thus San Marino has currently two sets of provisions, one regulating trusts and the other *affidamenti fiduciari*.

More recently, on 1 October 2011 the new Romanian Civil Code has come into force, introducing a new instrument named '*fiducia*' which can be established by contract or by law. The provisions regulating the *fiducia* seem to partly resemble those regulating the French *fiducie*, for instance, where they exclude its establishment for gratuitous purposes.[17] On 1 January 2014 the new Czech Civil Code will enter into force, containing a set of provisions on trusts. Finally, although Belgium has not ratified the Hague Trusts Convention, its Code of Private International Law provides for a set of rules concerning the law applicable to trusts that largely resembles the provisions of the Convention.[18]

[12] F. Barrière, 'The French *fiducie*, or the Chaotic Awakening of a Sleeping Beauty', in L. Smith (ed.), *Re-imagining the Trust: Trusts in Civil Law* (Cambridge University Press, 2011), p. 222.

[13] Law no. 37 of 17 March 2005. [14] Law no. 119 of 20 September 2004.

[15] Law no. 42 of 1 March 2010. [16] Law no. 43 of 1 March 2010. [17] Articles 773–91.

[18] P. Matthews, 'Trusts in Belgian Private International Law: Selected Provisions from the new Belgian Code of Private International Law, Translated into English, with an Introductory Note' (2005) 19 Trust L.I. 191.

To this list of countries, Italy and the Netherlands may be added in the future. Italy was among the first countries to ratify the Convention, which has led to the development of the so-called trusts *interni*, that is to say trusts that are placed in Italy but entirely regulated by foreign law.[19] Despite the success the use of trusts *interni* has met with in legal practice,[20] proposals were put forward aimed at adopting a domestic device called *fiducia*.[21] Quite like the French *fiducie*, the Italian *fiducia* is a fiduciary contract to be employed for both management and security purposes. Unlike the French *fiducie*, however, its provisions are more flexible, allowing a broader use of the device. Whether the proposal to introduce the *fiducia* will ever be implemented remains to be seen. In any event, the main motivation behind the envisaged legislation seems to lie in the desire to provide Italian practitioners with a device that has a sufficient degree of flexibility, while being framed in a language familiar to Italian lawyers.[22] This way, lawyers, notaries and financial advisers would no longer need to acquaint themselves with foreign law in order to set up a trust. Thus, the *fiducia* is principally intended as an alternative to trusts *interni* which are governed by foreign law, though without intending to prevent their continuing use in Italian legal practice.[23]

[19] For an analysis see A. Braun, 'Italy: The Trust Interno', in D. Hayton (ed.), *The International Trust*, 3rd edn (Bristol: Jordans, 2011), p. 787.

[20] Interestingly, Switzerland has followed the same path as Italy. Having ratified the Convention in 2007, it is now possible for Swiss citizens to set up a 'trust *interno*'. However, unlike Italy, Switzerland has decided not to transpose article 13 of the Convention into its national law. Hence, Swiss judges will not be able to deny the recognition of a trust *interno* on the basis of article 13.

[21] The Bill of the Community Law 2010 (no. 2284/2010) had authorized the Italian government to adopt one or more *decreti legislativi* regulating the *fiducia* (art. 11). The proposal, based on an earlier Bill (Bill no. 854 of 28 June 2008), aimed at introducing a new chapter into Title III of Book IV of the Italian Civil Code which deals with contracts. However, when in July 2011 the Bill was discussed by the Chamber of Deputies the provisions on the *contratto di fiducia* were eliminated from the Bill. Nonetheless, on 27 July 2011 a new Bill (no. 4554) containing the same text was presented to the Chamber of Deputies.

[22] M. Graziadei, 'Recognition of Common Law Trusts in Civil Law Jurisdictions in the Light of the Hague Trusts Convention of 1985 with Particular Regard to the Italian Experience', in Smith, *Re-imagining the Trust*, above, note 12, p. 20.

[23] See the 2010 report to the DDL (Delega al Governo per le modifiche al codice civile, in materia di disciplina della fiducia e del contratto autonomo di garanzia, ed al codice del consumo), available at www.giustizia.it/, last consulted 14 August 2012.

Not only Italy is considering the introduction of a national fiduciary device; the Netherlands too is currently working on the development of a domestic instrument.[24]

All these examples show how, in the aftermath of the adoption of the Convention, some civil law countries have tried (and are still trying) to pass a domestic device in order to 'swim against the tide of trusts rushing in from common law countries . . . if only to try to capture back some of the lucrative international financial work which has gone to common law jurisdictions'.[25] Also, as the *Exposé des motifs* to the French *fiducie* highlights, once some countries had decided to legislate in this area, others felt the need to follow.[26]

Thus, it can be said that in several countries the coming into force of the Hague Trusts Convention has provoked a discussion concerning the opportunity to reform substantive national laws so as to make them more in line with the needs that are taken care of by the law of trusts.[27] Although the fear of losing business to other countries has stopped some legislatures from ratifying the Convention, it has provided them with an incentive to amend their substantive law in this area and to introduce a device that would qualify as a 'trust' under the Hague Trusts Convention. It follows that although the Convention was not intended to introduce the trust concept into the domestic law of States that do not already have it, new trust or fiduciary devices have been developed in addition to those already in place. This is in line with developments outside the European Union where, as the examples of Quebec, China and Uruguay show, the Convention has had a similar impact.

Interestingly, however, the nature and scope of the devices enacted since the coming into force of the Hague Trusts Convention are quite varied.

[24] In view of the ratification of the Hague Trusts Convention, the Netherlands had considered adapting its *bewind* so as to fall within the definition of article 2 of the Hague Convention, but that never happened. A. Dyer, 'International Recognition and Adaptation of Trusts: The Influence of the Hague Convention' (1999) 32 Vander. J. Transnat'l L. 989, 1015. It should be noted that with effect from 1 January 2012, the Island of Curaçao (part of the Kingdom of the Netherlands) has its own law on trusts.

[25] P. Matthews, 'The New Trust: Obligations without Rights?', in A. J. Oakley (ed.), *Trends in Contemporary Trust Law* (Oxford: Clarendon Press, 1996), pp. 1, 22.

[26] 'La France ne peut pas rester insensible à la globalisation de cet instrument juridique.' See Proposition de Loi, no. 178 (2004–5). In Spain, there is an increasing interest of the legal profession in the introduction of a domestic trust. S. Cámara Lapuente, 'Trusts y patrimonios fiduciarios: acerca de sus posibles aplicaciones en el derecho de la persona, familia y sucesiones y su eventual regulación', La Ley 13923/2011, 3.

[27] In this sense, Graziadei, Mattei and Smith, *Commercial Trusts*, above, note 3, p. 15.

Although the French *fiducie*, like the Luxembourgish *contrat fiduciaire*, the Romanian *fiducie* and the potential Italian *fiducia* all represent contractual devices, they feature different connotations. And, whilst Austria has introduced a private foundation endowed with legal personality, San Marino has established not only a comprehensive trust law, resembling the trust of the English and international model,[28] but also the *affidamento fiduciario* which is civilian.[29] Thus, the various instruments are inspired by different conceptual structures.

B. *The effect of these developments*

The fact that some national legislatures have adopted trust or fiduciary devices is seen as beneficial not only to the functioning of the Hague Trusts Convention, but also to national conflict of law rules since courts can more easily recognize foreign trusts.[30] In fact, in those countries that have not ratified the Convention, the problem that arises is that they often fail to make specific provisions for the recognition and enforcement of foreign trusts because their system does not recognize trusts as such. As a consequence, courts of a Member State without conflict of law rules addressing trusts will characterize the device on the basis of their domestic legal categories.[31] Therefore, having a national trust or fiduciary device could actually render the operation of foreign trusts smoother.

At the same time, however, some scholars have pointed out that the establishment, in the aftermath of the Hague Trusts Convention, of new national devices has rendered the spectrum of existing trust law within Europe much more complex and, therefore, enhanced the difficulties of mutual recognition. It has been suggested that the lack of harmonization between all these different devices represents an obstacle to the proper

[28] Some of the provisions seem to resemble the trust law of Jersey and of Malta. See P. Panico, 'Trusts in a Civil Law Environment: The New Laws of San Marino' (2006) *Trusts & Trustees* 20.

[29] M. Lupoi, 'The New Law of San Marino on the "affidamento fiduciario"' (2011) 25 Trust L.I. 51.

[30] D. J. Hayton, S. C. J. J. Kortmann and H. L. E. Verhagen (eds.), *Principles of European Trust Law* (The Hague: Kluwer Law International, 1999), p. 10.

[31] For an account of the situation in countries that have not ratified the Hague Convention, see D. Hayton, 'International Recognition of Trusts', in Hayton (ed.), *The International Trust*, above, note 19, p. 161; J. Harris, *The Hague Trusts Convention: Scope, Application and Preliminary Issues* (Oxford: Hart, 2002), pp. 330–5 and K. Lipstein, 'Trusts', in K. Lipstein (ed.), *International Encyclopedia of Comparative Law, Private International Law* (Tübingen: JCB Mohr, 1994), vol. III, ch. 23, pp. 16ff.

functioning of the EU internal market, creating impediments not only to the free movement of services, but also to the freedom of establishment as well as the free movement of capital.[32] Thus, because new domestic devices have been developed alongside the many other national devices already in place, some trust lawyers have started advocating the need for uniform trust rules within the European Union.

III Attempts to render European trust law uniform

Considering that, unlike contract and company law, trust law represents an area of the law in which the EU legislature has hardly intervened, the proposals to introduce a uniform European trust law come as a little unexpected.[33] In fact, to this date, trust law has been largely immune from attempts to harmonize the law.

A first attempt at a unification of trust law was envisaged by UNIDROIT in the course of the 1950s, but not taken any further.[34] Nearly fifty years later, in 1999, a group of international experts published a set of uniform *Principles of European Trust Law*.[35] The *Principles* consist of eight articles only and do not therefore represent a comprehensive set of trust provisions. Instead, they outline the basic elements of the trust and, in doing so, mostly draw on the common law model. The declared goal of these *Principles* was not, however, to harmonize substantive law in the area, nor to advocate the adoption by civil law jurisdictions of a trust concept.

[32] S. C. J. J. Kortmann, D. J. Hayton, N. E. D. Faber, K. G. C. Reid and J. W. A. Biemans (eds.), *Towards an EU Directive on Protected Funds* (The Hague: Kluwer Law International, 2009), p. 2.

[33] References to trusts are found, for instance, in the Council Regulation (EC) no. 44/2001 of 22 December 2000 on jurisdiction and the recognition and enforcement of judgments in civil and commercial matters: Arts. 5(6), 23(4), 23(5) and 60(3) as well as the Regulation (EC) no. 805/2004 of 21 April 2004, creating a European enforcement order for uncontested claims. See further the Resolution of the European Parliament of 15 November 2001 on the approximation of civil and commercial law of the Member States, OJ C 140 E/538 of 13 June 2002, art. 14(a). It has to be noted, however, that the French version of the text refers to antitrust law. See M. Grimaldi and F. Barrière, 'Trust and *Fiducie*', in A. S. Hartkamp, M. W. Hesselink, E. H. Hondius, C. Mak and C. E. du Perron (eds.), *Towards a European Civil Code*, 4th edn (The Hague: Kluwer Law International, 2011), p. 1086.

[34] G. Hornsey, 'Report on Possible Uses of Certain Principles of the Trust in Civil Law Countries (I)', in *Unification of Law – Unidroit, Yearbook 1957*, p. 44 and L. M. Bentivoglio, 'Investment Trusts (I)', ibid., p. 105; M. Matteucci, 'The Activities of the International Institute for the Unification of Private Law', *Unidroit, Yearbook 1959*, p. 41 and Matteucci, ibid., 1960, p. 39.

[35] Hayton, Kortmann and Verhagen, *Principles of European Trust Law*, above, note 30.

Their objective was rather to serve as default rules parties may use, or as guidelines for practitioners in interpreting trust instruments.[36]

In 2005, a group of international scholars, working under the auspices of the Trento Common Core Project, produced a volume on *Commercial Trusts in European Private Law*.[37] Unlike the *Principles of European Trust Law*, this volume did not represent an attempt to outline principles. It rather draws a map of existing law with the aim of enhancing a better understanding of the legal regulation of devices that entrust wealth to others.

Thus, so far no real attempt at harmonizing or unifying this area of the law has been undertaken. This is perhaps not altogether surprising, considering that not all legal systems recognize trust devices and that only a few jurisdictions have a branch of the law dealing with trusts. Moreover, traditionally trust law has been seen as part of property law, an area that is often considered difficult to harmonize and that has hitherto been touched only indirectly by EU legislation.[38] Also, trusts have frequently been portrayed as tied to the common law tradition and in conflict with fundamental principles of civil law legal systems, such as the unity of patrimony and the *numerus clausus* of property rights. Hence the resistance of some continental lawyers against trusts and their increasing use in international affairs.

However, in 2009 two books were published which, contrary to the *Principles of European Trust Law*, suggest the adoption of two sets of uniform rules on trust law in all EU Member States. The method as well as the scope of the projects are different, and so is the device whose adoption they recommend. Nevertheless, they both proceed from the assumption that trust law within Europe needs to be rendered uniform. Before questioning this assumption, let us have a look at the set of rules put forward in these books. A detailed analysis of both projects will not be possible. I shall therefore focus on some of their essential features.

A. Book X on 'Trusts' of the Draft Common Frame of Reference

In 2003 the European Commission set out an 'Action Plan' for the elaboration of a Common Frame of Reference (CFR), the settled purpose of which is to ensure a 'greater coherence of existing and future *acquis* in

[36] Ibid., p. 11. [37] Graziadei, Mattei and Smith, *Commercial Trusts*, above, note 3.

[38] P.-C. Müller-Graff, 'EU Directives as a Means of Private Law Unification', in Hartkamp, Hesselink, Hondius, Mak and du Perron (eds.), above, note 33, p. 149.

the area of contract'.[39] Two international research groups, the 'Study Group on a European Civil Code' and the 'Acquis Group', working within a network partly funded by the European Commission, have produced a draft of the envisaged future Common Frame of Reference (DCFR). The final outline of the draft was published in March 2009 and included, among others, a book, Book X, on 'Trusts'.[40]

Thus, Book X forms part of a wider project aimed at creating a greater 'coherence' within European private law. The reason why there is a book on trusts, if the whole purpose of the exercise is to present a draft for the establishment of common principles on contract law is, of course, an interesting question.[41] Unfortunately the drafters have not provided us with any explanation as to the rationale of Book X. In fact, in contrast to most of the other books of the DCFR, Book X contains no notes explaining the propositions which it sets out by reference to the respective European legal systems, and the comments by the drafters of Book X cover only three of its ten chapters. In the absence of any indications from the drafters, one has to assume that the harmonization of trust law was perceived as directly or indirectly necessary, or at least desirable, for the establishment of a greater coherence of EU contract law.

Having clarified, as far as possible, the background of this initiative, let us now look at the nature of the instrument proposed by the drafters of Book X (the 'DCFR trust'). First, Book X of the DCFR sets out a uniform device entitled 'trusts'. Second, the trust proposed by Book X is largely based on the common law trust and in particular the English model. It follows that the trust, whose adoption the drafters recommend within Europe, is not based on principles common to existing trust and fiduciary devices in Europe. In other words, it is not an attempt at comparative legislation, but rather an attempt to extend the English model, or more specifically a somewhat modified version of it, to the rest of Europe. In fact, though predominately English the DCFR trust also shows signs of deviation from the model.

[39] European Commission, Communication to the European Parliament and the Council – A more coherent European Contract Law: An Action Plan, COM(2003) 68 final, OJ 2003 C 63/1. This Communication was followed by another Communication in 2004. European Commission, Communication to the European Parliament and the Council – European Contract Law and the Revision of the Acquis: The way forward, COM(2004) 651 final.

[40] C. von Bar and E. Clive (eds.), *Principles, Definitions and Model Rules of European Private Law: Draft Common Frame of Reference (DCFR)* (Oxford University Press, 2009).

[41] The author has addressed this question elsewhere, in A. Braun, 'Trusts in the Draft Common Frame of Reference: The "best solution" for Europe?' (2011) 70 CLJ 327, 348ff.

The English roots of the DCFR provisions can be seen in the fact that the DCFR trust does not have a contractual nature, but is conceived as a unilateral instrument. Moreover, its essential features consist of the need for: a trustee, trust assets, a beneficiary or a public benefit purpose, the segregation of the trust assets from the personal assets of the trustee and a court or administrative authority to whom considerable power has been given. In addition, the position of the trustee is seen as an office and he owes a core of duties towards the beneficiary, who is provided with relatively effective protection against the trustee and third parties. Further, several articles simply codify some of the English leading trust cases.[42]

At certain points, however, the model rules deviate from English trust law. There are, first of all, linguistic differences as exemplified by the use of the Scottish term truster instead of settlor. These deviations aside, there are some substantive differences concerning the nature of the trust. So, for example, and contrary to English law, the DCFR contains no provision concerning the duration of the trust. Also, although in principle only trusts for beneficiaries and for public benefit purposes are valid under the DCFR, private purpose trusts may take effect as long as the purpose is considered lawful. Further, until trust assets are segregated by the truster, the trust takes effect as a trust of the entire 'patrimony'.[43] Hence, what Book X of the DCFR aims to do is to transpose into European legal systems a modified version of the English trust.

Its rules are expressed in the context of 116 articles which are crafted by reference to trusts constituted by a 'juridical act',[44] that is to say express or voluntary trusts,[45] and which regulate every aspect of the life of the trust, from the creation to its termination. Article X.-1:201 Book X defines the 'trust' in the following manner: 'A trust is a legal relationship in which a trustee is obliged to administer or dispose of one or more

[42] This can be seen in provisions, such as, for instance, art. X.-9:104 which strongly resembles the rule expressed in *Saunders* v. *Vautier* (1841), 41 E.R. 482, or art. X.-2:103(1) which embraces a doctrine similar to that in *Re Rose* [1952] Ch 499, concerning the perfect constitution of a trust. For further examples, see Braun, 'Trusts in the Draft Common Frame of Reference', above, note 41.

[43] DCFR, art. X.-3:103(2). For further examples, see Braun, ibid.

[44] The drafters define the term in the following manner: 'A "juridical act" is any statement or agreement, whether express or implied from conduct, which is intended to have legal effect as such. It may be unilateral, bilateral or multilateral.'

[45] See art. X-1:101(2). For further explanations see von Bar and Clive, *Principles, Definitions and Model Rules*, above, note 40, pp. 5671–5.

assets (the trust fund) in accordance with the terms governing the relationship (trust terms) to benefit a beneficiary or advance public benefit purposes.' Hence, private purpose trusts are excluded from the scope of Book X, whilst charitable trusts fall within it. Other provisions disclose that Book X admits both *inter vivos* and testamentary trusts, whether set up for commercial or non-commercial purposes. In fact, Book X provides a partly different regulation for trusts that are set up for gratuitous purposes. Also, the provisions explicitly mention that the DCFR trust can be used for management and security purposes. It follows that Book X has a very broad scope, suggesting a fully-fledged trust law.

At this point the central question is what the function of Book X is. Unfortunately, its drafters are silent on the point. However, given that the whole structure of the DCFR is designed as a codification of a large part of private law, it would seem that the real motive behind the project was indeed a European Civil Code.[46] Meanwhile, in October 2011, the Commission published the proposal for an optional Common European Sales Law (CESL).[47] There seems therefore little prospect that the European legislature will turn Book X into a legislative text.

B. *The proposed Directive on protected funds*

Book X of the DCFR does not represent the only attempt to render the law in this area uniform. In 2009, a group of scholars who are part of the International Working Group on European Trust Law at the Business and Law Research Centre of the University of Nijmegen published a book containing an unofficial draft of a Directive on 'protected funds'. The same group, although with some different personnel, had previously produced the *Principles of European Trust Law*, of which the draft Directive is a developed version.[48]

[46] See S. Whittaker, *The 'Draft Common Frame of Reference': An Assessment, Commissioned by the Ministry of Justice, United Kingdom*, November 2008, www.justice.gov.uk/publications/eu-contract-law-common-frame-reference.htm, p. 6; N. Jansen and R. Zimmermann, '"European Civil Code in all but Name": Discussing the Nature and Purposes of the Draft Common Frame of Reference' (2010) 69 CLJ 98.

[47] COM(2011) 635 final.

[48] K. Reid, 'Conceptualising the Chinese Trust: Some Thoughts from Europe', in R. van Rhee and L. Chen (eds.), *Towards a Chinese Civil Code: Historical and Comparative Perspectives* (Leiden: Brill, 2012), p. 5.

The volume consists of twenty articles that express the proposal for a new EU Directive. In addition, it contains comments by the authors of the Directive as well as a set of National Reports explaining the current legal position and considering implementing the protected fund Directive into national law.

Unlike the drafters of Book X of the DCFR, the authors of the unofficial Directive on protected funds have provided us with a comprehensive explanation of the underlying goals of the project. According to them, more money is likely to be made available by lenders and investors if their interests are protected against the insolvency of the borrower. In other words, bank and business communities have a need for 'devices that make money work as hard as possible and to help maintain a competitive position in European financial markets'.[49] As the drafters point out, quite a few legal systems within Europe already recognize institutions that create such a 'ring-fenced' fund. However, since the devices already present in each European legal system are quite different from one another, problems of mutual recognition arise. In light of this, the proposed Directive aims at enhancing the functioning of the internal market by proposing a new device, a so-called 'protected fund'. According to the drafters, this 'protected fund' would provide a uniform alternative to the growing diversity and would allow mutual recognition of already established devices. As a consequence, the drafters envisage that the freedom of establishment and the free movement of services and of capital would increase.

This explains why the protected fund is intended to be used to 'further commercial investment and trading, with the aim of encouraging economic growth in the financial sectors of the EU'.[50] In other words, contrary to the DCFR trust, the protected fund is not to be employed for the purpose of managing family wealth through a number of generations, nor for charitable, religious or political purposes. What exactly commercial purposes comprise is not, however, clearly defined in the proposed draft, which instead lists a number of examples, such as: the financing of pensions for retired employees, the operation of collective investment schemes, collective debt financing and transfers of title to the administrator of particular property by way of security.[51]

[49] Kortmann, Hayton, Faber, Reid and Biemans, *Towards an EU Directive*, above, note 32, p. 1.
[50] Ibid., pp. 18–19. [51] Ibid., p. 8.

As to the nature of the 'protected fund', first, unlike the DCFR trust, the protected fund is not defined as a 'trust', but rather as a 'trust-like device'. According to the drafters, this is because it differs from a trust in respect of its structure, scope and method of constitution as well as extinction.[52] The choice not to define the device as a trust explains why the drafters have not employed terms such as trustee, trust fund or settlor or, indeed, other terms that are reminiscent of trust devices of common or civil law jurisdictions. Instead, the proposed language is that of 'protected fund', 'administrator', 'assets of a protected fund' and 'originator'. Second, it is said to be a new 'trust-like' device that has no direct equivalent in any existing institution. In fact, although it inevitably bears a certain resemblance to the common law trust, it also exhibits features of certain fiduciary devices that exist in some other European legal systems. Be that as it may, the protected fund shows some resemblance to the Scottish trust.[53] Thus, like Book X of the DCFR, the draft Directive does not attempt to identify principles common to already existing trust and fiduciary devices, but rather suggests a new uniform instrument for Europe, which allows parties to ring-fence assets for a specific purpose. Hence, unlike Book X, it adopts a functional approach.

That said, what are the essential features of this new device that represents neither a trust, nor a contract nor a company? As mentioned earlier, it can only be set up for commercial purposes. Further, such a fund can only be established during the originator's lifetime,[54] and only in favour of beneficiaries, thus excluding both funds for private and charitable purposes. It follows that the draft Directive is not as comprehensive as Book X which, as we have seen, proposes a fully-fledged trust law. Instead, the draft Directive suggests a minimum set of rules, laying out the principal elements of the fund, which Member States would have to implement, though with a certain degree of flexibility.

The proposed Directive requires the presence of an originator who establishes the protected fund, as well as an administrator who 'owns' and administers the assets in the interest of beneficiaries.[55] The protected fund will be regulated by the law chosen by the creator of the fund, which can be the law of any of the Member States and must be identified in the constitutive document. The assets composing the fund form a separate

[52] Ibid., p. 4.

[53] K. Reid, 'National Report for Scotland', in Kortmann, Hayton, Faber, Reid and Biemans, *Towards an EU Directive*, above, note 32, p. 257.

[54] Unofficial draft Directive, arts. 4, 5. [55] Ibid., art. 3.

'patrimony' (terminology employed by the drafters of the proposed Directive) that can be administrated only by a limited class of persons, displaying certain professional requirements.[56] In fact, administrators must be appointed from a restricted category of persons operating within the EU and regulated under the law of a Member State, such as a legal person having its registered office or an establishment in a Member State, or a natural person who is a resident of a Member State and belongs to the category of public notaries, lawyers admitted to the bar, accountants or bailiffs.

The relationship between the originator and the administrator, and the administrator and the beneficiary, does not seem to be a contractual one. In fact the originator cannot enforce the administrator's duties (though he may be given certain powers – see article 6) and the protection granted to the beneficiary is much wider than that of a contracting party. Further, the function of the administrator is treated as an office, meaning that his death does not bring the fund to an end. The administrator owns the fund and has certain duties towards the beneficiary, which either he or an enforcer can enforce.[57] It follows that the protected fund is not conceived of as a separate entity.

As for the position of the beneficiary, although he is protected against the administrator's insolvency, in case of misappropriation of assets belonging to the fund, he has no claim against the third party, whether of a proprietary or a personal nature. The drafters have instead opted for a strong protection of the third party who can claim moneys out of the fund unless he or she had actual knowledge of the administrator's breach of its duties or of special circumstances that would make such a breach obvious to an honest reasonable person.[58] In this way the authors hope to facilitate the use of protected funds in the commercial sphere.[59]

The protected fund is to be introduced into the EU by means of a Directive to be implemented in each Member State. Thus the authors of the volume have opted for a soft law, and suggested a harmonization of European trust law by way of an additional uniform device that coexists

[56] Ibid., art. 7. [57] Ibid., art. 8.

[58] Ibid., art. 10.2: it states that a creditor cannot claim out of the fund moneys due under an unauthorized obligation if he 'knew or ought to have known without inquiry' that the obligation was unauthorized. Kortmann, Hayton, Faber, Reid and Biemans, *Towards an EU Directive*, above, note 32, p. 33.

[59] However, in the note to the article it is specified that Member States may provide further remedies against the transferee, for example on the ground of fraud or (if the transfer was gratuitous) unjust enrichment. Ibid., p. 31.

along with other national devices already in place. If adopted, each Member State would be required to recognize the protected fund set up under the law of any other Member State.[60]

C. *Differences and commonalities*

Having examined the two academic initiatives, let us briefly summarize some of the main differences and commonalities. As mentioned before, the rationale of the projects is different, one being part of a broad framework for the harmonization of large parts of European private law, and the other being a specific project aimed at introducing a uniform ring-fenced fund into all EU Member States. However, both projects suggest a device that allows investors to create a segregated fund of assets that may be employed for management as well as for security purposes. In doing so, both projects have chosen not to identify principles common to the already existing trust and fiduciary devices in Europe, but rather to propose a 'new device'. But whereas the DCFR trust is strongly rooted in the common law tradition and in particular in English law, the unprotected fund does not seem to reflect the law of a specific legal system, though revealing a certain resemblance to the Scottish trust.

Whilst Book X of the DCFR contains 116 detailed provisions regulating a new European trust in all its facets, the proposed Directive aims at introducing a new trust-like device, called 'protected fund', for which it establishes basic elements in the context of twenty articles (of which only fourteen effectively regulate the protected fund). In fact, Book X provides a comprehensive and detailed set of rules that regulate the trust, whereas the proposed Directive establishes a set of minimum requirements, with the fund being regulated by the law chosen by the originator. And whereas Book X of the DCFR extends to both *inter vivos* and testamentary trusts, including charitable trusts, the proposed Directive only applies to *inter vivos* commercial trusts established for the benefit of one or more beneficiaries. Its scope is, therefore, much more limited.

However, the essence in both cases is that the assets of the DCFR trust or the protected fund form part of a separate patrimony which the trustee or administrator owns for the benefit of others and which is protected

[60] Unofficial draft Directive, art. 16.

against his insolvency, liquidation or death. Neither the protected fund nor the DCFR are thus a legal person or an ownerless patrimony. However, whilst the DCFR does not prescribe who can act as trustee, not everybody can be an administrator of a protected fund.

Interestingly, neither project foresees the need for a mandatory system of public registration, which may create difficulties in civilian legal systems. Also, neither prescribes a maximum duration, and thus allows for property to be segregated in perpetuity.[61] According to the drafters of the proposed Directive, this gives greater flexibility to the instrument. And the authors of the DCFR do not see the need for a maximum duration because the DCFR trust can be wound up by the beneficiaries as well as the trustee himself.[62] As for formality requirements, whilst the DCFR contemplates the possibility of an oral trust,[63] the draft Directive is created by way of a document which records on its face that a protected fund is to be established.[64] A qualification of the exact nature of the document establishing such a protected fund is remitted to each Member State, with the possibility of seeing it as a contract.[65]

Finally, whereas the protected fund would coexist alongside already established devices, it is not quite clear yet what the destiny of Book X will be. As mentioned earlier, it is unlikely that Book X will be transformed into European legislation. However, should the EU legislature decide differently, Book X could probably serve either as the basis for an optional instrument, or be turned into a mandatory legislative instrument imposing a European trust that could either replace present national instruments or coexist alongside them. In either case, a new branch dealing with trust law would be introduced into each European legal system.

In summary, although the ultimate function of the specific devices is similar, namely asset segregation in favour of a beneficiary, the nature of the instruments suggested, as well as their scope, is quite different.

[61] It is possible, however, for the constitutive document of a protected fund to limit the duration. Unofficial draft Directive, art. 5.1(b).

[62] Article X-9:108.

[63] DCFR, art. X.-2:203(1).

[64] Unofficial draft Directive, art. 4.

[65] Kortmann, Hayton, Faber, Reid and Biemans, *Towards an EU Directive*, above, note 32, p. 11.

IV Feasibility of the two academic proposals

A. Book X of the DCFR

Having examined both academic projects, let us now consider whether it would be feasible to transform them into EU legislation. What sort of difficulties might arise if they were to be embedded into national law, especially of non-trust countries? Looking at Book X of the DCFR, were it to operate as the basis for an optional instrument for the parties to choose, then that might not be too difficult a goal to achieve. At the same time, it would require an adjustment of conflict of law rules so as to allow settlors to choose non-State law to govern their trusts.

If, however, Book X in its current form were to function as the basis for a future set of mandatory rules, whether in order to replace or coexist along with current trust law, things would get more difficult. The introduction of a fully-fledged trust law into all Member States is inevitably problematic. This is even more so the case for Book X, as it proposes a codified, though somewhat modified, version of English statute and case law to function as the basis for a European trust. Both trust and non-trust countries within Europe might see that as a reason for resisting an attempt to transform this academic project into European legislation.

Also, because of its broad scope, if Book X were to be transformed into a mandatory set of rules, a significant conflict might arise with national provisions in the laws governing tax, insolvency, companies, civil procedure, the family, succession as well as property, especially in civil law jurisdictions.[66] For instance, testamentary trusts might not be able to operate in those civilian legal systems which possess succession laws and matrimonial property regimes capable of taking precedence over the law governing the trust. Moreover, several non-trust countries might see the model rules of Book X as being in conflict with their national property law, especially as far as publicity and formality requirements are concerned as well as the protection of third-party creditors. Furthermore, with the exception perhaps of Italy,[67] the extensive supervisory powers which the DCFR confers on courts could conflict with national rules governing judicial institutions and civil procedure in European countries which have not hitherto recognized the trust. Although such a jurisdiction is often granted in relation to certain institutions, such as

[66] For a detailed analysis of the potential problems see Braun, 'Trusts in the Draft Common Frame of Reference', above, note 41.

[67] Braun, 'Italy: The Trust Interno', above, note 19, pp. 807ff.

guardianship, curatorship and administratorship of deceased estates, it is questionable whether courts can be called upon to ensure that the purpose of the trust is carried out.[68] In France, for instance, courts have only a limited power to intervene with the management and the administration of the *fiducie*.[69] A reform of national rules concerning judicial supervision might therefore be needed in order to make the DCFR trust actually work.[70]

Finally, problems could arise with the translation of the model rules of Book X into the language of all Member States, something the drafters have envisaged.[71] Finding a terminology that captures the notion of trust in each legal system seems a rather difficult task.

B. *The draft Directive on protected funds*

Somewhat different remarks are to be made about the unofficial draft Directive on protected funds. First of all, as mentioned above, the draft does not suggest a fully-fledged trust law, limiting itself to outlining the essential elements of the suggested protected fund and leaving Member States a certain amount of flexibility in implementing them. For instance, as far as the protection of third parties dealing with the administrator is concerned, and in contrast with Book X, the proposed Directive foresees that Member States can establish a system of voluntary registration.[72] In other words, Member States can require disclosure on the register that the asset in question is held in a protected fund.

Because of this flexibility and the simplicity of the provisions, the drafters of the proposed Directive are of the view that the protected fund can be easily introduced in any legal system.[73] According to them, the proposed Directive would not affect tax, succession, property and

[68] See T. Honoré, 'On Fitting Trusts into Civil Law Jurisdictions', Oxford Legal Studies Research Paper No. 27/2008, p. 4.

[69] See *Code civil* (C. civ.), arts. 2027, 2028.

[70] U. Mattei, 'Should Europe Codify Trust?', in P. Birks and A. Pretto (eds.), *Themes in Comparative Law: In Honour of Bernard Rudden* (Oxford University Press, 2002), p. 235.

[71] Von Bar and Clive, *Principles, Definitions and Model Rules*, above, note 40, p. 29.

[72] According to the drafters, registration would not be necessary because the protection which, in some legal systems, is given by publicity, is given for protected funds in a different way; that is to say, by giving strong protection to third parties working with the administrator. In their view, the lack of mandatory registration renders the instrument more flexible and informal. See Kortmann, Hayton, Faber, Reid and Biemans, *Towards an EU Directive*, above, note 32, p. 11.

[73] Ibid., pp. 3, 15.

regulatory supervision law, and insolvency law would only be affected as far as the recognition of a 'fiduciary patrimony' is concerned.

It is certainly true that no conflict should arise with family and succession law given that the drafters only had in mind commercial trusts. As for property law, the proposed Directive does not grant the beneficiary any rights against third parties. This avoids a possible clash with principles of property law of civilian jurisdictions. Nevertheless, some of the rules foreseen in the draft Directive may still be seen as entering into conflict with national principles in the area of property law, such as the principle of the unity of patrimony. Also, some national legislatures might have a problem with the fact that the protected fund does not have a limited duration and that it does not require a notarial deed to be established. Further, conflicts are bound to arise in the area of insolvency law, which will have to be adapted accordingly. Moreover, as is the case with Book X of the DCFR, the proposed Directive would definitely require a reform of the provisions concerning the supervisory powers of courts in national legal systems.

Finally, linguistic problems may occur because of the need to draft the text in the languages of all Member States. This is particularly difficult in this area of the law where the language is so culturally sensitive. Also, the fact that the drafters have opted for a Directive may amplify this problem given that in case of minimum harmonization each Member State may choose to adopt a different technique when implementing the Directive. These range from a simple copy-out approach, with minimum elaboration, to the gold-plating technique, which may lead to an over-implementation of the Directive. And, given that each State can add further rules when implementing the proposed Directive, in the end the protected fund might not be that uniform throughout Europe.

C. A comparison

In the light of the above it is evident that both proposals on the table could potentially trigger difficulties. However, in comparing both projects it would seem from the way it is designed that the protected fund may be more easily embraced by countries which are not familiar with the trust concept. First of all, quite a few Member States recognize the existence of some sort of segregated fund.[74] Furthermore, the proposed

[74] See D. J. Hayton, *Extending the Boundaries of Trusts and Similar Ring-Fenced Funds* (The Hague: Kluwer Law International, 2002). See also the national reports in Kortmann,

draft Directive suggests a device that is not clearly rooted in any particular tradition. Member States, be it trust or non-trust law countries, might therefore be less reluctant to embrace it because it would not be perceived as the transplant of a concept belonging to a particular legal culture. This is facilitated by the choice of the authors not to employ terminology that resembles English trust law. Whether a translation of its terminology into the languages of the single Member States is therefore easier is another question. Also, compared to Book X, the proposed Directive is less ambitious. Because its scope is not as broad, the risk of a clash with national law is not as high. On the whole, therefore, the proposal of a Directive on protected funds might find less opposition from non-trust States.

This, however, does not in itself make the protected fund an instrument desirable to all Member States. It is by no means obvious that there is a need for such a device, nor that it would solve all the problems pointed out by its drafters. In fact, the Directive will not for instance remove the obstacle of mutual recognition of existing devices. Although mutual recognition of the protected fund would be guaranteed, the proposed Directive would do nothing about 'the scattered and diverse range of trusts and trust-like devices' denounced by the drafters themselves. As it stands, the Directive would leave current trust and fiduciary law unaffected. In fact, pre-Directive relationships would not be recognizable as a protected fund, given that they have to be explicitly designated in the constitutive document as a protected fund.[75]

Although the drafters suggest that national legislatures may decide to reform their domestic law while implementing the proposed Directive,[76] this may also not happen. In some countries, such as Switzerland, initiatives for the amendment of national law at the time of ratification of the Hague Trusts Convention were not successful.[77] Indeed, several

Hayton, Faber, Reid and Biemans, *Towards an EU Directive*, above, note 32, as well as Graziadei, Mattei and Smith, *Commercial Trusts*, above, note 3.

[75] Unofficial draft Directive, art. 4.

[76] See Kortmann, Hayton, Faber, Reid and Biemans, *Towards an EU Directive*, above, note 32, p. 3.

[77] Some Swiss authors have suggested using the opportunity of the ratification of the Convention in order to pass a legislative reform of 'fiduciary transfers' which are commonly recognized in Switzerland. See L. Thévenoz, *Trusts in Switzerland: Ratification of the Hague Convention on Trusts and Codification of the Law of Fiduciary Transfers* (Zurich: Schulthess, 2001), p. 306. According to the author, p. 311: 'there is a substantial risk that the transactions for which Switzerland's existing fiduciary transfers do not seem

European countries have such a variety of different devices, developed by legal practice or specific legislation, that it would be rather arduous, if not impossible, to bring all of them together under one heading. This means that if such countries decide not to bring their existing devices into line with this new protected fund, the mutual recognition of those devices will depend partly on whether they fall within the definition of article 2 of the Hague Trusts Convention and on whether the other States decide to ratify the Convention.

V Is there a need for a uniform European law of trusts?

Irrespective of whether one proposal is more feasible than the other, the question that arises is whether the two projects currently on the table should remain an academic exercise, or whether they should be transformed into European legislation. After all, both books were ultimately drafted for this purpose. This mainly depends on whether there is a need for a uniform European trust law. Though different in many ways, the two academic proposals seem to suggest that there is. But is that really the case, and are we ready for such a big step? The answer to either question is in my view negative, for reasons that I shall explain.

Any discourse about harmonization or unification of trust law at a European level has to take into account that trust law is different from other areas of private law. Not all European legal systems are familiar with trusts. Thus, a debate focusing on the harmonization of this area of the law necessarily requires a discussion about whether a trust or 'trust-like' device should be introduced into all EU countries. In fact, the upshot of both projects published in 2009 would ultimately be that of making such a device available in each European Member State.

But what are the justifications for that? Unfortunately the drafters of Book X do not provide us with a set of reasons that would explain its rationale. The drafters of the Directive, on the other hand, have advanced the following arguments in support of such an extension. First, it is suggested that every legal system would profit from a protected fund as money is likely to be made available by lenders and investors if their interests are protected.[78] Second, it is argued that the current situation creates barriers to cross-border operations, and third, that the plurality of

sufficiently reliable may be legitimately carried out by means of a trust governed by better-adapted and more modern foreign legislation'.

[78] Ibid., p. 1.

devices represents an obstacle to mutual recognition. Thus the drafters of the Directive see the justification of uniform rules mostly in economic arguments. Among the other economic considerations often indicated are that it would increase fair competition between countries.[79] It is further suggested that investors would have greater confidence when investing in civil law countries that have not hitherto embraced the trust in their legal system. Moreover, it is said that transaction costs could be diminished and the European market perhaps become more competitive.

But do we really have sufficient empirical evidence in support of these economic arguments? And is it really the case that economic arguments should prevail?[80] And even if the answer to both questions were to be positive, is the appropriate response to all the problems listed above necessarily a European trust imposed by the EU legislature?

There are a number of arguments that speak against the introduction into all Member States of a European trust or trust-like device. The question of competence of the EU legislature aside, if certain Member States have not already introduced a trust or fiduciary device they may have good reasons for not doing so. Why should the EU legislature interfere with their choice? Further, according to some authors, regulatory competition is more desirable than a top-down harmonization or unification.[81] Harmonization may in fact distort domestic law and there is a risk that cultural and linguistic plurality and diversity are compromised.[82] One could probably argue that the Directive on protected funds would still allow countries to compete against each other as it only sets minimum standards to be implemented by Member States. Thus, some differences will remain which means that transaction costs might not be necessarily diminished.

In any event, it is not self-evident that having yet another instrument, although a uniform one, alongside the already established instruments is

[79] In this sense, D. Hayton, 'The Developing European Dimension of Trust Law' (1999) 10 KCLJ 48, 70; Grimaldi and Barrière, 'Trust and *Fiducie*', above, note 33, pp. 1085, 1087. The authors clearly favour the expansion of trusts throughout Europe. See also M. J. de Waal, 'A European Law of Trusts?', in A. Vaquer (ed.), *European Private Law Beyond the Common Frame of Reference* (Groningen: Europea Law Publishing, 2008), p. 167.

[80] Hayton, 'The Developing European Dimension', above, note 79, p. 70.

[81] There is a voluminous literature on this point concerning different fields of law. See, in particular, K. Pistor, 'The Standardization of Law and its Effect on Developing Economies' (2002) 50 AJCL 97, 107ff.

[82] G. Teubner, 'Legal Irritants: Good Faith in British Law or How Unifying Law Ends Up in the New Divergences' (1998) 61 MLR 11.

beneficial in itself. There is no guarantee that citizens will actually make use of a new European trust. The experience of the *Societas Europaea* (SE) is significant here. It would, in fact, seem that so far only modest use has been made of the SE and that its use is not driven by the reasons that had led the EU legislature to establish this form of company.[83]

Moreover, this is not an area of the law in which there is a problem of incoherent piecemeal legislation by the EU legislature, nor is there an *acquis* to be consolidated. Finally, it is highly questionable that a uniform device would render the European financial market more competitive with the US or offshore jurisdictions.[84] As Donovan Waters has pointed out, settlors usually choose such jurisdictions not only on the basis of tax considerations, but also because they allow them to retain control over assets while maintaining complete confidentiality.[85]

Thus, apart from the fact that there is no clear evidence that would justify the allegations that there is a need for a European trust or trust-like device, the arguments that speak against a unification of the law in this area are tantamount to those in favour. Also, it is not obvious that a European trust or trust-like device is the only solution to the economic considerations listed earlier. At least as far as mutual recognition of the devices already in place is concerned, a wider ratification of the Hague Trusts Convention could probably solve the problem. Also, a fairer competition is not only to be achieved by means of a European trust. Member States could simply introduce their own domestic device. Thus a European trust might not be the only 'cure'.

VI The necessary steps for a unification of trust law in Europe

Even on the assumption that it would be a good thing to introduce a European trust or trust-like device, and this assumption awaits proper justification, it is rather questionable whether there is sufficient political consensus for a uniform solution. Further, a way would have to be found to overcome possible clashes between the trust concept and traditional features of the law of those jurisdictions which are not familiar with it.

83 See P. Davis, 'The European Private Company (SPE): Uniformity, Flexibility, Competition and the Persistence of National Laws', (2010) ECGI Working Paper 154/2010, p. 2. See also H. Eidenmüller, A. Engert and L. Hornuf, 'Incorporating under European Law: The Societas Europaea as a Vehicle for Legal Arbitrage' (2009) 10 *European Business Organization Law Review* 1.

84 See, for instance, the Regulation implementing the European Public Company.

85 In this sense, Waters, 'The Hague Trusts Convention', above, note 3, p. 85.

Moreover, there are several questions that would need to be addressed before proceeding any further.

First of all, it would be essential to establish a consensus about what we aim to achieve through the unification of trust law in Europe. Are we only concerned with increasing the level of mutual recognition of existing devices or do we intend to achieve other goals as well? Do we envisage an approximation of the different legal traditions or is what we ultimately want the introduction of the common law trust into all EU legal systems? And is it preferable to have an additional device or rather to render current law uniform? We further need to know whether the device is to be confined to the commercial context only or whether it should go beyond. Moreover, it is important to establish whether the instrument should serve a management purpose, or also, or principally, a security purpose. Finally, should charitable trusts become part of the project? Thus, it is essential to clarify which effect we want to achieve and what the intended rationale of the device is so as to be able to define the scope of the provisions to be developed.

And when a consensus over all these points is reached, it will be necessary to make a choice about the language, considering that it is necessary to draft a text accessible to common and civil lawyers alike. This is a difficulty the drafters of the Hague Trusts Convention had to tackle.[86] Furthermore, a decision as to the appropriate methodology has to be made. Here, there are different options.[87] One could identify a device from a particular national legal order. However, this would carry the risk of being perceived as a form of domination or legal imperialism, potentially clashing with the pre-existing legal and social concepts in the law-receiving countries. This seems to reflect the path taken by the drafters of the DCFR, though, as we said, the DCFR trust is not a purely English trust. Alternatively, one could also decide to identify the lowest common denominator among existing devices. This would not preclude diversity, but may lower the standards. And, thirdly, it is possible to develop a new legal concept. This third approach would seem to have been adopted by the drafters of the proposed Directive on protected funds. This way the negative effects of the other two approaches may be avoided, but the risk is that the device will not have been tested in any legal system and there is no guarantee that it will work. Thus, each of

[86] Graziadei, 'Recognition of Common Law Trusts', above, note 22.

[87] For an analysis of the possible ways of creating international standards and their consequences, see Pistor, 'The Standardization of Law', above, note 81, 107ff.

these three options has downsides and there is an inevitable price to be paid should a uniform device be imposed.

That aside, it is necessary to define which legislative technique to use in order to introduce the uniform device into the EU. Should harmonization of substantive law be achieved by means of a Regulation, a code or a Directive? Directives are usually employed in order to reach harmonization. However, if what is really intended is uniformity of solutions, then a Directive may not be the most effective instrument.[88] The text of a Directive runs the risk of being either too detailed or too vague, granting Member States too much leeway when implementing the rules. Further, in case of minimum harmonization as envisaged by the drafters of the Directive, each Member State can adopt different approaches in implementing Directives. Moreover, not only do implementing laws all have their own structure, each country also has different methods of interpretation. At the same time, however, Directives would seem the best way for 'combining the necessities for uniform Community standards on the one hand and the possibility to tolerate national individualities on the other'.[89] Such national individualities would get compromised if a Regulation or a code were to be enacted. At the same time, if we want a set of rules that are directly applicable and that render the law more coherent, then this is probably the way forward. However, as already mentioned, this solution may require an adaptation of national laws in several fields.

It seems thus clear, that a number of difficult questions would have to be addressed before we could proceed any further towards unification.

VII Conclusion

Although the Hague Trusts Convention principally aimed at establishing uniform conflicts of law rules, it led some European countries to reform their substantive trust law and to introduce their own domestic device. This, as we have seen, is clearly true of Luxembourg, France, San Marino, Romania and the Czech Republic and may become true also of Italy and the Netherlands. The fact that the number of trust instruments available within Europe has increased has paved the way for claims that there is a need for a uniform trust law not only at the level of conflict of law rules, but also at a substantive level. It would therefore seem that we have

[88] For an analysis of the pros and cons of harmonization through Directives see Müller-Graff, 'EU Directives', above, note 38, p. 77.

[89] Ibid., p. 83.

the common lawyer would recognize them. Let me be clear about what I mean by the term 'true trust'.

As defined in the American *Restatement (Third) of Trusts*,[6] the trust is 'a fiduciary relationship with respect to property, arising as a result of a manifestation of an intention to create that relationship and subjecting the person who holds title to the property to duties to deal with it for the benefit of charity or for one or more persons'. Several characteristics mentioned in this definition mark features that I take to be essential to the existence of a true trust, in view of the common law. First, a trust must involve a *fiduciary* relationship. The fiduciary concept, of course, is not unknown to the civil law and is not unique to the trust. However, the nature of the trust has been the subject of some controversy over the past several years. Drawing on the agency-relations theory in corporate law which subsumes the many and diverse fiduciary relationships into contracts, John Langbein has argued that the trust itself is a contract.[7] Other scholars have disagreed with him, but the contract theory of the trust has been very prominent in recent years.

Second, the *Restatement*'s definition holds that the trust is a *property-based* relationship. It is common to say that there is no trust without an existing and identifiable *res*.[8] The fiduciary duties must pertain to some specific asset or separate fund.

Third, and most important, the definition holds that legal title in the trust property, or *res*, must be held by a person or persons who has/have duties to deal with that property for the benefit of others. Here is the core of the common law trust – the separation of legal title from equitable ownership. The trustee may also be a beneficiary, of course, but there must be some additional beneficiary other than the trustee to whom the trustee owes fiduciary duties and against whom the beneficiary has rights that are enforceable in equity. It is this fragmentation of ownership that seems so strange, indeed well-nigh impossible, to the civilian, but so essential to the common lawyer. So, we must pursue this matter more if we are to get to the heart of the trust's dilution.

The definition also provides that the trustee must 'deal with [the trust *res*] for the benefit of charity or for one or more persons'. This part of the definition signals two important points. First, a trust requires that

[6] *Restatement of the Law Third, Trusts*, 4 vols. (St Paul: American Law Institute, 2003–12), §2.

[7] J. H. Langbein, 'The Contractarian Basis of the Law of Trusts' (1996) 105 Yale L.J. 625.

[8] E.g., *Brainerd* v. *Commissioner*, 91 F.2d 880 (7th Cir. 1937).

there be, at least for what common lawyers call a private express trust, one or more definite and validly ascertainable beneficiaries. Such beneficiaries, it is thought,[9] are necessary to enforce the trust. The second point signalled is that in dealing with the trust property, the trustee must act in the beneficiaries' interest. This is the principle that the Uniform Trust Code, picking up John Langbein's pithy expression,[10] calls the 'benefit the beneficiaries' principle.[11] It is an integral aspect of the idea that the trustee is acting in a fiduciary capacity and owing fiduciary duties.

This, then, is the core of the common law idea of the trust institution. How, then, is it diluting? To begin with, consider the two efforts at harmonization underway in Europe. The first, the Draft Common Frame of Reference (DCFR) Trust, involves the least amount of dilution. Alexandra Braun notes as one point of departure from English trust law that the DCFR provides no durational limit. This I do not find especially important for my purposes, as the same is true of trusts for family property settlements in several US jurisdictions these days, owing to the abolition of the rule against perpetuities as it applies to trusts in these states. And it really does not go to the heart of the trust form. As to that form, the DCFR Trust appears to be quite consistent on the whole with what I have called the 'true trust'. It requires a separate and identified trust *res*, so that it is a property-focused arrangement. It requires a trustee who owes duties of a fiduciary nature to beneficiaries who have enforceable rights against the trustee. All in all, the picture that emerges is remarkably like the common law trust.

The other European project leaves us with a quite different impression. The proposed Directive on 'protected funds' creates an institution that is a considerable distance from the common law trust. Its very title suggests that this is not a true trust but rather a 'ring-fenced' fund, created solely for commercial purposes. Now, the mere fact that its sole function is commercial does not itself rule out the possibility that it might be a true trust. As John Langbein has reminded us in a splendid article,[12] the common law trust form is used today for a variety of

[9] See, e.g., *Clark* v. *Campbell*, 133 A. 166 (N.H. 1926).

[10] See J. H. Langbein, 'Mandatory Rules in the Law of Trusts' (2004) 98 Nw. U. L. Rev. 1105, 1107.

[11] See Uniform Trust Code, §105(b)(3).

[12] See J. H. Langbein, 'The Secret Life of the Trust: The Trust as an Instrument of Commerce' (1997) 107 Yale L.J. 165.

important commercial purposes in the UK, the US and throughout the Commonwealth. The problem stems from the fact that the arrangement does not appear to involve a separation of legal title from equitable, or beneficial, ownership, which, as I have indicated, is the core of the common law trust form. Indeed, the authors of the proposed Directive themselves contemplate that the 'protected fund' device is not a true trust but only 'trust-like'. Perhaps they might call it 'trust-lite'.

Is the separation of legal title and equitable ownership indispensable for the creation of a true trust, such that any arrangement that does not strictly involve the separation of legal title and equitable ownership is a trust-lite? Not really. Professor du Toit's fascinating paper tells us why.[13] As we learn from his paper, the South African trust does not involve a strict separation between legal and equitable ownership as there is in the common law trust. As du Toit points out,[14] however, the South African trust is based on a functional substitute for the common law's approach of dual ownership, namely, a duality of estates. This arrangement appears to overcome the civilian's conceptual problem with divided ownership, yet it does virtually the same functional work, in terms of the beneficiaries' rights and remedies, that the common law idea does. Moreover, like the common law trust, South African trust law conceptualizes the trust beneficiaries' rights as stemming from the trustee's fiduciary duties rather than from contractual obligations, or at least not from contractual obligation alone. Tony Honoré has argued on more than one occasion that the essential mechanism of the true trust's operation is not the separation of legal and equitable ownership but the existence of the trusteeship as an office.[15] Professor du Toit's paper picks up this point by emphasizing that in South African law, not only does the trustee stand in a fiduciary relationship with the beneficiaries – obviously

[13] F. du Toit, 'Jurisprudential Milestones in the Reception and Development of Trust Law in South Africa's Mixed Legal System', Chapter 10 in this collection.

[14] Ibid., at pp. 258–9.

[15] See, e.g., T. Honoré, 'On Fitting Trusts into Civil Law Jurisdictions', unpublished Oxford Legal Studies Research Paper No. 27/2008, Oxford University (2008), p. 6; Honoré, 'Trust', in R. Zimmermann and D. Visser (eds.), *Southern Cross: Civil Law and Common Law in Southern Africa* (Oxford University Press, 1996), p. 849; Honoré, 'Obstacles to the Reception of Trust Law? The Examples of South Africa and Scotland', in A. M. Rabello (ed.), *Aequitas and Equity: Equity in Civil Law and Mixed Jurisdictions* (Jerusalem: Harry and Michael Sacher Institute for Legislative Research and Comparative Law, the Hebrew University of Jerusalem, 1997), p. 792.

not a sufficient condition for the existence of a true trust – but also trusteeship is an office.[16]

So, if the absence of a strict division between legal and equitable ownership is not at the heart of the dilution of the trust, as the South African example appears to show,[17] just exactly what features have contributed to the trust's dilution? Two examples from elsewhere in the world may illustrate the point. Consider first one of the newest trust-like arrangements to appear in the civil law world, the Chinese trust.

The first Trust Law of the People's Republic of China (PRC) was enacted in 2001.[18] It states that it applies to 'civil, business, or public interest' activities in the PRC. However, its objective is primarily commercial. Many aspects of the so-called trust under the 2001 Trust Law remain murky. However, it seems rather clear that it is not a true trust but rather a trust-like arrangement created largely for the reasons that underlay the European proposed Directive on 'protected funds'. The Chinese Trust Law does not categorize the trustee (whom the law does call a trustee) as 'owner' of the trust property. Indeed, the law does not state that the settlor must 'transfer' property to the trustee. Rather, it deliberately abandons the term 'transfer' and substitutes for it the term 'entrusts': it provides that the settlor 'entrusts the property rights in his property' to a trustee.[19] This is quite problematic.[20] To the common lawyer, the term 'entrusts' signals that the trustee's relationship with respect to the trust property is materially less than ownership. In Chinese law, the term carries basically the same meaning. It is used to create an agency relationship, in which possession but not ownership is transferred.[21] This is simply inconsistent with the core idea of the common law trust. As Tony Honoré states, 'The settlor may be the *constituent* of the trust, but the trust instrument is its *constitution*.'[22] Honoré goes on flatly to declare, 'In administering the trust the trustee cannot be the mere agent of the settlor or subject to his orders.'[23]

[16] Du Toit, 'Jurisprudential Milestones', above, note 13.
[17] See Honoré, 'On Fitting Trusts', above, note 15, 1–12 (footnote omitted).
[18] Trust Law, above, note 4. [19] Ibid., art. 2.
[20] For an excellent discussion of the merits and demerits of the entrustment approach, see L. Ho, 'The Reception of Trust in Asia: Emerging Asian Principles of Trust?' (2004) Sing. J.L.S. 287, 294–6.
[21] Ibid., 294.
[22] Honoré, 'On Fitting Trusts', above, note 15, 6 (emphasis in original).
[23] Ibid.

This is black letter law for common law trusts, but the Chinese Trust Law appears to violate it.

In the context of the Chinese Trust Law, the term 'entrusts' has proved to be controversial and troublesome. Some have argued that its contextual meaning is the same as 'transferred'. They point to the requirements that the trustee 'transfer' trust property to those entitled upon termination of the trust,[24] and that the trustee segregate trust property from the trustee's non-trust assets.[25] But these requirements would not seem to require that 'entrust' mean 'transfer'. The requirement that the trustee transfer trust property, for example, does not state that the trustee transfers *legal title*. If, as seems to be the case, 'entrust' means 'entrust', then this suggests that under the Chinese Trust Law it is possible to create a trust by entering into a contract with the trustee rather than by transferring legal title to the trustee.[26] From the perspective of the common law trust, this is very problematic conceptually, not to mention practically.

The Trust Law goes on to give the trustee powers to 'manage[]' and 'dispose[] of' trust property. Moreover, the law states that the trustee is to manage the trust property 'in his own name',[27] and although an exercise of the power of disposal is supposed to be according to the settlor's wishes, a disposal against the settlor's wishes is still valid unless the court revokes it upon the settlor's petition. The mere entrustment of the trust property in the trustee seriously complicates the trustee's management power. For if the settlor retains title, then whenever the trustee seeks to invest trust assets, it will be necessary not only to produce the trust instrument but, seemingly, to provide authorization from the settlor. And if the settlor, as the owner, can veto or affirm a proposed trust investment at will, then will the trustee's fiduciary duty of prudence be effectively undermined?

The picture that emerges from even a cursory review of the Chinese Trust Law is that it is indeed not a true trust but rather a 'trust-like' arrangement, or, if you will, 'trust-lite'.

How can we account for the global emergence of these trust-like arrangements? Rather clearly, I think, the reason is not the same as that which accounts for the remarkable success and popularity of the common law trust. As Tony Honoré noted, in the common law world trusts are used for a wide range of purposes, 'almost as a universal fix-it',

[24] Trust Law, above, note 4, art. 41. [25] Ibid., art. 16.

[26] See Ho, 'The Reception of Trust in Asia', above, note 20, 295.

[27] Trust Law, above, note 4, art. 14.

as he put it.[28] Many of the trust-like arrangements in civil law jurisdictions have limited purposes, usually commercial. That is almost certainly what accounts for their recent development throughout the world. As Alexandra Braun's paper points out, the proposed EU Directive on 'protected funds' was motivated by the perceived need for a device that would enable Continental European financial institutions to compete effectively by protecting lenders and investors against loss in the event of borrower insolvency.[29] In Japan, trusts, although permitted for personal as well as business purposes, are primarily used commercially, notably as a device for creditor protection but also for asset management.

Why have these jurisdictions limited the purposes of the trust-like devices? Why not seek to obtain the breadth of purposes that comes with the flexibility of the common law trust? Why not, in short, go for the real thing – the true trust, rather than its ersatz substitute? The answer, I think, is less a matter of fear of Anglo-American legal imperialism than it is the doctrinal problem with the *numerus clausus*. We have our own *numerus clausus*,[30] of course, but its contours and its conceptual underpinnings are different from those of the civil law, having no difficulty with two-dimensional fragmentation of ownership, between legal and equitable ownership and between presently possessory estates and future interests.

Along with the fragmentation of ownership, the availability of proprietary remedies to the beneficiaries of the common law trust further exacerbate the difficulty of reception of the full-fledged common law trust in civil law jurisdictions. Equitable tracing to recover trust assets in the hands of a third party and assertion of claims against the asset via a lien of constructive trust run deeply against the grain of civilian legal notions. As others have observed,[31] these obstacles can be overcome, and it is quite possible that at least in some jurisdictions they will be overcome. We may eventually come to view the trust-like arrangements as the first steps taken toward true trusts, an initial stage in an institutional development that somewhat resembles the development of the English trust itself.

Finally, it is worth asking what implications the emergence and spread of the trust-like arrangements – diluting the trust as they do – have or

[28] Honoré, 'On Fitting Trusts', above, note 15, 4.

[29] A. Braun, 'The Framing of a European Law of Trusts', Chapter 11 in this collection.

[30] See T. W. Merrill and H. E. Smith, 'Optimal Standardization in the Law of Property: The Numerus Clausus Principle' (2000) 110 Yale L.J. 1.

[31] See, e.g., Honoré, above, note 15.

may have for the common law trust. The short answer, I think, is absolutely nothing, at least nothing bad. I see very little threat that the emergence of the trust in diluted form in the civil law world will dilute the trust in its true form in the common law world. If there is such a threat – and I am not saying that there is – it is an internal threat. The development of new features added to trusts, such as the trust protector device,[32] pose a greater risk of dilution than do any external trust-like arrangements. If anything, trust-like arrangements give those of us in the common law world ideas for trust law reform, making the common law trust even more flexible and adaptable to a wide variety of uses. It might be useful, for example, to explore relaxing the common law requirement that the trustee hold legal title to the trust *res*. So long as the *res* is identified and segregated and the trustee has the power to administer it in the interest of the beneficiaries, we might treat the trust as in existence even though the trustee does not hold legal title to the *res*, at least for certain purposes where the settlor has a legitimate reason for not wanting to part with title. There may be other areas as well in which we can learn from these civilian innovations, without endangering the core common law idea of the trust. This would truly be a move toward harmonization.

[32] On the risks of the trust protector device in American trusts, see G. S. Alexander, 'Trust Protectors: Who Will Watch the Watchmen?' (2006) 27 Cardozo L. Rev. 2807; S. E. Sterk, 'Trust Protectors, Agency Costs, and Fiduciary Duties' (2006) 27 Cardozo L. Rev. 2761.

13

The compatibility of the trust with the civil law notion of property

PAUL MATTHEWS

'There are more things in heaven and earth, Horatio, than are dreamt of in your philosophy.'

– Shakespeare, *Hamlet*, Act I, Sc 5

'Le trust, c'est les autres'

– Not quite Jean-Paul Sartre

I Introduction

First of all, imagine that this chapter is a cigarette packet. Inside, I am going to suggest that the conceptual approach to the idea of property found in the civil law systems of the world has proved to be a difficulty in the development of a trust-like idea and of the acceptance of the common law trust. The converse is in my view also true. One of the characteristics of the common law that has facilitated the development and the growth of the trust institution has been its anti-conceptual approach to the idea of property. Instead of being a weakness, it has been a strength.

Before you remove the cellophane and open the packet, however, I draw your attention to what it says on the front. We must notice a particular problem which we must take into account in the discussion. This is the problem of language. This chapter is inevitably influenced by the choice of the language in which it is written, that is, English. In itself this would pose problems at any multinational and indeed multilingual conference. So, if this were a conference about medicine, or nuclear physics, or the art of Picasso, there would also be such problems. But we would hope that they could be solved for the most part by translation and by interpretation.

However, they are exacerbated here, almost exponentially, by the fact that the subject matter of the chapter is law. Because law, unlike medicine or nuclear physics or representational art, changes its methods of reasoning, its fundamental values and building blocks, from one legal system – in very approximate terms, one country – to another. This means the translation and interpretation may not only not be sufficient to get over the problem. Instead they may in fact make it worse. It is no good looking for an accurate translation into French or Italian or German of the English expression 'fee simple absolute in possession'. To say, as some do, that you can translate the French word '*patrimoine*' by the English word 'patrimony' or the Italian word '*usufrutto*' by the English word 'usufruct' is only to push the enquiry on a further stage, to ask what these peculiar English words mean. In fact they have no technical meaning in English law,[1] referring back to the concepts (whatever they are) in their original languages or their original legal systems. They are simply Anglicizations of foreign words.

Another translation problem is the French phrase *droit réel*, and its equivalents in other languages. When this phrase occurs in European Union texts it is translated into English as 'right *in rem*'.[2] But a better translation would be 'real right'. Unfortunately, that has no legal meaning in English law (though it has in Scots law).[3] So it is not used.

And, even where it seems that a translation can be obtained, it is often a 'false friend'. One of the most glaring examples, relevant to this chapter, concerns the English word 'property' and the French word '*propriété*' (Italian *proprietà*, Spanish *propiedad*). Whereas in English the word 'property' often signifies some *thing* which belongs to a person, in French (and Italian and Spanish and so on) the word usually[4] signifies the relation which a person has with the thing. The best translation into English is normally 'ownership'. Actually it is worse even than that. In English, the word property can be taken to refer to several ideas, including[5] (i) a tangible thing owned by a person ('When you leave the train, do not forget to take all your property with you'), (ii) *rights* in a tangible thing, and even (iii) property rights in nothing tangible at all (for example debts, company shares or intellectual property). A well-read

[1] They may have a particular meaning in mixed or civilian systems where English is the dominant language, like the Scottish system, for example.

[2] As in e.g. Brussels Convention on Jurisdiction and Enforcement of Judgments in Civil and Commercial Matters, Brussels, 27 September 1968, art. 16(1); see *Webb* v. *Webb* [1994] QB 696; P. Matthews, 'Review of Sparkes, *European Land Law*' (2007) 19 K.C.L.J. 661, 665–6.

[3] G. Gretton, 'Trusts Without Equity' (2000) 49 I.C.L.Q. 599, 607.

[4] But cf. e.g. the French *Code civil*, art. 644.

[5] See *Re Earnshaw-Wall* [1894] 3 Ch 156, 157.

civilian lawyer might justifiably accuse the English of committing all the mistakes of which the Pandectists accused Gaianism, in particular that of using a word to stand not only for a physical thing, but *also* for rights in the thing. Fortunately, most civilian lawyers are far too polite to do any such thing.

Of course, I do not mean to suggest that we should not try to discuss or to debate cross-border legal issues at as fundamental a level as I shall try to do now. International conferences in agreeable (preferably foreign, even exotic) surroundings should not be abandoned as easily as that. I mean only to say that, as with the humble cigarette packet, this chapter comes with a warning attached: you cannot believe everything you read. As Professor Gretton has very properly said, 'a system-neutral language is both necessary and impossible'.[6]

II Property and ownership

What distinguishes a property right from a personal right? In the common law world, there is no Gaius, no code or other legislation to tell us. There is not much in the way of judge-made law, either.[7] Even the doctrinal analysis is thin, and nearly all modern.[8] Essentially it comes to this. A property right is a right in relation to a thing – including an imaginary thing such as a debt, a share or a patent (all legal constructs) – and is binding, not only on the person creating it, but on third parties as well. Otherwise it is a personal right.

But as we see, in the common law world you do not own *things* (a 'physical' approach). You own *rights in things* (a 'metaphysical' approach). We call these bundles of rights[9] 'estates' or 'interests'. This apparently complex approach is a hangover from the medieval

[6] Gretton, 'Trusts Without Equity', above, note 3, 604.

[7] For a rare example, see e.g. *National Provincial Bank* v. *Ainsworth* [1965] AC 1175, 1247–8, followed in *R* v. *Toohey, ex p Meneling Station Pty Ltd* (1982) 158 CLR 327, 342. Scotland is far richer in this field: see e.g. *Sharp* v. *Thomson* 1995 SC 455, reversed 1997 SC (HL) 66.

[8] See e.g. P. Birks, 'Five Keys to Land Law', in S. Bright and J. Dewar (eds.), *Land Law, Themes and Perspectives* (Oxford University Press, 1998), pp. 472–5; L. Smith 'Transfers', in P. Birks and A. Pretto (eds.), *Breach of Trust* (Oxford: Hart Publishing, 2002), p. 111; W. T. Murphy, S. Roberts and T. Flessas, *Understanding Property Law*, 4th edn (London: Sweet & Maxwell, 2004), pp. 58–60; B. McFarlane, *The Structure of Property Law* (Oxford: Hart Publishing, 2008), pp. 137–9.

[9] Not all common lawyers accept the 'bundle of rights' view: see e.g. J. E. Penner, *The Idea of Property in Law* (Oxford University Press, 1997).

feudal system. But it makes it easy for ownership of the thing to be dismembered, and bits parcelled out to different people. For example, A has a life interest, B an interest in remainder conditional upon an event, C the interest in remainder in default, whilst D has a lease for 10 years and E has a right of way for 99 years, all in relation to the same piece of land. It is a market-based, client-driven approach (where the client is the original megalomaniac owner of all the rights in the thing, who wished to do lots of different things, and benefit different people in different ways).

III Two points about trusts

When a trust lawyer from the common law tradition embarks upon a comparativist discussion of the nature of the trust with a civil lawyer, he or she, in order to be sensible, will not try to explain all the detail. Instead he or she will go for the 'big picture'. This will consist of a small number of vital characteristics of the trust idea. Which ones are chosen will depend on the perspective of the comparative inquiry. In my view, for present purposes there are two of these that stand out above all the others. The first is that the person whom we in the common law know as the trustee is, according to our way of thinking, the *owner* of the trust assets in the most complete sense possible.[10] The trustee is *not* an agent or a representative of the settlor or the beneficiaries. Contrary to the views of many civilian writers[11] and indeed courts,[12] the trustee's ownership is no less than the ownership of a person who is not a trustee. In particular, there is no 'double property', where the trustee is legal owner, and the beneficiary is the equitable owner.[13]

[10] J. B. Ames, 'Purchase for Value Without Notice' (1887) 1 Harv. L. Rev. 1, 9. Even in Scotland, a mixed system, this is accepted: Stair, *Institutions of the Law of Scotland* (Edinburgh: Heir of Andrew Anderson, 1681), 1,13,7.

[11] E.g. P. Lepaulle, 'Réflexion sur l'expansion des trusts. Remarques à propos du livre de M. Claude Reymond sur "Le trust et le droit suisse"' (1955) 7 *Revue Internationale de Droit Comparé* 318, 319.

[12] *Tucker* v. *Royal Trust* [1982] 1 S.C.R. 250.

[13] P. Matthews, 'From Obligation to Property and Back Again? The Future of the Non-charitable Purpose Trust', in D. Hayton (ed.), *Extending the Boundaries of Trusts and Other Ring-fenced Funds* (The Hague: Kluwer Law International, 2002), p. 203; L. Smith, 'Trust and Patrimony' (2009) 28 E.T.P.J. 332, 342–7. Cf. M. Lupoi, *I trust nel diritto civile* (Turin: UTET, 2004), pp. 19–23; B. Mallet-Bricout, 'The Trustee: Mainspring, or Only a Cog, in the French *Fiducie*?', Chapter 7 in this volume, pp. 164–6, where the 'divided ownership' idea is put forward.

This means that, vis-à-vis the outside world, the trustee has all the powers which ownership confers. Only *inside* the trust are the powers limited to what is authorized (by the trust terms, the court or the beneficiaries).[14] So, as the trustee normally wants his actions to bind the beneficiaries, he sticks to authorized actions. But if he goes beyond this, the third party outside the trust is not concerned, and will obtain a perfect title, *unless* his conscience[15] is affected. So if, for example, he uses trust money to pay private debts, the creditors whose consciences are not affected obtain good title to the money, and the debts are discharged, but because the action is unauthorized within the trust structure the trustee incurs a personal liability to the beneficiary.[16] The common law trust is enhanced by this Janus-like approach of looking out as full owner but inwards as limited owner. The civil law systems – in their original forms, at least – do not have this possibility. Either you are the 'owner', or you are not.

The second point is that the position of the beneficiary affects the trustee's *conscience*. (Here, incidentally, is another word that is almost impossible to translate, at least in its technical sense, into other languages.)[17] The reason that the beneficiary can oblige the trustee to make the trust assets available to the beneficiary is because the conscience of the trustee as owner is so affected by the position of the beneficiary that the court considers that the trustee should act in that way.

14 Cf. R. Lee, 'Convergence and Divergence in the Worlds of the Trust: Duties and Liabilities of Trustees under the Chinese Trust', Chapter 17 in this volume, pp. 417–8.

15 Discussed below.

16 Cf. Lee, Chapter 17 in this volume, p. 411, referring to T. Honoré, 'Trusts: The Inessentials', in J. Getzler (ed.), *Rationalizing Property, Equity and Trusts: Essays in Honour of Edward Burn* (Oxford University Press, 2003), ch. 1, p. 9.

17 The idea of conscience in the context of the trust is based upon the notion that there exists a standard of behaviour which is higher than that required by law, and which more or less conforms to the standard of behaviour of a good Christian in a given situation, bearing in mind the moral precepts of his religion. It therefore pushes up the legal standard to a higher level, which is fixed and not variable: *Cook* v. *Fountain* (1767) 3 Swans 585, 600; *Re National Funds Assurance Co.* (1878) 10 Ch D 118, 128; *Re Telescriptor Syndicate Ltd* [1903] 2 Ch 174, 195. In this it rather resembles the way that Islamic and Jewish law deal with the regulation of behaviour beyond what Western systems would regard as the province of the law, i.e. so as to include matters of morality. In my view it is no coincidence that the word for law in both Islamic (*sharī'a*) and Jewish (*halakhah*) systems translates as 'the path to follow,' and covers matters of etiquette, everyday behaviour and morality, far beyond the limited Western notion of law. See also L. Smith, 'Philosophical Foundations of Proprietary Remedies', in R. Chambers, C. Mitchell and J. Penner (eds.), *Philosophical Foundations of the Law of Unjust Enrichment* (Oxford University Press, 2009), pp. 285–91.

The beneficiary's claim is not *competitive* with that of the trustee, but *derivative*.[18] And the consequence is not only that the trustee must allow the beneficiary to enjoy the benefit of the trustee's property. It is also that the beneficiary can attack the conscience of a third party who receives the trust assets from the trustee gratuitously or with notice of the trust, and can thus in effect both (i) trace the trust assets, in whatever form they have been converted (a form of real subrogation),[19] into the hands of third parties, and (ii) prevent the private creditors of the trustee from seizing the trust assets in satisfaction of the private debts. Both of these consequences are important from a comparative law point of view, and in particular in examining the notion of property.

IV Property in the civil law

When, with these two points in mind, we look at the notion of property in the civil law, we can see immediately that there is going to be a problem with the trust. The problem is not with the idea that property rights bind third parties. That was recognized in Roman law,[20] and is recognized in modern civil law[21] and also in Scots law.[22] Instead the problem lies in the width of the concept of ownership.

Perhaps the most well-known model for a civil law system in modern times is the French *Code civil* of 1804. Article 544 of the Code provides (my translation): 'Ownership is the right to enjoy and dispose of things in the most absolute manner, provided they are not used in a way prohibited by statutes or regulations.' This is a modern formulation of the Roman law principle of *dominium*.[23] On this, as on many other points,

[18] See e.g. N. Jones, 'Trusts in England after the Statute of Uses: A View from the 16th Century', in R. Helmholz and R. Zimmermann (eds.), *Itinera Fiduciae: Trust and Treuhand in Historical Perspective* (Berlin: Duncker & Humblot, 1998), p. 190, citing McLelland J. in *Re Transphere Pty Ltd* (1986) 5 NSWLR 309, 311.

[19] See e.g. V. Ranouil, *La subrogation réelle en droit civil francais* (Paris: LGDJ, 1985); A. N. Yiannopoulos, *Louisiana Civil Law Treatise: Property*, 4th edn (St Paul: West Group, 2001), vol. 2, ch. 8, para. 199; G. Gretton and A. Steven, *Property, Trusts & Succession* (Sussex: Tottel Publishing, 2009), para. 22.6.

[20] W. W. Buckland and A. D. McNair, *Roman Law and Common Law* (Cambridge University Press, 1936), pp. 66–8.

[21] J. Carbonnier, *Droit civil: Les biens*, 19th edn (Paris: Presses Universitaires de France, 2000), vol. 3, paras. 38–40.

[22] J. Erskine, *An Institute of the Law of Scotland*, 8th edn J. B. Nicolson (Edinburgh: Bell & Bradfute, 1871), III, i, 2; *Sharp* v. *Thomson* 1995 SC 455, 462–3.

[23] W. W. Buckland, *A Textbook of Roman Law*, P. Stein (ed.), 3rd edn (Cambridge University Press, 1963), pp. 186–95; B. Nicholas, *An Introduction to Roman Law*

the French Code has been copied in the codes of a large number of other civil law systems. If we needed to, we could refer to this as the 'Latin' school of civil law. Another important strand of civil law thinking is represented by German law. The German Civil Code, the *Bundesgesetzbuch*, or BGB, dates from almost a hundred years after the French Code, though of course there were codes in German-speaking countries (for example Prussia and Austria) at about the same time as the French Code. Section 903 of the BGB provides (again, my own translation): 'To the extent that it is not contrary to law or to the rights of third parties, the owner of a thing may deal with it as he pleases, and exclude others from any interference.'[24]

Given the essentially practical, even agricultural setting of the French Code of 1804, and all the romanticism and the *Sturm und Drang* of the nineteenth century, it is interesting to see that the two most important ideas in this section are the same as the two main ideas in the French article. The owner may deal with it as he pleases, but this is subject to enactments of positive law.

The French commentators analysed article 544 as dealing with three rights, expressed in the Latin words *usus, fructus, abusus*: the right to use the thing, the right to take its fruits, and the right to destroy or alienate it. This is still reflected in the modern law of Quebec. Article 947, first sentence, of the Civil Code of Québec[25] provides: 'Ownership is the right to use, enjoy and dispose of property fully and freely, subject to the limits and conditions for doing so determined by law.'[26]

Taken with the idea that property is both perpetual and exclusive,[27] together these three rights add up to the most complete power over the thing the subject of ownership. It is an absolutist view of property.[28] Paring back the concept of property to this view appealed to the draftsmen of the French Civil Code. For them it was part of the French

(Oxford University Press, 1961), pp. 153–7; J. A. C. Thomas, *Textbook of Roman Law* (Amsterdam: North-Holland Pub. Co., 1976), pp. 131–7.

24 In recent times a second sentence has been added, dealing with the sensibilities of animal rights activists. Such are the vagaries of modern German politics, that fundamental sections of the BGB have to be altered to keep governments in power. For our purposes we can ignore it.

25 Hereinafter cited as 'C.C.Q.'.

26 See also article 406 of the Civil Code of Lower Canada of 1866, and also (in relation to Scotland) Erskine, *An Institute of the Law*, above, note 22, II, i, 1.

27 See Mallet-Bricout, Chapter 7 in this volume, pp. 161–2.

28 J. Mazeaud et al., *Leçons de droit civil: Biens*, 8th edn (Paris: Montchrestien, 1994), vol. 2, paras. 1332–6.

revolutionary process itself, a negation of the aristocratic, feudal idea of property as an asset in which many different people had legitimate interests.[29] It was a retreat to a position which focused on the position of the individual, even if it did not give him *carte blanche*: he was still subject to limits imposed by the law.[30]

As a result, the principle is that in relation to any particular thing there should be a *single* person who has *all* the rights.[31] The fragmentation (or dismemberment) of property into different estates or interests of different values, each belonging to a different person, so characteristic of property law in the common law world (and especially in relation to land) finds no place in this system.[32] It is true that societal necessity forces the civil law to provide for a limited number of real rights which are less than ownership. This so-called *numerus clausus*[33] of lesser real rights includes rights such as the hypothec, the usufruct, the servitude and so on. But they are very much exceptions to the general principle. In the singular, they are usually each referred to as *ius in re aliena*: a right in a thing belonging to someone else.[34]

Indeed, French law as originally enacted in the Code of 1804 did not like the idea of co-ownership either. This is different from fragmentation into different estates and interests, because each co-owner has a share of the *same* ownership rights, rather than different ones from each other. But it still infringed the principle that there ought to be one person with

[29] T. G. Watkin, *An Historical Introduction to Modern Civil Law* (Aldershot: Ashgate, 1999), p. 227.

[30] J.-L. Halpérin, *The French Civil Code*, T. Weir (trans.) (London: UCL Press, 2006), pp. 38–40; Mazeaud et al., *Leçons de droit civil: Biens*, above, note 28, paras. 1337–46; Watkin, *Historical Introduction to Modern Civil Law*, above, note 29, pp. 255–6.

[31] Watkin, *Historical Introduction to Modern Civil Law*, above, note 29, p. 225.

[32] Though see the second sentence of article 947 of the C.C.Q.: 'Ownership may be in various modes and dismemberments.' This refers on to the two modes of co-ownership and superficies (arts. 1009–1118), and the four dismemberments of usufruct, use, servitude and emphyteusis (arts. 1119–1211).

[33] See e.g. A. Gambaro, *La proprietà* (Milan: Giuffrè, 1990), pp. 67–75; A. Fusaro, 'The Numerus Clausus of Property Rights', in E. Cooke (ed.), *Modern Studies in Property Law* (Oxford: Hart Publishing, 2001), vol. 1, pp. 309–17; T. W. Merrill and H. E. Smith, 'Optimal Standardization in the Law of Property: The Numerus Clausus Principle' (2000) 110 Yale L.J. 1; U. Mattei, *La proprietà* (Turin: UTET, 2001), pp. 16–18, 142–6; B. Akkermans, *The Principle of Numerus Clausus in European Property Law* (Oxford: Intersentia, 2008). Whether such a principle exists in the common law is a contentious question; see W. Swadling, 'Property', in A. Burrows (ed.), *English Private Law*, 2nd edn (Oxford University Press, 2007), paras. 4.09–4.12.

[34] D.-C. Lamontagne, *Biens et propriété*, 5th edn (Cowansville: Éditions Yvon Blais, 2005), para. 204; Watkin, *Historical Introduction to Modern Civil Law*, above, note 29, p. 256.

all the rights in a thing. Hence it was acceptable to have co-ownership only in one situation, namely where there was a plurality of heirs on the death of a property owner. The desire of the revolutionaries to have equality amongst the heirs trumped the desire of the drafting committee to align French law with what they saw as the stark simplicity of the Roman law idea of property.[35] But even then it was tolerated only in the short-term, and no co-owner could be required to remain in a state of co-ownership.[36] The same is true in Scotland.[37]

V The problem

When the common lawyer explains the trust to the civil lawyer, and says that the trustee is the owner of the trust assets, but must employ them for the benefit of, or make them available for use by, the beneficiary, he is saying no more than orthodox trust doctrine requires. But to the civil lawyer, used to the absolutist scheme of property outlined above, it is difficult to understand. If the trustee is the full owner (as the common lawyer says) then he must have all the property rights. Therefore the beneficiary does not have any.[38] Or, if the beneficiary has property rights, then the trustee does not have full ownership,[39] and the beneficiary must at least have one of the lesser property rights to be found in the *numerus clausus*. But it is not so found. Consternation. Perfidious Albion is lying again.

The common lawyer says that the trustee is an owner of assets *for the benefit of another*. But the civil lawyer considers this to be an oxymoron. If A is an *owner* of assets, it is for his *own* benefit.[40] If A holds assets for the benefit of B, then A is not the owner, at least not unless B has one of the bright line lesser real rights, such as usufruct, and A is the owner subject to that burden.

35 But in fact Roman law allowed co-ownership *inter vivos*: see Buckland and McNair, *Roman Law and Common Law*, above, note 20, p. 80; Buckland, *Textbook of Roman Law*, above, note 23, p. 539.

36 *Code civil*, art. 815, as originally enacted. Co-ownership can now be deliberately produced or prolonged by contract *inter vivos*.

37 *Morrison* v. *Kirk* 1912 SC 44; *Upper Crathies Fishings Ltd* v. *Barclay* 1989 SCLR 560.

38 Of course the beneficiary may have purely personal rights against the trustee, as is clear in the Scottish law of trusts: see the authorities referred to at note 66, below.

39 In *Royal Trust Co.* v. *Tucker* [1982] 1 S.C.R. 250. The Supreme Court of Canada held that the trustee's ownership was *sui generis*, a position criticized by civilian commentators, e.g. M. Cantin Cumyn, 'La propriété fiduciaire: Mythe ou réalité?' (1984) 15 R.D.U.S. 7.

40 See e.g. P. Decheix, 'La fiducie ou du sens des mots' (1997) *Recueil Dalloz* 35.

Attempts may be made to deal with this problem by legislation. The Bailiwick of Jersey, in the Channel Islands, is an offshore finance centre using common law institutions including the trust. But its law is based originally on Norman customary law. It may not be right to describe it today as a civil law jurisdiction, but like Scotland it is at least 'mixed'. This means that sometimes legislation has to take account of fundamental rules of civil law. The States of Jersey, in legislating for trusts, appear to have tried to deal with the problem of the trustee as owner in article 2 of the Trusts (Jersey) Law 1984. In its original form,[41] this read as follows:

> A trust exists where a person (known as a trustee) holds or has vested in him or is deemed to hold or have vested in him property (of which he is not the owner in his own right)
>
> (a) for the benefit of any person (known as a beneficiary) whether or not yet ascertained or in existence; or
> (b) for any purpose which is not for the benefit only of the trustee; or
> (c) for such benefit as is mentioned in sub-paragraph (a) and also for any such purpose as is mentioned in sub-paragraph (b).

The phrase 'of which he is not the owner in his own right' is a curious one. It seems to be intended to reflect the fact that the trustee is an owner for the benefit of another or for a purpose which is not (or not only) for his own benefit. But the common lawyer finds it strange, because the whole point about a trustee is that he *is* the owner in his own right, although admittedly not for his own (exclusive) benefit.

It may be that recent legislation in civil law systems introducing trust-like devices, such as the *fiducie*, in Quebec, Luxembourg and France, is to be treated as modifying the civil law conception of property.[42]

The problem illustrated is not confined to trusts. There is a similar degree of difficulty shown by civil law systems when it comes to other situations in which one person controls assets which are not intended for that person's sole benefit (or in some cases for that person's benefit at all).

[41] The first few lines of article 2 have since been rewritten in a fit of political correctness to read: 'A trust exists where a person (known as a trustee) holds or has vested in the person or is deemed to hold or have vested in the person property (of which the person is not the owner in the person's own right).' In all developed legal systems, there comes a tipping point when the lunatics threaten to take over the asylum.

[42] F. Barrière, 'The Security *Fiducie* in French Law', Chapter 6 in this volume, pp. 106–8; Y. Emerich, 'The Civil Law Trust: A Modality of Ownership or an Interlude in Ownership?', Chapter 2 in this volume.

Consider the case of a company director. He or she constitutes the directing mind of the company, and his or her consent or authority is what in effect makes the company do something. So if the company owns assets, and the director decides that the company should deal with those assets in a particular way, that is what happens. In part this helps to account for the comparative weakness of the position of the minority shareholder in civilian corporate capitalism, compared to that in common law systems. Of course, with the company, there is the legal fiction of a separate legal person to take account of. It is therefore not exactly the same as a trust. Hence civil lawyers can accept the result as compatible with the civil law principle of absolute ownership.

Less easy, perhaps, is the case of a public officer, say a government minister or the mayor of a town. If the Tour de France cycle race passes through his town and in front of the *mairie*, will the mayor be criticized for reserving the balcony for himself and his family and friends to view the race from? If a European Union Commissioner has a budget for allocating research funds to individuals, can she not allocate some to her dentist? Of course, once again we can see that this is not exactly the same as a trust. The mayor or the Commissioner controls the use of the town's or the Commission's assets, but is not the owner. In civil law countries as in common law ones there are rules about not abstracting public assets for one's own benefit. Yet my point is that so deeply ingrained in the civil lawyers' consciousness is the notion that an owner must be absolute, that there is an easy acceptance – or at least an enhanced tolerance – of the idea that a person who is the titleholder (*titulaire*) of a thing must be able to deal with it as he or she wishes, and therefore for his or her own benefit.

The second critical trust characteristic mentioned above was that of the effect of conscience. By this means the beneficiary makes good his claim against the trustee that he should be allowed to enjoy the trustee's assets. But the development and extension of the conscience idea to attack third parties meant that the rights of the beneficiary were no longer merely *in personam*. Instead they began to resemble property rights, in the sense that they bound not only the trustee, but also at least some – in practice, most of the relevant – third parties. The beneficiaries' rights failed only against a third party who could claim to be a purchaser in good faith for value of legal rights in the thing without notice of the trust. Perhaps paradoxically, this means that the rights of a beneficiary under a trust in the common law world are at least as strong as, if not stronger than, the rights of an ordinary owner of a thing in the civil law world. This is because in the civil law world many systems provide that a third party who in good faith acquires (not necessarily by purchase for value) an asset from a person who does not own it nonetheless acquires a good title.

As already stated, the civil law world knows little or nothing today of this idea of conscience.[43] What it does have is the idea of patrimony. When civil lawyers are trying to understand why it is that the beneficiaries can make claims against third parties for the return of trust assets, or that personal creditors of the trustee cannot seize trust assets in satisfaction of their claims, they often see an analogy with the patrimony idea.

VI Patrimony[44]

In broad terms, the notion of patrimony derives from the notion of personality. According to the classic French nineteenth-century theory of Aubry and Rau, every person must have a patrimony, and only one.[45] Not every civil code makes express provision for the patrimony. The French Code of 1804 certainly did not, forcing Aubry and Rau to rationalize its existence, rather like the Higgs boson, from everything else that they found in the text of the code.[46] The C.C.Q. does, however, mention it. Article 2, first sentence, baldly says: 'Every person has a patrimony.'

The theory of Aubry and Rau has been considerably criticized, and refined, by subsequent commentators,[47] but so far as I know no mainstream civilian writer has gone so far as to say that there is no such thing as patrimony. Patrimony is a theoretical construct comprising all items of economic value, both positive and negative, both present and future, appertaining to a particular individual.[48] In homely terms, it is like a

[43] For an excellent survey of *early* material see M. Lupoi, 'Trust and Confidence' (2009) 125 Law Q. Rev. 253.

[44] See Smith, 'Trust and Patrimony', above, note 13.

[45] C. Aubry and F. C. Rau, *Cours de droit civil français d'après la méthode de Zachariae*, 4th edn (Paris: Marchal et Billard, 1873), vol. 6, bk. 2, div. 1, para. 573. See the English translation by N. Kasirer, 'Translating Part of France's Legal Heritage: Aubry and Rau on the Patrimoine' (2008) 38 R.G.D. 453.

[46] Ibid., para. 573, fn 1.

[47] P. Cazelle, 'De l'idée de la continuation de personne comme principe des transmissions universelles', Thesis (Paris: Université de Paris, 1911); F. Gény, *Méthode d'interprétation et sources en droit privé positif*, 2nd edn (Paris: LGDJ, 1954), pp. 126–9; M. Planiol and G. Ripert, *Traité pratique de droit civil* (Paris: LGDJ, 1938), vol. 3, p. 22; Yiannopoulos, *Louisiana Civil Law Treatise*, above, note 19, at para. 192.

[48] Carbonnier, *Droit civil*, above, note 21, paras. 1–8.

bag, originally empty, which from time to time contains both assets and liabilities. In principle, therefore, it is the legal expression of the economic personality of a person. It has particular importance in relation to the rights of creditors and the rights of heirs. For creditors the patrimony of their debtor is a security for payment. Since it includes future assets, creditors can simply wait until the debtor becomes able to pay (maybe years later, when he or she has inherited from parents or others), and then attach the assets.

Hence the patrimony idea is inconsistent with the Anglo-Saxon idea of bankruptcy, in which current assets are applied in pro rata discharge of unsecured debts – and only those unsecured debts – proved by creditors, and at the end of which process the debtor is discharged from all his unsecured debts existing at the date of bankruptcy. Thus he may acquire assets in the future without any fear that the former creditors will be able to seize them. This encourages entrepreneurs to take risks and helps the economy grow. Civil law systems typically have a bankruptcy procedure for companies which become insolvent, and usually for individuals who carry on business (but only in relation to the business). In modern times, some civil law systems have even introduced a bankruptcy system for individuals in relation to non-business affairs. France for example introduced such a law in 2004, as part of its consumer code.[49] It will be noted that this is not contained in the commercial code, and is not for the purpose of encouraging entrepreneurs to take risks. It is instead for the purpose of relieving overburdened consumers of the debts into which wicked (and probably Anglo-Saxon) capitalists have led them.

Because patrimony is an expression of the economic personality of a property owner, it is of great significance on his death, when it comes to the question of inheritance by his heirs. In essence, the economic personality is transmitted intact to the heirs. And the civil law rule is that the transfer takes place immediately on death, without the intervention of any liquidation mechanism, such as the system of personal representatives employed by the common law. As the French say, '*Le mort saisit le vif, sans ministère de justice.*' If there is only one heir, he or she in effect *becomes* the deceased.[50] Common lawyers will need to be reminded that the transmission of the patrimony will include therefore the transmission of the *debts* of the deceased. This means that in principle the heir is

[49] Code de la consommation, Liv. III, Tit. III.

[50] Mazeaud et al., *Leçons de droit civil*, above, note 28, *Tome 4, vol. 2*, 'Successions-Libéralités', 5th edn (Paris: Montchrestien, 1999), paras. 1203–21.

personally liable for the debts, whether or not there are sufficient assets to pay them.[51] Of course, in practice there are mechanisms in civil law systems by which heirs can have a look before deciding whether to accept the inheritance. But the principle is plain. And there are occasions when the rule is critical.[52]

But patrimony is more than just a convenient bag to hand on to the heirs of the deceased property owner. It enables everyone to examine the question of what actually should be handed on in the first place. An important principle in the Latin versions of the civil law in the past was keeping assets – particularly land – in the family. The French referred to the principle of '*la conservation du bien dans la famille*'. In the common law world we have largely lost the dynastic attachment to particular assets. The Industrial Revolution separated people from the land, and unrestrained nineteenth-century capitalism enabled entrepreneurs to make far more money than they could ever have inherited. I say 'largely lost'. A few aristocrats and wealthy families keep it going, usually in relation to an ancient family seat and attached heirlooms. For this purpose they use trusts, and in some cases the old-fashioned so-called strict settlement or the marriage settlement. But the rest of us do not have the same sense of attachment to particular things. However, it is very different in the civil law world, where the Industrial Revolution came later and capitalism red in tooth and claw had more difficulty in taking off.

Thus there are and have been a number of rules in the civil law designed to prevent undue impoverishment of property owners and to ensure that the assets contained in the patrimony are retained there until the death of the property owner, when they are passed on intact to the heirs. Some of these rules have now gone. Some remain. A sale by that owner can be attacked after his death in some circumstances (e.g. *lésion d'outre-moitié*,[53] where a gross undervalue was paid), and if the sale is set

[51] Ibid., para. 1218; A. Torrente and P. Schlesinger, *Manuale di Diritto Privato*, 15th edn (Milan: Giuffrè, 1997), para. 546. Whether the principle applies in Scotland seems contentious: see e.g. J. McLaren, *The Law of Wills and Succession as Administered in Scotland*, 3rd edn (Edinburgh: Bell & Bradfute, 1894), ch. LXIX (Yes); Gretton and Steven, *Property, Trusts & Succession*, above, note 19, para. 25.35 (No).

[52] See e.g. *EL* v. *Switzerland* [2000] WTLR 873, where the European Court of Human Rights had to consider the compatibility of this rule (in Swiss law), in a criminal context, with article 6 of the European Convention on Human Rights.

[53] In France see arts. 1674ff *Code civil*; in Italy see art. 1448 *Codice civile*; in Jersey (where it is called *déception* rather than *lésion*), see *Snell* v. *Beadle* 2001 JLR 118; and in Guernsey see *Watson* v. *Trouteaud* (1987) 5 GLJ 6.

aside the thing returns to the patrimony and the purchase price is repaid. Formerly, at least, in one or two rare cases a sale could be set aside even where the sale by the deceased during his life was for the full market value (*retrait lignager*).[54]

As for inheritance itself, the rights of the family still predominate, and freedom of testation is still limited. In some systems spouses qualify for a share, or for a usufruct of a share, and in others they do not. Usually the proportion of the patrimony of the deceased that he may dispose of by will varies according to the number of children. And, importantly, *gifts* made during the deceased's lifetime, or during the last part of it, are taken into account in calculating the compulsory shares of the heirs.[55] This does not, however, restrict the freedom to alienate ownership itself. A gift is valid at the time, even though subject to possible[56] reduction after the donor's death. This may mean that the actual thing given away has to be returned to the patrimony (*réduction en nature*: still the law in Luxembourg, and formerly in France and Belgium), or it may simply mean that the value of the thing has to be paid back into the patrimony (*réduction en valeur*: as in Germany, and now also in France since 2007).

The notion of patrimony allows a civil lawyer to explain the trust to himself. He sees the trustee as owning two patrimonies.[57] One is his personal patrimony, and the other is the patrimony of the trust. The trustee's personal creditors can access the assets in the personal patrimony but not those in the trust patrimony. When assets leave the trust patrimony unlawfully, there are legal rules designed to ensure that they are returned to the patrimony.

There is only one difficulty with all this. It is that the common law never had, and never needed, the patrimony idea. It simply does not exist in the common law. It therefore cannot explain the common law trust. It is true that common lawyers use the idea of the 'estate'. But this is quite different. This is the notion of assets which at a given moment in time

[54] In France see e.g. former art. 841 *Code civil* (repealed 1976); *retrait lignager* in Jersey was abolished in 1834, but in Guernsey only in 2008.

[55] See e.g. the German BGB ss. 2303–38, French *Code civil* arts. 912–28; C. Castelein, R. Foqué and A. Verbeke (eds.), *Imperative Inheritance Law in a Late-Modern Society* (Antwerp: Intersentia, 2009).

[56] Only 'possible' because, whatever the position at the time of the gift, the deceased may die with no heirs close enough to demand reduction, or may before death become resident in or national of another state having no provision for such reduction.

[57] F. Sonneveldt and H. L. van Mens (eds.), *The Trust: Bridge or Abyss Between Common and Civil Law Jurisdictions?* (Denver, Boston: Kluwer Law and Taxation, 1992), p. 5.

belong to a particular person. In the common law it is in effect a snapshot of the economic position of a person on one of (usually) two events occurring, bankruptcy and death. But it looks only at the assets at that moment, and not at future assets. And it is almost always a positive concept: the notion of an 'insolvent estate' means only that whatever assets do exist will be distributed amongst creditors pro rata. The 'heirs' never have any personal liability for the debts of the deceased.

Some writers argue that the trust must be a kind of patrimonial concept because the personal creditors of the trustee cannot attach the assets belonging to the trust.[58] The latter statement is true, but the rule of law concerned is a rule developed by the *common law courts* in the context of the law of the execution of judgments, and not by the courts of equity in the context of the law of trusts. Indeed, the rule that trust assets are immune from execution of judgments actually proves the opposite of what it should be if the trust was a patrimonial concept. If the trust assets formed a separate patrimony from that of the trustee, one would of course expect that the assets of that patrimony should be immune from action by the personal creditors of the trustee. And it is so. What one would not expect is that the assets of the trust would also be immune from execution of judgments against the trustee *in respect of debts contracted as trustee and for the benefit of the trust*. Yet that is the law. The rule of the common law (at least in England) is that, with certain exceptions, judgments may only be executed against the *beneficial* property of the judgment debtor, here, the trustee.[59] This is because liability has been assumed *personally* by the trustee, so it is his own liability.[60] It underlines once again that the trustee is not a representative, but the true owner of the trust assets.

Of course the trust is not confined simply to common law systems. There is the example of Scotland to consider. The Scottish legal system is heavily influenced by the civil law.[61] On the other hand it is also influenced by English law, and is therefore generally referred to as a 'mixed' legal system. In that system the trust has existed for more than 300 years.

58 *Farr* v. *Newman* (1792) 4 TR 621, 645; *Cailland* v. *Eastwick* (1794) 2 Anst 381.

59 *Jennings* v. *Mather* [1901] 1 KB 108, affd [1902] 1 KB 1 (CA); Smith, 'Trust and Patrimony', above, note 13, 338–9.

60 Of course, the trustee who is not himself in breach of trust has the right to an indemnity out of the trust assets, but he takes the risk that they are sufficient, and liquid enough, for this purpose.

61 See e.g. W. Gordon, 'Roman Law in Scotland', in R. Evans-Jones (ed.), *The Civil Law Tradition in Scotland* (Edinburgh: The Stair Society, 1995), ch. 2.

It is true that Scottish legal scholars have in recent times made considerable use of the patrimony idea in seeing how the trust can coexist with the largely civilian property law in Scotland.[62] But this reliance upon patrimony appears to be anachronistic,[63] because so far as I can see the earliest trust cases in Scotland do not refer to patrimony or make use of any similar concept.

It is perhaps worth pausing at this point to see just how Scots law deals with the trust in the context of the absolutist property principle. First of all, there is no doubt that the uncodified Scots law does nevertheless see the concept of property more in Roman law rather than common law terms.[64] Accordingly there is the idea that in principle there should be an owner with all the rights, and that there exists a *numerus clausus* of exceptions to that principle.[65] Accordingly, the right of the beneficiary under a Scots trust has been held to be no more than a *ius crediti*, the right of a creditor.[66] Very good. This means there is no overt interference with the ownership of the trustee. And yet, when you consider the case of the trustee who in breach of trust alienates the trust property to a third party, in at least some cases the third party is bound by the trust (so the beneficiary's rights must to that extent be real rights).[67] Moreover, the rights of the beneficiary are not defeated by the insolvency of the trustee. So it seems to be a case of saying one thing but doing another.

[62] See Gretton, 'Trusts Without Equity', above, note 3, 608–15; K. Reid, 'Trusts in Scotland', in D. J. Hayton, S. C. J. J. Kortmann and H. L. E. Verhagen (eds.), *Principles of European Trust Law* (The Hague, Deventer: Kluwer Law International, 1999), pp. 68–9; but cf. G. Gretton, 'The Evolution of the Trust in a Semi-Civilian System', in Helmholz and Zimmermann, *Itinera Fiduciae*, above, note 18, pp. 525–6.

[63] In just the same way that the patrimony theory of Aubry and Rau is anachronistic.

[64] See Erskine, *An Institute of the Law*, above, note 22, III, i, 2; Gordon, 'Roman Law in Scotland', above, note 61.

[65] Gretton and Steven, *Property, Trusts & Succession*, above, note 19, paras. 1.4, 2.1–2.4, 2.9.

[66] Lord McLaren (ed.), *Bell's Commentaries on the Law of Scotland*, 7th edn (Edinburgh: T & T Clark, 1870), vol. 1, pp. 33, 35; *IRC* v. *Clark's Trustees* 1939 SC 11, 22, 26; W. A. Wilson and A. G. M. Duncan, *Trusts, Trustees and Executors*, 2nd edn (Edinburgh: Green, 1995), paras 1.42–51, 10.01; J. M. Thomson, 'The Role of Equity in Scots Law', in S. R. Goldstein (ed.), *Equity and Contemporary Legal Developments* (Jerusalem: Harry and Michael Sacher Institute for Legislative Research and Comparative Law, 1992), pp. 915–16; Reid, 'Trusts in Scotland', above, note 62, pp. 69–72; Gretton and Steven, *Property, Trusts & Succession*, above, note 19, para. 22.55.

[67] *Taylor* v. *Forbes* (1830) 4 W&S 444; *Bertram Gardner & Co's Trustee* v. *King's Remembrancer* 1920 SC 555, 562. Cf. *Airdrie Magistrates* v. *Smith* (1850) 12 D 1222 (purchaser in bad faith bound by trust): rule reversed by Trusts (Scotland) Act 1961, s. 2.

VII Preventive justice

Another important cultural difference between common law and civil law, relevant to the possible transplantation into civil law systems of the trust, is that of preventive justice. This is the idea that, if consensual transactions are declared by the parties in front of, and are recorded by, a public official, it is less likely that there will be litigation about them, or more especially their terms, at a later stage. The public official concerned is usually a notary. There is inevitably a higher cost per transaction (especially when notaries are entitled to charge their fees as a percentage of the value of the assets concerned), but – it is said – a lower incidence of litigation and hence (it is argued) lower cost overall.[68] The many who would in a non-notarial system never have any disputes about transactions in effect subsidize the few who would. The common law world does not use notaries in this way. In particular there is no register of trusts in the United Kingdom.

In order for this kind of system to work, however, there have to be rather stricter rules about formalities than are generally to be found in the common law world. In particular, it would not be acceptable to require that *legal* transactions involving land are carried out in front of notaries, but *trusts* involving land need not be. This is only one reason why trusts are regarded with suspicion, not only by civil law governments but also by civil law notaries, who can see an important revenue source disappearing. But it means that self-declared trusts, where the property does not change hands, and the wide range of informal transactions in land in common law systems, characterized by the cases of proprietary estoppel and common intention constructive trust,[69] would be very much restricted in a civil law environment. (It also makes it hard to understand how the draft EU Regulation on Wills and Successions currently being negotiated could work so as to require, say, a French court to decide on a proprietary estoppel claim over English land.)[70]

[68] I am not, however, aware of any robust studies on this point which would support such a hypothesis.

[69] And, in the context of trusts created by conduct rather than words, see *Paul* v. *Constance* [1977] 1 WLR 527, CA.

[70] Cf. P. Matthews, *Memorandum to House of Lords European Union Committee*, in 6th Report of Session 2009–10, paper 75, 54–65, paras. 46–7, 52–3.

VIII Bright line solutions

Of course, the functional needs which a legal system has to serve are not necessarily very different in a civil law environment from a common law one. So the civil law system, if it has no recourse to the trust, must provide an alternative. In the circumstances, it is unsurprising that civil law systems have developed a number of legal devices to fulfil at least some of the roles performed by the trust. All of these are compatible with the civil law notion of property. First and foremost, if a property owner wishes to entrust an asset to another, for the purposes of investment, or simply for management, and wishes to give that other ownership ability (which may be important as against third parties) the simplest device is for the asset to be 'sold' to the 'manager' subject to an option for instant repurchase at any moment at a nominal figure. This device may be combined with some form of fiduciary contract (mentioned below) or it may stand on its own. In that way the 'settlor/beneficiary' has the security of knowing that the asset can always be recovered by exercising the option.

There are also agency solutions, where the person in the role of 'trustee' is only a representative, a person with power over the property of another. It may be a particular mandate, or the *bewind* of Dutch and Roman-Dutch law, or it may be a species of legal office such as the tutor of a minor or the curator of a mentally incapable person may have. Or the solution may be one of a species of contracts, such as the fiduciary contracts developed in some civil law systems, essentially the descendants of the Roman law *fiducia*. The *fiducie* in Luxembourg[71] and in France[72] are, and the old *fiducie* of Quebec law[73] was, such a device. It may even involve the creation of a new legal person, with its own patrimony, such as a foundation. The modern *fiducie* of Quebec law[74] is more along these

[71] *Loi du 27 juillet 2003*; P. Matthews, 'Fiducia and the Hague Trusts Convention: The New Luxembourg Law' (2003) 17 T.L.I. 188.

[72] *Loi du 19 février 2007*; P. Matthews, 'The French *fiducie*: And Now for Something Completely Different?' (2007) 21 T.L.I. 17; J-P. Béraudo, 'La loi du 19 février créant une fiducie française', in *Trusts et fiducie, concurrents ou compléments?* (Geneva: Éditions Academy & Finance, 2008), pp. 123–46; F. Lefebvre et al., *La fiducie, mode d'emploi*, 2nd edn (Paris: Éditions Francis Lefebvre, 2009).

[73] Act respecting trusts, SQ 1879, c. 29; Civil Code of Lower Canada, arts. 981a–981n.

[74] Civil Code of Québec, art. 1261; M. Cantin Cumyn, 'The Trust in a Civilian Context: The Quebec Case' (1994) 3 *Journal of International Trust and Corporate Planning* 69; D. W. M. Waters, M. Gillen and L. Smith, *Waters' Law of Trusts in Canada*, 4th edn (Toronto: Thomson Carswell, 2005), pp. 1346–7, 1353–68.

lines, being a patrimony devoted to particular purposes. None of these, of course, addresses the absolutist property problem head-on. Instead, they appear to comply with it, though as some commentators have now pointed out, the ownership of the *fiduciaire* must surely be somewhat diminished by the restrictions to which he is subject.[75]

The only devices which get close to confronting the problem are (i) use and habitation, (ii) the usufruct and (iii) the descendant of the Roman law *fideicommissum*,[76] the *substitution fidéicommissaire*. The first two reflect the desire of their creator to restrict the beneficial enjoyment of an asset for a particular beneficiary, so that the beneficiary cannot destroy or alienate the asset, and in the first case cannot enjoy the fruits either, but can only enjoy the thing itself in specie. The beneficiary in the first case has *usus* only, or in the second case *usus* and *fructus* (hence the name), but not *abusus*. From the common law perspective, it looks rather like a life interest trust, or, better, an old-fashioned common law life estate and remainder, without the interposition of a trust at all. But with these there is no fragmentation of property into different estates. The person that common lawyers would call the remainderman is known as the bare owner (*nu-propriétaire*), having the bare ownership (*nue-propriété*) of the thing. The usufructuary has no estate. His real right is good against third parties to whom the bare owner may transfer the thing, but it is in legal terms relegated to the status of a burden upon the bare owner's ownership.[77] The absolutist civil law analysis of property is thus (just) satisfied.

The *substitution fidéicommissaire* is in a way more complicated. Whereas the use or usufruct idea does not seem for the common lawyer to have enough estates, the *substitution fidéicommissaire* seems to have too many. In Roman law, the *fideicommissum* was a testamentary device in which initially the heir would be charged to keep the property during his own life and pass it (or some portion of it) to the beneficiary on his own death. The fundamental idea was that fiduciary and beneficiary had entirely separate interests, which each beneficially owned. Unlike a trust (which originally was *inter vivos*

[75] See e.g. Mallet-Bricout, Chapter 7 in this volume.

[76] See generally D. Johnston, *The Roman Law of Trusts* (Oxford University Press, 1988); D. W. M. Waters, 'The Institution of the Trust in Civil and Common Law', in *Collected Courses of the Hague Academy of International Law*, vol. 252 (Dordrecht: Martinus Nijhoff, 1995), pp. 136–59; D. Johnston, 'Trusts and Trust-like Devices in Roman Law', in Helmholz and Zimmermann, *Itinera Fiduciae*, above, note 18.

[77] In Scotland, see, Erskine, *An Institute of the Law*, above, note 22, II, i, 1.

only), a *fideicommissum* could *only* arise on death, never through a transaction *inter vivos*.[78] This was because it was originally an extension of testamentary power, i.e. in being able to give property on death to persons who could not legally be instituted as heirs.[79] There was less need for such an extension in the case of *inter vivos* gifts, because the power of donation *inter vivos* could be exercised amongst a wider class anyway.[80] Modern civil law systems, however, developed an *inter vivos fideicommissum*, in French known as the *substitution fidéicommissaire*.

The characteristic of this device was that both the fiduciary and the beneficiary were regarded as the full owners of the asset at the time at which they each owned it. It was only that the fiduciary was not allowed to alienate it to anyone other than the beneficiary. One might have thought that this removed a fundamental part of the civil law notion of ownership (i.e. '*abusus*'). However, the difference from, say, usufruct, is that the usufructuary never has the ownership of the property at all (unless he was also the settlor). His real right is always less than ownership.[81] But the fiduciary in a *fideicommissum* receives the full ownership from the settlor and then passes it on to the beneficiary at the appropriate moment (usually his own death). As the French might say, '*Un propriétaire peut en cacher un autre.*'

This poses a problem of restraint on alienation. If the device works, the first owner cannot alienate the property at all, even to a bona fide purchaser for value.[82] When the first transmits it to the second designated owner, he (being full owner) may impose his own *substitution* on the second owner, charging him to keep it and to pass it on to a third owner, with the effect that the property is inalienable for another generation. And, certainly, this is what seems to have happened in early Rome.[83] Indeed, it seems that some Roman testators managed

78 Johnston, *The Roman Law of Trusts*, above, note 76, p. 15; Johnston, 'Trusts and Trust-like Devices in Roman Law', above, note 76, pp. 46–7.

79 Buckland, *A Textbook of Roman Law*, above, note 23, p. 353; Thomas, *Textbook of Roman Law*, above, note 23, p. 511.

80 Thomas, ibid., p. 192.

81 Cf. *Batthyany* v. *Walford* (1887) 36 Ch D 269, 281, dealing with an Austrian *Fideikommiss*.

82 *Abdul Hameed Sitti Kadija* v. *De Saram* [1946] AC 208, PC; *Abeyawardene* v. *West* [1957] AC 176, PC.

83 W. W. Buckland, *Equity in Roman Law* (University of London Press, 1911), pp. 84–5; Thomas, *Textbook of Roman Law*, above, note 23, pp. 513–14; cf. Johnston, *The Roman Law of Trusts*, above, note 76, pp. 78–9.

to create perpetual *fideicommissa*.[84] In this way great families could conserve their wealth and their lands. The Emperor Hadrian tried to curb the excesses, by prohibiting *fideicommissa* in favour of unascertained persons (*personae incertae*).[85] In the late Roman law Justinian went back on this, but then forbade *fideicommissa* beyond the fourth generation.[86]

Nonetheless, *substitutions* were still being created *inter vivos* of immovables under Norman customary law in the sixteenth century.[87] Until 1560 there were no limits on substitutions in French law, which could accordingly be perpetual.[88] French efforts[89] to deal with this problem did not succeed until the introduction of the *Code civil* in 1804, when all *substitutions* (both testamentary and *inter vivos*) were, subject to certain limited exceptions, abolished by French law.[90] In fact, Napoleon almost immediately brought them back in 1806, as *majorats*, to support his new nobility, and it was only after the Restoration that they were abolished

[84] Buckland and McNair, *Roman Law and Common Law*, above, note 20, p. 138.

[85] Ibid., p. 139.

[86] Justinian, Nov. 159, c. 2; C. F. Thevenot, *Traité des Substitutions* (Paris: Moutard, 1778), ch. LXXIII, s. 1; Buckland, *A Textbook of Roman Law*, above, note 23, p. 364; Thomas, *Textbook of Roman Law*, above, note 23, p. 514; Johnston, *The Roman Law of Trusts*, above, note 76, p. 111; Waters, 'The Institution of the Trust in Civil and Common Law', above, note 76, pp. 143–4; Johnston, 'Trusts and Trust-like Devices in Roman Law', above, note 76, pp. 49–50.

[87] See G. Terrien, *Commentaires du Droit Civil*, 2nd edn (Paris: Jacques Du Puys, 1578), liv. 6, ch. 1, pp. 193–4.

[88] C. Serres, *Explication de l'ordonnance* (Avignon: François Girard, 1766), p. 163; Thevenot, *Traité des Substitutions*, above, note 86, pp. 376–7. This may also be the position in Andorra, where the *ius commune* still has effect, and at least one view is that there is no limit on substitutions, which can accordingly still be perpetual: see J.-A. Brutails, *La coutume d'Andorre*, 2nd edn (Andorra la Vella: Editorial Casal I Vall, 1965), pp. 150–1; cf. A. M. Borrell, *Dret civil vigente a Catalunya* (Barcelona: Impremta de la Casa de caritat, 1923), para. 454, and L. Puig i Ferriol et al., *Fonaments de dret privat Andorrà* (Sant Julià de Lòria, Principat d'Andorra: Fundaciâo Juliáa Reig, 2005), vol. 4, ch. 27, para. 4.2, pp. 805–6, both of which seek to apply Justinian's limit of four degrees.

[89] *Ordonnance d'Orleans*, 1560, art. 59 (restricting the validity of testamentary and *inter vivos substitutions* to the second degree removed from the creator, not including the original donee); *Ordonnance de Moulins*, 1566, art. 57 (expressly permitting substitutions predating 1560 to continue to the fourth degree); *Ordonnance de Substitutions*, 1747, arts. 30, 31 (restricting them to a maximum of two degrees for the future, but otherwise confirming the earlier *Ordonnances*); art. 32 expressly preserved the privilege of certain provinces to permit infinite substitutions.

[90] Art. 896; C. de Wulf, *The Trust and Corresponding Institutions in Civil Law* (Brussels: Établissements Emile Bruylant, 1965), pp. 130–5.

(but only for the future) once more.[91] And now very recently they have been brought back once again,[92] under the new title of *libéralités graduelles*, but subject to strict limits. And it is not just France, either. In Italy the *sostituzione fedecomissaria* still exists, but is severely restricted, essentially to the case of a mentally handicapped child.[93] But the fiduciary substitution is still found in the laws of Switzerland,[94] Denmark,[95] Spain,[96] Andorra,[97] Greece[98] and elsewhere.[99]

IX The trust as fuzzy line solution

When one contrasts all these civilian solutions, with their bright line compliance with the absolutist property principle, the trust looks distinctly strange. In effect, it is a fuzzy line solution. It is the case of the owner who must act in the interests of another person or persons. The ownership of the trustee is not quite complete, not quite *full* enough.[100] That such a person can exist is a reflection of the fact that English law, being

91 Mazeaud et al., *Leçons de droit civil*, above, note 28, para. 1431; any still remaining were bought out by the French State in 1905: see also A. Castaldo, 'Les Majorats napoléoniens' (1997) 2 *Revue de recherche juridique* 479.

92 *Loi no 2006-728 du 23 juin 2006*, inserting *Code civil*, arts. 1048–56.

93 See the Italian *Codice civile*, art. 692. Since the ratification by Italy of the Hague Trusts Convention, such cases are now more commonly dealt with by using the trust: see e.g. P. Lebano, 'Il trust Mevio', in I. Beneventi and G. Alpa (eds.), *I trusts in Italia oggi* (Milan: Giuffre, 1996); A. Palazzo, 'Trust e successioni', in S. Buttà (ed.), *Introduzione ai trust e profili applicative* (Milan: Ipsoa, 2002), pp. 39–40.

94 *Code civil suisse*, arts. 488–92; A. von Overbeck, 'Switzerland', in J. Glasson (ed.), *International Trust Laws* (Bristol: Jordan, 2002), para. A52.51; J. Guinand and M. Stettler, *Droit civil II*, 2nd edn (Fribourg: Éditions Universitaires, 1992), paras. 186–91.

95 R. Feldthusen, 'National Report for Denmark', in Hayton, Kortmann and Verhagen, *Principles of European Trust Law*, above, note 62, p. 173.

96 See the *Código civil*, arts. 781–6; in Catalonia, see Book IV of the *Codi civil de Catalunya, relatiu a les successions*, Cap VI, *Els fideicomisos*, formerly the *Codi de successions*, Llei 40/1991, Cap VII.

97 Borrell, *Dret civil vigente a Catalunya*, above, note 88, paras. 453–66; Brutails, *La coutume d'Andorre*, above, note 88, pp. 149–51; Puig i Ferriol, *Fonaments de dret privat Andorrà*, above, note 88, ch. 27.

98 Civil Code 1941 (in force 1946), arts. 1923–41.

99 As to Scotland, see G. Gretton, 'Fideicommissary Substitutions: Scots Law in Historical and Comparative Perspective', in K. Reid, M. J. de Waal and R. Zimmermann (eds.), *Exploring the Law of Succession* (Edinburgh University Press, 2007).

100 See e.g. M. Lupoi, *Trusts: A Comparative Study*, Simon Dix (trans.) (Cambridge University Press, 2000), pp. 81–2, 179–83 and *Trusts*, 2nd edn (Milan: Giuffrè, 2001) (Italian only), pp. 134–5, 287–90; Lupoi, *I trust nel diritto civile*, above, note 13, pp. 19–23, 294; Mallet-Bricout, Chapter 7 in this volume.

anti-conceptual, never had a Gaius to lay down in advance a rigid framework for the development of the law. Instead, the law developed on a case-by-case basis, a little like creating a mosaic or a pointillist painting. Thus the structure and the categories of the law appeared afterwards, as a result of the decisions, rather than the other way round.

An excellent example of this phenomenon is the nineteenth-century English case of *De Mattos* v. *Gibson*.[101] This case could never have been decided as it was if English law had adopted the structure laid down by Gaius, and there would have been no need for litigation at all if it had adopted any other structure. A owned a ship and chartered it to B to carry a full cargo. Before the voyage was completed, A mortgaged the ship to C, and committed a breach of its terms entitling C to sell the ship. The question was whether B could obtain an injunction against C to restrain C from selling the ship inconsistently with the charterparty to B. On an application for an interim injunction, Knight Bruce LJ said:

> Reason and justice seem to prescribe that, at least as a general rule, where a man, by gift or purchase, acquires property from another, with knowledge of a previous contract, lawfully and for valuable consideration made by him with a third person, to use and employ the property for a particular purpose in a specified manner, the acquirer shall not, to the material damage of the third person, in opposition to the contract and inconsistently with it, use and employ the property in a manner not allowable to the giver or seller.[102]

As it happens, the plaintiff failed to prove the necessary facts at trial, and thus lost the case. But the statement of principle given on the earlier application sets out the law very clearly. There are cases in which B, who has rights *in personam* only against A, can nevertheless enforce those rights against C, with whom he had no relationship whatever previously. It is important to notice that there is no suggestion that the rights of B against C depend in any way upon the law of property. This is exactly the problem which English litigants faced in the post-medieval period. Having established a good right against the 'trustee' for acting against conscience, they sought to make *the same right* good against the third party who had dealt with the trustee. It was at this point that the rights which the beneficiary had *in personam* against the trustee became rights against third parties, *in effect* property rights.[103]

[101] (1858) 4 De G & J 276, 45 ER 108. In modern times, see e.g. *Manchester Airport* v. *Dutton* [2000] 1 QB 133, CA (licence to occupy land).

[102] 4 De G & J 282, 45 ER 110.

[103] E.g. Smith, 'Trust and Patrimony', above, note 13, 342–7.

X Fuzzy lines for all

My purpose in mentioning this case here is not to suggest that the trust phenomenon was here reinventing itself, or indeed taking over parts of shipping law. Instead, it is to draw attention to the fact that the context in which this particular problem arose was one which would inevitably arise also in civil law countries. There were always going to be cases in which one person (B) had a contractual relationship with another (A), and a third person (C) interfered with this. What should the response of the legal system be? It is not going to be based on a property right because B has no property right, at least so far as the legal system currently knows that. So it has to be based on the idea that there is a personal right against A, which is also good – at least potentially – against C, D, E and so on. And yet (for a common lawyer at least) that is the primary characteristic of a *property* right.[104]

It is a curiosity of European legal history that this kind of case *does* occur in civil law systems, but comes to prominence only after the Second World War, that is, approximately a century after it did in England. And, unsurprisingly, the civil law systems come to a similar conclusion to English law. If the third party (C) knows about the contract and deliberately interferes, then the rights that B has against A can be enforced against C.[105] The consequence is that the rigid barrier between property and obligation drawn by Gaius is shown to be porous. There are cases where a person (B) has rights against a third party (C), even though these are not categorized by the civil law system in question as property or real rights. Yet the test – or at any rate the most important test – of whether a right is real or personal is whether it is good against third parties. So by definition such rights should be real.

[104] Of course, the claim to such a right fails against the good faith purchaser of a legal estate without notice. But that important limitation should not deter the analogy with civil law property rights, since, as pointed out earlier in the text, in most civil law systems the good faith acquirer (even without payment) of another's goods takes free of the original owner's claim, an even more far-reaching limitation.

[105] S. Ginossar, *Liberté contractuelle et respect des droits des tiers: émergence du délit civil de fraude* (Paris: LGDJ, 1963); J. Ghestin, *Traité de droit civil, les effets du contrat*, 2nd edn (Paris: LGDJ, 1994), pp. 443ff; Corte di Cassazione, 30 marzo 1942, no. 882, G. Alpa, *Diritto di responsabilità civile* (Bari/Rome: Laterza, 2003), pp. 252–60; B. S. Markesinis, *The German Law of Torts*, 3rd edn (Oxford University Press, 1994), pp. 894–8, cases cited at p. 898 no. 3; P.-G. Jobin, *Les Obligations*, 6th edn (Cowansville: Édition Yvon Blais, 2005), pp. 523–6; Y. Emerich, *La propriété des créances: approche comparative* (Cowansville: Édition Yvon Blais, 2006), pp. 435–55.

This chapter is not – and is not intended to be – an exercise in ritual humiliation of civil law systems for their inadequate categorization of legal rights. All that I am seeking to show is that the trust, and the rights of the beneficiaries under a trust, cannot be so easily categorized in the way that Gaius wanted. And it is the anti-conceptualist approach taken by the common law that allows this to happen.

XI Civil law developments

In modern times, the increasing importance of cross-border transactions (not just commercial, but also involving persons from one country who go to live, marry and have children, then die, in another) has meant that it has been necessary to create legal institutions having even more of the characteristics of the trust. These have almost necessarily involved partial derogation from the principle of patrimony as laid down by Aubry and Rau. This theory was never so strongly adopted by German law, and hence the derogations in the Germanic school have been perhaps easier than they might have been otherwise. But we have seen not only increasing use of the foundation, but also of the one-person company, the fiduciary contract with ring-fencing of assets, the *patrimoine affecté* (also known in Quebec because of the new *fiducie*), and in French law, the new legal status of *entrepreneur individuel à responsabilité limitée.*[106]

What these developments show is that there is a much greater acceptance of the idea in modern civil law that the owner of an asset may hold it for the benefit of others rather than for his own.[107] More than that, there is the acceptance of the idea that in some cases at least he should prefer the interests of others to his own. Of course there are already some such ideas in civil law systems. For example, in Guernsey law (like Jersey law, based originally on Norman customary law) it is well understood that in some circumstances the owner of property should act *en bon père de famille* – like the good father of a family. Indeed, this expression even appears in the Guernsey trust law, in considering the standard of behaviour required of a trustee: 'A trustee shall, in the exercise of his functions, observe the utmost good faith and act en bon père de famille.'[108]

[106] *Loi 2010-658 du 15 juin 2010.*

[107] D.-C. Lamontagne, *Biens et propriété*, 5th edn (Cowansville: Édition Yvon Blais, 2005), p. 202.

[108] Trusts (Guernsey) Law 2007, s. 22(1).

In fact, the likelihood is that the classical Roman law approach to property and ownership was never as absolute as the draughtsmen of the French *Code civil* of 1804 had considered.[109] Roman law was never a finished product, frozen in aspic. It was a work in progress for something like a thousand years, from the time of the Twelve Tables through to the Digest of Justinian. For much of this time there was no overarching conceptual design into which all legal development had to fit. On the contrary, development was for much of this time in the hands of the judges themselves.[110] Ironically, this is also the story of the development of English law. It is instead the modern civil law countries, taking Roman law all of a piece in the late Middle Ages, who have a different story to tell. It is about time that the story of property in the civil law was reconsidered. The increasing international acceptance of the trust and the general liberalization of property law are going some way towards achieving this.

But, for those civil lawyers who are opposed to all revisionism, all that I can say in my defence was well said already by William Shakespeare in the words he gave to the character Puck at the end of his play, *A Midsummer Night's Dream*:

> If we shadows have offended,
> Think but this, and all is mended,
> That you have but slumber'd here
> While these visions did appear.
> And this weak and idle theme,
> No more yielding but a dream . . .

[109] Buckland, *A Textbook of Roman Law*, above, note 23, p. 187; Buckland and McNair, *Roman Law and Common Law*, above, note 20, pp. 71–80.

[110] P. Stein, *Roman Law in European History* (Cambridge University Press, 1999), pp. 8–12.

14

Categorically different: unintended consequences of trust taxonomy

MICHAEL LUBETSKY

Your client, in Quebec, wants to create a trust which will be used exclusively for the education of his descendants. He asks how long such a trust can legally last. Answering this question requires determination of the trust category under the Civil Code of Québec (C.C.Q.). If the trust is 'social' or 'private', the trust can potentially last perpetually;[1] if it is 'personal', its maximum duration will be limited.[2]

As this example illustrates, the classification of a trust can have profound legal consequences and practitioners need to give informed advice – *today* – on the category into which a proposed trust may fall. However, the definitions of the three trust categories in the C.C.Q. largely overlap, making it extremely difficult – if not impossible – to say *a priori* where one category ends and another begins. The courts in Quebec have yet to provide any guidance on the classification of trusts and they may well not have occasion to do so for another hundred years or so, when settlors' heirs may be motivated to seek the disbursement of assets held by social and private trusts on the grounds that they are actually personal trusts that have remained in existence beyond the maximum time.

A number of Quebec authors have considered trusts for the education of members of a particular family, although they have disagreed (interestingly, along language lines) on their classification. Authors writing in French have tended to consider them 'private trusts' (Beaulne,[3] Brierley[4] and Bruneau[5]), whilst those writing in English have found the 'personal

[1] Civil Code of Québec (C.C.Q.), art. 1273. [2] Ibid., arts. 1271–2.

[3] J. Beaulne, *Droit des fiducies*, 2nd edn (Montreal: Wilson & Lafleur, 2005), para. 112.

[4] J. E. C. Brierley, 'De certains patrimoines d'affection', in A. Laprise and D. Vaugeois (eds.), *La réforme du Code civil: Textes réunis par le Barreau du Québec et la Chambre de notaires du Québec* (Sainte-Foy: Les Presses de l'Université Laval, 1993), vol. 1, p. 758.

[5] D. Bruneau, 'La fiducie et le droit civil' (1996) 18:4 R.P.F.S. 755, 765.

trust' category more appropriate (Claxton[6] and McClean[7]). Perhaps more interestingly, none of these authors, in making their assessments, considered it necessary to consider the treatment of such trusts in the common law.

In the face of this ongoing uncertainty, the present debate among scholars will likely play a vital role in shaping how the codal trust categories evolve. This chapter aims to advance this discussion by identifying and tracing the common law origins of the three C.C.Q. trust categories, and discussing the degree to which common law jurisprudence on classifying trusts can help inform their interpretation.

To this end, this chapter first reviews the classification of trusts in the common law (Part I) and the C.C.Q. (Part II), then outlines how the common law jurisprudence can inform the C.C.Q. regime (Part III). After considering the special case of non-charitable purpose trusts (Part IV), the chapter concludes with a plea for greater trans-systemic dialogue.

I The classification of trusts in the common law

Figure 14.1 illustrates, in a simplified manner, the classification of intentional trusts[8] in the common law:

First, intentional trusts divide into charitable and non-charitable. To qualify as charitable, a trust must provide a 'public benefit' and its object(s) must fall exclusively into the four nominate categories developed by the jurisprudence: education, religion, relief of poverty, and general public utility.[9] Charitable trusts have a number of well-known advantages that make them particularly attractive to settlors: they qualify for perpetual existence, they can benefit from the cy-près rule, and they typically enjoy preferable taxation.[10]

Non-charitable trusts, also known as 'private' trusts, bifurcate into trusts for persons and trusts for purposes. A trust for persons has one

[6] J. B. Claxton, *Studies on the Quebec Law of Trust* (Toronto: Thompson Canada, 2005), n. 5–5.

[7] A. J. McClean, 'The Trust in the Civil Code of Quebec', in Canadian Institute for Advanced Legal Studies, *Conférences sur le nouveau Code civil du Québec* (Cowansville: Yvon Blais, 1992), pp. 94–5.

[8] This chapter leaves to future scholarship the question of trusts arising by operation of law.

[9] D. W. M. Waters, M. Gillen and L. Smith, *Waters' Law of Trusts in Canada*, 4th edn (Toronto: Thomson Carswell, 2012), pp. 721–2; A. H. Oosterhoff et al., *Oosterhoff on Trusts: Text, Commentary and Materials*, 7th edn (Toronto: Thomson Carswell, 2009), p. 382.

[10] Waters, ibid., pp. 664, 666, 680–720; Oosterhoff, ibid., pp. 376–9, 462–503.

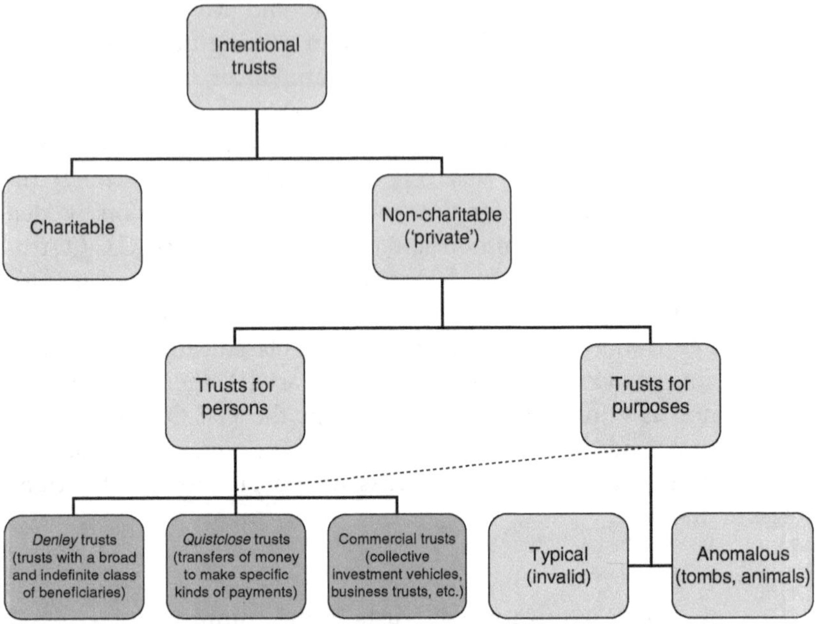

Fig. 14.1 Classification of intentional trusts.

or more identifiable individuals as its objects, whilst a trust for purposes aims to promote an activity or initiative.

Non-charitable trusts for purposes in the common law are prima facie invalid[11] – celebrated examples of such invalid trusts include a trust to endow a prize for an annual yacht race (*Re Nottage*)[12] and a trust to promote the conversion of English to a new phonetic alphabet (*Re Shaw*).[13] However, a non-charitable trust for purposes can be saved if it falls into one of the 'anomalous cases' recognized in the jurisprudence, primarily trusts for the care of specific animals or for the maintenance of graves.[14]

[11] Waters, ibid., pp. 163, 625–6; Oosterhoff, ibid., pp. 523–9. The jurisprudence has identified four reasons for the presumptive invalidity of purpose trusts: (a) want of a party with standing to enforce its terms, (b) violation of the rule against perpetuities, (c) uncertainty of objects and (d) improper delegation of testamentary powers. (*Re Russell Estate* [1977] 6 WWR 273, 1 ETR 285, 20 (Alta SC (TD))).

[12] *Re Nottage* [1895] 2 Ch 649 (Ch. Div.).

[13] *Re Shaw* [1957] 1 All ER 745 (CA), settled on appeal [1958] 1 All ER 245n.

[14] Waters, *Waters' Law of Trusts*, above, note 9, p. 667; Oosterhoff, *Oosterhoff on Trusts*, above, note 9, pp. 530–5.

Because of the presumptive invalidity of trusts for purposes, common law jurists often engage in considerable (if not heroic) intellectual gymnastics to characterize what are essentially trusts for purposes as trusts for persons.[15] The jurisprudence has generally taken a permissive attitude to what might be called 'quasi-purpose' trusts, with *Re Denley's Trusts*[16] and *Barclays Bank Ltd* v. *Quistclose Investments Ltd*[17] establishing themselves as classic (and still controversial) cases. *Denley* involved an employer who transferred land to a trust, with instructions that it be maintained as a campground for its employees and their guests. *Quistclose* involved the transfer of a sum of money on trust to pay specific kinds of expenses. The courts eventually upheld both trusts, holding either that there exists an identifiable (if diffuse) class of beneficiaries (the company employees in *Denley*) or else that the trust has an identifiable beneficiary in the person of the settlor himself (the transferor of the funds in *Quistclose*).

'Commercial trusts', such as collective investment vehicles, special-purpose entities for financing transactions, income trusts (like real estate investment trusts) and business trusts, although not a formal category, differ sufficiently from other forms of trusts in their constitution, governance and regulation that they tend to be treated as a distinct group.[18] Although commercial trusts have largely managed to escape the theoretical controversies that have dogged other forms of trusts,[19] they also straddle the line between trusts for purposes and trusts for persons[20] and potentially raise challenging theoretical issues about their fundamental nature and validity.[21]

15 Oosterhoff, *Oosterhoff on Trusts*, above, note 9, pp. 556–83.

16 *Re Denley's Trusts* [1968] 3 All ER 65. For discussion, see Waters, *Waters' Law of Trusts*, above, note 9, pp. 670–2.

17 *Barclays Bank Ltd* v. *Quistclose Investments Ltd* [1970] AC 567. See also *Twinsectra Ltd* v. *Yardley*, 2002 UKHL 12.

18 A. W. Scott et al., *Scott and Ascher on Trusts*, 5th edn (New York: Aspen Publishers, 2006), vol. 1, pp. 34–5; K. Fan Sin, *The Legal Nature of the Unit Trust* (Oxford: Clarendon Press, 1997), pp. 2–3.

19 The primary conceptual debate before the courts on commercial trusts has been whether to assimilate them with corporations for purposes of corporate and tax legislation. See e.g. *Smith* v. *Anderson* (1880), 15 Ch D 247 (CA) and *Eliot* v. *Freeman*, 220 US 178 (1911).

20 Fan Sin, *The Legal Nature of the Unit Trust*, above, note 18, p. 72.

21 Ibid., devotes an entire monograph to this subject.

II The classification of trusts in the C.C.Q.

The Civil Code of Lower Canada, in force in Quebec until 1994, only recognized a small subset of all the trusts permitted by the common law. Trusts for persons could only be established by will or donation – a formulation that essentially excluded all commercial trusts.[22] Charitable trusts (technically not trusts at all, but a *sui generis* institution dating back to old French law) could be established only by will.[23] Quebec had no provision at all for the anomalous graveyard and animal care trusts.[24]

During the recodification, the legislature sought to give Quebeckers access to most of the trusts available in other jurisdictions,[25] and therefore posited a trust regime with three new trust categories: the 'personal trust', corresponding roughly to the gratuitous trusts for persons previously recognized under the former Code (article 1267 C.C.Q.),[26] the 'social trust', analogous to the common law charitable trust (article 1270 C.C.Q.), and the 'private trust', a uniquely Quebec institution encompassing a broad range of trusts not previously permitted (articles 1268–9 C.C.Q.):

1267. A personal trust is constituted gratuitously for the purpose of securing a benefit for a determinate or determinable person.	1267. La fiducie personnelle est constituée à titre gratuit, dans le but de procurer un avantage à une personne déterminée ou qui peut l'être.
1268. A private trust is a trust created for the object of erecting,	1268. La fiducie d'utilité privée est celle qui a pour objet l'érection, l'entretien

[22] For a summary list of the relevant jurisprudence, see J. L. Baudouin and Y. Renaud, *Code civil annoté* (Montreal: Wilson & Lafleur, 1989), vol. 1, pp. 543–4. Note that separate legislation in Quebec provided for 'security trusts' (Beaulne, *Droit des fiducies*, above, note 3, para. 7, n. 19) as well as trusts held by pension plans and trust companies (Claxton, *Studies on the Quebec Law of Trust*, above, note 6, pp. 11–12).

[23] Civil Code of Lower Canada (C.C.L.C.), art. 869; G. Brière, *Donations, substitutions et fiducie* (Montreal: Wilson & Lafleur, 1988), pp. 266–7.

[24] Although there apparently was some discussion about whether such trusts were contemplated by art. 869 C.C.L.C. Ibid., para. 88; Brière, *Donations*, above, note 23, p. 271; Brierley, 'De certains patrimoines d'affection', above, note 4, p. 759.

[25] Claxton, *Studies on the Quebec Law of Trust*, above, note 6, p. 25; Brière, *Donations*, above, note 23, p. 270. Note, however, that the recodification maintained the bar against purely self-constituted trusts (viz., trusts created by a 'unilateral declaration of trust') (C.C.Q. art. 1275). But see Claxton, *Studies on the Quebec Law of Trust*, above, note 6, pp. 80–1.

[26] D. C. Lamontagne, *Biens et propriété*, 5th edn (Cowansville: Yvon Blais, 2005), para. 187; Beaulne, *Droit des fiducies*, above, note 3, para. 82.

maintaining or preserving a thing or of using a property appropriated to a specific use, whether for the indirect benefit of a person or in his memory, or for some other private purpose.

1269. A trust constituted by onerous title, particularly one created for the purpose of allowing the making of profit by means of investments, providing for retirement or procuring another benefit for the settlor or for the persons he designates or for the members of a partnership, company or association, or for employees or shareholders, is also a private trust.

1270. A social trust is a trust constituted for a purpose of general interest, such as a cultural, educational, philanthropic, religious or scientific purpose. It does not have the making of profit or the operation of an enterprise as its main object.

ou la conservation d'un bien corporel, ou l'utilisation d'un bien affecté à un usage déterminé, soit à l'avantage indirect d'une personne ou à sa mémoire, soit dans un autre but de nature privée.

1269. Est aussi d'utilité privée la fiducie constituée à titre onéreux dans le but, notamment, de permettre la réalisation d'un profit au moyen de placements ou d'investissements, de pourvoir à une retraite ou de procurer un autre avantage au constituant ou aux personnes qu'il désigne, aux membres d'une société ou d'une association, à des salariés ou à des porteurs de titre.

1270. La fiducie d'utilité sociale est celle qui est constituée dans un but d'intérêt général, notamment à caractère culturel, éducatif, philanthropique, religieux ou scientifique. Elle n'a pas pour objet essentiel de réaliser un bénéfice ni d'exploiter une entreprise.

A closer look at articles 1268 and 1269 C.C.Q. reveals three distinct kinds of 'private trust':

(a) a trust for erecting, maintaining or preserving a thing ('*un bien corporel*') (article 1268 C.C.Q. *in inceptum*);
(b) a trust for using a property ('*un bien*'), which can include a sum of money, appropriated to a specific use (article 1268 C.C.Q. *in fine*); and
(c) a trust created 'by onerous title' (article 1269 C.C.Q.).[27]

[27] For an enumeration of various kinds of trusts allowable under art. 1269 C.C.Q., see Beaulne, *Droit des fiducies*, above, note 3, paras. 94–108; Claxton, *Studies on the Quebec Law of Trust*, above, note 6, pp. 99–100.

The *Commentaires du ministre*, issued by the Quebec government during the recodification, illustrate the kinds of trusts covered by the three sub-categories:

> Il vise plusieurs situations. Il permet, d'une part, d'englober les fiducies constituées même à titre onéreux, où aucune personne physique ou morale n'est vraiment bénéficiaire, mais dont le but revêt un caractère purement privé. C'est le cas, par exemple, de la fiducie constituée dans le but *d'ériger et d'entretenir un monument funéraire* à la mémoire du défunt ou des membres de sa famille, ou encore d'assurer la *survie des animaux préférés* du défunt.
>
> Il permet, d'autre part, de couvrir les fiducies constituées dans le but de procurer un avantage indirect à une personne ou à un groupe, en lui permettant d'utiliser un bien affecté à un usage déterminé, par exemple *une somme destinée à l'achat de médicaments, d'appareils médicaux, fauteuil roulant etc.*, ou *un immeuble destiné à servir de lieu de villégiature aux salariés d'une entreprise.*[28]
>
> L'article 1269 vise ainsi les fiducies d'investissement en matière immobilière ou relatives à des valeurs mobilières, les fiducies établissant des fonds de retraite et autres fiducies à titre onéreux, de même que les fiducies constituées à l'occasion d'une émission d'obligations.[29]

The examples given in the *Commentaires du ministre* evoke classic cases in the common law jurisprudence and leave no doubt about the inspiration behind the different private trust categories. The first kind of private trust comes from the 'anomalous trust for purposes' of the common law ('dans le but d'ériger et d'entretenir un monument funéraire . . . ou encore d'assurer la survie des animaux préférés'). The second kind corresponds to *Quistclose* trusts ('une somme destinée à l'achat de médicaments, d'appareils médicaux, fauteuil roulant etc.') and *Denley* trusts ('un immeuble destiné à servir de lieu de villégiature aux salariés d'une entreprise'). The final kind corresponds to the various commercial trusts that have become commonplace in common law jurisdictions, including business trusts, special-purpose entities and collective investment vehicles.

Considerable overlap exists between the codal definitions of 'personal trust' and 'private trust'. Difficulties in classification occur when (a) a gratuitous trust has a 'purpose' which directly benefits identifiable individuals (such as a trust to provide for the education of the settlor's

[28] Quebec, Ministère de la justice, *Commentaires du ministre de la justice* (Quebec: Publications du Québec, 1993), vol. 1, p. 754 (*Commentaires du ministre*) (emphasis added).

[29] Ibid., p. 755.

descendants), or (b) it is not clear whether the trust has been established 'by onerous title'. A number of Quebec authors have discussed how to characterize such ambiguous trusts[30] and have even speculated on whether a trust can change its classification over time and/or be both 'personal' and 'private' simultaneously.[31] However, the courts have yet to provide any guidance on these matters and, as discussed above, it may take decades before they have occasion to do so.

The new definition of 'social trust' also creates ambiguity insofar as a trust can simultaneously advance some kind of 'general interest' while still 'securing a benefit for a determinate or determinable person' or 'using a thing for a particular purpose' – such as a building fund for a particular educational institution. The C.C.Q. provides for no hierarchy between the trust categories and, as in the case of private trusts, no clear line delineates where the personal or private trusts end and social trusts begin.[32]

III Relevance of common law classifications in Quebec

The common law has seen no shortage of cases on the classification of trusts that straddle the line between charitable and non-charitable, or

[30] The most complete discussion on characterizing gratuitous 'private' trusts that benefit identifiable individuals comes from Beaulne, who argues that classification of the trust requires the identification of its '*finalité*'. Does the beneficiary 'only benefit from the trust through realization of the trust purpose' (in which case the trust is private), or does the beneficiary 'himself represent the trust purpose' (in which case it is personal). Such characterization essentially constitutes a question of fact. (Beaulne, *Droit des fiducies*, above, note 3, pp. 110–12.)

In a similar vein, Bruneau has considered the question of 'onerous title', and has observed that trusts constituted through onerous title fall into three broad categories: (a) cases where the settlor receives something in return for setting up the trust, (b) cases where the beneficiaries buy into the trust, and (c) cases where the trust has the vocation to generate income and profits 'sur une base commerciale [plutôt que] personnelle'. By operation of art. 1269, such trusts necessarily qualify as 'private' regardless of whether they benefit identifiable individuals (Bruneau, 'La fiducie et le droit civil', above, note 5, 795–801).

See also McClean, 'The Trust in the Civil Code of Quebec', above, note 7, p. 94.

[31] Claxton, *Studies on the Quebec Law of Trust*, above, note 6, p. 108; L. Jeannotte and S. D'Aoust, 'La fiducie de protection du capital, de sa mise en place à sa liquidation', in *Cours de perfectionnement du Notariat* (Montreal: Chambres des notaires du Québec, 2005), para. 260, n. 205.

It is very difficult to see how a trust can be simultaneously personal and private, given that the C.C.Q. expressly states that a personal trust cannot last perpetually (C.C.Q. art. 1272) while a private trust can (C.C.Q. art. 1273).

[32] See Claxton, *Studies on the Quebec Law of Trust*, above, note 6, p. 105.

between trusts for persons and trusts for purposes. To the extent that the C.C.Q. trust categories trace their origins to common law trust categories, the common law jurisprudence can potentially offer useful guidance on trust categorization in Quebec.

As discussed above, the C.C.Q. social trust traces its origins to the common law charitable trust. A charitable trust must satisfy a two-part test: (a) it must confer a 'public benefit' and (b) its object(s) must fall exclusively into the nominate categories of charity. The C.C.Q. social trust has largely retained the first prong of this test ('a trust constituted for a purpose of general interest'), although it has not retained the second ('*such as* a cultural, educational, philanthropic, religious or scientific purpose').

Consequently, it stands to reason that the common law jurisprudence on the first prong of the test – namely, whether a putative charitable trust actually confers a 'public benefit' – should meaningfully inform the application of article 1270 C.C.Q. For example, common law courts in Canada and the United Kingdom have repeatedly held that trusts for the education of members of a particular family or for employees of a particular company do *not* provide a public benefit and thus do *not* qualify as charitable.[33] These cases would seem to provide persuasive authority for the proposition that such trusts likewise do not qualify as 'social trusts' under the C.C.Q.

That said, a question remains whether 'general interest' ('*intérêt général*') captures a slightly different scope of activity than 'public benefit'. In the common law, for example, trusts to promote political causes have been routinely found non-charitable primarily on the grounds that the Court cannot assess the 'benefit' such causes bring to the community.[34] A political charity, however, might pass a 'general interest' test more readily than a 'public benefit' test. It therefore remains to be seen whether a trust to promote a particular political point of view will qualify in Quebec as a social trust.[35]

The common law jurisprudence on the categories of charity offers more limited usefulness in the Quebec context. A trust to promote amateur sport, for example, might conceivably qualify as a social trust

[33] *Re Compton, Power* v. *Compton* [1945] 1 All ER 198 (CA), discussed in Oosterhoff, *Oosterhoff on Trusts*, above, note 9, pp. 395–6. See also Waters, *Waters' Law of Trusts*, above, note 9, pp. 743–6 and accompanying notes.

[34] *McGovern* v. *Attorney-General* [1981] 3 All ER 493 (Ch D). For a more complete review of jurisprudence, see Waters, *Waters' Law of Trusts*, above, note 9, p. 742; Oosterhoff, *Oosterhoff on Trusts*, above, note 9, pp. 398–401.

[35] Claxton, *Studies on the Quebec Law of Trust*, above, note 6, pp. 104–5.

in Quebec even though common law courts have traditionally found such trusts non-charitable for failing to fall into a nominate charitable category.[36] That said, Quebec jurists should not completely discount the common law jurisprudence on categories of charity, since it could indirectly contribute to the assessment of 'public interest'. A trust to promote the development and implementation of a new phonetic alphabet in Quebec, for example, could conceivably fail to qualify as a social trust on the grounds that it advances no genuine 'public interest', with *Re Shaw* serving as persuasive authority for the result if not the reason.

It bears note that a number of common law jurisdictions (particularly in Canada) have also started tentatively moving away from nominate categories of charity, viewing them more as simply examples of the kinds of trusts that confer a genuine public benefit.[37] For this reason, the decision to dispense with the nominate categories in the C.C.Q. may represent not so much a departure of the common law but more a reinterpretation of previous case law and an anticipation of how the law will be understood in the future.

Although the common law courts have repeatedly held that a charitable trust's objects must be exclusively charitable, no such language appears in article 1270 C.C.Q., potentially raising the question of whether a social trust can legitimately have a mixture of general and private objects. The common law jurisprudence would seem to provide persuasive authority that the phrase 'a purpose of general interest' includes an exclusivity element, although it remains to be seen whether the Quebec courts will emend article 1270 C.C.Q. accordingly.

Distinguishing a personal from a private trust requires a more nuanced analysis. The C.C.Q. private trust encompasses various kinds of trusts which clearly constitute trusts for persons in the common law. Consequently, although a trust to provide for the education of one's descendants incontrovertibly constitutes a 'trust for persons' under the common law, it does not immediately follow that it constitutes a 'personal trust' under the C.C.Q.

That said, it is important to remember that the private trust, as defined in articles 1268 and 1269 C.C.Q., represents an amalgam of four well-known kinds of trust that have long proven conceptually challenging and/or controversial in the common law: anomalous trusts for purposes

[36] Oosterhoff, *Oosterhoff on Trusts*, above, note 9, pp. 443–52.

[37] Ibid., p. 444; *Cassano* v. *Toronto-Dominion Bank*, 2009 CanLII 35732 (Ont Sup Ct), para. 27.

(graveyards and animals), trusts for a diffuse and variable class of beneficiaries (*Denley* trusts), trusts to make certain kinds of payments on behalf of the settlor (*Quistclose* trusts) and commercial trusts. A trust for the education of one's descendants does not fall into any of these broad groupings. To the contrary, such a trust presents absolutely no conceptual difficulty in the common law and exemplifies a discretionary trust for persons with the settlor's descendants as its objects. It stands to reason that such a trust should likewise constitute a 'personal trust' under article 1267 C.C.Q.[38]

IV The non-anomalous, non-charitable trust for purposes under the C.C.Q.

Parts II and III of this chapter traced the three C.C.Q. trust categories to their common law antecedents. A review of Figure 14.1, however, reveals one common law category which remains unaccounted for: the non-commercial, non-anomalous, non-charitable trust for purposes which, under the common law, is presumptively invalid. Is such a trust also invalid in Quebec, and if so, why?

By construction, such a trust could not constitute a social trust (since not charitable), a personal trust (since it lacks a beneficiary) or an article 1269 private trust (since not commercial). Such a trust, therefore, could only constitute an article 1268 private trust. A careful look at article 1268 C.C.Q., however, reveals that it contains internal limits in the words 'thing' ('*bien corporel*') and 'specific' ('*déterminé*'). Both of these words seem to import a certainty requirement; a private trust cannot have a completely abstract and imprecise purpose, but must relate to a tangible piece of property or else have a purpose identified with some degree of precision.

As Scott et al. have observed, the common law jurisprudence on trusts for purposes (including graves, animals, *Quistclose* and *Denley* trusts) can be essentially reconstrued as a specificity test. According to this theory, a trust for purposes only fails when the trust purpose is 'general and indefinite'.[39] Otherwise, the trustee holds the *corpus* on trust for the

[38] It also bears noting that such a trust would certainly have been lawful under the former Code, which only recognized what are now called trusts for persons. Indeed, perhaps the simplest way to distinguish a personal from a private trust is simply to ask whether the trust would have been allowed under the former Code. If 'yes', then the trust is personal; if 'no', then it must be private.

[39] Scott et al., *Scott and Ascher on Trusts*, above, note 18, vol. 2, p. 735.

settlor (or his heirs) with a *power* to spend trust funds in fulfilment of the specific purpose. Consistent with this theory, a number of common law jurisdictions (including Ontario, Alberta and British Columbia) have enacted legislation to the effect that a trust purpose, if articulated with sufficient specificity, is to be reconstrued as a power[40] – an approach also endorsed by the United States *Restatement (Third) of Trusts*.[41] Since under the common law, the validity of a power is subject to a certainty test,[42] a trust purpose which fails the power certainty test cannot be reconstrued as a power and thus precipitates the immediate failure of the trust.

Quebec doctrine and jurisprudence have paid scant attention to the question of uncertainty in trust formation[43] – which is particularly surprising given how prominently the issue features in common law trust theory.[44] However, it seems that the certainty test as developed by the common law courts could meaningfully inform the interpretation of 'specific' in article 1268 C.C.Q. If adopted, this approach would result

[40] Waters, *Waters' Law of Trusts*, above, note 9, p. 175. For example, in Ontario's Perpetuities Act, R.S.O. 1990, c. P.9, s. 16(1).

[41] American Law Institute, *Restatement of the Law Third: Trusts* (St Paul: American Law Institute Publications, 2003), vol. 2, s. 47.

[42] According to which the court must be able to 'say that a given application of the money does or does not fall within its terms' (*Twinsectra*, above, note 17, para. 16). See also *Russell*, above, note 11, paras. 30–5; *Dionisio* v. *Mancinelli* [2004] O.J. No. 4354 (S.C.J.) (review of jurisprudence); Waters, *Waters' Law of Trusts*, above, note 9, pp. 105–8.

[43] A body of doctrine and jurisprudence under the former Code considered wills that give executors and trustees the power to distribute, as they see fit, an estate among a class of heirs. Generally speaking, the jurisprudence evidenced a fairly permissive approach to evaluating whether such powers fail for uncertainty, upholding clauses instructing executors to distribute an estate 'to the poorest' or 'most needy' heir. However, in such cases, the courts have insisted either that (a) the trust be charitable, or (b) the *class of potential recipients* be identified with sufficient certainty (Claxton, *Studies on the Quebec Law of Trust*, above, note 6, pp. 284–96 (review of jurisprudence)). Given that a private trust under the C.C.Q. does not require a clearly identified class of potential recipients, this older jurisprudence would seem to have only limited relevance today.

[44] A number of authors (Brierley, 'De certains patrimoines d'affection', above, note 4, pp. 750–1; Claxton, *Studies on the Quebec Law of Trust*, above, note 6, pp. 393–4; Beaulne, *Droit des fiducies*, above, note 3, para. 77, n. 267) and a handful of cases (*Sécurité Saglac (1992) Inc. (Syndic de)* [1997] R.J.Q. 2448 at 2453 (CA); *Chibou-vrac inc. (Syndic de)* [2003] R.J.Q. 2809, 2821–3; *Ateliers Dominique inc. (Syndic de)* [1995] R.J.Q. 2165, 2173; *Multisens inc. (Syndic de)* [1995] R.J.Q. 1876, 1880; *Droit de la famille – 071938*, 2007 QCCS 3792, para. 49; *Laporte* v. *Lauzon*, 2007 QCCS 6226, n. 38) have opined that the 'three certainties' of the common law apply to Quebec trusts. However, as Beaulne has lamented, there is very little foundation in the C.C.Q. for saying so (Beaulne, *Droit des fiducies*, above, note 3, para. 77).

however, the combined effect of articles 1268 and 1273 C.C.Q. – which amorphously define the 'private trust' and endow it with perpetual existence – negates these principles entirely and arguably makes Quebec even more accepting than the common law has ever been of reserved property-holding.

There is no suggestion that the legislature ever intended such a radical reconceptualization of its property regime, and unless the legal community in Quebec adopts a more restrictive view on what kind of trusts can qualify as 'private', the private trust may well prove a particularly subversive institution. A greater awareness of and willingness to refer to the common law origins of the private trust can help set workable limits for the institution and keep it largely in line with its counterparts in other jurisdictions. It remains to be seen, however, whether such awareness and willingness will be forthcoming.

15

Why civil law countries might forego the individual trustee: provocative insights from the new-to-the-fold

IRIS J. GOODWIN

I Introduction

Over the last century a number of civil law countries have taken the bold step of adopting the common law trust, but have restricted the office of trustee to banks and similar financial service institutions. Having had an opportunity to consider the trust anew, these countries represent a challenge to the common law where the individual – indeed the untutored individual – can still qualify as trustee (and serve in this capacity alone). This permissive common law regime obtains notwithstanding the size of the trust endowment or the number of beneficiaries whose interests might be at stake. Indeed, in some common law countries individuals can qualify as trustee not only of a personal trust (for transmission of family wealth), but also of a pension trust holding assets under a retirement plan sponsored by a large employer, or even of an indenture for holders of significant corporate debt. While it may be a rare individual who would be nominated to serve in these latter situations, nothing in the law directly precludes an individual from qualifying as sole trustee of even these trusts.

That an untutored individual can still qualify as trustee in common law jurisdictions is especially interesting considering the movement over the last thirty years, spearheaded by the American academic bar,[1] to bring about a doctrinal reformation in the law of trusts and otherwise propel the trust into the modern era. One of the larger themes in this

[1] If led by the American academy, it was embraced in other jurisdictions. Regarding the change in the fiduciary standard of care from Prudent Man to Prudent Investor, for the history of the American doctrine, see, e.g., S. Sterk, 'Rethinking Trust Law Reform: How Prudent is Modern Prudent Investor Doctrine?' (2010) 95 *Cornell Law Review* 851. For the similar Canadian doctrine, see D. W. M. Waters et al., *Waters' Law of Trusts in Canada*, 4th edn (Toronto: Thomson Carswell, 2012), pp. 1006–9.

multi-faceted movement has been to recognize the trust in its essential identity as an investment vehicle, whether it is used as an instrument of commerce or for family wealth transmission. Part and parcel of this effort to usher the trust into the modern era has been the professionalization of the office of trustee. Nevertheless, scant attention has been paid in this literature to whom or what type of entity should be able to qualify as trustee. Rather, the effort to professionalize the office has largely centred on the duties incumbent upon the fiduciary (and, further, the status of these requirements as mandatory or default rules). And there is no doubt that evolving standards for the investing of trust assets coupled with widening discretion in choosing appropriate vehicles is to the uninitiated a powerful caveat. But the question raised for common law jurisdictions remains: if the goal is to professionalize the office of trustee, why continue to allow the untutored individual to qualify and, moreover, serve alone?

The decision by these civil law countries to preclude the individual from serving is provocative in deeper ways as well – ways that implicate fundamental aspects of this effort at doctrinal reformation by common law academics. While little attention has been paid in this literature to the prerequisites of the fiduciary office, the movement to see the trust into the modern era has hardly been neutral with respect to whom or what entity might be selected as trustee. In fact, at some level, this movement has lent new vitality to the individual trustee. Beyond the effort to secure the identity of the trust as an investment vehicle, this literature has set about to recover for the trust its historic role as a vehicle of innovation under the common law, in any era a device that can circumvent – even subvert – onerous and possibly dysfunctional aspects of the property regime.[2] To secure the trust in this historic dimension, this literature has sought to recast the weight of much legal authority away from the prevailing view: first, that the trust was an institution founded in property (so that the constitutive act was the transfer of assets from the property-holder to the trustee) and, second and as a corollary to the first, that the essential rules incumbent upon the trustee were mandatory rules.[3] This literature has offered instead a view of the trust as a creature of contract such that the constitutive act is an agreement between the settlor and the trustee and, again with a corollary as to the status of the rules, that virtually all the fundamental precepts of fiduciary duty are default rules, to be embraced or not in

[2] See Section IV below. [3] See Section IV below.

line with the settlor's agreement with the trustee. In this way, the trust is to be reinvigorated as a flexible and innovative device for the transfer and administration of property as the settlor exercises wide discretion in crafting trust terms.

But this new rubric harbours an implication with respect to the choice of a trustee: if the settlor is to exercise his freedom of contract to create a trust consistent with his preferences (potentially opening new avenues with respect to the stewardship of property), he must have a counterparty for whom his terms are congenial. In short, if the settlor is to craft the trust as he sees fit, he needs broad discretion in selecting a trustee. But further, as it works out, the magnitude of this discretion – and the potential for innovation – is likely to be larger if the settlor contracts with an individual trustee. As between an individual and a bank or other financial services institution, the settlor's latitude in negotiating trust terms is almost certainly greater with an individual trustee as a counterparty. Because financial services institutions are enmeshed in a regulatory framework that operates with an eye to the overall health of the institution as well as the larger banking sector, such institutions tend to be risk-averse, looking over their shoulders for that court that would adhere to some precept drawn from the regime of mandatory rules, even where the trust terms might invoke a different rubric. For this reason, banks and other financial services institutions often decline to serve as trustee where an agreement contains innovative terms, insisting instead on trust terms that, absent doctrinal reformation, align with rules long believed mandatory. From the settlor's perspective, where the terms of the trust are particularly innovative, the individual trustee winds up being not merely a choice, but a preferable one.

Securing this core capacity for innovation by reliance upon the individual trustee comes at a price, however. And it is this cost that is brought to the fore by statutes in those civil law countries that eliminate the individual trustee. Allowing the settlor to name an individual as trustee jeopardizes trust property by potentially subjecting it to the unprepared or unscrupulous. And while the risk attendant upon the settlor's discretion might be mitigated where the beneficiary can recover against the trustee upon breach of fiduciary duty, the potential for recovery is mitigated by the possibility (especially in the case of the individual trustee) that an errant trustee does not have the resources to make the trust whole. If banks and other financial institutions are embedded in a regulatory apparatus, that apparatus is calculated to ensure capital resources against which an aggrieved beneficiary can recover.

But those civil law countries that allow only a bank or similar financial service institution to qualify also pay a price. If there is a trade-off between capacity for innovation and security of trust assets, what adopting jurisdictions gain in predictability and institutionalized accountability by restricting the fiduciary office to regulated entities must be set off against lost flexibility in a vehicle for the management of wealth for which flexibility is a primary appeal. While there is an increased likelihood of recovery against the errant trustee where the trustee is a regulated entity, such a regime effectively becomes a creature of mandatory rules and the trusts that emerge from it will almost inevitably be formulaic. Any innovation with respect to the trust itself must then emanate from the state regulatory authority, as the initiative of private individuals is rendered nugatory. But further, when the donor's options in drafting trust terms are limited, the trust loses that historic potential, where aspects of the property regime have grown untimely, to draw upon individual initiative to challenge and indeed circumvent dysfunctional elements.

The discussion in this chapter is in three sections. Section II centres on the common law requirements for undertaking the office of trustee and focuses on the fundamental rules and doctrines that are constitutive of the fiduciary office. This inquiry lays the groundwork to appreciate the hold that the individual trustee continues to exert over the common law imagination. Section III turns to laws recently adopted in certain civil law jurisdictions that preclude the individual from qualifying and instead require a bank or other regulated entity to serve in the office. This resistance to the individual trustee is considered against the background of an historical distaste for the trust in the civil law. Section IV returns to the common law and surveys aspects of the American literature of doctrinal reformation where the permissive posture of the common law with respect to the individual trustee stands unchallenged. This literature of reform indicates that there are deep normative biases in the common law that underpin the continued vitality of the individual trustee there.

II The common law requirements of the fiduciary office

The hold that the individual trustee exerts over the common law imagination has historical roots and survives into this era in doctrines that remain constitutive of the fiduciary office. To qualify as a common law trustee, the candidate must have two fundamental legal capacities. First, the would-be fiduciary needs to be capable of the full sweep of legal agency attendant upon fee simple ownership. Second, the trustee must be of a character such that he can be responsive in equity.

A. *Fundamental requirements of the common law fiduciary office*

Owner in fee simple. Under the common law, the trust itself has never been deemed a legal person and, accordingly, the trust (as distinct from the trustee) has never been able to effectuate any legal act.[4] Indeed, as the trust has developed under the common law, the entire edifice came to hang on the legal persona of the trustee and, specifically, his capacity to act with respect to the property as a fee simple owner. For this reason, the common law has demanded that the would-be occupant of the fiduciary office meet several requirements calculated to ensure the officeholder the full sweep of legal agency attendant upon fee simple ownership.[5] These requirements appear in all the common law commentaries but they are perhaps most concisely put forth in the American treatises. For example, both Bogert and Scott summarize these fundamental necessities in a threefold requisite for the office:[6] first, with respect to any property that is to be transferred into the trust, the would-be trustee must be able to take title; second, assuming title can pass, this candidate must be able to hold the title that has been received; and third, going forward, the would-be trustee must be able to administer the property in the trust.[7]

4 While the trustee may be a corporate entity, the transfer of property in trust to a trustee – be it an individual or a corporation – does not create a corporation or any other entity deemed a person under the law. See F. W. Maitland et al., *Equity, also The Forms of Action at Common Law: Two Courses of Lectures* (Cambridge University Press, 1929).

5 G. G. Bogert et al., *The Law of Trusts and Trustees*, 3rd edn (St Paul: Thomson West, 2006; supplement 2009), para. 125.

6 For the requirements under English law, see D. J. Hayton, *Underhill and Hayton: Law Relating to Trusts and Trustees*, 16th edn (London: Butterworths, 2003), art. 13 at p. 268 ('Who may be a settlor or trustee. Every person, male or female, married or unmarried, human or corporate, who has power to hold and dispose of any legal or equitable estate or interest in property can create a trust in respect thereof, and can be a trustee thereof.'). For English law, see also J. Mowbray et al., *Lewin on Trusts*, 18th edn (London: Thomson Sweet & Maxwell, 2008), p. 31. For Canadian common law, see Waters et al., *Law of Trusts in Canada*, above, note 1, pp. 121–3.

7 M. L. Ascher et al., *Scott and Ascher on Trusts*, 5th edn (New York: Aspen Publishers, 2006; supplement 2009), para. 11.1; see also *Restatement (Third) of Trusts*, 4 vols. (St Paul: American Law Institute, 2003–12), para. 32(b): 'A person who lacks capacity to contract or make a conveyance ... cannot serve in a capacity, because such a person cannot properly fulfill the duties of a fiduciary ... ' Of course, there may be additional statutory requirements in any particular jurisdiction.

At a practical level, these distinctions, first between taking title and holding it and then between holding title and administering the property, seem needlessly subtle. But these three requisites of the office speak to doctrines and statutes from diverse areas of the law that govern aspects of legal capacity integral to exercising the legal agency entailed in fee simple ownership. They also reflect the nuanced view that the law takes with respect to legal capacity for some persons. For example, neither infants[8] nor the insane[9] have been able to qualify as trustee because contracts or deeds made by such persons can be voided.[10] This means that, while an infant or an insane person can receive and hold property, such a person will inevitably encounter obstacles in administering this property. At an earlier point in history, aliens could not qualify as trustee because, while they were able to take title to real property, they could not hold it against the sovereign.[11] Similarly, until the advent of the Married Women's Property Act, a married woman could receive property but she could not hold it against her husband (or more specifically, his creditors).[12]

Responsive in equity. So much does the legal operation of the trust depend on the legal persona of the trustee (expressed as a fee simple owner) that the test for the requisite capacity is whether the trustee can take, hold and administer property *for his own benefit*. And there's the rub. While the edifice of the trust is erected on the trustee's fee simple capacity to act for his own benefit, there is an agreement appurtenant to the transfer of property from the settlor to the trustee stipulating that this agency in all its potential is to be exercised for the benefit of someone else, the beneficiary. Once this beneficial interest is introduced and made the object of the trust, erecting this trust on the trustee's fee simple right would appear to create little else than a ready instrument of exploitation.[13]

[8] Ascher et al., *Scott and Ascher on Trusts*, above, note 7, para. 11.1.1; Bogert et al., *Law of Trusts and Trustees*, above, note 5, para. 127; Hayton, *Law Relating to Trusts and Trustees*, above, note 6, p. 269; Mowbray et al., *Lewin on Trusts*, above, note 6, p. 33.

[9] Ascher et al., *Scott and Ascher on Trusts*, above, note 7, para. 11.1.2; Hayton, *Law Relating to Trusts and Trustees*, above, note 6, p. 269.

[10] Bogert et al., *Law of Trusts and Trustees*, above, note 5, para. 127.

[11] Ibid., para. 126.

[12] Of course, even if the person named as trustee does not have capacity to take title, the intended trust does not fail, but the court will simply appoint someone to serve who can qualify. Ascher et al., *Scott and Ascher on Trusts*, above, note 7, para. 11.1; Bogert et al., *Law of Trusts and Trustees*, above, note 5, para. 126; Mowbray et al., *Lewin on Trusts*, above, note 6, p. 33; Waters et al., *Law of Trusts in Canada*, above, note 1, p. 114.

[13] R. A. Pearce and J. Stevens, *The Law of Trusts and Equitable Obligations*, 3rd edn (London: Butterworths, 2002), p. 683.

The common law provides an antidote, however:[14] for the person who would qualify as a trustee, there is an additional requirement layered on to the necessary capacity in fee simple. As important as is the legal ability to take, hold and administer property in fee simple, the trustee must also be capable of embracing a standard of meticulous probity anchored in the jurisdiction of the court of equity and the jurisprudence spawned there. In short, to forestall the potential for abuse, the common law again looks to the trustee, but this time to predicate the trust not merely on his legal persona, but on his moral persona as well. The common law trustee must not merely be amenable but, most importantly, he must be susceptible to the subtle supervision of the court of equity – to be willing and able to exercise his right of fee simple subject to standards particularly attuned to evaluating the exercise of discretion. The court of equity will supervise only those that are amenable to its supervision. In this way, the trustee's fee simple discretion is not attenuated, but rather any potentially self-serving purposes for which this discretion might be exercised are redirected, courtesy of the agreement between the settlor and the trustee and subject to the supervision of the court.[15] This equitable oversight gives rise to the beneficiary's unique right, one that runs not against the trust property (such as to diminish the trustee's fee simple interest), but against the trustee personally.

[14] The contemporary legal imagination can conjure up various alternative ways of conceiving the office of trustee and the relationship between the trustee and the beneficiary, any of which would avoid or at least mitigate this potential for abuse. For various reasons, alternative formulations did not materialize when the trust was in its nascence. While the common law could have vested the beneficiary with a legal right in the trust property, the venerable Frederic Maitland argues that such a right would almost certainly have had to have been grounded in the contract between the settlor and the trustee (for which the beneficiary could have been conceived a third-party beneficiary), but that the common law contract was itself nascent in this period and was thus limited in ways that precluded founding the trust in the contract: Maitland et al., *Equity*, above, note 4, pp. 28–30. In the alternative, the common law could have subjected trustees to intense, perhaps day-by-day, regulatory scrutiny (something now done in the case of charitable and pension trusts which exist for important public purposes). But again, in the era in which the trust developed, the apparatus of government was not sufficiently mature to render such oversight: ibid., pp. 29–30.

[15] This requirement of probity is coupled with draconian remedies that operate to deprive a trustee of any gain made through abuse of his position. See Pearce and Stevens, *Law of Trusts and Equitable Obligations*, above, note 13, p. 686.

This requisite moral agency has been famously rendered rhapsodic in the phrase, 'a punctilio of an honor the most sensitive'.[16] Historically, this moral agency has operated as a categorical disqualification for certain individual candidates whose lives bespoke a lack of rectitude – like felons and bankrupts. And there are common law jurisdictions that still prohibit felons from qualifying.[17] But even those that do not exclude particular categories of people as inherently unfit continue to reserve discretion in the court to deny appointment to individuals that are deemed to be fundamentally unsuitable, including the dishonest, the improvident, and candidates with other defects of character suggesting that they will not be amenable to equitable supervision.[18]

B. Corporations as trustees

Throughout much of the history of the common law trust, corporations have been unable to qualify as trustees. The essential attributes deemed to inhere in those individual candidates that succeeded in qualifying for the fiduciary office – the full sweep of agency attendant on fee simple ownership together with a capacity to be responsive in equity – were found lacking in corporations. In the early centuries of the trust, judges refused to allow a corporation to be seized to a 'use' (the aboriginal common law trust) because, while a corporation could take title to property, it could not, consistent with its corporate purposes, hold and administer it in trust. In that event, attempting to do so was inevitably an *ultra vires* act. As an artificial person in the law, the corporation had no capacity to act beyond those express objects set forth in its charter (plus any implied powers incidental to the realization of these express purposes).[19] And early in the history of the corporation purposes tended to be specific and, read narrowly, they precluded the holding and administering of property in trust. Further, beyond the limitations emanating from a corporate charter, some judges resisted the idea that a corporation could be responsive in equity.

[16] But within the jurisprudence of equity, this 'punctilio of an honor' consists in far more than mere moral finesse, and has been rendered legally choate in the duties of loyalty and prudence. See *Meinhard* v. *Salmon*, 249 NY 458, 164 NE 545 at 546 (N.Y. 1928).

[17] New York Surrogate's Court Procedure Act § 707(1)(d) (McKinney 2010) [NYSCPA].

[18] NYSCPA § 707(1)(e); see also Uniform Trust Code § 706 (2006) [UTC]. In addition to the draconian tort remedies (see above, note 15), some abuses, particularly the misappropriation of trust property, constitute criminal offences. See Pearce and Stevens, *Law of Trusts and Equitable Obligations*, above, note 13, p. 685.

[19] Hayton, *Law Relating to Trusts and Trustees*, above, note 6, pp. 270–2.

The corporation was deemed a 'dead body' and, as such, could not be made subject to the *in personam* jurisdiction of a court of equity.[20]

By the eighteenth century, however, judicial rhetoric about the corporation being a 'dead body' with its implications with respect to equitable jurisdiction was set aside.[21] And the constraints of the narrowly drawn corporate charter were a problem that abated in the late nineteenth century. At that point a movement emerged to lessen the legislative strictures on corporations so that they ceased to be created for stipulated and narrow purposes but the grant of authority became typically broad.[22] Then, whether a corporation had the capacity to hold and administer property in trust came to turn on whether the trust according to its terms furthered the purposes of the corporation as set out in its charter and whether the essential endeavours undertaken were consistent with the charter (and other constitutive documents).[23] So, for example, as the jurisprudence moved forward here, it was readily apparent that a corporation could, consistent with its corporate charter, serve as trustee of a trust holding retirement funds or otherwise benefiting employees.[24]

C. *Fiduciary regulation*

But even if a broad grant of authority might address per se reservations with respect to the corporate trustee, in many common law jurisdictions corporate trustees have yet to obtain an equal footing with the individual trustee when it comes to qualifying for the office. This is because, a broad grant of authority notwithstanding, corporations remain creatures of legislative grace and, where a corporation would qualify as trustee, regulatory requirements for the office potentially overlay those the common law imposes. In some common law jurisdictions this regulatory authority has been particularly exigent for corporations that would enter

[20] Bogert et al., *Law of Trusts and Trustees*, above, note 5, para. 131.

[21] Ascher et al., *Scott and Ascher on Trusts*, above, note 7, para. 11.1.6.

[22] See J. D. Cox and T. L. Hazen, *Cox & Hazen on Corporations*, 2nd edn (New York: Aspen Publishers, 2003), ss. 2.02–2.06.

[23] The nature of the property to be held in trust could also present a stumbling block under the charter of the would-be corporate trustee: Bogert et al., *Law of Trusts and Trustees*, above, note 5, para. 131; see also *Restatement (Third) of Trusts*, above, note 7, para. 33: 'A corporation has capacity to take and hold property in trust except as limited by law, and to administer trust property and act as trustee to the extent of the powers conferred upon it by law.'

[24] Hayton, *Law Relating to Trusts and Trustees*, above, note 6, pp. 270–2.

into the business of being a trustee. Indeed, where common law jurisdictions have come to differ quite significantly is in the degree to which they subject to regulation corporations conducting a fiduciary business. For these professional corporate trustees, the additional requirements of office are calculated to ensure solvency as well as other elements of fiduciary integrity – appropriate risk management (including investment of trust assets), custody of assets, segregation of assets, and liability of bank property with respect to trust losses.[25] Note that, however reasonable such requirements might be, given the opportunity for abuse inherent in the trust, individual trustees have never been subjected to such *ex ante* supervision. Typically in common law jurisdictions, if individual trustees are supervised at all, it occurs after the fact, upon breach of fiduciary duty, when the errant trustee is held accountable pursuant to tort standards by disgruntled beneficiaries either in court or in negotiations occurring under the threat of litigation.[26]

Jurisdictions within the United States regulate corporations engaging in the business of being a trustee. In these jurisdictions, such corporations must have 'trust powers' which can be acquired only as a term (express or implied) of a bank or trust company charter.[27] Chartering occurs either at the state or the federal level, but in every instance requires that the institution meet and maintain certain capital requirements. For banks chartered at the state level, it is the legislature in the state where the bank has its principal place of business that authorizes the corporation to enter into the banking business in that state and (if trust powers are sought) to offer fiduciary services to the public there. States can also charter trust companies.[28]

[25] 12 Code of Federal Regulations § 9.13(a) (2010) [CFR] requires that, with respect to each trust account, investments shall be kept separate from the assets of the bank and shall be placed in the joint custody or control of the bank with officers in control of these assets adequately bonded.

[26] For consideration of this issue in the English context, see A. Hudson, 'The Regulation of Trustees', in M. Dixon et al., *Contemporary Perspectives on Property, Equity and Trusts Law* (Oxford University Press, 2007), p. 163.

[27] In order to protect the public, it is now often provided by statute that only corporations authorized to do a trust business can use the words 'trust' or 'trustee' in their corporate names. See Bogert et al., *Law of Trusts and Trustees*, above, note 5, para. 131.

[28] While state-chartered banks typically offer services as trustee alongside a larger package of banking services (checking and savings accounts, lending, investment vehicles, etc.), state-chartered trust companies are chartered for the purpose of administering trusts and other fiduciary relationships with banking services available as ancillary offerings: ibid., para. 136.

Banks can also be chartered at the federal level in the United States, historically under the Federal Reserve Act, under which approval could be granted for undertaking trust services (in addition to banking activities).[29] In 1962, this authority was transferred to the Comptroller of the Currency,[30] who now promulgates rules and otherwise supervises the exercise of trust powers by national banks under Regulation 9.[31] In exercising trust powers, national banks must segregate trust property and comply with state regulations regarding the deposit of securities, filing of bond, etc., so far as these requirements are also laid down for state banks and trust companies in the state.[32] Where conduct is continuously improper, the Comptroller can revoke a national bank's authority to provide trust services.[33]

In the United States, this regulatory framework has operated to allow banks and state-chartered trust companies to edge out non-bank corporations that would engage in the business of being a trustee.[34] A well-known

[29] Until 1962, regulatory authority with respect to nationally chartered banks arose under the Federal Reserve Act of 1913 that, pursuant to Regulation F, authorized national banks to act as trustees (among other banking services): Federal Reserve Act of 1913 § 11(k), 12 United States Code § 248(k) (1913) [USC] (repealed 1962).

[30] 12 *United States Code Annotated* (St Paul: West Group, 2010), § 92a [USCA].

[31] 12 CFR §§ 9.1–9.101 (2010) [Reg. 9].

[32] 12 USCA § 9(c), (f)–(g). If the laws of the state in which the national bank is located permit the exercise of trust powers by state banks or trust companies, the granting to and exercise of a power to act by a national bank are not deemed in contravention of state law: Bogert et al., *Law of Trusts and Trustees*, above, note 5, para. 134.

[33] This can be done without going into court at the state level and asking a court of equity to remove the trustee: 12 USCA § 9(c), (f)–(g).

[34] The regulatory framework surrounding the United States banking industry has been in flux for two decades. The goal has been to deregulate the industry 'to eliminate statutory and regulatory barriers that segmented the banking industry between commercial banks and thrift institutions and that created a noncompetitive environment between these industry segments'. J. J. Norton, 'The 1982 Banking Act and the Deregulation Scheme' (1983) 38 *Business Lawyer* 1627. Under the 1980 Omnibus Banking Act, federal savings and loan associations were authorized to make application to the Federal Home Loan Banking Board to secure trust powers: Depository Institutions Deregulation and Monetary Control Act of 1980 § 403 (Pub. L. No. 96–221, 94 Stat. 132) [DIDMCA] (codified as amended in scattered sections of 12 USC and 15 USC). A federal savings and loan association may be authorized to exercise trust and fiduciary powers. See 12 USCA § 1464. By DIDMCA § 704, the provisions of the national banking laws regarding the power of the Comptroller to revoke trust powers for the unlawful or unsound exercise of powers or for failure to exercise powers were amended. See 12 USCA § 92a (developments authorizing interstate banking). Further, savings banks and savings or savings and loan associations have recently become eligible by statute to act as trustees. See Bogert et al., *Law of Trusts and Trustees*, above, note 5, para. 135; see also 12 USCA § 1464(a).

exception to this stranglehold can be found in Massachusetts where corporations – 'limited purpose trust companies' – may conduct trust and fiduciary business where the commissioner of banking is 'satisfied that public convenience and advantage will be promoted and that competition among banking institutions will not be unreasonably affected'. Other state statutes afford the commissioner of banking or such other state official similar discretion, but such authorities in other states are typically unable to satisfy themselves that the introduction of these non-bank trustees will indeed serve 'public convenience and advantage.'[35]

In Canada, corporations in the business of being a trustee are also subject to a highly restrictive regulatory regime, but not via the banking laws. Historically, in Canada neither banks nor insurance companies have been permitted to enter into the business of being a trustee. Instead, Canada has regulated those corporations that would enter into this business as special purpose financial companies, institutions peculiar to Canada and known as 'trust companies'. These requirements for corporations that would serve as trustee still obtain.[36] Any Canadian trust company is subject to the jurisdiction of both federal authorities and those provincial authorities where the trust company is incorporated.[37]

Until quite recently, England and Wales have had an exceedingly liberal regulatory regime where corporate trustees are concerned. In fact, in England and Wales (which are effectively one regime for purposes of the law of trusts and trustees), there has been no requirement either of registration or of licensure. A corporation that is neither a bank nor a trust company has been able to enter into the business of being a trustee of personal trusts for members of the public without being subject to any regulatory regime. This liberal regime endures, with the exception of two recent statutory additions – first, the Financial Services and Markets Act 2000 and, second, the Money Laundering Regulations 2007 (Statutory Instrument 2007 No. 2157). The Financial Services Act introduces only modest burdens into the enduring liberal regime. First, the 2000 Act

[35] See for example *Massachusetts General Laws Annotated* (Massachusetts: West, 2010), ch. 172, § 9A.

[36] Waters et al., *Law of Trusts in Canada*, above, note 1, pp. 125–6. Regulatory changes and market pressure in recent years have resulted in discretionary fiduciary services being provided primarily by trust companies that are subsidiaries of banks. Independent trust companies, while still an important part of the market for discretionary fiduciary services, are much less significant than they were in the past.

[37] Ibid.

applies only to a trustee that engages in investing, requiring that this trustee be authorized to undertake this activity and then be subject to a regulatory regime administered by the Financial Services Authority (which is created under this Act).[38] This statute would appear to apply to virtually any professional trustee, as any professional trustee effectively holds itself out as offering investment management as part and parcel of being a professional trustee. Nevertheless, a corporate trustee can avoid the 2000 Act if it does not hold itself out as offering investment services and does not receive remuneration for investment services in addition to fees charged for serving as trustee. What must be avoided is seeking to draw business to the corporation by advertising expertise in investments. And the second exception may be satisfied if the corporate fiduciary only takes its fees as a percentage of assets under management.[39]

The 2007 Money Laundering Regulations require only that a corporate trustee register with Her Majesty's Revenue & Customs, an agency that has discretion to reject entities deemed at risk with respect to money laundering activities or terrorist financing. The 2007 Act can also be satisfied by registering with the Financial Services Authority created under the Financial Services and Markets Act 2000 (treated in the preceding paragraph). The Regulations impose due diligence measures, monitoring and record-keeping requirements, all of which facilitate the monitoring of sources and recipients of funds.

D. Continued appeal of the individual trustee under the common law

The common law fiduciary office was developed on the legal persona of the individual. But if at some point the common law doctrines governing the fiduciary office have matured in such a way as to permit the corporation to qualify, the individual trustee has in no way been legally jettisoned or even sidelined in the course of these changes. There are multi-layered reasons that the individual trustee endures in common law jurisdictions and the deepest of these will be addressed in Section IV of this chapter.

[38] The specific language is 'deals in investments or arranges deals in investments or manages investment or safeguards and administers assets belonging to another': Financial Services and Markets Act 2000, c. 8 (UK).

[39] See D. J. Hayton, *Underhill and Hayton: Law Relating to Trusts and Trustees*, 17th edn (London: Lexis Nexis/Butterworths, 2007; supplement 2009), pp. 271–2. For consideration of this issue in the English context, see Hudson, 'The Regulation of Trustees', above, note 26.

At this juncture, however, suffice it to note that, for certain settlors, because the corporate trustee is almost certain to be regulated *ex ante*,[40] the appeal of the individual trustee has endured. While regulation *ex ante* may remove certain risks to beneficiaries (particularly the risk of the insolvent trustee),[41] settlors attracted to the flexibility of the trust and seeking wide discretion in crafting trust terms often have reason, when choosing a trustee, to avoid financial services institutions enmeshed in a regulatory framework.[42] When asked to serve under trust agreements with innovative terms, such institutions tend to be risk-averse and fear liability with respect to duties considered (by some lights) to inhere in the office even where the trust agreement, consistent with innovative terms, directs otherwise.[43] In the individual trustee, the common law continues to afford the settlor a comparatively free hand and, as we shall see in Section IV, secures the long-standing innovative potential of the trust where fundamental property norms are concerned.

III The civil law trustee

In contrast to the common law where the individual remains the quintessential trustee, civil law jurisdictions that have adopted the common law trust over the last sixty or so years evidence a clear preference not merely for the corporate trustee, but a corporate trustee subject to regulation *ex ante*, such as a bank or insurance company. But to the extent that this apparent distaste for the individual trustee might constitute a challenge to the common law, it is instructive to locate this civil law

[40] Certain common law jurisdictions have of late seen the advent of trust companies that are exempt from regulation (in the United States, these are state-chartered entities). These new entities are not addressed in the body of this article because, as they are restricted to serving only a related group of people, they remain a relatively minor phenomenon and, further, their appeal to settlors validates the larger argument of this piece. In establishing a 'family trust company,' settlors are seeking to use the corporate form to minimize the liability of the trustee without losing the discretion that the unregulated individual trustee has long afforded the settlor. See I. J. Goodwin, 'How the Rich Stay Rich: Using a Family Trust Company to Secure a Family Fortune' (2010) 40 Seton Hall L. Rev. 467.

[41] C. Harrington and R. M. Harding, 'Private Trust Companies and Family Offices: What Every Estate Planner Needs to Know', in *Sophisticated Estate Planning Techniques: ALI-ABA Course of Study Materials* (Philadelphia, Penn.: American Law Institute–American Bar Association, 2008), p. 689.

[42] See Goodwin, 'How the Rich Stay Rich', above, note 40, 487–8.

[43] See Section IV.D below.

preference in the context of the long-standing and quite fundamental ideological discomfort with the trust.

A. Historical discomfort

As a prelude to considering the particulars of the civil law challenge to the common law on the point of the individual trustee, it is worth noting that for centuries now the civil law has exhibited considerable discomfort with the trust itself. In particular, the civil law has shown discomfort with bifurcated ownership as well as the attendant successive beneficial substitutions that commonly occur within any property settlement (like the trust) lasting multiple decades.[44] This chapter suggests that, where the choice of a trustee is concerned, any civil law predilection for an entity regulated *ex ante* bespeaks a continuing discomfort with the trust in general, a discomfort that bespeaks certain core principles embedded in the civil law, especially with respect to property. These ideas came to the fore in the legal reforms of the French Revolution, ideas that, in the wake of the Revolution, were exported via the *Code Napoléon*, first to European countries occupied by the French during the Revolution and later to regions throughout the world as these areas were subjected to colonial rule by European countries.

Whether the civil law could have ultimately produced an institution equivalent to the common law trust remains a matter of some controversy.[45] There is no doubt that, with a binary judicial system, England provided especially fertile ground for the realization of this particular institution in all its vitality. The dual judicial apparatus of common law courts standing side-by-side with courts of equity made for two distinct forms of pleadings, each ultimately recognizing two distinct but coextensive types of ownership embedded in the trust.[46] Nevertheless, under the Roman law (the precursor to the civil law in Continental Europe), there

[44] This discomfort is of a piece with the legendary early twentieth-century story where the illustrious common law scholar Frederic Maitland attempted to explain the trust to the equally illustrious civil law scholar Otto von Gierke only to have the great German jurist confess that the idea still made no sense to him. Maitland recounts the story and clearly takes it to be evidence of the uniqueness of the trust, a validation of the trust as a quintessentially common law institution. Maitland, *Equity*, above, note 4, pp. 23–4.

[45] For a subtle view of the civil law tradition, see V. Bolgar, 'Why No Trusts in the Civil Law?' (1952) 2 Am. J. Comp. L. 204; see also F. Weiser, *Trusts on the Continent of Europe* (London: Sweet & Maxwell, 1936).

[46] N. Malumian, *Trusts in Latin America* (Oxford University Press, 2009), p. xxvi.

did emerge certain agency relationships and other types of transfers similar at least to the common law trust in its early, medieval guise. Like the nascent common law trust, these Roman law stratagems operated as measures of limited application, devised to circumvent laws limiting disposition at death or (with respect to the Roman law in particular) to navigate idiosyncratic circumstances not contemplated within the governing legal rubrics. For example, under the Roman *fideicommissum*,[47] if a transfer to a particular donee was proscribed (such as a transfer to a foreigner), a donor could make the transfer instead to a third party with a direction to convey the property at the donor's death to the designated recipient.[48] Of course, consistent with the primitive simplicity of this particular finesse, the intended recipient of the property had no legal recourse in the event the property was not delivered.[49]

None of these Roman law stratagems ever developed sufficiently as a legal institution to invite – like the mature common law trust – the management of significant wealth over an extended period on behalf of diverse legal interests with respect to the assets. Nevertheless, by the eighteenth century, the French aristocracy had made the most of a stratagem akin to the Roman *fideicommissum*, what in this later era was termed the *substitution fidéicommissaire* – a gift to one person with an understanding that he convey it to a third – to entail property over multiple generations. But as the French often employed the *substitution*, the initial transferee had ceased to be a strawman (as was the case with the Roman law *fideicommissum*), but was a bona fide recipient in his own right – at least for his lifetime. Typically, the *paterfamilias* transferred his patrimony to his eldest son on condition that the son transfer it to his firstborn son and so on. The nobility used the *substitution* in this way to sustain the institution of primogeniture, ensuring thereby that wealth remained concentrated in aristocratic hands.

Whether the *substitution* would have continued to develop into something akin to the full-blown common law trust is hard to know. With the French Revolution, *substitutions* (and by implication, similar institutions such as the common law trust) became anathema in the civil law.

47 W. W. Buckland and A. D. McNair, *Roman Law and Common Law* (Cambridge University Press, 1952), 173ff.

48 In a similar vein were the *fiducia* and the *pactum fiduciae*. In the case of the *fiducia* there was actually a transfer of property to a party who had an obligation (based on trust) to transfer the property to a third party after a period of time had passed or a condition was met, ibid., p. 177.

49 Ibid.

In 1792 the Legislative Assembly prohibited such arrangements as undermining the pursuit of equality throughout the larger body politic.[50] To ensure the appropriate legal underpinnings to a bourgeois republic, the Revolution put in place a property regime in which transparency with respect to title was key. Ownership was co-extensive with the legal interest of that person who had an immediate right to the asset (for example, to be on the land).[51] The simplicity of this regime ensured that someone was always legally empowered to transfer the property and, further, that this person was readily discoverable. Land could come into the stream of commerce where it could change hands frequently like any other asset. The new property regime fostered equality by quite literally cutting the ground from feudalism.[52]

When the *Code Napoléon* was drafted, this prohibition against *substitution* (with the attendant distaste for the common law trust) deeply informed the precepts of law promulgated there. This attitude was exported to countries occupied by the French during the Napoleonic Wars. Influence spread further as French, Spanish and Portuguese colonies around the world tracked the French canons in drafting their own codes at independence. Finally, the influence of the *Code Napoléon* became virtually global as modernizing non-Western countries with little historical connection to Continental Europe – indeed, some of them former British colonies[53] – modelled their statutes on the civil law. At a premium in these modernizing countries has been a legal system characterized by lucid precepts solidly grounded in the legitimating provenance of a democratically elected legislature. Such nascent polities could scarcely afford the luxury of a legal system such as the historic common law, maturing by accretion over decades, even centuries, as judges layered one nuanced, fact-intensive holding upon another. In these jurisdictions this quest for legal simplicity further militated against the trust, a creature of seeming legal contradictions, a rich stew of apparent incompatibles predicated upon the competing jurisdictions of law and equity.

[50] The Civil Code codified the proscription at article 896. See R. Hyland, *Gifts* (Oxford University Press, 2009), paras. 448–50. As Hyland notes, there were a number of exceptions: ibid.; see also P. Matthews, 'The French *Fiducie*: And Now for Something Completely Different?' (2007) 21 *Trust Law International* 17.

[51] 'Cultural Variations on Property Law' in F. H. Lawson (ed.), *Encyclopedia of Comparative Law* (New York: Oceana, 1978), vol. VI, para. 10.

[52] Hyland, *Gifts*, above, note 50.

[53] See Section III.A above.

B. *The trust nevertheless*

Whatever civil law norms with respect to the institution of property might be, however, from early in the twentieth century, civil law jurisdictions have struggled to reconcile the essential elements of the trust with these fundamental principles as a first step to assimilating this quintessential common law institution.[54] Any discomfort with the trust notwithstanding, in the twentieth century civil law jurisdictions began to discern its significant utility. First, while there are a few essential rights and obligations with respect to property that must be present for a structure to be deemed a trust, few devices for holding and administering property are so flexible as to form as the trust. In establishing a trust, a settlor has enormous discretion in formulating managerial duties and creating beneficial rights. And as modern economies saw increasingly sophisticated forms of intangible property, this flexibility made the trust an attractive device to hold such interests, for purposes of making intra-family transfers of wealth but also for myriad other purposes. Indeed, in a significant number of civil law jurisdictions, the trust became an expedient to utilize in securitizing certain assets, making it a vehicle for the creation of such complex financial instruments.[55] Second, if the requisites to formation are minimal, once the trust is formed, its terms are almost impossible to change (absent authority in the contract or application to court or some supervisory authority). Such legal barriers to reformation offer settlors assurance of desired outcomes, especially for any trust the object of which can be realized only over an extended period of time. The trust thus stands in marked contrast to the corporation where the imprimatur of the state is a prerequisite to formation and many terms (such as certain shareholders' rights) can be required. And once a corporation is established, corporate boards can have a much freer hand in altering corporate purposes.

Of course, the challenge for these jurisdictions has been, without positing the concurrent jurisdictions of law and equity or otherwise relying on judicial nuance, to draw together into one legal rubric the nexus of very minimal but altogether essential interests and obligations with respect to property that together make the trust. The civil law has

[54] The history of the reception varied jurisdiction by jurisdiction. With respect to Mexico, see for example R. M. Pasquel, 'The Mexican Fideicomiso: The Reception, Evolution and Present Status of the Common Law Trust in a Civil Law Country' (1969) 8 Colum. J. Transnat'l L. 54.

[55] Malumian, *Trusts in Latin America*, above, note 46, ch. 3, 'Securitization'.

struggled, without violating its fundamental principle with respect to unity of title, to render a legal account of the authority of the trustee holding and disposing of property subject to terms stipulated by the settlor, terms that typically vest beneficiaries with rights with respect to trust property. (Indeed, in this vein beneficiaries must be able to hold trustees accountable for misapplied assets and in particular they must be legally empowered to pursue trust property which has been transferred in breach of trust.) Further, this empowerment of the trustee must be expressed in such a way as not to jeopardize the autonomy of the trust estate: the property conveyed to the trustee must somehow be rendered legally secure from both the creditors of the trustee (notwithstanding the status of the trustee as owner) and the creditors of the settlor (notwithstanding the settlor's stipulations in the foundational document).

The civil law has made numerous attempts to articulate these rudimentary requirements in a legal idiom consistent with its core values. First, in the early twentieth century, civil law jurists resorted to age-old civil law ideas and tried to cognize the trust as an agency relationship – a modern *fideicommissum*. Unfortunately, while this idea captured the obligation to manage the trust estate in accordance with the settlor's terms, it failed to clarify who actually owned the property. Also, if the trust was to be understood as a conventional agency relationship so that the trustee remained subject to the settlor after the conveyance, this formulation jeopardized the autonomy of the trust estate, especially with respect to the settlor's creditors.[56] Later civil law jurists characterized the trust as an entity in the law, like the corporation. Unfortunately, while this characterization secured the autonomy of the trust estate, it also rendered the trust a creature of the state, inviting regulation and even regimentation. Still others simply tried to bite the bullet and concede that the trust entailed a twofold ownership – 'juridical ownership' in the trustee and 'economic ownership' in the beneficiary. While this characterization empowered beneficiaries to secure and defend their interest in the trust estate, it flew in the face of the principle of unitary ownership. To date, perhaps the most successful attempt to characterize the trust consistent with fundamental precepts of the civil law has tempered technical legal terminology with metaphor, describing the trust as a 'special-purpose patrimony'. The term captures the status of the

[56] Also, as an agency relationship, the *fideicommissum* would not survive the settlor's death, ibid., p. 184.

trustee as owner of the trust property at the same time as, in the idea of an inherent 'special purpose', it tips its hat to the interests of beneficiaries created in the settlor's stipulations at conveyance. The idea of a special purpose also lays the groundwork for securing the trust estate vis-à-vis the trustee's creditors. If the devil is in the details, however, the idea of a special purpose patrimony provides only the broad outlines within which the real work must ensue.[57]

C. *Who or what can serve*

In civil law jurisdictions adopting the trust, the trustee is no less an essential element of the institution than it has been under the common law.[58] If the trust is not to be deemed an entity in the law, then the institution has to be developed around the office of the fiduciary. And a significant cohort of these civil law jurisdictions has precluded the individual trustee from qualifying. These jurisdictions restrict the office of trustee to an entity regulated *ex ante*.

Of all the regions comprised of civil law countries, none has so embraced the common law trust as has Latin America. In 1932 Mexico became the first Latin American jurisdiction to adopt the common law trust, '*el fideicomiso*'.[59] After Mexico adopted the trust, the institution migrated south over subsequent decades to be adopted by other Latin American countries.

[57] For a critique, see Matthews, 'The French *Fiducie*', above, note 50.

[58] Note that we are not concerned here with those civil law jurisdictions that have adopted the trust in order to develop an offshore trust business, to offer a tax haven and potentially asset protection for non-citizen non-residents. We are concerned instead with those civil law jurisdictions that have introduced the trust so that it can be used by their own citizens in ordering their affairs. We are also not concerned with countries (such as Italy) that have accepted the trust into the property regime not by introducing specific legislation but rather by ratifying the Hague Convention and recognizing the trust as a consequence, so that citizens who with Italian-*situs* property establish trusts pursuant to foreign law then benefit from the choice of law provisions under article 11 of the Convention. For Italy, see M. Lupoi, *Trusts: A Comparative Study* (Cambridge University Press, 2000), p. 368. For the Hague Convention, see Hague Convention on the Law Applicable to Trusts and on Their Recognition, The Hague, 1 July 1985, in force 1 July 1992, 23 ILM 1389 (1984).

[59] The 1932 General Law of Securities and Credit Transactions (*Ley General de Títulos y Operaciones de Crédito*) arts. 346–59 under the heading of *Del fideicomiso*, which was developed under the influence of the jurists Ricardo Alfaro and Pierre Lepaulle. See Pasquel, 'The Mexican Fideicomiso', above, note 54, 57–67.

If Mexico adopted the common law trust, however, this country nevertheless repudiated the individual trustee. Indeed, in Mexico, the fiduciary must be an authorized *institución fiduciaria*. Perhaps because, as in most Latin American jurisdictions, the trust is used primarily in financial operations and real estate matters, *instituciones fiduciarias* are limited to credit institutions, insurance companies and similar entities regulated *ex ante*. Of these, credit institutions have the broadest purchase, while insurance companies can qualify only with respect to trusts whose object is related to their corporate purposes. Where guarantee trusts are concerned, almost any of these fiduciary entities can serve, as can general depositaries and credit unions.[60]

After Mexico adopted the common law trust, the institution moved south in guises of various degrees of similarity.[61] Colombia adopted the trust in 1941 and there only trust companies can be trustees. These trust companies must be authorized by the superintendent of banking to undertake the role of fiduciary and must be engaged solely in the business of being trustee.[62] In Honduras, where the trust was adopted in 1950, trustees also must be authorized banking institutions.[63] Venezuela adopted the trust in 1956 and allows only banking institutions and insurance companies to be trustees.[64] Guatemala put in place a statute permitting trusts to be created in 1970 but permits only Guatemalan banks, credit institutions and those private investment companies authorized by the Junta Monetaria to qualify as trustees.[65] El Salvador adopted the trust in the same year and requires that a trustee be either a bank or authorized credit institution.[66] Bolivia adopted the trust in 1977 and there only banks can be trustees.[67]

Ecuador put in place legislation authorizing the trust in 1993, restricting the office of trustee to fund and trust management companies with the state bank and the National Finance Corporation also permitted to qualify.[68]

[60] *Ley General de Títulos y Operationces de Crédito* 1932, c. V, art. 350, *Diario Oficial de la Federación* (Mexico).

[61] Malumian, *Trusts in Latin America*, above, note 46, p. 19.

[62] *Codigo de Comercio*, tit. IX, art. 1226 (Colombia).

[63] *Ley de la Comision National de Bancos y Seguros* (Decree No. 155/95) (Honduras).

[64] *Ley de Fideicomisos* 1956, art. 12 (Venezuela).

[65] *Codiga Comercia*, c. 5, ss. 766–93; Financial Supervision Decree No. 18–2002 (Guatemala).

[66] *Codiga Comercia*, ss. 1233ff; *Ley de Bancos* ss. 67ff (El Salvador).

[67] *Codiga Comercia*, tit. VII, c. IV, s. 11, arts. 1409–27; *Ley de Bancos y Entidodes Financieros*, arts. 3, 9; Circular SB/254/93 (12 July 1993) (Bolivia).

[68] *Ley de Mercado de Valores* (No. 367/1998); Decree No. 390 (No. 87/1998) (Ecuador).

Peru adopted the trust in 1996 and opened the office to a variety of banking institutions. A state-owned financial institution, the *Corporación Financiera de Desarrollo*, can qualify, as can banking companies, financial companies, municipal savings and credit banks, municipal people's credit banks, entities for the development of small- and micro-sized companies and credit cooperatives authorized to raise resources from the public, rural savings and credit banks, exchange services companies and funds transfer companies, fiduciary services companies (corporations that have as sole object and activity to be trustees) and insurance companies.[69] Finally, Paraguay adopted the trust the same year as Peru and permits to qualify as trustee only banks and corporations organized for the exclusive purpose of being trustees and authorized by the Central Bank of Paraguay.[70]

On the European Continent, Luxembourg introduced the *contrat fiduciare* into law in 1983.[71] There, the office of trustee is limited to banks.[72]

Quite recently, in 2007, the wellspring of the *Code Napoléon*, France, amended its civil code to introduce the *fiducie*. Significantly, the French *fiducie* is quite restricted in its application, both in the creation of a trust and in filling the office of trustee. Individuals and partnerships cannot settle a trust, but only corporations subject to the corporation tax can create a *fiducie*. Further, only banks and insurance companies can be trustees.[73] These restrictions would seemingly bespeak an enduring discomfort with *substitutions* – and the trust – in France.[74]

D. *Exceptions*

There are exceptions, however. Not every civil law jurisdiction adopting the trust has rejected the individual trustee. In these cases, however, even if the legal regime is at base a civil law regime, each of these jurisdictions has in some way been subject to common law influence that has been

[69] *Ley General de Instituciones Bancarias, Financieras y de Seguros* (No. 770/1993), sub-ch. IX, art. 315 (Peru).

[70] *Ley de Negocios Fiduciarios* (No. 921/96) and Resolution No. 6 (22 November 2004); *Ley General de Bancos, Financieras y Otras Entidades de Crédito* (No. 861/96), ss 40, 73 (Paraguay).

[71] Lupoi, *Trusts*, above, note 58, p. 281.

[72] Grand Ducal decree of 19 July 1983, art. 1 (Luxembourg).

[73] *Loi 2007-211 du 19 février 2007 instituant la fiducie, Journal Officiel de la République Française*, 19 February 2007, art. 2051.

[74] See Matthews, 'The French *Fiducie*', above, note 50.

especially resonant with respect to the trust. For example, some of these jurisdictions were once British or American colonies. Belize (known as British Honduras in the colonial era)[75] and Panama (where the United States' domination began in the early years of the twentieth century)[76] are civil law countries that allow the individual to qualify as trustee. Further, India adopted the trust in the Indian Trust Act of 1882 and permits any individual, limited company or other corporation capable of holding property and able to enter into contracts to become a trustee. Israel discovered the trust in 1924, during the British mandate, and permits an individual to qualify as trustee.[77] South Africa can also be added to this list of former colonies that have adopted the trust and embrace the individual trustee.[78]

Other civil law jurisdictions that allow the individual to qualify as trustee either are presently or have in the past been semi-autonomous regions within common law countries. Both Scotland (governed by Roman-Scots law, a regime with deep ties to the legal tradition of Continental Europe) [79] and Quebec[80] fit this description. Louisiana with a legal regime closely connected to the *Code Napoléon* only adopted the trust in all its applications in 1964, but did so allowing the individual to qualify.[81]

75 Trusts Act, s. 17 (2000) (Belize).

76 Trust Law (No. 1/1984); Executive Decree (No. 16/1984) (Panama). See also R. J. Alfaro, 'The Trust and the Civil Law with Special Reference to Panama' (1951) 33:3/4 J. Comp. Legis. & Int'l Law (Third Series) 25; see also Lupoi, *Trusts*, above, note 58, p. 285.

77 Trust Law, 5739–1979, ch. 2, § 21; for compensation, see Trust Law, 5739–1979, ch. 1, § 8(a) (Israel). See also Lupoi, *Trusts*, above, note 58, pp. 279–80.

78 Trust Property Control Act 55 of 1988 § 1 (as amended) (South Africa).

79 Trusts (Scotland) Act 1961; Law Reform (Scotland) Act 1968. See also R. Evans-Jones, 'Civil Law in the Scottish Legal Tradition', in R. Evans-Jones (ed.), *The Civil Law Tradition in Scotland* (Edinburgh: The Stair Society, 1995); D. M. Walker, *A Legal History of Scotland* (Edinburgh: W. Green & Son, 1988–95); R. Burgess, 'Thoughts on the Origins of the Trust in Scots Law' (1974) *Juridical Review* 196.

80 The trust finally entered the Quebec civil code in 1994 on the heels of a great controversy as to whether the trust in its quintessential aspects could be assimilated, consistently with civil law property principles (as derived from the French legal tradition). Civil Code of Québec, art. 1274 (Canada); see also Lupoi, *Trusts*, above, note 58, p. 287.

81 *Louisiana Statutes Annotated: Revised Statutes* (St Paul, Minn.: West, 2005) § 9:1783. See also J. M. Wisdom, 'A Trust Code for the Civil Law, Based on the Restatement and Uniform Acts' (1938) 13 Tulane L. Rev. 79. The trust was originally introduced in Louisiana in 1882 in the form of public interest (or charitable) trusts. The impetus to the introduction of this legislation was to permit Paul Tulane to create an endowment for Tulane University.

Finally, other civil law jurisdictions adopting the trust and allowing the individual to qualify have developed their trust laws either by directly appropriating a statute from a common law jurisdiction or by relying on a common law adviser to draft their respective statute. Examples include the Russian Federation where English and American law firms have been responsible for drafting code provisions relating to the trust as part of an ongoing process of economic privatization.[82] In Ethiopia, draftspersons relied heavily on the English Trustee Act of 1925 in creating the trust provisions of the Ethiopian civil code of 1960.[83] Liechtenstein relied on the English Trustee Act of 1925 to draft the *Personen- und Gesellschafts-recht*,[84] which introduced the trust or *Treuhanderschaft*.[85]

[82] *Sobranie aktov Prezidenta i Pravitelstva, Sobranie Zakonodatel'stva Rossiiskoi Federatsii* 1993, No. 2296, Item 1 § 6, para. 100 [Decree No. 2296]. Note that trust beneficiaries cannot be trustees under Decree No. 2296, which was followed by regulations dated 1 February 1994.

[83] Civil Code of Ethiopia 1960, ss. 516–37. See also N. C. Vosikis and R. David, *Le Trust dans le code civil ethiopien* (Geneva: Droz, 1975).

[84] *Liechtenstein, Personen- und Gesellschaftsrecht*, 1926 (amended 1980), art. 897 (Liechtenstein). In 1928, section 932a on trust enterprises or *Treuunternehmen*, which are legal entities, consisting of 170 articles, was added. See Lupoi, *Trusts*, above, note 58, p. 280; see also Guido G. Meier and O. Schmidt, 'Liechtenstein', in A. Kaplan et al., *Trusts in Prime Jurisdictions*, 3rd edn (London: Globe Law and Business, 2010), p. 275. Art. 897(1) provides that the trustee can be an individual or a legal entity ('Treuhänder (Trustee oder Salmann) im Sinne dieses Gesetzes ist diejenige Einzelperson, Firma oder Verbandsperson').

[85] Five civil law countries might be deemed outliers within the analysis promoted here. Four of these non-conforming jurisdictions – Costa Rica, Argentina, Uruguay and, outside Latin America, China – permit the individual to qualify, even though none of these countries has been colonized by a common law country or has ever been a semi-autonomous jurisdiction within a common law country. *Ley* 24.441, 9 January 1995, art. 5 (Argentina); Trust Law of the People's Republic of China (Order of the President No. 50) *Zhonghua Renmin Gongheguo Xintuo Fa* [Trust Law of the People's Republic of China] (promulgated by President, 28 April 2001, effective 1 October 2001) art. 2474 *St. Council Gaz.* 16 § 2, art. 24 (China), available at www.gov.cn/english/laws/2005-09/12/content_31194.htm (China); *Código de Comercio* arts. 633–62 (Costa Rica); *Ley Organica del Sistoma Bancario Nacional*, c. 10 (Costa Rica); Law No. 17703 (26 November 2003) (Uruguay); see also Lupoi, *Trusts*, above, note 58, p. 273. Further, with respect to these jurisdictions, there is no evidence of a common law adviser nor is there evidence that any of these countries relied closely upon a common law statute as they themselves attempted to draft legislation authorizing the trust. Finally, a fifth country, Japan, is non-conforming in ways that are the flip-side of the other four. Even though Japan (like Liechtenstein and Ethiopia) relied on a common law statute to amend its code to include the trust, Japan precludes the individual from qualifying and permits only banks (six banks in particular) to serve: *Shintakuo Ho* [Trust Law], Law No. 62 of 1922 (Japan); see also 'Japan', in J. Glasson and A. Gore, *International Trust Laws* (Colorado Springs: John Wiley & Sons, 2003), A21.9–A21.11.

E. *Appeal of the regulated trustee in civil law jurisdictions*

The frequent civil law requirement that the trustee be a regulated entity is noteworthy in light of the long-standing distaste that the civil law has shown for the trust. Recall that the political values associated with the French Revolution and embedded in the *Code Napoléon* rendered the common law trust anathema, a threat to the bourgeois Republic that potentially allowed wealthy landowners to circumvent aspects of the new property regime deemed integral to the new order.[86]

If there are civil law jurisdictions that have now seen the utility of the trust, the requirement that the trustee be a regulated entity suggests that these jurisdictions remain unprepared to embrace the institution completely and that in fact they are prepared to forego some of the inherent flexibility of the trust in order to constrain the uses to which it can be put. If the trust is seen as potentially a way to avoid or indeed thwart essential elements of the civil law property regime, subjection of trustees to a regulatory apparatus vests those authorities with enormous power to constrain the settlor's discretion by denying him a counter-party where trust terms would otherwise circumvent fundamental norms.

IV Insights from the common law reformation

While many civil law countries have been busy precluding the individual from qualifying as trustee, the American academic bar has undertaken to reform the core doctrines that inform the concept of the trust and govern fiduciary duty, but with seemingly scant attention to the perquisites of fiduciary office.[87] Although this literature has acknowledged the

[86] See Section III.A above.

[87] The primary exponent of this movement has been Professor John Langbein, but others have participated as well. See J. Langbein, 'Reversing the Nondelegation Rule of Trust-Investment Law' (1994) 59 Mo. L. Rev. 105; J. Langbein, 'The Contractarian Basis of the Law of Trusts' (1995) 105 Yale L.J. 625; J. Langbein, 'The Mandatory Rules in the Law of Trusts' (2003–4) 98 Nw. U.L. Rev. 1105; J. Langbein, 'The Secret Life of the Trust: The Trust as an Instrument of Commerce' (1997) 107 Yale L.J. 165; J. Langbein, 'The Uniform Prudent Investor Act and the Future of Trust Investing' (1996) 81 Iowa L. Rev. 641. Other scholars involved in this movement include Frank H. Easterbrook, Daniel R. Fischel, Robert H. Sitkoff and Melanie B. Leslie. See F. H. Easterbrook and D. R. Fischel, 'Contract and Fiduciary Duty' (1993) 36 J.L. & Econ. 425; M. B. Leslie, 'Trusting Trustees: Fiduciary Duties and the Limits of Default Rules' (2005) 94 Geo. L.J. 67; R. H. Sitkoff, 'An Agency Costs Theory of Trust Law' (2004) 89 Cornell L. Rev. 621.

utility of the professional trustee on prudential grounds (especially in light of the change in the typical modern *res* from land to financial assets), this body of work contains no suggestion that the law should constrain the settlor's ultimate discretion in choosing an individual trustee, professional or otherwise. The reason for this omission is clear upon consideration of the essential nature of the trust that this movement explicitly promotes. But beyond the concerns for the contemporary applications of the trust that are at the forefront of this movement, aspects of this literature indicate more fundamental reasons why the common law has always taken a permissive posture toward the individual trustee, reasons that go far beyond any contemporary requirements of the institution. Like many movements advocating change, this literature is as much about renewal as reform and what it advocates is at base the recovery and restoration of essential elements of the authentic common law trust. As this literature points to those age-old elements of the institution, it provides a window into deep normative biases in the common law understanding of property that underpin and indeed require the continuing vitality of the individual trustee. In short, in this literature the individual trustee remains an option – and an important one – for reasons consistent with the doctrine advocated and indeed the one recovered.

A. *Trust as contract*

This recent American literature of reform has promoted a cluster of ideas, the most important of which is that the trust is founded in contract. The trust is a 'deal', it is said, 'a bargain about how the trust assets are to be managed and distributed'.[88] This claim is offered as the final sortie in a long-running battle concerning the fundamental nature of the trust – whether it is a creature of contract or of property. The modern chapter in the controversy dates at least from the era before the first *Restatement of Trusts* when the central figures were Frederic W. Maitland, the great scholar of the common law, and Austin W. Scott, the author of the *Restatement*. In his venerated lectures on Equity, Maitland allowed that the trust was in essence a contract. As early as the fourteenth century, observed Maitland, when the English Chancellor began to enforce the trust it was as 'a contractual right, a right created by

[88] Langbein, 'The Contractarian Basis of the Law of Trusts', above, note 87, 627. Equity interests would then arise as third-party beneficiaries of the contract.

a promise'.[89] Be this as it may, however, several decades later, in 1917, Scott published an article in which, while recognizing 'that in the creation of a . . . trust there are often found all the elements . . . of a contract', [90] it is nevertheless the 'undertaking' of fiduciary obligation and responsibility, Scott maintained, that is the basis of the trust. 'A fiduciary is a person who undertakes to act in the interest of another person' and whether the role emerges from the quid pro quo of the contract or in a gratuitous act is immaterial. It is the presence of the role – with the set of attendant obligations – that matters. A trust exists when a trustee is in place and acting in the role – that is, when the settlor has transferred to the trustee a *res* to manage subject to the requirements of fiduciary responsibility.[91]

As the author of the *Restatement*, Scott had the last word, at least until recent times. The language of the first *Restatement* (published in 1935) in the ordinary course found its way into the second *Restatement* (published in 1959) so that for many subsequent decades attorneys were encouraged to take Scott's view as authoritative. Throughout much of the twentieth century, in common law jurisdictions the trust was taken as a matter of law to be founded in a transfer of property subject to fiduciary duty.[92]

In making the case that the trust is a bargain, the intent of this contemporary literature is to cut the ground from Scott's position and restore the advantage to Maitland once and for all. But this recent literature of doctrinal reformation does not resurrect the colloquy between Maitland and Scott and parse the elements of it in the mere pursuit of analytical integrity. At base, in the modern literature, the question of the nature of the trust – whether it is a creature of contract or of property – is important because it bears upon the requirement of particular terms that, in the ascendancy of Scott, were taken as necessary to the creation of the fiduciary office and thus the trust itself.

[89] F. W. Maitland et al., *Equity: A Course of Lectures*, 2nd edn (Cambridge University Press, 1936), pp. 28–9, 110. The beneficiary of the trust enters as beneficiary of third-party-beneficiary contract.

[90] A. W. Scott, 'The Nature of the Rights of the *Cestui Que* Trust' (1917) 17 Colum. L. Rev. 269, 270.

[91] A. W. Scott, 'The Fiduciary Principle' (1949) 27 Calif. L. Rev. 539, 540–1.

[92] *Restatement (First) of Trusts* (St Paul: American Law Institute, 1935) § 197 cmt. b states: 'The creation of a trust is conceived of as a conveyance of the beneficial interest in the trust property rather than as a contract.' *Restatement (Second) of Trusts* (St Paul: American Law Institute, 1959) § 197 cmt. b adds: 'Although the trustee by accepting the office of trustee subjects himself to the duties of administration, his duties are not contractual in nature.' Note also in *Restatement (Second)* § 74 the requirement of a *res*: 'A trust cannot be created unless there is trust property.'

An argument could be made that, in truth, the trust sits at the intersection between contract and property, incorporating elements of both. That is to say, any trust will include essentialist terms (a core list of fiduciary duties that are together constitutive of the office) as well as other terms that are included as a matter of agreement between the parties. From the perspective of the recent literature, however, this solomonic view misses the point. With respect to any particular trust provision, whether the analytical vector toggles toward 'contract term' or 'property term' governs the amount of discretion the settlor has in including it in any given trust agreement. If terms are essentialist, they are required if what results is to be a trust. If they are not, then they are included at the discretion of the parties. By revisiting the disagreement between Maitland and Scott and taking Maitland's part, the modern literature lays the foundation to secure broad discretion in the settlor for purposes of crafting trust terms.

B. *Default rules*

That the objective of the contemporary literature is to free the hand of the settlor becomes evident upon review of the second in the cluster of ideas promoted by the recent common law literature. Closely allied to the idea that the trust is a contract is a second claim – that virtually all elements of fiduciary duty, components of the heretofore 'punctilio of honor', are simply default rules.[93] Most of those elements of fiduciary duty previously deemed essential are not required terms in any trust agreement. Rather, properly understood, these rules have the normative status of terms in a hypothetical bargain, the agreed-upon objectives of a hypothetical settlor and hypothetical trustee establishing a garden-variety trust.[94] Because these elements of fiduciary duty are only default rules, settlors can opt out with respect to all terms except the most minimal (for example, that the resultant agreement benefit the beneficiary). As a further implication of the position that the trust is essentially a contract, the claim that most of the historical components of fiduciary duty are default rules leaves enormous discretion in the hands of the settlor in determining which terms are included – and which are not.

[93] Langbein, 'The Contractarian Basis of the Law of Trusts', above, note 87, 628, 634.
[94] Easterbrook and Fischel, 'Contract and Fiduciary Duty', above, note 87.

C. *Civil law alignment*

The claim in this recent literature that the trust is a creature of contract would seem to align the common law trust with the civil law model.[95] (We will return to the question of default rules in a moment.) In civil law jurisdictions, core principles of property embedded in the civil law courtesy of the French Revolution (such as unity of title) have meant that, if the trust was to be introduced, it could not be conceived as a property institution but could only be understood to arise by means of contract, one between the settlor and the trustee. Thus, in this common law literature the effort to reinvigorate Maitland's view of trust-as-contract would appear to draw the common law alongside the civil law with respect to the conceptual foundation of the trust.

Other ideas promoted in this recent American literature would also seem to make the common law trust of a piece with the new civil law version. For example, this literature seems to announce a certain similarity between the two trusts – at least in this era – with the claim that, just as the civil law trust is in some jurisdictions used exclusively for commercial transactions, the present day common law trust is commonly an investment vehicle.[96] Indeed, this literature takes another step here and tries to raise the legal profile of what was previously only a bit-part player in the annals of the common law: the commercial trust, the form of the common law trust that appears (as in civil law countries) in the quid pro quo of the marketplace.[97] But further, this literature continues, pressing yet another point: that, of late, even the intra-familial donative trust is, like the commercial trust, best understood as an entity operating in the stream of commerce. No longer is the intra-familial trust born of paternalism, erected to conserve assets and otherwise secure the fortunes of the vulnerable within the family, but this trust is now commonly established to implement sophisticated tax strategies and holds a portfolio of complex financial instruments.[98] Once only an asset-conservation vehicle,[99] the intra-familial trust is now best understood like the

[95] Langbein, 'The Contractarian Basis of the Law of Trusts', above, note 87, 629.

[96] J. Langbein and R. A. Posner, 'Market Funds and Trust Investment Law' (1976) 1:1 Am. B. Found. Res. J. 1. See also Langbein, 'The Secret Life of the Trust', above, note 87; Langbein, 'The Uniform Prudent Investor Act', above, note 87.

[97] This is also part of the legacy of Scott. See Langbein, 'The Secret Life of the Trust', above, note 87, 166.

[98] See Goodwin, 'How the Rich Stay Rich', above, note 40, 487–8.

[99] Until the late twentieth century, the trust and attendant fiduciary duties were formed on a medieval model where the trust facilitated the conveyance of land within the family and

commercial trust as operating in the stream of commerce and taking risks accordingly. Whether the common law trust is to be used for family financial purposes or as a trust established purely as a vehicle in the marketplace, today the common law trust is likely to be operating – like the civil law trust – in the stream of commerce.

D. *Settlors rule*

In claiming that the prototypical trust today is created to serve as an investment vehicle operating in the stream of commerce, the common law literature of reform seeks to register a paradigm shift. The law is no longer appropriately framed around the intra-familial donative trust where, historically, the lack of parity between beneficiary and trustee justified Scott's rigorous view of fiduciary duty as an antidote to exploitation. Rather, the paradigmatic common law trust is now an investment vehicle holding complex financial interests – perhaps established for family reasons, perhaps to function in the larger marketplace – but in all events operating in the stream of commerce.[100]

This particular paradigm shift – registering a change both in the nature of the *res* and in what is to be done with it – might seem to herald a commensurate sea-change in thinking about the fiduciary. A *res* of complex financial assets operating in the stream of commerce would seem to call for regulations *ex ante* applicable to trustees, requirements for the office that would potentially preclude the individual from qualifying. While this literature of reform recognizes that, given the modern *res*, a professional trustee is a prudent choice, there is no suggestion here that the law should stipulate criteria of fiduciary competence to govern the selection of trustees *ex ante* or that the office should be restricted (as in many civil law countries) to regulated entities.[101] Indeed, rather than upping the ante for the would-be trustee, in this literature the location of the trust in the stream of commerce serves instead as yet another reason to attenuate Scott's view of the fiduciary role as born of vulnerability and entailing an unyielding set of duties. So attenuated, the

the fiduciary posture was one of risk-aversion: F. Pollock and F. W. Maitland, *The History of English Law Before the Time of Edward I*, 2nd edn (Cambridge University Press, 1898), pp. 1, 231, 237–8. See also Langbein, 'The Contractarian Basis of the Law of Trusts', above, note 87, 633; Sterk, 'Rethinking Trust Law Reform', above, note 1.

[100] See Langbein, 'The Secret Life of the Trust', above, note 87, 166; see also Goodwin, 'How the Rich Stay Rich', above, note 40, 488.

[101] Langbein, 'The Contractarian Basis of the Law of Trusts', above, note 87, 638–9.

common law standards of fiduciary duty – and indeed the concept of fiduciary duty itself – stand ready to be framed in the expectation that market mechanisms will dissuade the fiduciary from most forms of opportunistic behaviour. [102]

The reason that this literature does not constrain the settlor's discretion regarding the individual trustee, paradigm shift notwithstanding, becomes evident upon placing this paradigm shift alongside those other ideas promoted by the reform movement – that the trust is a creature of contract and that almost all rules of fiduciary duty are default rules. Taken alone with the view that the trust is a contract, the claim that in these times the typical trust is most likely an investment vehicle might appear to bring the common law trust alongside the civil law version. But when taken together with the view of the trust as contract and fiduciary duty as largely consisting of default rules, a profounder implication arises. It starts to appear that those ideas promoted in the movement of doctrinal reform are calculated to free the settlor's hand in shaping trust terms and indeed in devising fiduciary duties appropriate to the specified terms.

If the settlor's hand is to be free in any meaningful sense, however, he needs a willing counterparty. The individual trustee continues to appeal because he is more likely to agree to serve under a trust agreement incorporating innovative terms than is a corporate entity subject to governmental regulation. Regulations are put in place to minimize risk to particular institutions and to the entire financial services industry. Consequently, regulated trustees tend to be risk-averse and develop internal policies accordingly. Settlors can include cutting-edge terms, but in deciding whether to serve under such instruments, regulated trustees often construe existing laws against themselves, in the expectation that courts will continue to take the elements of fiduciary duty as mandatory and impose upon them the draconian remedies that have been part and parcel of the rigorous regime. And this reluctance often persists even where the trust agreement explicitly releases the fiduciary from duties previously thought absolute.[103]

[102] This means that, for example, the long-embraced 'no-further-inquiry rule', the legal undergirding of the previously sacrosanct proscription against trustee self-dealing, readily gives way to the standard for corporate directors and even this becomes a default rule. See Leslie, 'Trusting Trustees', above, note 87, 79.

[103] Goodwin, 'How the Rich Stay Rich', above, note 40, 479–81.

Ideas at the heart of this reformation suggest deep normative biases in the common law that underpin the continued vitality of the individual trustee. The most important of these biases is a willingness in the common law to tolerate – indeed to embrace – the trust as a vehicle by which a settlor, adopting innovative trust terms, can manipulate aspects of the property regime and precipitate change. Indeed, during the period in which this literature of reformation has appeared, settlors in the United States using the trust have produced a reconsideration of assumptions underlying the recent movement to eliminate the rule against perpetuities. Until quite recently this rule limiting the time horizon of a trust was thought a needless vestige of the era when the typical trust asset was land and assets were rarely traded. Elimination of the rule was thought a mark of progress – until states started repealing it. Immediately upon its repeal, wealthy settlors embraced the reform, establishing 'Dynasty Trusts', perpetual trusts that use the repeal of the rule to avoid the transfer tax regime, creating family endowments of a magnitude and permanence that potentially jeopardize the rough equality that is a background condition to healthy democracy.[104] The advent of the Dynasty Trust has summoned the academic bar to reconsider the rule and, rather than advocate its repeal, recognize anew the reasons to limit the time horizon of trusts.[105]

That the trust is a catalyst to legal change is not a new idea. In fact, the trust was born as a catalyst to change, a point not overlooked by Maitland:

> Feudalism had ceased to be useful, it had become a system of capricious exactions – it was very natural and not dishonourable that men should attempt to free themselves from the burdens or reliefs and wardships and marriages, from the terribly severe law of forfeiture and escheat for crime, that they should wish to make wills of land or go very near to making them.[106]

Maitland clearly views the trust here as a progressive instrument, a tool where outmoded elements of the legal regime could be circumvented. Of course, the impetus at work here – settlors seeking to avoid inconvenient or unprofitable aspects of the law – is the same agency that was in play in the *substitution fiduciaire*, a device the French viewed as

104 Ibid.

105 *Restatement (Third) of Property: Wills and Other Donative Transfers*, Tentative Draft No. 6 (Philadelphia: American Law Institute, 2010), ch. 27.

106 Maitland et al., *Equity*, above, note 4.

thwarting fundamental principles of justice. The question is whether the trust – the instrumentality to which the common law has long given quarter – is ultimately a progressive instrument or a reactionary one. As with most libertarian agencies, the exercise of individual discretion produces outcomes that are as difficult to predict as they are hard to control. Settlor's discretion is effectively a wild card and, whether in any given circumstance it serves progressive or reactionary purposes, turns on where this agency falls on the arc of history.

the *New York University Law Review*. The second – an 'abridgment'[10] of the first – appeared in the *American Journal of Comparative Law* (*AJCL*). These articles are classics and very worth a careful reading. The *AJCL* article, in particular, is likely to be known in countries outside the Anglo-American legal tradition.[11]

The articles assess the 'special contribution'[12] of the law of trusts, both within the US legal system and from the perspective of comparative law. The assessment is striking. Hansmann and Mattei argue that trust law's 'most important contribution'[13] is what other scholars have called 'ring-fencing':[14] separating trust assets from the personal assets of the trustee, thereby defining the rights of third-party creditors. In contrast, Hansmann and Mattei argue, the role of trust law in fiduciary governance – 'the creation and enforcement of [the trustee's] fiduciary duties' – is 'relatively unimportant'.[15] The argument is noteworthy because much of Anglo-American trust law *is* fiduciary law, defining and regulating the trustee's powers and obligations with respect to trust administration.

Prompted by the articles by Hansmann and Mattei, this chapter offers some reflections on the current contributions, and the potential for future contributions, of trust fiduciary law. The analysis of trust doctrine herein is descriptive and normative,[16] and proceeds in three parts.

[10] Hansmann and Mattei, 'Basic Study', above, note 9.

[11] The *American Journal of Comparative Law* is the scholarly journal of the American Society of Comparative Law, which has foreign members, individual and institutional, around the globe. If I understand Professor Sitkoff's commentary rightly, Professor Hansmann (but not Professor Mattei?) has subsequently modified or clarified his views in US law journals as these 'early writing[s]' were developed into a 'more mature corpus'. See R. H. Sitkoff, 'Trust Law as Fiduciary Governance Plus Asset Partitioning', Chapter 18 in this volume. This is good for readers of this volume to know. But the original articles remain cited and read, particularly the *AJCL* article abroad. Labelling an accurate summary of these articles as a 'straw man' does not withstand scrutiny.

[12] Hansmann and Mattei, 'Basic Study', above, note 9.

[13] Ibid., p. 134. See also Hansmann and Mattei, 'Functions', above, note 9, 438 (same words).

[14] See, e.g., D. Hayton, *Extending the Boundaries of Trusts and Similar Ring-Fenced Funds* (The Hague: Kluwer Law International, 2002).

[15] Hansmann and Mattei, 'Basic Study', above, note 9, 134. See also Hansmann and Mattei, 'Functions', above, note 9, 438 (same words).

[16] Observers with a transatlantic lens will readily notice that law professors in England take legal doctrine seriously. The contrast with the elite legal academy in the US is striking. See generally J. H. Langbein, 'Scholarly and Professional Objectives in Legal Education: American Trends and English Comparisons', in P. B. H. Birks (ed.), *What Are Law Schools For?*, vol. 2 in *Pressing Problems in the Law* (Oxford University Press 1996), pp. 5–6.

Section II explicates the argument made by Hansmann and Mattei in order to facilitate the proper assessment of it. Section III embarks on that assessment and reflects on the uses and contributions of fiduciary law within the Anglo-American law of trusts. Section IV explores the current and future role for trust fiduciary law in legal systems outside the common law.

II Hansmann and Mattei's argument

The two classic and influential articles published by Professors Hansmann and Mattei seek to provide a 'better understanding of the functions of [Anglo-American] trust law'.[17] They ask: 'What is the role of the law of trusts? Does that body of law perform a vital function . . . [o]r is the law of trusts just an anachronism . . .?'[18] After raising these questions, they pose a distinct, narrower question: 'What useful relationships can be established under the law of private trusts that cannot as easily be established using just the general law of contract and agency?'[19] The articles then address this narrower question. The answer begins with the following observation: 'At its core, a trust involves contractual relationships. The institution of the trust offers a set of standard terms for those relationships – in effect, default terms that will be implied in the absence of explicit language to the contrary in the parties' contract.'[20] Viewing the trust as a contract, the authors make the following statements about the role of trust fiduciary law:

> If the law of trusts did not exist, the Transferor and the Manager could still establish . . . all of the obligations that are at the core of the private trust . . . The simplest approach to creating such a contractual version of the trust law duties . . . would just be to insert into the contract . . . the same language concerning the Manager's duties that presently appears in the sections of the Restatement of Trusts describing a trustee's duties . . .
>
> That is not to deny that, providing default rules concerning the Manager's obligations, the law of trusts offers some real efficiencies . . . The practical

[17] Hansmann and Mattei, 'Functions', above, note 9, 435. [18] Ibid.

[19] Hansmann and Mattei, 'Functions', above, note 9, 445–6. See also Hansmann and Mattei, 'Basic Study', above, note 9 (initially describing the inquiry as 'the general economic functions served by a separate law of trusts' but then narrowing the question to 'what the law of trusts adds to the law of contract and agency').

[20] Hansmann and Mattei, 'Functions', above, note 9, 446. See also Hansmann and Mattei, 'Basic Study', above, note 9, 135 (same words).

> importance of these efficiencies is difficult to assess. It is not obvious, however, that – today at least – they are particularly large. Privately prepared standard form contracts would seem to offer efficiencies nearly as great.[21]

This line of thinking leads the authors to their central observation, namely that trust law's significance does not rest on the rules it provides to govern the rights and duties of the parties to the trust, but in the rules it provides to govern the rights of third parties. These third parties are the 'personal creditors' [22] of the settlor, trustee and beneficiaries, as well as the creditors with claims 'that arise out of transactions with the Managed Property itself'.[23] The authors summarize their findings in the following words:

> In sum, it appears that the important contribution of trust law lies not in its ordering, via default rules of contract, of the relationships among the three principal parties to a trust-like relationship ... but rather in its ordering of the relationships between those persons and third parties with whom they deal. It is the latter relationships that, owing to high transaction costs, cannot be rearranged easily by contractual means.[24]

III Assessment of the argument

There is much to praise in the articles by Professors Hansmann and Mattei,[25] but I have always been troubled by some aspects. Four points should be mentioned.

First, the articles' emphasis on trust fiduciary law as default law strikes me as too strong. The shorter article in the *American Journal of Comparative Law*, with a worldwide readership, treats trust fiduciary law as entirely a system of default rules.[26] The longer article in the *NYU Law*

21 Hansmann and Mattei, 'Functions', above, note 9, 448–9. See also Hansmann and Mattei, 'Basic Study', above, note 9, 136: 'These default terms are unquestionably a convenience. But that is all they are. If the law of trusts did not exist, the Settlor and the Trustee could still establish between themselves the obligations that are at the core of the private trust.'

22 Hansmann and Mattei, 'Functions', above, note 9, 451. 23 Ibid., 459.

24 Ibid., 466. See also Hansmann and Mattei, 'Basic Study', above, note 9, 147 (same words).

25 I fully agree that the 'ring-fencing' function of trust law is important. See G. L. Gretton, 'Trusts Without Equity' (2000) 49 *International Comparative Law Quarterly* 599, 606–7; D. Hayton, 'Commercial Counterparts', above, note 2, 24–5. I do not agree with the assessment that trust fiduciary law is 'relatively unimportant'.

26 Proving a negative is a *probatio diabolica*, I have read the article (Hansmann and Mattei, 'Basic Study', above, note 9) multiple times and find many references to trust

Review is more careful on this point and acknowledges that some rules of trust fiduciary law are mandatory.[27] On this point of doctrine, the longer article, not the shorter, is correct. Each of the trustee's fiduciary duties[28] has a mandatory core that cannot be eliminated by the terms of the trust. With respect to the duty of prudence, for example, the *Restatement (Third) of Trusts* is clear that 'trust terms may not altogether dispense with the fundamental requirement that trustees not behave recklessly but act in good faith, with some suitable degree of care, and in a manner consistent with ... the interests of the beneficiaries'.[29] Similarly, with respect to the duty of loyalty, the *Restatement (Third) of Trusts* is explicit that 'no matter how broad the provisions of a trust may be in conferring power to engage in self-dealing or other transactions involving a conflict of fiduciary and personal interests, a trustee violates the duty of loyalty to the beneficiaries by acting in bad faith or unfairly'.[30] A third example will drive home the point. With respect to the duty to furnish information about the trust to at least some of its beneficiaries, the *Restatement (Third) of Trusts* emphasizes that 'the duty to provide information to certain beneficiaries ... may not be dispensed with entirely or to a degree or for a time that would unduly interfere with the underlying purposes or effectiveness of the information requirements'.[31]

How significant are the mandatory rules of trust fiduciary law? Any question about something as unquantifiable as 'significance' does not lend itself to a precise answer; the response will be a matter of opinion and judgment. In the longer article, Professors Hansmann and Mattei conclude that 'the mandatory nature of these [fiduciary] duties is a relatively modest contribution of the law of trusts'.[32] In this assessment,

fiduciary law as 'default terms' or 'default rules' (e.g., 135, 136, 147) but no acknowledgement that some trust fiduciary rules are mandatory.

27 Hansmann and Mattei, 'Functions', above, note 9, 449–50.

28 The specific duties of trusteeship, as formulated in the *Restatement (Third) of Trusts*, 4 vols. (St Paul: American Law Institute, 2003–12), are: the duty to administer the trust in accordance with its terms and applicable law (§76); the duty of prudence (§77); the duty of loyalty (§78); the duty of impartiality (§79); the duty with respect to delegation (§80); the duty with respect to co-trustees (§81); the duty to furnish information to beneficiaries (§82); the duty to keep records and provide reports (§83); the duty to segregate and identify trust property (§84).

29 Ibid., §77, cmt. d.

30 Ibid., §78, cmt. c(2).

31 Ibid., §82, cmt. a(2).

32 Hansmann and Mattei, 'Functions', above, note 9, 449. In the longer of the two articles, the authors say that 'the mandatory nature of these duties is a relatively modest contribution of the law of trusts ... [in part because] the elements of trust law fiduciary duties that are mandatory is quite limited ... [and in part because] [i]n the absence of trust law, the parties would still have available to them the fiduciary duties offered by agency law'

the authors are in good company: Professor John Langbein has written that the mandatory rules of the law of trusts 'barely intrude on ordinary practice'.[33] In my view, some mandatory rules do not intrude on ordinary practice, but others do – and significantly so.[34] For an example of a significant intrusion, I would point to the mandatory duty to furnish information about the trust and its activities to the trust's beneficiaries. The existence of that mandatory rule in the Uniform Trust Code has met with such a frosty reception that the Uniform Law Commission ultimately decided to place the provision in brackets, thereby indicating that uniformity is not expected.[35]

The second aspect of the articles that is of concern to me is that the authors' estimates of transaction costs sometimes have the air of *ipse dixit*. On the one hand, the authors suggest that there is no need for a separate body of trust fiduciary law because a contract between the settlor and the trustee could simply contain 'the same language . . . that presently appears in the sections of the Restatement of Trusts describing a trustee's duties'.[36] On the other hand, when the authors are confronted with the suggestion that the law of contract could *also* replace the 'ring-fencing' function of trust law, at least with respect to the trustee's voluntary creditors, the authors respond: 'In principle, even without the law of trusts the same insolvency rule concerning the Manager's personal creditors could be established by contractual means . . . The transaction costs of this approach, however, would be prohibitively high.'[37] Why high in the second example but low in the first? The black letter and official commentary of the *Restatement (Third) of Trusts* on the trustee's fiduciary duties – from Section 76 on the duty to administer the trust in accordance with the trust's terms and applicable law to Section 84 on the

(ibid., 449–50). But see the authors' admission in the shorter article that 'the duty of loyalty . . . in trust law is slightly more rigorous than that implied by the law of agency'. Hansmann and Mattei, 'Basic Study', above, note 9, 137.

33 J. H. Langbein, 'Mandatory Rules in the Law of Trusts', (2004) 98 *Northwestern University Law Review* 1105, 1126.

34 See, e.g., T. P. Gallanis, 'The Trustee's Duty to Inform' (2007) 85 *North Carolina Law Review* 1595, 1617–23.

35 The uproar over Uniform Trust Code Section 105(b)(8) and (b)(9), on the trustee's mandatory duty to provide information, forced the Uniform Law Commission to retreat by bracketing the provisions as optional. See Uniform Trust Code §105 cmt: 'These subsections have generated more discussion in jurisdictions considering enactment of the UTC than have any other provisions of the Code . . . [T]he provisions were placed in brackets out of a recognition that there is a lack of consensus on the extent to which a settlor ought to be able to waive reporting to beneficiaries . . .'.

36 Hansmann and Mattei, 'Functions', above, note 9, 448.

37 Ibid., 457.

duty to segregate and identify trust property – cover approximately 70 printed pages.[38] On top of this would have to be added the many other pages on the trustee's powers and duties[39] and the consequences of fiduciary breach.[40] Trust fiduciary law is not a list of five or ten commandments but rather a sophisticated and detailed body of law. So I would imagine that the negotiation between a settlor and a prospective trustee about all of these rules could readily be as complex and costly as (if not more so than) the negotiation between a trustee and a prospective creditor on the single question of which assets the creditor may reach in the event of the trustee's liability.

Third, I worry that the articles' thought-experiment, while valuable in so far as it goes, does not sufficiently recognize the extent to which it is extremely unrealistic. More specifically: while a settlor and prospective trustee *could* agree to the current rules of trust fiduciary law, they are extremely unlikely to do so. In the real world, the settlor is likely to agree only to the rules of trust fiduciary law which effectuate the settlor's intention. But some rules of trust fiduciary law are not intent-effectuating. This is true of some mandatory rules and some default rules.

With respect to mandatory rules, some of them may be consistent with what the particular settlor wishes, and *in these instances* the mandatory rules can be called intention-effectuating.[41] But where the particular settlor wants to provide less protection to the beneficiaries than the mandatory rules require, the mandatory rules are intention-defeating – and deliberately so, in order to reinforce the fundamental requirement that a trust and its terms must be for the benefit of the beneficiaries.[42] As the Uniform Trust Code explains in a related context:

[38] In the hardcover published version, Section 76 starts on page 68 and Section 84 concludes on page 218. *Restatement (Third)*, above, note 29, vol. 3. These pages include the black letter, official commentary, and reporter's notes; subtracting the reporter's notes (approximately 81 pages) leaves approximately 70 pages.

[39] See, e.g., ibid., §§70–5 (trustee powers and duties: general principles), §§85–9 (extent and exercise of trustee powers), §§90–2 (investment of trust funds).

[40] See, e.g., ibid., §§93–102.

[41] Compare Langbein, 'Mandatory Rules', above, note 33, 1125–6, with Gallanis, 'Trustee's Duty to Inform', above, note 34, 1620–1.

[42] See Uniform Trust Code, above, note 35, §105(b)(3): describing as mandatory 'the requirement that a trust and its terms be for the benefit of its beneficiaries', §404: 'A trust and its terms must be for the benefit of its beneficiaries'. For discussion, see Gallanis, 'Trustee's Duty to Inform', above, note 34, 1621.

> Although the settlor is granted considerable latitude in defining the purposes of the trust, the principle that a trust have a purpose which is for the benefit of its beneficiaries precludes unreasonable restrictions on the use of trust property. An owner's freedom to be capricious about the use of the owner's own property ends when the property is impressed with a trust for the benefit of others.[43]

With respect to the default rules of trust fiduciary law, they are in most instances designed to effectuate intention.[44] But not in all instances. In some cases, the aim of the default rule is to push the parties (particularly the settlor) to *articulate* an intention.[45] An example is the rule governing the extent to which an exoneration clause inserted into the trust instrument by, or at the direction of, the trustee will insulate the trustee from liability for breach of a fiduciary duty. In the words of the *Restatement (Third) of Trusts*:

> If the terms of the trust were drafted by the trustee, or if the exculpatory clause was caused to be included in the trust by the trustee, the clause is presumptively unenforceable. The presumption is rebuttable, and the clause will be given effect if the trustee proves that the exculpatory provision is fair under the circumstances (including, when applicable, the fiduciary risks to be assumed) and that the existence, contents, and effect of the clause were adequately communicated to or otherwise understood by the settlor.[46]

This default rule – rendering the exoneration clause unenforceable absent evidence of the settlor's informed agreement to it – encourages the trustee to disclose the clause's existence and effect and encourages the settlor to make a knowing and reasoned choice about whether to

[43] Uniform Trust Code, above, note 35, §412 cmt. (administrative deviation).

[44] See *Restatement (Third)*, above, note 28, §10.1: 'The donor's intention is given effect to the maximum extent allowed by law'; J. H. Langbein, 'The Contractarian Basis of the Law of Trusts' (1995) 105 *Yale Law Journal* 625, 664: 'What was the intention of the parties to the trust deal respecting this point, and if they did not articulate their intention on this matter, which default rule captures the likely bargain they would have struck had they thought about it?'

[45] On the so-called 'penalty' or 'information-forcing' default rule, see the classic article by I. Ayres and R. Gertner, 'Filling Gaps in Incomplete Contracts: An Economic Theory of Default Rules' (1989) 99 *Yale Law Journal* 87, 94.

[46] *Restatement (Third)*, above, note 28, §96, cmt. d. See also Uniform Trust Code, above, note 35, §1008(b): 'An exculpatory term drafted or caused to be drafted by the trustee is invalid as an abuse of a fiduciary or confidential relationship unless the trustee proves that the exculpatory term is fair under the circumstances and that its existence and contents were adequately communicated to the settlor.'

accept the provision.[47] This 'information-forcing' default rule is an important part of the law governing the trustee's fiduciary obligations and would not be replicated in the real world by intention-effectuating contractual provisions.

Fourth and finally, the rhetoric of the articles strikes me as going too far in downplaying the role of trust fiduciary law. I share the view, expressed in the title of Professor Sitkoff's commentary, that trust law involves both 'fiduciary governance' and 'asset partitioning'.[48] I do not see the need to downplay the former. The essential structure of a trust, in which managerial power is divorced from beneficial ownership, creates the danger that the trustee will act for his own benefit, not for the benefit of the beneficiaries. As I have written elsewhere, trust fiduciary law 'remains a vital aspect of modern trust law ... [because] [t]he powers of trust administration are held by the trustees, who have no personal stake in the effect of their decisions on the trust corpus; conversely, the beneficiaries who do bear the risk of asset loss have no control over the trust's administration'.[49] The central aim of trust fiduciary law is to guard against the danger that the trustee 'will not work as hard as he would do if he were also [the beneficiary] – indeed [the trustee] may even breach his duties to [the beneficiary]'.[50] Doctrinally and functionally, therefore, trust fiduciary law is an important component of the Anglo-American law of trusts. Indeed, the leading American treatise on trust law offers the view that '[t]he most important and perhaps the most interesting questions of the law of trusts are those that relate to trust administration'.[51]

IV The role of trust fiduciary law outside the common law

Trust fiduciary law is a well-developed and sophisticated body of doctrine, rooted in a distinguished history yet modernized for contemporary legal practice. The rules of trust fiduciary law – some mandatory, some default – serve a variety of functions as they perform the important task of governing the administration of the trust. Doctrinally and

[47] For discussion, see R. H. Sitkoff, 'An Agency Costs Theory of Trust Law' (2004) 89 *Cornell Law Review* 621, 645.

[48] Sitkoff, 'Trust Law as Fiduciary Governance', Chapter 18 in this volume.

[49] See Gallanis, 'Trustee's Duty to Inform', above, note 34, 1615. [50] Ibid., 1616.

[51] M. L. Ascher, W. F. Fratcher, A. W. Scott, *Scott and Ascher on Trusts*, 5th edn (New York: Aspen, 2007), p. 1021.

functionally, trust fiduciary law makes a significant contribution within the Anglo-American law of trusts. For the same reasons, trust fiduciary law is making, or has the potential to make, important contributions to other legal systems that adopt the trust or a trust-like device.

Let us consider, by way of example, two countries outside the common law, both of which are economic powerhouses: China and France.

A. *China*

The People's Republic of China has become one of the world's great economic powers. China's gross domestic product (GDP) ranks the country second in the world, exceeded only by the United States.[52] This is a remarkable achievement for a country that became a member of the IMF and the World Bank only thirty years ago.[53] Economic modernization became possible in China after 1976, as Deng Xiaoping emerged as the country's leader, repudiated the Cultural Revolution and the Gang of Four, and set in motion a series of programmes known collectively as 'Reform and Opening' (*Gaige kaifang*) or colloquially as 'socialism with Chinese characteristics'. Deng also presided over the revival of China's civil law tradition,[54] with the enactment of the General Principles of Civil Law (*Zhonghua renmin gongheguo minfa tongze*) in 1986.[55]

Within this civil law tradition is the Chinese Trust Law (*Zhonghua renmin gongheguo xintuo fa*), enacted on 28 April 2001, and effective on 1 October 2001.[56] Consisting of seven chapters and 74 articles, the Trust Law comprehensively introduced the trust into China's civilian legal system.[57] The process of drafting the Trust Law was begun in 1993 by

[52] See http://data.worldbank.org/indicator/NY.GDP.MKTP.CD.

[53] See W. Klatt, 'Chinese Statistics Up-Dated' (1980) 84 *China Quarterly* 737, 737.

[54] On China's civil law tradition from the late Qing dynasty to the Property Code of 2007, see L. Chen, 'The Historical Development of the Civil Law Tradition in China: A Private Law Perspective' (2010) 78 *Legal History Review* 159.

[55] The General Principles of Civil Law were enacted on 12 April 1986, and effective 1 January 1987. Ibid., 176.

[56] Xintao Fa [Trust Law] (promulgated by the Nat'l People's Cong., 28 Apr. 2001, effective 1 Oct. 2001). (An official English-language translation of the Trust Law is available at www.gov.cn/english/laws/2005-09/12/content_31194.htm.)

[57] Prior to the Trust Law, Chinese law had some limited provisions on trusts. See W. Hutchens, 'The PRC's First Trust Law: Trusts Without Chinese Characteristics?' (2001) 15 *China Law & Practice* 18 (observing, however, that 'no prior statute spelled out the basic parameters of trust relationships'). After the enactment of the Trust Law,

the Financial and Economic Committee of the Chinese National People's Congress (NPC or *Quanguo renmin daibiao dahui*) and was completed during the twenty-first session of the Standing Committee (*Changwu weiyuanhui*) of the Ninth NPC in 2001.[58]

The Trust Law transplanted the common law trust into China's civilian legal tradition.[59] In the words of the first annotated commentary on the Trust Law, the statute is a '"fruit tree" that has come across the ocean to another shore . . . [and that has been] altered to fit China's water and soil'.[60] Focusing on the provisions of the Trust Law governing the fiduciary duties of the trustee, we can see that these were drawn heavily from Anglo-American law. The Trust Law requires the trustee to:

- 'abide by the provisions of the trust documents';[61]
- 'handle trust business for the best interests of the beneficiary';[62]
- 'be careful in performing [the trustee's] duties';[63]
- 'fulfill [the trustee's] obligations with honesty, good faith, prudence, and efficiency';[64]

China adopted additional legislation and administrative regulations 'to provide for the use of the trust in numerous financial arrangements . . . such as securities investment funds, collective capital trusts, occupational pension funds ("enterprise annuities"), and asset securitization'. L. Ho, 'The People's Republic of China', in J. Glasson and G. Thomas (eds.), *The International Trust*, 2nd edn (Bristol: Jordans, 2006), p. 825.

58 C. Z. Qu, 'The Doctrinal Basis of the Trust Principles in China's Trust Law' (2003) 38 *Real Property Probate & Trust Journal* 345, 348.

59 See Z. Tan, 'The Chinese Law of Trusts: A Compromise Between Two Legal Systems' (2001) 13 *Bond Law Review* 224.

60 F. H. Foster, 'American Trust Law in a Chinese Mirror' (2010) 94 *Minnesota Law Review* 602, 621–2 (translating W. Quig & G. Ce, *Zhonghua Renmin Gongheguo Xintuo Fa Tiaowen Quanshi* [Annotated Articles of the Trust Law of the People's Republic of China] 1 (2001)).

61 Trust Law, above, note 56, art. 25. Cf. *Restatement (Third)*, above, note 28, §76(1): 'The trustee has a duty to administer the trust, diligently and in good faith, in accordance with the terms of the trust and applicable law.'

62 Trust Law, above, note 56, art. 25. Cf. *Restatement (Third)*, above, note 28, §78(1): 'a trustee has a duty to administer the trust solely in the interest of the beneficiaries'. On the distinction between 'sole interest' and 'best interest', see J. H. Langbein, 'Questioning the Trust Law Duty of Loyalty: Sole Interest or Best Interest?' (2005) 114 *Yale Law Journal* 929 (arguing that the 'sole interest' standard should be replaced by 'best interest'); M. Leslie, 'In Defense of the No Further Inquiry Rule: A Response to Professor John Langbein' (2005) 47 *William & Mary Law Review* 541 (arguing in favour of the traditional 'sole interest' standard).

63 Trust Law, above, note 56, art. 25. Cf. *Restatement (Third)*, above, note 28, §77(2): 'The duty of prudence requires the exercise of reasonable care, skill, and caution.'

64 Trust Law, above, note 56, art. 25. Cf. *Restatement (Third)*, above, note 28, §76(1) (requiring diligence and good faith); ibid., §77 (duty of prudence).

- 'administer the trust property separately from his own property and keep separate accounting books';[65]
- 'keep complete records of the trust business';[66] and
- 'at regular intervals each year, report to the settl[o]r and beneficiary on the administration and disposition of the trust property and income and expenses relating to the property'.[67]

In addition, the trustee must avoid:

- 'seek[ing] interests for himself by using the trust property';[68]
- 'convert[ing] the trust property into his own property';[69] or
- 'conduct[ing] ... transaction[s] between his own property and trust assets or between the trust assets of different settl[o]rs, unless it is otherwise stipulated in the trust documents or is consented by the settl[o]rs or beneficiary and the ... transaction is conducted at fair market price'.[70]

The similarity between these provisions and their Anglo-American counterparts is no accident. During the process of drafting the Trust Law, Chinese authorities consulted many foreign experts on trusts, including experts from the United States.[71] Moreover, Chinese scholarship in the field of trusts often cites and discusses American trust law statutes, cases, treatises, Restatements, casebooks and law review articles.[72]

65 Trust Law, above, note 56, art. 29. Cf. *Restatement (Third)*, above, note 28, §84: 'The trustee has a duty to see that trust property is designated or identifiable as property of the trust, and also a duty to keep the trust property separate from the trustee's own property and, so far as practical, separate from other property not subject to the trust.'

66 Trust Law, above, note 56, art. 33. Cf. *Restatement (Third)*, above, note 28, §83: 'A trustee has a duty to maintain clear, complete and accurate books and records regarding the trust property and the administration of the trust. . .'.

67 Trust Law, above, note 56, art. 33. Cf. *Restatement (Third)*, above, note 28, §83: 'A trustee has a duty ... at reasonable intervals on request, to provide beneficiaries with reports or accountings.' See also ibid., §82 (duty to furnish information to beneficiaries).

68 Trust Law, above, note 56, art. 26. Cf. *Restatement (Third)*, above, note 28, §78(1): 'A trustee has a duty to administer the trust solely in the interest of the beneficiaries.'

69 Trust Law, above, note 56, art. 27. Cf. *Restatement (Third)*, above, note 28, §78 cmt. b: '[a] trustee ... commits a breach of trust by purchasing trust property, even as the highest bidder at a public auction'.

70 Trust Law, above, note 56, art. 28. Cf. *Restatement (Third)*, above, note 28, §78 cmt. c(2) (authorization in the terms of the trust); ibid., §97 (beneficiary consent).

71 For example, some members of the Uniform Law Commission's Joint Editorial Board for Uniform Trust and Estate Acts were consulted.

72 See Foster, 'Chinese Mirror', above, note 60, 624–6 (collecting examples).

There are some differences, of course, between Chinese and Anglo-American trust fiduciary law. For example, the Chinese Trust Law is explicit that some of the trustee's fiduciary duties run not only to the beneficiaries but also to the settlor.[73] These duties include the duty to report 'at regular intervals every year ... on the administration and disposition of the trust property'.[74] Moreover, the settlor is given powers of enforcement: article 23 of the Chinese Trust Law provides that, in the event of a fiduciary breach, 'the settl[o]r shall have the right to dismiss the trustee according to the provisions in the trust documents or apply to the People's Court for dismissing him'.[75] Another difference appears in the trustee's duty with respect to delegation. Here, the Chinese Trust Law is more restrictive than the modern American rule: article 30 requires the trustee to 'handle trust business himself ... [except] where the trust documents provide otherwise or [the trustee] has to do so for reasons beyond his control'.[76] A third difference is that the duty of impartiality in the Chinese Trust Law is phrased in terms of concurrent, rather than successive, beneficial interests: article 45 provides that '[t]he co-beneficiaries shall enjoy the benefits from a trust according to the provisions in the trust documents. Where no percentage or methods for distribution of the benefits from the trust are specified in the documents, all the beneficiaries shall enjoy the benefits equally.'[77] This approach is consistent with the traditional civilian understanding of property rights, in which ownership is not divided into present and future estates,[78] and also with China's Property Law (*Zhonghua renmin gongheguo wuquan fa*),

[73] For a discussion of the enhanced role of the settlor in Chinese trust law, ibid., 638–42.

[74] Trust Law, above, note 56, art. 33.

[75] Ibid., art. 23. The settlor also has the power to redress misconduct by a *beneficiary*: 'the settler [*sic*] may replace the beneficiary or dispose of his right to benefit from the trust ... [if] (1) the beneficiary commits a major tort against the settler; [or] (2) the beneficiary commits a major tort against the other co-beneficiaries'. Trust Law, art. 51. Cf. *Restatement (Third)*, above, note 28, §94 (authorizing the settlor to sue to enforce a charitable trust, but not to enforce a private trust).

[76] Trust Law, above, note 56, art. 30. Cf. *Restatement (Third)*, above, note 28, §80(1): 'A trustee has a duty to perform the responsibilities of the trusteeship personally, except as a prudent person of comparable skill might delegate those responsibilities to others.'

[77] Trust Law, above, note 56, art. 45. Cf. *Restatement (Third)*, above, note 28, §79 (duty of impartiality); see also ibid., cmt. B: 'It would be overly simplistic, and therefore misleading, to equate impartiality with some concept of "equality" of treatment or concern...'.

[78] See J. H. Merryman, 'Ownership and Estate (Variations on a Theme by Lawson)' (1974) 48 *Tulane Law Review* 916, 925: 'Even in the civil law, land can be "owned" simultaneously by two or more persons *in comune* [sic] ... [But] a temporal division into present and future estates, simply does not exist.'

effective 1 October 2007,[79] which provides for concurrent but not successive ownership.[80]

Many of the differences between Chinese and American trust law have already been insightfully analysed by Professor Frances Foster.[81] For this reason, and for present purposes, it is the similarities that are the focus here.

Most of the rules of Anglo-American trust fiduciary law have been transplanted into China. Why did China borrow so heavily in this area of the law? Anglo-American trust fiduciary law is able to make a substantial contribution in China for the same reasons it makes a substantial contribution at home. The law is well-developed and sophisticated, and suited to modern legal practice. The law combines appropriate mandatory and default provisions that go beyond, and serve purposes that cannot easily be replicated in the real world by, the terms of any particular trust instrument. And the law performs – effectively and appropriately – the crucial function of governing the trust's administration. Chinese legislators, having decided to import the institution of the trust, observed the role of fiduciary law within the law of trusts, and recognized the benefits of importing the fiduciary law, while altering it 'to fit China's water and soil'.[82]

B. France

China illustrates the current contribution of Anglo-American fiduciary law to a country within the civilian legal tradition. Let us now turn to France, as an example of a civil law country where Anglo-American fiduciary law has the *potential* to make a contribution in the future. France is squarely within the tradition of the civil law, and economically prominent, ranking fifth among nations in GDP for 2011.[83]

The French *fiducie*[84] was introduced by statute in 2007.[85] Under this legislation, both the settlor (*constituant*) and the trustee (*fiduciaire*) had

[79] Wuquan Fa [Property Rights Law] (promulgated by the Nat'l People's Cong. 16 March 2007, effective 1 October 2007). (An official English translation is available at www.npc.gov.cn/englishnpc/Law/2009-02/20/content_1471118.htm.)

[80] Ibid., art. 93. [81] See for example, Foster, 'Chinese Mirror', above, note 60.

[82] See Sitkoff, 'Trust Law as Fiduciary Governance', Chapter 18 in this volume. See also Foster, 'Chinese Mirror', above, note 60, 636 (providing an example of Chinese scholarship proposing further amendments to the fiduciary provisions of the Trust Law).

[83] See http://data.worldbank.org/indicator/NY.GDP.MKTP.CD.

[84] For a treatise on the subject, see A.-L. Blandin et al., *La Fiducie: mode d'emploi* (Levallois: Francis Lefebvre, 2007).

[85] Law No. 2007-211 of 19 February 2007, online: Legifrance www.legifrance.gouv.fr/home.jsp. For a discussion of the legislative history of the 2007 statute, see P. Matthews, 'The

to be 'legal entities, subject to corporate income tax'.[86] In August 2008, amending legislation made the *fiducie* open to individual *constituants*, and it authorized members of the legal profession to serve as *fiduciaires*.[87] In January 2009, an ordinance (*ordonnance*) later ratified by the French legislature provided 'additional details on the legal and tax regime' governing the *fiducie*.[88] Despite this liberalization, the *fiducie* is currently designed for commercial purposes, not for family wealth transmission.[89] For example, the *fiducie* automatically terminates at the death of the settlor (*constituant*).[90] Moreover, a *fiducie* is void if it results in a gift to the beneficiary (*bénéficiaire*).[91]

The fiduciary laws governing the French *fiduciaire* lack the breadth and depth of the law governing the Anglo-American trustee.[92] The principal obligation is to fulfil the mission of the *fiducie* as provided in the instrument,[93] without misconduct.[94] The *fiduciaire* must also avoid self-dealing,[95] disclose its fiduciary capacity to third parties,[96] and

French *Fiducie*: And Now for Something Completely Different?' (2007) 21 *Trust Law International* 17, 19. See also J.-P. Béraudo, 'La loi du 19 février créant une fiducie française', in Tirard, *Trust & Fiducie*, above, note 3.

86 J. Saiac and D. Gutmann, 'The French "*Fiducie*": A Missed Opportunity or a Work in Progress?' (April 2010) *European Taxation* 149.

87 Law No. 2008-776 of 4 August 2008. For discussion, see Saiac and Gutmann, 'The French "*Fiducie*"', above, note 86, 149.

88 Saiac and Gutmann, 'The French "*Fiducie*"', above, note 86, 149 (citing Ordonnance No. 2009-112 of 30 January 2009, ratified by art. 138 of Law No. 2009-526 of 12 May 2009). See also M. Gdanski and T. Pichardo-Angadi, 'Recent Changes to French Law Affecting Fiducie and Rights of Secured Creditors' (2009) 24 *Journal of International Banking and Regulation* 262.

89 For a discussion of the purposes to which the *fiducie* is currently put, see M. Gdanski and T. Pichardo-Angadi, 'The French Law on *Fiducie* and its Application to Banking and Finance Transactions' (2007) 22 *Journal of International Banking and Regulation* 434.

90 Art. 2029 *Code civil* (C. civ.): 'Le contrat de fiducie prend fin par le décès du constituant personne physique.'

91 Art. 2013 C. civ.: 'Le contrat de fiducie est nul s'il procède d'une intention libérale au profit du bénéficiaire. Cette nullité est d'ordre public.'

92 See, for example, Blandin et al., *La Fiducie: mode d'emploi*, above, note 84, pp. 121–4 (devoting approximately three pages of text, in a book of 274 pages, to 'obligations et responsabilité du fiduciaire').

93 Art. 2018 C. civ.: 'Le contrat de fiducie détermine . . . [l]a mission du ou des fiduciaires.'

94 Art. 2026 C. civ.: 'Le fiduciaire est responsable, sur son patrimoine propre, des fautes qu'il commet dans l'exercice de sa mission.'

95 Art. 1596 C. civ.: 'Ne peuvent se rendre adjudicataires, sous peine de nullité, ni par eux-mêmes, ni par personnes interposées: . . . [l]es fiduciaires, des biens ou droits composant le patrimoine fiduciaire.'

96 Art. 2021 C. civ.: 'Lorsque le fiduciaire agit pour le compte de la fiducie, il doit en faire expressément mention. De même, lorsque le patrimoine fiduciaire comprend des biens

provide reports to the settlor (*constituant*) and beneficiary (*bénéficiaire*) as provided in the instrument.[97]

Current French law seems to suffice for the present purposes of the *fiducie*. But there is the potential for Anglo-American fiduciary law to make a contribution in the future, because this trust-like device has the potential to reach beyond its current functions. The French *fiducie*, in the few years since its introduction as a device limited to entities paying corporate income tax, has already been opened to individual settlors.[98] The further extension of the *fiducie* to enable its use for family wealth transfer is now being urged by French lawyers.[99] As the range of uses widens, and particularly if the institution is able to last over multiple generations for unborn or unascertained beneficiaries (as is the Anglo-American trust), the thin fiduciary rules in French law will come under increasing strain. Thus the door opens for a contribution from the well-developed, time-tested and recently modernized rules of Anglo-American fiduciary law.

This chapter does not argue that such a transplant will happen or that it will work. Within the field of comparative law, there is a substantial body of scholarship – yet no real agreement – on the reasons why legal transplants succeed or fail.[100] The example of Chinese law shows that the rules of Anglo-American trust fiduciary law can make a substantial contribution within a civil law country. My judgment is that we shall soon see the expansion of the French *fiducie*, with the potential for considerable borrowing from our fiduciary law. Admittedly, this is speculative. The points to remember are what Anglo-American fiduciary law contributes at home, and what it contributes or has the potential to contribute abroad.

ou des droits dont la mutation est soumise à publicité, celle-ci doit mentionner le nom du fiduciaire ès qualités.'

97 Art. 2022 C. civ.: 'Le contrat de fiducie définit les conditions dans lesquelles le fiduciaire rend compte de sa mission au constituant. [. . .] Le fiduciaire rend compte de sa mission au bénéficiaire et au tiers désigné en application de l'article 2017, à leur demande, selon la périodicité fixée par le contrat.'

98 For discussion, see S. Prigent, 'L'ouverture de la fiducie aux personnes physiques' (April 2009) R.F. Compt. 420, 14.

99 Saiac and Gutmann, 'The French "*Fiducie*"', above, note 86, 151 ('The hope of French tax practitioners is that this is not the end of the story and that the French government will finally accept that a French trust may be used for gift/inheritance purposes and will define an acceptable tax treatment for such operations').

100 For a recent discussion and summary, see Foster, 'Chinese Mirror', above, note 60, 614–18.

V Conclusion

Maitland, the great historian of English law, described the practitioner of the common law as someone who 'knew nothing and cared nothing for any [legal] system but his own'.[101] Subsequent historical research has yielded a more nuanced account. The law of England borrowed from the law of the Continent,[102] and – importantly – vice versa. Continental law has borrowed from English law before.[103] Today, to the extent that countries outside the heritage of the common law embrace the trust or a trust-like device, there is much of value that these countries will find in Anglo-American trust fiduciary law.

[101] F. Maitland, 'Why the History of English Law is not Written', in Fisher, *The Collected Papers*, above, note 1, vol. I, pp. 480, 488.

[102] See, for example, R. H. Helmholz, 'Continental Law and Common Law: Historical Strangers or Companions?' (1990) *Duke Law Journal* 1207.

[103] See, for example, A. Padoa-Schioppa, 'Common Law e Civil Law: *Uno Scambio Biunivoco*', in R. H. Helmholz and V. Piergiovanni (eds.), *Relations Between the Ius Commune and English Law* (Soveria Mannelli: Rubbettino, 2009).

17

Convergence and divergence in the worlds of the trust: duties and liabilities of trustees under the Chinese trust

REBECCA LEE

I Introduction

The trust is a familiar tool for asset management in the English common law world. Yet it is less well known in most civil law jurisdictions. That being so, there are naturally legitimate concerns in adapting a trust institution to civilian jurisdictions. These include the vesting of trust property in the trustee, the enforceability of the arrangement against third parties, and compatibility with indigenous civil law concepts. Despite these conceptual difficulties, China embraced the trust by enacting a Trust Law[1] in 2001 in an attempt to regulate its emerging financial trust services industry. This chapter examines certain operational aspects of the Chinese trust to see if they may shed light on its nature and juridical basis.

Part II of this chapter considers whether the common law method of creating a trust by the settlor transferring ownership of trust property presents any obstacle to the reception of trust law in China, which apparently does not so mandate. It suggests that, properly understood, this method merely enables the imposition of additional rights and duties on the trustee and the beneficiary so as to create the necessary tension between them to ensure division of management and enjoyment, and so is functionally equivalent to the substantive feature of granting rights and

I am grateful to George Gretton, Lusina Ho, Paul Matthews, Kenneth Reid and participants at the 'The Worlds of the Trust' Conference for their invaluable comments on an earlier draft of the chapter, and to Lionel Smith for inviting me to participate in this conference. All errors remain mine.

[1] Adopted at the 21st session of the Standing Committee of the Ninth National People's Congress on 28 April 2001; promulgated and came into force on 1 October 2001 (hereafter 'Chinese Trust Law'). Official translation by the National People's Congress of the PRC available at www.npc.gov.cn/englishnpc/Law/2007-12/10/content_1383444.htm (last accessed on 1 April 2013).

duties to trustees and beneficiaries in a trust. Thus, a trust is still functionally a trust so long as requisite rights and duties are imposed on trustees and beneficiaries. Part III then evaluates such control mechanisms under the Chinese trust against the notion of an 'irreducible core content of trusteeship' in English law and, in turn, the feasibility of implementing a trust without transferring ownership of the trust property. It argues that while there is functional convergence between an English and a Chinese trust, the absence of transfer of trust property in a Chinese trust means that the 'irreducible core content of trusteeship' needs to be refined. Finally, Part IV considers briefly whether the operational rules under examination may shed light on the conceptual basis of the Chinese trust. It is submitted that the prominent status of the settlor, as well as the potential application of contractual doctrines to determine the efficacy of trustee exemption clauses, may suggest a contractual conceptualization of the Chinese trust. Nonetheless, the proprietary effects of the Chinese trust must also be accounted for before a contractual conceptualization can be fully accepted.[2]

II Functional convergence: transfer of ownership of trust property as an obstacle to the reception of trusts?

Until very recently, it has been perceived that one of the major technical obstacles to the reception of trusts in civilian jurisdictions is the common law rule that there is split ownership of trust property in a common law trust, with the trustee having legal ownership and the beneficiary equitable ownership.[3] However, the notion of 'equitable ownership' has been challenged because of its difficulties in explaining, inter alia, the trust beneficiary's ability to assert a right against third parties,[4] and so it has

[2] Note that this chapter focuses on the core content of *trusteeship*, as opposed to the core content of a *trust*. The presence of these core duties on trustees is only one of the core elements of a trust, and hence their mere presence does not mean that there is a fully functional trust. For an exposition of the core elements of a trust, see, e.g., Lusina Ho, 'The Reception of Trust in Asia: Emerging Asian Principles of Trust?' (2004) *Singapore Journal of Legal Studies* 287; M. J. de Waal, 'In Search of a Model for the Introduction of the Trust into a Civilian Context' (2001) 12 *Stellenbosch Law Review* 63; Maurizio Lupoi, 'Civil Law Trust' (1999) 32 *Vanderbilt Journal of Transnational Law* 967.

[3] See, e.g., *Abdul Hameed Kadija* v. *De Saram* [1946] AC 208, 217: 'the distinction between the legal and the equitable estate is of the essence of the trust', quoting R. W. Lee, *Introduction to Roman-Dutch Law*, 3rd edn (Oxford: Clarendon Press, 1931), p. 372.

[4] See Lionel Smith, 'Trust and Patrimony' (2008) 38 *Revue générale de droit* 379; Ben McFarlane, *The Structure of Property Law* (Oxford: Hart Publishing, 2008).

been suggested that the beneficiary's rights are not some form of equitable ownership, but are rights held in the rights of the trustee or rights against the trustee's rights (labelled 'persistent rights').[5] Nonetheless, irrespective of whether there is a system of split ownership in a trust, transfer of trust property to the trustee is seen to be one of the core elements of a trust.[6] In order to create a valid (express) trust under English law, both declaration of trust and constitution of the trust by vesting of legal title to the trust property in the trustee are essential unless the settlor declares himself to be the trustee.[7] Civilian jurisdictions that have transplanted the trust institution also generally mandate transfer of the trust property to the trustee.[8] The question for these jurisdictions which adhere to the concept of indivisibility of ownership is rather the location of ownership of the trust property upon the transfer, whether in the hands of the trustee, the beneficiary,[9] a separate juristic person[10] or even nobody.[11]

A. *The Chinese trust*

China also adheres to the notion of indivisibility of ownership. However, the Chinese trust presents a unique, and perhaps unusual, feature in that

[5] See Smith, 'Trust and Patrimony', above, note 4, para. 15; McFarlane, *Structure of Property Law*, above, note 4, pp. 25–32.

[6] See e.g., Lupoi, 'Civil Law Trust', above, note 2, which suggests that the core elements of a trust are: (i) transfer of property to trustee; (ii) separation of trust property and trustee's estate; (iii) loss of settlor's power over trust; (iv) existence of beneficiaries; (v) trustee in fiduciary position.

[7] See David Hayton et al. (eds.), *Underhill and Hayton: Law Relating to Trusts and Trustees*, 18th edn (London: LexisNexis, 2010), para. 9.

[8] See, for example, the Trust Law of Taiwan (promulgated by the President 26 January 1996, amended on 30 December 2009), art. 1, which requires the settlor to 'transfer or dispose of a right of property' to the trustee.

[9] See, e.g., the Dutch-style *bewind* trust in South Africa in which ownership is in the beneficiary but the property is placed under the control of the trustee: Trust Property Control Act 1988 (Act No. 57 of 1988), § 1(b).

[10] This was considered but rejected by the Scottish Law Commission in its 'Discussion Paper on the Nature and Constitution of Trusts' (Discussion Paper No. 133, Edinburgh, The Stationery Office, October 2006), para. 2.39.

[11] See, e.g., the Quebec trust where trust property is ownerless. Article 1261 of the Civil Code of Québec (C.C.Q.) provides that '[t]he trust patrimony, consisting of the property transferred in trust, constitutes a patrimony by appropriation, autonomous and distinct from that of the settlor, trustee or beneficiary and in which none of them has any real right'.

it appears that it does not contemplate any transfer of the trust property. A Chinese trust is defined in article 2 of the Chinese Trust Law as follows:

> For purposes of this Law, trust refers to that the settlor, based on his faith in [the] trustee, *entrusts* his property rights to the trustee and allows the trustee to, according to the will of the settlor and in the name of the trustee, administer or dispose of such property in the interest of a beneficiary or for any intended purposes. (emphasis added)

Thus, in order to create a trust, the settlor 'entrusts'[12] trust property to the trustee, and this differs from the general requirement of a *transfer* of trust property to the trustee in common law jurisdictions.[13] The use of the word 'entrust' in defining a Chinese trust seems to suggest an absence of vesting of property in the trustee. This view is in fact supported by a number of provisions of the Chinese Trust Law. For example, article 30 permits a trustee to 'entrust' others to handle the trust affairs on his behalf,[14] notwithstanding that that 'entrustment' appears to refer to a simple authorization of delegation of trust administration to others, with no transfer of property contemplated. Besides, after stipulating for the settlor's act of 'entrustment' in article 2, article 15 still requires separation of trust property from private property of the settlor.[15] The requirement of separation of trust property from the settlor's own property would have been superfluous if property had already been transferred to the trustee. Consequently, entrustment of trust property does not entail any transfer of property from the settlor to the trustee. In fact, article 8 of the Chinese Trust Law provides that a trust becomes effectively established once a trust contract is entered into, without mandating any transfer of trust property to the trustee.

12 Cf. article 3 of the Trust Law of Japan 2006 (Act No. 108 of 2006) where a trust is created when a settlor 'assigns' property to the trustee: official translation by the Ministry of Justice of Japan available at www.japaneselawtranslation.go.jp/law/detail/?id=1936&vm=04&re=02 (last accessed on 1 April 2013). It is unclear whether an absence of transfer of ownership of the trust property is contemplated though.

13 Hayton et al., *Underhill and Hayton*, above, note 7.

14 Chinese Trust Law, art. 30: 'The trustee shall handle trust business himself, but may entrust another person to handle such affairs on his behalf where the trust documents provide otherwise or he has to do so for reasons beyond his control.'

15 Ibid., art. 15: 'The trust shall be differentiated from other property that is not put under trust by the settlor. . .'.

B. *Necessity of transfer of ownership of trust property*

A common law trust arises where the settlor transfers his property to the trustee who holds and manages it for the benefit of the beneficiary. Fundamental to this conception of transfer of ownership is that a trustee holds property belonging (beneficially) to another. The Chinese trust, however, does not mandate transfer of ownership of the trust property. Two questions arise: first, whether arrangements that are structurally trusts can be set up notwithstanding the absence of transfer of ownership of the trust property; and second, whether this has created any difficulties in practice. While it is true that a Chinese trust that does not mandate transfer of trust property may give rise to many difficult conceptual questions, it appears that it has not created significant problems in practice. According to article 10 of the Chinese Trust Law,[16] where trust property is registrable, there needs to be trust registration before the trust would become effective. In China, most trusts established so far involved trusts of money, which are not registrable. The trust thus takes effect when the trust contract is entered into. The settlor almost invariably has to transfer (by physical delivery) ownership of the trust money to the trustee in order that the trustee may exercise the rights of administration and disposal granted to him under the Chinese Trust Law.[17] Thus, even though transfer of ownership of the trust property is not required, this is carried out in most cases. On the other hand, where trust property is registrable, such as land, the trust will only have effect if the registration formalities have been complied with. No detailed guidelines have been provided on how such registration is to be done. But it is likely that at least the fact that the property is subject to a trust has to be disclosed upon registration. Third parties dealing with the trust will therefore not be subject to its hidden proprietary effect.

Notwithstanding the above, the conceptual question remains. Besides, there may still be circumstances where the settlor retains ownership and is managing the trust property as if he were the trustee, so that the conceptual difficulties raised by the absence of transfer of ownership of trust property still need to be addressed. This

[16] Ibid., art. 10: 'Where laws or administrative regulations stipulate that registration formalities shall be gone through for the creation of a trust, such formalities shall be gone through accordingly. Anyone who fails to go through the registration formalities prescribed in the preceding paragraph shall go through the formalities as required; otherwise, the trust shall have no effect.'

[17] See, e.g., arts. 2, 14, 25 and 29.

issue relates to the function served by transfer of ownership, and hence the substantive feature to which it corresponds.

Honoré considers the trustee's (legal) ownership of the trust property 'inessential', because even if assets are vested in the trustee, they must still be separated in law from the trustee's private assets in order that the beneficiaries are to be protected. The function of vesting (legal) title in the trustee is to enable management.[18] Unlike full ownership, a trustee who has merely legal title cannot deal with the property as he pleases. He cannot, for example, use trust property which is legally owned by him to satisfy the claims of his private creditors. Instead, he only has the right to manage the trust property while the beneficiary has the right to enjoy it. Transfer of ownership merely enables the imposition of additional rights and duties on the trustee and the beneficiary so as to create the necessary tension between them to ensure division of management and enjoyment. This protects beneficiaries from the trustee's insolvency or misapplication of trust property.[19] Transfer of (legal) ownership to the trustee is only the most convenient arrangement for the common law in light of its historical equity heritage. It is but a structural feature of the English trust that corresponds to the substantive feature of rights and duties of trustees and beneficiaries in it.[20]

Hence, it is the transfer of ownership which enables the imposition of additional rights and duties on the trustee and beneficiary that is essential to the trust. At common law, control mechanisms are then imposed to prevent abuse of the trustee's (legal) ownership and, in turn, protection of the beneficiaries' (equitable) ownership. Viewed this way, civil law jurisdictions can introduce a trust without violating the indigenous principle of indivisibility of ownership so long as this tension is sustained by, inter alia, imposing sufficient control mechanisms on the powers and discretions of the trustee (and correspondingly, granting sufficient rights to beneficiaries). The Chinese Trust Law has no difficulties imposing

[18] Tony Honoré, 'Trusts: The Inessentials', in Joshua Getzler (ed.), *Rationalizing Property, Equity and Trusts: Essays in Honour of Edward Burn* (Oxford University Press, 2003), ch. 1 at p. 9. See also Tony Honoré, 'On Fitting Trusts into Civil Law Jurisdictions'; available at http://users.ox.ac.uk/~alls0079/chinatrusts2.PDF (last accessed on 1 April 2013).

[19] See, e.g., de Waal, 'In Search of a Model', above, note 2, 67. See also Patrick Parkinson, 'Reconceptualising the Express Trust' (2002) 61 *Cambridge Law Journal* 657 at 680: 'Equity protects the trust by means of tension', although he takes the view that beneficiaries (or enforcers) must have an interest in the trust property.

[20] Cf. section 402 of the American Uniform Trust Code: '(a) A trust is created only if . . . (4) the trustee has duties to perform'.

control mechanisms on the managerial powers of the trustee. The question becomes one of sufficiency of the control mechanisms in light of the absence of transfer of trust property. This calls for an evaluation of the operational rules on the duties and liabilities of the trustee under the Chinese trust.

III Duties and liabilities of trustees under the Chinese trust and the 'irreducible core content of trusteeship'

A. *Irreducible core content of trusteeship*

Hayton, in his influential article,[21] proposes that at the heart of the trust lie the trustee's duties to the beneficiaries. He identifies two such core duties, namely:

(1) the duty to account to beneficiaries: '[t]he beneficiaries' right to enforce the trust and make the trustees account for their conduct with the correlative duties of the trustees to the beneficiaries are at the core of the trust';[22] and
(2) the duty to act honestly and in good faith: '[t]he duty to act in good faith (i.e. honestly and consciously) in respect of any trust matter cannot, of course, be excluded. To do so would make a nonsense of the trust relationship as an obligation of confidence.'[23]

Millett LJ (as he then was) also echoed an irreducible core of trusteeship in *Armitage* v. *Nurse*.[24] While his Lordship reckoned that 'if the beneficiaries have no rights enforceable against the trustees there are no trusts', the core duty of trustees was only to 'perform the trusts honestly and in good faith for the beneficiaries'.[25]

What follows is an examination of these two aspects of the core content of trusteeship to see if they are present in the Chinese trust. The purpose is twofold: first, to see whether, insofar as fiduciary management of trust property is concerned, a Chinese trust is functionally

[21] David Hayton, 'The Irreducible Core Content of Trusteeship', in A. J. Oakley (ed.), *Trends in Contemporary Trust Law* (Oxford: Clarendon Press, 1996), ch. 3.

[22] Ibid., p. 47. Although Millett LJ did not state that the duty to provide accounts was an irreducible core obligation of a trustee, his Lordship did agree that '[e]very beneficiary is entitled to see the trust accounts, whether his interest is in possession or not': *Armitage* v. *Nurse* [1998] Ch 241, 261.

[23] Hayton, 'Irreducible Core', above, note 21, p. 57.

[24] *Armitage*, above, note 22.

[25] Ibid., para. 253.

equivalent to an English one notwithstanding the absence of transfer of ownership of trust property; and if so, secondly, the implications of such functional equivalence for the 'irreducible core content of trusteeship' and conceptual basis of the Chinese trust.

B. Duty to account to beneficiaries

1. Duty to account and provide information under English and Chinese trusts laws

According to Hayton, the essential ingredient of trusteeship is 'the duty to account which affords the beneficiaries a correlative right to have the court enforce the trustees' fundamental obligation to account'.[26] What does this 'duty to account' entail? It seems that this core duty comprises at least (i) the duty to inform beneficiaries that they are beneficiaries;[27] (ii) the duty to keep accounts;[28] and (iii) the duty to provide information.[29] Accordingly, the trustee must (i) take steps to ensure that (discretionary) beneficiaries[30] know that they are such, so that they can hold trustees accountable for their stewardship of the trust property; (ii) keep clear and accurate accounts of the trust property;[31] and (iii) give beneficiaries full and accurate information as to the amount and state of the trust property, and to permit inspection of the relevant accounts and vouchers.[32]

Modern commonwealth decisions have also confirmed the trustee's duty to account, and hence the beneficiary's correlative right to information, on the basis of the trustee's core accountability to beneficiaries.[33]

[26] Hayton, 'Irreducible Core', above, note 21, pp. 49–50. See also Hayton et al., *Underhill and Hayton*, above, note 7, para. 56.2: 'The rights of a beneficiary to monitor and protect his interest by obtaining accounts from the trustee so that they can then be falsified or surcharged is at the very core of the trust concept.' In a similar vein, see also section 173 of the Restatement (Second) of Trusts which stipulates a trustee's duty to account.

[27] See Hayton, 'Irreducible Core', above, note 21, p. 49. [28] Ibid., p. 57.

[29] Ibid., p. 49. Note that the reasons for the trustees' exercise of distributive powers in favour of beneficiaries need not be disclosed.

[30] Ibid., p. 50. Hayton suggests that this right to information does not extend to objects of a fiduciary power. This has been criticized, see Jonathan Hilliard, 'The Rights to Information of an Object of a Fiduciary Mere Power' (2003) 10 *Journal of International Trust and Corporate Planning* 209.

[31] Hayton et al., *Underhill and Hayton*, above, note 7, para. 56.1.

[32] Ibid., para. 56.1. Accordingly, the settlor cannot require his trustees to withhold information without which the beneficiaries cannot vindicate the rights that the settlor purported to give them: see Hayton, 'Irreducible Core', above, note 21, p. 53.

[33] See, e.g., *Hartigan Nominees Pty Ltd* v. *Rydge* [1992] 29 NSWLR 405; *Re Rabaiotti's Settlement* [2000] WTLR 953.

For example, the Privy Council in *Schmidt* v. *Rosewood Trust Ltd*[34] opined that the basis of disclosure was the court's inherent jurisdiction to supervise, and if necessary intervene in, the administration of the trust.

In China, trustees are subject to a range of duties. The overriding duty is that a trustee must manage the trust property 'for the best interests of the beneficiary', rather than for his personal benefit.[35] Accordingly, he must segregate trust property from property of his own, and administer trust property separately from his own.[36] In order to ensure segregation of trust property, the trustee is under a duty to keep and provide accounts as set out in article 33 of the Chinese Trust Law:

> The trustee shall keep complete records of the trust business handled.
>
> The trustee shall, at regular intervals every year, report to the settlor and beneficiary on the administration and disposition of the trust property and the income and expenses relating to the property.
>
> The trustee shall, in accordance with law, have the obligation to keep confidential minutes relating to the settlor, the beneficiary and trust business handled.

Article 20 of the Chinese Trust Law correspondingly states that the settlor shall have the right to know the administration, use and disposition of the trust property, and the right to request the trustee to give explanations in this regard. Article 49 grants the same right to beneficiaries. Therefore, in brief, the Chinese Trust Law imposes on the trustee two main duties to provide information: (1) duty to keep accounts and furnish reports on the management, use and disposition of trust property; and (2) duty to provide explanations upon request. Although it is not expressly stated, it is generally accepted that documents relating to trust accounts, including supporting vouchers and accounting books and other relevant data, are disclosable.[37]

2. Sufficiency of the control mechanisms: refining the content and scope of the core duties

By giving trustees appropriate powers of management subject to preventive control mechanisms for abuses, the Chinese trust could be regarded

[34] *Schmidt* v. *Rosewood Trust Ltd* [2003] UKPC 26; [2003] 2 AC 709. Cf. *Breakspear* v. *Ackland* [2008] EWHC 220; [2008] 3 WLR 698.

[35] Chinese Trust Law, art. 25: 'The trustee shall abide by the provisions in the trust documents and handle trust business for the best interests of the beneficiary…'. See, further, discussion in Part III.C below.

[36] Ibid., art. 16 and art. 29.

[37] Zhong Ruidong and Chen Xiangcong, *Xintoufa* [*Trust Law*], 2nd edn (Xiamen Daixue Chubanshe [Xiamen University Press], 2007), pp. 89–90.

as functionally equivalent to an English trust insofar as fiduciary management of trust property is concerned. However, as mentioned above, that a trustee should be mandated to account to beneficiaries is premised on the settlor's transfer of trust property to the trustee. As Hayton recognizes:

> unaccountability to the beneficiaries arising from the trustees not letting them know that they are beneficiaries is inconsistent with, and repugnant to, the purposes for which the settlor *transferred* the trust property to the trustees . . .[38]

The transfer of ownership to both the trustee and the beneficiary in English law is significant because this ensures that checks on the managerial powers of the trustee need not depend solely on the duties imposed on him, but also on the (equitable) ownership interest of the beneficiary, in that the beneficiary's ownership also operates to bolster the protection to him in order to support the necessary tension between the trustee and the beneficiary. This can be illustrated by the principle in *Saunders* v. *Vautier*.[39] By virtue of the beneficiaries' indefeasible equitable ownership in the trust property, all beneficiaries, being *sui juris* jointly, are entitled to direct the trustees to convey the trust property to them notwithstanding any express constraints on the gift. This underlies a pro-beneficiary principle that empowers beneficiaries to shape the way in which trustees exercise their discretions.[40]

Chinese law diverges. Although trustees are subject to comparable core duties, the beneficiary is in a relatively weak position: while articles 43 and 44 of the Chinese Trust Law stipulate that beneficiaries enjoy the 'right to benefit' from a trust, the Property Law[41] does not recognize a property right known as the beneficial right of enjoyment. The *numerus clausus* principle[42] also requires that new property rights can only be

[38] See Hayton, 'Irreducible Core', above, note 21, p. 49 (emphasis added).

[39] *Saunders* v. *Vautier* [1841] 4 Beav 115.

[40] Joshua Getzler, 'Transplantation and Mutation in Anglo-American Trust Law' (2009) 10(2) *Theoretical Inquiries in Law* 355, 369.

[41] Property Law of the People's Republic of China 2007 (Order of the President of the People's Republic of China No. 62), adopted at the fifth session of the Tenth National People's Congress on 16 March 2007 and came into effect on 1 October 2007. Official translation by the National People's Congress of the PRC available at www.npc.gov.cn/englishnpc/Law/2009-02/20/content_1471118.htm (last accessed on 1 April 2013).

[42] The *numerus clausus* principle is embodied in Chinese law by virtue of article 5, ibid., which requires '[t]he categories and contents of the property right [to] be stipulated by law'.

created by law. Thus, the beneficiary does not own the trust property. Moreover, it is the settlor who retains or is granted extensive powers; and the core trust obligation to account is not only owed to the beneficiary, but also to the settlor. These features necessitate modification of the core duties to accommodate the special features of the Chinese trust to ensure more stringent control mechanisms in the trust to protect the beneficiaries. It is submitted that, first, in light of the lack of ownership interest on the part of the beneficiaries to influence the trustees' exercise of their discretions, the core duties of trustees will need to be augmented to enhance protection of the beneficiaries. Second, in view of the prominent status of the settlor, the scope of application of these core duties will need to be expanded to cover settlors as well. A detailed discussion of each of the above is in order.

(a) Refining the content of the duty to account The role of the duty to account and provide information is to ensure that the trustee's decisions are known or discoverable to the beneficiaries so as to sustain the tension between the trustee and the beneficiary. The Chinese Trust Law has already stipulated that the trustee should be under a duty to provide sufficient information to enable beneficiaries to monitor and evaluate the trustee's performance, or to make an informed request if necessary. In order to make the duty to account meaningful, what it should additionally state is that trustees are under a duty to inform beneficiaries that they are such.

One question arises. If the type of information requested falls outside the scope of disclosable documents (i.e. they do not relate to 'the administration, use and disposition of, and the income and expenses relating to [the] trust property' under article 20), do the settlor and beneficiary enjoy an unlimited right to information over and above the scope delineated in article 20? It would be useful to include a provision to deal with such exceptional circumstances. It is submitted that the beneficiary's (and settlor's) right to information should only be subject to minimal restrictions so as to enhance protection to the beneficiaries. Thus, all documents should prima facie be disclosable if they are relevant to the interests of the beneficiaries (or settlor), unless disclosure may have an adverse effect on the trust,[43] subject to the court's exercise of supervisory discretion to the contrary.

[43] E.g., if the beneficiary is, say, a member of the managerial staff of a company that competes with the one the trust fund has been investing in, disclosing the details of the investment to the beneficiary may enable him to act in a way that jeopardizes the trust.

(b) Expanding the scope of application of the core duties to settlors

Second, and more significantly, what distinguishes the Chinese trust from an English trust is that under the Chinese trust the settlor is granted rights of enforcement that are commensurate with those of the beneficiaries. In fact, apart from the right to inspect trust documents, the settlor is also granted other extensive powers to intervene in the trustee's management of the trust property, including the power to manage the trust property, and even the right to request the trustee to adjust the methods of management.[44]

The prominence of the settlor's status shows that the Chinese trust is, from beginning to end, a relationship among three parties, and so there also needs to be an optimal balance between the settlor and the trustee's rights.[45] This, however, gives rise to a few problems. First, the focus on the settlor's right to monitor the Chinese trust may be incompatible with the very tension between the trustee and the beneficiary that is necessary to sustain the trust. The continued ownership of trust property by the settlor and the powers retained by him without corresponding duties being imposed fail to ensure that he will not misappropriate the trust property or act in a way inconsistent with the best interests of the beneficiaries. This is exacerbated by the fact that although beneficiaries have rights against trustees, they have no rights against settlors. In fact, in certain circumstances, the settlor has stronger rights than the beneficiaries, such as the power to replace the beneficiary or dispose of his right to benefit from the trust if the beneficiary commits a major tort against the settlor.[46] Second, the settlor's prominent status also runs counter to Hayton's view that the irreducible core content of trusteeship is to '[set] limits to the free will of the settlor',[47] as well as the principle in *Saunders* v. *Vautier* which demonstrates that not even the settlor might impose conditions or restraints on the trust property to interfere with the beneficiary's interest.[48] Hence, it is submitted that, first, when the settlor

44 Chinese Trust Law, arts. 20–3.

45 Frances H. Foster, 'American Trust Law in a Chinese Mirror' (2010) 94 *Minnesota Law Review* 602, 641.

46 Chinese Trust Law, art. 51(1).

47 Hayton, 'Irreducible Core', above, note 21, p. 49.

48 The English position may be contrasted with the American one which places slightly fewer restrictions on settlor autonomy. American courts followed the English rule in *Saunders* v. *Vautier* until the Supreme Judicial Court of Massachusetts in *Claflin* v. *Claflin* 149 Mass 19, 20 N.E. 455 (1889) refused termination of a trust notwithstanding consent of all beneficiaries in favour of the testator's contrary intent and freedom to dispose of his

exercises powers to intervene in the trustee's management of the trust property, he should be subject to similar duties as the trustee; and second, there should be restraints on the extent to which the Chinese Trust Law may allow deference to the settlor's wishes. This latter point will become evident when we examine the ability of the settlor to allow trustees to detract from their core duty of honesty and good faith performance.

C. *Duty to act honestly and in good faith and the efficacy of trustee exemption clauses in relieving a trustee's liabilities*

As mentioned above, Hayton also suggests that the duty to act honestly and in good faith is part of the 'irreducible core of obligations' owed by trustees. This aspect of the duty has particular relevance to the permissible scope of exemption clauses.

1. Duty to act honestly and in good faith under English and Chinese trusts laws

In modern trust practice, trustee exemption clauses are almost invariably inserted into the trust instrument by professional trustees or their solicitors. English law now permits exemption clauses to validly exonerate trustees from liability for all non-fraudulent breaches of trust. Millett LJ in *Armitage* v. *Nurse*[49] rejected the proposition that a trustee exemption clause which purported to exclude all liability except for actual fraud was void, either for repugnancy or as contrary to public policy. The duty of the trustees to perform the trusts honestly and in good faith for the benefit of the beneficiaries was both necessary and sufficient to give substance to the trusts. Thus, he permitted an extremely generous exemption of liability: clauses exempting trustee liability for gross negligence were not incompatible with the fundamental tenets of trusteeship.[50]

In China, it is unclear whether a settlor may create a trust in which the trustees are not liable for gross negligence or reckless breach of trust. At

property. This is now known as the material purpose doctrine, which maintains that trust beneficiaries cannot compel a trust's premature termination unless all beneficiaries consent *and* such termination will not defeat a material purpose of the trust (see section 411(b) of the Uniform Trust Code).

49 Hayton, 'Irreducible Core', above, note 21, p. 47.

50 See also Hayton, who takes the view that liability arising from negligence (whether ordinary or gross negligence) may be exempted, but not liability arising from recklessness in the sense of deliberate indifference to one's responsibilities, because the latter would enable the trustees to act in bad faith and negate a core duty of the trustees ('Irreducible Core', above, note 21, p. 59).

the moment, the Trust Law does not contain any regulation of trustee exemption clauses, nor does it prohibit them. In fact, articles 28 and 30 of the Chinese Trust Law, which regulate dealings with trust property and non-delegation of the trustee's duties, permit parties to contract out from these duties. Control of exemption clauses, however, can only be found in the Contract Law,[51] alongside a principle of good faith and fairness in contracting contained in the General Principles of Civil Law.[52]

There are, however, difficulties applying the Contract Law to determine the efficacy of trustee exemption clauses in a Chinese trust. It is not surprising that the scope of statutory control under articles 39–41 of the Contract Law is confined to contractual parties. Besides, they apply only to exemption clauses that take the form of a standard clause inserted by one party without giving the other any room to negotiate.[53] This means that the statutory rules are inapplicable to contracts fully negotiated between two commercial parties of equal bargaining power. A (trust) contract entered into between the settlor and the trustee is very different in form and substance from, say, a consumer contract between parties of unequal bargaining power. In any case, there is also an apparent inconsistency between article 39 and article 40. Whereas article 39 permits exemption clauses to remain valid if the party providing it brings the clause to the reasonable attention of the other,[54] article 40 suggests that they will most likely be void.[55]

[51] Contract Law of the People's Republic of China, adopted at the second session of the Ninth National People's Congress on 15 March 1999 and came into force as of 1 October 1999. Official translation by the National People's Congress available at www.npc.gov.cn/englishnpc/Law/2007-12/11/content_1383564.htm (last accessed on 1 April 2013).

[52] General Principles of the Civil Law, adopted at the fourth session of the Sixth National People's Congress on 12 April 1986 and promulgated by Order No. 37 of the President of the People's Republic of China on 12 April 1986. Official translation by the National People's Congress available at www.npc.gov.cn/englishnpc/Law/2007-12/12/content_1383941.htm, arts. 4 and 5 (last accessed 1 April 2013).

[53] Contract Law of China, above, note 51. Standard clauses are defined in article 39 to mean 'clauses that are formulated in anticipation by a party for the purpose of repeated usage and that are not a result of consultation with the other party in the making of the contract'.

[54] Ibid., art. 39: 'If standard clauses are used in making a contract, the party that provides the standard clauses shall determine the rights and obligations between the parties in accordance with the principle of fairness, and shall call in a reasonable manner the other party's attention to the exemptible and restrictive clauses regarding its liability, and give explanations of such clauses at the request of the other party.'

[55] Ibid., art. 40. Article 40 of the Contract Law provides that a standard clause exempting the party inserting it from liability, imposing greater liability on the other party, or precluding the other party from its main rights will be invalid.

The trustee's duty to provide information is owed not only to the beneficiaries, but also to the settlor. The provisions of the Chinese Trust Law conferring extensive rights on the settlor reinforce a conception of trust arising from the contractual undertaking by the trustee towards the settlor for the benefit of a third party beneficiary. The settlor, being a party to the contract, has the right to demand proper performance of the contract from the trustee.[60] As regards the trustee's duty of honesty and good faith, whereas the Chinese Trust Law does expressly specify such a duty in administering the trust property absent any express provisions on regulation of exemption clauses in the Chinese Trust Law, it is unclear whether the settlor may allow the trustee to detract from this duty. In any case, if the efficacy of a trustee exemption clause is going to be tested by reference to a similar clause in a contract, the trust institution is likely to be analysed as a form of contract. In fact, Chinese courts are also inclined to characterize the trust as a form of contract.[61]

Consequently, it seems that there is doctrinal divergence between English and Chinese views on the conceptualization of the trust. A contractual understanding of the Chinese trust is consistent with Professor Langbein's suggestion that trust law's contractarian elements predominate.[62] The trust is a deal about how trust property is to be managed and distributed. The distinguishing feature is not transfer of property from the settlor to the trustee, but the trust deal that defines the powers of the trustee in managing the property, as well as the duties of the trustee in protecting beneficiaries from the risk of trustee misbehaviour.

parties agree that the debtor shall discharge the debts to a third party and where the debtor fails to do so or fails to meet its liability as contracted, the debtor shall bear the liability for breach of contract to the creditor'), a third party who benefits from the performance of a contract cannot sue the debtor/contracting party directly for non-performance under article 64. Accordingly, article 64 does not give the third party any independent legal right, and so does not actually provide for the establishment of a contract for benefit of third parties.

60 See also Ho, 'The Reception of Trust', above, note 2, 296. Indeed, article 8 of the Trust Law of China requires written forms such as trust contracts to be adopted for the establishment of a trust, thus anticipating the trust to be created by virtue of a contract.

61 See, e.g., *Yanxin Co. Ltd* v. *Huabao Trust and Investment Co. Ltd*, Shanghai High People's Court, 16 March 2005, Decision No. 226 of 2004 where the Court invoked the Contract Law to deal with assignment of the settlor's rights under a trust. For details see Lusina Ho, 'Trust Laws in China: History, Ambiguity, and Beneficiaries' Rights', in Lionel Smith (ed.), *Re-imagining the Trust: Trusts in Civil Law* (Cambridge University Press, 2012), ch. 5.

62 John H. Langbein, 'The Contractarian Basis of the Law of Trusts' (1995) 105 *Yale Law Journal* 625, 627: 'the deal between settlor and trustee is functionally indistinguishable from the modern third party beneficiary contract. Trusts are contracts.'

Nevertheless, analysing the trust as a form of contract between the settlor and the trustee does not confer unrestrained freedom of contract (trust) on either the trustee or the settlor. The trustee remains subject to an irreducible core content of trusteeship, which includes the duties of account and good faith performance to protect the beneficiaries' interest.[63] On the other hand, while a contractual approach may give the settlor more autonomy, it is likely that deference to his wishes will be limited by prohibiting him from inserting trust terms that permit trustees to derogate from good faith administration of the trust.[64] Hence, the duty of honesty and good faith performance should operate to limit the permitted scope of exemption clauses.

B. *Conceptualizing the Chinese trust as a contract*

Not only does the experience of China show that it is possible to embrace a trust by contract, an examination of the irreducible core content of trusteeship also shows that 'contractualizing' the trust is gaining favour even in traditional common law jurisdictions.[65] For example, it has been argued that the reasoning in *Armitage* v. *Nurse* suggested that trust terms are merely a matter of agreement between the settlor and the trustee to deal with property for the benefit of third parties, hence permitting inclusion of provisions to relieve trustee liability. Such reasoning emphasizes the obligational aspect of trusts over their proprietary aspect, the latter of which recognizes the beneficiary as the property owner and treats the trust terms as running with the trust property.[66]

[63] According to Langbein, these should more precisely be regarded as mandatory rules applicable to both the trustee and the settlor. These mandatory rules implement the settlor's intent of benefiting the beneficiaries (a settlor who has contrary intent would need to articulate this clearly). Without these rules, the trust obligation would be illusory, effectively allowing the trustee to loot the trust. See, further, John H. Langbein, 'Mandatory Rules in the Law of Trusts' (2004) 98 *Northwestern University Law Review* 1105 at 1126.

[64] See also Langbein, 'Rembrandt', above, note 56, arguing that a settlor is not allowed to direct the trustee to make investment decisions that are harmful to the beneficiaries' interests.

[65] See, e.g., Langbein, 'Contractarian Basis of Trusts', above, note 62; Parkinson, 'Reconceptualising the Express Trust', above, note 19; D. J. Hayton, 'Developing the Obligation Characteristic of the Trust' (2001) 117 *Law Quarterly Review* 96.

[66] James Penner, 'Exemptions', in Peter Birks and Arianna Pretto (eds.), *Breach of Trust* (Oxford: Hart Publishing, 2002), ch. 8; Bryan, 'Contractual Modification', above, note 58. If the trust is a form of property ownership, the beneficiary is the property owner and the

If a trust is understood as a (contractual) obligation, what distinguishes this trust obligation is, therefore, not the settlor's transfer of his interest in the trust property to the trustee, but rather duties of the trustees to the beneficiaries in managing the trust property as defined by the terms of the trust. However, the rights and duties of the various parties to a trust represent only the internal aspect of the trust, namely fiduciary management of trust property. The external aspect of the trust – which deals with the trust's relationship with third parties (e.g. trust property being unavailable to satisfy claims of the trustee's personal creditors, and enforceability of the trust arrangement on third party transferees) – must also be accounted for before a contractual conceptualization can be fully accepted.[67] It is submitted that if a trust is conceptualized as an obligation, the primary role of the trust obligation is to subject the trustee to obligations to account and act honestly and in good faith. But it does not mean that the arrangement produces no proprietary effects. Rather, the proprietary effects of the trust obligation are more limited and merely secondary, in the sense that they are merely instituted to help ensure the trustee's compliance with his primary obligations to account and act honestly and in good faith.

In the case of the Chinese trust, beneficiaries do not seem to have any (equitable) proprietary interest in the trust to provide foundation for any *in rem* explanation of the proprietary effects of a Chinese trust against third parties. Nonetheless, they may be explicable along the lines of the above suggestion. Two such proprietary features (identified above) merit further discussion. First, trust property is usually not available to satisfy claims of the trustee's personal creditors. In this regard, article 16 of the Chinese Trust Law creates a separate trust fund which would not be available to satisfy claims of the trustee's personal creditors or successors.[68] Significantly, this separate trust patrimony comprises not only the initial trust property, but also its substituted assets, for article 26 stipulates that

trust terms are not a matter of agreement between the settlor and the trustee but run with the trust property, thus rendering trustee exemption clauses conceptually impossible.

[67] See, e.g., Henry Hansmann and Ugo Mattei, 'The Functions of Trust Law: A Comparative Legal and Economic Analysis' (1998) 73 *New York University Law Review* 434, 471: 'the important contribution of trust law lies . . . in its ordering of the relationships between those persons and third parties with whom they deal'. The ring-fencing function of the trust is significant in distinguishing it from other legal devices.

[68] Chinese Trust Law, art. 16: '[t]he trust property shall be segregated from the property owned by the trustee . . . Where the trustee dies . . . or is declared bankrupt . . . the trust property shall not be deemed his legacy or liquidation property.'

(unauthorized) profits made by the trustee by using the trust property will be disgorged and integrated into the trust property.[69] While the beneficiary's right to trust property that is immune from claims of the trustee's personal creditors or successors may still be regarded as a personal right against the trustee's duty to segregate trust property, the appropriation of disgorged profits into the trust property is akin to imposing proprietary (constructive trust) liability on the trustee. Nonetheless, such proprietary effects are limited (in that the beneficiary's right is enforceable against the trustee only), and secondary in nature (in that it is a remedy consequent on the trustee's unlawful disposition of the trust property for personal benefit) to ensure the trustee's compliance with his primary obligation to account to the beneficiaries.

The other typical proprietary feature is that beneficiaries have a right to claim against unauthorized transferees or recipients of misappropriated trust property. In the context of the Chinese trust, the beneficiary has (limited) secondary rights to claim the misapplied trust property against an indeterminate class of persons. If the trustee misapplies trust property and transfers it to third parties, the beneficiary will be able to claim against the third-party transferee. The beneficiary's claim is, however, subject to two restrictions: [70] first, his claim is only enforceable against a third party who accepted the trust property 'knowing' that the disposition violates the purpose of the trust; and second, the transferee would only be subject to the more limited personal remedies of compensation or restitution of the trust property to its original state (as opposed to the full breadth of proprietary liability by way of constructive trust against all transferees consequent on an equitable tracing process at common law). This ensures the transferee's personal creditors or successors will not be subject to hidden proprietary effects under a Chinese trust.

Thus, while the primary role of the trust is to subject the trustee to obligations of accountability and good faith, such obligations do produce (limited) secondary proprietary effects to help ensure that these primary obligations are met. To this end, it may not be implausible to adopt an

[69] Chinese Trust Law, art. 26: 'Where the trustee . . . seeks interests for himself by using the trust property, the interests gained therefrom shall be integrated into the trust property.'

[70] Ibid., art. 22: 'Where a transferee of the [trust property disposed of in breach of the purposes of the trust] accepts the property while knowing the violation of the purposes of the trust, he shall return the property or make compensation.'

'obligation' view of the Chinese trust to explain the limited proprietary effects arising from the beneficiary's right to trustee accountability under the trust arrangement.

V Conclusion

This chapter has examined China's experience with transplanting the common law trust. It reveals that the transplantation is not a process of replication. Rather, in order to avoid conflicts with indigenous legal concepts, some orthodox English trust doctrines are disregarded. Nonetheless, the core trustee duties are not displaced. This shows that arrangements that are structurally trusts can be set up notwithstanding the absence of transfer of ownership of trust property, so long as the substantive features that correspond to the common law mode of creating a trust and the essential functions it serves are preserved. Accordingly, when one looks beyond the jurisdictional roots, the creation of a common law trust by transfer of ownership of the trust property can be explained in civilian terminology, and a trust can be established no matter where the ownership of the trust property is located. It is therefore possible for civil law jurisdictions to embrace a trust so long as the core elements of a trust are present, one of which is the imposition of duties on the trustee to protect the beneficiary.

This chapter considers the function served by the transfer of ownership, namely the trustee–beneficiary tension it sustains through the imposition of rights and duties on the trustee and the beneficiary, and the implications on the core duties of trustees. It suggests that there is functional convergence on the core content of trusteeship between an English and a Chinese trust, in that both require duties of accountability and good faith performance. Nonetheless, these duties must be refined in order to cater for the special features of the Chinese trust. The point of divergence arises in relation to the conceptual basis of the trust. In the case of the Chinese trust, the examination of the two core duties points towards a contractual understanding of the trust.

What remains to be seen is how far such a contractual conceptualization can go. Insofar as it explains the internal relationships between the settlor, the trustee and the beneficiary, a contractual conceptualization of the trust suffices. This is because the internal aspect of the trust, namely fiduciary management of trust property, is akin to a contractual arrangement. However, the distinctiveness of the trust also lies in the nature of the trust property being ring-fenced, and this relates to the external aspect of the trust, namely the proprietary effects of a trust against third parties. This asset-partitioning function of the trust must also be accounted for before a contractual understanding of the trust can be fully endorsed.[71]

[71] Indeed, the fact that trust assets are segregated from all other assets of the trustee, in that they are immune from the claims of the trustee's heirs and personal creditors under articles 16 and 17 of the Chinese Trust Law, distinguishes the Chinese trust from a contract for the benefit of third parties. Thus, it seems that the functions of the trust can neither be fully explained nor replaced by contract. For an alternative, illuminating view, see Kenneth Reid, 'Conceptualizing the Chinese Trust: Some Thoughts from Europe', in Chen Lei and C. H. van Rhee (eds.), *Towards a Civil Code: Comparative and Historical Perspectives* (Leiden: Martinus Neijhoff, 2012), pp. 209–23.

18

Trust law as fiduciary governance plus asset partitioning

ROBERT H. SITKOFF

I Introduction

Organizational law – a category that includes the law of corporations, limited liability companies, partnerships and trusts – has two core functions. First, organizational law supplies a set of contractarian rules, some of a fiduciary character, that provide for the *internal governance* or *administration* of the organization. These are the rules that provide for the powers and duties of the managers and the rights of the beneficial owners.

Second, organizational law supplies a set of proprietary rules that provide for *asset partitioning* or *ring-fencing* or *entity shielding*. These are the rules that provide for the separation of the property of the organization from the property of the organization's managers, beneficial owners and other insiders. Asset partitioning requires rules of agency to establish the authority of the managers to bind the organization in dealings with third parties, and rules of court procedure to establish the ability of the organization and third parties to sue each other.

Reconciliation of the contractarian governance and proprietary asset partitioning features of trust law is the theme that ties together the chapters for this volume by Thomas P. Gallanis and by Rebecca Lee.[1]

The author thanks Joshua Getzler, Henry Hansmann, Daniel Kleinberger, Reinier Kraakman and John Langbein for helpful comments and suggestions, and Greg Dihlmann-Malzer, Ronnie Gosselin and Jeffrey Hughes for excellent research assistance. Portions of this chapter derive from R. H. Sitkoff, 'The Economic Structure of Fiduciary Law' (2011) 91 *Boston University Law Review* 1039. In accordance with Harvard Law School's policy on conflicts of interest, the author discloses certain outside activities, one or more of which may relate to the subject matter of this chapter, at http://www.law.harvard.edu/faculty/COI/2012_Sitkoff_Robert.html.

[1] T. P. Gallanis, 'The Contribution of Fiduciary Law', Chapter 16 in this volume; R. Lee, 'Convergence and Divergence in the Worlds of the Trust: Duties and Liabilities of Trustees under the Chinese Trust', Chapter 17 in this volume.

Gallanis argues for the importance of the governance features of trust law, chiefly trust fiduciary law. He frames his argument as a reply to scholars of organizational law whom he believes have mistakenly emphasized the significance of trust law's asset partitioning features and unfairly disparaged the importance of trust fiduciary law. Gallanis argues that trust fiduciary law is as important as its asset partitioning rules, and that Anglo-American trust fiduciary law provides a suitable template for civilian jurisdictions that are assimilating the trust concept.

Lee treats the Chinese enactment in 2001 of a systematic law of trusts as a natural experiment on the nature and function of trusteeship. Because China follows the civilian tradition of indivisible property ownership, the assimilation of Anglo-American trust law into Chinese law required replicating trust law's governance and asset partitioning functions without the express bifurcation of legal and beneficial ownership that is characteristic of the common law trust. Lee's thesis is that the Chinese law of trusts therefore provides a window on the essential characteristics of trusteeship.

The remainder of this essay, a commentary on the Gallanis and Lee chapters from an American perspective, is organized as follows. Part II develops further the idea that, the lack of juridical personality notwithstanding, trust law follows the governance and asset partitioning pattern of organizational law. Part III comments on the Gallanis essay. Part IV comments on the Lee essay. Part V concludes. The underlying theme of this essay is that trust law is not a species of property law or contract law, but rather is a species of organizational law.

II Trust law as organizational law

The hallmark characteristic of the common law trust is bifurcation: the trustee holds legal title to the trust property and the beneficiaries have the equitable, or beneficial, interests. Two categories of issues arise from this splitting of legal and equitable ownership: (1) the powers and duties of the trustee and the corresponding rights of the beneficiary with respect to the trust property and against the trustee (*governance*), and (2) the effect on the rights of third parties with respect to the trust property versus the personal property of the trustee (*asset partitioning*). These issues – governance and asset partitioning – are together the core domain of organizational law.[2]

[2] See, e.g., R. H. Sitkoff, 'An Agency Costs Theory of Trust Law' (2004) 89 *Cornell Law Review* 621, 624–34.

A. *Fiduciary governance: powers and duties*

The underlying purpose of governance rules is to enable an organization's managers to act expeditiously on behalf of the organization and its beneficial owners while minimizing the agency costs arising from the separation of management and beneficial ownership.[3] In the context of trust governance, the focus is on safeguarding the beneficiary's interest from mismanagement or misappropriation by the trustee in circumstances in which the trustee must have discretionary powers of administration.

The traditional but now outmoded governance strategy for protecting the beneficiary's interests was to negate the agency problem by disempowering the trustee. Under traditional law, the trustee had no default powers to engage in market transactions over the trust property. The trustee's powers were limited to those granted expressly in the trust instrument. The problem with this disempowerment strategy is that in protecting the beneficiary from mis- or malfeasance by the trustee, the law also disabled the trustee from undertaking transactions useful for the beneficiary.

As trusts have come increasingly to be funded with liquid financial assets that require alert management in the face of swiftly changing financial markets, modern trust law has come to give the trustee broad *powers* to undertake any type of transaction, subject to the trustee's fiduciary *duties*.[4] Modern law gives the trustee 'all of the powers over trust property that a legally competent, unmarried individual has with respect to individually owned property'.[5] However, 'in deciding whether and how to exercise the powers of the trusteeship, [the trustee] is subject to and must act in accordance with the [trustee's] fiduciary duties'.[6]

What has happened, in other words, is that modern trust law has come to substitute empowerment subject to fiduciary obligation for simple disempowerment as the preferred means for safeguarding the beneficiary's interests. The settlor need not spell out with specificity what the trustee should do in all possible future circumstances, an impossible task given transaction costs and the settlor's lack of clairvoyance. Instead, trust law

[3] Ibid., 627–48; see also R. H. Sitkoff, 'The Economic Structure of Fiduciary Law' (2011) 91 *Boston University Law Review* 1039, 1040–5.

[4] This thematic observation has been sounded most prominently by John Langbein. See J. H. Langbein, 'The Contractarian Basis of the Law of Trusts' (1995) 105 *Yale Law Journal* 625, 640–3; J. H. Langbein, 'Rise of the Management Trust' (October 2004) *Trusts & Estates* 52.

[5] *Restatement (Third) of Trusts,* 4 vols. (St Paul: American Law Institute, 2003–12), §85(1)(a); see also Uniform Trust Code §815(a)(2)(A) (2000) [UTC].

[6] *Restatement (Third) of Trusts*, ibid., §86; see also §70, cmts. a, d.

provides the trustee with expansive default powers of administration, the trustee's exercise of which is subject to review *ex post* for compliance with the open-ended fiduciary duties of loyalty and prudence.[7]

The fiduciary obligation thus minimizes transaction costs.[8] Instead of trying in advance to reduce to writing provisions for every future contingency, the parties need only address expressly those contingencies that are important and likely enough to warrant the transaction costs of express provision. For all other contingencies, the fiduciary obligation fills the gap. A similar evolutionary pattern toward empowerment subject to fiduciary governance is apparent in the modern law of agency, partnerships and corporations – all fields in which the agency problem arising from incomplete contracting in the separation of management and beneficial ownership is likewise prominent.

Viewed in this manner, the fiduciary governance strategy of modern law is intuitive. The functional core of fiduciary law is deterrence.[9] The fiduciary is induced to act in the best interests of the beneficiary by the threat of after-the-fact liability for breach of the fiduciary standards of conduct. The core fiduciary duties are the duties of loyalty and prudence (or care). The duty of *loyalty* proscribes misappropriation and regulates conflicts of interest by requiring the fiduciary to act in the 'best' or even 'sole' interests of the principal. The duty of *prudence* or *care* prescribes the fiduciary's standard of care by establishing an objective 'prudence' or 'reasonableness' standard in which the meaning of prudence or reasonableness is informed by industry norms and practices.

Although the duties of loyalty and prudence are formulated in terms of open-ended standards, the normal accretive process of the common law has produced a rich body of interpretive authority on fiduciary matters. This mass of authority includes not only decades of case law, but also generations of treatises, restatements and statutory codifications. Such authority improves predictability and reduces decision costs by providing instructive guidance on what the otherwise expansive duties of loyalty and prudence require of the trustee in particular circumstances.

7 The *Restatement* characterizes this structure as 'a basic principle of trust administration', namely, that 'a trustee presumptively has comprehensive powers to manage the trust estate and otherwise to carry out the terms and purpose of the trust, but that all powers held in the capacity of trustee must be exercised, or not exercised, in accordance with the trustee's fiduciary obligations'. *Restatement (Third) of Trusts,* above, note 5, §70, cmt. a.

8 See Sitkoff, 'Economic Structure', above, note 3, 1040–1, 1044.

9 See F. H. Easterbrook and D. R. Fischel, 'Corporate Control Transactions' (1982) 91 *Yale Law Journal* 698, 702.

Accumulated experience with recurring, common sets of facts and circumstances has also led to the development of *subsidiary* or *implementing rules* regarding the application of the duties of loyalty or prudence to those circumstances. The trust law no-further-inquiry rule (and its proliferating exceptions) is an example of such a rule.[10] Other common examples from across the fiduciary fields are specific rules on disclosure, earmarking, record-keeping, competition with the principal, theft of the principal's opportunity, and commingling funds.

Operating in tandem, the broad duties of loyalty and prudence plus the specific subsidiary rules provide the decision costs advantage of rules and the error costs advantage of standards.[11] The subsidiary or implementing rules simplify application of the fiduciary obligation to cases that fall within their terms. But if the trustee acts in a manner that is inimical to the beneficiary's interests yet does not fall within one or another subsidiary rule, the beneficiary may still invoke the broad, open-ended duties of loyalty and prudence.[12]

Most fiduciary obligations are *default rules* that yield to the contrary agreement of the parties. This is true not only in trust law but across the fiduciary fields. The default character of most fiduciary rules follows from the nature of fiduciary governance as a system of deterrence meant to reduce agency costs in circumstances in which the fiduciary must have broad discretion. If the parties specify what the fiduciary should do in a particular contingency, the default fiduciary standards of conduct no longer pertain with respect to that contingency. Even the fiduciary duty of loyalty is subject to modification. If the principal gives informed consent to certain self-dealing by the fiduciary, the rationale for the duty of loyalty's prophylactic rule against self-dealing falls away. In such circumstances, the fiduciary may engage in the specified self-dealing, provided that she acts in good faith and that the transaction is objectively fair and in the best interests of the principal.[13]

[10] See *Restatement (Third) of Trusts,* above, note 5, §78, cmts. b–d.

[11] See, e.g., L. Kaplow, 'Rules Versus Standards: An Economic Analysis' (1992) 42 *Duke Law Journal* 557.

[12] See Sitkoff, 'Agency Costs Theory', above, note 2, 682–3. I have elsewhere characterized this mode of legal governance as a 'standard tempered by presumptions', in comparison to a 'rule tempered by exceptions'. J. Dukeminier, R. H. Sitkoff and J. Lindgren, *Wills, Trusts, and Estates*, 8th edn (Frederick, MD: Aspen Publishers, 2009), pp. 386–7.

[13] See, e.g., *Restatement (Third) of Trusts,* above, note 5, §78, cmts. c–d; *Restatement (Third) of Agency,* 2 vols. (St Paul: American Law Institute, 2006), §8.06(1); *Principles of Corporate Governance: Analysis and Recommendations,* 2 vols. (St Paul: American Law Institute, 1994), §5.02.

To be sure, there is a mandatory core to fiduciary obligation that cannot be overridden by agreement. A fiduciary may not be authorized to act in bad faith.[14] Even if the principal authorizes self-dealing, fiduciary law provides substantive and procedural safeguards. The fiduciary must always act in good faith and deal fairly with and for the principal, and the fiduciary must apprise the principal of the material facts in securing the principal's informed consent to a conflicted action or self-dealing transaction.[15] But such *mandatory rules* are not a serious impediment to the parties' reasonable refinement of the fiduciary obligation to be applied in their fiduciary relationship. Rather the mandatory core of fiduciary law serves an internal protective or cautionary function and an external categorization function.

With respect to the internal *protective* or *cautionary function*, the mandatory core insulates fiduciary obligations that the law assumes would not be bargained away by a fully informed, sophisticated principal. True, in an individual case a particular principal might be fully informed and have good reason to want to bargain away something from the mandatory core. But such circumstances are infrequent enough that a prophylactic (if paternalistic) mandatory rule may be justified nonetheless, at least in the traditional fiduciary fields such as trust and agency, in which the principal is commonly not sophisticated and fully informed.

With respect to the external *categorization function*, the mandatory core addresses the need for clean lines of demarcation across forms of property holding to minimize third-party information costs and to protect third-party rights. This standardization function has been much discussed in the contemporary learning in property theory.[16] On this view, the mandatory core of fiduciary law polices the line that differentiates a fiduciary relationship on the one hand from a fee simple or other such arrangement on the other. A person may give property to another person and authorize the other person to act whimsically with respect to

[14] See, e.g., *Restatement (Third) of Trusts,* above, note 5, §78, cmt. c(2); *Restatement (Third) of Agency*, above, note 13, §8.06(1)(a), (2)(a); Uniform Power of Attorney Act §114(a)(2) (2006); UTC §105(b)(2); see also J. H. Langbein, 'Mandatory Rules in the Law of Trusts' (2004) 98 *Northwestern University Law Review* 1105.

[15] See, e.g., *Restatement (Third) of Trusts,* above, note 5, §78, cmt. c(2) (2007); *Restatement (Third) of Agency*, above, note 13, §8.06.

[16] See H. Hansmann and R. Kraakman, 'Property, Contract, and Verification: The *Numerus Clausus* Problem and the Divisibility of Rights' (2002) 31 *Journal of Legal Studies* S373; T. W. Merrill and H. E. Smith, 'Optimal Standardization in the Law of Property: The *Numerus Clausus* Principle' (2000) 110 *Yale Law Journal* 1; T. W. Merrill and H. E. Smith, 'The Property/Contract Interface' (2001) 101 *Columbia Law Review* 773; see also Sitkoff, 'Agency Costs Theory', above, note 2, 643.

the property. But this mode of transfer is an absolute gift, and this mode of holding property is fee simple.[17]

In summary, the purpose of the governance rules of trust law is to facilitate expeditious management of the trust property while minimizing the agency costs arising from separating management (the trustee) and beneficial ownership (the beneficiary). To that end, modern law supplies an expansive set of default powers that enable the trustee 'to engage in every conceivable transaction that might wrest market advantage or enhance the value of trust assets'.[18] However, modern law subjects the trustee's exercise or non-exercise of those powers to fiduciary duties of loyalty and prudence as well as a set of implementing fiduciary sub-rules. The fiduciary obligation consists generally of default rules that are alterable in the trust instrument, though there is a mandatory core that serves protective and categorization functions.

B. *Asset partitioning: toward entitization*

The core function of asset partitioning rules in organizational law is to separate the personal property and obligations of the organization's insiders from the property and obligations of the organization.[19] Such separation reduces monitoring costs and facilitates productive transactions by making the organization itself a transactional party separate from its managers and beneficial owners. For example, a prospective

[17] The Delaware Supreme Court has put the point thus: 'A trust in which there is no legally binding obligation on a trustee is a trust in name only and more in the nature of an absolute estate or fee simple grant of property': *McNeil* v. *McNeil*, 798 A.2d 503, 509 (2002); see also *Armitage* v. *Nurse* [1997] 2 All ER 705, [1998] Ch 241, 253 (Millett LJ) ('[t]here is an irreducible core of obligations owed by the trustees to the beneficiaries and enforceable by them which is fundamental to the concept of a trust. If the beneficiaries have no rights enforceable against the trustees there are no trusts').

The categorization, third-party information costs explanation for the mandatory core is strongest as regards fiduciary relationships for which there is no public notice filing upon creation such as agency and common law trusts. The explanation is weaker as regards filing entities such as corporations and limited liability companies, because the public filing that brings the entity into existence also provides notice to third parties of the existence of the organization. For this reason, and because the parties in such contexts are more likely to be fully informed and sophisticated, the mandatory core for filing fiduciary entities is both less robust and more contentious than in agency and trust law. See Sitkoff, 'Economic Structure', above, note 3, 1047–8.

[18] Langbein, 'Contractarian Basis', above, note 4, 641.

[19] The seminal exposition is H. Hansmann and R. Kraakman, 'The Essential Role of Organizational Law' (2000) 110 *Yale Law Journal* 387.

lender to the organization need examine the finances of the organization only, acting without regard to the solvency of the organization's managers or beneficial owners.[20] To be effective, asset partitioning also requires rules of agency to establish the authority of the managers to bind the organization, and rules of procedure to establish the ability of the organization and its counterparties to sue each other.[21]

For an organization that enjoys juridical personality, such as the corporation, strong asset partitioning is uncomplicated. The organization's property is held in the name of the entity, the insiders' personal property is held in the name of each insider, and the parties' respective obligations follow accordingly. The fact of the organization and its separateness from its managers and beneficial owners is easily verifiable in the notice-filing records of the jurisdiction in which the entity was formed. There was a clean and obvious line between the personal property and obligations of Steve Jobs, on the one hand, and the property and obligations of Apple, the corporation for which he was the chief executive officer, on the other. Each could sue or be sued with regard to the separate property of each.

For a common law trust, such straightforward asset partitioning is not possible. Formally a trust is not a freestanding juridical entity but rather a relationship created by private agreement without a filing with the state. A trust cannot sue, be sued, hold property or transact in its own name. Instead, the trustee sues, is sued, holds property and transacts with respect to trust property in the trustee's fiduciary capacity as trustee. Both substantive and semantic consequences ensue.

As a substantive matter, because the trustee holds legal title to the trust property, under traditional law the trustee was personally liable for the debts and other obligations arising from ownership of the trust property. The trustee's personal liability was offset, however, by a right to indemnification out of the trust corpus. A plumber who repaired a broken toilet in a rental building held in trust could recover his fee from the trustee personally, but the trustee would then indemnify himself for the expense out of the trust fund. This clumsy and formalistic ritual,

[20] Ibid., 399–405.

[21] For a clear discussion, see J. Armour, H. Hansmann and R. Kraakman, 'What is Corporate Law?' paras. 1.2.1, 7–8, in R. Kraakman et al. (eds.), *The Anatomy of Corporate Law: A Comparative and Functional Approach*, 2nd edn (Oxford University Press, 2009), pp. 6–9.

which is codified in authorities as late as the Second *Restatement of Trusts*, published in 1959, served no functional purpose.[22]

Prevailing American trust law has since been revised to provide that a creditor of the trustee in the trustee's fiduciary capacity as such recovers directly from the trust fund without recourse against the trustee's personal property.[23] Likewise, even though the trustee has legal title to the trust property, a personal creditor of the trustee has no recourse against the trust property.[24] Accordingly, from the perspective of third parties (i.e. persons outside of the settlor–trustee–beneficiary triangle), modern law in effect splits the trustee into 'two distinct legal persons: a natural person contracting on behalf of himself, and an artificial person acting on behalf of the beneficiaries'.[25]

As a semantic matter, Americans have come to reify the trust, referring to it as if it were an entity (e.g. 'an agent owes a duty to the trust'[26]). When we do so, we are making use of a convenient shorthand for the more awkward locution of the trustee acting in his fiduciary capacity as trustee.[27] This simplification accords with prevailing American trust doctrine, which gives the trust relationship strong entity-like asset partitioning. Because modern law sharply separates the property of the trustee personally from the property of the trust, the contemporary American trust is in function (though not in juridical form) an entity. Reifying the trust in expression is an embrace of substantive function over technical form.

Three features of the asset partitioning rules require further elaboration. First, such rules tend to have a mandatory character with respect to the preservation of third-party rights. Just as the governing organizational documents of a corporation, limited liability company or

[22] See *Restatement (Second) of Trusts* (St Paul: American Law Institute, 1959), §§244, 261–5; see also A. W. Scott, W. F. Fratcher, and M. L. Ascher, *Scott and Ascher on Trusts*, 5th edn (New York: Aspen Publishers, 2006), §§26.1–26.7.

[23] See *Restatement (Third) of Trusts*, above, note 5, §§105–6 (2012); UTC §1010.

[24] See *Restatement (Third) of Trusts*, above, note 5, §42, cmt. c (2003); UTC §507.

[25] Hansmann and Kraakman, 'Role of Organizational Law', above, note 19, 416; see also H. Hansmann and U. Mattei, 'The Functions of Trust Law: A Comparative Legal and Economic Analysis' (1998) 73 *NYU Law Review* 434. For a similar discussion rooted in the concept of a separate patrimony, see G. L. Gretton, 'Trusts Without Equity' (2000) 49 *International & Comparative Law Quarterly* 599, 608–13.

[26] Uniform Prudent Investor Act §9(b) (1994); see also *Restatement (Third) of Trusts*, above, note 5, §80, cmt. g.

[27] This discussion is thus a brief answer to Lionel Smith's criticism in 'Mistaking the Trust' (2010) 40 *Hong Kong Law Journal* 787, 799–800; see also L. Smith, 'Trust and Patrimony' (2008) 38 *Revue générale de droit* 379.

partnership could not validly foreclose recovery against the organization's property by a third party in satisfaction of the third party's claim against the organization,[28] a trust instrument cannot validly foreclose recovery against trust property by a third party in satisfaction of the third party's claims against the trust.[29] Regardless of whether an organization has formal juridical personality, in creating what is in effect an artificial person separate from the organization's insiders, the law requires this artificial person to be responsible for claims against it by third parties.

Second, the effectiveness of the mandatory protection of third-party rights in the asset partitioning rules is in part dependent on the mandatory rules of fiduciary governance. Such mandatory rules serve a categorization or standardization function in the *numerus clausus* sense by providing notice and clean lines of demarcation across and within types of property holdings.[30] Organizational property, which is always available to a creditor of the organization unless the creditor waives that right,[31] must be earmarked and administered as such.

Third, unlike fiduciary governance, which is in theory (though not always in fact) replicable by contract, the asset partitioning of organizational law is categorically not replicable by contract. Persons cannot create a ring-fenced fund, protecting their personal assets against future claimants, by a web of contracts among themselves without also invoking the asset partitioning rules of trust or other organizational law. This insight, which has been developed most extensively by Henry Hansmann and Reinier Kraakman,[32] reflects the inability to limit by contract the rights

[28] See, e.g., Revised Uniform Limited Liability Company Act §110(c)(1), (c)(11) (2006); Uniform Limited Partnership Act §110(b)(1), (b)(13) (2001); Revised Uniform Partnership Act §103(b)(10) (1997). In the words of the official comment to Uniform Limited Partnership Act §110(b)(13): 'The partnership agreement is a contract, and this provision reflects a basic notion of contract law – namely, that a contract can *directly* restrict rights only of parties to the contract and of persons who derive their rights from the contract'.

[29] See UTC §105(b)(11).

[30] See above, note 16, and text accompanying.

[31] An interesting encroachment on this principle is the rise of the series organization. For an example, see article 4 of the Uniform Statutory Trust Entity Act (2009).

[32] The principal work is Hansmann and Kraakman, 'Role of Organizational Law', above note 19, previewed in H. Hansmann and R. Kraakman, 'Organizational Law as Asset Partitioning' (2000) 44 *European Economic Review* 807, and applied to trust law in Hansmann and Mattei, 'Functions of Trust Law', above, note 25. See also Armour et al., 'What is Corporate Law?', above, note 21, para. 1.2.1; H. Hansmann, R. Kraakman and R. Squire, 'Law and the Rise of the Firm' (2006) 119 *Harvard Law Review* 1333; H. Hansmann, R. Kraakman and R. Squire, 'The New Business Entities in Evolutionary

of third parties not privy to the contract. By contrast, because fiduciary law creates rights and imposes duties only on the parties to the fiduciary relationship or their privies, there is no legal impediment to those parties replicating the applicable fiduciary rules by contract. This latter point is the premise of John Langbein's argument that, as regards the trustee's powers and the role of trust fiduciary law in governing the exercise of those powers, trust law is predominantly contractarian.[33]

To be sure, fiduciary law serves a crucial role in minimizing transaction costs. Without the ability to absorb an existing set of fiduciary governance rules tailored to the particulars of the agency problem in the undertaking the parties intend, the parties would need to think up and then spell out such rules in detail. In some circumstances, the associated transaction costs would be insuperable, suppressing otherwise beneficial deals. For those deals in which the transaction costs would otherwise be insuperable, fiduciary law is essential. This transaction costs minimizing function, in which the state supplies the public good of standard-form fiduciary contracts, has been discussed extensively in the literature, particularly of corporate law.[34] Standard-form fiduciary contracts include agency, partnership, trust, corporation and limited liability company.

There is, however, a difference in kind between the utility of organizational law in reducing transaction costs by offering standard-form fiduciary contracts versus the necessity of organizational law to overcome the limited reach of contract law by offering asset partitioning as against third parties. Without the ability to absorb the default fiduciary governance rules of organizational law, the question in each prospective deal would be whether the parties had enough to gain from the deal to warrant incurring the costs of creating such rules from scratch by contract. Even if fiduciary law is in fact essential in a particular deal,

Perspective' (2005) *University of Illinois Law Review* 5; Hansmann and Kraakman, 'Property, Contract, and Verification', above, note 16. Hansmann and Kraakman previously questioned the necessity of corporate limited liability in tort. See H. Hansmann and R. Kraakman, 'Do the Capital Markets Compel Limited Liability? A Response to Professor Grundfest' (1992) 102 *Yale Law Journal* 427; H. Hansmann and R. Kraakman, 'A Procedural Focus on Unlimited Shareholder Liability' (1992) 106 *Harvard Law Review* 446; H. Hansmann and R. Kraakman, 'Toward Unlimited Shareholder Liability for Corporate Torts' (1991) 100 *Yale Law Journal* 1879.

[33] See Langbein, 'Contractarian Basis', above, note 4.

[34] See, e.g., F. H. Easterbrook and D. R. Fischel, *The Economic Structure of Corporate Law* (Cambridge, MA: Harvard University Press, 1991), pp. 34–5; see also L. E. Ribstein, 'Making Sense of Entity Rationalization' (2003) 58 *Business Lawyer* 1023.

fiduciary law is not essential as a matter of categorical legal necessity. There is no legal disability, as opposed to a transaction costs obstacle, to replicating the rules of trust or other fiduciary law by way of an ordinary contract.

By contrast, the asset partitioning rules of trust and other organizational law are categorically essential as a matter of legal necessity. The parties to a prospective deal cannot validly replicate the third-party effects of organizational law's asset partitioning rules by way of ordinary contracts. Without organizational law, one cannot create a ring-fenced fund of certain property that is enforceable against third parties. It is in this sense that Hansmann and Kraakman and other scholars of organizational law speak of the 'essential role of organizational law'.[35] No one denies the utility of trust law and other species of organizational law as 'standard-form contracts among the parties who participate in an enterprise'.[36] Rather, the claim is that the 'essential' role of organizational law is 'the creation of relationships that could not practicably be formed by contract alone'.[37]

In summary, the core function of asset partitioning rules in organizational law is to separate the personal property and obligations of the organization's insiders from the property and obligations of the organization. Such separation reduces monitoring costs and facilitates productive transactions by creating a separate counterparty for deals pertaining to the organization's property. In the context of trust law, asset partitioning allows the trustee to deal separately with his personal creditors and with creditors in respect of trust property.[38] Because prevailing modern American trust law gives creditors of the trust (i.e. creditors of the trustee in his fiduciary capacity as such) direct recourse against the trust property and no rights against the trustee's personal property, the modern American trust is in function (though not in form) an entity separate from the trustee and the beneficiary. Unlike the rules of fiduciary governance, which could in theory be replicated by contract subject only to the constraint of transaction costs, the rules of asset partitioning, which reorganize the rights of third parties to the trust property, could not likewise be replicated by an ordinary contract owing to the inability of a contract to limit the rights of non-privies.

[35] Hansmann and Kraakman, 'Role of Organizational Law', above, note 19.
[36] Ibid., 390. [37] Ibid. [38] See Sitkoff, 'Agency Costs Theory', above, note 2, 631–3.

III Gallanis and the contribution of fiduciary law

In his chapter in this volume, Thomas Gallanis undertakes to identify what Anglo-American trust law might usefully contribute to other legal systems. From this point of departure, Gallanis argues for the importance of trust fiduciary law. Gallanis's underlying purpose is to urge the suitability of Anglo-American trust fiduciary law as a model for jurisdictions that seek to assimilate the trust concept. To this end, Gallanis advances two claims. First, to establish the significance of trust fiduciary law, he argues against what he perceives to be a mistaken analysis by scholars of organizational law who emphasize the significance of trust law's asset partitioning features and, in Gallanis's view, needlessly 'downplay'[39] the important contribution of trust fiduciary law. Second, having established the importance of trust fiduciary law by rebutting those who he thinks have challenged its importance, Gallanis points to the development of trust law in France and China as illustrations of the potential for Anglo-American trust fiduciary law to serve as a model for jurisdictions lacking indigenous trust law.

A. Fiduciary law and asset partitioning

Gallanis's overarching claim is that trust fiduciary law makes an important welfare contribution. He does not advance this claim with a theoretical or empirical model, however. Instead he makes his affirmative case for the significance of fiduciary law by way of a critical discussion of recent work in the literature of organizational law as applied to trust law. According to Gallanis, this work has mistakenly identified asset partitioning as the essential contribution of trust law and wrongly disparaged the contribution of fiduciary law as 'relatively unimportant'.[40]

Gallanis takes as his foil a paper published in 1998 by Henry Hansmann and Ugo Mattei.[41] That paper is an early writing in what is now a more mature corpus on asset partitioning by Hansmann and various co-authors, principally Reinier Kraakman.[42] The underlying

[39] Gallanis, 'The Contribution of Fiduciary Law', Chapter 16 in this volume, p. 397.

[40] Ibid., p. 390.

[41] See Hansmann and Mattei, 'Functions of Trust Law', above, note 25. Hansmann and Mattei published an abridged version of this paper as H. Hansmann and U. Mattei, 'Trust Law in the United States: A Basic Study of Its Special Contribution' (1998) 46 *American Journal of Comparative Law* 133.

[42] See above, note 32.

thesis of this body of work is that unlike fiduciary governance, which does not affect the rights of third parties and hence in theory could be replicated by contract, asset partitioning rules reorganize the rights of third parties and therefore could not be replicated by contract. On this view, the essential contribution of organizational law is asset partitioning, with the term 'essential' used to describe that which is categorically impossible without organizational law.

Gallanis is 'troubled' by Hansmann and Mattei's analysis.[43] His discontent is rooted in the observations that fiduciary law includes mandatory as well as default rules; that some fiduciary rules are penalty defaults rather than majoritarian or market-mimicking defaults; and that the nuance and complexity of the web of rules and standards that comprise trust fiduciary law resist easy (read: low-transaction-cost) replication by private agreement.

These observations and Gallanis's broader claim that fiduciary law makes a significant contribution are surely correct. But I don't see how these points, with which I am certain Hansmann and his collaborators would agree, undermine their claim of the categorical necessity of organizational law to achieve asset partitioning. The Hansmann and Mattei paper should be read in the context of the subsequent asset partitioning literature that has elaborated on the theory,[44] and against the transaction costs fiduciary law literature that the asset partitioning work was meant to enrich.[45] Contextualized in this way, it seems evident that the aim of the project by Hansmann and his collaborators was to identify the essential core of organizational law that could not ever, even with an assumption of zero transaction costs, be replicated by way of contract or other law.[46] Accordingly, no language in those papers should be read to imply that the authors believe that fiduciary law lacks real-world significance.

Start with the point that fiduciary law includes mandatory as well as default rules. As Gallanis acknowledges, Hansmann and his collaborators do not deny that fiduciary law includes mandatory rules or that the mandatory character of such rules serves useful policies.[47] Rather their point is that whatever the rules of governance supplied by fiduciary law, whether those rules are default or mandatory, in theory such rules could be replicated in a contract binding on those privy to the contract.

[43] Gallanis, 'Contribution of Fiduciary Law', Chapter 16 in this volume, p. 392.
[44] See above, note 32. [45] See text accompanying, above, note 34 and, below, note 60.
[46] See Hansmann and Kraakman, 'Role of Organizational Law', above, note 19, 437.
[47] Ibid., 437–8, 440.

A similar answer can be given to the point that some fiduciary rules are penalty defaults. Because such rules are meant to induce explicit contracting, perforce there is no legal impediment to the parties replicating the outcome of that negotiation by way of a contract rather than a trust agreement.[48] True, without the fiduciary law superstructure the information-forcing benefit would be lost. But this is to say that the structure of fiduciary law usefully alters the negotiation dynamic in setting the terms of the parties' contract,[49] not that private contract is categorically impossible.

This brings us to the most substantial issue – transaction costs. To illustrate the point that trust fiduciary law could be replicated by contract, Hansmann and Mattei suggested that a prospective settlor and a prospective trustee could execute a contract containing the relevant sections of the *Restatement of Trusts*.[50] Such a contract would be valid, providing for powers and duties perfectly tracking those of trust law, both default and mandatory. By contrast, the asset partitioning effect of trust law, good against third parties not privy to the contract, could not likewise be replicated. In this sense the asset partitioning effect of trust law, but not the law of powers and duties, is essential.

Gallanis's answer to the *Restatement*-incorporation heuristic, a thought experiment, is to say that it is 'extremely unrealistic'.[51] Gallanis explains: 'While a settlor and prospective trustee *could* agree to the current rules of trust fiduciary law, they are extremely unlikely to do so.'[52] This critique reflects a mistaken view of the project of Hansmann and his collaborators. Their core claim, with which Gallanis appears to agree, is that no rule of contract law (as compared to preferences or transaction costs) would interfere with a prospective settlor and a prospective trustee entering into a valid contract reproducing the entirety of the current *Restatement of Trusts* and providing that those provisions are to be interpreted in accord with the prevailing interpretation of the *Restatement*. Such a contract would, by force of contract law, create among the putative settlor, trustee and beneficiary the same rights, powers and duties as under trust law – but there would be no third-party

[48] Ibid., 437 (discussing rules that put the parties on notice of non-standard governance provisions).

[49] See Sitkoff, 'Economic Structure', above, note 3, 1049.

[50] See Hansmann and Mattei, 'Functions of Trust Law', above, note 25, 447–8.

[51] Gallanis, 'Contribution of Fiduciary Law', Chapter 16 in this volume, p. 395.

[52] Ibid.

asset partitioning.[53] The Restatement-incorporation thought experiment thus brings into sharp relief the categorical impossibility of achieving asset partitioning without organizational law.

Gallanis's real point, I think, is that even if fiduciary law pertains only within the settlor–trustee–beneficiary triangle, such law makes important contributions by protecting the unsophisticated (read: mandatory rules); by altering the negotiating dynamic (read: penalty defaults); and, perhaps most importantly, by reducing transaction costs (read: no need to dicker over expensive, nuanced and complex rules). As is made clear in their subsequent work, Hansmann and his collaborators agree. In the centrepiece paper of this line of work, Hansmann and Kraakman argue that 'aspects of organizational law other than asset partitioning are not "essential" in the sense that workable substitutes for them [exist] elsewhere in the law. This is not to say, however, that elements of organizational law other than asset partitioning are trivial and could be dispensed with costlessly'.[54] To the contrary, the 'efficiencies offered by the various detailed rules governing standard-form legal entities are important'.[55] Nevertheless, asset partitioning 'is the only important feature of [organizational law] for which substitutes could not be crafted, at any price that is even remotely conceivable, using just the basic tools of contract, property, and agency law'.[56]

Reworking Gallanis's critique of Hansmann and Mattei into an explanation of trust fiduciary law rooted in transaction costs reconciles Gallanis's disagreement with Hansmann and his collaborators and makes clearer the sensible core thesis of Gallanis's essay. The cleavage between Gallanis and the asset partitioning literature is not in the *fact* of transaction costs in replicating fiduciary law by private agreement, but rather in the *magnitude* of the costs involved in doing so. Hansmann and his co-authors regard the contribution of organizational law in minimizing such costs as being 'not of the same order'[57] as the contribution of

[53] The beneficiary would become that species of contract party called a third-party donee beneficiary. See *Restatement (Second) of Contracts* (St Paul: American Law Institute, 1981), §302, cmt. c.

[54] Hansmann and Kraakman, 'Role of Organizational Law', above, note 19, 437.

[55] In a subsequent writing, Hansmann suggested that the ability of the legislature simultaneously to modify the governance of all firms making use of one or another form of entity is yet another cost saving from state-supplied standard-form entities. See H. Hansmann, 'Corporation and Contract' (2006) 8 *American Law & Economics Review* 1.

[56] Hansmann and Kraakman, 'Role of Organizational Law', above, note 19, 437.

[57] Ibid.

organizational law in providing for asset partitioning. In response, Gallanis says that Hansmann and Mattei's 'estimates of transaction costs sometimes have the air of *ipse dixit*'.[58] To illustrate, he points to the expansive and discursive fiduciary provisions of the 2007 volume of the Third *Restatement of Trusts.* Given the breadth and depth of those provisions, Gallanis suggests that 'the negotiation between a settlor and a prospective trustee about all of these rules' might well be 'complex and costly'.[59]

Viewed in this manner, Gallanis has undertaken to rehabilitate the prior generation of fiduciary contractarians, most obviously Frank Easterbrook and Daniel Fischel, who argued that the primary function of organizational law is to minimize transaction costs by providing a menu of standard-form fiduciary contracts.[60] Unlike Easterbrook and Fischel, Gallanis does not state expressly that fiduciary terms are 'public goods' that warrant public provision.[61] But his argument about the transaction costs of replicating by private agreement the nuances of fiduciary law maps onto the Easterbrook and Fischel analysis quite neatly.

The affirmative case for the importance of trust fiduciary law should not rest on a critical analysis of Hansmann and Mattei, but rather on a functional explanation of the purpose of fiduciary law – that is, minimizing transaction costs in establishing terms that will suppress agency costs.[62] For persons wishing to create a trust, the existence of trust fiduciary law provides a ready-made web of rules and standards to govern the trustee's exercise of the trustee's discretionary powers of administration. This web of rules includes a few that are mandatory, with protective and categorical purposes, and a few that are penalty defaults, to encourage disclosure and precise articulation of intention. But otherwise the rules are market-mimicking defaults, which economizes on transaction costs. Overall, trust fiduciary governance provides for expeditious management of the trust property while minimizing the agency costs arising from separating management (the trustee) and beneficial ownership (the beneficiary).

58 Gallanis, 'Contribution of Fiduciary Law', Chapter 16 in this volume, p. 394.
59 Ibid., p. 395.
60 See Easterbrook and Fischel, *Economic Structure of Corporate Law*, above, note 34, pp. 34–5.
61 Ibid., p. 35.
62 See above, notes 3, 8 and 34, and text accompanying.

B. *Exporting fiduciary law abroad*

Having undertaken to establish the importance of trust fiduciary law, Gallanis points to the development of trust law in China and France as illustrations of the potential for Anglo-American trust fiduciary law to serve as a template for foreign jurisdictions interested in assimilating the trust concept. Gallanis's treatment is largely descriptive. He starts with China and then moves to France.

The Chinese trust law, an adaptation of the common law trust for the Chinese civilian system, includes many fiduciary rules that closely resemble those of Anglo-American law. Gallanis schedules a host of examples and explains that the similarity is deliberate. Gallanis also remarks upon several differences, chiefly in the trustee's duties to the settlor, delegation by the trustee, and in impartiality among concurrent beneficiaries without provision for impartiality when administering successive beneficial interests. Gallanis points to the Chinese tradition of undivided ownership in explanation for the focus on concurrent rather than successive interests. But Gallanis does not say clearly whether the terms of the trust can provide for successive interests and modify the duty of impartiality accordingly.

Gallanis celebrates the similarities between Chinese trust law and Anglo-American trust fiduciary law. To Gallanis, the similarities evidence how 'well-developed and sophisticated, and suited to modern legal practice', is trust fiduciary law.[63] Here it is noteworthy that Hansmann and his collaborators agree. In the centrepiece paper of the asset partitioning corpus, Hansmann and Kraakman took notice of 'the fact that most developed market economies provide for standard-form legal entities that are similar in their basic features'.[64] To Hansmann and Kraakman, like Gallanis, this fact is evidence that the governance rules of organizational law provide real-world benefits such as economizing on transaction costs.

A more interesting question is how to explain the differences between Anglo-American and Chinese trust law. A common observation in the economic literature on fiduciary law is that the precise contours of the fiduciary obligation vary across fiduciary applications.[65] This observation about the doctrine fits nicely the agency and transaction costs theory of fiduciary law, in which the fiduciary obligation operates as an after-the-

[63] Gallanis, 'Contribution of Fiduciary Law', Chapter 16 in this volume, p. 402.
[64] Hansmann and Kraakman, 'Role of Organizational Law', above, note 19, 437.
[65] See Sitkoff, 'Economic Structure', above, note 3, 1045.

fact completion of what is necessarily an incomplete contract,[66] because agency problems vary across contexts. For example, the fiduciary obligation in American trust law is generally stricter than the fiduciary obligation in American corporate law. But those differences reflect the different contexts. The agency problem in a family trust in which the beneficiaries have no exit option and that is managed by a corporate fiduciary that cannot easily be replaced differs significantly from the agency problem in a large, publicly traded corporation from which a shareholder can separate easily by selling his shares in a thick securities market (the 'Wall Street rule').[67]

So a pressing question, not addressed in Gallanis's discussion (but elsewhere discussed by Frances Foster[68]), is why the Chinese authorities opted to deviate in certain respects from the Anglo-American model. Do those deviations reflect material differences in the underlying agency structure of the Chinese trust? Are such trusts predominantly managed by professional fiduciaries? Is the Chinese system of adjudication more or less reliable than the Anglo-American courts? The fact of the settlor's enforcement right and the absence of successive interests, for example, would seem to bear on the nature and scope of the agency problem to be ameliorated by the Chinese fiduciary law.

Gallanis's treatment of the French trust fiduciary law is more functional. According to Gallanis, the French counterpart to the Anglo-American trust, the *fiducie*, is meant for commercial purposes, not donative wealth transfer. To Gallanis, the *fiducie* thus has a narrower purpose than the Anglo-American trust, and this explains why its accompanying fiduciary law is less detailed. But French lawyers have begun to urge that the *fiducie* be used in family wealth transfer. If this idea comes to fruition, Gallanis argues, then Anglo-American trust fiduciary law could provide a useful template for expanding French fiduciary law accordingly.

The underlying insight is that Anglo-American trust fiduciary law evolved out of long experience with the agency costs that arise in separating management and beneficial ownership in a donative transfer 'projected on the plane of time'.[69] Gallanis's point, which seems quite

[66] F. H. Easterbrook and D. R. Fischel, 'Contract and Fiduciary Duty' (1993) 36 *Journal of Law & Economics* 425, 432–4.

[67] See R. H. Sitkoff, 'Trust Law, Corporate Law, and Capital Market Efficiency' (2003) 28 *Journal of Corporation Law* 565; see also S. M. Bainbridge, 'The Case for Limited Shareholder Voting Rights' (2006) 53 *UCLA Law Review* 601, 619.

[68] See F. H. Foster, 'American Trust Law in a Chinese Mirror' (2010) 94 *Minnesota Law Review* 602, 621–50.

[69] B. Rudden, 'Book Review' (1981) 44 *Modern Law Review* 610, 610.

sensible, is that if the French are to make use of a transactional structure for which we have centuries of experience, they would do well to examine the governance regime we developed out of that experience.

But Gallanis's focus on critiquing Hansmann and Mattei obscures deeper questions. What are the commercial purposes to which the French trust is put? Why hasn't the agency problem in those applications already strained 'the thin fiduciary rules in French law'?[70] American corporate law, used routinely in commercial transactions, has a rather detailed fiduciary law, including extensive rules on corporate opportunities, executive compensation and ratification of conflicted transactions.[71] If agency costs in the commercial applications of the *fiducie* have been minimized other than with fiduciary law, perhaps the same techniques would be available in a donative application? Gallanis takes as a given that commercial applications do not require much fiduciary law, but this assumption does not follow from an immutable rule of organizational dynamics.

Gallanis's discussion of the function of fiduciary law is stimulating and generative, and in my view largely sound. His discussion of Chinese and French trust law is interesting and also impressive inasmuch as neither jurisdiction uses English as its primary language. But Gallanis's organizing motivation, critiquing Hansmann and Mattei, needlessly distracts from the deeper issues to which his chapter points and from his sensible core thesis that trust fiduciary law improves social welfare by minimizing transaction costs.

IV Lee and the transplantation of trust law

In her chapter for this volume, Rebecca Lee takes the Chinese enactment in 2001 of a systematic law of trusts as a natural experiment on the nature and function of trusteeship. Because China follows the civilian tradition of indivisible ownership, the Chinese assimilation of Anglo-American trust law required replicating trust law's governance and asset partitioning features without an express bifurcation of legal and beneficial ownership. The idea that animates Lee's essay is that the resulting Chinese law of trusts provides a window on the essential characteristics of trusteeship. Lee's thesis is that, to the extent the Chinese law

70 Gallanis, 'Contribution of Fiduciary Law', Chapter 16 in this volume, p. 404.

71 See, e.g., *Principles of Corporate Governance: Analysis and Recommendations*, above, note 13, §§4.01–6.02 (1992).

But the English view does not follow inexorably from immutable first principles of trust law. In the American tradition, illustrated by *Claflin* v. *Claflin*[80] and by the recognition of spendthrift trusts,[81] the trust is a conditional gift. The beneficiary takes his interest in the trust subject to any restrictions imposed by the settlor. Constrained only by anti-dead-hand public policy rules such as the rule against perpetuities and the rule against capricious purposes, the American settlor is free to impose conditions on the beneficiary's enjoyment of the trust property.[82] Viewed in this manner, the puzzle is not so much that the Chinese give the settlor standing to enforce the trust, but rather the American reluctance, outside of recent reform in trustee removal and in charitable trusts, to do the same.[83] As Langbein has suggested, settlor standing is consistent with a contractarian understanding of trust governance,[84] a point I have elaborated on elsewhere from an agency costs perspective.[85]

In Lee's telling, however, the settlor has more than an enforcement right akin to the rights of a party to a third-party beneficiary contract. The settlor 'is also granted other extensive powers to intervene in the trustee's management of the trust property, including the power to manage the trust property, and even the right to request the trustee to adjust the methods of management'.[86] To an American trust lawyer, this passage evokes the contemporary revocable trust, which has come to be conceptualized in American practice as a will substitute for posthumous transfer outside of the probate system. Under modern American trust law, the trustee of a revocable trust is subject to the control of the settlor, and the trustee's fiduciary duties run only to the settlor, for so long as the settlor retains the power of revocation.[87]

The analogy to the revocable trust is imperfect. Nothing in Lee's discussion implies that the Chinese trust was meant to be a will substitute. Even so, the analogy brings into focus the need to get a grip on the purpose and uses of the Chinese trust. American trust law has fractured

80 20 N.E. 454 (Mass. 1889).

81 Compare Dukeminier, Sitkoff and Lindgren, *Wills, Trusts, and Estates*, above, note 12, pp. 614–16, with *Brandon* v. *Robinson*, (1811) 18 Ves. Jr. 429, 34 E.R. 379 (Ch.).

82 See *Restatement (Third) of Property: Wills and Other Donative Transfers*, 3 vols. (St Paul: American Law Institute, 1999–2011), §10.1, cmt. c.

83 See *Restatement (Third) of Trusts*, above, note 5, §94; UTC §§706(a), 405(c).

84 Langbein, 'Contractrian Basis', above, note 4, 664.

85 Sitkoff, 'Agency Costs Theory', above, note 2, 666–9.

86 Lee, 'Convergence and Divergence', Chapter 17 in this volume, p. 417.

87 See *Restatement (Third) of Trusts*, above, note 5, §74; UTC §603(a).

into three distinct branches: (1) business trusts, now dominated by the Delaware statutory business trust, a juridical entity with capacity to sue, be sued, and hold property in its own name;[88] (2) revocable trusts, a will substitute over which the settlor remains in control and in which the beneficiary has no rights; and (3) irrevocable trusts, the traditional trust in which a segregated pool of assets is held by a trustee subject to a fiduciary governance regime for the benefit of one or more beneficiaries.[89] Lee's discussion, in particular her worry about the lack of clarity in the Chinese law respecting exoneration clauses, implies that the Chinese trust is not a will substitute but rather a business trust or a donative irrevocable trust.

The revocable trust analogy also points to the question of whether the settlor's creditors have recourse against the trust property as in the American revocable trust.[90] The American rule follows from the role of the revocable trust as a will substitute; in truth, in a revocable trust the trust property still belongs to the settlor. Lee's discussion, including her reference to a 'separate trust patrimony' and the rules requiring the settlor to segregate the trust property,[91] implies that the settlor's creditors cannot reach the trust property. But Lee does not address this issue expressly. Instead, following Hansmann and Mattei's analysis of asset partitioning in trust law, which Lee calls the 'external aspect' of the trust,[92] Lee focuses on the inability of the trustee's personal creditors to reach the trust property.

Lee's focus on asset partitioning for the trustee is incomplete. In the Chinese trust, the settlor, not the trustee, is the technical owner of the trust property. Recall that at the outset of Lee's essay, she tells us that in the Chinese trust there is no required conveyance of the trust property to the trustee. Instead the settlor remains the owner, subject to a duty to keep the trust property separate from the settlor's other property. The asset partitioning literature that Lee follows emphasizes the separateness from the trustee's personal obligations because in the Anglo-American

[88] See Delaware Statutory Trust Entity Act §3804 (2011); Uniform Statutory Trust Entity Act §§307–8 (2009); see also R. H. Sitkoff, 'Trust as "Uncorporation": A Research Agenda' [2005] *University of Illinois Law Review* 31.

[89] In this taxonomy, which I intend to develop in future work, I am putting to the side the constructive trust, which is a remedy, and the resulting trust, which is an equitable reversionary interest.

[90] *See Restatement (Third) of Trusts,* above, note 5, §25, cmt. e; UTC §505.

[91] Lee, 'Convergence and Divergence', Chapter 17 in this volume, p. 424.

[92] Ibid., pp. 424, 427.

tradition the trustee is the legal owner of the trust property. This is the feature of trust law – in effect, the splitting the trustee into two separate persons – that cannot be replicated by mere contract. But if the settlor and not the trustee owns the trust property, then the locus of the partitioning or separateness issue shifts to the settlor, and the question is whether the settlor becomes in effect two separate persons.

Lee's discussion of the Chinese assimilation of the trust concept is provocative and interesting. Although China follows the civilian tradition of indivisible ownership, the Chinese were able to replicate the fiduciary governance of Anglo-American trust law by direct imposition of rights, powers and duties that parallel those of Anglo-American trust law. In this sense, the Chinese experience lends support to the contractarian model of trust law. But we also find in the Chinese trust the existence of the asset partitioning rules that separate organizational law, of which trust law is a species, from mere contract law. Although Lee emphasizes the Chinese replication of Anglo-American trust governance, her essay suggests an equally interesting replication of asset partitioning, though this point is not as well developed and is lacking with respect to the settlor's continued ownership of the trust property and the rights of the settlor's personal creditors.

V Conclusion

Organizational law supplies a set of contractarian rules, some of a fiduciary character, that provide for the governance of the organization. These are the rules that provide for the powers and duties of the managers and the rights of the beneficial owners. Organizational law also supplies a set of proprietary rules that provide for asset partitioning. These are the rules that provide for the separation of the property of the organization from the property of the organization's managers, beneficial owners and other insiders. Because trust law follows this pattern, supplying both fiduciary governance and asset partitioning, the law of trusts is a species of organizational law.[93]

The chapters for this volume by Thomas P. Gallanis and by Rebecca Lee both emphasize the importance of the fiduciary governance rules of trust law. Gallanis argues that trust fiduciary law makes an important contribution. I have suggested that this contribution can be understood

[93] See Sitkoff, 'Agency Costs Theory', above, note 2, 627–34.

primarily as minimizing transaction costs through provision of a standard-form contract suited to the agency problem underlying the trust structure. Fiduciary law also supplies mandatory rules that serve protective and categorization functions, and penalty default rules that are meant to alter the parties' negotiation dynamic. Lee argues that the Chinese experience with assimilating the trust, in which the Chinese have replicated Anglo-American trust fiduciary law without separate concepts of law and equity, shows that the governance rules but not legal and equitable ownership are part of the irreducible core of trusteeship. I have suggested several follow-up questions for Lee, in particular about the nature of asset partitioning in the Chinese trust given the settlor's continued ownership of the trust property.

More than fifteen years ago, John Langbein suggested that '[t]rust is a hybrid of contract and property, and acknowledging contractarian elements does not require disregarding property components whose convenience abides'.[94] The claim that runs through this chapter, a commentary on those by Gallanis and Lee, is that such hybrids are properly regarded as organizations. Trust law is organizational law.

[94] Langbein, 'Contractarian Basis', above, note 4, 669.

19

Parallels between the civilian separate patrimony, real subrogation and the idea of property in a trust fund

MAGDA RACZYNSKA

I Introduction

One of the essential characteristics of the common law[1] trust is that the trust property constitutes a segregated fund.[2] It has been argued that the existence of a separate trust fund in common law helps to explain why a trust does not fail for want of a trustee, and crucially, why creditors of the trustee have no claim on it.[3] This emphasis on the importance of a separate fund, coupled with the expansiveness of trusts in non-common law jurisdictions, has inevitably led to a quest for functional equivalents of the trust fund within the civilian taxonomy. In civilian jurisdictions, the concept of a separate patrimony has transpired as a suitable candidate to mirror the operation of the common law trust fund. Separate patrimonies have been known since Roman times (*peculium*) and are also present in modern civil law jurisdictions: for instance, the French *patrimoine d'affectation* and the German *Sondervermögen*.[4] Professor Lawson commented that 'a *Sondervermögen* can easily be created by means of a trust'[5] but the question considered here is different: can a trust be created by a *Sondervermögen*? The separate patrimony has become the basis of the civilian versions of the trust in France[6] and Liechtenstein,[7] and the Hague

[1] 'Common law' is used here as the obverse of 'civil law', rather than 'equity'.

[2] D. W. M. Waters, M. Gillen and L. Smith, *Waters' Law of Trusts in Canada*, 4th edn (Toronto: Thomson Carswell, 2012), p. 9.

[3] G. Gretton, 'Trusts without Equity' (2000) 49 I.C.L.Q. 599, 614.

[4] Ibid., and literature cited there.

[5] Ibid., 614, note 75.

[6] See French Civil Code, art. 2011: 'la fiducie est l'opération par laquelle un ou plusieurs constituants transfèrent des biens (. . .) à un ou plusieurs fiduciaires qui, les tenant séparés de leur patrimoine proper. . .'. See also art. 2025.

[7] Principality of Liechtenstein Trusts Law, art. 915: 'the trust estate is to be treated as a separate patrimony and the creditors of the trustee have no claim on it', cited in Gretton, 'Trusts without Equity', above, note 3, 614, note 73.

Convention on the Recognition of Trusts in its article 2 refers to trust assets as constituting a 'separate fund', which Professor George Gretton equates with a 'special patrimony'.[8]

Immunity from execution of claims of the trustee's creditors is a necessary, but not a sufficient condition for producing a functional equivalent of a common law trust fund in the civil law. It is important that new assets acquired with the exchange value of the assets within the fund be protected against the creditors' claims, an effect to be ensured by real subrogation.[9] Although the extent to which real subrogation is inherent in the notion of a separate patrimony is debatable,[10] both separate patrimony and real subrogation have been included in the list of 'core elements' that a civilian construct would need to display in order to structurally and functionally match the common law trust.[11] There is therefore a temptation to equate the separate patrimony with the trust fund and tracing with real subrogation. The inclination to do so is strong because, firstly, the immunity of the fund/patrimony from claims of the trustee's creditors is prima facie ensured by the segregation of the fund/patrimony from the rest of the assets of the trustee. Secondly, the beneficiary's ability to assert a claim to assets acquired with the exchange value of the original trust assets seems to be explicable as much by tracing as it is by real subrogation. If one of the crucial features of the common law trust is that beneficiaries can assert a proprietary claim to traceable proceeds against third parties, the question then is whether real subrogation and separate patrimony can provide as much, or justify a comparable claim in civil law.

This chapter deals with some of the misconceptions that exist when exploring the parallels that can be drawn between the separate patrimony and real subrogation in civil law systems, and the trust fund, tracing and claims contingent on tracing in common law systems. Firstly, it challenges the views that reify patrimonies and trust funds, and will argue that a patrimony is not a *res*. An attempt is made to explain how separate

8 Gretton, 'Trusts without Equity', above, note 3, 614.

9 M. de Waal, 'In Search of a Model for the Introduction of the Trust into a Civilian Context' (2001) 12 *Stellenbosch Law Review* 63, 67.

10 See in particular Gretton, 'Trusts without Equity', above, note 3, 613, note 67.

11 The other two being the fiduciary position of a trustee; the office of a trustee. See de Waal, 'In Search of a Model', above, note 9, 66–7; T. Honoré, 'Obstacles to the Reception of Trust Law? The Examples of South Africa and Scotland', in A. Rabello (ed.), *Aequitas and Equity. Equity in Civil Law and Mixed Jurisdictions* (Jerusalem: Harry and Michael Sacher Institute for Legislative Research and Comparative Law, The Hebrew University of Jerusalem, 1997), p. 793.

patrimonies work in civil law and how it is possible to overcome the objection to the trust fund as a separate patrimony that the trustee is liable for trust debts in his own capacity, not in the capacity as a trustee.[12] Secondly, the chapter goes on to explain the mechanisms of real subrogation and challenges the common assumption that real subrogation is an equivalent to tracing.[13] Thirdly, it shows that the exercise of the trustee's powers of disposition achieves an outcome similar to the type of real subrogation that operates within separate patrimonies. This is true of authorized dispositions of assets. When the dispositions by the trustee or a manager of a separate patrimony are unauthorized, both real subrogation and the trust concept struggle to explain the rights of the fund beneficiaries and it may be necessary to turn to other mechanisms for claiming.

The approach developed in this chapter is based primarily, although not exclusively, on the English trust as an example of a common law trust, and the Polish doctrine of real subrogation. The choice of Polish law has been dictated by insights it offers as a civil law jurisdiction derived from mixed French and German legal traditions. References to Roman law are crucial because a misunderstanding of the original sources inhibits the comprehension of present-day concepts.

II The concept of a separate patrimony

A. The meaning of the segregation

In civil law, every person has a patrimony, even if it is an empty one.[14] *Sensu largo* it comprises everything one owns, is owed and owes;[15] *sensu stricto* it covers only assets, not liabilities.[16] The purpose of treating all of a person's assets as a juridical universality is so that the creditors of that

[12] L. Smith, 'Trust and Patrimony' (2008) 38 R.G.D. 379, para. 9; (2009) 28 E.T.P.J. 332.

[13] See G. Gretton, 'Constructive Trusts' (1997) 1 Ed. L. Rev. 281, 291, 297–8; V. Sagaert, 'Cour de Cassation Française, 26 Avril 2000 – Priority Conflict Between the Seller Under Title Retention and the Assignee of the Resale Claim' (2002) 10 E.R.P.L. 823, 823.

[14] Smith, 'Trust and Patrimony', above, note 12, para. 13.

[15] Z. Radwański, *Prawo Cywilne – Część Ogólna* (Warsaw: C.H. Beck, 2007), p. 139; Smith, 'Trust and Patrimony', above, note 12, para. 13; see also Scottish Law Commission, *Discussion Paper on the Nature and the Constitution of Trusts* (Edinburgh: The Stationery Office, 2006), p. 10, para. 2.16.

[16] Radwański, *Prawo Cywilne*, above, note 15, p. 139; see also A. Dyoniak, 'Pojęcie Majątku W Prawie Cywilnym' (1985) 11–12 PiP 119, 139 (favouring the narrower interpretation of the patrimony in Polish civil law).

person can enforce their claims against all these assets.[17] Thus, any liabilities incurred by A are enforceable against A's patrimony, which means that A's assets are available for seizure and sale to satisfy claims of the judgment creditors (universal patrimonial liability).[18] The French[19] and Quebec Civil Codes[20] refer to this as *gage commun*, a right of general pledge on all the assets of A where the creditors are the pledgees.

Polish law, following German scholarship, has also recognized the concept of a separate patrimony (or a separate fund),[21] defined as a particular set of assets[22] which is segregated from another set of assets (usually the patrimony) in the following way. Even though both sets of assets belong to the same person, the separation of one set from another enables exchanges between the two sets of assets, as if they belonged to two different persons.[23] Although there is no definition of

[17] This theory of general patrimony was developed by French scholars Aubry and Rau, see C. Aubry and C. Rau, *Cours de droit civil français*, 7th edn (Paris: Imprimerie et Librairie Générale de Jurisprudence, 1919).

[18] H. Hansmann, R. Kraakman and R. Squire, 'Law and Rise of the Firm' (2006) 119 Harv. L. Rev. 1335, 1337; see N. Kasirer, 'Translating Part of France's Legal Heritage' (2008) 38 R.G.D. 453, 463; French Civil Code, art. 2284 (former art. 2092): 'Quiconque s'est obligé personnellement, est tenu de remplir son engagement sur tous ses biens mobiliers et immobiliers, présents et à venir.' The same principle exists in Polish law but it has not been codified, see W. Czachórski et al., *Zobowiązania* (Warsaw: LexisNexis, 2003), p. 61; see also Civil Code of Québec, art. 2645: 'Any person under a personal obligation charges, for its performance, all his property, movable and immovable, present and future, except property which is exempt from seizure or property which is the object of a division of patrimony permitted by law.'

[19] French Civil Code, art. 2285: 'Les biens du débiteur sont le gage commun de ses créanciers; et le prix s'en distribue entre eux par contribution, à moins qu'il n'y ait entre les créanciers des causes légitimes de préférence.' The concept of 'gage commun' is not present in Polish law.

[20] Civil Code of Québec, art. 2644: 'The property of a debtor is charged with the performance of his obligations and is the common pledge of his creditors.'

[21] Polish *majątek odrębny*, German *Sondervermögen*, *Sondergut*. This chapter does not draw linguistic differences between a separate patrimony and a separate fund.

[22] Polish definition uses the phrase 'valuable right' meaning a right of value, transferable (assignable) right. This includes rights to assets, such as an ownership of an asset. A collection of bikes is thus perceived as a collection of rights to bikes. It seems that in English the term 'assets', which covers intangibles including rights, conveys the meaning better than the civilian 'right'.

[23] E. Kitłowski, *Surogacja Rzeczowa w Prawie Cywilnym* (Warsaw: Wydawnictwo Prawnicze, 1969), p. 14; A. von Tuhr, *Der Allgemeine Teil des Deutschen Bürgerlichen Rechts* (Berlin: Duncker und Humblot, 1957), p. 340: 'Die Selbstständigkeit des Songerguts gegenüber dem allgemeinen Vermögen des Subjekts zeigt sich besonders deutlich daran, dass zwischen beiden Massen Rechtsbeziehungen möglich sind, wie sie sonst nur zwischen verschiedenen Personen vorkommen.'

a separate fund in Polish legislation, a number of provisions refer to it: for instance the Civil Code provisions on the separate fund of spouses,[24] the partnership fund[25] or the inheritance fund before it is split between heirs and becomes a part of their respective patrimonies.[26]

1. Protection of separate patrimonies from otherwise enforceable claims

Matrimonial regimes are a good example to illustrate the workings of separate patrimonies. In Poland, from the moment a marriage is concluded, a community of property is formed.[27] Assets acquired by either or both spouses during the marriage, in particular collected wages or pension,[28] are owned jointly and become a part of the so-called 'common patrimony'. Assets which fall outside of the common patrimony form separate property of each of the spouses (H and W).[29] These include assets acquired before marriage or assets inherited during marriage. This means that H's own assets are immune from W's creditors and, analogously, W's own assets cannot be claimed by H's creditors. If one spouse (say H) agreed to W's debt, then W's creditors could resort to the property owned by H and W jointly to pay the debt (the common patrimony),[30] but they still could not claim against H's separate patrimony. The Polish law on matrimonial property regimes changed significantly on 17 June 2004.[31] Prior to the reform, a creditor of only one spouse (say W) could resort to W's separate patrimony *and* to the common patrimony even if H did not expressly consent. After the reform, creditors of W's debts could only enforce their claims against W's separate patrimony. This had significant consequences for banks. Typically, before the reform, if H borrowed money from a bank, the bank could enforce the claim against H's assets as well as H and W's common assets. After the reform, the bank must seek consent from W in order to claim against the spouses' common assets. If the bank fails to do so, it can only claim against H's own assets. The reform is also significant to our understanding of separate patrimonies for other reasons, which are discussed below. For the moment, the key observation is that even before

[24] Polish Code of Family and Tutelage of 25 February 1964, Official Journal 1964/9/59, arts. 31–51, later amended.
[25] Polish Civil Code, arts. 863–75.
[26] Ibid., art. 1030.
[27] Polish Code of Family and Tutelage, above, note 24, art. 31 s.1.
[28] Ibid., art. 31 s.2.
[29] Ibid., art. 31 s.1.
[30] Ibid., art. 41 s.1.
[31] Law reform of 17 June 2004, OJ 162/1691, in force from 20 January 2005.

the reform the separate patrimony of H would have been immune from claims by W's creditors. This supports the view that separate patrimonies protect assets within them from execution of claims of creditors of another person. In other words, when we talk about a separate patrimony of a person entitled to it (H), what is usually meant is that this separate patrimony will be immune from another person's creditors (e.g. claims of W's creditors), who could, were it not for the separate patrimony, seize the assets within the separate patrimony.[32] However, there is not necessarily a corresponding liability of the separate patrimony (*and only* the separate patrimony) to pay debts made in connection to it.

2. Liability for debts incurred with respect to separate patrimonies

In Polish law, the liabilities incurred with respect to assets belonging to a separate patrimony tend to be enforceable against that patrimony. For instance, if a spouse is a liable to pay 1000 PLN for redecorating her own house (which does not belong to the common patrimony), and she does not pay, the decorating company will be able to claim against the house or other assets in the spouse's separate patrimony, but not against the assets within the common patrimony.[33] This does not have to be the case, however. It is not inherent in the definition of a separate patrimony that debts incurred with respect to the separate patrimony must be paid, voluntarily or through enforcement, from the separate patrimony. As mentioned above, under the pre-17 June 2004 law, a wife's personal creditor could look to both the wife's own assets and the assets she owned jointly with her husband. The creditor was limited to seizure and sale of assets belonging only to the wife's patrimony. Yet, this did not defeat the existence of the wife's separate patrimony. This observation should be kept in mind when we look at Lionel Smith's objection to Lepaulle's characterization of the trust fund as a separate patrimony.

[32] Following this definition, W's own patrimony can only be labelled as a 'separate patrimony' if we agree that W would otherwise be (at least perceived as) liable for H's debts, i.e. H's creditors could direct their claims against W and (all) W's assets. If there is no basis on which to say that W and H share debts, their debts remain separate and a situation when one spouse's creditors would claim against another spouse's assets would never arise. In such cases there is no point in talking about their respective 'separate patrimonies' because there is nothing these would be 'separate' from.

[33] Polish Code of Family and Tutelage, above, note 24, art. 41 s.2. If it were the husband dealing with the decorator, however, the unpaid decorators would be able to enforce the claim against the common patrimony as the husband will be deemed to have consented.

Lepaulle understood the trust as a patrimony appropriated to a destination or purpose, which belittled the role of trustees and beneficiaries.[34] Smith rightly questioned this approach on the basis that the common law trust cannot exist without the beneficiaries or the trustee.[35] Smith also made a point that the fact that the creditors of the trust could claim against the trustee as a person and not the trustee *in the capacity of trustee* indicates that the trust cannot be equated with a separate patrimony. Yet, the evidence from Polish law on debts arising from matrimonial property regime law helps to explain that the two are not mutually exclusive: an owner of a separate patrimony does not necessarily need to be sued in such capacity for there to be a separate patrimony. We have seen that in Poland debts relating to a debtor's separate patrimony can be enforced against both the separate patrimony of a spouse (the debtor) and against the common patrimony.[36] Thus a separate patrimony remains a meaningful concept even if that separate patrimony is not exclusively liable for debts relating to it.

The concept of a separate patrimony remains relevant for the purposes of excluding claims by the other spouse's creditors. Therefore, it is argued that the existence of a separate patrimony could be seen as functionally equivalent to the trust fund insofar as the protection from a certain group of creditors (trustee's creditors) is concerned.

B. *Exchangeability of the assets as an element of the separate patrimony*

Assuming that functional parallels can be drawn between a trust fund and a separate patrimony, as the previous section has attempted to show, we must now turn to their rationale, which is to enable a person to enjoy continuing rights in a fluctuating group of assets.[37] The question is whether the exchangeability of contents within a patrimony is essential for the patrimony to be separate. The content of patrimonies is rarely static: perhaps a collection of old paintings held only for the enjoyment of

34 P. Lepaulle, *Traité théorique et pratique des trusts en droit interne, en droit fiscal et en droit international* (Paris: Rousseau et Cie, 1931), p. 31, cited in Smith, 'Trust and Patrimony', above, note 12, para. 11.

35 Ibid., para. 14.

36 After 17 June 2004 only if the other spouse consented, see above.

37 R. Nolan, 'Property in a Fund' (2004) 120 Law Q. Rev. 108, 109; E. McKendrick (ed.), *Goode on Commercial Law*, 4th edn (London: Penguin Books, 2010), pp. 65–6; F. H. Lawson and B. Rudden, *The Law of Property*, 3rd edn (Oxford University Press, 2002), pp. 44–6.

the paintings themselves could be an example of such a rare 'static' patrimony. In most patrimonies assets are sold, exchanged or otherwise disposed of, producing proceeds; this gives rise to the question whether the patrimony can only be considered truly separate if the proceeds of such dispositions are automatically treated as falling into it.

In Poland, article 33(10) of the Polish Code of Family and Tutelage provides that assets acquired with means from the personal patrimony of one of the spouses belong to that patrimony.[38] This provision has been in existence only since the Family and Tutelage Code reform of 17 June 2004.[39] Prior to this, the wording was to the opposite effect: assets acquired after the marriage with a spouse's own means did not enter the personal patrimonies of the spouses but the common patrimony, the result being a progressive shrinkage of the 'size' (value) of personal patrimonies. Even though the reform reversed the effect of a transfer of assets from the personal patrimonies, it has not been questioned that both before and after the reform the spouses had personal (separate) patrimonies. This suggests that exchangeability of assets within a patrimony is not a crucial element of a separate patrimony. Patrimonies can be separate, irrespective of whether the substitutes are caught automatically by a patrimony.

An argument to the contrary draws on the German concept of *fiduziarische Treuhand*.[40] If the *Treuhänder* becomes insolvent, the assets held by him in *Treuhand* fall into his bankrupt estate unless they have been transferred to him directly by the settlor,[41] pursuant to the court-affirmed *Unmittelbarkeitsprinzip*.[42] This principle developed gradually. According to the early twentieth-century *Reichsgericht* jurisprudence, the

[38] Polish Code of Family and Tutelage, art. 33(10). See e.g. resolution of the Polish Supreme Court of 11 September 2003, III CZP 52/03.

[39] See Section II.A.1 above.

[40] Gretton, 'Trusts without Equity', above, note 3, note 67, and remarking that it is irreconcilable with a notion of a special patrimony because 'if there is a special patrimony then there must be real subrogation'.

[41] Since most 'trusts' in Germany are said to be *inter vivos* for the settlor's own benefit, some German authors refer to settlors as having the beneficial ownership (as distinct from legal ownership) but it seems that even if that is the case it is conceptually clearer to use the different terms – beneficiary and settlor – as non-synonymous.

[42] Decisions of *Reichsgericht* RGZ 84, 214, at 217; RGZ 91, 12, at 16; RGZ 133, 84, at 87; decision of *Bundesgerichtshof* BGHZ 1959, Entscheidungen des Bundesgerichtshofes in Zivilsachen p. 1223, cited in C. Rounds and A. Dehio, 'Publicly-Traded Open End Mutual Funds in Common Law and Civil Law Jurisdictions: A Comparison of Legal Structures' (2007) 3 N.Y.U.J.L. & Bus. 473, note 85. The term *Unmittelbarkeitsprinzip* (principle of immediacy of transfer) was coined by Friedmann, 36 DJT 1930, vol. I, 805 at 862, as cited

creditors of the 'trustee' could not seize 'trust' property if it was 'properly ear-marked' and therefore distinguishable[43] because it would have been considered as a windfall for these creditors.[44] Courts subsequently limited this to property transferred directly from the settlor to the 'trustee',[45] which meant that the traceable proceeds of the original property fell within the 'trustee's' own estate (*Surrogationsverbot*). Thus, even if trust property was regarded as belonging to a separate patrimony it was not regarded as including accessions, replacements or proceeds of sale of the original assets, unless these had been conveyed to the settlor and resettled.[46] This excludes transfers from third parties, particularly when bank accounts are involved and held in 'trust' by a notary or a lawyer.[47] There are views advocating the return to the original principle: that the beneficial interest be protected each time the property can be distinguished from other assets (*Bestimmtsheitsgrundsatz*).[48]

The *Unmittelbarkeitsprinzip* is, however, disapplied in the German mutual fund context. Where there is a mutual fund under German law on the basis of *Treuhand*,[49] which is particularly useful in the case of collective investments in real property,[50] the investors transfer monies to the KAG (*Kapitalanlegegesellschaft*) and KAG administers the underlying assets of a mutual fund (*Sondervermögen*).[51] KAG is then the titleholder to the underlying assets.[52] The separate investment fund

in S. Grundmann, 'Trust and Treuhand at the End of the 20th Century: Key Problems and Shift of Interests' (1999) 47 Am. J. Comp. L. 401, 408, note 34.

43 Grundmann, 'Trust and Treuhand', above, note 42, 407, citing (at note 32) RGZ 45, 80 at 83–7 and RGZ 79, 121 at 122ff, described as the principle of certainty (*Bestimmtsheitsgrundsatz*).

44 Ibid., note 33.

45 Ibid., 408, note 34 and see literature there.

46 A. Honoré, 'Book Review: The British Commonwealth in International Law by JES Fawcett' (1964) 13 I.C.L.Q. 713, 736.

47 Grundmann, 'Trust and Treuhand', above, note 42, 408, note 35.

48 Ibid., 408–9, and see also other proponents of this view cited there.

49 Under German law, a mutual fund can be construed as the *Treuhandlösung* – an imperfect common law trust, or the *Miteigentumslösung* – an imperfect common law tenancy in common, see Rounds and Dehio, 'Publicly-Traded Open End Mutual Funds', above, note 42, 496.

50 Every ownership transfer of real property must be registered in the land register (*Grundbuch*) in order to take effect (*Offenkundigkeitsprinzip*). Without a single entity to hold the title, such as the KAG, each investor would have to be registered in the *Grundbuch* to effect their pro rata share of the collective ownership (*Bruchteilsgemeinschaft*), rendering the investment process, which it was designed to achieve, impracticable. Ibid., 498.

51 §2 II German *Investmentgesetz*. KAG has a special banking licence issued by the German Federal Banking Agency. Ibid., 496.

52 *Investmentgesetz*, §30 I.

is segregated from KAG's own assets.[53] According to the *Unmittelbarkeitsprinzip* only the monies initially paid in the fund by investors would be protected from creditors of the *Treuhänder*. The effect would be incompatible with the concept of an open-ended mutual fund, hence the principle was neutralized legislatively in Section 30 II of the German Investment Law.[54] All investments within the *Sondervermögen* accrue to the *Sondervermögen* and are protected from a *Treuhänder*'s creditors.

It has therefore been argued that the German mutual fund investor is essentially endowed with a 'quasi-property interest in *Sondervermögen*, the title to which is in the KAG'.[55] The parallels with a common law beneficiary's equitable title should not be drawn too hastily, however. Unlike the common law beneficiary in the breach of trust by the trustee, the 'beneficiary' of a German *Treuhand* has merely contractual remedies in case of harm done to the *Sondervermögen* by the *Treuhänder*.

It seems that exchangeability of assets is not an indispensable element of a separate patrimony. A patrimony may still be separate even if proceeds of a disposition of patrimonial assets fall outside of the patrimony. However, there is a good argument that in order to achieve a particular outcome within a separate patrimony traceable proceeds must inhere within the patrimony. Simply because a patrimony is separate does not mean that its contents may not change: assets may be both taken out or added in. Further, the *Unmittelbarkeitsprinzip*, coupled with the *Surrogationsverbot*, does not seem to be incompatible with a separate patrimony. If, however, the separate patrimony is managed for the benefit of another person, these principles are likely to undermine the efficacy of the patrimonial structure.

C. *Types of separate patrimonies*

It is suggested that the extent to which separate patrimonies are 'separate' varies in civil law. At one end of the spectrum lies the type of patrimony where assets are segregated from the other assets of a person (A) in such a way that A's personal creditors have no access to them and any

[53] Ibid., §30 I Abs. 2: 'Das Sondervermögen ist von dem eigenen Vermögen der Kapitalanlagegesellschaft getrennt zu halten.'

[54] Ibid., §30 II: 'Zum Sondervermögen gehört auch alles, was die Kapitalanlagegesellschaft auf Grund eines zum Sondervermögen gehörenden Rechts oder durch ein Rechtsgeschäft erwirbt, das sich auf das Sondervermögen bezieht, oder was derjenige, dem das Sondervermögen zusteht, als Ersatz für ein zum Sondervermögen gehörendes Recht erwirbt.'

[55] Rounds and Dehio, 'Publicly-Traded Open End Mutual Funds', above, note 42, 500.

liabilities arising from that pool of assets are satisfied by seizing and selling these assets. Creditors of such a separate patrimony cannot seek enforcement of their claims from A's own assets unless they form a part of the separate patrimony. As it is known in the US, this can be described as 'asset independence', or affirmative asset partitioning:[56] assets are subtracted from the common pledge of A's personal creditors as each pool of assets is bonded to a different purpose.[57] Such a fund could be called a separate patrimony *par excellence*, or a stronger version of a separate patrimony. An example of such a patrimony is the Italian 'committed funds' introduced in the Italian Civil Code in 2003.[58] An Italian corporation may partition up to 10 per cent of its assets in order to commit them to a specific business purpose. These assets are pledged only to those creditors whose claim is related to a specific business purpose ('specialized creditors'). The general creditors of the corporation have no recourse against this separate fund (affirmative asset partitioning). Equally, the specialized creditors cannot claim against the corporation's assets which are not part of the committed fund (defensive asset partitioning).[59] The functional equivalent of this type of separate patrimony is a corporate subsidiary.[60]

A weaker version of the separate patrimony insulates the assets from A's creditors, but the liabilities incurred with respect to this patrimony may be satisfied by enforcement not only against the assets within the separate patrimony but also against A's own assets. This pattern seems to be followed by the French *fiducie*.[61] An independent patrimony (*patrimoine fiduciaire*) is created, which is separate from the patrimonies of both the settlor (*constituant*) and the fiduciary (*fiduciaire*) and thus immune from claims of either the settlor's or fiduciary's creditors. No assets can be seized from the fiduciary patrimony to satisfy claims other than those arising from the management or preservation of the fiduciary patrimony.[62] However, if the assets within the fiduciary patrimony are insufficient to pay the creditors, the latter can seize assets

[56] G. R. Elgueta, 'Divergences and Convergences of Common Law and Civil Law Traditions on Asset Partitioning: A Functional Analysis' (2010) 12 U. Pa. J. Bus. L. 517.

[57] Ibid., 525. [58] Italian Civil Code, arts. 2447 *bis* – 2447 *decies*.

[59] Elgueta, 'Divergences and Convergences', above, note 56, 534.

[60] A subsidiary can be incorporated for other reasons too.

[61] French Civil Code, art. 2011 *et seq*.

[62] French Civil Code, art. 2025(1): 'Sans préjudice des droits des créanciers du constituant titulaires d'un droit de suite attaché à une sûreté publiée antérieurement au contrat de fiducie et hors les cas de fraude aux droits des créanciers du constituant, *le patrimoine*

within the patrimony of the settlor,[63] unless the contract creating the *fiducie* provides otherwise.

III Real subrogation as a mechanism for asset exchangeability

Even though asset exchangeability falls short of a condition *sine qua non* of every separate patrimony, it may play a crucial role if the effect that we are after is a fluctuating fund of assets. Exchangeability (or substitution) of assets in civil law systems is usually linked with real subrogation.

Real subrogation developed in Roman law to operate within collections of assets.[64] On the basis of Roman law, the following Pandectist maxims have been developed to illustrate the process of asset substitution within funds:[65] *in universalibus res succedit loco pretii et pretium loco rei* (in the context of collections of assets a thing takes the place of the price and the price takes the place of the thing); *in singularibus res non succedit loco pretii nec res loco rei* (where particular assets are concerned neither is the price substituted for the asset nor the asset substituted for the price).[66] Thus the second maxim excluded the application of subrogation where entitlements to particular assets were concerned.[67] The third maxim pertains to the effects of real subrogation: *subrogatum capit naturam subrogatii*: the substitute takes the nature of the substituted asset. The meaning of '*capit naturam*' is far from clear.

The application of real subrogation has been extended not only to explain rights to substitutes within separate patrimonies or general

fiduciaire ne peut être saisi que par les titulaires de créances nées de la conservation ou de la gestion de ce patrimoine' (emphasis added).

63 There is a *gage commun* over the patrimony of the settlor, French Civil Code, art. 2025(2).

64 A prototype mechanism for asserting rights in substituted assets developed in Greek law in connection with a contract of sale. See L. Winkel, 'Some Remarks on Substitution of Property and Unjust Enrichment in European Legal History', in E. Schrage (ed.), *Unjust Enrichment and the Law of Contract* (The Hague: Kluwer Law International, 2001), p. 442 citing F. Pringsheim, *Der Kauf mit fremdem Geld* (Leipzig: Verlag von Veit, 1916); F. Pringsheim, *The Greek Law of Sale* (Weimar: H. Böhlaus Nachfolger, 1950).

65 V. Ranouil, *La subrogation réelle en droit civil français* (Paris: Bibliothèque de Droit Privé, 1985), pp. 58–9 (explaining all three maxims); Kitłowski, *Surogacja Rzeczowa*, above, note 23, p. 8.

66 The origins seem to be in D. 5,3,22 Paulus libro vicensimo ad edictum; see A. Santos, *Subrogación real y patrimonios especiales en el derecho romano clásico* (Universidad de Valladolid: Secretariado de Publicaciones e Intercambio Cientifico, 1997), p. 90; J. Flach, *De la subrogation réelle* (Paris: A. Durand et Pedone-Lauriel, 1870), p. 21.

67 Ranouil, *La subrogation réelle*, above, note 65, p. 58. Exceptions are when legislative provisions allow asset substitution without any separate fund.

patrimonies (such as rights to common pledge),[68] but also to explain how particular rights could apply to substitutes when a collection of assets was not involved, thus contradicting the second Pandectist maxim. As a result, subrogation within separate funds[69] has been traditionally distinguished[70] from subrogation outside of such funds.[71]

A. *Two types of real subrogation*

1. Real subrogation within separate funds (*in universalibus*)

Real subrogation of assets within collections of assets is the archetype of real subrogation, reflected in the first Pandectist maxim. It is controversial whether this type of real subrogation may operate within any separate fund or solely when so provided by law. There is an argument that whenever means from (any) separate fund are used to acquire an asset, the asset should fall into that separate fund, notwithstanding the lack of a specific legislative provision.[72] This seems right but it is important to remember that the presence of a legislative provision that takes new assets outside of the scope of a separate patrimony, when assets inhering in it have been exchanged for the new assets, does not preclude the existence of a separate patrimony.[73]

Separate funds serve to fence off the assets and make them *unavailable* to a certain group of potential creditors. Real subrogation preserves that quality in assets newly acquired with the means from separate funds. The result is that if the old asset was immune from some creditors' claims, the new asset will also be protected against such creditors' claims. Real subrogation in separate funds does not operate to subject substitutes

[68] Real subrogation was key to Aubry and Rau's concept of general patrimony. Aubry and Rau, *Cours de droit civil*, above, note 17, pp. 340ff.

[69] Polish *surogacja w składzie majątku odrębnego*, German *Universalsurrogation*.

[70] Kitłowski, *Surogacja Rzeczowa*, above, note 23, p. 13; S. Grzybowski (ed.), *System prawa cywilnego. Część ogólna* (Warsaw: Ossolineum, 1985), vol. I, p. 472.

[71] Polish *surogacja poza majątkiem odrębnym*, German *Singularsurrogation*.

[72] A. Ohanowicz, 'Case Comment to Supreme Court Ruling of 18 October 1961, 4 Cr 957/60' (1962) 8–9 PiP 465. A view to the contrary was presented by S. Szer, 'Case Comment to Supreme Court Ruling of 24 November 1963' (1963) OSPIKA 1963/240/538, 538. To give a brief example, the Civil Code does not provide expressly for asset substitution within a fund of a partnership running a business. Yet, it seems that if real subrogation was not allowed, notwithstanding the lack of a specific provision, it would impede the partnership's performance.

[73] See Polish matrimonial regime before the reform of 17 June 2004, discussed above, see section II.B.

to the same *right* as the original asset but rather it transfers a particular attribute that the previous right had. Therefore, where separate funds are involved, it is wrong to say that a new asset becomes subject to the same right as the old asset.[74]

The new asset must be sufficiently linked with the old one so as to become an element of the separate fund: a transactional link is necessary but not sufficient. It is not clear whether a causal link, or some other link, is needed. In German law, this additional requirement is epitomized in the phrase 'acquired with the means from' the separate fund,[75] supplemented by an intention that the substituting act relates to the separate fund.[76] What is clear is that it is insufficient for one event to be only a pretext for another to happen (i.e. a mere causal link is insufficient), as for instance where a gift from A to B of an asset from her separate fund provokes a gift in reciprocation from B to A. Likewise, if an asset is excluded from the fund, and by reason of this exclusion a new asset arises for the benefit of a *third party* (not the fund owner), the new asset will not be considered a substitute for the old one. To illustrate: if a thief stole an antique clock from a separate fund (such as an inheritance fund) and subsequently sold it, the only right that will arise within the separate fund will be a tort claim against the thief,[77] not the thief's right to claim a purchase price, which the thief might have obtained if he had entered into a sale contract and the other party had not yet performed his part of the bargain.[78] The situation may change if the separate fund is in the hands of a third party possessor, for instance when an administrator

[74] Similar conclusion on different arguments. Kitłowski, *Surogacja Rzeczowa*, above, note 23; what I refer to in this chapter as the transfer of particular attributes has led some authors to argue that real subrogation in civil law is in fact a method of primary, rather than derivative, acquisition (*mode originaire d'acquisition*), see E. Savaux, 'Subrogation Réelle' (March 1998) Rep. civ. Dalloz (I am very grateful to Rafael Ibarra Garza for providing me with this source).

[75] German Civil Code BGB, §2019: 'Als aus der Erbschaft erlangt gilt auch, was der Erbschaftsbesitzer durch Rechtsgeschäft *mit Mitteln der Erbschaft* erwirbt' (emphasis added).

[76] German law seems to require that the substituting act relate to the separate fund, e.g. that the person doing the substituting act does so with the intention that the substitute enters the separate fund. See R. Beyer, *Surrogation bei Vermögen* (Marburg: N. G. Elwert, 1905), p. 222, cited in Kitłowski, *Surogacja Rzeczowa*, above, note 23, p. 21.

[77] The use of 'tort claim' can be confusing. By 'tort claim' in this context is meant that the person whose asset was stolen will be able to demand that the wrongdoer make up for the loss. This in turn can be achieved by financial compensation or restitution (*restitutio ad integrum*). See Czachórski et al., *Zobowiązania*, above, note 18, pp. 107–8.

[78] Kitłowski, *Surogacja Rzeczowa*, above, note 23, p. 22.

compensation claim he may have. Thus the creditor would acquire a new right in the substitute. The new asset would serve the creditor in the same way as the old asset did: by providing a realizable value.[88] Consequently, real subrogation outside of separate funds may be better characterized as a process that allows the entitled person (e.g. the disenriched or the chargee) to use the proceeds for the same purpose which the original asset was to fulfil.

It follows that real subrogation is different from the evidentiary process of identifying misappropriated value, which is tracing.[89] Whether operating *in universalibus* or *in singularibus*, real subrogation ensures that the person availing herself of real subrogation is left with a claim (or right) to the new asset. It may not necessarily be the same right which one had to the original asset; it simply means that if A was entitled to an original asset, real subrogation will enable A to *claim* the new asset as long as it is at least transactionally linked to the original asset.[90] It must be remembered that real subrogation operates in a limited number of circumstances. Even though real subrogation within separate patrimonies does not transfer rights *per se*, it seems to be doing more than tracing. It subjects new rights to substitutes to a certain framework of enforceability. Therefore, it is suggested tracing and real subrogation cannot be equated.

IV Property in a fund and in a patrimony

The question remains whether one has a property right to the fund/patrimony or to the assets within it.

A. *Property in a patrimony as a collection of assets*

A group of assets held in the hands of a person gives rise to the question of whether the person has a property right to the assets within the collection or whether the collection is itself the subject matter of a property right.

[88] Kitłowski, *Surogacja Rzeczowa*, above, note 23, p. 35.

[89] L. Smith, *The Law of Tracing* (Oxford: Clarendon Press, 1997); *Foskett* v. *McKeown* [2001] 1 AC 102, 128 (Millett LJ); *contra*, e.g., C. Rotherham, 'The Metaphysics of Tracing: Substituted Title and Property Rhetoric' (1996) 34 Osgoode Hall L.J. 321.

[90] This may be more difficult in real subrogation outside of separate funds, see section above.

Roman law, under the influence of the stoic doctrine,[91] distinguished between things as singular, complex and collections.[92] Singular things,[93] such as an animal, a beam (*tignum*) or a stone, constituted a unity both legally and economically and, consequently, were unproblematic for questions of transfer of property.[94] The difficulties that arose were with respect to complex or composite things. Complex things, or *corpora ex cohaerentibus*, referred to in medieval writings as *universitas rerum cohaerentium*, were things composed of a number of elements joined in a lasting manner, so that they became unified both legally and economically (e.g. a building or a ship). Once a beam (*tignum iunctum*) became a part of a building it lost its independent character. The owner of a beam could not vindicate it although he could demand double its value.[95] Collections, on the other hand, were different. Referred to in the Digest as *corpora ex distantibus*, and labelled later as *universitas rerum distantium*, collections were groups of things, each of which retained their physical character whilst existing as one whole (e.g. libraries or herds of animals). The owner of a herd could vindicate both an entire herd (*vindicatio gregis*) or particular animals within it.[96] The reason for allowing vindication of an entire collection in Roman law was clearly convenience in cases such as the transfer of a testator's legacy.[97] In other situations, the important unit was the individual animal, not the herd.[98] It seems that a number of authors later confounded the two types of *universitas rerum* with each other, thus blurring the crucial difference in

[91] W. Wołodkiewicz and M. Zabłocka, *Prawo Rzymskie (Roman Law)* (Warsaw: C.H. Beck, 2001), p. 120.

[92] D. 6,1,23,5; D. 41,3,30.

[93] Referred to in later writings as *res singulae* although the Digest does not call them by this name. See e.g. C. K. Allen, 'Things' (1940) 28 Cal. L. Rev. 421, 429.

[94] D. 41,3,30 *in fine*: 'usucapione quaestionem non habet'. *Usucapio* is understood here broadly as relating to the issues of transfer of property, although it was more often associated with acquisition of property regardless of the owner's title, i.e. in the case of adverse possession. See e.g., 'The Operation of Usucaption in Roman Law' (1920) 1 *The Law Coach* 23; R. Yaron, 'Reflections on Usucapio' (1967) 35 *Tijdschrift voor Rechtsgeschiedenis* 191.

[95] Established as early as XII Tables, Table 6, 8 (an owner of a stolen beam was prevented from taking the beam out from a building, into which it had been incorporated).

[96] D. 41,3,30; J. 2,20,18.

[97] A. Watson, *Studies in Roman Private Law*, 1st edn (London: Hambledon Press, 1991), p. 139. Note the permissive rather than declarative language of J. 2,20,18: 'vindicari potest', which seems to indicate perhaps that there were other ways of vindication (i.e. vindication of each individual element) that were the norm.

[98] See ibid., pp. 139–40.

the method of vindicating each type.[99] The distinctions drawn by the Romans can be of particular use when discussing property in a fund.

Polish property law has not recognized the concept of *universitas rerum*. Unlike in Roman law, *universitas rerum* is not a *res*: selling a collection of books requires transfer of property of each and every book within the library,[100] unless a statute provides otherwise.[101] Likewise, a *universitas iuris* (a collection of rights, claims and sometimes also things) is not a *res*. Thus, a patrimony, an enterprise or a fund within an enterprise cannot be treated as a legally distinct subject matter of property rights, notwithstanding its economic (functional) integrity or its grouping (or segregation) for a specific purpose.[102] Yet, it can be subject to contractual and obligational relationships (including an obligation to transfer property) as an *ensemble*.[103] Property is, however, transferred separately to each asset. One can therefore never have a property right to a separate patrimony in civil law, but merely to assets that fall within it.

Bearing in mind that the separate patrimonies protect assets from certain creditors, we can consider the position of A, who is entitled to certain assets held by B within a patrimony separate from B's general patrimony. If A wants to transfer the property rights to any of the assets in the special patrimony, A must do so separately with respect to each asset. At no point can B's creditors seize any of those assets. A's own creditors may or may not have access to those assets.

B. *Property in a trust fund in English law*

If we are to draw functional parallels between the separate patrimony and the trust fund, the characterization of a separate patrimony as a sum of assets rather than a *res* sits uncomfortably with the view of a reified trust fund advanced by James Penner.

[99] Allen, 'Things', above, note 93, 429; Gretton, 'Trusts without Equity', above, note 3, 615–16.

[100] J. Ignatowicz and K. Stefaniuk, *Prawo Rzeczowe*, 2nd edn (Warsaw: LexisNexis, 2006), p. 20; similarly – Dutch law, see L. von Vliet, 'The Boundaries of Property Rights: Netherlands National Report 2006' (2007) 11 E.J.C.L. 1.

[101] See e.g. Polish Civil Code, art. 257 s. 1 (concerning usufruct); Polish Law on Registered Charge and the Charge Register, art. 7(2)(3).

[102] Ignatowicz and Stefaniuk, *Prawo Rzeczowe*, above, note 100, p. 20; Dutch law is similar in this respect. See Vliet, 'The Boundaries of Property Rights', above, note 100; see also e.g. *Investmentgesetz*, §30 I Abs 1: 'Die zum Sondervermögen gehörenden Vermögensgegenstände.'

[103] E. Gniewek, *Prawo Rzeczowe* (Warsaw: C.H. Beck, 2003), pp. 4–5.

Penner conceives of a fund as a distinct property interest, not merely as an interest in multiple items of property.[104] Penner observes that the whole point of a fund is to facilitate the exchange of assets.[105] Therefore, 'an interest in a fund is an interest not only in the assets in it at the moment but in those assets to the extent they become realized via exchange'.[106] Although the beneficiary has no interest in any assets presently comprising the fund, he has rights given under the terms of his interest in the fund.[107] It is part of the beneficiary's interest in a fund to have an option of electing to accept or reject wrongful transactions of the trustee. Based on this analysis, tracing claims are simply an aspect of the beneficiary's property right in a fund. Penner's conceptualization of property in a fund has been met with an objection by Sheehan,[108] who builds on Nolan and Fox's view of funds, to show that at no point can the beneficiary of a trust have an interest in a fund reified separately from assets within it.[109] As Sheehan points out, the starting point is that a trustee holds specific assets for the benefit of the beneficiary, which he must keep safe and from which he may not derive any personal benefit.[110] If the trustee is to invest trust property, as is usually the case, to generate a return for the beneficiaries, his investment powers will lead to existing assets being (from time to time) substituted for new ones. The beneficiaries will then continue to have the same interest in the new asset. For this to work, the trustee, as the fund-holder, has a power to alienate the assets free from the fund-beneficiary rights (the overreaching power).[111] The beneficiary acquires the same right, in whatever asset the trustee acquires as a result of the exercise of the trustee's overreaching power, as he had in the asset before the exchange. Otherwise, the exercise

[104] J. Penner, 'Duty and Liability in Respect of Funds', in J. Lowry and L. Mistelis (eds.), *Commercial Law: Perspectives and Practice* (London: LexisNexis, Butterworths, 2006), p. 212, para. 12.16. See also McKendrick, *Goode on Commercial Law*, above, note 37, pp. 45, 65.

[105] J. Penner, 'Value, Property and Unjust Enrichment: Trusts of Traceable Proceeds', in R. Chambers, C. Mitchell and J. Penner (eds.), *Philosophical Foundations of the Law of Unjust Enrichment* (Oxford University Press, 2009), p. 315: 'the history of the fund is the history of the exchanges of its assets'. It may be said that Penner views the fund as an 'exchange facilitator'.

[106] Ibid., p. 315. [107] Ibid., p. 314.

[108] D. Sheehan, 'Property in a Fund, Tracing and Unjust Enrichment' (2010) 2 *Journal of Equity* 225.

[109] Ibid., p. 226. [110] Ibid., p. 226; *Pickering* v. *Pickering* (1839) 2 Beav 31.

[111] Nolan, 'Property in a Fund', above, note 37, 108; R. Nolan, 'Understanding the Limits of Equitable Property' (2006) 1 *Journal of Equity* 1820; D. Fox, 'Overreaching', in P. Birks and A. Pretto (eds.), *Breach of Trust* (Oxford: Hart, 2002), pp. 95–6.

of the trustee's power would lead every time to a new separate trust over a new asset.[112] The beneficiary's interest may also expire without there being any replacement entering the trust fund. This takes place when the trustee (the manager) transfers an asset to a third party in an authorized way and receives nothing in return.

For as long as the trustee acts within his powers and the dispositions of trust property are authorized by the trust instrument, on Nolan's analysis, the right to claim substitute assets derives solely from the bargain or undertaking which establishes the beneficiaries' rights in the individual items of trust property. For Penner, the interest which the fund beneficiary has is not in the individual assets comprising the fund, the elements of which 'may fluctuate because of the exercise of the powers of the fund manager',[113] but rather 'his interest is only in whatever rights are given under the terms of his interest in the fund'.[114] For Penner, when the trustee acts within his powers, the beneficiary's rights with respect to property are legally protected by the trustee's enforcement of his legal rights to the trust property and the beneficiary does not have any rights to enforce legal rights himself.[115] Thus, for Penner, the beneficiary's interest falls short of proprietary, although the beneficiary can at any point be said to have a distinct kind of property interest in the fund itself.[116] Whether the beneficiary's interest is proprietary is controversial and clearly depends on what makes a right proprietary.[117] This question is not explored here. Suffice it to say that Nolan's view is that the beneficiaries' proprietary rights consist in their negative rights to exclude non-beneficiaries from the unencumbered enjoyment of trust property.[118] This conceptualization also works in the case of discretionary trusts and, as Sheehan shows,[119] beneficiaries of a discretionary trust may also be said to have proprietary interest in the individual assets.

[112] C. Rickett, 'Old and New in the Law of Tracing', in S. Degeling and J. Edelman (eds.), *Equity in Commercial Law* (Syndey: Lawbook Co., 2005), p. 136.

[113] Penner, 'Duty and Liability', above, note 104, p. 212, para. 12.16.

[114] Ibid. [115] Ibid.

[116] Ibid.; Penner, 'Value, Property and Unjust Enrichment', above, note 105, p. 314.

[117] Sheehan, 'Property in a Fund', above, note 108, 232.

[118] R. Nolan, 'Equitable Property' (2006) 122 Law Q. Rev. 232, 236–8; see also K. Gray, 'Property in Thin Air' (1991) Cambridge L.J. 252, 292–5.

[119] Sheehan, 'Property in a Fund', above, note 108, 231–4 and cases cited there: *Federal Commissioner of Taxation* v. *Vegners* (1989) 90 ALR 547, 552 (Gummow J); *Chief Commissioner of Stamp Duties* v. *Buckle* (1998) 192 CLR 226, 234.

It is worth pointing to a particular type of non-beneficiary which the beneficiary has a negative right to exclude, namely the trustee's creditors. The segregation of the trust assets from the trustee's other assets insofar as his creditors' claims are concerned is explained by the proprietary right of the beneficiary to *exclude* these creditors from seizing and selling the trust assets. Notice that on this analysis of segregation it is not relevant that the creditors of the trust sue the trustee in his own capacity.[120]

Before moving on to the discussion of rights of a beneficiary when a trust is breached, let us pause to sketch a parallel between the rights of a common law trust beneficiary and those of a patrimony owner.

V Convergence of the trust fund and separate patrimony[121]

A. *Authorized dispositions: exercise of trustees' powers and real subrogation parallel*

For as long as a civilian patrimony is not a *res* but merely a collection of assets, which appears to have been the case in Roman law and is now the case, for instance, in Poland, no one has a property right to a civilian (separate) patrimony. Penner's trust fund view as a distinct property interest diverges from the way the civilian separate patrimony has been understood.

For a separate patrimony to be comparable to a common law trust fund, two aspects must be considered: (1) segregation of the fund from the manager's assets, and (2) exchangeability of the assets within the fund. First, a separate patrimony is by its very nature, as discussed above, segregated from other assets of the patrimony-holder/manager (A), so that A's creditors cannot seize the assets within the separate patrimony to satisfy their claims. Assuming that the common law trust beneficiaries can be said to have proprietary rights in individual assets, the effect of the beneficiaries' negative rights to exclude trustees' creditors is exactly the same.

[120] See Smith, 'Trust and Patrimony', above, note 12, paras. 18–19. The liabilities incurred by the trust fund are usually satisfied from the trustee's own funds. The trustee then will have a right of recourse against the trust assets but the creditors can enforce the claim against both the trust assets and trustee's own assets.

[121] The idea of convergence is itself controversial in its principle, although this is not discussed here. See e.g. B. Markesinis, 'Learning from Europe and Learning in Europe', in B. Markesinis (ed.), *The Gradual Convergence: Foreign Ideas, Foreign Influences, and English Law on the Eve of the 21st Century* (Oxford: Clarendon Press, 1994), p. 1, and his critic P. Legrand, 'European Legal Systems Are Not Converging' (1996) 45 I.C.L.Q. 52.

The second aspect of the fund/patrimony is more complicated. The exchangeability of the assets within a trust fund is achieved by the exercise by the trustee of the power to make investments. The necessary corollary of powers in the trustee is overreaching, which means that a purchaser of property takes free from any interests or powers, which instead attach to the proceeds of sale.[122] Exchangeability of assets is not inherent in the concept of a separate patrimony. If substitute assets are retained in the trust fund, it happens due to the exercise of powers of the trustee. Real subrogation operating within separate patrimonies renders a similar result. It allows for the asset to be protected from A's creditors' claims in the same way as the previous asset was. It does not, however, necessarily create in the new asset an identical right. Nor does it imply that it cannot. Real subrogation within separate patrimonies ensures that the person entitled to the original asset within the separate patrimony will have the right to exclude certain creditors from claiming against the new asset inasmuch as they were excluded from claiming against the old asset. Yet, bearing in mind how both types of real subrogation operate, and that the effect of the exercise of the trustee's powers is that the beneficiary has the same right in the new asset, it is necessary to consider whether the model of real subrogation outside of separate funds would not be a better candidate for drawing parallels with the trust fund. If a beneficiary has a particular right against the asset in the trustee's hands then in order to ensure that the beneficiary has the same right in the new asset, real subrogation operating *in singularibus* seems better cut out to do the job. Clearly, our choice of real subrogation model depends on the right which the beneficiary is thought to have in the trust asset. Assuming that beneficiaries' proprietary rights consist in their negative rights to exclude non-beneficiaries from the unencumbered enjoyment of trust property (in particular to exclude a trustee's personal creditors from seizing trust assets), then the right in the new asset, which arises upon the exercise of the trustee's overreaching power, will also be a right to exclude the trustee's creditors from seizing that property in execution. The effect of applying the real subrogation model within separate funds would have the same effect in this case as applying real subrogation outside of separate funds. We must recall, however, that real subrogation *in singularibus* is only allowed on the basis of a specific provision,

[122] Fox, 'Overreaching', above, note 111; Rickett, 'Old and New in the Law of Tracing', above, note 112; Sheehan, 'Property in a Fund', above, note 108.

which is not true for a real subrogation *in universalibus*. If we were looking for a ready-to-use doctrine to apply in a civilian 'trust', which would ensure that the 'beneficiary' continues to have rights in the proceeds of an authorized disposition of the property originally settled on 'trust', then real subrogation *in universalibus* would be a better candidate because it is likely that it could operate within a collection of assets perceived as a separate patrimony without a prior intervention from a legislator, at least where there is no explicit *Surrogationsverbot*. This has potential consequences for the extent to which a 'trust-like' instrument could be used in civil law countries. The potential application of real subrogation *in universalibus* is subject to certain assumptions. First, as soon as the right of the beneficiary is perceived otherwise than as a right to exclude non-beneficiaries from the enjoyment of trust property, real subrogation *in universalibus* will struggle to provide the civil law 'beneficiary' with a continuing right to a new asset. Second, we would need to ensure that real subrogation *in universalibus* overcomes its difficulties with multiple substitutions at least as well as real subrogation *in singularibus*.[123] Therefore, even though real subrogation *in singularibus* is a better parallel to draw with the power of the trustee to dispose of the asset, under certain assumptions real subrogation *in universalibus* may achieve the same results.

B. *Unauthorized dispositions by the trustee*

In unauthorized transactions, the contract power of the manager of the trust fund does not exist. The right of the beneficiary to substitute cannot therefore derive from the bargain. Nolan's analysis does not explain this, nor does it claim to. However, Nolan indicates that remedial interests over a fluctuating class of assets are constructs of law, the role of which is different from property in a fund.[124] The latter is a product of a consensual stipulation whilst the former arise to fill the gaps beyond such a consenual ordering of affairs.[125]

To Penner, on the other hand, it is not until the trust is breached that the beneficiary's proprietary interest comes to light.[126] Only then may the beneficiary elect to enforce a direct proprietary interest in individual items of the fund. In such a case the beneficiary's claim to substitute assets is 'part and parcel of the nature of the property interest that

[123] See Section III.A above. [124] Nolan, 'Property in a Fund', above, note 37, 110, 131.
[125] Ibid., 131. [126] Penner, 'Duty and Liability', above, note 104, p. 212, para. 12.16.

the beneficiaries have, that is an interest in a fund'.[127] Sheehan convincingly argues that 'we can only identify a breach of trust obligation if we can identify the asset misused. Indeed we cannot identify a fund without identifying assets within it.'[128] Consequently, the view of a reified trust fund cannot explain claims of a beneficiary to traceable proceeds of a trustee's unauthorized dispositions.

The basis for claiming traceable proceeds of an unauthorized disposition, particularly in the hands of third parties, is a thorny issue. Much ink has been spilt in English law on arguing that the beneficiary's right arises to reverse an unjust enrichment,[129] or because of the law of property as a vindication of existing rights,[130] or yet for some other reason.[131] This chapter does not seek to contribute to this debate but it is a proper forum for considering how, if at all, real subrogation could operate in such cases.

First, however, a digression may be of interest here. Peter Birks drew a parallel between the vindication approach assumed in *Foskett* v. *McKeown*[132] and real subrogation.[133] Birks compared it to a fishing line which hooks onto different assets as they 'swim' past.[134] To him it was a

[127] Penner, 'Value, Property and Unjust Enrichment', above, note 105, p. 314.

[128] Sheehan, 'Property in a Fund', above, note 108, 231.

[129] P. Birks, *Unjust Enrichment*, 2nd edn (Oxford University Press, 2005), p. 35; Birks, 'Receipt', in Birks and Pretto, *Breach of Trust*, above, note 111, pp. 216–22; Birks, 'On Taking Seriously the Difference between Tracing and Claiming' (1997) 11 Trust L. Int'l 2, 7–8; Birks, 'Property and Unjust Enrichment: Categorical Truths' (1997) *New Zealand Law Review* 623, 661; Birks, 'On Establishing a Proprietary Base' (1995) 3 RLR 83, 91–2; A. Burrows, 'Proprietary Restitution: Unmasking Unjust Enrichment' (2001) 117 Law Q. Rev. 412; Burrows, *The Law of Restitution*, 2nd edn (London: Butterworths, 2002), p. 64; Smith, *The Law of Tracing*, above, note 89, p. 300, but see Smith, 'Restitution: The Heart of Corrective Justice' (2001) 79 Tex. L. Rev. 2115 which represents a more nuanced approach leaning towards the vindication view.

[130] G. Virgo, *The Principles of the Law of Restitution*, 2nd edn (Oxford University Press, 2006), pp. 11–17; Penner, 'Value, Property and Unjust Enrichment', above, note 105, pp. 313–14; J. Penner, *The Law of Trusts* (Oxford University Press, 2008), paras. 2.32, 11.89–95, 11.116–23; *Foskett*, above, note 89; P. Millett, 'Proprietary Restitution', in S. Degeling and J. Edelman (eds.), *Equity in Commercial Law* (Sydney: Lawbook Co., 2005), p. 314. See also L. Smith, 'Unjust Enrichment, Property and the Structure of Trusts' (2000) 116 Law Q. Rev. 412, 413; Smith, 'Transfers', in Birks and Pretto, *Breach of Trust*, above, note 111, p. 121, note 42.

[131] Such as a wrong of misappropriation, or a wrongful interference; see S. Worthington, 'Justifying Claims to Secondary Profits', in E. Schrage (ed.), *Unjust Enrichment and the Law of Contract* (The Hague: Kluwer Law International, 2001), pp. 451, 455 (rejecting property and unjust enrichment analyses).

[132] *Foskett*, above, note 89.

[133] Birks, *Unjust Enrichment*, above, note 129, p. 35.

[134] Ibid.

fiction that a beneficiary could assert the same property right in the substitute as the right in the original trust asset because it meant that the event from which the right in the substitute arose was the original declaration of express trust.[135] The way Birks viewed real subrogation corresponds better to the way the doctrine operates *outside* of separate funds, although in such cases the right over new assets may turn out to be a new right rather than a continuing interest, as we have seen.[136]

In Polish law it is not clear whether a person entitled to a separate patrimony managed by another could claim that proceeds of an unauthorized disposition by the manager fall in the separate patrimony by means of real subrogation. As mentioned above, it is controversial, at least in Polish law, whether real subrogation can operate within separate patrimonies on the basis of an agreement of the parties or whether a legislative provision is needed every time. If real subrogation is based on a specific provision that any assets acquired with the means from a separate patrimony fall within that patrimony, the question whether or not the manager of the fund was authorized to do so becomes irrelevant. As long as the disposition involved assets from the separate patrimony, any proceeds of such a disposition would fall within the separate patrimony. Issues of mixed substitutions are not discussed here but, it is submitted, they are unlikely to change the principle that any substitutes acquired with the means from the separate patrimony would inhere in that patrimony.

If we accept that real subrogation can also be agreed on by the parties, unauthorized dispositions fall outside of the parties' bargain and the problem is analogous to that of unauthorized trustee dispositions in English law: the property in the trust fund/separate patrimony is neither here nor there as far as an explanation of claims to traceable proceeds of unauthorized transactions is concerned. It seems that in order to ensure that proceeds of such unauthorized dispositions are held by the manager, the parties would need to explicitly agree to such a result. Otherwise the owner of the assets within the separate patrimony, which were disposed of contrary to the bargain, would normally have a contractual claim against the manager. It is uncertain whether any proprietary (such as *vindicatio*) or contractual (such as unjust enrichment) claim would arise. The causes of action would, however, be independent from the separate patrimony or real subrogation.

[135] Ibid. [136] Section III.A.2 above.

It seems that the lack of ability to provide an answer to unauthorized disposition claims with the concepts of separate patrimony and real subrogation is another point of functional similarity with the trust fund and the exercise of powers by the trustee. This correlation may well imply that there is a potential for convergence of the concepts of separate patrimony and real subrogation on the one hand, and trust fund and the exercise of trustees' powers on the other.

VI Conclusions

This chapter suggests that a parallel between the trust and a civilian separate patrimony could be drawn without any insistence on a purpose fund. It has been argued that a trust can be understood in civil law terms as a separate patrimony. Neither the trust fund nor the separate patrimony are distinct property interests. The trust beneficiary and the person entitled to the separate patrimony have rights to individual assets within the fund or within the patrimony. It has also been shown that parallels can be drawn with the way real subrogation operates in Polish law. In English law, assets vary within a trust fund as a result of the exercise of the trustee's powers of disposition according to the trust instrument, whilst in Polish law this function is performed by real subrogation. The application of the doctrine cannot be viewed as an equivalent of tracing, because tracing is merely an evidential process. Real subrogation either transfers rights, if outside of separate patrimonies, or it places rights to new assets within a particular framework of enforceability of separate patrimonies. Functional parallels can be drawn between the trustee's exercise of powers with both types of real subrogation, although it is the real subrogation *in singularibus* that better reflects structurally the exercise of powers by the trustee. When the trustee misappropriates a trust asset, he acts outside of the authority granted by the trust instrument and neither real subrogation nor the exercise of powers by the trustee can explain the rights which the beneficiary might have against the third party.

It also follows that a mere existence of a separate patrimony, even with a mechanism ensuring that exchangeability of assets takes place, such as the German mutual fund built on *Treuhand*, is not sufficient to say that the beneficiary of such an arrangement has a proprietary right. Just as in English law, the lawyers operating in civilian systems with 'trust-like' tools must find a different way of explaining the nature of the beneficiary's interest, not with reference to the trust fund or the separate patrimony.

20

Rights against rights and real obligations

REMUS VALSAN

I Introduction

The classical statement regarding the problems that the common law trust poses for civilian jurisdictions wishing to implement a trust-like arrangement can be enunciated as follows: on the one hand, in a legal system where the property law derives from Roman law, the unity of the concept of ownership and the *numerus clausus* of real rights prevent the beneficiary's right to be regarded as a special real right over the trust *res*. On the other hand, the fixed rules regarding the priority of creditors make it difficult to regard the beneficiary's right as a super-protected personal right.

Recent theories have demonstrated that the premise of these debates is inaccurate. The equitable ownership that the beneficiary is said to enjoy over the trust *res* is only a metaphor that does not offer a correct image of the trust beneficiary's right. This right could be more accurately conceived of as a persistent right, or a right against the trustee's right over the trust *res*.

This new understanding of the trust scheme opens up new perspectives for comparative trust lawyers. Many civil law scholars have already attempted to introduce the concept of right against right, most notably in the form of ownership of a claim. Such attempts, however, have been met with severe criticism by traditionalists, who discard the concept of right over another right as incompatible with the fundamentals of civil law. This chapter proposes a new avenue of research for the civilians struggling to fathom a right over a right. First, it is shown that the bare title and the emolument (the legal benefit) of a subjective right could be conceived as two separate elements. Consequently, the concept of right against a right could be understood as a right against the emolument of another right. Second, it is argued that through the mechanism of the obligation *propter rem*, or 'real obligation', the split between bare title and benefit can be rendered binding on the transferee of the encumbered subjective right.

II The nature of the trust beneficiary's right

The problem of identifying the nature of the trust beneficiary's right is as old as the trust mechanism itself. Starting off as a mere entitlement to the profits of the land 'by the hands of the feoffee', the trust beneficiary's interest has been judicially modelled and strengthened continually throughout the centuries. The desire to reinforce the beneficiary's position and to make the trust a more flexible institution obscured the original conceptual structure of the trust. Furthermore, the use of legal metaphors, such as equitable ownership, set the stage for unremitting disagreements as to the proprietary or obligational nature of the trust, and rendered this institution hazy for non-common law traditions. Against this backdrop, the persistent rights theory proposes a more accurate understanding of the trust mechanism, one that arguably could render the trust compatible with the civil law principles.

A. *Historical insights*

The genesis of the modern trust is an often-told story. The trust is the offspring of the use, an arrangement whereby a landholder conveys freehold land to one or several trusted persons for the benefit (*ad opus*) of the grantor or a third party (*cestui que use*).[1] At the end of the thirteenth century, putting lands in use was a fairly common practice.[2] By the fifteenth century, uses were created for four main reasons: to avoid the consequences of fraud (such as forfeiture of lands to the Crown in case of treason); to avoid feudal dues; to obtain a *de facto* devise of land; and to facilitate the creation of settlements of land.[3]

As a rule, the common law did not have a remedy for the *cestui* of a use of freehold land. Although transfers *ad opus* of chattels and money had remedies at common law,[4] uses of freehold land simply could not be

[1] As Coke put it, uses were invented by fear and fraud: 'fear in times of troubles and civil wars to save their inheritances from being forfeited; and fraud to defeat due debts, lawful actions, wards, escheats, mortmains, etc.' (*Chudleigh's Case*, [1589–95] 1 Co Rep 120a, 121b, in Sir Edward Coke et al., *The Reports of Sir Edward Coke, Knt: In Thirteen Parts* (London: J. Butterworth, 1826), vol. I, parts 1–2.

[2] A. W. Brian Simpson, *A History of the Land Law*, 2nd edn (Oxford University Press, 1986), p. 173.

[3] Ibid., p. 175.

[4] See N. G. Jones, 'Uses, Trusts and a Path to Privity' (1997) 56:1 Cambridge L.J. 175.

fitted into the common law system of actions.[5] The doctrine of estates and the doctrine of seisin, whereby the landowner's interest was protected through the protection of seisin, left no room for forms of action able to protect a beneficial interest divorced from seisin.

The inadequacy of the common law system of actions did not leave the *cestui* completely unprotected. There is evidence that relief against dishonest feoffees was granted since early times in ecclesiastical courts,[6] before the Chancellor started to intervene in the name of good conscience, and later equity, to compel the feoffee to hold the land for the benefit of the *cestui*. By the end of the fifteenth century, the frequency of petitions for the protection of uses allowed for the articulation of principles based on which the Chancellor intervened.[7]

As uses became more popular, they were increasingly employed to evade feudal dues and to defraud creditors. The royal attempts to curb fraudulent uses culminated with the adoption of the Statute of Uses in 1536.[8] This statute 'executed' uses by transferring the seisin of land from the feoffees to the *cestui*. Not all uses, however, fell within the scope of the Statute.[9] Active uses where the feoffees had duties to perform, uses of property other than freehold land, and the use upon a use survived to acquire 'the true name which the use had at first – which is "trust and confidence"'.[10]

The conventional description of the formative stages of the trust often overlooks the essential differences between the use and the trust's arrangements. Use and trust are habitually described as non-sacramental terms, the latter being employed, as a matter of convenience, to refer to uses that were not executed by the Statute. While correct, this statement obscures

[5] In some instances the *cestui* could obtain protection at common law under the actions of breach of condition, trespass or assumpsit. Such remedies, however, were of limited value (Simpson, *A History of the Land Law*, above, note 2, pp. 175–6).

[6] See R. Helmholz, 'The Early Enforcement of Uses' (1979) 79 Colum. L. Rev. 1503.

[7] Simpson, *A History of the Land Law*, above, note 2, p. 177.

[8] Statute of Uses, 27 Hen. VIII, c. 10.

[9] See J. H. Baker, *An Introduction to English Legal History*, 3rd edn (London: Butterworths, 1990), pp. 328–9; Simpson, *A History of the Land Law*, above, note 2, pp. 194–6.

[10] H. Sherfield, reading on the Statute of Wills, 32 Hen. VIII, c.1, Lincoln's Inn 1632, printed in J. H. Baker and S. F. C. Milsom, *Sources of English Legal History* (London: Butterworths, 1986), p. 126. Although the unexecuted uses were often referred to as trusts, to differentiate them from the executed uses, there were no clear dividing lines between the words 'use' and 'trust'. Pre-Statute uses were sometimes described as trusts; after the Statute, the word 'use' was still employed to describe unexecuted uses (see N. G. Jones, 'The Use upon a Use in Equity Revisited' (2002) 33 *Cambrian Law Review* 67, 67–8).

the structural differences between uses and trusts. Such differences cast a new light on the use upon a use, and on the nature of the *cestui*'s right.

A deeper analysis of the 'use' and 'trust' brings to light several different meanings of the term 'use'.[11] A meaning often overlooked, but key to a proper understanding of the trust structure, is use as a conceptually distinct part of title to freehold land. Before and after the Statute of Uses, title to freehold land was regarded as being composed of two elements: the seisin (or possession) and the use.[12] Possession and use may be conjoined in one person's hands, or may be held by separate persons.

The pre-1539 use was predominantly a separated use. The seisin, which was the core of the legal title, was in the feoffee's hands while the use, carrying with it occupation of the land, was in the *cestui*'s hands. Therefore, the separated use that the *cestui* enjoyed came to be regarded by some common lawyers as 'thing-like', as something in the nature of the land.[13]

The separation between use and possession, or seisin, did not occur in all situations where a use was said to exist. In some instances, such as active or charitable uses, the two elements of the title remained conjoined in the feoffee's hands, who nonetheless held the land not for himself but for the *cestui*'s benefit. A well-known note in Brooke's Abridgment, one of the oldest authorities on the doctrine of active uses, illustrates the difference between the separated and the conjoined use: if a man 'makes a feoffment in fee to his use for term of life, and that after his death ... the feoffees shall take the profits and deliver them to J. N., that does not make a use in J. N. for he does not have [the profits] except by the hands of the feoffees'.[14]

[11] See Jones, 'Uses, Trusts and a Path to Privity', above, note 4, 175; Jones, 'Trusts in England After the Statute of Uses: A View from the 16th Century', in R. Helmholz and R. Zimmermann (eds.), *Itinera Fiduciae: Trust and Treuhand in Historical Perspective* (Berlin: Duncker & Humblot, 1998), p. 173; Jones, '*Tyrrel's Case* (1557) and the Use Upon a Use' (1993) 14 J. Legal Hist. 75.

[12] A passage from St German's *Doctor and Student* offers an illustrative pre-1536 example of this dichotomy: 'Every man that has lands has thereby two things in him, that is to say, the possession of the land which after the law of England is called the frank tenement or the free hold, and the other is authority to take thereby the profits of the land' (C. St German, *Doctor and Student*, T. F. T. Plucknett and J. L. Barton (eds.) (London: Selden Society, 1974), p. 222).

[13] See Jones, 'Uses, Trusts and a Path to Privity', above, note 4, 179–80 and the examples cited therein.

[14] Notice the contrast between the use for the benefit of the settlor (a separated use) and J. N.'s entitlement to the profits of the land 'by the hands of the feoffees', a conjoined use. See Brooke's Abridgment, Feffment al Uses, pl. 52, cited in Jones, '*Tyrrel's Case*', above, note 11, p. 81.

This insight into the structure of the title to lands and the distinctiveness of the separated and the conjoined uses are prerequisites for an accurate understanding of the way in which the Statute of Uses operated, of the survival of the use upon a use, and of the structure of the trust. The Statute of Uses was deemed applicable only to situations where the two elements of title, use and possession, had been separated. The aim of the Statute was to rejoin the two elements by bringing the possession to the use.[15] The relation between possession and use as constituents of title also helps elucidate the basis of the rule that there cannot be a use upon a use.[16] The use separated from possession cannot act as foundation for another use. Only a full legal and beneficial title, or the seisin element of the title, can create the foundation for another use. In other words, 'uses cannot depend on one another, but must each in turn derive their validity from the seisin on which they are mounted'.[17] The impossibility to found a use on another use separated from possession explains why, in a use upon a use arrangement, only the first use was executed by the Statute of Uses. Having no valid foundation, the second use was inexistent for the purposes of the Statute. Unlike the common law, the Court of Chancery recognized the second use and enforced it as a trust. After the Statute of Uses, the word 'use' started to be employed predominantly to describe the separated uses that were executed by the statute, while the word 'trust' was used primarily to refer to the conjoined use in the hands of those who held otherwise than for their own benefit.[18]

Acknowledging the distinction between the separated use (executed by the Statute of Uses) and the conjoined use (the basis of the Chancery trust) is indispensable for creating a proper framework for understanding the difficult issue of the nature of the trust beneficiary's interest after the Statute of Uses. The essential difference between use and trust was that, while in the former the *cestui* had a thing-like right over the land, in the latter both use and seisin were in the trustee, the beneficiary having only an entitlement to the profits *through the trustee's hands*. The understanding of the beneficiary's interest evolved with the Chancery practice, from an unassignable personal right of action in Coke's time, to an equitable ownership right during Nottingham's Chancery tenure.

15 Ibid., p. 82. 16 Rule established by *Jane Tyrrel's Case* (1557), Dyer 155a.

17 D. E. C. Yale, 'The Revival of Equitable Estates in the Seventeenth Century: An Explanation by Lord Nottingham' (1957) Cambridge L.J. 72, 76.

18 Jones, 'Uses, Trusts and a Path to Privity', above, note 4, 82.

B. *The classical debate:* in rem *or* in personam?

Over the last centuries, the doctrinal debates concerning the nature of the trust started from the premise that all private law rights are either personal or proprietary, and therefore the *cestui*'s right must find a place within one of these two categories.

The classic viewpoint on the nature of the trust beneficiary's interest was articulated by Maitland. In his view, the historical evolution of the beneficiary's rights demonstrates that such rights were personal in nature – they were at all times rights against persons.[19] Maitland's theory ignited a controversy that culminated in 1917, with the exchange of opinions between Austin Scott and Harlam Stone. Scott pointed out that the *cestui*'s rights are complex. The beneficiary has a number of personal rights, both positive and negative, available against the trustee alone and, as equitable owner, a right against the world at large to insist that it respect his ownership.[20] Stone took issue with Scott's division between legal and equitable ownership in the trust context. He contended that to say that the *cestui* has a property right in the trust *res* against the world at large would be inaccurate. What the *cestui* has, he believed, is a right *in personam* against the trustee with regard to the trust *res*. This right has a corresponding personal obligation incumbent on the trustee to hold the legal estate for the *cestui*'s benefit. The liability of a third person springs into life whenever he interferes not with the trust *res*, but with the *cestui*'s right *in personam* against the trustee.[21] In contrast with the trustee's obligation, which arose from his undertaking to become a trustee, the third party's *in personam* obligation is imposed on him by law, regardless of his consent, because of his equitable wrong of knowingly interfering with the *cestui*'s right *in personam.*[22]

Subsequent theories tended to emphasize either the personal or the proprietary nature of the trust arrangement. Nevertheless, it appears that the theories placing the trust within the law of obligations have gained primacy. The trust is increasingly defined as a duty or set of

[19] F. W. Maitland, *Equity; Also, the Forms of Action at Common Law: Two Courses of Lectures* (Cambridge University Press, 1929), p. 120.

[20] A. W. Scott, 'The Nature of the Rights of the *Cestui que Trust*' (1917) 17 Colum. L. Rev. 269, 290.

[21] H. F. Stone, 'The Nature of the Rights of the *Cestui que Trust*' (1917) 17 Colum. L. Rev. 467, 470.

[22] Ibid., 496.

duties with relation to property. The oft-cited text of Millett LJ in *Armitage* v. *Nurse* is illustrative of this theory: '[T]here is an irreducible core of obligations owed by the trustees to the beneficiaries and enforceable by them which is fundamental to the concept of a trust. If the beneficiaries have no rights enforceable against the trustees there are no trusts.'[23]

The idea of an obligation-based trust appeals to civil law jurisdictions wishing to implement a trust-like arrangement. Conceptualizing the trust as an obligation-based relation appeared as a by-pass to the insurmountable problem of *numerus clausus* of real rights, which prevented the creation of a trust-like arrangement whereby the trustee and the beneficiary had competing proprietary rights over the trust *res*.

Understanding the relation between the trustee and the beneficiary as personal in the classical meaning of a personal right solves the *numerus clausus* issue, but raises numerous other difficulties.[24] The trustee cannot be characterized as the beneficiary's debtor in the traditional sense. A traditional contractual arrangement cannot explain the continuance of the trust despite the trustee's resignation, mental illness or death. A creditor of a personal right cannot normally demand accounting from his debtor or the latter's judicial replacement.

Therefore, it seems that neither the concept of a real right nor that of a personal right, in the classical civil law meaning, are able to capture the relationship between the parties to a trust and between these parties and the trust property. An innovative approach articulated recently has the potential to solve both problems. Regarding the core of the trust as a right against another right, this new theory offers intriguing new tools for understanding this institution and for translating it into civil law concepts.

[23] *Armitage* v. *Nurse* [1998] Ch 241 (CA) 253. The modern trust law texts comprise similar, obligation-based definitions. See e.g. J. Mowbray et al. (eds.), *Lewin on Trusts*, 18th edn (London: Sweet & Maxwell, 2008), p. 6; A. H. Oosterhoff et al., *Oosterhoff on Trusts*, 7th edn (Toronto: Carswell, 2009), p. 18; D. J. Hayton, 'Developing the Obligation Characteristic of the Trust', in D. J. Hayton (ed.), *Extending the Boundaries of Trusts and Similar Ring-Fenced Funds* (The Hague: Kluwer Law International, 2002), p. 200.

[24] See R. A. Macdonald, 'Reconceiving the Symbols of Property: Universalities, Interests and Other Heresies' (1994) 39 McGill L.J. 761, 792–3; K. Reid, 'National Report for Scotland', in D. Hayton et al., *Principles of European Trust Law* (The Hague: Kluwer Law International, 1999), p. 71; M. Milo and J. Smits, 'Trusts in Mixed Legal Systems: A Challenge to Comparative Law' (2000) 3 *European Review of Private Law* 421.

C. The persistent right theory

Modern commentators increasingly recognize that the *in rem* versus *in personam* debate on the nature of the beneficiary's right is more likely to confuse than to illuminate the issue.[25] The modern approach is that the beneficiary has claims against the trustee with regard to the benefit of the rights that the latter holds in trust. In other words, the trustee is the legal holder of the right in trust, while the beneficiary's right encumbers the right of the trustee. Therefore, the trustee's right and the beneficiary's right have different objects: while the object of the trustee's right is the trust *res*, the object of the beneficiary's right is the trustee's right.[26]

Building on the insight that the beneficiary's right is neither strictly personal nor strictly proprietary, but a right attached to the trustee's right, a recent theory has re-conceptualized this right as a third type of right: a 'right against a right' or 'persistent right'.[27] According to this theory, the notion of 'persistent right' is more apt to illustrate the nature of the trust beneficiary's right. First, it eliminates the misleading association of the beneficiary's right with a property right that the term 'equitable property right' created. Second, it captures the fact that the beneficiary's right relates to a specific right held in trust by the trustee and 'persists' against any transferees that acquire a right depending on the trustee's right.[28]

A right having as object another right (for convenience, I shall refer to the latter as 'the principal right') cannot be fitted in the classical Roman dichotomy of rights *in personam* and rights *in rem*, since it is neither a right against a thing nor a right against a person. This new type of right is 'persistent', since it is prima facie binding on anyone who acquires a right deriving from the principal right.[29] A persistent right arises whenever

[25] L. Smith, 'Trust and Patrimony' (2008) 38 R.G.D. 379, 381; (2009) 28 E.T.P.J. 332, 333; Oosterhoff, *Oosterhoff on Trusts*, above, note 23, p. 37.

[26] Oosterhoff, *Oosterhoff on Trusts*, above, note 23, p. 38.

[27] B. McFarlane and R. Stevens, 'The Nature of Equitable Property' (2010) 4 *Journal of Equity* 1; B. McFarlane, *The Structure of Property Law* (Oxford: Hart Publishing, 2008); B. McFarlane 'Equity, Obligations and Third Parties' (2008) Sing. J. Legal Stud. 308; Smith, 'Trust and Patrimony', above, note 25, 332; L. Smith, 'Unravelling Proprietary Restitution' (2004) 40 Can. Bus. L.J. 317; L. Smith, 'Transfers', in P. Birks and A. Pretto (eds.), *Breach of Trust* (Oxford: Hart Publishing, 2002), p. 111; R. Chambers, *An Introduction to Property Law in Australia*, 2nd edn (Sydney: Lawbook Co., 2008), para. 13.90.

[28] McFarlane, 'Equity', above, note 27, 312–22.

[29] McFarlane and Stevens, 'The Nature of Equitable Property', above, note 27, 1.

one person holds a specific claim-right or power, coupled with a duty towards another, relating to the claim-right or power. In this case, the beneficiary of the duty is deemed to have a persistent right.[30]

In order for a persistent right to arise, several conditions need to be fulfilled. First, the principal right must be susceptible to be burdened with a duty to another person. For certain rights, such as the right to physical integrity, the law does not allow their holder to come under a duty to another in relation to that right.[31] Second, according to Hohfeld's classification of rights, the principal right must be a claim-right or a power.[32] Third, the principal right must be specific (i.e. its object must be individualized, such as the promise to give a specific thing), distinct (i.e. its object must be distinct; for instance, a persistent right cannot exist over an indistinct part of an object, such as the paint of a bike) and present (in existence). Furthermore, the duty must concern the entirety of the principal right, without time or subject-matter limitations.[33]

The duty to use the principal right for another's benefit can be deconstructed into one negative duty and one or several positive duties. The negative duty, which is the core trust duty that attaches to the principal right, is the duty not to use that right for the benefit of its titulary. This is the only duty that is attached to the right and that follows it into the hands of third parties. The core trust duty is accompanied by a duty to use the right for the benefit of certain beneficiaries. Both the negative and the positive duties must cover the entire benefit of the right.

The core trust duty gives the beneficiaries entitled under the positive duty the power to impose the core duty on whoever is titulary of the principal right. For instance, if the initial trustee transfers the right to another person, the beneficiary can enforce against the transferee the duty not to use that right for the transferee's benefit. In such a case, the court can order the transferee to convey that right to another person, who had agreed to hold it subject to the duties created by the initial trust.[34] The holder of the principal right may also be one of the beneficiaries of the positive trust duties. Nevertheless, he will partake to the benefit of the right *qua* beneficiary, not *qua* titulary, of the principal right.

[30] McFarlane, *The Structure of Property Law*, above, note 27, p. 206.
[31] Ibid., p. 207.
[32] See W. N. Hohfeld, *Fundamental Legal Conceptions* (New Haven: Yale University Press, 1923).
[33] McFarlane, *The Structure of Property Law*, above, note 27, pp. 207–8.
[34] Ibid., pp. 216–17.

Consequently, in the light of the persistent rights theory, a trust will arise whenever the holder of a right:

(i) expresses his intention to use his right, in some way, for another's benefit; and
(ii) expresses his intention not to use his right for his own benefit, unless and to the extent that he is also a beneficiary of the trust.

Similarly, a trust arises whenever a person attempts to impose the core trust duty and the positive duties on someone else, for the benefit of a third party. In this scenario, a trust will be created only if the second party consents to bear the negative and positive duties.[35]

By demystifying the concept of equitable ownership and returning to the original understanding of the trust as a duty attached to a right, the persistent rights theory opens new perspectives for non-common law jurisdictions that wish to import the trust. More precisely, by accommodating the concept of persistent right, such jurisdictions would make a decisive step towards creating a right that closely resembles the right held by the beneficiary of a common law trust. The following section will explore the possibility of creating a persistent right in the civil law.

III Real–personal division of patrimonial rights in the French civil law: classical approach and contemporary challenges

The traditional understanding of patrimonial rights in French civil law has been facing a growing pressure to innovate. This pressure has been generated by the creation of hybrid types of rights that respond to the increasing complexity of legal relations, but do not fit the classical real–personal mould.

A. *The classical approach*

The classical civil law theory of rights regards as 'fundamental' the distinction between real and personal rights.[36] The classical theory, attributed generally to Aubry and Rau, regarded the real right as a right that gives its holder a direct and absolute power over a thing, and which can be asserted against the world. In contrast, a personal right derives

[35] Ibid., pp. 228–9.
[36] M. Planiol and G. Ripert, *Traité pratique de droit civil français*, 2nd edn (Paris: GDJ, 1953), vol. 3, p. 47.

from a jural relation between two determined persons, and is normally enforceable only against the contractual creditor and those who are bound by his engagements.[37]

This materialist theory based the real–personal dichotomy on the following criteria:

(i) the object of a real right is always an individualized thing, while the object of the personal right is a positive or negative prestation;
(ii) the titulary of a real right can pursue the thing in the hands of others, while the holder of a personal right can normally pursue only the debtor;
(iii) in case of concurrency of several real rights of the same nature over a thing, the prior right trumps all subsequent rights; in the case of competition between personal rights, the general rule is that no creditor has priority.[38]

The survey of the classical understanding of real and personal rights shows that, in this framework, it is very difficult, if not impossible, to conceptualize a right against another right using only the real and personal labels. If real rights can only bear on individualized corporeal things, then no real right may be asserted over another real or personal right. Similarly, since a personal right bears directly upon the activity of another person, it is impossible to fathom a personal right over another personal or real right.

B. *Attempts to collapse one category into the other*

The conceptual and practical difficulties that the classical materialist understanding of real and personal rights posed led to various attempts to re-characterize the patrimonial rights. Initially, these attempts aimed to collapse one category into the other.

1. Planiol's obligation-based approach to patrimonial rights

The materialist analysis of rights has been subjected to severe criticism by the promoters of the 'personalist' approach. The personalist view, attributed generally to Planiol, rejected the idea that a jural

[37] C. Aubry and C. Rau, *Cours de droit civil français d'après l'ouvrage allemand de C.-S. Zachariae*, 3rd edn (Paris: Imprimerie et Libraire Générale de Jurisprudence, 1863), vol. 2, pp. 42–3.

[38] Ibid., pp. 42–3.

relationship could exist directly between a person and a thing. The fundamental and axiomatic truth, on which the entire legal science is built, Planiol argued, is that all jural relations are relations between persons. A real right, just like any other right, needs an active subject, a passive subject and an object.[39]

Planiol defined the real right as a right imposing on the world, as passive subject, the purely negative obligation to abstain from interfering with the peaceful possession of a thing by the active subject. Thus, the jural relation generating the real right is obligation-based: it has a determined active subject, the holder of the real right, an unlimited number of passive subjects, and an object, the passive obligation with regard to a thing. Therefore, in Planiol's view, all rights were essentially personal rights.[40] Nevertheless, despite their common foundation, real and personal rights had distinct features and consequences.[41]

Planiol's personalist theory has made numerous adepts.[42] Among them, Demogue put forth a theory that pushed Planiol's ideas to their limit by arguing that there are no relevant differences between real and personal rights. He observed that, similar to the real rights, the personal rights were opposable *erga omnes*, because everybody is bound to respect their existence. He concluded that the distinction between real and personal rights is justified only as a didactic tool for law beginners: 'Consequently, the separation between real and personal rights is only a pedagogic distinction, used at the beginning of legal studies for understanding and conceptualizing basic situations.'[43]

Subsequent efforts at reconciling the materialist and personalist views of real rights have been made. Planiol and Ripert, for instance, have proposed

[39] M. Planiol, *Traité élémentaire de droit civil*, 11th edn (Paris: LGDJ, 1928), vol. 1, paras. 2158ff.

[40] Ibid., Planiol's thesis was further developed by H. Michas, *Le droit réel considéré comme une obligation passivement universelle* (Paris: A. Pedone, 1900). For a critique of the theories assimilating the real right into the personal right see G. Baudry-Lacantinerie, *Traité théorique et pratique de droit civil*, vol. 5, *Supplément* by J. Bonnecase (Paris: Librairie du Recueil Sirey, 1930), p. 49 (arguing that the assumption of a universal obligation is a fiction; in the absence of any interference with the real right, it is not logical to define the nature of a right by reference to an unknown number of debtors).

[41] Planiol, *Traité élémentaire*, above, note 39, paras. 2158ff.

[42] See e.g. Michas, *Le droit réel*, above, note 40; M. Teissier, *Essai d'une théorie générale sur le fondement de la responsabilité* (Aix: Librairie Nouvelle de Droit et de Jurisprudence, 1901); R. Queru, *Synthèse du droit réel et du droit personnel* (Paris: Giard et Brière, 1905).

[43] R. Demogue, *Les notions fondamentales de droit privé* (Paris: Librairie Nouvelle de Droit et de Jurisprudence, 1911), p. 430, author's translation.

a dualist approach to real rights: externally, a real right imposes a universal obligation to respect the position of the real right-holder. The universal passive obligation becomes active and individualized when a certain person interferes with the real right, and falls under a duty to restore possession of a thing to the holder of the right. Internally, the real right appears as legal power that the holder of a real right has over a thing.[44]

2. The *in rem* approach to patrimonial rights

Opposite to Planiol's personalist approach, a number of authors have attempted to define all subjective rights as rights against things. Gaudemet argued for the modernization of the classical understanding of the personal right: 'The personal right is no longer a right against a person; it is a right against things: *jus ad rem*. The only difference from the real right is that it does not bear on a determined thing, but on an entire patrimony.'[45] Saleilles attempted to collapse personal rights into real rights by proposing a similar re-conceptualization of personal rights. Analogous to a real right, which is a right as against a thing, a personal right is a right against another person's patrimony, and attaches itself to that person's assets rather than to the debtor's personality.[46]

3. Emergence of new categories of rights

Despite the efforts to understand rights within the real–personal *summa divisio*, an increasing number of rights emerged that could not easily be reconciled with the classical labels. The intellectual rights and the personality rights (*droits de personnalité*), for instance, resist facile characterization as personal or real rights.

Furthermore, some rights that nominally belong to one category, display features that are characteristic for the other category.[47] Some

[44] Planiol and Ripert, *Traité pratique*, above, note 36, pp. 45–6; A. N. Yiannopoulos, 'Real Rights in Louisiana and Comparative Law: Part I' (1963) 23:2 La. L. Rev. 161, 173.

[45] E. Gaudemet, *Étude sur le transport de dettes à titre particulier* (Paris: A. Rousseau, 1898), p. 30, author's translation.

[46] R. Saleilles, *Étude sur la théorie générale de l'obligation d'après le premier projet de Code civil pour l'empire allemand* (Paris: F. Pichon, 1901). Similar 'realist' theories have been proposed by other authors. See e.g. O. Jallu, *Essai critique sur l'idée de continuation de la personne, considérée comme principe des transmissions à titre universel* (Paris: A. Rousseau, 1902), vol. 1; H. Gazin, *Essai critique de la notion de patrimoine dans la doctrine classique* (Paris: A. Rousseau, 1910).

[47] See R. A. Macdonald, 'Reconceiving the Symbols of Property: Universalities, Interests and Other Heresies' (1994) 39 McGill L.J. 761; R. A. Macdonald, 'Enforcing Rights in Corporeal Moveables: Revendication and Its Surrogates – Part Two' (1986) 32 McGill L.J. 1.

rights that are nominally personal are reinforced with *in rem* features. Such is the case of the right of the lessee of an immovable, whose right could be enforced against the purchaser of the immovable, or of the right of retention, which confers an attenuated right to follow.[48] Conversely, some rights on things (such as the quasi-usufruct) present personal features, since the consumable thing is substituted by its pecuniary value.[49] The nature of both these types of hybrid rights – reinforced personal rights and defective real rights – has led some authors to characterize them as mixed rights.[50]

4. Conclusion

This section shows that the needs of the practice have created several categories of rights that cannot be easily fitted into the classical civil law 'real–personal' division. This demonstrates that there is room for new categories of rights. A right can no longer be considered incompatible with the civil law simply because it does not fit the classical taxonomy.

IV Rights against rights and the French civil law

The idea of a right having as object another right is not alien to French civil law. The majority of discussions where forms of a right against a right have occurred belong to the broader issue of defining real rights and separating them from personal rights.

A. Rights against rights in the existing theories

The various attempts to redefine real rights have led to theories that involve a right against another right. The strong critiques that such theories have encountered demonstrate the conceptual difficulties that the idea of a right against another right poses for a civilian mind.

48 Ibid.

49 For the nature of the quasi-usufruct, see e.g. M. Cantin Cumyn, 'De l'usufruit', in *Répertoire de droit: Biens*, 2nd edn (Montreal: Chambre des notaires du Québec, 1990), paras. 59–61.

50 See e.g. R. Savatier, 'La nature juridique et les caractères nouveaux du droit à un bail rural' (1946) *Recueil Dalloz* (Chronique) 41–5. See also C. D. Lamontagne, *Biens et propriété* (Cowansville: Editions Y. Blais, 2009), paras. 105–7 (discussing the category of mixed rights in Quebec civil law).

1. The transfer of real rights according to Planiol

In Planiol's view, the ownership right in itself authorizes the right-holder to perform only material acts of use or consumption of the thing. The disposal of ownership in a juridical way, by transfer, creation of a hypothec or a servitude, is beyond the object of the ownership right. Such juridical acts are in fact acts over the ownership right, rather than on the material object of ownership.[51] In other words, the right of alienation and the ownership right are distinct rights: the object of the former is the ownership right, whereas the object of the latter is the thing. The distinction between the right of alienation and the ownership right applies to all real rights, with only minor exceptions.

Planiol's view attracted strong criticism from his peers. Most notably, De Vareilles-Sommières took strong issue with Planiol's suggestion that a right can be the object of another right:

> Does any right, in general, and the ownership right in particular, have an individuality, a substance, a materiality on which juridical acts can be performed and effects produced? Is there anything immaterial, yet real, which the human actions can affect and transfer, outside the owner and the thing, or outside the creditor and his debtor?[52]

De Vareilles-Sommières qualified this idea as 'contrary to the whole doctrinal tradition', 'against the common sense and the universal patterns of thought and language'.[53] He concluded that, since a right cannot exist independently from a titulary, but only as an external manifestation of the latter's legal capacity, Planiol's affirmation that a right can be exercised over another right amounts to saying that a right can be exercised over the titulary's or the transferee's person.[54]

2. The juridical real rights according to Prodan

Prodan classified the real rights into material, intellectual, juridical and general.[55] Juridical real rights are real rights over other rights. They are: the juridical ownership, the pledge and the hypothec, the usufruct of rights and the lease of rights.[56]

[51] Planiol, *Traité élémentaire*, above, note 39, para. 2337.

[52] Marquis de Vareilles-Sommières, 'La définition et la notion juridique de la propriété' (1905) 4 R.T.D. civ. 443, 452, author's translation.

[53] Ibid., 451.

[54] This conclusion is founded on De Vareilles-Sommières' division of rights into rights over one's own person, rights over another's person, and rights over things (ibid., 453).

[55] C. Prodan, *Essai d'une théorie générale des droits réels* (Paris: Impr. H. Jouve, 1909).

[56] Ibid., pp. 154ff.

Juridical ownership is 'a complete real right that grants the mediate possession and juridical enjoyment of a thing in perpetuity'.[57] In contrast with the material ownership, which is a real right over corporeal things, the juridical ownership is a real right over another real right (such as the material ownership, the servitudes, the usufruct, the pledge) or over a personal right. In other words, the juridical ownership is a second-degree right since it is a right against a right, which gives its titulary a judicial enjoyment (administrative or dispositive acts) of a thing. The category of rights that can make the object of juridical ownership is broad: real or personal rights, actual or eventual rights, rights on the titulary's things or on the property of another.

Bonnecase rejected Prodan's concept of juridical ownership in harsh terms: 'Prodan's innovations belong to the realm of wild fantasy and are shrouded in the utmost obscurity and vagueness.'[58] 'From a practical and scientific point of view', Bonnecase added, 'it is inconceivable that a real right could have as object another right in itself, be it a real or a personal right.'[59] Bonnecase offered as possible justification for this fallacy a distorted comprehension of the distinction between corporeal and incorporeal things. Many authors misapplied this classification of things to oppose the rights, as incorporeal things, to their objects, as material things. This is a false opposition, Bonnecase argued, because it does not compare two concepts of the same nature. The real rights have nothing 'real' in themselves, but are simple technical notions that conceptualize the appropriation of wealth. The confusion between the nature of the right and the nature of the thing may be a Roman legacy. The Romans identified the ownership with the thing owned, and thus labelled ownership as a corporeal thing in opposition to other rights, considered incorporeal things.[60] This misconception led some authors to think that rights, as incorporeal things, could constitute the object of other rights.

Bonnecase's argument is based on Aubry and Rau's concept of ownership as a right in a corporeal thing. Since a right cannot exist in any meaningful way outside the personality of its titulary, it is impossible to

57 Ibid., author's translation.

58 Bonnecase, *Supplément*, above, note 40, p. 119, author's translation.

59 Ibid., p. 134, author's translation.

60 G.2.12–14. Gaius placed tangible things in the category of corporeal things and the rights, in general, in the category of incorporeal things. The ownership right, however, was not expressly placed with the incorporeal things, but was identified with the thing owned (H. F. Jolowicz and B. Nicholas, *Historical Introduction to the Study of Roman Law*, 3rd edn (Cambridge University Press, 1972), p. 412).

conceive an ownership right over another real right, independently of the thing on which the latter bears. A real right over a personal right poses even more serious problems. Quite apart from the impossibility of fathoming a service as something that could be owned, Bonnecase contended that allowing this possibility to exist would lead to the resurrection of the personal servitudes of the *ancien régime*.[61] Bonnecasse concluded his lengthy dismissal of the concept of right over a right, or juridical ownership, by pointing out the destructive effects that this concept could have on the foundations of civil law:

> We regret having had to embark on such a lengthy analysis of the so-called juridical real rights. In truth, this theory is so impertinent and exorbitant that it was important to strive to ban it from the realm of legal possibilities, lest it obscured completely the classification of rights and their specific nature. We hope it will remain settled that the existence of juridical real rights is a pure fantasy.[62]

3. The ownership of rights according to Ginossar

Perhaps the most well-known civilian theory of rights against rights belongs to Shalev Ginossar. For Ginossar, ownership describes a relationship of appropriation of corporeal or incorporeal things.[63] The ownership of corporeal things is identified with the *res* themselves. The appropriation of incorporeal things is conceptualized as ownership of relative rights or intellectual rights. The relative rights are the personal rights, the real rights on someone else's thing (the accessory real rights and the classical dismemberments of the ownership right) and the mixed rights (rights both real and personal). The relation of appropriation or attachment is the same for all subjective rights. All subjective rights therefore are absolute rights; they are all ownership rights over corporeal things or over other rights.

The legal relations generated by the ownership of rights have a double nature. The personal rights comprise two distinct, but coexistent legal relations: a relative relation, between the creditor and a specified debtor, and an absolute relation, between the creditor (*qua* owner of a personal right) and the rest of the world.[64] Similarly, the real rights other than ownership can be deconstructed in two legal relations. The first is a relative relation between the creditor–titulary of the relative real right

[61] Bonnecase, *Supplément*, above, note 40, p. 137. [62] Ibid., p. 154.
[63] S. Ginossar, *Droit réel, propriété et créance* (Paris: LGDJ, 1960). [64] Ibid., p. 85.

and the debtor–owner of the encumbered thing; the second is an absolute relation between the owner of the relative right and all other legal subjects, debtors of the universal passive obligation.

Thus, the ownership right creates the attachment to a person's patrimony of all subjective rights, and protects their enjoyment against the world by imposing a universal passive obligation to respect such rights. This universal passive obligation is doubled by a personal obligation (in the case of a personal right), by a real obligation (in the case of the relative real rights), or by a mixed obligation for mixed rights. What distinguishes real from personal rights is the liability of the passive subject of the legal relation: the personal right creates a personal obligation that binds the patrimony of the contracting party and his universal and general transferees; the relative real rights create real obligations that encumber specified things and bind their actual owners.[65]

Ginossar's theory was met with strong criticism, especially with regards to the replacement of the idea of appropriation or titularity of a right with ownership of a right. Mazeaud pointed out that claiming that a person is owner of a personal or a real right is 'an abuse of language'.[66] Flour and Aubert argued that Ginossar's thesis neglects the differences of substance and exercise between personal and real rights.[67] Ghestin and Goubeaux pointed out that inviolability and transmissibility are characteristics of all patrimonial subjective rights that have been recognized without the aid of the notion of ownership of a personal right.[68]

The most detailed criticism, however, comes from Jean Dabin. Dabin rejected the ideas of ownership of personal rights and the relative and obligational nature of the *jura in re aliena*. Concerning the first idea, Dabin contended that making both real and personal rights objects of ownership obscures the particularities of each of these types of rights, while rendering futile the concept of ownership: 'If everything is ownership, there is no longer ownership; the ownership right in its technical sense disappears.'[69] Concerning the second idea, Dabin pointed out that all real rights over another's thing encumber the thing itself, rather than the person of the owner. Moreover, in the case of dismemberments of the

[65] Ibid., p. 124.

[66] H. Mazeaud, *Leçons de droit civil*, 3rd edn (Paris: Monchrestien, 1963), vol. 1, p. 425, para. 266.

[67] J. Flour and J.-L. Aubert, *Les obligations*, 13th edn (Paris: A. Colin, 1994), b. 1, p. 11.

[68] J. Ghestin and G. Goubeaux, *Traité de droit civil: Introduction générale*, 4th edn (Paris: LGDJ, 1994), pp. 185–6.

[69] J. Dabin, 'Une nouvelle définition du droit réel' (1962) 60 R.T.D. civ. 20, 27.

ownership right, the bare owner has no positive 'real' obligation, only a duty of abstention that is the same as the universal passive duty to respect another's right.[70]

B. *Conclusion*

The classical theory of patrimonial rights opposed real rights, understood as direct and immediate powers over things, to personal rights, construed as powers to claim a service or abstention from someone. After nearly two centuries of legislative developments and continuous doctrinal refinement of ideas, a number of inadequacies of the classical theory have been brought to light. At the same time, the increasing complexity of civil relations has generated hybrid rights that resist classification according to the classical standards. These developments have exposed the incompleteness of the classical real–personal divide, and called for more adequate classifications. The severe criticism that many new theories have faced, however, shows that the classical understanding of the real and personal rights is too fundamental for the civilian mind, or too entrenched in the doctrine, to be swept away or reinvented. At the same time, the ample debates generated by these theories have evidenced that within the framework established by the classical real–personal *summa divisio* of rights there may be room for innovation and fine-tuning of concepts. The following section will attempt to conceptualize the right over a right without completely breaking off with the classical framework.

V Conceptual tools that could accommodate the persistent right

A. *Conceptualizing the right against a right: separation between title and enjoyment*

The right has been the object of many civil law theories. Some authors attempted to reduce the subjective right to a single element: the will or the interest.[71] Other authors, influenced by the positivist philosophy, contested its utility altogether.[72] The modern theories regard the subjective right as a complex legal prerogative founded on both the will and the

[70] Ibid., 33–43.

[71] For a review of these theories see J. Dabin, *Le droit subjectif* (Paris: Dalloz, 1952).

[72] See e.g. L. Duguit, *L'État, le droit objectif et la loi positive* (Paris: Fontemoing, 1910).

interest of its holder. Within the latter current of thought, some theories have decomposed the right into two elements: the title and the emolument.[73] The title is a capacity of an individual, created either by law (such as the capacity of legitimate child of heir) or by juridical act (such as the capacity of creditor or usufructuary). The emolument is the legal benefit that results from the title, consisting in the exercise of the powers granted by a right and the benefit created by such exercise.[74]

The title and the emolument are two distinct elements of the subjective right. In most instances, the emolument is attached to the pre-existing title from which it springs. In other instances, however, the title and the emolument are dissociated. In such situations the title alone is sufficient to constitute the right. Based on the principle of freedom of contract, with its established limits (such as the need for a licit cause, the provisions of mandatory law, and public order), the individuals are free to create and transfer a right while restricting or suppressing altogether the entitlement of the right-holder to the benefit deriving from such right. This hypothesis could accommodate an arrangement whereby the holder of a subjective right agrees to grant to another person a right over the emolument of the subjective right.

Historically, the Romans used arrangements whereby the holder of a personal right ceded the benefit deriving from such a right to another person, while formally remaining the right-holder, in order to achieve a de facto transfer of a personal right. The modern civil law already recognizes various situations where the title and benefit of a right are in the hands of different persons.

B. *Separation between the title and the benefit of a claim in Roman law*

Because a personal right was not transferable under the Roman law, the Romans created several arrangements whereby instead of a transfer of the whole right, the title of a personal right was separated from its emolument, and only the latter was transferred to third parties.[75]

[73] See J.-P. Sortas, *Titre et émolument* (Paris: LGDJ, 1961). [74] Ibid., pp. 12–16.

[75] See generally R. Zimmermann, *The Law of Obligations: Roman Foundations of the Civilian Tradition* (Oxford University Press, 1996), pp. 58–67; J. H. P. Costes, *Vente de créances* (Paris: Typographie de Gaittet, 1855); E. David, *De la cession des créances en droit romain et en droit français* (Paris: E. Thunot, 1856) (who rejects the Roman distinction between title and benefit of a right as 'too erudite and too subtle' to be of any use for the modern times, when practical concerns should replace the interest for legal philosophy (p. 54)).

The non-transferability of personal rights was a consecrated principle of Roman law. Thus, Gaius, after enumerating the modes of transmission of ownership, specified that none of them were applicable to personal rights:

> Obligations, no matter how they may have been contracted, cannot be transferred in either of these ways; for if anything is due from someone to me, and I wish to transfer the claim to you, I cannot do this in any of the ways by which corporeal property is transferred to a third party.[76]

Notwithstanding the rigour of this principle, social and economic progress rendered claims an increasingly significant part of a person's assets, and created a pressing need to include them in the commercial exchange.

For a long time, novation was the only way to achieve a result similar to a transfer of claim. Novation, however, did not involve a transfer of claim, but the replacement of the debtor's obligation towards the transferor with a new obligation towards the transferee. As Gaius wrote, in order to replicate the transfer of a claim, 'it will be necessary for you to stipulate with the debtor under my direction, with the result that he will be released by me and becomes liable to you, which is called the novation of an obligation'.[77]

This mode of achieving a transfer of claims had several important shortcomings. First, it led to the extinguishment of the initial personal right, which entailed the loss of any security that guaranteed this right. Second, the arrangement depended on the consent and participation of the debtor. These drawbacks compelled the Roman jurists to seek a more efficient way to transfer the benefits of a personal right. The solution came from the rules of judicial procedure, which allowed a person to be represented in court by a procurator. A creditor who wanted to transfer his claim authorized the transferee, through a mandate *ad litem*, to pursue the debtor in court and to retain the proceeds. Through this type of mandate, the creditor transferred not the claim itself (that would have been contrary to the law), but the exercise of this claim and the resulting benefit. Thus, the transferee was formally only a procurator, but since he acted for his own benefit, he was referred to as *procurator in rem suam*, by contrast with the ordinary mandatary, who was a *procurator in rem alienam*. Further legal developments allowed an extra-judicial transfer of the benefit of a personal right, through an *actio utilis*. An *actio utilis* gave the transferee a right to pursue the debtor and retain the benefit of the

[76] G.2.38. [77] Ibid.

claim, without amounting to a transfer of the claim itself. The initial creditor kept the right to a direct action against the debtor, and the latter could be liberated by a payment to his initial creditor.[78]

In conclusion, the principle of non-transferability of a claim established by the Roman law compelled the Romans to use various legal institutions to achieve a de facto transfer. In order to accommodate the growing needs of commercial life, the jurists used the institution of mandate and *actio utilis* to create a separation between the title and the benefit of a personal right. Thus, the principle of non-transferability was formally observed: the initial creditor remained at all times the holder of the personal right, albeit a bare right, while the emolument resulting from the claim was introduced into commercial exchange.[79]

C. *Separation between title and benefit in the French law*

The French civil law has always recognized several instances where a certain legal title or position could be dissociated from the benefits accruing thereto.

The sale of inheritance rights is one example. This sale is a transfer of the benefits deriving from the capacity of the heir, not a transfer of the title or capacity of the heir: *semel heres semper heres* (once an heir, always an heir). Thus, the sale of the emolument of an inheritance dissociates the title of heir and the whole of the emolument associated with this capacity.

According to Pothier,

> A sale of an inheritance is not a sale of the title or capacity of heir: such a title and capacity are attached to the heir's person, and cannot be dissociated from it ... What is it, then, that is transferred in a sale of inheritance? When I sell my rights to someone's succession, I sell the whole emolument that I have drawn and that I could draw from the succession.[80]

The sale of a usufruct is another example. The right of usufruct being *intuitu personae* is unassignable. Therefore, a sale of usufruct can only transfer the accrued and future benefits that the usufruct generates:

[78] This arrangement had its own disadvantages. See Zimmermann, *The Law of Obligations*, above, note 75, pp. 62–7.
[79] See Costes, *Vente de créances*, above, note 75, pp. 69–70.
[80] A. M. J. J. Dupin (ed.), *Oeuvres de Pothier* (Paris: Pichon-Béchet, 1827), vol. 2, p. 232.

> A usufructuary can sell to a third party his right of usufruct: the object of this sale, however, is the emolument that the usufruct could generate, rather than the right itself; since this right is attached to the usufructuary's person, it is non-assignable.[81]

Another example is the life annuity (*rente viagère*). As Carbonnier observed, in a life annuity contract the quality of creditor could be dissociated from the entitlement to the benefit of the claim. Thus, in a transfer of a life annuity, only the entitlement to arrears could be assigned to a third party. The title of the right remains attached to the annuitant for the duration of his life.[82] These examples show that the separation between the title and the benefit of a subjective right is not a mere doctrinal construct. It has existed since Roman law, and could be extended to accommodate new legal institutions, such as a right over another right.

The separation between title and emolument could be a useful starting point to conceptualize a right over another right. As the previous sections illustrate, the various civil law theories that featured a right over another right faced repeated criticisms arguing the logical impossibility of this concept: since a subjective right cannot be separated from its titulary, and since there is no intermediary figure between a thing and a person, a right over another right, in isolation from the holder or the object of the second right, is unfathomable. Therefore, there could be no logical addition to the division between a claim over a thing and a claim over a person. The separation between a right and its value, it is hoped, casts a new light onto this controversy.

D. *Ensuring the persistency of the separation between title and benefit of a right: the* obligatio propter rem

As shown in the previous sections, the classical theory of patrimonial rights opposes the personal rights to the real rights. The real right is a direct power over a corporeal thing that authorizes its holder to draw all or part of the utility of the thing.

In certain cases, however, the titulary of a real right cannot legally exercise his power over the thing in the absolute independence that *plena in re potestas* would suggest. A duty to perform certain actions for the

[81] Ibid., p. 243.

[82] J. Carbonnier, *Droit civil: Les obligations*, 22nd edn (Paris: Presses Universitaires de France, 1994), vol. 4, p. 564.

benefit of an adjacent thing could be imposed on the owner of a particular thing, either by the physical contiguity of the two things belonging to different owners, or, in limited cases, by the human will. An obligation imposed on the owner of a specified corporeal thing for the benefit of another owner is called a real obligation, or an obligation *propter rem*. Such obligations are 'real' in the sense that they are attached in perpetuity to a right over a thing, for the benefit of the holder of another real right, and are transferred automatically with the encumbered real right. In other words, in contrast to the non-transferability of personal obligations, real obligations are binding against the transferee of the encumbered real right.

The concept of obligation *propter rem* has been regarded with scepticism by many authors. Rigaud, for instance, referred to it as a 'clumsy concept, whose only purpose is to conceal the existence of real rights *in faciendo*'.[83] A great number of the authors rejecting the existence, or the generalization of the obligations *propter rem*, invoked the concern that the authors of the French Civil Code had towards a potential resurrection of the feudal land tenures. This concern led to a restrictive legal regime of rights over immovables, and to the prohibition of any arrangement that might resemble a personal servitude.[84]

Nevertheless, the real obligations gradually became the subject of many comprehensive studies. Far from promoting a unitary point of view on real obligations, these studies demonstrate that the civilians are increasingly interested in this hybrid concept. Whether attempting to assimilate it to a real or a personal right, or proclaiming its conceptual autonomy, these studies recognize that the obligation *propter rem* is an extant civil law concept that allows the transfer of the burden of an obligation to a transferee of the encumbered real right.

1. Michon's theory (1891)

Michon was one of the first French scholars to write a comprehensive study of the obligation *propter rem*.[85]

[83] L. Rigaud, *Le droit réel: histoire et théories: son origine institutionnelle* (Toulouse: A. Nauze, 1912), p. 432.

[84] P. A. Fenet, *Recueil complet des travaux préparatoires du code civil* (Paris: Videcoq, 1836), b. 11, p. 33; Yiannopoulos, 'Real Rights in Louisiana and Comparative Law', above, note 44, 168.

[85] L. Michon, *Des obligations propter rem dans le code civil* (Nancy: A. Nicolle, 1891).

Michon commenced his analysis by observing that certain obligations do not fit the profile of a standard personal obligation, i.e. an obligation binding on a person and enforceable against his patrimony. The obligations *propter rem* appear as encumbrances of a right that the debtor holds over a thing. Such obligations, although owed by a person, are attached to a right over a thing and bind a person only in his capacity as holder of the encumbered right. In contrast to the personal obligation, the real obligation is transferred *ipso iure* with the right over the thing, and can be extinguished by renunciation of the encumbered right, to the benefit of the creditor of the real obligation.

The author makes a systematic inventory of the cases in which positive charges were imposed on the owner of a real right. Such obligations have as legal cause the titularity of the real right, and follow the right in the hands of its transferees. He notices that the obligations *propter rem* are attached only to a real right over a corporeal thing and are imposed for the benefit of the property of another. Such restrictions to real rights, although similar to the servitudes established by the right-holder's will (*servitudes établies par le fait de l'homme*), are legal servitudes and cannot be established outside the limitative cases provided by law.

One set of cases when real obligations are imposed concerns the dismemberments of the ownership right. In these cases the real obligations that attach to the real rights over another's thing arise as a compensation for the use or enjoyment of the bare owner's property. In the case of a servitude consisting in a right of way on another's land, the parties can change the attachment of the duty to maintain the passageway, from an accessory of the ownership of the superior fund to an accessory of the ownership of the inferior fund (articles 698–9 *Code civil* (C. civ.)). This conventional relocation of the real obligation is an application of the principle set forth by article 686 C. civ.:

> Owners are permitted to establish over their property, or in favor of their property, such servitudes as they deem proper, provided however that the services established are laid neither on a person nor in favor of a person, but only on a tenement and for a tenement, and provided that those servitudes moreover are not in any way contrary to public policy. The use and extent of the servitudes thus established are regulated by the instrument which creates them[86]

[86] English version via Legifrance.

In this case, the real obligation established by law is only shifted from one real right to another. The rule remains that the parties cannot freely create positive real obligations that encumber in perpetuity a real right.[87]

Michon's analysis is limited to a description of the obligations *propter rem* established expressly by law. Neither did he inquire into the juridical nature of the real obligation nor was he preoccupied with the possibility of establishing a general legal regime for the real obligations.

2. Bonnecase's theory (1930)

Bonnecase believed that the obligations *propter rem* form an autonomous and unitary category of obligations.[88] They display both real and personal features, but do not fall into either of the two types of rights.

The obligations *propter rem* are autonomous in the sense that they form a distinct category of legal relations. They share with the general category of obligations the fact that the real debtor is bound to a positive performance. This resemblance to a personal obligation, however, is superficial. Actually, the real and the personal obligations are radically different and mutually exclusive. A core feature of the personal obligation is that it continues to bind the debtor and the ensemble of his assets until it is performed or extinguished in another way. In contrast, the debtor of a real obligation can liberate himself and his patrimony by the abandonment or transfer of the encumbered real right. As an exception to this rule governing the real obligations, a certain type of real obligation, the obligation *scripta in rem*, continues to bind the transferor of an immovable. The main application of the obligation *scripta in rem* is article 1743 C. civ., which provides that a lease concluded in authentic form or whose date is indisputable is enforceable against the purchaser of the leased immovable. The lessor's obligation is an obligation *scripta in rem*. Its effect is to bind the transferee of the immovable, without releasing the initial lessor. Consequently, the lessee acquires another debtor, and has the right to claim the fulfilment of the lease from any of the two real debtors. With the exception of the obligations *scriptae in rem*, however, the debtor of a real obligation can liberate himself through transfer or abandonment of the real right.

The obligations *propter rem* are also distinct from the real rights, notably from the real right of servitude. The first difference resides in the nature of these two concepts: the servitude is a principal real right,

87 Michon, *Des obligations*, above, note 85, p. 65.

88 Bonnecase, *Supplément*, above, note 40, pp. 393–436.

while the obligation *propter rem* has an accessory nature, being attached to a principal real right. Second, the number of real obligations is fixed by the legislator, while article 686 C. civ. allows the creation of various servitudes, as long as they do not contravene the public order, and are a burden and a benefit to properties not to persons. Beside conceptual autonomy, another characteristic of Bonnecase's notion of obligation *propter rem* is its homogeneity. Bonnecase rejected the theories that distinguished between the real obligations attached to principal real rights and those dependent on real rights of guarantee. In his view, the so-called real obligations attached to the real rights of guarantee do not exist independently from the right itself – they are simply the right viewed from another side.[89]

Based on these characteristics, Bonnecase defined the obligation *propter rem* as 'an obligation that, despite its nature as accessory to a principal real right, is an autonomous concept placed halfway between the real and the personal right; the positive duty that the real obligation imposes on its debtor and on the successive owners of the thing, exclusively by virtue of their possession of the thing, does not transform this concept into a real or a personal right'.[90]

3. Juglart's theory (1937)

Juglart was among the first authors to attempt a generalization of the concept of real obligation. He described the real obligation as an autonomous concept situated between real and personal rights. The real obligation is 'a juridical relation real and personal at the same time: real, since its purpose is the appropriation of wealth; personal, since it is accomplished only by a positive or a negative utilization of a service, subject to the right of abandonment'.[91]

A distinguishing feature of the real obligation, which illustrates its accessorial character and separates it from a personal obligation, is the possibility for the debtor to liberate himself by the unilateral juridical act of abandonment. This possibility is expressly provided for by article 656 C. civ., which allows a co-owner of a common wall to liberate himself from the duty to contribute to the reparation and reconstruction

[89] Ibid., pp. 395–404. [90] Ibid., p. 394, author's translation.
[91] M. de Juglart, *Obligation réelle et servitudes en droit privé français* (Bordeaux: Fredou et Manville, 1937), p. 284.

expenses by abandoning the common ownership.[92] Juglart noticed that the doctrine and the case law extended the application of this article to other real obligations, and rendered the right of abandonment a general right that applies to all real obligations.[93]

Because of the right of abandonment, the real obligation resembles an alternative obligation. The real debtor's rejection of the right to abandon and his acceptance of responsibility for the real obligation shift the accent of the real obligation towards the debtor's person and his patrimony. In such a case, 'a patrimony is bound towards another patrimony, and the personal pre-empts the real'.[94] In contrast, the refusal to fulfil the real obligation triggers the loss of the right over the thing, and brings the real obligation closer to the real right.[95]

Understood along these coordinates, the real obligation appeared to Juglart as a concept susceptible of generalization. The real obligation as a general concept could help fill in the normative gaps left by the insufficiency or desuetude of some legal provisions. More precisely, the real obligation in its positive or negative form could attach as an accessory obligation to an enlarged concept of servitude established by human will, replacing the antiquated notions of natural and legal servitudes. In this capacity, the real obligation could find diverse applications outside of relations between neighbours, such as ensuring that obligations created by agreements could be enforceable against transferees of the encumbered rights.[96]

Consequently, the general concept of real obligation proposed by Juglart was designed to act as a bridge between the law of obligations and that of real rights, by allowing the transmission of positive or negative obligations to transferees of encumbered rights, in the form of accessory to a servitude established by human will.

4. Aberkane's theory (1957)

In Aberkane's view, the purpose of the real obligation is to mitigate the conflicts that may arise between real rights over the same thing (such as the rights of co-owners on the common thing, the usufruct and the bare

[92] 'However, any co-owner of a party wall may excuse himself from contributing to repairing and reconstructing by waiving the right in common, provided the party wall does not support a building which belongs to him' (art. 656 C. civ., English version via Legifrance).

[93] De Juglart, *Obligation réelle et servitudes*, above, note 91, p. 278.

[94] Ibid., p. 283.

[95] Ibid.

[96] Ibid., pp. 323–53.

ownership, or a right of way on another's land and the ownership of that land) or real rights over adjacent things (such as conflicts between ownership rights over neighbouring plots of land concerning the boundary line). In such cases, the obligation *propter rem* allows the peaceful coexistence and the simultaneous exercise of competing real rights.[97]

The mitigating function of the obligation *propter rem* expresses the legal nature of this concept. By assuring the exercise of a real right, the real obligation ensures the opposability of the right to the holder of a rival right. From the standpoint of the debtor, the real obligation appears as a reinforced application of the universal passive obligation that a real right imposes on all legal subjects. Therefore, the real obligation and the universal passive obligation have the same legal nature. In contrast with the latter, the former may impose positive duties on the holder of a rival right.

Aberkane rejects the hypothesis of a mixed or hybrid legal nature of the universal passive obligation and of the real obligation. In his view, since there is no middle notion between things and persons an intermediary concept is inconceivable. The real obligation has the nature of a personal right, because it is directed against persons and it compels them to various actions.[98]

The obligation *propter rem* is not restricted to its legally or judicially recognized applications. Based on the principle of the autonomy of the will that rules the civil law, Aberkane argued that the real obligations could be freely established, modified or extinguished contractually, within the general limits imposed by the civil code for private agreements. The creation of an obligation *propter rem*, therefore, requires the presence of two conflicting real rights and the parties' will to solve the conflict by allocating the burdens and establishing the limits to the enjoyment of their rights. The real obligations must be established solely in the consideration of the protected real right, and not in the consideration of its holder.[99]

In contrast with Juglart, in whose view the concept of obligation *propter rem* is independent from, albeit closely linked to, the legal servitude, for Aberkane the servitude is only a particular species of the genus represented by the real obligations. The reluctance to recognize the generality of the obligation *propter rem*, Aberkane believes, is founded on

[97] H. Aberkane, *Essai d'une théorie générale de l'obligation propter rem en droit positif français* (Paris: LGDJ, 1957).
[98] Ibid., p. 27. [99] Ibid., paras. 128–9.

a misguided interpretation of article 686 C. civ. This article allows the free establishment of obligations *propter rem* in the form of servitudes. The reference to the obligation and benefit of property rather than person contained in this article has been misinterpreted as excluding positive obligations from the ambit of servitudes established by human will, through a confusion of this article with the principle *servitus in faciendo consistere nequit* (servitudes cannot impose positive duties).[100] An accurate interpretation of the requirement that the duty be imposed on the property and not on the person is that the debtor is bound to perform only by virtue of his right in the thing. The public order reasons advanced for a strict interpretation of this article, namely the fear of resurrection of the feudal land tenures, are 'chimerical' in contemporary social and economic conditions.[101]

5. *Obligatio propter rem* and the persistency of rights

The various theories on the obligation *propter rem* presented above show that the doctrine is far from having a unitary view on the nature, scope and utility of this concept. At minimum, all points of view seem to converge on the fact that the real obligation is an accessory to a right over a thing and binds transferees of such a right. This is enough to suggest the utility of this concept for a civilian form of the persistent right.

Recalling the common law concept of persistent right in the trust context, we have seen that the core trust duty was the trustee's duty not to use his right over the trust *res* for his own benefit. This duty can be construed in civilian terms as an obligation *propter rem* attached to the trustee's right over the trust assets, which follows the right in the hands of the subsequent transferees. Such transferees can never get more than a bare right, since the duty that follows the right ensures the opposability of the separation between title and emolument that the trustee or the settlor had created. The only exception to this rule is when the purchaser without notice of the trust arrangement acquires the right for valuable consideration. In this case the trust arrangement is not affected, since the positive trust duties can continue with regard to the value of the consideration.

[100] Aberkane, *Essai d'une théorie générale*, above, note 97, n. 93–6. For the meaning of this principle, see e.g. W. W. Buckland, *A Textbook of Roman Law: From Augustus to Justinian*, 3rd edn (Cambridge University Press, 2007), p. 256.

[101] Aberkane, *Essai d'une théorie générale*, above, note 97, n. 99.

The bona fide transfer without notice for consideration poses an obvious problem of real subrogation (i.e. it is not obvious that the consideration that the trustee receives automatically takes on the affectation that the transferred right and its emolument had). This is an issue that needs further development.

VI Conclusion

The common law trust appears discouragingly complex to a civilian legal mind attempting to translate it into civil law concepts. This complexity is the result of over five centuries of evolution, throughout which layers upon layers of rules and exceptions have been added by doctrinal interpretation and case-by-case judicial fine-tuning. Stripped of metaphors and technicalities, however, the core of the trust concept appears surprisingly intelligible for the civilian: it is an obligation in relation to particular property.

Building on the insight that the trust has obligational roots, modern theories have re-conceptualized the right of the beneficiary as a 'persistent' right having as object the trustee's right. This arrangement could be replicated within the civil law traditions if the concept of *obligatio propter rem* is brought from the fringes of civil law to the forefront of legal theory. The real obligation, in conjunction with a dual understanding of the subjective right (title and emolument), can lay the foundation for a civilian persistent right.

A trust-like arrangement based on a civilian equivalent of the persistent right cannot solve all the difficulties that the common law trust poses for civil jurisdictions. This concept alone cannot replicate all features of the trust, such as temporary survival without a trustee or the judicial scrutiny of the trust. Nonetheless, it could represent a promising starting point for the attempt to integrate the trust into the civil law conceptual system.

21

The trust and its civilian analogues

BEN MCFARLANE

A comparison of the common law trust and its possible civilian analogues may shed new light on each of the trust and the civilian concepts to which it is compared. Such a comparison, depending on its outcome, may also assist a civilian jurisdiction wishing to introduce a trust-like structure. To be truly valuable, however, any such comparison must move from the functional to the conceptual. Whilst a similarity of function may cause a particular civilian idea to be compared to the trust, the comparison must consider not only *what* can be achieved by using that idea or the trust, but also *how* each achieves that outcome. This can be seen even if we look for common law analogues of the trust. For example, asset protection is an important function of the trust: rights held by a trustee on trust are not available to the general creditors of the trustee. Yet, even within the common law, other legal devices can perform the same function: one may do business through a company, for example, in order to protect one's own assets from business debts. To see the difference between a trust and a company, it is necessary to consider *how* each achieves such asset protection. In this case, the crucial difference is that the setting up of a company involves the creation of a new legal personality, and debts are then incurred by that legal entity, rather than by the parties who established the company. This comparison demonstrates an important and distinctive feature of a trust: the trust permits a situation where rights are held by a particular legal person (the trustee) but are not available to meet the debts of that person. The possible conceptual justifications for this exceptional situation will be discussed further below.

A willingness to progress from the functional to the conceptual is a particular virtue of each of Magda Raczynska and Remus Valsan's contributions to this volume.[1] Between them, they examine three of

[1] Magda Raczynska, 'Parallels Between the Civilian Separate Patrimony, Real Subrogation and the Idea of Property in a Trust Fund', Chapter 19 in this volume; Remus Valsan, 'Rights Against Rights and Real Obligations', Chapter 20 in this volume.

the most striking aspects of the trust. First, the fact, considered above, that rights subject to a trust are immune to the general creditors of the trustee, and are instead liable to execution only for the benefit of creditors of the trust beneficiaries. Second, that this immunity extends beyond the initial trust assets, and even beyond rights acquired by a trustee through an authorized use of those initial trust assets, to include any rights acquired by a trustee through an *unauthorized* use of trust assets. Third, that a trust beneficiary may be able to assert a trust interest against a stranger who acquires a trust asset, even if that stranger does not knowingly acquire the asset in the capacity of a trustee. Raczynska considers whether the civilian concept of real subrogation can assist our understanding of the first two of those three features of the trust. Valsan, meanwhile, asks if a generalization of the concept of an obligation *propter rem* may be a means for a civilian system to mimic that third feature of the trust.

Raczynska's chapter is of special interest to a common law audience. Consider a case where a trustee, acting without authority, uses trust money to acquire, for himself, company shares. The power of a beneficiary to claim a trust in relation to those shares is a well-established feature of the common law; its conceptual basis, however, remains a matter of controversy. In the debates about this common law power, the civilian concept of real subrogation has featured: for example, Professor Birks argued that the analysis of the House of Lords in the leading case of *Foskett* v. *McKeown*[2] (an analysis with which he disagreed) implicitly equated the common law power with the civilian doctrine of real subrogation.[3] Such observations, of course, can be considered only if we have a clear understanding of real subrogation. Raczynska provides us with this and helpfully emphasizes the distinction, made by German and Polish scholars, between two different forms of the doctrine: universal subrogation and singular subrogation.

The universal form may occur only within a distinct and separate fund, such as the collection of rights and liabilities left by an individual on his death. The function of universal subrogation is to transmit a quality of an asset held within such a fund to a new asset acquired by the fund-holder. This function is crucial in those exceptional cases where the fund-holder is recognized as having more than one patrimony. An asset that lies outside the fund-holder's general patrimony, and thus inside

2 *Foskett* v. *McKeown* [2001] 1 AC 102 (*Foskett*).
3 P. Birks, *Unjust Enrichment*, 2nd edn (Oxford University Press, 2005), p. 35.

a special patrimony devoted to a particular purpose, will be immune from the claims of the general creditors of the fund-holder. Universal subrogation, where it operates, may transmit that immunity to a new asset acquired by the fund-holder. Whilst a common lawyer would not be familiar with the concept of a patrimony, the notion of a deceased's estate provides a very close analogy. If E is an executor, for example, the rights he holds include both his general assets and those rights he holds in his capacity as executor. The latter rights will not be available to E's general creditors; and the former rights will not be available to existing creditors of the deceased. When E acquires a new right (for example by receiving money as a birthday present, or as a result of selling crops on the deceased's land), there must be a mechanism to decide whether that new right falls into the former or latter group. If, as in the case of the proceeds of the crops, the right falls within the group held in his capacity as executor, this could be seen as the result of universal subrogation. Singular subrogation, in contrast, does not depend on the prior existence of a separate fund or distinct patrimony. Its function is to subject an asset newly acquired by a particular person to the same legal relationship as an asset formerly held by that person. For example, consider a case where A has granted B a security right in relation to A's chattel, and that chattel is then destroyed in a fire. If a matching, but new, security right is imposed over the insurance pay-out received by A, this will be an example of singular, rather than universal, subrogation.

In *Foskett* v. *McKeown*, the House of Lords explained a beneficiary's power to claim a trust of a right acquired by the unauthorized use of a trust asset as a matter of 'hard-nosed property rights'.[4] The analysis seems to be that the newly-acquired asset is held subject to the same property right – that of the beneficiary – which affected the initial trust asset. As noted by Raczynska, if this view is to be compared to a form of real subrogation, it is closer to singular subrogation. Raczynska then argues that this observation strengthens Professor Birks' criticism of the *Foskett* approach – after all, the question in that case was whether a particular asset acquired by a trustee should best be seen as falling within the trust fund, or instead within the general assets of the trustee, available to all his creditors. If any form of real subrogation is to be useful in answering that question, it must be universal, rather than singular, subrogation. Whilst our analysis can thus be clarified, the central

[4] *Per* Lord Browne-Wilkinson in *Foskett*, above, note 2, p. 109.

problem, however, remains. For universal subrogation, as applied in Polish law, has important limits. It seems that it cannot explain why an asset acquired through an *unauthorized* use of a fund should be immune from the general creditors of a fund-holder; nor can it explain why such immunity should also arise when such an asset is held by someone other than the initial fund-holder. Yet these are two of the three key features of the trust set out above.

Importantly, Raczynska's conclusion – that the concept of universal subrogation is of limited use in explaining the operation of the trust – applies equally to a concept that is frequently used, but less often analysed, by common law commentators: that of the fund. This reader shares Raczynska's scepticism about the broad concept of a fund, in which a beneficiary of a trust is seen as having a property right in a fund. The problem is that a fund comprising, as it must, unascertained future assets lacks the specificity required of an object of property rights. This concern does not apply to the more limited notion of a fund employed by, for example, Nolan:[5] it is that concept which, on Raczynska's analysis, is functionally and conceptually similar to the separate patrimony permitted, in some circumstances, by Polish law. This similarity means that the notion of a fund has no more explanatory power, when considering the key features of the trust, than the concept of universal subrogation within a separate patrimony. This is no surprise when we consider the very limited scope and effect of Nolan's concept of a fund: it is limited to cases where the fund-holder has undertaken to hold a distinct fund; and its effect is principally to explain why, when a fund-holder makes an authorized disposition of fund assets, the recipient of those assets takes free of any pre-existing rights of the beneficiary of the fund. It is clear that, so defined, the concept of a fund does not explain any of the three features of a trust set out above. Indeed, it is important to note that each of those three features can exist even in the absence of any undertaking by a fund-holder, as each of the features applies to non-express trusts as well as to express trusts.[6]

The comparison made between the trust and the notion of a distinct fund or patrimony prompts further reflections which may assist in our

[5] R. Nolan, 'Property in a Fund' (2004) 120 L.Q.R. 108.

[6] For example, in *Attorney-General of Hong Kong* v. *Reid* [1994] 1 AC 324, the Privy Council held that Reid held money received as a bribe on a non-express trust for his employer. As a result, his employer was able to claim that a trust also existed in relation to rights acquired with that money and held by third parties.

understanding of the first special feature of the trust outlined above: the immunity of trust assets from claims of a trustee's general creditors. It has been persuasively argued by, for example, Gretton,[7] that a civilian or mixed jurisdiction may replicate this feature by allowing for the recognition of separate patrimonies, each held simultaneously by the same legal person. The problem is that, on one view at least, the principle that each legal person has a single, indivisible patrimony is fundamental to civilian systems. Raczynska's chapter suggests that the principle's importance lies in the guarantee it provides that all of a person's assets will be available to meet his debts. It is vital to note that the very same principle exists in the common law. Indeed, it is the fundamental nature of this guarantee that may lie behind Penner's doubts about the usefulness of the concept of a patrimony:[8] it may be that the guarantee seems so obvious, that we do not need to explain it through the adoption of the further concept of a patrimony. There are a number of contexts in English law where we can see the effect of the principle that all one's assets are available for the satisfaction of one's debts, no matter in what capacity any debt is incurred. For example, consider a case where A and B are joint owners of a legal estate in land and C, a visitor to the land, is injured because, due to the carelessness of A and B, a building on the land has been left in a careless state. Each of A and B is jointly and severally liable to C, and, if C obtains judgment against either A and/or B, then all of A's assets, including but not limited to A's potential share of the jointly owned estate (and/or all of B's assets, including but not limited to B's potential share of the jointly owned estate), are available to meet the debt. Neither A nor B can argue that, as the liability was incurred in their capacity as joint owners, *only* their jointly held assets are available to meet the debt. The same analysis applies where A and B are partners, and a debt is incurred in the course of the business carried on through the partnership.[9] Of course, if the liability is a contractual one, and the contract expressly states that the creditor can make execution only against certain assets, then that contractual term will protect the debtor. The general rule, however, is just the same as in

[7] G. Gretton, 'Trusts Without Equity' (2000) 49 I.C.L.Q. 599.

[8] J. Penner 'Duty and Liability in Respect of Funds', in J. Lowry and L. Mistelis (eds.), *Commercial Law: Perspectives and Practice* (London: LexisNexis, 2006), pp. 211–12, 214.

[9] In English law, the position is different if a limited liability partnership has been set up: like a company, a limited liability partnership is a distinct legal entity with its own legal personality: see the Limited Liability Partnerships Act 2000, section 1.

a civilian system: the difference is that it has not been deemed necessary to explain the rule by reference to the concept of patrimony.

The basic principle, then, is that, in the absence of an express contractual stipulation with a creditor, one cannot both hold a right and immunize that right from execution for all or any of one's debts. The principle provides one important motivation for setting up a company or limited liability partnership: the principle is upheld but a new legal entity is created which can incur debts on its own behalf, and have its own assets exposed to execution for those debts. The first special feature of the trust, of course, breaches this general principle. If A holds rights on trust, then, even though those assets are held by A, they will *not* be available to A's creditors. The first point to make, therefore, is that the existence of the trust does not show that the common law allows separate patrimonies, or (in other words) does not adopt the fundamental principle that all one's assets must be available to meet all of one's debts. Rather, the existence of the trust shows that, if a legal system wishes to enjoy all the benefits the trust may offer, it must be prepared to allow an exception to that fundamental principle. The second point to make is that the extent of the trust exception is more limited than might first be thought. Crucially, if a trustee incurs a liability in his capacity as trustee, *all* of the trustee's general assets (i.e. the assets he does not hold on trust) are available to meet the debt.[10] Allowing the trust, then, does not force a system to recognize that a trustee has two separate capacities, or two separate patrimonies: just as any rights held on trust are indeed held by the trustee, so are any debts incurred by the trustee the debts *of* the trustee, and execution is possible against any and all of the trustee's general assets.

This, of course, leads us back to the conceptual question set out at the very start of these comments: why should the trust be allowed to breach the general principle that any right held by a person is available to meet the debts of that person? One answer would be that if an asset is held on trust, the trustee no longer has the right to benefit from that asset – the right to benefit instead belongs to the beneficiaries, and so the trust asset is available to meet the debts of the beneficiaries, and not those of the trustee. As Valsan shows in his chapter, this view fits well with the original conception of a passive use, in which the *cestui que use* was seen as entitled to a distinct and severable part of the trust property. As Valsan

[10] The importance of this point is highlighted by L. Smith, 'Trust and Patrimony' (2008) 38 R.G.D. 379; (2009) 28 E.T.P.J. 332.

notes, however, that analysis cannot be applied to the trust, as it came to exist after the Statute of Uses 1536. A crucial point is that the existence of a trust does not change the content of the right held by the trustee. For example, if A has a contractual right against Z, and then declares that he holds that right on trust for B, it is still only A (and not B) who can enforce the contractual right against Z.[11] It is not possible for Z to resist such a claim by arguing that the 'right to benefit' from the contractual right is no longer held by A. Similarly, if A has a property right, such as an estate in land, and declares a trust of that right, it is still only A (and not B) who can sue X if X interferes with that land.[12] As Professor Matthews notes in his chapter in this volume,[13] the existence of the trust does not involve a fragmentation of the initial right of the trustee; it is in fact critical to the operation of a trust that the trustee retain his right, but comes under a duty to the beneficiary or beneficiaries in relation to that right.

The analysis of Professor Matthews is consistent with what Valsan refers to as the 'obligational' analysis of the trust. On this view, the special immunity of trust assets from general creditors of the trustee must be seen as a consequence of the special nature of the duty owed by the trustee. At the core of the trust is the trustee's duty not to use a right for his own benefit (unless and to the extent that the trustee is also a beneficiary of the trust). The content of this duty, combined with the commitment of judges in courts of equity to the specific enforcement of duties, may go a long way to explaining the special features of the trust. For example, if a trustee can be prevented from using a particular right for his own benefit, it is difficult to see why that right should be available for general creditors of the trustee. The point is that a beneficiary of a trust is in a different position from a creditor to whom the trustee, for example, promised to pay £100. As the trustee simply promised to perform a particular action (payment of the sum), the duty owed to the creditor does not relate to any specific right held by the debtor. The content of the duty, therefore, does not prevent the debtor using any of

[11] As noted by the Court of Appeal in *Barbados Trust Co. Ltd* v. *Bank of Zambia* [2007] 2 All ER (Comm) 445; [2007] 1 Lloyd's Rep 495; [2007] EWCA Civ 148.

[12] See e.g. *The Lord Compton's Case* [1587] 3 Leo 197; *Leigh & Sillivan Ltd* v. *Aliakmon Shipping Co. Ltd* [1986] AC 785; *MCC Proceeds Inc.* v. *Lehman Bros. International (Europe)* [1998] 4 All ER 675 CA. The recent decision of the Court of Appeal in *Shell UK Ltd* v. *Total UK Ltd* [2010] 3 All ER 793; EWCA Civ 180 appears to conflict with these authorities.

[13] Paul Matthews, 'The Compatibility of the Trust with the Civil Law Notion of Property', Chapter 13 in this volume.

his rights for his own benefit – as noted by Penner, and quoted in Raczynska's chapter, the creditor cannot complain if the debtor enlists his rich aunt to pay the £100.[14] On this view, the obligation of a trustee is distinguished from a personal obligation by its content: in particular, by its relation to a specific right held by the trustee.

This analysis of the trust is the foundation of the 'persistent rights' theory discussed by Valsan. A particular advantage of this theory – in contrast to the more common view that a beneficiary of a trust has a property right – is that it can explain what occurs when a personal right, such as a bank account, is held on trust. It is not the case that a beneficiary then acquires a property right in the bank account; rather, the trustee holds the account, and has a personal right against the bank, and the beneficiary has a right in relation to that personal right. A claim sometimes made by those who favour the persistent rights theory is that it may assist in the incorporation of trust-like structures in civilian systems.[15] The chief basis of this claim is simply that the persistent rights view is less obviously problematic, from a civilian perspective, than any view which sees the trust as dependent on the existence of equitable property rights, or on the fragmentation of rights into legal and equitable title. As Valsan demonstrates, however, it certainly cannot be said that the persistent rights theory is a magic wand which will dispel all difficulties. Indeed, Valsan's chapter very usefully discusses some of the reactions from civilian commentators to theories which, whilst different from the persistent rights theory, similarly attempted to break away from the strict and exclusive duopoly of personal and property rights. The basic difficulty, apparent for example in the analysis of Aubry and Rau, seems to be the assumption that the subject matter of a right must be an entity in the real, non-legal world, such as a person or a thing. On this view, the concept of a right relating to another right is deeply problematic. A civilian sceptic might, for example, quote Aberkane: 'An intermediary concept is inconceivable, since there is no middle notion between things and persons';[16] or harness Bonnecase's view that a right with another right as its object takes us into the 'realm of wild fantasy'.[17]

[14] Penner, 'Duty and Liability in Respect of Funds', above, note 8.

[15] See e.g. B. McFarlane and R. Stevens, 'The Nature of Equitable Property' (2010) 4 *Journal of Equity* 1, 28.

[16] H. Aberkane, *Essai d'une théorie générale de l'obligation propter rem en droit positif français* (Paris: Librairie générale de droit et de jurisprudence, 1957), p. 27.

[17] G. Baudry-Lacantinerie, *Traité théorique et pratique de droit civil*, 3rd edn, vol. 5, supplement by J. Bonnecase (Paris: L. Larose and L. Tenin, 1905–9), p. 199.

The vituperative nature of these reactions makes clear that a civilian system may not easily accept the transplantation of the concept of a persistent right. It may be possible, however, to meet some of the objections. First, as Valsan usefully notes, it is a mistake to think that the duopoly of personal and property rights can adequately account for *all* forms of rights currently permitted in civilian systems – for example, neither intellectual property rights, nor the lease of an immovable, falls easily into either of the two categories. Second, Valsan suggests that the concept, known to civilian systems, of an obligation *propter rem* may form a useful analogy to that of a persistent right and may thus be a means to give effect to the third feature of a trust set out above: the ability of a beneficiary to bring a claim against certain strangers to the trust, who have acquired a right from a trustee. It is interesting to note that, as Valsan shows, the debate amongst civilian commentators as to the proper categorization of an obligation *propter rem* has many similarities with the ongoing controversy as to the nature of a beneficiary's interest under a common law trust.

It should be emphasized, however, that the analogy between an obligation *propter rem* and a persistent right is not exact. First, the category of such obligations is currently limited: in particular, it seems that despite the arguments made by commentators such as Juglart,[18] an obligation *propter rem* cannot be freely created by the parties but can arise only in a limited number of factual situations recognized by the law. Second, it seems that such an obligation must relate to a specific, physical thing (such as land): one of the key features of a persistent right, as discussed above, is that its object may be a personal right, such as a bank account. Third, it seems that the class of parties bound by such an obligation consists of those with ownership of a specific thing. The class of parties potentially bound by a persistent right is instead defined by the *right* acquired by such a party. This makes that class in some ways wider, and in some ways narrower, than that caught by an obligation *propter rem*. Wider, because a stranger may be bound by a persistent right if he receives *either* the very right that is the object of the persistent right (as where a trustee holds a legal freehold of land on trust, and then transfers that freehold, without authority, to the stranger) *or* a new, different right that depends on the object of the persistent right (as where a trustee holds a legal freehold on trust and then, without authority, grants the

[18] M. de Juglart, *Obligation reélle et servitudes en droit privé français* (Bordeaux: Fredou et Manville, 1937), p. 284.

stranger a limited property right in the land, such as a lease or charge). Narrower, because a stranger may only be bound where he acquires a right that depends on the object of the initial persistent right. For example, if a trustee holds a legal freehold on trust, and a stranger, by entering the land and possessing it adversely, acquires an independent estate in the land, then that stranger is not bound by the beneficiary's right under the trust: in such a case, the right acquired by the stranger does not depend on the right initially held on trust. Finally, if a stranger receives property burdened by an obligation *propter rem*, it seems that the stranger is bound by that obligation independently of his knowledge of it. In contrast, the stranger's knowledge of a pre-existing persistent right plays a significant role in determining whether (and, if so, when) the stranger is bound by that right. For example, if a trustee, without authority, makes a gift of a right held on trust to a stranger, and the stranger then disposes of that right without retaining any traceable proceeds of it, and before having acquired knowledge of the initial trust, it seems that, under common law systems, the beneficiary can make no claim against the stranger.[19]

Each of the chapters by Raczynska and Valsan vividly demonstrates the many benefits of comparing the trust with its civilian analogues: any reader will be left with a much deeper understanding not only of the trust, but also of the civilian concepts of real subrogation and of obligations *propter rem*. Of course, neither chapter concludes that there is an existing civilian concept through which the trust, or a trust-like structure, can be easily accommodated: indeed, such a simplistic conclusion would be incompatible with the sophisticated and careful analysis of each chapter. Moreover, the very interest of any civilian or mixed jurisdiction considering the introduction of a trust-like structure will generally be founded on the current absence of any such structure within that system. The difficulty of finding true analogues of the trust is also significant as it helps a common lawyer to see just how remarkable the trust truly is. It also raises the question of whether the trust can ever be successfully transplanted if wrenched away from its origins in courts of equity.

In particular, it may be that each of the three special features of the trust noted above is a product of the particular concerns and techniques of courts of equity.[20] For example, the features discussed in Raczynska's

[19] See e.g. *re Montagu's Settlement Trusts* [1987] Ch 264; *BCCI* v. *Akindele* [2001] Ch 437.

[20] For a consideration of the special concerns of equity, see L. Smith, 'Fusion and Tradition', in S. Degeling and J. Edelman (eds.), *Equity in Commercial Law* (Sydney: Thomson, 2005), ch. 2.

chapter (the immunity of trust assets from the general creditors of a trustee, as well as the power of a beneficiary to make a claim in relation to a right acquired by a trustee through the unauthorized use of trust assets) may each depend on equity's concern for the most direct and effective enforcement of the trustee's duty not to use a right held on trust for his own benefit. As noted by Valsan, the notion of a right against a right is problematic for any civilian commentator who adopts the assumption that a right must have as its object something external to the legal system, such as a thing or a person. A key feature of equity, however, is that it often operates as a secondary jurisdiction, presupposing the existence of a general common law jurisdiction. It may not be surprising, therefore, that courts of equity could view rights (such as rights acknowledged by the common law system) as a proper object of equitable rights. Valsan also notes that commentators, such as De Vareilles-Sommières,[21] have objected to the notion that a right can be separated from its holder: on this view, a right against a right cannot be distinguished from a right against a person. The concept of a persistent right, as developed by equity, precisely allows this separation. This can be seen not only in the third feature of a trust set out above (the ability of the beneficiary to assert his right against particular strangers to the initial trust relationship) but also in the phenomenon, referred to by Valsan at the conclusion of his chapter, of the trust as office. This latter phenomenon allows, for example, for the replacement of a trustee, and so for a trust to continue despite the death or removal of an initial trustee. This depersonalization of the trust obligation is permitted by the trust's focus on the duties of a trustee *in his capacity as* holder of a particular right. After all, the defining feature of a trustee is that he both holds a right and has a duty not to use that right for his own benefit. The personality, or creditworthiness, of the trustee is not critical to the performance of that core duty: its negative nature thus permits its extension to strangers to the trust, provided that such a stranger also holds the right initially held on trust, or a product of that right. This may finally account for the fact that the right of a beneficiary occupies an awkward position between property and obligation. The trust requires a relationship between beneficiary and trustee; unlike the ancient use, the trust does not permit a beneficiary to have a direct, unmediated relationship with an asset. Yet the *particular identity* of the trustee is not critical to the relationship, as the relationship is

[21] M. de Vareilles-Sommières, 'La définition et la notion juridique de la propriété' (1904) 4 R.T.D. civ. 443, 452.

defined by the holding of a right subject to a negative duty. On the view that a beneficiary of a trust has a right against a right (the 'persistent rights' theory), the trustee is necessary; but only because the object of a trust must be a right, and all rights must be held by someone.

The two thorough and thought-provoking chapters considered here therefore lead this reader to two chief conclusions. First, the very advantages of a trust, which may be sought by a civilian or mixed system wishing to introduce a trust-like device, stem from its power to break fundamental rules of the legal system within which it operates. In the common law, for example, the trust breaks the rule that all of the rights held by a person are available to meet his debts. If, therefore, a civilian or mixed system wishes to capture the advantages of the trust, it must be prepared to accept the breach of one or more of its fundamental rules. Second, to understand not only what a trust does, but more precisely *how* a trust operates, it is necessary to reflect on its origin in courts of equity. The key features of a trust discussed here can exist in a jurisdiction which has never benefited from the productive paradox of courts of equity; but only if that system replicates the particular concerns and techniques of those courts.

22

Up there in the *Begriffshimmel*?

GEORGE GRETTON

I Introduction

'I can't understand your trust.' So wrote Otto von Gierke to Maitland.[1] Elsewhere Maitland conjures up an imaginary continental friend who asks him: 'You might tell us what sort of thing is this wonderful Trust of yours . . . See, here is our general scheme of Private Law. Are we to place this precious *Rechtsinstitut* under the title of *Sachenrecht* or should it stand under *Recht der Schuldverhältnisse*, or, to use a term which may be more familiar, *Obligationenrecht*?'[2]

More than a hundred years later the picture is much the same. Common lawyers are comfortable with the trust.[3] Civil lawyers are uncomfortable with the trust. This is, in itself, simply an empirical observation, not a doctrinal one. But it also calls for a doctrinal explanation.

On the common law side – that is, the question of why common lawyers do not agonize, or do not agonize much, about the nature of the trust – I have little to offer. One might remark that common lawyers seldom concern themselves greatly with architectonics anyway, so it is not surprising if they seldom worry about the nature of the trust. Or it may be that in the common law the trust is, as Lionel Smith puts it, 'a fundamental legal institution'.[4]

1 F. W. Maitland, *Equity: Also the Forms of Action at Common Law: Two Courses of Lectures* (Cambridge University Press, 1909), p. 23.

2 F. W. Maitland, 'Trust and Corporation', in H. A. L. Fisher (ed.), *The Collected Papers of Frederic William Maitland* (Cambridge University Press, 1911), vol. III, p. 323. '*Sachenrecht*' means property law. '*Recht der Schuldverhältnisse*' means the law of debtor/creditor relationships.

3 Generally speaking. Of course there are exceptions.

4 L. Smith, 'Trust and Patrimony' (2008) 38 R.G.D. 379, paras. 2, 24; (2009) 28 E.T.P.J. 332. I think that for Lionel Smith the trust is a fundamental legal institution wherever it is adopted, so that for him it is a fundamental legal institution not only in the common law

This chapter looks at the question mainly from the civil law standpoint, including the standpoint of the mixed systems, for the latter all have the trust, and the agonizing over the 'what is a trust?' question affects jurists in the mixed systems as it does the jurists in the unmixed civilian systems.[5]

II Locating the trust in the framework of civilian private law

Where does one locate the trust in the framework of civilian private law? This is a large and much-discussed question. I am not going to embark on a full examination, but merely offer a few thoughts, some of them relevant to Quebec law. It seems to me that the trust is at or near a gravitational mid-point between three massive bodies, each with its own *vis attractiva* (see Figure 22.1).

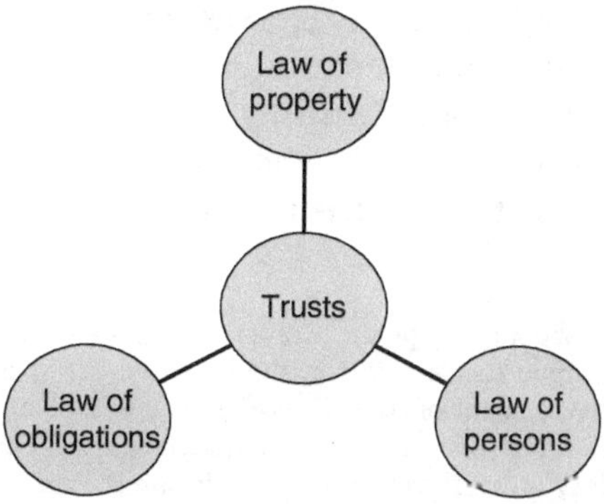

Fig. 22.1

A. *The gravitational pull of the law of obligations*

The gravitational pull of the law of obligations is apparent. John Langbein has rightly stressed the 'contractarian' aspect of trusts.[6] It is

systems. There is much that I agree with in Smith's profound paper, but the present chapter represents a partial disagreement with it.

5 'Unmixed' is shorthand. I do not wish to assert any idea of purity. 'Common law', 'civil law' and 'mixed' are vague concepts, but not so vague, in my view, as to be altogether useless.

6 'The deal between settlor and trustee is functionally indistinguishable from the modern third-party-beneficiary contract. Trusts are contracts.' J. H. Langbein, 'The Contractarian Basis of the Law of Trusts' (1995) 105 *Yale Law Journal* 625, 627.

worthwhile asking, for any legal system, to what extent ordinary contract law can establish something like a trust. Assets can be vested in X with X being bound to A, B, C and so on to use the assets for their benefit. This is all the easier if a legal system recognizes the possibility of a contract having third-party beneficiaries – the *stipulatio alteri.*[7] Contract can create what might be called a 'quasi-trust' not only for specific assets but also for a fund of assets.

But contract law cannot go all the way. In particular it cannot protect the 'quasi-beneficiaries' from the creditors of the quasi-trustee, i.e. the holder of the assets. Contractual ring-fencing can mimic the trust, but contractual ring-fencing cannot achieve the type of ring-fencing achieved by the trust.

And there are other aspects of trusts that do not fit into the law of obligations. For example, in contract law if a debtor behaves badly, there can be no question of the creditors asking the court to give them a new and better debtor.[8] But precisely that is possible in trust law, when a court replaces a misbehaving trustee. As Honoré puts it, trust is an *office.*[9] The supervisory role of the court demarcates what have been called 'private fiduciary institutions'[10] from the trust.

For 'purpose trusts' such as charitable trusts, a contractual approach may work for the settlor/trustee relation but it does not work for

[7] Which English law did not, until the Contracts (Rights of Third Parties) Act 1999. Indeed, one might argue that a factor in the development of English trust law might have been under-development of contract law, i.e. the lack of *stipulatio alteri.*

[8] One qualification to this is that in most legal systems unpaid creditors can apply to the court for a bankruptcy order, the effect of which is that the creditors obtain, in a sense, a new and better debtor, namely the bankruptcy administrator.

[9] This point has been particularly prominent in South Africa. See e.g. T. Honoré, 'Obstacles to the Reception of Trust Law? The Examples of South Africa and Scotland', in A. M. Rabello (ed.), *Aequitas and Equity: Equity in Civil Law and Mixed Jurisdictions* (Harry and Michael Sacher Institute for Legislative Research and Comparative Law, the Hebrew University of Jerusalem, 1997); M. de Waal, 'The Core Elements of the Trust: Aspects of the English, Scottish and South African Trusts Compared' (2000) 117 *South African Law Journal* 548; E. Cameron et al. (eds.), *Honoré's South African Law of Trusts*, 5th edn (Landsowne: Juta, 2002). Article 1299 of the Civil Code of Québec in its English version says that a trustee holds an 'office' (the French text is not so strongly expressed). In South Africa the 'office' nature of trusteeship has led to the view that, to quote Honoré, the trust 'is not a purely private institution'. See T. Honoré, 'Trusts: the Inessentials', in J. Getzler (ed.), *Rationalizing Property, Equity and Trusts: Essays in Honour of Edward Burn* (London: LexisNexis UK, 2003).

[10] Cameron et al., *Honoré's South African Law of Trusts*, above, note 9, p. 23. They give as examples *fiducie, Treuhand, bewind.*

the trustee/beneficiary relation, for in a purpose trust there are no beneficiaries in the narrow sense.[11]

B. The gravitational pull of the law of property

The gravitational pull of property law is even stronger. Indeed, trust law is commonly thought of as a branch of property law. The assets held in trust are dyed with the colour called 'trust'. In Quebec the trust has sometimes been described as constituting a 'modality' of property.[12] Common lawyers often speak[13] of divided ownership, with the trustee being owner 'in law' and with the beneficiaries being owners 'in equity'. For the civilian *duplex dominium* is, speaking in broad terms, not an acceptable concept.[14]

Scots lawyers too tend to think of trusts as belonging to property law. Indeed, that approach has quasi-constitutional force. Gaius's division of law into *personae* and *res* and *actiones* lives on in Scotland, and is to be found in the Scotland Act. That Act splits the Gaian *res* into two: law of obligations and law of property, and it allocates trusts to the law of property.[15] But the location of trusts within property law has never been a secure one.

Civilian property law knows of the *ius in re aliena*, the limited real right, and the rights of the beneficiaries look rather like that, with the trustee being owner and the beneficiaries having limited real rights. Such a conceptualization (equitable ownership in the common law tradition

[11] A private purpose trust such as a STAR trust can be for the benefit of persons. Such persons are beneficiaries in a broad sense – people who benefit – but not in the narrow sense. See in particular Part VIII of the Cayman Islands Trust Law.

[12] 'The right of ownership is not the traditional one, since, for example, it is temporary and includes no *fructus*. It is a *sui generis* property right.' *Tucker* v. *Royal Trust* [1982] 1 S.C.R. 250, a case that predates the present code. As I understand it, this does not reflect current thinking.

[13] But not always, and not all of them.

[14] One must beware of speaking in too dogmatic terms. For example, German law has for long been prepared to speak of *wirtschaftliches Eigentum* (economic ownership), which has some likeness to beneficial ownership in the common law tradition. See also A. J. van der Walt and D. G. Kleyn, 'Duplex Dominium: The History and Significance of the Concept of Divided Ownership', in D. P. Visser (ed.), *Essays on the History of Law* (Cape Town: Juta, 1989).

[15] The Scotland Act 1998 gave Scotland limited autonomy. It was found necessary to define 'private law' and this was done in section 126. Private law is said to consist of persons, obligations, property and actions, with the addition of a preliminary general part. Thus there are five divisions in all, but the Gaian core is obvious.

and limited real right in the civilian tradition) could explain, for example, why the rights of the beneficiaries trump the rights of the trustee's creditors.

Some legal thinkers have developed an idea that is in some ways similar. Lionel Smith has argued that 'the essence of the common law trust lies not in any division of ownership of the trust property . . . Rather it lies in the fact that the trust beneficiaries hold rights in the rights that the trustee holds as trust property.'[16]

This idea can be called that of the 'duty-burdened right'.[17] The rights held in trust are all burdened by the obligations of the trust. The idea has parallels with the concept of the limited real right, but it is not the same concept. The duty that burdens the right goes beyond what could be attained through the limited real right of the civilian tradition. The duty that burdens the right is rather like another, much less developed, civilian concept, the *obligatio propter rem*. The 'duty-burdened right' theory explains why a trust asset, when coming into the hands of another party, may bind that third party, because the duty is stuck to the right with glue. Trust law is the law of glue.

This theory seems to me a powerful one. Whether it is adequate to explain the common law trust perhaps remains to be seen. (Whether *any* theory is adequate to explain the common law trust remains to be seen.) The theory perhaps under-explains the *unity* of the trust estate. It may also – though perhaps this is the same thought in another manifestation – under-explain the real subrogation that happens in the administration of a trust estate.

And there is the fact that the glue is a weak glue, for when the trustee alienates a right that is subject to the trust, the duty that burdens that right almost always gets detached. That happens in two cases, but those two cases cover virtually all cases in real life. The first is where the alienation is an unlawful one but the transferee is a purchaser in good faith. The second is where the alienation is a lawful one. Much theoretical discussion of trust law seems to assume that sales by trustees are generally in breach of trust. This is the tail wagging the dog. In practice sales in

[16] Smith, 'Trust and Patrimony', above, note 4, para. 2. Nevertheless he sees the trust as originating in 'a distortion of the law of obligations' (para. 15) and refers to 'the obligational roots of the common law trust' (para. 17).

[17] The contribution in this volume from Remus Valsan is along these lines (Chapter 20, R. Valsan, 'Rights Against Rights and Real Obligations'). And see in particular Ben McFarlane and Robert Stevens, 'The Nature of Equitable Property' (2010) 4 *Journal of Equity* 1.

breach of trust are rare – not because sales are rare but because sales by trustees are almost always permitted sales. It seems to me that from a practical standpoint what protects beneficiaries is 99% real subrogation and only 1% glue.

Other difficulties may dog property-based approaches to trusts. One is the fact that a trust is an *office*: a point noted above in relation to the law of obligations.

C. *The gravitational pull of the law of persons*

Trusts often behave like persons. Of course, trusts do not *always* behave like persons. Sometimes trustees are passive, merely holding the title to an unchanging single asset. But they can and often do behave like persons; that potentiality inheres in them. The single unchanging asset trust is merely a sluggish trust.

Trusts are in practice usually *spoken of* in the same way as persons. For example 'they could sue the trust' or 'these shares belong to the XYZ trust' and so on. Trusts often play the same role as persons. For example, it is often a merely technical matter as to whether a charity is established as a trust or as a juristic person.[18] There is what is sometimes called the Massachusetts trust, i.e. a trust that is a commercial enterprise, and thus does the same job as a commercial corporation. In many countries tax law treats a trust as a juristic person.[19] In some countries[20] a trust can be made bankrupt. I sometimes wonder whether trust law developed in England because in English law it was too difficult to create juristic persons, but this hypothesis would call for a good deal of historical-comparative research to test it.

It sometimes happens that juristic persons call themselves 'trusts'. One type of case is probably attributable to the fact that the English language lacks any established term to mean a non-profit juristic person, so that the word 'trust' is borrowed to perform this linguistic task. A good example is the National Trust for Places of Historic Interest or Natural

[18] In the UK, smaller charities tend to be trusts and larger charities tend to be juristic persons. The distinction is mainly a matter of administrative convenience. It is easier to run a small charity as a trust, and it is easier to run a large one as a juristic person.

[19] For example, the Canadian Income Tax Act, RSC 1985, c 1 (5th Supp), s. 104(2) says: 'A trust shall, for the purposes of this Act, . . . be deemed to be in respect of the trust property an individual . . .'.

[20] Including Scotland: see the Bankruptcy Act 1985, s. 6(1)(a) (Scotland). This does not even speak of trustees in their capacity as such: the subject of bankruptcy is the 'trust'.

Beauty, which is incorporated under special legislation by the UK Parliament.[21] There are also some profit-making financial institutions that call themselves 'trusts' perhaps to support an impression of probity. In the UK the main example is the 'investment trust', such as the Scottish Investment Trust plc. The 'plc' contradicts the 'trust', and in truth the company is not a trust but a commercial enterprise incorporated under the UK companies legislation. (A company of this sort is the converse of a Massachusetts trust. A Massachusetts trust is a trust that calls itself a company. An investment trust is a company that calls itself a trust.) A particularly remarkable example of this second type is the 'trust' under the Uniform Statutory Trust Entity Act in the USA.[22] This is simply a type of commercial corporation: 'A statutory trust is an entity separate from its trustees and beneficial owners.'[23]

Pierre Lepaulle thought that 'la solution la plus efficace et la plus simple est de doter le trust de la personne morale'.[24] In 2005 the Scottish Law Commission consulted on the idea that all Scottish trusts should be juristic persons.[25] To turn trusts into persons is to abolish the trust, while at the same time adding an extra item to the list of species of the genus 'juristic person'. The gravitational mass of the law of persons would have swallowed up the trust, like a star gulping down an errant planet. Is that an objection? It seems to me that that is not an easy question. We teach our students that a trust is not a person, and we say the truth, but if we are asked what the differences are, what do we say? This is even more difficult in Scotland and certain other countries, such as Quebec, because there the trust has, I think, gone even further than the common law trust has gone towards personality. The Quebec and Scottish trusts are planets perilously near to the star of personality.

[21] National Trust Act 1907 plus subsequent amendments. This is a private statute and so not printed among the public general statutes. The same is true of the National Trust for Scotland, incorporated by another private statute, the National Trust for Scotland Order Confirmation Act 1935, plus subsequent amendments.

[22] Once again I am indebted to Lionel Smith. See L. Smith, 'Mistaking the Trust' (2011) 40 *Hong Kong Law Journal* 747.

[23] Uniform Statutory Trust Entity Act, s. 302. As far as I can see the word 'person' is used neither in the Act nor in the official commentary. This may tell us something about legal thinking in the USA.

[24] 'The simplest and most effective solution would be to endow the trust with juristic personality.' P. Lepaulle, 'Review of Roberto Pasqual's *La Propriété dans le Trust*' (1952) 4 *Revue internationale de droit comparé* 377, 378.

[25] Scottish Law Commission, *Discussion Paper on the Nature and the Constitution of Trusts* (2006). The idea was rejected.

III Patrimony

A. General

The concept of patrimony is linked with the law of persons. There can be no person without a patrimony, for personality implies patrimony: the patrimony is the totality of assets and liabilities of that person. Quebec and Scotland both have come to regard a trust as a patrimony. In both that development has been fairly recent. In Quebec the step was taken in the new civil code, i.e. in the 1990s. In Scotland the idea that the trust should be conceptualized as a patrimony also happened in the 1990s, and quickly gained acceptance without legislation, no doubt because it merely put old law into new words.[26] In both jurisdictions the idea drew its inspiration from Lepaulle. The two approaches are wonderfully similar, but they are not quite the same. In Scotland the trust is a special patrimony. But in Quebec the trust patrimony is an autonomous patrimony, *un patrimoine d'affectation autonome*.[27]

B. Scotland

In Scots law if Jack is a trustee then he has two patrimonies, his ordinary or general patrimony and his special, or trust, patrimony. The asset side of the trust patrimony consists of rights, and it is he who holds those rights, though in his capacity as trustee. In a nutshell: one person but two patrimonies. For example, if there is land in the trust, Jack owns the land, i.e. has the real right of ownership, albeit not for his own benefit.

[26] The story begins with one of my articles. See G. Gretton, 'Trust and Patrimony', in Hector MacQueen (ed.), *Scots Law into the 21st Century* (Edinburgh: W. Sweet/Sweet & Maxwell, 1996), a volume in honour of the late Professor W. A. Wilson, a scholar who made valuable contributions to many areas of law, including trusts. See further K. Reid, 'Patrimony Not Equity: the Trust in Scotland' (2000) 8 *European Review of Private Law* 427; G. Gretton, 'Trusts without Equity' (2000) 49 *International and Comparative Law Quarterly* 599.

[27] In C. von Bar and E. Clive (eds.), *Principles, Definitions and Model Rules of European Private Law: Draft Common Frame of Reference (DCFR)* (Oxford University Press, 2009), art. X-1:202(1) says that 'the trust fund is to be regarded as a patrimony distinct from the personal patrimony of the trustee and any other patrimonies vested in or managed by the trustee'. This part of the DCFR was to some extent influenced by Scots law. But the apparent equation of 'patrimony' with 'fund' may be questioned. A patrimony is arguably more than a fund. In some respects the DCFR trust may be nearer the English than the Scottish trust: see e.g. art. X-10.201. The DCFR trust is more fully discussed in A. Braun, 'The Framing of a European Law of Trusts', Chapter 11 in this volume.

The principle that a title is vested in the trustee goes back a long way. Already in the seventeenth century Lord Stair, a dominating figure in Scottish legal history, laid down that 'the property of the thing intrusted, be it land or moveables, is in the person of the intrusted, else it is not a proper trust'.[28] Over time, there have been occasional wobbles, but the law has always reverted to this position. Lionel Smith has written:

> It is important to notice that the Scots solution does not presuppose a kind of *sui generis* ownership. The trustee is the full, civil law owner, with *usus*, *fructus* and *abusus*. The beneficiary has only personal rights against the trustee – more precisely, against the trustee in his quality as trustee, since these rights are exigible only against the trust patrimony. There is nothing in this that is contrary to civilian thinking about property.[29]

Scotland is the home of heather, haggis, golf, tartan, uisge beatha, mountain mists, the kilt, the pibroch, and the trust as a special patrimony.

C. *Quebec*

Quebec law is fascinatingly similar – nearly but not quite the same. There is a distinct trust patrimony, but it belongs to no one. Jack does not own the assets. He has no rights at all, but only powers to administer the elements of the patrimony.

The Aubry/Rau theory of patrimony which has been so influential in France and many other jurisdictions has four principles: (i) Every person has a patrimony. (ii) Every person has only one patrimony. (iii) Every patrimony belongs to a person. (iv) Two persons cannot have the same patrimony. Scots law is incompatible with the second principle, because a person who is a trustee has two patrimonies. It is also incompatible with the fourth principle, because where there are joint trustees they have a joint patrimony. Quebec law has chosen to adhere to those two principles, but to break another, the third – a principle that Scots law observes.[30]

[28] Stair, *Institutions of the Law of Scotland*, 2nd edn (Edinburgh: Heir of Andrew Anderson, 1693), 1,13,7.

[29] Smith, 'Trust and Patrimony', above, note 4, 379.

[30] Subject to the problem of what happens if all trustees die. In the interval before a new trustee can be appointed, is there a patrimony that belongs to no one? It is a difficult question, and could perhaps be used as a criticism of the Scots conception of trust, and in favour of the Quebec conception. It is an issue that can arise outwith the context of trusts. When anyone dies, to whom does the patrimony belong immediately after the death? The Roman law tradition at one stage seems to have considered the *patrimonium* to be itself a

And there is another reason, too, why in Quebec the trust patrimony is autonomous. As Lepaulle states: 'Il est … impossible de traduire les droits du trustee comme étant ceux d'un "propriétaire" dans notre conception de la propriété. Le trustee n'a ni l'*usus* … ni le *fructus* … ni l'*abusus*.'[31] Likewise, for Madeleine Cantin Cumyn, a right (*droit*) is 'une prérogative juridique reconnue à son titulaire dans son intérêt propre'.[32] Thus the Quebec trust patrimony, unlike the Scottish trust patrimony, does not belong to the trustee. The trustee has powers, but not rights. And here we come to article 1261 of the Quebec Civil Code:

Le patrimoine fiduciaire, formé des biens transférés en fiducie, constitue un patrimoine d'affectation autonome et distinct de celui du constituant, du fiduciaire ou du bénéficiaire, sur lequel aucun d'entre eux n'a de droit réel.	The trust patrimony, consisting of the property transferred in trust, constitutes a patrimony by appropriation, autonomous and distinct from that of the settlor, trustee or beneficiary and in which none of them has any real right.

To summarize: the Quebec trust patrimony is an autonomous patrimony (*un patrimoine d'affectation autonome*): such a patrimony is nobody's patrimony. By contrast, the Scottish trust patrimony is not an autonomous patrimony, but a special patrimony. It belongs to the trustee, alongside the general patrimony, and if there is more than one trustee it belongs to them all, as a joint patrimony.

In the language of the place where the underlying theory comes from, the Quebec patrimony is a *Zweckvermögen* whilst the Scots trust patrimony is a *Sondervermögen*. German law *de lege lata* recognizes

person, or at least a juridical subject, under the name of the *hereditas jacens*. One is reminded of Madeleine Cantin Cumyn's theory, discussed below. The subject of death is too vast for discussion here. For valuable discussion see M. de Waal, 'The Strange Path of Trust Property at a Trustee's Death: Theory and Practice in the Law of Trusts' (2009) *Journal of South African Law* (TSAR) 84.

31 'It would be impossible to render the rights of a trustee as being those of an owner within our (French) conception of property. A trustee has neither *usus* nor *fructus* nor *abusus*.' P. Lepaulle, 'Réflexion sur l'expansion des trusts' (1955) 7 *Revue Internationale de Droit Comparé* 318, 319 (author's translation).

32 'A juridical prerogative in favour of the holder (titulary) *for the benefit of that holder*'. M. Cantin Cumyn, 'La fiducie en droit québécois', in J. Herbots (ed.), *Le trust et la fiducie: implications pratiques* (Brussels: Bruylant, 1997), p. 75. See also Cantin Cumyn, 'Le pouvoir juridique' (2007) 52 *McGill Law Journal* 215.

the *Sondervermögen* (special patrimony), but not the *Zweckvermögen* (purpose patrimony, i.e. autonomous patrimony).

> There has been a widespread misunderstanding (linguistically based) of the German legal position: the purpose patrimony, held by nobody, and the special patrimony, held by a person, have both been rendered into the French language by the same term: *patrimoine d'affectation.* Purpose patrimonies, without a holder, are not admitted in Germany, whereas the possibility of a special patrimony is nowadays uncontroversial.[33]

Most of us are imperialists – generally unconscious imperialists – for our own legal systems. Perhaps the criticism that I am about to put forward of the Quebec conceptualization of the trust patrimony is mere imperialism.

In the first place, the 'one person, one patrimony' doctrine is not a doctrine of the civil law tradition in general, but rather a doctrine developed for French law by Aubry and Rau in the nineteenth century, and taken thence by Quebec. In the second place, the view that a right must be held in the interest of the right-holder is again not a doctrine of the civil law tradition in general and seems to me lacking in merit. I see no difficulty in saying that Jack has a right that he holds solely in the interests of another. Lepaulle says that Jack has neither *fructus, usus* nor *abusus.* Suppose a trust holds land which it lets out. Can the tenant say 'you, dear landlord, have not *fructus* so I am not paying you'? On the contrary, the trust works only because the trustee *does* have *fructus.* Without it, the trust would be paralysed. Far from being inconsistent with *fructus*, it presupposes it. Lepaulle, for all his genius, seems to me wrong on this point.

When beginning to study the Quebec trust, I was unsure which of the following was a correct statement of the law: (i) The trust patrimony does not contain rights. (ii) The Quebec trust patrimony contains rights, both

[33] R. Becker, *Die Fiducie von Québec und der Trust* (Tübingen: Mohr Siebeck, 2007), pp. 178–9 (author's translation). The issue has been noted by others, such as J. Beaulne, *Droit de fiducies*, 2nd edn (Montreal: Wilson & Lafleur, 2005), p. 25. The first to make the point may have been K. W. Ryan, 'The Reception of the Trust' (1961) 10 *International and Comparative Law Quarterly* 265 who listed Lepaulle's mistakes, concluding (at p. 271) that 'above all, he [Lepaulle] confused the two distinct notions of the "separate patrimony" (*Sondervermögen*) and the "purpose patrimony" (*Zweckvermögen*)'. Despite Lepaulle's mistakes, he was a scholar of wonderful insight and clarity, from whom there is even now still much to learn. It may be added that the 'purpose patrimony' (*Zweckvermögen*), while it has much in common with the 'purpose trust' of the common law world, is not to be identified with it.

real and personal. Thus if the trust has land, there is a real right of ownership, and that right is in the trust patrimony, but no person holds that real right. Trust rights have no holder, no *titulaire*. As to power to deal with those rights, the trustees have that power. The trustees thus have powers but not rights. Nevertheless, the rights do exist, within the trust patrimony.

The latter is, I believe, the right interpretation.[34] I exhibit my early-stage confusion because I think it helps to show up the lights and shades of the picture. Take a trust asset such as a house. A right exists. It is, I think, a right of ownership, because I do not see what other right it could be. (And if it is not a right of ownership, the right of ownership vanished when the trustee acquired the property, and will re-appear if the trustee sells it to a third party, or transfers it to a beneficiary. That would be strange.) There is a right of ownership, but no owner. This is different from the ordinary case of ownerless property, where there exists neither an owner nor a right of ownership. Nevertheless it is hard to see why it does not engage the Quebec rules about ownerless property passing to the state,[35] for those rules, as I read them, are triggered not by the lack of a right of ownership, but by a lack of owner.

As a matter of *theory*, the difference between the Quebec trust and the Scottish trust lies in titularity. In the Scottish trust, the trustee is titulary (holder) of the rights that lie in the trust patrimony. In the case of, say, land, that means that the trustee, being titulary of the right of ownership, is the owner of the land.[36] That is not the position in the Quebec trust. But this difference seems to me to be, in *practical* terms, microscopic.

It is sometimes said that in modern Quebec law there is no link between trust and property.[37] It might be more precise to say that in modern Quebec law, there is no link between trust and titularity. For the elements of the trust patrimony are (if I understand the position

[34] I am grateful to Madeleine Cantin Cumyn and to Michael McAuley for their help, via email correspondence, on this and other matters.

[35] Civil Code of Québec (C.C.Q.), arts. 935, 936. Cf. S. Pluskat, *Der Trust im Recht von Québec und die Treuhand: Probleme der Rezeption einer englischen Rechtsfigur in einer Civil-Law-Rechtsordnung* (Berlin: Logos, 2001), pp. 203–4.

[36] It is not necessary here to discuss whether one can be owner of rights, rather than things.

[37] 'La fiducie créée par le Code civil du Québec semble avoir évité le lien entre fiducie et propriété.' J. E. C. Brierley, 'De certains patrimoines d'affectation (De la fondation; De la fiducie)', in Barreau du Québec and Chambre des notaires du Québec, *La réforme du Code civil*, vol. 1 (Sainte-Foy: Presses de l'Université Laval, 1993). I owe this quotation to Yaëll Emerich's valuable contribution to this volume (Chapter 2).

correctly) the same as the elements of a non-trust patrimony – rights of ownership, other real rights, personal rights and intellectual property rights. The difference between the elements of a trust patrimony and the elements of a non-trust patrimony lies in the lack of titularity in the former case.

In the Quebec trust, the trustees have no rights, but they have powers. Thus Jack has power to sell or to buy. If money is owed to the trust and not paid, Jack has the power to sue the debtor. Suppose the debtor is Paul. Paul has a duty to pay Jack, and Jack can compel him to perform that duty. There exists a right to be paid – but no one has that right. To me this looks odd. How does this situation differ from the situation in which Paul simply owes money to Jack? To Paul there is no difference: the quality of his obligation to pay is the same as if he had owed the money to a non-trustee. In short, I do not find it easy to see what *work* the right/power distinction is doing.

Let us return to article 1261 to consider the words 'in which'. The end of the article tells us that nobody has a real right in . . . *in what*? In the English text, there is an ambiguity. The reference could, grammatically speaking, be either to 'the property' or to 'the trust patrimony'. Turning to the French text, there is no ambiguity. Whereas the English text has 'the property' in the singular, the French text has '*les biens*' in the plural. Accordingly '*sur lequel*', being grammatically singular, cannot refer to '*les biens*' but must refer to the '*patrimoine fiduciaire*'. Now, once one has settled the textual meaning, there is surely something odd about this statement. The concept of patrimony refers to the container, not to the contained. The question whether someone has or does not have a real right in an item in a patrimony is a question that makes sense. But to ask whether someone has a real right in a *patrimony* makes no sense.[38]

One might add that whereas article 1261 mentions only *property* as being in the patrimony, a patrimony comprises debts as well as rights, and whoever could seriously debate whether debtors might have 'real rights' in their own debts?

[38] See also DCFR art. X-3: 203 which speaks of patrimony having an 'owner'. And consider this: 'En droit québécois, un patrimoine autonome peut donc être constitué sans que personne ne puisse en revendiquer la titularité. Ceci heurte la conception personnaliste qui clamait haut et fort la nécessité absolue de l'existence d'un droit de propriété sur les biens.' S. Normand, *Introduction au droit des biens* (Montreal: Wilson & Lafleur, 2000), p. 25. The object of a *rei vindicatio* could never be a titularity. *Rei vindicatio* presupposes a titularity that predates the action. *Ubi rem meam invenio, ibi vindico*. What is vindicated is always an object of property.

Article 1261 says 'in which none of them has any *real* right', but then it falls silent. One is half-expecting the words 'nor any *personal* right', but those words are not there. Perhaps the word 'property' refers only to corporeal property, and not to other trust assets, such as money owed by debtor Paul to trustee Jack?[39] The monetary claim is a trust asset but it is a personal right, so denying that anyone has a real right in it says little. And it does not seem to exclude Jack from *having* the personal right. For a personal right against Paul exists. The only question in Quebec law is whether anyone *has* that personal right. And article 1261 does not seem to exclude that. This line of reasoning seems to lead to the odd result that in the case of, say, land, there is a real right but the trustee does not have it (neither does anyone else), but for a monetary claim, there is a personal right and the trustee has it.

It might be replied that personal rights are themselves real rights: that one owns every asset in the patrimony (not just corporeal property) and that accordingly when article 1261 says that nobody has a real right, what it is saying is that none of the trust assets – whether corporeal or incorporeal – belong to the patrimonies of the 'settlor, trustee or beneficiary'. Or, put another way, the meaning of article 1261 may be 'no real rights, and therefore no personal rights either'. That approach would cohere with the Ginossarian tendencies that can be discerned in Quebec.[40] Not being a Ginossarian,[41] that would leave me uncomfortable. My discomfort does not matter. But the meaning of article 1261 does. And I think that article 1261 is, in fact, not clarified by Ginossarianism. In the Ginossarian scheme, a person who has a personal right has the real right of ownership in that personal right. Article 1261 strips out the real right of ownership. The trustee has no real right of ownership in the personal right they have against the bank. But they still have that personal right. That lands us, once again, with a strange asymmetry. The trustee has no real right in the trust land but has (it seems) a personal right against the trust debtor.

[39] It may be that the 'no real right' provision was designed to exclude the 'divided real right' or 'dismemberment of property' approach that has sometimes been suggested as an analysis of the trust. On this, see M. Cantin Cumyn, 'La fiducie, un nouveau sujet de droit?', in J. Beaulne (ed.), *Mélanges Ernest Caparros* (Montreal: Wilson & Lafleur, 2002), p. 135, note 11. But article 1261 of the C.C.Q. goes beyond, saying 'no divided real rights'.

[40] See for instance Y. Emerich, *La propriété des créances* (Paris: L.G.D.J., 2007), p. 469.

[41] My own views on this controversial, and difficult, issue of the civilian patrimonial structure are developed in G. Gretton, 'Ownership and its Objects' (2007) 71 *Rabels Zeitschrift* 802.

In Scots law, just as the rights of the trust are the rights of the trustees (*as* trustees), so the obligations of the trust patrimony are the obligations of the trustees (*as* trustees). Article 1261 speaks of the assets, but not of the liabilities too. If the trustees do not hold the rights that are within the trust patrimony, do they owe the obligations that lie within the trust patrimony? Or are the trust obligations owed by nobody?[42] If in Quebec law a right must be for the benefit of the right-holder, is it also the case that an obligation must be for the detriment of the obligation-holder? If not, then why? Or if the trust patrimony is itself a subject of law, perhaps it itself owes the obligations?[43] This leads us to the next topic.

IV The patrimonial theory: collapsing into personhood?

Madeleine Cantin Cumyn has argued that the Quebec trust is itself a *sujet de droit*, but not a *personne morale*,[44] a distinction not easy to translate into English, and, indeed, perhaps not a distinction easy to draw in French itself.[45] She offers two points of distinction from the true juristic person.[46] The first is that a trust cannot have extra-patrimonial rights. The other is that a trust, unlike a juristic person, cannot be an administrator, a trustee or a mandatary. The stability of this point of view may be debated. Juristic persons can have broader or narrower capacities,[47] and what Professor Cantin Cumyn describes could equally be described as a juristic person with limited powers. That the Quebec trust is a juristic person is the view of one outside observer.[48] The pressure in that direction – the pressure to turn the trust into a juristic person – is stronger in Quebec law than it is in

[42] See D. W. M. Waters, M. Gillen and L. Smith, *Waters' Law of Trusts in Canada*, 4th edn (Toronto: Thomson Carswell, 2012), p. 1428. The issues arise both for trust debts and for beneficiaries' rights.

[43] As suggested by Y. Rossier, 'Étude comparée de certains aspects patrimoniaux de la fiducie' (1988/1989) 34 *McGill Law Journal* 817, 870.

[44] Cantin Cumyn, 'La fiducie, un nouveau sujet de droit?', above, note 39.

[45] Or, I think, in other European languages.

[46] Cantin Cumyn, 'La fiducie, un nouveau sujet de droit?', above, note 39, 142.

[47] Thus one could imagine a legal system establishing a juristic person, or a class of juristic persons, lacking the power to be a mandatary. In the United Kingdom, and I dare say elsewhere too, there are many things that a local authority lacks power to do, such as some types of financial transactions (a dramatic example is *Hazel* v. *Hammersmith & Fulham LBC* [1992] 2 AC 1). Yet a local authority is a juristic person.

[48] Pluskat, *Der Trust im Recht von Québec und die Treuhand*, above, note 35. She calls the Quebec trust a '*Rechtssubjekt*' (see p. 204), i.e. a *sujet de droit*, but I take it that for Pluskat '*Rechtssubjekt*' and '*juristische Person*' mean the same.

Scots law, because of Quebec's decision to make the trust patrimony an autonomous patrimony[49] rather than a special patrimony,[50] for the former has, as it seems to me, greater conceptual problems.

And yet it seems to me an open question whether the idea of a separate patrimony of either kind is really capable of conceptual stability. The patrimonial theory recognizes the powerful pull of personality, but seeks to establish the trust at a point outside the sphere of personality. Can it remain there, or must it be sucked in? I do not know. In the light of a recent Quebec appellate decision on partnership law, I offer one reflection. It has been held that under Quebec law, a general partnership has a distinct patrimony.[51] Scots law has gone even further: since the late eighteenth century it has taken the view that a general partnership is a separate juristic person.

The common law trust seems to be more distant from personality than are trusts that are patrimonies. Lionel Smith has argued this point cogently, his position being that in the common law trust the liabilities are the trustee's personal liabilities, albeit normally with a right of recoupment out of the trust assets, whereas in a patrimonial trust the liabilities are normally the liabilities of the trustees as trustees.[52] In the patrimonial system the position of the trustees comes near to the position of the director of a corporation.

Some legal systems offer the foundation as a functional equivalent to the trust.[53] Some offer both trusts and foundations. In broad terms a foundation is a trust with personality. It seems to me that almost nothing, practically speaking, separates (i) a trust that is conceptualized as a patrimony, whether on the Quebec lines or the Scottish lines, and (ii) the foundation.

[49] *Zweckvermögen.* [50] *Sondervermögen.*

[51] *Ferme CGR enr., s.e.n.c. (Syndic de)* 2010 QCCA 719.

[52] Smith, 'Trust and Patrimony', above, note 4.

[53] There is a terminological issue here. In the Quebec code, 'foundations' are of two types: trusts and juristic persons. That differs from the predominant terminology used elsewhere, which is that a foundation is a person, with the consequence that a trust, not being a person, is not a foundation. (Article 1257 C.C.Q. says: 'The property of the foundation constitutes either an autonomous patrimony distinct from that of the settlor or any other person, or the patrimony of a legal person. In the first case, the foundation is governed by the provisions of this Title relating to a social trust, subject to the provisions of law; in the second case, the foundation is governed by the laws applicable to legal persons of the same kind.') Somewhat similar to the Quebec approach as expressed in article 1257 C.C.Q. is German law, in which the *Stiftung* (foundation) is divided into the autonomous (*selbständige*) and the non-autonomous (*unselbständige*). The former is, whilst the latter is not, a juristic person.

We commonly think of juristic personality as something that has to be conferred by public authority, and that involves publicity, typically registration. Often there is a requirement to file annual accounts. The trust sidesteps such requirements. This is not necessarily a criticism. In Scots law a general partnership has personality without any need for registration, and the Scottish Law Commission has recommended that not-for-profit associations should also have personality without registration.[54]

V Gravitational stability?

Does the trust have gravitational stability, or is it sucked in by *vis attractiva* of property, obligations or persons? I doubt whether any confident answer can be given, and what answers can be offered no doubt vary according to the legal system in question. But certainly the Scottish trust is near to personhood, and the Quebec trust is nearer still, having even perhaps crossed the line.[55] The common law trust is further from personhood, but I am unconvinced that it is in a stable point in conceptual space. The common law trust is more explicable than are the Quebec and Scottish trusts by means of the law of obligations and the law of property. But the common law trust also has some person-like qualities that are hard to explain through the law of obligations or the law of property. Perhaps that simply means that it remains comfortably independent. I do not know.

[54] Scottish Law Commission, *Report on Unincorporated Associations* (Scot. Law Com. No. 217) 2009.

[55] In UK law, trade unions tremble at the margin of personality. '(1) A trade union is not a body corporate but (a) it is capable of making contracts; (b) it is capable of suing and being sued in its own name, whether in proceedings relating to property or founded on contract or tort or any other cause of action; and (c) proceedings for an offence alleged to have been committed by it or on its behalf may be brought against it in its own name.' Thus speaks section 10 of the Trade Union and Labour Relations (Consolidation) Act 1992. So in what respect is it not a person? Section 11 says that 'all property belonging to a trade union shall be vested in trustees in trust for it'. So it is a trust, or perhaps it is a person that is inseparably linked to a trust, as a lichen is two interdependent species. But section 11 goes on to say that 'a judgment, order or award made in proceedings of any description brought against a trade union is enforceable, by way of execution, diligence, punishment for contempt or otherwise, against any property held in trust for it to the same extent and in the same manner as if it were a body corporate'. So is a trade union a person? Who can say?

VI A fundamental legal institution?

What has been said so far has been fairly narrow in focus, asking whether the trust can avoid being sucked into one or other of the three great stars of the law of property, the law of obligations and the law of persons. Much more could be said. But in the remainder of this chapter there will be a change of focus. So far the focus has been on the gravitational pulls of other areas of law, assuming the trust itself to be a recognizable single entity, Planet Trust.

In the remainder of this chapter the focus is on the interior of Planet Trust. Is there really a single entity? Or, to put it another way, do we really know what a trust is? There are problems in pinning down the trust even within the common law world, and once one steps outside that world there is a plethora of institutions which more or less resemble the trust. Where does one draw the line between 'trusts' and 'trust-like institutions'? For example, on which side of the line is the French *fiducie* or the German *Treuhand* or the *sharīʿa waqf*? Might even the Quebec and Scottish trusts not be 'real' trusts because they are conceptualized as patrimonies? Perhaps we should forget about drawing lines and instead accept a boundaryless savannah of possibilities?

Is a trust something capable of being used for donative purposes? In the common law that would probably be regarded as an essential feature. But in many countries the trust (or whatever it may be called) cannot be so used. France is an example: 'Le contrat de fiducie est nul s'il procède d'une intention libérale au profit du bénéficiaire.'[56]

Must the trust assets be owned by the trustee? Not in Quebec.[57]

Must there be a transfer from the settlor? Yet in South Africa there is the '*bewind* trust' in which title remains in the settlor. On one view the trust in China functions, or at least can function, like the *bewind*.[58] On

[56] 'A trust is invalid if it operates as a donation to a beneficiary.' *Code civil* (C. civ.), art. 2013.

[57] The fact that in many legal systems trustees can vest title in a nominee is not, I think, a fact of more than technical significance. Under such an arrangement, there is still a trust fund vested in the trustees. The fund consists of rights in relation to the nominee.

[58] In the Chinese Trust Law of 2001, article 2 says that the settlor 'entrusts his property rights to the trustee'. The word 'entrusts' (*weituo*) refers to an agency relationship (official translation, for which see http://english.gov.cn/laws/2005-09/12/content_31194.htm). See L. Ho, *Trust Law in China* (Hong Kong: Sweet & Maxwell Asia, 2003), p. 41; R. Lee, 'Conceptualizing the Chinese Trust' (2009) 58 *International and Comparative Law Quarterly* 655 and L. Ho, 'Trust Laws in China', in Lionel Smith (ed.), *Re-imagining the Trust* (Cambridge University Press, 2012), pp. 183–221. Maltese law hedges its bets.

one view the Hague Trusts Convention does not unambiguously exclude the *bewind*. Indeed, legal systems that allow a settlor to declare that some asset or group of assets is constituted as a trust fund are permitting something rather akin to the *bewind*.[59]

Many people would say that at the same time the trust assets belong in equity to the beneficiaries, so that there is divided ownership. But that is not the position in Scotland or in many other countries where equitable ownership is not recognized.[60] Even in English law, in the case of a charitable trust there is no equitable ownership held by beneficiaries.

Does a trust need a settlor,[61] a trustee and a beneficiary? In fact all these seem dispensable. Firstly: must trusts have settlors? An English bankruptcy is a trust, but it does not have a settlor. Must a trust have trustees? But all trustees may die, or, if juristic persons, may be dissolved, and yet the trust survives. What about beneficiaries? Charitable trusts have no beneficiaries, at least in the ordinary sense of that term. Some legal systems in the common law world do not require beneficiaries even for private trusts.[62]

Trusts are not juristic persons? For this question, see above.

Must the trust be insolvency-proof, meaning that the beneficiaries are, in principle at least, protected from the general creditors of the trustee? Perhaps. But the trust had long existed in South Africa before this point was settled in 1988,[63] while in Germany the insolvency protection operates only in relation to the original trust assets, and not to substituted

Chapter 331 of the Malta Civil Code, article 3(3): 'The trust property is held by or in the name or under the control of the trustee'. But see also article 3(1).

59 Scotland allows this, as does the DCFR. But Quebec does not.

60 It is often said that the doctrine of the *numerus clausus* of real rights excludes the possibility of recognizing the trust in civil law systems. This argument is not one I am able to grasp. It is not necessary to classify the rights of beneficiaries as being a type of real right. That is so even if the trust assets consist of land, and even more so if the assets are stock market investments. No system with civilian property law has such a long experience of trusts as Scotland, for trusts appeared in Scots law in the seventeenth century. Scots law has a *numerus clausus* of real rights, but Scots law shows how the law of trusts does not interact at all with the doctrine of *numerus clausus*. The *numerus clausus* argument rests on a category mistake, caused by the misleading rhetoric of 'divided ownership'.

61 The Scots term is 'truster'. (It has been adopted by the DCFR.)

62 Such as the STAR trust of the Cayman Islands. See, inter alia, P. Matthews, 'The New Trust: Obligations without Rights?', in A. J. Oakley (ed.), *Trends in Contemporary Trust Law* (Oxford: Clarendon Press, 1996).

63 Trust Property Control Act 1988.

trust assets.[64] Does that mean that the German *Treuhand* is not 'really' a trust 'in the true sense of that term' but only 'trust-like'?[65]

Must a trust be capable of holding assets of any kind? Some trust laws exclude land, yet land lies at the historic heart of the English trust.

Can a trust be established only by *inter vivos* act? Here too there is much variation. Is one to say that a legal system that does not have the *mortis causa* trust does not have the trust?

Is any case where one person administers property for the benefit of another a trust? Then all commercial corporations are trusts. (Some would hesitate before reaching that conclusion. Can one say why corporate directors are, in the common law tradition, commonly called trustees?) Another consequence might be that fideicommissary substitution should be classified as a trust. Indeed, David Johnston's well-regarded work on that subject is called *The Roman Law of Trusts*.[66]

'An obligation to do an act with respect to property creates a trust', an English judge once said in the House of Lords in relation to Scots law.[67] That was untrue then and is untrue now. If it is true of English law[68] then the Scottish 'trust' should perhaps be regarded as being merely a 'trust-like institution'.

Some authors have sought to list features that are *not* essential to the concept of trust, aiming their blows chiefly at specific aspects of English law, such as the concept of equitable property. Professor Honoré has

64 The *Unmittelbarkeitsprinzip*.

65 In Scotland, there used to be an exception to the general principle that a trust is insolvency-proof: if the registered title to land did not disclose that the person registered held in trust, the insolvency protection did not apply to such property. This exception was removed by the House of Lords in *Heritable Reversionary Company Ltd* v. *Millar* (1892) 18 R 1166, a case that reveals a good deal of muddle on the part of their Lordships about the nature of the trust in Scots law. The question of precisely *how* trust-held property appears in land registries, or registers of other assets, such as company share registers, would be a fruitful area for comparative study. Some legal systems require the fact of the trust to be omitted. Others permit it but do not require it. Others require it. Those that permit or require do not always agree as to the manner in which the fact of trust is to be disclosed. For example, there is the 'X Y and Z as trustees . . .' approach. There is the 'trustees from time to time . . .' approach. There is the 'ABC trust' approach. Some of these approaches come close to treating the trust as a person. Perhaps there are other approaches.

66 D. Johnston, *The Roman Law of Trusts* (Oxford: Clarendon Press, 1988).

67 *Fleeming* v. *Howden* (1868) 6 M (HL) 113, 121 *per* Lord Westbury.

68 I am unqualified to judge, but it seems to be true in some cases (e.g. contracts for the sale of immoveable property) but not in others (e.g. contracts for the sale of tangible moveable property).

written a paper wittily called 'Trusts: the Inessentials'.[69] In the first chapter of his book, *Trusts*, Professor Lupoi has a barrage of such *non verum est*[70] statements:

> It is not true that a trust involves three persons . . . It is not . . . true that the establishment of a trust is the consequence of a transfer in favour of the trustee . . . It is not true . . . that the rights of a beneficiary of a trust fall within the notion of 'ownership' . . . It is not true that where the trust calls for the existence of beneficiaries they need necessarily be 'equitable owners' . . . It is not the case that the trustee must necessarily have a legal status which is recognised by common law . . . It is not true that the trust is a fiduciary *negotium*, as the concept is understood in civil law legal systems . . . It is not true that . . . the basis of a trust is a contract between the settlor and the trustee . . . It is not true that the law of trusts is a specialized and archaic field which has become rigid . . . It is not true that the supplementary or complementary function of equity is a historical legacy . . . It is not true to say that the trust is a legal device which is found exclusively in common law systems.[71]

Such comments may tell us what is not essential to the trust. But even if they are accepted, there is still the question: what *is* the essence of the trust considered as an autonomous institution? Can one demarcate between true trusts on the one hand, and mere trust-like devices on the other?

One possibility would be to declare the common law trust to be the true trust and everything else at best trust-like. On that basis, the trusts of the 'mixed systems' such as Quebec, Scotland and South Africa would not be real trusts. That approach is quite common. For example, writing in the *International Encyclopaedia of Comparative Law*, Professor Fratcher opens the chapter on trusts with these words: 'The trust is a legal device developed in England whereby ownership of property is split . . .'[72]

[69] T. Honoré, 'Trusts: The Inessentials', in J. Getzler (ed.), *Rationalizing Property, Equity and Trusts: Essays in Honour of Edward Burn* (London: LexisNexis UK, 2003).

[70] Or rather, as Lupoi says in the Italian original *Trusts, 'non è vero'*. M. Lupoi, *Trusts*, 2nd edn (Milan: A. Giuffrè, 2001).

[71] M. Lupoi, *Trusts: A Comparative Study* (Cambridge University Press, 2000). The whole passage extends from pp. 1–4, so this quotation is very selective. I might add that, valuable though this work is, it is not always clear to me when Professor Lupoi is writing about modern English trust law and when he is writing of the trust in a more system-neutral sense. This is no doubt my fault.

[72] W. F. Fratcher, 'Trust', in R. David et al. (eds.), *International Encyclopaedia of Comparative Law* (Tübingen: J. C. B. Mohr 1973), vol. 6, chap. 11, para. 1. This could of course be questioned even for the common law. In an English charitable trust, is the ownership split?

I do not know the answer. Is the trust up there in von Jhering's *Begriffshimmel*?[73] If in this life we are very, very good lawyers, can we hope, when we die, and are conducted, by a juridical Beatrice, around the Paradiso of Concepts, to meet the Pure Spirit of the Trust? Could that be so in a trans-systemic[74] sense? Could that be true even for the common law? I do not know.

[73] R. von Jhering, *Scherz und Ernst in der Jurisprudenz* (Leipzig: Breitkopf & Härtel, 1885), satirizing what he saw as the excessive conceptualism of the Pandectists.

[74] This word should perhaps be regarded as © McGill University Faculty of Law.

INDEX